HARRY C. TREXLER LIBRARY

The Japan Foundation

Library Support Program

1993

MUHLENBERG
COLLEGE

Productivity Growth in Japan and the United States

Studies in Income and Wealth
Volume 53

National Bureau of Economic Research
Conference on Research in Income and Wealth

Productivity Growth in Japan and the United States

Edited by   Charles R. Hulten

The University of Chicago Press

Chicago and London

CHARLES R. HULTEN is professor of economics at The University of
Maryland, chairman of the executive committee of the Conference on Re-
search in Income and Wealth, and a research associate of the National
Bureau of Economic Research

The University of Chicago Press, Chicago 60637
The University of Chicago Press, Ltd., London
© 1990 by the National Bureau of Economic Research.
All rights reserved. Published 1990
Printed in the United States of America
99 98 97 96 95 94 93 92 91 90   5 4 3 2 1

Library of Congress Cataloging-in-Publication Data

Productivity growth in Japan and the United States / edited by Charles
R. Hulten.
    p.   cm. — (Studies in income and wealth ; v. 53)
   Includes bibliographical references and index.
   ISBN 0-226-36059-8 (alk. paper)
   1. Industrial productivity—Japan—Congresses. 2. Industrial pro-
ductivity—United States—Congresses. I. Hulten, Charles R. II.
Series.
HC106.3.C714 vol. 53
[HC465.I52]
330 s—dc20
[338'.06'0952]   90-46002
                                                                        CIP

⊚ The paper used in this publication meets the minimum requirements of
the American National Standard for Information Sciences—Permanence
of Paper for Printed Library Materials, ANSI Z39.48-1984.

Contents

Prefatory Note

Preliminary versions of the papers and discussions contained in this volume were presented at the Conference on Productivity Growth in Japan and the United States held in Cambridge, Massachusetts, 26–28 August 1985. Funds for this conference were provided to the National Bureau of Economic Research by the National Science Foundation through grant PRA-8414535. Funding of the Conference on Research in Income and Wealth series is now provided by the Bureau of the Census, the Bureau of Economic Analysis, the Bureau of Labor Statistics, Statistics Canada, and the Statistics Division of the Internal Revenue Service. We are indebted to all of them for their support. We also thank Charles R. Hulten, who served as an organizer of the conference and as editor of this volume, and the other members of the organizing committee, Mieko Nishimizu and John R. Norsworthy. Laurits R. Christensen had an early organizing role.

Volume Editor's Acknowledgments

I would like to thank Mieko Nishimizu and John R. Norsworthy who, as members of the organizing committee, were instrumental in shaping and organizing the conference program. The financial support of the National Science Foundation, grant PRA-8414535, is also gratefully acknowledged. Special thanks are due Kathi Smith of the NBER for her considerable efforts with the administrative arrangements and for seeing that all went smoothly at the 26–28 August 1985 conference. Finally, thanks are due to Mark Fitz-Patrick, also of the NBER, and to Judy Xanthopoulos and Gregorio Arevalo of the University of Maryland, for invaluable assistance in the editorial process.

Introduction

Charles R. Hulten

The Japanese "miracle" is one of the remarkable economic events of the last 50 years. Emerging from the ruins of World War II, the Japanese economy grew at double-digit rates through the 1950s and 1960s and, when the oil crises of the 1970s slowed growth throughout the industrialized world, Japanese growth rates continued to be relatively strong. Japan has emerged as the second largest economy in the noncommunist world and one of the most formidable trade competitors.

There have been many attempts to explain this remarkable history. A wide variety of hypotheses, which range over a number of academic disciplines, have been offered about the Japanese experience. Some explanations stress cultural factors (the Japanese have always been a frugal and industrious people), while some are essentially historical (the destruction of World War II provided an opportunity to "catch up" to the United States by building a new capital stock and by importing the best-practice technology). Other explanations are institutional in nature (the war reduced the power of special interest groups like labor unions and trade cartels, which tend to impede growth), or organizational (Japanese managers keep their eye on long-run growth while their American counterparts stress short-run profitability), or fiscal (Japanese tax policy was more conducive to saving and investment than that of the United States).

Some of these explanations are surely correct, if only in part and in combination with other factors. The problem is to assign the correct weight to the various alternatives. This is not an easy task, since there is no accepted model that encompasses the full range of cultural, political, and economic factors. Without such a model, it is virtually impossible to sort out the true causal factors from those that correlate well with the phenomenon of rapid growth, but are not true explanatory variables, or those that are truly causal but of limited significance.

1

Quantitative analyses of economic growth have tended to explore the more limited, but also more tractable, question of *how* Japan was able to grow so rapidly. Any sustained increase in real gross national product (GNP) must be due either to an increase in the quantity of capital and labor used in production or to the more efficient use of these inputs (e.g., technical and organizational progress). Empirical models have been developed that sort out the separate contribution of each factor and that indicate the weight of each in the process of output growth. This, in turn, provides a limited explanation of how growth was achieved but falls short of a complete explanation since the factors causing the growth of capital, labor, and technology are not explained.

The papers presented in this volume belong to this tradition of growth analysis and range over a variety of topics related to the measurement of economic growth. Early versions were originally given at the 26–28 August 1985 meeting of the Conference on Research in Income and Wealth and are, for the most part, quite technical. However, the reader who is more interested in substantive issues rather than issues of technique will find much of interest. To facilitate reading this volume from that point of view, the following section provides an overview of the basic methods commonly used in empirical growth analysis. Those familiar with these methods may want to proceed directly to the "Summary of the Conference Proceedings" below.

Introduction to the Measurement of Economic Growth[1]

Theory

The neoclassical analysis of aggregate economic growth starts with the assumption of a stable relationship between output, $Q(t)$, and inputs of capital, $K(t)$, and labor, $L(t)$:

$$(1) \qquad Q(t) = F[K(t),L(t),t].$$

The production function $F(\cdot)$ represents the technological possibilities open to an economy at any point in time; a time trend t is included to allow for the changes in the function due to improvements in technology or in managerial efficiency. If an economy remains on its technological frontier, the production function is a constraint on the rate of economic growth, and any hypothesis about the fundamental causes of growth must be consistent with this constraint.

The analysis of growth can proceed directly from equation (1). The early work used a parametric form for (1)—the famous Cobb-Douglas production function, $Q(t) = e^{\lambda t}K(t)^\alpha L(t)^\beta$—which characterized the production possibility set in terms of three parameters: the rate of change of technical efficiency (λ) and the elasticities of output with respect to capital (α) and labor (β).

Estimation of the parameters (α,β,λ) yields complete information about the technology and permits a decomposition of the growth rate of output into

(2) $$\dot{q}(t) = \hat{\alpha}\dot{k}(t) + \hat{\beta}\dot{\ell}(t) + \hat{\lambda}.$$

This equation indicates that the growth rate of output, $\dot{q}(t)$, must be equal to the growth rate of capital, $k(t)$, weighted by its estimated output elasticity, plus the growth rate of labor input, $\dot{\ell}(t)$, also weighted by its elasticity of output, plus the estimated rate of technical change, $\hat{\lambda}$. This decomposition highlights the relative importance of each factor in explaining the growth of output and thus provides clues about the underlying mechanisms of economic growth.

An alternative approach assumes a competitive equilibrium in which prices are related to the marginal products. This assumption, along with a more general and flexible parametric representation of technology (typically the translog functional form), is used to estimate the production function. The resulting parameter estimates can be used to decompose the growth rate of output into its components in a manner analogous to (2), but without the restriction that the capital and labor weights are constant. Another variant of this approach allows for even more flexibility by dropping the assumption that the economy adjusts to price changes instantaneously. In this variant, costs of adjustment are assumed to prevent capital from varying by the extent necessary to equate marginal products to relative factor prices at each point in time.

The assumption of competitive equilibrium is also used to characterize technology (1) in terms of its minimum cost function. The minimum cost of producing a given level of output $Q(t)$ when the prices of capital and labor services are $P_K(t)$ and $P_L(t)$ is denoted by

(3) $$C(t) = C(P_K(t),P_L(t),Q(t),t).$$

Since technical change in the sense of equation (1) is equivalent to a reduction in the quantity of inputs needed to produce a given level of output, technical change can equally be represented as a reduction in the minimum cost of producing that output, given input prices. The t in (3) is thus analogous to the t in (1), and the rate of technical change, along with other characteristics of technology, can be estimated by specifying a parametric representation of (3)—the translog cost function, for example. A decomposition of the change of minimum cost into its components, along the lines of (2), is also possible, and adjustment costs can be taken into account.

Estimation of (1) or (3) is termed the *parametric* approach to measuring the sources of economic growth. An alternative model, which does not involve parametric representation of the technology or econometric analysis, has been developed from *index number* theory. This model starts with the "adding-up" identity between the value of output and the value of input:

(4) $$P_Q(t)Q(t) = P_K(t)K(t) + P_L(t)L(t),$$

where $P_Q(t)$ represents the price of output. Differentiation of the prices and quantities in (4) yields, with some manipulation, the following expression for the growth rates of prices and quantities:

(5) $\dot{q}(t) - s_K(t)\dot{k}(t) - s_L(t)\dot{\ell}(t) = \dot{p}_Q(t) - s_K(t)\dot{p}_K(t) - s_L(t)\dot{p}_L(t) = \dot{a}(t),$

where $s_K(t)$ and $s_L(t)$ are the shares of capital and labor in the value of output, that is $s_K(t) = P_K(t)K(t)/P_Q(t)Q(t)$ and $s_L(t) = P_L(t)L(t)/P_Q(t)Q(t)$. The far left-hand side of (5) defines the residual growth rate of output not explained by the share-weighted growth rates of inputs, and is interpreted as the growth rate of output per unit input. This index, termed "total factor productivity" and denoted by $\dot{a}(t)$, is also seen to be equal to the (negative) growth rate of output *price* not explained by the share-weighted growth rates of the input prices.[2] This is the "dual" form of the growth accounting model.

The estimate of total factor productivity derived from (5) is based only on prices and quantities and is thus a pure index number—nothing is said about the parameters of an underlying technology or even the existence of such a technology. However, it was demonstrated by Solow (1957) and Diewert (1976) that, under the conditions assumed above, there is a fundamental unity between the parametric and index number approaches, in the sense that both are derived from the production function (1).[3] The share-weighted growth rates of the inputs are interpreted, by Solow, as a movement along the aggregate production function, while the TFP residual is interpreted as a shift in that function.

The analysis of individual industries within the aggregate economy is also important for understanding the process of economic growth. The techniques for analyzing aggregate growth outlined above can also be applied on an industry-by-industry basis, with appropriate modification for interindustry flows of materials and services. This modification involves the use of real gross output rather than real value added as the measure of output and requires that the list of inputs in (5) be extended to include intermediate goods. The main complication arises when the resulting industry-based estimates of TFP growth are aggregated into an economywide measure of TFP. The appropriate weights for this aggregation sum to a quantity greater than one because of the magnifying effects of the intermediate inputs. The industry-level TFP estimates computed using gross output thus tend to be smaller than TFP estimates based on value added.[4]

We note, finally, that the analysis of equation (5) involves rates of growth. The study of the corresponding levels is also of interest, for at least two reasons. First, one of the major explanations of the high rate of Japanese economic growth emphasizes Japan's ability to grow by "catching up." In this view, the devastation of World War II put Japan far below her production possibility frontier, and the national effort to rebuild industry, along with the ability to import technology from abroad, created an opportunity for an abnormally high rate of growth. This opportunity has diminished over time as the level of technology in Japan has approached that of the best-practice countries.

The measurement of relative TFP levels is also important for explaining the pattern of international trade. The price competitiveness of U.S. and Japanese products depends, in part, on the relative efficiency with which these goods are produced. Other things equal, a relatively higher level of TFP in one country will result in a relatively lower product price.[5] When exchange rates adjust to balance trade flows, comparative advantage will be influenced by relative TFP levels.

A method of estimating relative TFP levels using index number procedures was developed by Jorgenson and Nishimizu (1978). For any industry, the index of relative TFP is defined as the difference in the natural logarithms of output in each country minus the share-weighted difference in the logs of the inputs, where the weights are the cost shares averaged across the two countries. As such, the Jorgenson-Nishimizu TFP index is a variant of the translog method of estimating the growth rate of TFP over time applied to the problem of estimating TFP differences across countries (with appropriate adjustment of prices to insure comparability).[6]

The Sources of Growth

A number of empirical studies have used the index-number approach to compare the sources of output growth in Japan to those in the United States. The paper by Nishimizu and Hulten (1978) compares the results of 12 studies undertaken prior to 1978, and more studies have been published since then. The results of several studies are shown in table 1, thereby providing a sample of the kinds of numbers generated by the sources of growth approach. These results are supplemented by table 2 below, which places Japanese economic growth in an international context. Table 1 shows the decomposition of the

Table 1   **The Sources of Aggregate Economic Growth in Japan (in percentages)**

	Denison & Chung (1976) for 1953–71	Nishimizu & Hulten (1978) for 1955–71	Christensen, Cummings, & Jorgenson (1976)	
			1952–60	1960–73
Growth rate of:				
Output	10.0	11.5	8.1	10.9
Capital[a]	2.2	5.9	1.6	4.8
Labor[a]	2.0	1.9	3.1	1.6
TFP	5.9	3.7	3.4	4.5

Note: TFP = Total factor productivity.
[a]Weighted by income share.

growth rate of output into its components: total factor productivity and the *share-weighted* growth rates of capital and labor. Table 2 presents similar estimates, but input growth rates are not weighted by cost shares.

It is readily apparent from these tables that the Japanese economy has performed very well. Japan grew rapidly (at or near double-digit rates) throughout much of the post–World War II period and still managed to outperform Europe and the United States even after the energy crisis slowed economic growth nearly everywhere. The sources of this superior performance are less readily apparent. The relative importance of each factor varies from study to study and from year to year but, for the period before 1973, a rough estimate would assign somewhat more than one-half of Japan's economic growth to TFP and most of the balance to capital input, with only a small fraction attributed to labor input. After 1973, growth slowed dramatically, and the importance of TFP growth declined while that of capital increased, a phenomenon that also occurred in a number of other countries listed in table 2. Japan experienced a more rapid rate of growth of output and capital input than other countries, while Canada and the United States experienced the strongest growth in labor input. However, while the magnitude of the Japanese numbers is large, the *pattern* of growth (i.e., the relative importance of each source of growth) is not all that different from the other countries of table 2.

These tables also provide some support for the catching-up hypothesis. Total factor productivity grew at a slower rate in the United States over the period 1960–73 than in any other country listed in Table 2. Englander and Mittelstadt (1988) report that these data show a steady process of catch-up and convergence. However, critics of the convergence hypothesis point to a breakdown of this hypothesis when more countries are added to the list.[7]

The study of relative labor productivity levels at the industry level of detail has also been quite active in recent years. Table 3 reports the results of one such study, by Dollar and Wolff (1988), which tracks the level of labor productivity in 13 countries for the years 1963, 1970, 1976, and 1982. They conclude that there has been a convergence in labor productivity over this period, both in aggregate manufacturing and in individual manufacturing industries. They also note that of all the countries in their study, Japan started with the lowest productivity level relative to the United States. However, they also note that convergence was stronger in the aggregate than in the separate industries, suggesting an added degree of complexity to the catching-up process.

In contrast to the Dollar-Wolff paper, which studies labor productivity in manufacturing industries, Jorgenson and Nishimizu (1978) present estimates of relative TFP levels in the aggregate economies of Japan and the United States. Using the translog method developed in that paper (described above), they find that the catching-up process was largely completed by 1973. However, a subsequent study by Christensen, Cummings, and Jorgenson (1981), using revised data, reported that, in 1973, Japanese technology still lagged behind that of the United States by about 20%.

Table 2   **Real Gross Product, Factor Inputs, and Productivities in the Business Economies of Nine Countries, 1960–1973 and 1973–1979 (average annual percentage rates of change)**

Country	Real Gross Business Product	Factor Inputs			Factor Productivities		
		Total	Labor[a]	Capital[a]	Total	Labor	Capital
United States:							
1960–73	3.8	2.3	1.7	3.5	1.5	2.2	.3
1973–79	2.8	2.9	2.5	3.7	−.1	.3	−.9
1979–86	2.2	2.2	1.6	3.3	.0	.6	−1.0
Canada:							
1962–73	5.7	3.5	2.8	4.6	2.2	2.9	1.1
1973–79	4.9	3.7	2.9	5.2	1.1	2.0	−.3
1979–86	2.5	2.9	1.5	5.2	−.3	1.1	−2.6
Japan:							
1967–73	9.7	3.5	1.0	12.1	6.1	8.6	−2.4
1973–79	3.8	2.0	.6	6.8	1.8	3.2	−3.0
1979–86	3.8	2.1	1.0	5.8	1.7	2.8	−2.0
United Kingdom:							
1960–73	3.2	1.2	−.1	3.9	2.0	3.3	−.7
1973–79	1.1	.9	−.1	3.0	.2	1.3	−1.9
1979–86	1.4	.3	−.6	2.1	1.1	1.9	−.8
France:							
1965–73	6.4	2.1	.5	5.7	4.3	5.9	.6
1973–79	3.5	1.4	.0	4.7	2.1	3.5	−1.2
1979–86	1.5	.2	−1.0	3.0	1.3	2.5	−1.4
West Germany:							
1961–73	4.6	1.8	−.3	5.6	2.8	4.9	−1.1
1973–79	2.4	.6	−1.0	3.5	1.8	3.4	−1.1
1979–86	1.6	.8	−.4	2.9	.8	2.0	−1.3
Italy:							
1961–73	5.6	.9	−.9	5.2	4.7	6.5	.4
1973–79	2.9	1.3	.5	3.4	1.6	2.4	−.4
1979–86	1.9	1.1	.6	2.5	.7	1.2	−.7
OECD average:							
1960–73	5.2	2.4	1.1	5.6	2.8	4.1	−.4
1973–79	2.9	2.2	1.3	4.4	.7	1.6	−1.4
1979–86	2.3	1.7	.9	3.6	.6	1.4	−1.3

Source: Englander and Mittelstadt (1988), based on the national source data and Organization for Economic Cooperation and Development estimates.
Note: Errors due to rounding.   [a]Unweighted.

Finally, it should be noted that the results summarized in these tables contain an important lesson for "consumers" of growth analysis. There is substantial variation across studies, and the reader should be careful to note the following characteristics of any study: the time period covered, the scope of the economic activity covered, the methods used, and the definitions of output

Table 3   Value Added per Workhour in Manufacturing in 12 Industrial
            Countries Relative to the United States, 1963–1982 (index numbers,
            United States = 100)[a]

	1963	1970	1976	1982
United States	100	100	100	100
United Kingdom	52[b]	60	94	88
Italy	45[c]	50	58	88
Sweden	52	68	72	78
Canada	77	80	77	76
Germany	54[d]	68	70	68
France	53	64	59	67
Japan	26	49	50	61
Denmark	41	54	54	59
Australia	47	53	55	56
Finland	34	48	45	51
Austria	37	47	45	49
Norway	46	58	54	49
Coefficient of variation	.36	.24	.26	.23
Unweighted average (excluding United States)	47	58	61	66

Source: Dollar and Wolff (1988).
[a]Calculated from aggregate data for all manufacturing.
[b]1968 data
[c]1967 data
[d]1965 data

and input. Denison (1962), for example, uses national income as the definition of output, while the other studies use gross product. When combined with a measure of capital stock that is heavily weighted to gross stock, a national income measure of real product tends to reduce the apparent importance of capital as a source of growth. On the other hand, studies that include the residential and household sectors of the economy tend to increase the apparent importance of capital and reduce the importance of TFP.

Summary of the Conference Proceedings

Overview

The papers included in this volume cover a variety of subjects and techniques. To facilitate reading, they are grouped into two general categories. The first contains papers dealing with the measurement of productivity in Japan and the United States. The first two papers in this group present results based on the conventional index-number and econometric approaches to estimating the structure of production. The next four papers introduce capacity utilization and adjustment costs into the analysis: some treat some inputs—principally capital—as being fixed in the short run, while the fourth investigates the complementarity of capital and energy and its impact on measured TFP growth. The last paper discusses the measurement of TFP in an open-economy context.

The second category of papers discusses various issues in the measurement of, or market for, capital and labor. The first set of four papers range over the application of the perpetual inventory method to Japanese investment data, the taxation of income from capital in Japan, the measurement and interpretation of Tobin's Q, and the relationship between R&D capital and productivity growth. The last three papers deal with labor input and include a discussion of quality change in the Japanese labor force, investment in firm-specific labor skills, and the effects of work attitudes on production costs in the two countries. Comments that were prepared by conference discussants are included when available.

The Structure of Production in Japan and the U.S.

The paper by Jorgenson and Kuroda presents estimates of the relative levels of TFP in a variety of industries in Japan and the United States that are based on the translog index method developed by Jorgenson and Nishimizu (1978). This paper is an updated version of the original paper presented at the 1985 conference—Jorgenson, Kuroda, and Nishimizu (1987), which covered the period 1960–79—and extends the estimates of relative TFP levels to the period 1960–85. Since the comparison of relative TFP levels sheds light on the "catching-up" hypothesis (the idea that Japan was able to grow rapidly by importing foreign technology) and provides partial insight into the pattern of comparative advantage in bilateral trade, the extension of the original study to these additional years is particularly important.

The authors reported in the original conference paper that the level of TFP in Japan had passed or reached that of the United States in nine of the 28 industries studied, and that Japan was expected to close the gap in six others. In the revised and updated version of this paper, Japan has reached or surpassed the United States in 12 industries and is expected to close the TFP gap in three others. Thus, in both 1979 and 1985, Japan has or is expected to have technological leadership in half of the industries studied. The United States is expected to have an efficiency advantage in the remaining half.

These results suggest that catching up is an uneven process, if it is operative at all. Some industries seem to catch up and others do not, and the catch-up pattern appears to change from period to period. This may reflect industry-level differences in the ability to "play catch-up," or it may reflect differences in measurement procedures or measurement difficulties during periods of macroeconomic turbulence, such as occurred after 1973. Or it may reveal that the notion of catching up is too simplistic or that the catch-up effect had worked itself out by the mid-1970s. In any event, there is little evidence in this paper to complement the Dollar-Wolff (1988) finding of a general convergence of labor productivity at the industry level in Japan and the United States. That is, the convergence of labor productivity was apparently not caused by a convergence in one of the factors explaining the growth rate of labor productivity, that is, total factor productivity.[8]

Jorgenson and Kuroda also present estimates of relative product prices, adjusted for purchasing power parity. They report that, by 1985, the relative price of labor input in Japan was only 50% of the U.S. level, the relative cost of capital was 75% of the U.S. level, and that relative product prices in Japan were only 83% of those of the United States. They also find that a lower product price in one country is generally associated with a higher level of TFP in that country, suggesting that the TFP level is an important determinant of relative product price.

The paper by Jorgenson, Sakuramoto, Yoshioka, and Kuroda is a companion piece to the original TFP-level comparison paper presented at the conference. This second paper presents econometric estimates of the parameters of a translog production function and thus represents the second of the two major approaches to analyzing the structure of production (the index-number approach of the first paper is the other). The translog production function is parameterized so as to jointly estimate the structure of production in the United States and Japan for each of the 28 industries included in the study. Parameter estimates for each industry are presented for the time period 1960–79, but partial elasticities of substitution are not presented.

The principal results can be summarized briefly. The factor substitution parameters and biases in technical change are distributed rather heterogeneously across industries, implying diversity in the structure of production. Production in Japan is also shown to differ from production in the United States with Japanese industry generally found to be more capital intensive and material-input intensive and U.S. industry more labor intensive. That is, if input prices were the same in both countries, Japanese industries would tend to have higher capital-labor and materials-labor ratios (though actual ratios depend on differences in input prices). It is interesting to note, in this regard, that Japan had a significantly higher savings rate during the period in question while the United States had a higher growth rate of labor input. However, it must also be noted that the authors report that technical change was predominantly capital saving *and* laborsaving, but materials using, in both countries.

The next group of papers extend the conventional framework for measuring productivity change to allow for the possibility that some factors cannot adjust rapidly or costlessly to shifts in relative prices. This possibility introduces a variety of potential biases into conventional analyses of economic growth, which uses relative price ratios as a surrogate for the corresponding marginal rate of substitution.[9] And, even when bias is not present, the short-run fixity of some factors (termed "quasi-fixed" factors) leads to a distinction between changes in TFP due to improvements in technology and changes due to variation in the degree of utilization of these factors.

This distinction is central to the paper by Fuss and Waverman, who present a translog cost function analysis of the Canadian, Japanese, and U.S. auto industries over the period 1970–84. In the Fuss-Waverman framework, the growth in unit production costs is decomposed into the weighted growth rates of input prices and the growth rate of TFP (this is the economic dual of the decomposition of output into the weighted growth rates of input and TFP). The growth rate of TFP is then decomposed into three further components: technical change, capacity utilization, and scale economies, thus adding structure to the conventional TFP residual.

The empirical results reveal the role of TFP growth, and its individual components, in the evolution of unit costs and price competition in this important industry. Measured in yen, the average cost of producing autos grew at an average annual rate of 2.5% over the period 1970–84.[10] This rate is the sum of two effects: an increase in input prices drove costs up to 5.5%, and TFP growth offset 3% of this increase. Most of the increase in TFP was due to technical change (over four-fifths), while scale economies accounted for the rest of TFP growth. Changes in capacity utilization accounted for almost nothing.

In contrast, the average cost of auto production in the United States grew at an average annual rate of 6.3% over this period, measured in dollars. The growth of input prices increased cost by 7.4%, and this was offset by TFP growth of 1.3%. Technical change accounted for 0.8% of the TFP number, while scale economies accounted for 0.2% and capacity utilization for 0.3%. However, variations in capacity utilization are seen to be far more important when subperiods are considered: from 1970 to 1980, technical change proceeded at an annual rate of 1.1%, but this was offset by deteriorating utilization of 0.7% a year; this turned around during the 1980–84 period, with technical change proceeding at only 0.2% while increases in capacity utilization reduced costs at a rate of 2.7% per year. This effect was so strong that overall average cost did not grow at all during the 1980–84, and the U.S. auto industry actually outperformed the Japanese auto industry in this dimension of competitiveness over this period.

However, for the 15-year period as a whole, the average cost of producing autos in Japan grew at a significantly slower rate than in the United States (the differential was 3.8% a year), and the source of this advantage was split equally between a slower growth of input prices and improvement in efficiency due to scale economies and technical change.[11] This cost advantage was largely offset, however, by an appreciation in the value of the yen relative to U.S. and Canadian dollars. When this appreciation is taken into account, the authors find that the Japanese cost advantage grew at only 0.7% per year, as measured in Canadian dollars.

The paper by Nadiri and Prucha analyzes productivity change in another important industrial sector: the electrical machinery industries of Japan and the United States. This industry is a major success story in both countries. In the United States, the electrical machinery industry outperformed the manufacturing sector as a whole by growing at 4.2% a year from 1968 to 1973, and 4.9% from 1973 to 1979. In Japan, output grew at 16.9% during the first period, and then fell to 6.4% during the second period. However, despite this drop-off in output growth, Japan managed to increase its share of free-world exports in electrical machinery from 22% in 1971 to 48% in 1981.

Nadiri and Prucha develop a dynamic factor demand model of the electrical machinery industry in which capital and R&D are treated as quasi-fixed inputs. The technology is modeled in terms of a restricted cost function that explicitly incorporates dynamic costs of adjustment, and that is fitted to annual U.S. data for the period 1960–80 and Japanese data for the period 1968–80. Parameter estimates are presented, as are price and output elasticities distinguished by the short run, intermediate run, and long run. The short-run estimates are found to be significantly more inelastic than the longer-run counterparts and, while this is not surprising, it does suggest that the quasi fixity of some inputs is of economic importance and that short-run adjustments to price changes may be very different than long-run adjustments. The authors also note that the pattern of elasticities is quite similar in the two countries, with the own-price elasticities of capital and R&D somewhat larger in Japan and the own-price elasticities of labor and materials somewhat larger in the United States. The cost shares of each are also very similar in the two countries.

The estimated cost function is then used to decompose the growth rate of output into the contributions of inputs (capital, R&D, labor, materials), the direct effect of adjustment costs, technical change, and a residual. The bulk of U.S. and Japanese growth over the periods 1968–73 and 1973–79 is accounted for by the contribution of the inputs. For the United States, the average rate of technical change over the two periods is 0.73% and 0.86%, and for Japan the corresponding figures are 1.55% and 2.55%. Furthermore, the direct adjustment cost effect is small, except for the higher growth era before 1973 in Japan. However, this does not imply that the adjustment cost model is largely irrelevant, since adjustment costs also affect the weights assigned to the various inputs.

Of the input effects, the materials effect is shown to be the most important source of growth in the electrical machinery industries of both countries. Capital formation is seen to play a more important role in Japan than in the United States, but R&D is somewhat more significant in the United States over the period 1968–73. It is perhaps relevant to note that the authors show that the ratio of tangible capital investment to gross output is higher in Japan, but the ratio of R&D spending to gross output is higher in the United States.[12]

The authors also present an analysis of the conventionally measured TFP residual similar to the one carried out by Fuss and Waverman, although the latter is done with respect to the cost "dual" and does not model adjustment costs explicitly. The growth rate of TFP is decomposed into a scale effect, technical change, temporary equilibrium and adjustment cost effects, and an unexplained residual. The scale effect is shown to predominate, and, combined with the technical change effect, it explains most of the conventional TFP residual (a somewhat different pattern than observed in the auto industry). There is no simple relationship between this decomposition and the previous decomposition of the pseudo–TFP residual.

The paper by Morrison continues the analysis of quasi-fixed inputs in U.S. and Japanese manufacturing industries. In this paper, however, both capital and labor are treated as fixed in the short run, and energy and materials inputs are treated as variable. The parameters of a generalized Leontief cost function are estimated using annual data for total manufacturing over the period 1952–81 for the United States and 1957–81 for Japan.

The results of this analysis are similar to those of the preceding two papers. The parameters characterizing production in the two countries are, with a few exceptions, quite similar. Also, the short-run price elasticities tend to be significantly less elastic than their long-run counterparts, suggesting that production plans are less flexible in the short run (and that the extension of the conventional analysis to allow for the quasi fixity of some inputs is empirically important). The author also reports that capital and energy appear to be even stronger complements in Japan than in the United States, in contrast to some previous studies, and that labor and energy were less substitutable. This, in turn, suggests that Japanese manufacturing industries were not necessarily in a better position to absorb the energy price shocks of the 1970s.

Morrison also presents estimates of capacity utilization and corrected TFP. The trends in capacity utilization are similar in the two countries, but with Japan displaying a larger decline after 1970. The implied adjustment to the TFP residual is, however, rather small. For the United States, TFP growth is found to average 0.77% per year for the period 1956–81 using the author's "quantity variant," and this is adjusted downward to an average annual rate of 0.74%. For Japan, the corresponding figures are 1.30% and 1.00%, implying that the adjustment for capacity utilization is somewhat more significant, but nonetheless of a second order of importance. This finding is also generally valid for the year-to-year changes in TFP.

The study by Berndt, Mori, Sawa, and Wood also examines the implications of capital-energy complementarity for the measurement of capital and TFP growth. Although energy's share of total cost (and thus its weight in the sources of growth equation) is small, the close link between energy use and capital utilization could result in a situation in which an increase in energy prices would render energy-inefficient capital obsolete and thereby reduce the effective amount of capital input obtained from a given stock of capital.[13] In order to examine this effect, the authors develop a putty-clay model in which each vintage of capital is built with a particular energy intensity based on the relative energy-capital prices prevailing at the date the capital was placed in service. Each vintage can be operated at a different intensity by switching labor from one vintage to another. Since energy and capital are "bundled," a rise in the cost of energy will cause those vintages designed under the assumption of lower energy prices to be operated less intensively.

In this framework, utilization is defined as the ratio of effective capital input to the stock of capital. Utilization is then shown to depend on the relative prices of capital services and energy expected to prevail in the future and on the ex ante elasticity of substitution between capital and energy. Changes in the rate of utilization are shown to introduce biases in the measurement of total factor productivity: the TFP measured by conventional procedures for estimating capital input is equal to the "true" TFP measure plus the rate of change of utilization weighted by capital's cost share.

This model is simulated for different values of the elasticity of substitution between energy and capital, using data on Japanese and U.S. manufacturing for the years 1958–81. The authors find that their index of utilization is roughly constant in both countries up to 1973 and that a large reduction occurs thereafter (for the largest value of the elasticity, the reduction is 25% for the United States and 22% for Japan). This result leads to an increase in the "true" TFP residual of up to 0.13% per year for the U.S. for the period 1973–81, and a corresponding annual increase of up to 0.48% for Japan. The U.S. figure is too small to account for much of the decline in TFP occurring after 1973, but the number for Japan is substantially larger and does explain about a third of the growth slowdown in TFP after 1973.

The paper by Morrison and Diewert shifts direction and offers a novel extension of the standard productivity model. A distinction is made in the standard model between movements along a production function and shifts in that function. Since the shift in the function implies an increase in output from given inputs, the shift effect represents a way for an economy to increase its welfare from a given resource base. Morrison and Diewert point to two additional ways that welfare in any given year can be improved in an open economy: an improvement in the economy's terms of trade (a fall in the price of imported goods relative to exports) and an increase in the trade deficit. As with a shift in the production function, these two mechanisms allow for increased domestic consumption and investment from a given amount of resources (albeit a transitory increase).

Morrison and Diewert develop a model, in which the trade effects are embedded in the standard sources-of-growth model, and present estimates of the three effects for Japan and the U.S. for the years 1967–82. They report that the annual growth rate of TFP averaged 3% for Japan and 0% for the United States (which is not surprising or necessarily inconsistent with other studies, since the starting year of the analysis was near a peak in the business cycle and the end year near a trough). The terms-of-trade effect for Japan is found to be rather small over the entire period (0.5% per year) but shows considerable year-to-year variation. The trade effect is found to be far less important for the United States, presumably reflecting the greater importance of foreign trade in the Japanese economy. The deficit effect also appears to be more important for Japan, although it appears to be highly transitory. However, while the terms of trade and deficit effects are rather small during the 1967–82 period, the recent changes in the value of the dollar and the massive U.S. trade deficit might well enhance the importance of the these effects in an updated version of this paper.

Capital and Labor

The paper by Dean, Darrough, and Neef considers one of the most important issues in empirical growth analysis: the problem of measuring capital stocks. While almost all economic measurement is problematic, the measurement of capital is especially subject to ambiguities and difficulties. A stock of capital provides a flow of services over a number of years, and this flow is, for the most part, not directly observable because capital is largely owner utilized. For the same reason, the price of capital services—the implicit rent that the owner must charge himself for the use of the asset—is also not observed directly. The measurement of this key variable must therefore proceed by indirect procedures, like the perpetual inventory method (PIM) and the Hall-Jorgenson user cost formula.

These procedures start with an estimate of the nominal value of investment spending in each year, $P_I(t)I(t)$. An estimate of the price of investment goods—the "investment deflator" $P_I(t)$—is then used to split nominal investment spending into price and quantity components. The quantity of investment is then cumulated into an estimate of capital stock using the PIM: with a constant rate of depreciation δ, this can be written as

$$(6) \qquad K(t) = I(t) + (1-\delta)K(t-1),$$

which states that capital stock in period t is the sum of investment in period t and the undepreciated amount of capital carried forward from the preceding period. This approach requires a benchmark value for $K(t)$ or a sufficiently long time series on $I(t)$ that the initial level of $K(t)$ can be ignored.[14]

The price of capital services can be imputed using the formula developed by Jorgenson (1963) and Hall and Jorgenson (1967). With perfect foresight and no taxation, this formula is written as

$$(7) \qquad P_K(t) = (r(t) + \delta)P_I(t) - \Delta P_I(t),$$

which states that the implicit rent charged on owner-utilized capital must cover the opportunity cost of capital (the discount rate r times the investment deflator) and depreciation (the rate of depreciation δ times the deflator) less any revaluation of the asset. Given data on the δ used in the PIM, the investment deflator, and an estimate of the discount rate r, this equation can be used to impute a value for the service price.

The paper by Dean, Darrough, and Neef describes how this framework can be implemented for Japanese manufacturing industry. Data on nominal investment from four sources—the Census of Manufactures, the Economic Planning Agency, the Annual Report on the Corporate Sector, and the Report on the Corporate Industry Investment Survey—are described and compared (their Table 5 provides a detailed comparison of these sources). A procedure for estimating the rate of depreciation, δ, from these sources and from capital benchmarks derived from the National Wealth Surveys is then described, and estimates of δ are reported for several types of assets. Deflators, user costs, and aggregation procedures are also discussed.

The authors conclude that the Census of Manufactures is the most reliable source of investment data. More important, they demonstrate that there is considerable variation in estimated capital stocks and depreciation rates calculated from the different data sets: estimates of the growth rate of capital stock based on census data average 3.9% per year over the period 1973–81, while Economic Planning Agency data yielded an estimate of 2.3% and Annual Report data implied a growth rate of 4.2%. These are significant differences considering that they represent growth rates compounded over eight years. Such a finding serves to reinforce the crucial point that different data sources and procedures can lead to very different results.

The paper by Kikutani and Tachibanaki examines the impact of the Japanese tax code on taxation of income from capital. This is an important problem for Japan-U.S. productivity comparisons, which attempt to apply a common analytical framework (e.g., the user cost of capital—eq. [7]) to the different institutional settings of two countries. The accurate specification and modeling of the relevant institutions in each country is often the most difficult part of such international comparisons. The tax codes of Japan and the United States bear witness to this problem: not only are the tax codes of both countries exceedingly complex, the resulting tax treatment of capital income is also very different in the two countries.

Kikutani and Tachibanaki present estimates of the marginal effective tax rate on income from capital, building on earlier work by Shoven and Tachibanaki (1988) and King and Fullerton (1984). The current paper extends the coverage of the Shoven and Tachibanaki paper from 1980 to the trio of years 1961, 1971, and 1980 and also takes into account additional features of the tax code like the "special depreciation" and "tax-free reserve" provisions. The tax treatment of the banking sector is also discussed in detail. Marginal effective tax rates are calculated at various rates of inflation and presented by class of asset, industry, source of finance, and owner. It is shown that the overall effective tax rate decreased from 24.7% in 1961 to 15.0% in 1970, and finally to 9.6% in 1980. The comparable U.S. figures are 48.4%, 47.2%, and 37.2%, respectively.

Several conclusions emerge from these results. The combined effects of the corporate and individual incomes taxes imply a heavier burden on capital income in the United States than in Japan over the period 1961–80, and effective tax rates fell in both countries over this period.[15] The authors show that this can be attributed in large part to the greater use of debt finance in Japan and the lower effective tax rate on interest income. Indeed, it is interesting to note that the effective tax rate associated with debt finance is − 55% in 1980, while the tax rate on equity-financed capital is around 70%. The average of the two is 9.6%, so it is apparent that the debt-equity ratio is a critical determinant of the average rate. Furthermore, the authors present a simulation for the year 1980 in which they replace the Japanese debt-equity ratio with the U.S. figure and show that the overall Japanese tax rate rises from 9.6% to 29.0% (furthermore, if Japanese interest income is subjected to U.S. tax treatment, the overall Japanese tax rate rises from 9.6% to 40.3%, which is larger than the overall U.S. tax rate of 37.2%).

The authors also explore the impact of inflation on effective tax rates in both countries. They show that effective rates rise with inflation in the United States, but fall with inflation in Japan. This curiosity is attributed to the greater use of debt finance in Japan and to the lower effective tax rate on interest income.

The next paper, by Fumio Hayashi, continues the analysis of the Japanese tax code within the framework of Tobin's Q analysis. Tobin's marginal Q is conventionally defined as the present value of the income accruing to an additional unit of capital (as reflected by the financial value of the firm or industry) divided by the cost of purchasing that unit. With competitive markets and the absence of adjustment costs and taxes, a value of Q greater than one indicates that an additional unit of capital is worth more than it costs, implying that the capital stock should be expanded. Conversely, a Q less than one signals that the capital stock is too large; equilibrium occurs when Q equals one. This is equivalent to the neoclassical condition that the user cost (eq. [7]) should be equal to the value of the marginal product of capital.

When adjustment costs are present, a variant of this optimal investment rule must be used. Adjustment costs introduce a gap between the value of the marginal product of capital and the user cost, and Hayashi derives a version of Q that is shown to be equivalent to the present value of this gap. This version is adjusted for various features of the Japanese tax code, including the special depreciation and tax-free reserve provisions discussed by Kikutani and Tachibanaki.

Hayashi describes the steps necessary to implement his model, including the problem of using average Q to measure the marginal value of Q. He presents estimates for the years 1956–81, and shows that Q is a significant factor in explaining Japanese investment up to 1974. He also notes that Q fails to provide a good explanation of investment behavior after this time, that is, after the OPEC oil crisis, and speculates that the failure may be due to mismeasurement or omitted variables. It may be noted, however, that a similar pattern occurs in the U.S. data: Q theory explains U.S. investment behavior fairly well up to the energy crisis, and does poorly for the rest of the 1970s. Thus, while mismeasurement of key variables in both countries cannot be ruled out, it seems more likely that omitted variables or specification errors are the source of the problem.

While the preceding papers have dealt primarily with the accumulation of tangible capital, the paper by Griliches and Mairesse examines the role of another type of capital: intangible "knowledge" capital. The concept of a "stock of technical knowledge" is a departure from the conventional Solow (1957) dichotomy, since advances in technical knowledge are associated with systematic changes in a measured input (the accumulated stock of R&D investment) and not with residual shifts in the production function. Indeed, the attempt to estimate a stock of knowledge may be regarded as an attempt to build additional structure into the sources of growth model.[16]

Griliches and Mairesse begin by comparing aggregate data on R&D spending in Japan and the United States. They observe that there is little difference in the level or sectoral distribution of company-financed R&D investment in the two countries (although there is a larger difference in government-financed R&D spending). They also note that most of the company-financed R&D is done in three industries—electrical equipment, transportation, and chemicals—and that large firms account for almost all of the U.S. R&D spending but only three-quarters of Japanese R&D. These data are then compared with the firm-level data used in the subsequent analysis. The authors find that the U.S. company data are roughly consistent with the aggregate data but report that the Japanese data appear to under report R&D spending.

These data, which cover the years 1973–80, are used to estimate the parameters of a Cobb-Douglas production function expressed in growth rate form (recall eq. [2]). The authors find that the estimated R&D coefficients are of similar size in both countries and statistically significant (except for Japan when industry dummy variables are introduced). They also report that estimated coefficients imply that R&D contributed around 0.5% per year to the growth of labor productivity in both countries. The principal finding, however, is that R&D investment cannot account for the mean difference in the growth rates of Japan and the United States. That is, the generally superior performance of labor productivity and TFP in Japan cannot be attributed either to the intensity or "fecundity" of R&D expenditures. While this may be due to the measurement problems described by the authors, it nevertheless casts doubt on one possible explanation of U.S.-Japan productivity growth differentials.

The last three papers deal with the measurement of labor input. The first of the three, by Hajime Imamura, presents an analysis of the sources of "quality" change using the Divisia index framework. As noted above, the growth rate of output can be decomposed into the growth rates of capital and labor, weighted by their cost shares, plus the growth rate of total factor productivity. This decomposition can be taken a step further by allocating the growth rate of labor input into a component due to the growth rate of total hours worked and a component due to the shift in the composition of the work force.

The nature of the compositional changes can be seen by the following example. Suppose that there are two types of worker, Y (young) and O (old), that the growth rate of hours worked by young and old is $\dot{\ell}_Y$ and $\dot{\ell}_O$ percent a year, respectively, and that the corresponding wage-shares are s_Y and s_O. The Divisia index of labor input is defined as the share-weighted average of these two growth rates:

(8)
$$\dot{\ell} = s_Y \dot{\ell}_Y + s_O \dot{\ell}_O.$$

This expression can be modified to account for shifts in the composition of the work force by simultaneously adding and subtracting the (unweighted) growth rate of total hours worked, $\dot{h}$, in the right-hand side of this equation (it can be introduced in this way because the wage-shares sum to one):

(9)
$$\dot{\ell} = \dot{h} + s_Y(\dot{\ell}_Y - \dot{h}) + s_O(\dot{\ell}_O - \dot{h}).$$

In this form, the growth rate of the Divisia index of labor input is the sum of the growth rate of total hours plus the share-weighted sum of the shifting fraction of total hours worked by each type of worker. The latter measures the impact on output growth if the composition of the work force shifts toward the category with the smallest output elasticity (as measured by the cost shares).[17] For this reason, the composition effect is termed "quality change."

Imamura applies a more complex version of this framework to Japanese labor-force data and compares his results to corresponding results for the United States. Japanese workers are classified according to gender, age, education, and occupation, and the Divisia index of quality change is for the period 1960–79 by major industry. The principal findings include: (1) quality change was an increasingly important source of growth in Japanese labor input and, after 1970, served as an offset to the negative growth rate of hours worked; (2) the age category had by far the most important direct effect of quality change, with education and occupation sharing a distant second and the gender category in the last place; (3) quality change was a more important source of economic growth in Japan than in the United States, according to a comparison with the study by Chinloy (1980); (4) where age was the most important quality dimension in Japan, education was the most important dimension in the United States.

The importance of the age dimension in Japan is hardly a major surprise, in view of the tendency toward seniority-based labor compensation in that country. If wage differentials are interpreted as wholly due to productivity differences (as they are in the Divisia framework), a seniority-based wage system combined with an aging work force will necessarily produce a strong labor-quality effect. One must therefore question whether wages are based entirely on current productivity or whether they reflect other factors like implicit contracts, in which wages are back loaded in order to attract workers with low quit rates and to reduce incentives to shirk. Or, are the seniority-based wages largely due to a cultural respect for age and seniority?

The paper by Hong Tan investigates some of these issues. Tan hypothesizes that a higher rate of technical change induces firms to want workers with firm-specific skills, which in turn increases the incentive to induce low quit rates by rewarding job tenure. In this model, workers and firms share training costs through low initial wages; training results in higher productivity, and thus wages will rise with job tenure. Tan then compares his model with the competing model of implicit contract theory, in which workers initially accept wages that are less than their marginal product in order to obtain job tenure and higher wages in the future.

The paper presents evidence on these competing models, using U.S. data from the May 1979 Current Population Survey and Japan's 1977 Employment Status Survey. These data show that American workers tend to have shorter job tenure (8.1 years) than their Japanese counterparts (12.2 years) but more schooling (12.9 vs. 11.0 years). The wage in each country (in logarithmic form) is regressed on age (a surrogate for experience), tenure, schooling, total factor productivity growth, and output growth. Wage-experience and wage-tenure profiles are found to rise more rapidly in Japan than in the United States, and the latter is found to be steeper than the former. The difference between the return to experience is interpreted as a return to firm-specific training, and the author concludes that Japanese firms invest more in firm-specific skills than do American firms.

The hypothesis that the observed difference in firm-specific skills is positively related to the difference in TFP growth rates is clearly supported by aggregate data on the growth of the U.S. and Japanese economies. However, the hypothesis is not confirmed when interindustry variations in TFP are linked to variations in skill investment within the United States and Japan. While there is a positive association between the two variables among U.S. industries, the Japanese data do not reveal a significant association. Since this finding leaves room for other explanations, Tan compares his explanation of seniority-based wages with a leading competitor, the implicit contract explanation. Using U.S. data from the National Longitudinal Survey, he finds a correlation between a direct measure of training and TFP growth and concludes that the evidence favors his hypothesis. In sum, these results suggest a link between wage differentials and differences in worker productivity, and thus they tend to support the use of the Divisia labor-quality adjustments.

Differences in age, experience, education, and training of the labor force are not the only source of difference between workers in Japan and the United States. There is a widespread view that the Japanese simply work harder and more diligently than their American counterparts. While this view may be supported largely by casual empiricism, it is amusing to note that the Japanese government has recently proposed a new holiday, "Happy Couple Day," in an effort to reduce the perceived workaholic tendencies of the Japanese labor force.

The paper by Lam, Norsworthy, and Zabala attempts to probe this issue by examining differences in worker attitudes in the United States and Japan. Although attitude and effort are not necessarily the same thing, differences in attitude may serve as a proxy for differences in the intensity of work effort and commitment to product quality. With this in mind, Lam et al. collected data on strikes, labor disputes, and quit rates in both countries, with the rationale that labor unrest is related to worker attitude. These variables are added to a conventional translog cost function analysis of the manufacturing sectors of both countries. The authors find that strikes and grievances have a larger impact on costs in the United States than in Japan. In the United States, these factors increased the cost of production by around 8% in the 1950s and 1960s, and this increased to 12% in 1980. On the other hand, production costs in Japanese manufacturing were higher by only 7% in 1965 and this fell to about 3% in 1978. These results suggest that a significant cost advantage accrues to Japanese manufactured goods as a result of conditions in the workplace.

Conclusions

The last two decades have been a steady advance in the methods of empirical productivity analysis: the development of flexible functional forms, like the translog, for use in estimating the structure of production; the introduction of duality theory into empirical analyses of production and growth; the extension of conventional models to allow for the possibility that capital cannot adjust immediately or costlessly to changes in input prices or desired output levels; and, the elaboration of the index-number approach to measuring economic growth and the linkage of this approach to the corresponding parametric procedures. The papers in this volume may be regarded as an application of these new developments to the comparison of U.S. and Japanese economic growth.

The results presented in the various papers generally confirm the conventional view that Japan experienced an extraordinary surge of growth, from the mid-1950s through 1973, that far exceeded the rate of U.S. growth, which was itself quite strong. After 1973, growth slowed in both countries and the relative growth rates narrowed. However, while there is widespread acceptance of this pattern, there is no agreement about its cause. No single causal factor—no "smoking gun"—emerges from these papers to explain why Japan was able to grow so fast. Indeed, several authors comment on the similarity of the structure of production in the countries. By the same token, there is little agreement about the factors causing the post-1973 slowdown in Japan and the United States. There is similarly a lack of agreement about "catching up" as an explanation of comparative growth trends. This notion is intuitively appealing and, in light of recent analyses of labor-productivity growth, is surely part of the answer. However, several papers in this volume suggest that the process is more complex than the simple convergence of labor productivity at the industry level. According to Jorgenson and Kuroda, the total factor productivity levels in some U.S. industries are increasing relative to the corresponding Japanese levels, while Japan has already surpassed the U.S. in other industries. And, while they do not examine the time trends in comparative TFP levels, the Nadiri and Prucha industry study finds little evidence of convergence in TFP growth rates after the 1973 dropoff.

That there remain many puzzles and unresolved issues is hardly surprising. The papers in this volume are essentially limited to the analysis of one subset of equations governing the economic system: that is, the production function and associated equilibrium conditions. Even complete knowledge of this subsystem could not lead to a complete understanding of the growth process, and our knowledge of the production subsystem is far from complete. Much more work needs to be done on the data used to test the structure of production, with particular emphasis on the development of better measures of capital in all its forms—tangible, intangible, and human. The formal modeling of production also needs attention. It would be, for example, desirable to move away from the paradigm of pure competition that underlies much of the conventional analysis of growth and move toward models that incorporate a more realistic description of market structure, account for uncertainty and expectation-formation, and allow for differences in institutions across countries and regions. Further progress in the modeling of productivity change is also desirable, since the residuals and time trends of many, if not most, conventional analyses are poor substitutes for direct measures of technical and organizational progress. Finally, our understanding of the process of economic growth at the level of plants and firms needs to be integrated with our analyses of growth (and fluctuations) at the industry and economywide level of aggregation.

Work on this agenda is underway, and the papers in this volume are part of this trend. They present many interesting facts and ideas (far more than have been reviewed in this introduction), but they also remind us that, while much progress has been made, there is much still to learn about the processes of economic growth.

Appendix

Logarithmic differentiation of production function (1) yields

$$(1')\qquad \dot{q}(t) = \varepsilon_K(t)k(t) + \varepsilon_L(t)l(t) + \dot{a}(t),$$

where $\dot{a}(t)$ is the rate of change of the production function $F(\cdot)$ with respect to time, holding capital and labor constant: $[\partial F/\partial t)/F]$. It is evident that $(1')$ is a generalization of (2) where $\dot{a}(t) = \lambda$, $\varepsilon_K(t) = \alpha$, and $\varepsilon_L(t) = \beta$. It is also true that if input prices are equated to marginal products, the output elasticities, $\varepsilon_K(t)$ and $\varepsilon_L(t)$, are equivalent to the value shares, $s_K(t)$ and $s_L(t)$, since the conditions $P_Q(\partial Q/\partial K) = P_K$ and $P_Q(\partial Q/\partial L) = P_L$ imply

$$\varepsilon_K = \frac{\partial Q}{\partial K}\frac{K}{Q} = \frac{P_K K}{P_Q Q} = s_K,$$

and

$$\varepsilon_L = \frac{\partial Q}{\partial L}\frac{L}{Q} = \frac{P_L L}{P_Q Q} = s_L.$$

This being true, it follows immediately that the total factor productivity index defined on the right-hand side of $(1')$ is equivalent to $\dot{a}(t)$, leading to a geometric interpretation of the total factor productivity index as the shift in the production function (1), and the index $s_K(t)\dot{k}(t) + s_L(t)\dot{\ell}(t)$ as a movement along the production function. Note the right-hand side of (4) is related to the cost function (3) when price equals marginal cost.

Notes

1. There are numerous sources that provide a more detailed description of the procedures used in growth analysis. Solow (1957), Kendrick (1961), Denison (1962), and Jorgenson and Griliches (1967) set forth the basic sources of growth framework. The surveys by Nadiri (1970), Hulten (1986), Maddison (1987), and Griliches (1987) provide more recent descriptions of the relevant issues and methods, as does the material presented in the Bureau of Labor Statistics publication *Trends in Multifactor Productivity* (U.S. Department of labor 1983). However, this list hardly exhausts the relevant literature. *Asia's New Giant* (Patrick and Rosovsky 1976) is a key source for comparative economic studies of the United States and Japan.

2. The term "total factor productivity" is used to denote the collective productivity of all inputs taken together and is synonymous with "multifactor productivity" and "joint productivity." This concept of productivity must be distinguished from single-factor measures like labor productivity. The latter is defined as rate of change of output per unit labor and, in the notation of equation (5), can be written as

$(5')$ $\qquad\qquad\qquad \dot{q}(t) - \dot{\ell}(t) = s_K(t)(\dot{k}(t) - \dot{\ell}(t)) + \dot{a}(t),$

under the assumption of constant returns to scale. In this form, the sources-of-growth equation states that the growth rate of labor productivity is equal to the share-weighted growth rate of the capital-labor ratio plus the growth rate of total factor productivity.

3. A derivation of this key result is given in the appendix below.

4. The issues involved in aggregation with intermediate goods are reviewed in Hulten (1978). It may be noted that industry-level estimates of TFP growth can be computed using a value-added measure of real output. However, the resulting estimates are theoretically correct only if the underlying production function exhibits the property of weak separability in the primary inputs. When this holds, aggregation can proceed with weights that sum to one.

5. Under constant returns to scale in production and Hicks-neutral technical change, eq. (3) can be written in such a way that the price of output is equal to a function of input prices (w) times the index of TFP (A), i.e., $p = A^{-1}\phi(w)$. Differences in product price, measured in domestic currency units, must therefore be due to differences in the relative level of TFP or due to differences in $\phi(w)$.

6. The nature of the relative TFP index can be illustrated in the following example. If a good is produced in the United States with a technology $Q_u = A_u F(X_u)$, where A_u is an index of TFP and X_u a vector of inputs, while the same good is produced in Japan with the technology $Q_J = A_J G(X_J)$, the translog index of relative TFP measures the ratio A_J/A_U. In actual applications, the technology is assumed to have the translog form and technical change is not restricted to Hicks neutrality.

7. See Baumol, Blackman, and Wolff (1989) for a detailed discussion of this issue and references to the relevant literature.

8. Recall, here, that the growth rate of labor productivity is equal to the growth rate of the capital-labor ratio, weighted by capital's share of total factor cost plus the materials-labor ratio and the energy-labor ratio, weighted by their cost shares, plus the growth rate of TFP. The time path of labor productivity can thus be quite different from the path of TFP. Moreover, Dollar and Wolff (1988) use a value added framework for estimating labor productivity, while Jorgenson and Kuroda (in this volume) use a gross output framework. One consequence of this difference is that the estimated growth rates of TFP are typically quite a bit smaller than the corresponding rates generated by the value-added approach.

9. First, capital is almost invariably measured as a stock and not a flow, so that variations in the latter may go undetected and be suppressed into the TFP residual. This problem is widely thought to account for the procyclical variation in TFP over the business cycle. However, Berndt and Fuss (1986) have shown that, in the absence of adjustment costs, the conventional framework does embody a degree of correction for factors that are fixed in the short run: if firms react along their short-run marginal cost curves, utilization is increased by the application of more variable input to the quasi-fixed input, and this increased utilization is accurately reflected in relative prices. If, on the other hand, firms shut down in response to changes in demand, or these changes are not expected, then the Berndt-Fuss approach does not solve the stock-flow problem. Furthermore, when adjustment costs are present, prices are not proportional to marginal products and the conventional productivity model yields biased results.

10. The TFP estimates of this paper are somewhat higher than those reported in the Jorgenson-Kuroda paper. This difference is not surprising given the difference in data, methodology, and time period. It does, however, highlight the problem noted at the beginning of this introduction that different procedures can yield very different conclusions about the process of economic growth.

11. It is interesting to note that the superior rate of technical change in Japan was apparently not associated with a greater degree of flexibility in production. The authors show that own-factor price elasticities were roughly similar in all three countries and rather inelastic. Partial elasticities of substitution showed less commonality, but not dramatically so.

12. It is also worth noting that R&D spending is subtracted from other inputs in order to avoid a double counting of inputs. This adjustment is not made in most studies, so the impact of R&D is either embodied in the weighted growth of the other inputs (e.g., labor or capital) or, if there are economic rents or if the social return to R&D exceeds the private return, suppressed into the conventional TFP residual.

13. Recall, again, that capital input is typically measured as a stock rather than as a flow (using, as we shall see, a perpetual inventory method that does not allow for an acceleration in the rate of retirement of old capital or for variations in the rate of utilization of existing stock). This method results in biased estimates in situations where an

increase in the price of a complementary input, like energy, reduces the demand for capital services when stocks cannot adjust rapidly.

14. This procedure yields an estimate of the *stock* of a given type of capital asset, but not the *flow* of services of that asset. Several of the preceding papers in this volume have dealt with this issue under the guise of quasi fixity and endogenous capacity utilization. Other procedures include the assumption that service flows are proportional to stocks and the use of an exogenous estimate of capital utilization.

15. Those who believe that differential tax burdens are a key determinant of relative economic performance may find some comfort in these numbers, given the lower effective tax rate on capital income in Japan and the more rapid rate of capital formation and economic growth. However, the time pattern of tax rates is not so favorable to this view. The percentage cut in the Japanese effective tax rate was roughly equal between the 1961–70 and 1970–80 eras, but the rate of capital formation fell dramatically in the second period. And, in the United States, the period of high growth came during the 1960s, when the fall in the effective tax rate was negligible, and not in the 1970s, when it was substantial.

16. In this view, the residual shift in the production function is due to unmeasured inputs like the stock of knowledge, and accurate measurement of all inputs should reduce the residual to zero (Jorgenson and Griliches 1967). This is, of course, very difficult to accomplish since unobserved variables like the stock of knowledge cannot be measured with complete accuracy. Knowledge, for example, can be accumulated systematically through R&D investment, or it can be the result of learning by doing, pure inspiration, or imitation. The TFP residual may thus incorporate advances in knowledge through spillovers and non-R&D generated increments to knowledge even when a separate R&D stock is included in the analysis.

17. Suppose, for example, total hours worked is growing at 3% a year, while the hours worked by the young and old are growing at 4% and 2% a year, respectively. If the wage-share of the young workers is .25 and the share of the older workers is .75, the Divisia index of labor input grows at 2.5% per year. The relative increase in younger workers has the effect of decreasing the effect of hours worked on output.

References

Baumol, William J. 1986. Productivity growth, convergence, and welfare. *American Economic Review* 76 (December):1072–85.

Baumol, William J., Sue Anne Batey Blackman, and Edward N. Wolff. 1989. *Productivity and American leadership: The long view.* Cambridge, Mass.: MIT Press.

Berndt, Ernst R., and Melvyn A. Fuss. 1986. Productivity measurement with adjustments for variations in capacity utilization, and other forms of temporary equilibrium. *Journal of Econometrics* 33:7–29.

Chinloy, Peter. 1980. Sources of quality change in labor input. *American Economic Review* 70 (March):108–19.

Christensen, Laurits R., Dianne Cummings, and Dale W. Jorgenson. 1976. Economic growth, 1947–1973: An international comparison. In *New developments in productivity measurement,* ed. John W. Kendrick and Beatrice Vaccara. Studies in Income and Wealth, no. 44, National Bureau of Economic Research. New York: Columbia University Press.

———. 1981. Relative productivity levels, 1947–1973. *European Economic Review* 16 (May):61–94.

Christensen, Laurits R., Dale W. Jorgenson, and Lawrence J. Lau. 1973. Transcendental logarithmic production frontiers. *Review of Economics and Statistics* 55 (February):28–45.

Denison, Edward F. 1962. *The sources of economic growth in the United States and the alternatives before us.* New York: Committee for Economic Development.

Denison, Edward F., and William K. Chung. 1976. *How Japan's economy grew so fast, the sources of postwar expansion.* Washington, D.C.: Brookings.

Diewert, W. E. 1976. Exact and superlative index numbers. *Journal of Econometrics* 4, no. 4 (May): 115–46.

Dollar, David, and Edward N. Wolff. 1988. Convergence of industry labor productivity among advanced economies. *Review of Economics and Statistics* 70 (November):549–58.

Englander, A. Steven, and Axel Mittelstadt. 1988. Total factor productivity: Macroeconomic and structural aspects of the slowdown. *OECD Economic Studies* 10 (Spring):8–56.

Griliches, Zvi. 1987. Productivity: Measurement problems. *The new Palgrave dictionary of economics,* ed. John Eatwell, Murray Milgate, and Peter Newman, 1010–13. New York: Macmillan.

Hall, Robert E., and Dale W. Jorgenson. 1967. Tax policy and investment behavior. *American Economic Review* 57:391–414.

Hulten, Charles R. 1978. Growth accounting with intermediate inputs. *Review of Economic Studies* 45 (October):511–18.

———. 1986. Productivity change, capacity utilization and the sources of efficiency growth. *Journal of Econometrics* 33:31–50.

Jorgenson, Dale W. 1963. Capital theory and investment behavior. *American Economic Review* 53 (May):247–59.

Jorgenson, Dale W., and Zvi Griliches. 1967. The explanation of productivity change. *Review of Economic Studies* 34 (July):349–83.

Jorgenson, Dale W., Masahiro Kuroda, and Mieko Nishimizu. 1987. Japan-U.S. industry-level comparisons, 1960–79. *Journal of the Japanese and International Economies* 1 (March):1–30.

Jorgenson, Dale W., and Mieko Nishimizu. 1978. Japanese economic growth, 1952–1974: An international comparison. *Economic Journal* 88 (December):707–26.

Kendrick, John. 1961. *Productivity trends in the United States.* New York: National Bureau of Economic Research.

———. 1981. International comparisons of recent productivity trends. *Essays in contemporary economic problems: Demand, productivity, and population,* ed. William Fellner, 125–70. Washington, D.C.: American Enterprise Institute.

King, Mervyn, and Don Fullerton. 1984. *The taxation of income from capital: A comparative study of the United States, the United Kingdom, Sweden, and West Germany.* Chicago and London: University of Chicago Press.

Maddison, Angus. 1987. Growth and slowdown in advanced capitalist economies: Techniques of quantitative assessment. *Journal of Economic Literature* 25 (June):649–98.

Nadiri, M. Ishaq. 1970. Some approaches to the theory and measurement of total factor productivity: A survey. *Journal of Economic Literature* 8 (December):1137–77.

Nishimizu, Mieko, and Charles R. Hulten. 1978. The sources of Japanese economic growth, 1955–71. *Review of Economics and Statistics* 60 (August):351–61.

Patrick, Hugh, and Henry Rosovsky, eds. 1976. *Asia's new giant.* Washington, D.C.: Brookings.

Shoven, John, and Toshiaki Tachibanaki. 1988. The taxation of income from capital in Japan. In *Government policy towards industry in the United States and Japan,* ed. John Shoven. Cambridge and New York: Cambridge University Press.

Solow, Robert M. 1957. Technical change and the aggregate production function. *Review of Economics and Statistics* 39 (August):312–20.

Törnqvist, L. 1936. The Bank of Finland's consumption price index. *Bank of Finland Monthly Bulletin* 10:1–8.

U.S. Department of Labor, Bureau of Labor Statistics. 1983. *Trends in multifactor productivity, 1948–81*. Bulletin no. 2178. Washington, D.C.: Government Printing Office (September).

1 Productivity and International Competitiveness in Japan and the United States, 1960–1985

Dale W. Jorgenson and Masahiro Kuroda

1.1 Introduction

The political relationship between Japan and the United States has become increasingly preoccupied with "trade frictions." These disputes over trade issues have accompanied the massive expansion of Japanese exports to the United States. Explanations for the resulting trade imbalance must include variations in the yen-to-dollar exchange rate, changes in the relative prices of capital and labor in the two countries, and the relative growth of productivity in Japanese and U.S. industries. We analyze the role of each of these factors in explaining the rise in competitiveness of Japanese industries relative to their U.S. counterparts.

At the outset of our discussion it is essential to define a measure of international competitiveness. Our measure of international competitiveness is the price of an industry's output in Japan relative to the price in the United States. Japanese exports are generated by U.S. purchases from Japanese industries, while U.S. exports result from Japanese purchases from U.S. industries. The relative price of an industry's output enters the decisions of purchasers in both countries and the rest of the world. In order to explain changes in international competitiveness we must account for changes in the determinants of this relative price.

Dale W. Jorgenson is a professor of economics at Harvard University. Masahiro Kuroda is a professor of economics, Faculty of Business and Commerce, Keio University.

This paper was prepared for presentation at the Social Science Research Council Conference on International Productivity and Competitiveness, held at Stanford, California, 28–30 October 1988. We are grateful to Paul David and Bert Hickman for their comments on an earlier draft of the paper and advice about presentation of the final manuscript. Obviously, they do not share our responsibility for any remaining deficiencies in the paper. We are also indebted to Mieko Nishimizu for her collaboration on earlier phases of the research that we report in this paper. Financial support for this research has been provided by the Harvard-MITI World Oil Project and the Program on Technology and Economic Policy of Harvard University.

The starting point for our analysis of the competitiveness of Japanese and U.S. industries is the yen-to-dollar *exchange rate*. This is simply the number of yen required to purchase one U.S. dollar in the market for foreign exchange. Variations in the yen-to-dollar exchange rate are easy to document and are often used to characterize movements in relative prices in the two countries. However, movements in relative prices of goods and services do not coincide with variations in the exchange rate. To account for changes in international competitiveness a measure of the relative prices of specific goods and services is required.

To assess the international competitiveness of Japanese and U.S. industries it is necessary to carry out price comparisons for industry outputs in the two countries. These comparisons are hampered by the fact that the makeup of a given industry may differ substantially between Japan and the U.S. For example, the steel industry produces an enormous range of different steel products. The relative importance of different types of steel differs between the two countries. The composition of the output of the steel industry in each country also changes over time. These differences must be taken into account in comparing the relative prices of steel between Japan and the United States.

Relative prices between Japanese and U.S. industries can be summarized by means of purchasing power parities. The purchasing power parity for a specific industry's output is the number of yen required in Japan to purchase an amount of the industry's output that would cost one dollar in the United States. The dimensions of purchasing power parities are the same as the yen-to-dollar exchange rate, namely, yen per dollar. However, the purchasing power parities reflect the relative prices of the goods and services that make up the industry's output in both countries.

The most familiar application of the notion of purchasing power parity is to the relative prices of such aggregates as the gross domestic product. This application has been the focus of the landmark studies of Kravis, Heston, and Summers (1978). As a consequence of their research, it is now possible to compare the relative prices of gross domestic product for a wide range of countries, including Japan and the United States. Kravis, Heston, and Summers have based their purchasing power parities for gross domestic product on relative prices for 153 commodity groups.

In this study we estimate purchasing power parities for 29 industries in Japan and the United States for the period 1960–85. These are relative prices of the outputs of each industry in the two countries in terms of yen per dollar. We divide the relative price of each industry's output by the yen-to-dollar exchange rate to translate purchasing power parities into relative prices in terms of dollars.[1] We find it convenient to employ relative prices in dollars as measures of international competitiveness. Variations in the exchange rate are reflected in the relative prices of outputs for all 29 industries.

To account for changes in international competitiveness between Japanese and U.S. industries, we have compiled purchasing power parities for the inputs into each industry. By analogy with outputs, the purchasing power parities for inputs are based on the relative prices of the goods and services that make up the inputs of each industry. We have disaggregated inputs among capital and labor services, which are primary factors of production, and energy and other intermediate goods, which are produced by one industry and consumed by other industries. We can translate purchasing power parities for inputs into relative prices in dollars by dividing by the yen-to-dollar exchange rate. We describe purchasing power parities for output and inputs in 29 industries of the United States and Japan in section 1.2 below.

Our final step in accounting for international competitiveness between Japanese and U.S. industries is to measure the relative levels of productivity for all 29 industries. For this purpose we employ a model of production for each industry. This model enables us to express the price of output in each country as a function of the prices of inputs and the level of productivity in that country. We can account for the relative prices of output between Japan and the United States by allowing input prices and levels of productivity to differ between countries. We have compiled data on relative productivity levels in Japan and the United States for the period 1960–85. For this purpose we have revised and extended the estimates for 1960–79 reported by Jorgenson, Kuroda, and Nishimizu (1987).

The methodology for our study was originated by Jorgenson and Nishimizu (1978). They provided a theoretical framework for productivity comparisons based on a bilateral production function at the aggregate level. They employed this framework in comparing aggregate output, input, and productivity for Japan and the United States.[2] This methodology was extended to the industry level by Jorgenson and Nishimizu (1981) and employed in international comparisons between Japanese and U.S. industries. The industry-level methodology introduced models of production for individual industries based on bilateral production functions for each industry. This methodology was used in Jorgenson, Kuroda, and Nishimizu (1987), which involved comparisons between Japan and the United States at the industry level for the period 1960–79.[3] We discuss the theoretical framework for international comparisons briefly in the appendix to this paper.

We present comparisons of productivity levels between the United States and Japan by industry in section 1.3. Jorgenson, Kuroda, and Nishimizu (1987) have presented a taxonomy of Japanese and U.S. industries, based on the development of relative productivity levels over the period 1960–79. They have used this taxonomy to project the likely development of relative productivity levels for each industry. We can now assess the validity of these projections on the basis of developments during the period 1960–85. We find that the taxonomy has been very useful in forming expectations about future developments in productivity. Finally, we employ changes in relative productivity levels and relative prices of inputs in accounting for changes in international competitiveness between Japanese and U.S. industries over the period 1960–85. Section 1.4 provides a summary and conclusion.

1.2 Purchasing Power Parities

We treat data on production patterns in Japan and the United States as separate sets of observations. We assume that these observations are generated by bilateral models of production for each industrial sector presented in detail in the appendix. We can describe the implications of the theory of production in terms of production functions for each industry. These production functions give industry outputs as functions of capital, labor, energy, and other intermediate inputs, a dummy variable equal to one for Japan and zero for the United States, and time as an index of technology.

In our bilateral models of production, the capital, labor, energy, and other intermediate input prices are aggregates that depend on the prices of individual capital inputs, labor inputs, energy inputs, and other intermediate inputs in Japan and the United States. The product of price and quantity indices must equal the value of all the components of each aggregate. We define price indices corresponding to each aggregate as ratios of the value of the components of the aggregate to the corresponding quantity index. In international comparisons, the price indices represent purchasing power parities between the yen and the dollar. For example, the price index for labor input represents the Japanese price in yen for labor input costing one in the United States.

Our methodology for estimating purchasing power parities is based on linking time-series data sets on prices in Japan and the United States. Suppose that we observe the price of the output of the ith industry in Japan and the United States, say $q_i(\text{JAPAN})$ and $q_i(\text{US})$, in the base period, where these prices are evaluated in terms of yen and dollars, respectively. We can define the *purchasing power parity* for the output of the ith industry, say PPP_i, as follows:

$$(1) \qquad \text{PPP}_i = \frac{q_i(\text{JAPAN})}{q_i(\text{US})}, \quad (i = 1, 2, \ldots, I).$$

The purchasing power parity gives the number of yen required in Japan to purchase an amount of the output of the ith industry costing one dollar in the United States in the base period.

To estimate purchasing power parities for outputs of all industries in Japan and the United States, we first construct a time series of prices for the output of each industry in both countries in domestic currency. To obtain price indices for industry outputs in the United States, we normalize the price index for each industry, say $q_i(\text{US}, T)$, at unity in the base period. We normalize the corresponding price index for Japan, say $q_i(\text{JAPAN}, T)$, at the purchasing power parity in the base period. We obtain estimates of purchasing power parities for all years, say $\text{PPP}_i(T)$, from these price indices and the purchasing power parity for the base period from the equation

$$(2) \quad \text{PPP}_i(T) = \text{PPP}_i(0) \frac{q_i(\text{JAPAN}),T)q_i(\text{US},0)}{q_i(\text{JAPAN},0)\, q_i(\text{US},T)}, \quad (i = 1, 2, \ldots, I).$$

where PPP$_i$(0) is the purchasing power parity in the base period and q_i(JAPAN,0) and q_i(US,0) are the prices of outputs of the ith industry in Japan and the United States in the base period.

Finally, we define the *relative price* of the output of the ith industry in Japan and the United States in dollars, say p_i(JAPAN,US), as the ratio of the purchasing power parity for that industry to the yen-to-dollar exchange rate, say E:

$$(3) \qquad p_i(\text{JAPAN,US}) = \frac{\text{PPP}_i}{E}, \quad (i = 1, 2, \ldots, I).$$

The relative price of the output of the ith industry in Japan and the United States is the ratio of the number of dollars required in Japan to purchase an amount of the industry's output costing one dollar in the United States. This index is our measure of international competitiveness between the Japanese industry and its U.S. counterpart.

In order to construct purchasing power parities and the corresponding relative prices between Japanese and U.S. industries, we require an estimate of the purchasing power parity for each industry in the base period. For this purpose we have developed purchasing power parities for industry outputs based on the results of Kravis, Heston, and Summers (1978). They have provided purchasing power parities between the yen and the dollar for 153 commodity groups for the year 1970. These commodity groups are components of the gross domestic product of each country, corresponding to deliveries to final demand at purchasers' prices.

We construct purchasing power parities for industry outputs, energy inputs, and other intermediate inputs by mapping the 153 commodity groups employed by Kravis, Heston, and Summers (1978) into the industry classification system shown in table 1.1. Unfortunately, a complete correspondence between the two systems is impossible, since not all intermediate goods delivered by the different industrial sectors are included among the 153 commodity groups delivered to final demand. We have eliminated the gap between the two systems by utilizing the purchasing power parities of close substitutes for a given industry's deliveries to intermediate demand.

To obtain purchasing power parities for industry outputs from the producer's point of view, we adjust the price indices for commodity groups in Japan and the United States by "peeling off" the indirect taxes paid and trade and transportation margins for each industry. We estimate these margins from the interindustry transactions table for 1970 for each country. To obtain the purchasing power parities for industry outputs, we aggregate the results for commodity groups, using as weights the relative shares of each commodity in the value of industry output from the 1970 interindustry transactions tables. Similarly, to obtain purchasing power parities for components of intermediate input in each industry, we aggregate purchasing power parities for goods and services delivered by that industry to other industries. We employ relative

Table 1.1   **List of Industries**

Number	Industries	Abbreviation
1.	Agriculture, forestry, & fisheries	Agric.
2.	Mining	Mining
3.	Construction	Construct.
4.	Food & kindred products	Foods
5.	Textile mill products	Textiles
6.	Apparel & other fabricated textile	Apparel
7.	Lumber and wood products, except furniture	Lumber
8.	Furniture & fixtures	Furniture
9.	Paper & allied products	Paper
10.	Printing, publishing, & allied products	Printing
11.	Chemical & allied products	Chemical
12.	Petroleum refinery & coal products	Petroleum
13.	Rubber & miscellaneous plastic products	Rubber
14.	Leather & leather products	Leather
15.	Stone, clay, & glass products	Stone
16.	Primary metal products	Prim. Metal
17.	Fabricated metal products	Fab. Metal
18.	Machinery	Machinery
19.	Electric machinery	Elec. Mach.
20.	Motor vehicles & equipment	Mot. Veh.
21.	Transportation equipment, except motors	Trsp. Eqpt.
22.	Precision instruments	Prec. Inst.
23.	Miscellaneous manufacturing	Mfg. Misc.
24.	Transportation & communication	Trsp. Comm.
25.	Electric utility & gas supply	Utilities
26.	Wholesale & retail trade	Trade
27.	Finance, insurance, & real estate	Finance
28.	Other service	Service
29.	Government services	Gov. Serv.

shares in the value of deliveries of intermediate input from other industries from the 1970 interindustry transactions tables as weights.

For both Japan and the United States, capital stocks are divided among seven types of depreciable assets and two types of nondepreciable assets for each industry. These assets are further subdivided among legal forms of organization. We employ the equality between the price of an asset and the discounted flow of future capital services to derive service prices for capital input. Although we estimate the decline in efficiency of capital goods for each component of capital input separately for Japan and the United States, we assume that the relative efficiency of new capital goods in a given industry is the same in both countries. The appropriate purchasing power parity for new capital goods is the purchasing power parity for the corresponding component of investment goods output. To obtain the purchasing power parity for capital input, we multiply the purchasing power parity for investment goods by the

Table 1.2   **The Japanese Price Index Transformed by the Purchasing Power Parity Index at 1970 (United States Price = 1.000)**

Industry	Output Price	Capital Price	Labor Price	Energy Price	Material Price
Agric.	1.04556	.90835	.21352	1.48236	.91204
Mining	.72125	.88095	.21263	1.44013	.70573
Construct.	1.03487	.92127	.18607	1.42641	.72203
Foods	1.03569	.9219	.21894	1.26554	.88483
Textiles	.77898	.90871	.24099	1.18329	.76975
Apparel	.76952	.86037	.18975	1.24298	.74821
Lumber	.79154	.84363	.22805	1.2268	.90165
Furniture	.67945	.84214	.22952	1.22178	.74429
Paper	.58858	.89567	.2217	1.18606	.65664
Printing	.78107	.86742	.21251	1.12482	.65975
Chemical	.6621	.91711	.25039	1.3363	.712
Petroleum	1.59952	.89588	.21846	1.31298	.88291
Rubber	1.06186	.86013	.24042	1.22499	.76731
Leather	.71273	.82076	.23569	1.31561	.81086
Stone	.69603	.89998	.23083	1.31627	.72567
Prim. Metal	.81706	.91205	.252	1.37079	.80318
Fab. Metal	.81514	.90205	.21072	1.32346	.77507
Machinery	.61327	.9202	.22564	1.28346	.71093
Elec. Mach.	.68127	.92036	.22308	1.24327	.71054
Mot. Veh.	.78627	.91647	.18581	1.1729	.76428
Trsp. Eqpt.	.94794	.87722	.21944	1.24063	.76549
Prec. Inst.	.71912	.86402	.2315	1.22607	.71774
Mfg. Misc.	.69473	.88034	.22549	1.27395	.71238
Trsp. Comm.	.47247	.91027	.22713	1.43624	.68624
Utilities	1.02936	.90389	.26605	1.4949	.78528
Trade	.66155	.93094	.26889	1.35118	.73683
Finance	.86176	.833	.30796	1.1449	.77297
Service	.56751	.91719	.25592	1.22718	.73724
Gov. Serv.	.30797	0	.19482	1.35489	.68436

Note: See table 1.1 for key to industry abbreviations.

ratio of the price of capital goods for Japan relative to the United States. The resulting price index represents the purchasing power parity for capital input.

For both Japan and the United States, labor inputs are cross-classified by employment status, sex, age, education, and occupation. Given the detailed classification of labor input for each industry in our data base, we construct purchasing power parities for labor input on the basis of relative wage levels for each component of labor input in each industry. Purchasing power parities for industry output, capital, labor, energy, and other intermediate inputs in 1970 are shown in table 1.2.

According to our purchasing power parities for industry output in 1970, prices in Japan were higher than those in the United States in only six sectors—agriculture-forestry-fisheries, construction, food and kindred products, petroleum refinery and coal products, rubber products, and electricity and gas. The purchasing power parities for labor input in 1970 represent substantially lower costs of labor input in Japan relative to the United States. In that year, hourly wages in Japan were 30% or less of U.S. hourly wages. By contrast, the cost of capital in Japan averaged about 80% of that in the United States in 1970. The purchasing power parities for intermediate inputs are calculated as a weighted average of the purchasing power parities of industry outputs. The cost of intermediate inputs in Japan, other than energy, is 60%–90% of the cost in the United States in 1970. On the other hand, the purchasing power parities for energy inputs in 1970 are greater than unity, implying that the cost of energy in Japan was higher than that in the United States.

We have estimated purchasing power parities between the yen and the dollar in 1970 for the 29 industries listed in table 1.1 above. We have also compiled price indices for industry outputs and inputs in both countries for the period of 1960–85. We obtain indices of prices of outputs and inputs for each industry in Japan relative to those in the United States for each year from equation (2) above. Table 1.3 presents time series for price indices of value added and capital and labor inputs for the period 1960–85 in Japan and the United States. Column 1 of the table represents the yen-dollar exchange rate. The second and third columns represent price indices for Japan. The second column gives the domestic price index with base equal to the purchasing power parity in 1970. The third column gives this price index, divided by an index of the yen-dollar exchange rate, equal to one in 1970. The fourth column gives the corresponding price index in the United States with base equal to one in 1970.

According to the results presented in table 1.3, the price deflator for aggregate value added in Japan was 0.49401 in 1960, while that in the United States was 0.78454 in that year. This implies that the Japanese aggregate price index in 1960 was only 63% of that in the United States. Under the fixed yen-dollar exchange rate of 360 yen to the dollar that prevailed until 1970, the ratio of the Japanese price index to the U.S. price index rose to 76% in 1970. With the collapse of the fixed-exchange-rate regime in 1970 and the beginning of the energy crisis in 1973, the price index in Japan, denominated in dollars, exceeded the corresponding U.S. price index. This was a consequence of more rapid inflation in Japan and a substantial appreciation of the yen through 1973. The competitiveness of U.S. industries relative to their Japanese counterparts reached a temporary peak in that year.

After 1973 the U.S. inflation rate continued at a high level, while Japan underwent a severe deflation, accompanied by depreciation of the yen. This had the short-run effect of restoring the competitiveness of Japanese industries. Inflation resumed in Japan after 1974, and the yen was allowed to appreciate again, reaching an exchange rate of 210 yen to the dollar in 1978. Once again, Japanese prices, denominated in terms of dollars, exceeded U.S. prices. This situation continued until 1980 as inflation in the United States

Table 1.3   **Comparison of Trend of Value-added Price Index between Japan and the United States**

Year	(1) Exchange Rate	(2) Value-added Japan (1)	(3) Value-added Japan (2)	(4) Value-added United States
1960	360	.49401	.49401	.78454
1961	360	.53183	.53183	.79409
1962	360	.55298	.55298	.80279
1963	360	.57685	.57685	.80636
1964	360	.59492	.59492	.81536
1965	360	.61978	.61978	.83047
1966	360	.64779	.64779	.86174
1967	360	.67604	.67604	.88078
1968	360	.69657	.69657	.91007
1969	360	.72318	.72318	.95491
1970	360	.75878	.75878	1
1971	348	.77834	.80517	1.0476
1972	303.1	.80947	.96143	1.09325
1973	271.7	.92428	1.22466	1.16623
1974	292.1	.8719	1.0746	1.29731
1975	296.8	.99093	1.20194	1.42734
1976	296.5	1.05665	1.28294	1.49954
1977	268.3	1.10367	1.48088	1.60448
1978	210.1	1.18892	2.03717	1.73642
1979	219.5	1.21565	1.99378	1.89859
1980	203	1.27198	2.25573	2.09651
1981	219.9	1.30588	1.13787	2.29653
1982	235	1.34193	1.05572	2.43595
1983	232.2	1.36365	2.11418	2.51156
1984	251.1	1.37795	1.97556	2.59771
1985	224.05	1.38862	2.23121	2.66754

Note: Col. 1 is the observed exchange rate (yen/dollar); col 2 is the Japanese price index transformed by the purchasing power parity (PPP) index; col 3 is the Japanese PPP-based price index denominated by exchange rate; col. 4 is the U.S. corresponding price index.

continued at high rates. In the 1980s U.S. prices in dollars rose to well above the level of Japanese prices due to the rapid appreciation of the U.S. dollar relative to the Japanese yen. By 1985 the Japanese price level in dollars was only 83% of the U.S. price, which implies that Japanese industries had a substantial competitive advantage relative to their U.S. counterparts.

According to the international comparison of capital input prices shown in table 1.4, the cost of capital in Japan in 1960 was almost 78% of that in the United States and gradually rose to within 89% of the U.S. level by 1970. After the energy crisis in 1973 the cost of capital in Japan increased relative to the United States, exceeding the U.S. level by almost 11% in 1978. The appreciation of the U.S. dollar reversed this trend. By 1985 the relative cost of capital in Japan had fallen to only 75% of the U.S. level, which is below

Table 1.4   Comparison of Trend of Capital Input Prices between Japan and the United States

Year	(1) Exchange Rate	(2) Capital Japan (1)	(3) Capital Japan (2)	(4) Capital United States
1960	360	.62499	.62499	.79723
1961	360	.7001	.7001	.80034
1962	360	.64268	.64268	.87577
1963	360	.62544	.62544	.9131
1964	360	.68795	.68795	.96814
1965	360	.68865	.68865	1.05671
1966	360	.71741	.71741	1.08764
1967	360	.7829	.7829	1.06235
1968	360	.86281	.86281	1.07711
1969	360	.88634	.88634	1.09371
1970	360	.89842	.89842	1
1971	348	.81956	.8478206	1.07581
1972	303.1	.83773	.9949943	1.16855
1973	271.7	.9224	1.2221715	1.22005
1974	292.1	.99464	1.2258486	1.12504
1975	296.8	.9234	1.1200269	1.29908
1976	296.5	.94393	1.1460870	1.42287
1977	268.3	.96151	1.2901364	1.63368
1978	210.1	1.15219	1.9742427	1.78198
1979	219.5	1.21611	1.9945312	1.82541
1980	203	1.00809	1.7877458	1.85044
1981	219.9	.98245	1.6083765	2.00438
1982	235	1.04394	1.5992272	1.96229
1983	232.2	1.06156	1.6458294	2.13968
1984	251.1	1.10386	1.5825949	2.43909
1985	224.05	1.1502	1.8481231	2.46379

Note: Col. 1 is the observed exchange rate (yen/dollar); col 2 is the Japanese price index transformed by the purchasing power parity (PPP) index; col 3 is the Japanese PPP-based price index denominated by exchange rate; col. 4 is the U.S. corresponding price index.

the level that prevailed almost a quarter century earlier, in 1960. The rise in the cost of capital in Japan relative to that in the United States after the energy crisis was a consequence of the appreciation of the yen. The fall of this relative price in the 1980s resulted from the appreciation of the dollar.

Finally, a comparison of labor input prices in table 1.5 shows that the Japanese wage rate in 1960 was only 11% the U.S. wage rate. By 1970 the Japanese wage rate had reached 23% of the U.S. level. Rapid wage increases in Japan during the 1970s and the sharp appreciation of the yen raised wage rates in Japan to 60% of the U.S. level in 1980. The subsequent appreciation of the dollar and rapid wage increases in the United States resulted in a decline in Japanese wage rates relative to the United States. The relative price of labor input in Japan was only 50% of the U.S. level in 1985.

Table 1.5   **Comparison of Trend of Labor Input Prices between Japan and the United States**

Year	(1) Exchange Rate	(2) Labor Japan (1)	(3) Labor Japan (2)	(4) Labor United States
1960	360	.06759	.06759	.60926
1961	360	.07795	.07795	.64391
1962	360	.08871	.08871	.65408
1963	360	.10203	.10203	.66726
1964	360	.10864	.10864	.68739
1965	360	.12425	.12425	.70308
1966	360	.13732	.13732	.74533
1967	360	.15215	.15215	.79066
1968	360	.17714	.17714	.8549
1969	360	.20104	.20104	.90917
1970	360	.23211	.23211	1
1971	348	.26643	.2756172	1.07431
1972	303.1	.30113	.3576601	1.14898
1973	271.7	.38076	.5045034	1.24142
1974	292.1	.46834	.5772078	1.36978
1975	296.8	.55019	.6673463	1.49983
1976	296.5	.59518	.7226468	1.62713
1977	268.3	.6492	.8710846	1.73529
1978	210.1	.67337	1.1537991	1.84918
1979	219.5	.70365	1.1540501	2.00071
1980	203	.75423	1.3375507	2.21758
1981	219.9	.79732	1.3052987	2.39774
1982	235	.8339	1.2774638	2.54319
1983	232.2	.83456	1.2938914	2.64133
1984	251.1	.85129	1.2204874	2.73005
1985	224.05	.89202	1.4332836	2.864

Note: Col. 1 is the observed exchange rate (yen/dollar); col 2 is the Japanese price index transformed by the purchasing power parity (PPP) index; col 3 is the Japanese PPP-based price index denominated by exchange rate; col. 4 is the U.S. corresponding price index.

Our international comparisons of relative prices of aggregate output and inputs show, first, that the Japanese economy has been more competitive than the U.S. economy throughout the period 1960–85, except for 1973 and 1978–79. Second, lower wage rates have contributed to Japan's international competitiveness throughout the period, especially before the energy crisis in 1973. Lower costs of capital have also contributed to Japan's international competitiveness for most of the same period with important exceptions in 1973 and 1978–80.

We turn next to international competitiveness of Japanese and U.S. industries. Exchange rates play the same role in relative price comparisons at the industry level as at the aggregate level. However, industry inputs include energy and other intermediate goods as well as the primary factors of production—capital and labor inputs. The price of energy inputs in each industrial sector is an aggregate of inputs of petroleum and coal products and electricity and gas products. The relative prices of the outputs of these two industries in Japan and the United States are given in table 1.6

The energy crisis of 1973 had an enormous impact on the prices of energy in both Japan and the United States. Prices of petroleum and coal products in Japan were almost double those in the United States, while prices of electricity and gas were about 1.3 times those in the United States in 1985. By comparison petroleum and coal products in Japan were only 1.6 times as expensive as those in the United States in 1970, while electricity and gas were only slightly more expensive in Japan than in the United States in that year.

Table 1.7 gives average annual growth rates of input prices in Japan and the United States in the 1960s, 1970s, and 1980s at the industry level. Differences in the growth rates of the cost of capital between Japan and the United States

Table 1.6   Relative Prices of Outputs in Two Energy Industries

	Petroleum & Coal		Electricity & Gas	
Year	Japan	United States	Japan	United States
1960	1.71118	.97477	.83247	.94299
1965	1.51919	.94523	1.00311	.96430
1970	1.59952	1.00000	1.02936	1.00000
1975	5.34666	2.51780	2.26813	1.78555
1980	14.75987	6.46713	5.99713	3.45804
1985	13.28313	5.98764	6.25211	5.04334

Table 1.7   Annual Growth Rate of Prices

		Price Increase (%)	
Period	Source	Japan	United States
1960–70	Capital service	2.8435	2.2153
	Labor service	12.2062	4.5325
	Energy input	.5881	.4513
	Material input	2.1515	2.0432
1970–80	Capital service	− .5899	6.3782
	Labor service	11.6868	8.0232
	Energy input	13.8936	15.1777
	Material input	7.7005	8.1342
1980–85	Capital service	.0777	5.9044
	Labor service	3.8273	5.2741
	Energy input	1.2662	4.3062
	Material input	.5704	3.2437

Note: Annual growth rates of each price are estimated in terms of a simple average of an annual growth rate by industry in each item.

were negligible in the 1960s. Since 1970, average rates of growth in the United States have been considerably higher. The rates of growth of wage rates in Japan were substantially higher than U.S. rates throughout in the 1960s and 1970s. During the 1980s, however, annual rates of growth of wages in the United States exceeded those in Japan by about 1.5% per year.

The movements of energy input prices were similar in the two countries in the 1960s. We have already described these movements during the energy crisis of the 1970s. Rates of growth of energy prices in the United States during the 1980s were about 3% per year higher than those in Japan. This implies that differences between energy prices in the two countries have been decreasing since 1980, in spite of the relatively high level of energy prices in Japan. The growth rates of other intermediate input prices in the United States were also higher than that in Japan after 1980. The higher growth rates of input prices in the United States since 1980—including capital, labor, energy, and other intermediate inputs—have resulted in a substantial deterioration of international competitiveness of U.S. industries relative to their Japanese counterparts.

1.3   Relative Productivity Levels

In this section we estimate relative levels of productivity in Japan and the United States for each of the 29 industries included in our study. Jorgenson, Kuroda, and Nishimizu (1987) have reported relative productivity levels for the two countries for the period 1960–79. All Japanese industries had lower levels of productivity than their U.S. counterparts in 1960. However, there were nine industries in which productivity gaps between the two countries had closed during the period 1960–79. In 19 industries, differences in productivity levels between Japan and the United States remained in 1979.

Jorgenson, Kuroda, and Nishimizu (1987) have divided Japanese and U.S. industries into seven categories. Type 1 included four industries in which productivity gaps between Japan and the United States were expected to increase in the future—agriculture-forestry-fisheries, textiles, printing and publishing, and trade. Type 2 includes industries in which the productivity gaps were decreasing before 1973, but increasing after 1973. These industries were food and kindred products, apparel, furniture, rubber, stone and clay, other transportation equipment, utilities, and other services. Type 3 includes industries in which the United States had an advantage in productivity in 1979, but productivity gaps between Japan and the United States were expected to close in the near future. This category contains investment-goods industries such as nonelectrical machinery, electrical machinery, and motor vehicles.

Paper and allied products constitute type 4; in this industry U.S. productivity levels increased relative to those in Japan before 1973, but the productivity gap was decreasing afterward due to deterioration of productivity in the U.S. industry. Petroleum and coal products with a constant productivity gap, favoring the United States, and construction with negative growth rates of productivity in both countries are classified as type 5 and type 6, respectively. Finally, type 7 includes the nine industries in which Japan had a productivity advantage in 1979. The Japanese advantage was expected to increase in the future. These include mining, lumber, chemicals, primary metals, fabricated metals, precision instruments, miscellaneous manufacturing, transportation and communication, and finance and insurance.

In order to assess the validity of this taxonomy in projecting future patterns of relative productivity growth in Japan and the U.S. we consider additional observations for the period 1979–1985. However, we must take note of the following revisions in the data base. First, we have revised U.S. intermediate input measures by constructing a time series of interindustry transactions tables for the period 1947–85. The methodology is consistent with the approach used for constructing a time series of Japanese interindustry transactions tables for the period 1960–85.[4] Second, we were able to obtain more detailed information on wage differentials between full-time employees and other employees in Japan. We used this information to improve our estimates of labor compensation for temporary employees, day laborers, and unpaid family workers in Japan.

The earlier estimates of purchasing power parities for labor input were based on relative wage levels for full-time workers in Japan and the United States. In the agricultural sector in Japan, however, there is a substantial number of irregular and part-time workers, especially unpaid family workers. Taking the labor compensation of these workers into account, we find that we overestimated the purchasing power parity of labor input in the agricultural sector in our earlier work. We have revised the purchasing power parity index of labor input in the agriculture-forestry-fisheries industry in 1970 from 0.60588 to 0.21352, as shown table 1.2. This is much closer to results for other industries, where we only take account of ordinary full-time employees in estimating the purchasing power parity index for labor input.

The three revisions in the data base have resulted in two substantial changes in the taxonomy of industries presented for the period 1960–79 in Jorgenson, Kuroda, and Nishimizu (1987). The fabricated metal products industry was moved to type 1 from the type 7 classification of Jorgenson, Kuroda, and Nishimizu (1987). Second, the trade sector was classified in type 1 and is now classified in type 7 in the revised version. The remaining 26 industries were classified in the same way as in the industrial taxonomy of the earlier paper.

A new industrial taxonomy, based on our revised data base for the period 1960–1985, is given in table 1.8. Industries in which the United States has a substantial advantage in productivity in 1980 and productivity gaps between Japan and the United States are expected to persist into the future include agriculture-forestry-fisheries, textile products, and printing and publishing industries. These industries coincide with type 1 in Jorgenson, Kuroda, and Nishimizu (1987). Productivity growth since 1980 has added three industries to this category—petroleum and coal products, construction, and food and kindred products. These industries were classified in types 2, 5, and 6 in the earlier paper.

Type 2 includes those industries in which the United States had a productivity advantage in 1980 after productivity gaps had been closing during the 1960s and 1970s, but the U.S. productivity advantage was expected to grow in the future. The industries in this category in the 1987 paper included furniture and fixtures, rubber products, stone, clay and glass and other transportation equipment. Motor vehicles was added to this category in the 1980s. In the previous paper this industry was classified as type 3, where the technology gaps were expected to close in the near future.

According to new evidence on the productivity gap in the motor vehicle industry during the period 1980–85, the gap between Japan and the United States had closed by 1982, as we expected from our earlier observations. After 1983, however, the gap increased again due to rapid productivity growth in the U.S. industry. The index of productivity in motor vehicles in Japan and the U.S. during the period 1979–1985 is given in table 1.9.

Type 3 includes industries in which productivity gaps are expected to close in the near future, even though the United States had an productivity advantage in 1980. Three industries included in this category in Jorgenson, Kuroda, and Nishimizu (1987)—leather, nonelectrical machinery, and electrical machinery—had already attained U.S. levels of productivity by 1980, as we expected. In table 1.8 we have reclassified these industries in type 7. Industries added to type 3 in the 1980s were apparel, miscellaneous manufacturing, and finance, insurance, and real estate, previously classified as type 2 and type 7. These are three industries in which we were unable to project relative trends in productivity during the 1980s. Finally, type 7 includes industries in which Japan had a productivity advantage that we expected to increase in the future. Three industries previously classified in type 3 were added to this category in the 1980s, so that 12 industries of the 29 are included in type 7.

In evaluating the usefulness of the industrial taxonomy presented in Jorgenson, Kuroda, and Nishimizu (1987), we find only four industries in which the trend of technology gaps was not projected. The U.S. productivity advantage was expected to increase in apparel and miscellaneous manufacturing. The Japanese advantage was expected to increase in motor vehicles and finance. We conclude that the predictive power of the Jorgenson-Kuroda-Nishimizu taxonomy is substantial. We can also draw attention to the findings from new observations during the period 1980–85. According to table 1.9, industries with a clear advantage in productivity in Japan or the United States fall into two groups. Type 1 includes seven industries with a U.S. advantage, while Type 7 includes 12 industries with a Japanese advantage.

To analyze the trend of productivity differences between Japan and the United States, we have estimated the mean and variance of relative productivity by industry during the period 1960–85. The results are shown in figures

Table 1.8   An Industrial Taxonomy in Terms of Technology Gaps

Type of Technology	Industry	Technology Gaps, 1980	Average Annual Growth Rate of Productivity						Technology Gaps, 1985
			1960–70		1970–80		1980–85		
			Japan	United States	Japan	United States	Japan	United States	
Type 1	(1) Agric.	U > J	.452	1.178	−1.641	.673	−.274	4.431	U > J
	(3) Construct.	U > J	.854	.228	.717	−1.07	−1.707	.516	U > J
	(4) Foods	U > J	−.155	.556	.37	.208	−.917	.8	U > J
	(5) Textiles	U > J	.526	1.437	−1.22	.187	.188	.309	U > J
	(10) Printing	U > J	.858	.647	−1.469	.218	.02	.979	U > J
	(12) Petroleum	U > J	−1.358	1.616	−3.889	−4.56	−1.29	3.422	U > J
	(17) Fab. Metal	U > J	2.668	.293	.837	.618	.009	.376	U > J
Type 2	(8) Furniture	U > J	1.405	.03	1.364	.792	1.02	1.475	U > J
	(13) Rubber	U > J	1.499	.868	.55	.981	2.623	3.502	U > J
	(15) Stone	U > J	2.794	.339	−1.248	.555	.414	2.443	U > J
	(20) Mot. Veh.	J > U	.086	.155	.512	.282	−1.286	2.553	U > J
	(21) Trsp. Eqpt.	U > J	6.649	1.395	.706	−4.26	2.107	3.456	U > J

Type 3	(6) Apparel	U > J	2.294	.625	1.414	1.16	.42	.203	U > J
	(28) Service	U > J	1.378	.7	-3.033	.018	.502	-1.179	U > J
	(27) Finance	U > J	1.81	.535	.15	.181	3.311	-1.179	U > J
Type 5	(25) Utilities	U > J	3.222	2.111	-2.991	-1.497	.603	-1.668	U > J
Type 7	(2) Mining	J > U	1.662	1.084	1.722	-5.584	.301	.045	J > U
	(7) Lumber	J > U	2.781	.965	2.032	.738	3.522	1.211	J > U
	(9) Paper	J > U	1.616	.338	.505	.233	1.982	1.207	J > U
	(11) Chemical	J > U	3.343	1.501	.731	-1.517	2.671	1.63	J > U
	(14) Leather	U > J	.926	.452	.713	1.066	.552	-4.352	J > U
	(16) Prim. Metal	J > U	.915	.088	.781	.534	.624	-2.294	J > U
	(18) Machinery	J > U	2.212	.809	.377	.693	-1.073	.785	J = U
	(19) Elec. Mach.	J > U	3.304	.093	3.663	.693	3.222	.5	J > U
	(22) Prec. Inst.	J > U	1.943	.729	3.626	.13	1.513	3.105	J > U
	(23) Mfg. Misc.	J > U	1.741	.647	1.257	.795	.252	.23	J > U
	(24) Trsp. Comm.	J > U	3.056	1.085	.49	.995	1.186	.251	J > U
	(26) Trade	J > U	2.507	.077	.838	.316	.607	2.6	J = U

Note: For industry abbreviations, see table 1.1 above. U = United States; J = Japan. Type 1: the United States had still an advantage in the 1980 technology. The technology gaps are expected to continue to expand in the future. Type 2: the United States had an advantage in the 1980 technology. Before 1980, the technology gaps partly were closing. But they, however, were expanding in 1980's and are expected to expand in the future. Type 3: the United States had an advantage in the 1980 technology. The technology gaps were expanding in 1980's. The technology gaps are expected to close in the near future. Type 5: the United States had an advantage in the 1980 technology. The technology gaps were mostly constant during the period 1960–85. Type 7: Japan had an advantage in the 1980 technology. The technology gaps are expected to continue to expand in the future.

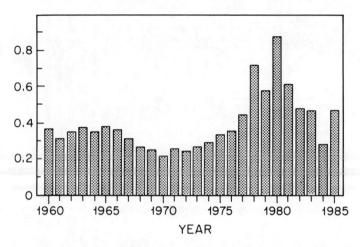

Fig. 1.1. Average of proportional gap of the technology between the United States and Japan

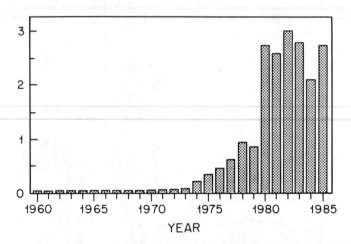

Fig. 1.2 Variance of proportional gap of the technology between the United States and Japan

1.1 and 1.2. The mean of relative productivity levels between the two countries remained fairly stable during until 1973 and then rose through the 1970s. This movement peaked in 1980. Since that time, the trend has reversed with gains in productivity levels for the United States during the 1980s. The variance of the relative productivity levels shown in figure 1.2 was stable until the oil crisis in 1973 and has expanded rapidly since.

We conclude that the energy crisis had a very substantial impact on patterns of productivity growth by industry. Both the mean and the variance of relative productivity levels between Japan and the United States expanded during the period 1974–80. In the 1980s the mean of the relative productivity levels has fallen, while the variance has increased rapidly. This implies that the relative productivity levels in the two countries have tended to differ substantially among industries, as shown in table 1.9.

Finally, we turn to international competitiveness between Japan and the United States. We can account for movements in the relative prices of industry outputs in the two countries by changes in relative input prices and changes in relative productivity levels. Figures 1.3a and 1.3b show the relative prices of industry outputs between Japan and the United States in terms of dollars. We have expressed these prices in logarithmic form so that a negative difference implies that the U.S. output price is below the Japanese price, while a positive difference implies the Japanese price is below the U.S. price.

Figure 1.3a includes plots of the relative prices of industries in which the United States has a higher level of productivity in 1985. In the 1960s the Japanese output prices were relatively low, due primarily to lower labor costs. Although lower relative wage rates in Japan helped to reduce relative prices of output, they were almost totally offset by the lower levels of productivity in Japan during the 1960s.

After the energy crisis of 1973, U.S. output prices in the industries plotted in figures 1.3a fell relative to Japanese prices until 1980 due to much greater increase in energy prices in Japan and appreciation of the yen relative to the dollar. During the 1980s the international competitiveness of Japanese industries has been increasing in spite of the productivity gains in the United States. This is because of the more rapid increase in U.S. wage rates and costs of capital and the appreciation of the dollar. It is especially interesting that output prices in textile products, motor vehicles, and fabricated metals industries have been almost the same in Japan and the United States since 1980, notwithstanding the increasing U.S. productivity advantage in these industries.

In figures 1.3a–1.3b, we present plots of the relative output prices of industries in which Japan had a productivity advantage in 1985. The time trends of relative prices in these industries during the period 1960–85 are very similar to those of industries in which the United States had a productivity advantage.

Table 1.9   **Index of Productivity in Motor Vehicles**

Year	Japan	United States
1979	.91639	.97490
1981	.89246	.88842
1983	.85502	.95674
1985	.85379	.98393
1980	.91050	.53853
1982	.86165	.84402
1984	.85545	1.02915

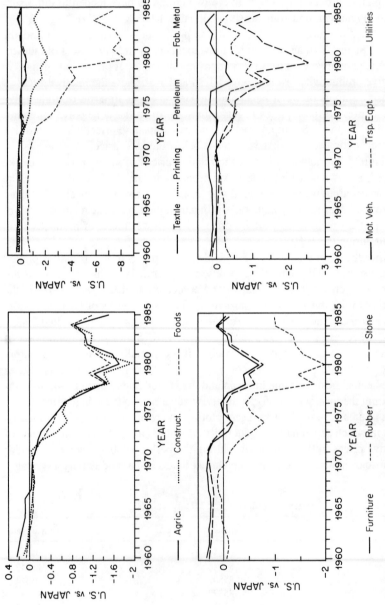

Fig. 1.3a Trends of proportional gap of denominated output prices

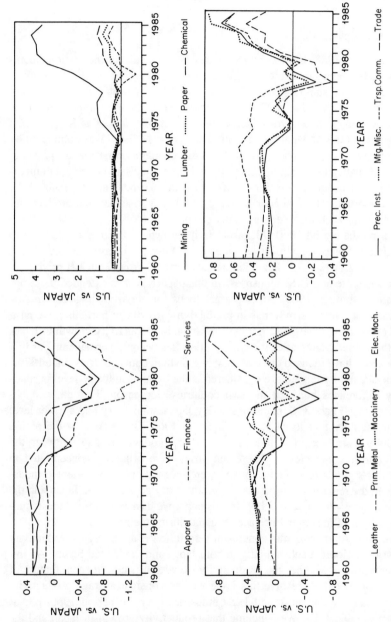

Fig. 1.3b   Trends of proportional gap of denominated output prices

However, the price levels are lower in Japan, so that Japan has a clear advantage in international competitiveness. These features are especially evident in industries classified as type 7 in our industrial taxonomy.

1.4   Conclusion

Jorgenson (1988) has recently summarized the results of international comparisons between Japan and the United States. The period 1960–73 was characterized by substantial economic growth in the United States and very rapid economic growth in Japan. Capital input was by far the most important source of growth in both countries, accounting for about 40% of U.S. economic growth and 60% of Japanese growth. The period 1973–79 was dominated by the energy crisis, which began with drastic increases in petroleum prices in 1973. Growth slowed significantly in the United States and declined dramatically in Japan during this period. The growth of capital input remained the most important source of economic growth in both countries, but productivity growth at the sectoral level essentially disappeared.

During the period 1960–73, productivity growth in Japan exceeded that in the United States for almost all industries. After the energy crisis in 1973, there were very few significant differences between growth rates of productivity in Japanese and U.S. industries. In this paper we have extended these observations through 1985. An important focus for our work has been the assessment of longer-term trends in productivity growth. In particular, we have tried to establish whether or not the slowdown in productivity growth in Japan and the United States after the energy crisis has become permanent. For this purpose we have focused on productivity growth in both countries since 1979.

The second issue we have considered is the trend of industry-level productivity differences between the two countries. Jorgenson, Kuroda, and Nishimizu (1987) showed that almost every Japanese industry had a lower level of productivity that its U.S. counterpart in 1960. By the end of the period 1960–79 there were nine industries in which productivity gaps between the two countries had closed. These industries were primarily concentrated in producer's goods manufacturing and were focused on export-oriented industries. In the remaining 19 industries, productivity gaps between Japan and the United States remained in 1979. In this paper we have reexamined these findings in light of the experience accumulated during the period 1979–85.

We can summarize our conclusions as follows: after 1970, productivity growth deteriorated substantially in both Japan and the United States. An important issue is whether the productivity slowdown is a permanent feature of both economies. To resolve this issue we can consider average productivity growth rates in Japanese and U.S. industries over the period 1960–85, as shown in table 1.10. We conclude that productivity growth in Japan and the United States has revived somewhat since 1980. However, the growth rates

Table 1.10   **Average Productivity Growth Rates in Japan and the United States**

	Japan (%)	United States (%)
1960–65	1.478	1.993
1965–70	1.946	− .985
1970–73	.686	.941
1973–75	− 1.481	− 3.064
1975–80	.178	− 1.058
1980–85	.760	.448

for the period 1980–85 are well below those for the period 1960–73, especially in Japan.

A second issue is whether productivity levels in Japan and the United States have tended to converge. While the mean of relative productivity levels between Japan and the United States has fallen since 1980, the variance has expanded rapidly. This implies that convergence of Japanese and U.S. levels of productivity during the 1960s has given way to sharply divergent trends in relative productivity by industry during the 1970s and, especially, during the 1980s. Figures 1.3a–1.3b provide our results on international competitiveness between Japan and the United States. The competitiveness of U.S. industries has been declining since 1980, due to more rapid growth of input prices in the United States and the appreciation of the dollar relative to the yen.

The industrial taxonomy presented by Jorgenson, Kuroda, and Nishimizu (1987) has proved to be relatively robust. The productivity trends by industry that was projected on the basis of earlier results have materialized with only a few exceptions. While the United States retains an overall advantage in relative productivity levels, there is a substantial number of industries where Japan has gained an advantage and seems likely to increase it. Perhaps equally important, the increase in the variance of relative productivity levels among industries has created opportunities for both countries to benefit from the great expansion in Japanese-U.S. trade that has already taken place. However, this increase is also an important source of "trade frictions" and will require continuing efforts at coordination of trade policies in the two countries.

Appendix

The industries in our data base for Japan are classified into 31 industrial sectors. For the United States, the industries are classified into 35 industrial sectors.[5] For international comparisons we have aggregated these industries to the 29 sectors given in table 1.1. To represent our bilateral models of production we require the following notation:

$$q_i = \text{price of the output of the } i\text{th industry;}$$

$$p_{Ki}, p_{Li}, p_{Ei}, p_{Mi} = \text{prices of capital, labor, energy, and other intermediate inputs in the } i\text{th industry;}$$

$$v_{Ki}, v_{Li}, v_{Ei}, v_{Mi} = \text{value shares of capital, labor, energy and other intermediate inputs in the } i\text{th industry.}$$

We represent the vector of value shares of the ith industry by v_i. Similarly, we represent the vector of logarithms of input prices of the ith industry by $\ln p_i$. We employ a time trend T, as an index of technology, and a dummy variable D, equal to one for Japan and zero for the United States, to represent differences in technology between the two countries. Under competitive conditions we can represent technology by a price function that is dual to the production function relating each industry's output to the corresponding inputs, the level of technology, and differences in technology between the two countries:

$$\ln q_i = \ln p_i' \alpha^i + \alpha_t^i T + \alpha_d^i D + \tfrac{1}{2}\ln p_i' B^i \ln p_i + \ln p_i' \beta_t^i T$$

(A1)
$$+ \ln p_i' \beta_d^i D + \tfrac{1}{2}\beta_{tt}^i T^2 + \beta_{td}^i T D + \tfrac{1}{2}\beta_{dd}^i D^2,$$
$$(i = 1, 2, \ldots, I).$$

For each industry the price of output is a transcendental or, more specifically, an exponential function of the logarithms of the input prices. We refer to these functions as *translog price functions*.[6] In this representation the scalars—$\alpha_t^i, \alpha_d^i, \beta_{tt}^i, \beta_{dd}^i$—the vectors—$\alpha^i \beta_t^i, \beta_d^i$—and the matrices, B^i, are constant parameters that differ among industries. These parameters reflect differences in technology among industries. Within each industry, differences in technology among time periods are represented by time as an index of technology. Differences in technology between Japan and the United States are represented by a dummy variable, equal to one for Japan and zero for the United States.

In analyzing differences in each industry's production patterns between Japan and the United States, we combine the price function with demand functions for inputs. We can express these functions as equalities between shares of each input in the value of the output of the industry and the elasticity of the output price with respect to the price of that input. These elasticities depend on input prices, dummy variables for each country, and time as an index of technology. The sum of the elasticities with respect to all inputs is equal to unity, so that the value shares also sum to unity.

For each industry the value shares are equal to the logarithmic derivatives of the price function with respect to logarithms of the input prices:

(A2) $$v_i = \alpha^i + B^i \ln p_i + \beta_t^i T + \beta_d^i D, \quad (i = 1, 2, \ldots, I).$$

We can define *rates of productivity growth*, say v_{Ti}, as the negative of rates of growth of the price of output with respect to time, holding the input prices constant:

(A3) $-v_{Ti} = \alpha_t^i + \beta_t^{i'} \ln p_i + \beta_{tt}^i T + \beta_{dt} D$, $(i = 1, 2, \ldots, I)$.

Similarly, we can define *differences in technology* between Japan and the U.S., say v_{Ti}, as the negative of rates of growth of the price of output with respect to the dummy variable, holding the input prices constant:

(A4) $-v_{Di} = \alpha_d^i + \beta_d^{i'} \ln p_i + \beta_{td}^i T + \beta_{dd}^i D$, $(i = 1, 2, \ldots, I)$.

The price of output, the prices of inputs, and the value shares for all four inputs are observable for each industry in the period 1960–85 in both countries. The rates of productivity growth are not directly observable, but average rates of productivity growth between two points of time, say T and T-1, can be expressed as the difference between a weighted average of growth rates of input prices and the growth rates of the price of output for each industry:

(A5) $-\bar{v}_{Ti} = \ln q_i(T) - \ln q_i(T-1) - v_i'[\ln p_i(T) - \ln p_i(T-1)]$,
$(i = 1, 2, \ldots, I)$,

where the average rates of technical change are:

$$\bar{v}_{Ti} = \tfrac{1}{2}[v_{Ti}(T) + v_{Ti}(T-1)],$$

and the weights are given by the average value shares:

$$v_i = \tfrac{1}{2}[v_i(T) + v_i(T-1)].$$

We refer to the index numbers (A5) as *translog price indices* of the rates of productivity growth.[7]

Similarly, differences in productivity v_{Di} are not directly observable. However, the average of these differences for Japan and the United States can be expressed as a weighted average of differences between the logarithms of the input prices less the difference between logarithms of the output price:

(A6) $-\hat{v}_{Di} = \ln q_i(\text{JAPAN}) - \ln q_i(\text{US}) - \hat{v}_i'[\ln p_i(\text{JAPAN}) - \ln p_i(\text{US})]$,
$(i = 1, 2, \ldots, I)$,

where the average differences in productivity are

$$\hat{v}_{Di} = \tfrac{1}{2}[v_{Di}(\text{JAPAN}) + v_{Di}(\text{US})],$$

and the weights are given by the average value shares

$$\hat{v}_i = \tfrac{1}{2}[v_i(\text{JAPAN}) + v_i(\text{US})].$$

We refer to the index numbers (A6) as *translog price indices* of differences in productivity.

Notes

1. Equivalently, these prices could be expressed in terms of yen.
2. Christensen, Cummings, and Jorgenson (1980, 1981) have compared aggregate outputs, inputs, and productivity levels for nine countries, including Japan and the United States. Their estimates of relative productivity levels are based on the methodology for multilateral comparisons developed by Caves, Christensen, and Diewert (1982a, 1982b). An alternative approach is presented by Denny and Fuss (1983).
3. A similar approach is employed by Conrad and Jorgenson (1985) in comparisons for 1960–79 among the Federal Republic of Germany, Japan, and the United States. This methodology is also used by Nishimizu and Robinson (1986) in comparisons among manufacturing industries in Japan, Korea, Turkey, and Yugoslavia.
4. The methodology was originated by Kuroda (1981).
5. This classification is a consolidation of that used by Jorgenson, Gollop, and Fraumeni (1987).
6. The translog price function was introduced by Christensen, Jorgenson, and Lau (1971, 1973).
7. Diewert (1976) showed that the index numbers employed by Christensen and Jorgenson (1973) are exact for the translog price function of Christensen, Jorgenson, and Lau (1971, 1973).

References

Caves, D. W., L. R. Christensen, W. E. Diewert. 1982a. Multilateral comparisons of output, input, and productivity using superlative index numbers. *Economic Journal* 92, no. 365 (March):73–86.
———. 1982b. The economic theory of index numbers, and the measurement of input, output, and productivity. *Econometrica* 50, no. 6 (November):1393–1414.
Christensen, L. R., D. Cummings, and D. W. Jorgenson. 1980. Economic growth, 1947–1973: An international comparison. In *New developments in productivity measurement*, ed. J. W. Kendrick and B. Vaccara, 595–698. Chicago: University of Chicago Press.
———. 1981. Relative productivity levels, 1947–1973. *European Economic Review* 16, no. 1 (May):61–94.
Christensen, L. R., and D. W. Jorgenson. 1973. Measurement of economic performance in the private sector. In *The measurement of economic and social performance*, ed. M. Moss, 233–351. New York: Columbia University Press.
Christensen, L. R., D. W. Jorgenson, and L. J. Lau. 1971. Conjugate duality and the transcendental logarithmic production function. *Econometrica* 39, no. 4 (July) 255–56.
———. 1973. Transcendental logarithmic production frontiers. *Review of Economics and Statistics* 55, no. 1 (February):28–45.
Conrad, Klaus, and Dale W. Jorgenson. 1985. Sectoral productivity gaps between the United States, Japan, and Germany, 1960–1979. In *Probleme und Perspektiven der Weltwirtschaftlichen Entwicklung*, ed. Herbert Giersch, 335–47. Berlin: Duncker and Humblot.
Denny, M., and M. Fuss. 1983. A general approach to intertemporal and interspatial productivity comparisons. *Journal of Econometrics* 23, no. 3 (December):315–30.

Diewert, W. E. 1976. Exact and superlative index numbers. *Journal of Econometrics* 4, no. 4 (May):115–46.

Jorgenson, D. W. 1988. Productivity and economic growth in Japan and the United States. *American Economic Review* 78, no. 2 (May):217–22.

Jorgenson, D. W., F. M. Gollop, and B. M. Fraumeni. 1987. *Productivity and U.S. economic growth.* Cambridge, Mass.: Harvard University Press.

Jorgenson, D. W., M. Kuroda, and M. Nishimizu. 1987. Japan-U.S. industry-level productivity comparisons, 1960–1979. *Journal of the Japanese and International Economies* 1, no. 1 (March):1–30.

Jorgenson, D. W., and M. Nishimizu. 1978. U.S. and Japanese economic growth, 1952–1974: An international comparison. *Economic Journal* 88, no. 352 (December):707–26.

———. 1981. International differences in levels of technology: A comparison between U.S. and Japanese industries. In *International Roundtable Congress Proceedings*. Tokyo: Institute of Statistical Mathematics.

Kravis, I. B., A. Heston, and R. Summers. 1978. *International comparisons of real product and purchasing power.* Baltimore: Johns Hopkins University Press.

Kuroda, M. 1981. Method of estimation for updating the transactions matrix in input-output relationships. Discussion Paper no. 1. Keio Economic Observatory, Keio University, Tokyo.

Nishimizu, M., and S. Robinson. 1986. Productivity growth in manufacturing. In *Industrialization and growth,* ed. H. Chenery, S. Robinson, and M. Syrquin, 283–308. Oxford: Oxford University Press.

Comment   Robert M. Schwab

This paper is an ideal contribution to a volume on U.S. and Japanese productivity. It presents careful estimates of prices, inputs, outputs, and productivity for 31 Japanese and 35 U.S. industries for the period from 1960 to 1985. These estimates allow Jorgenson and Kuroda to ask and answer a wide range of interesting and important questions. Did the differences between Japanese and U.S. productivity growth rates narrow or widen during this period? Have levels of productivity converged? What can we learn by looking at patterns across industries?

The productivity estimates are derived in the sources-of-growth framework. In that framework, productivity growth over time within a country equals the difference between the growth rate of output and the share-weighted growth rates of inputs. Similarly, the difference in the level of productivity across countries at a point in time equals the difference in output less the share weighted differences in inputs. This approach is well developed in the literature, and many of the often-heard objections to growth accounting can be raised once again. For example, payments to capital are interpreted as the

Robert Schwab is an associate professor of economics at the University of Maryland.

value of the marginal product of capital, ignoring capital utilization issues, adjustment costs, and so on. Growth accounting imposes an assumption of constant returns to scale at the industry level; if this assumption is wrong, then the paper's estimates of productivity growth include scale economies.

The paper's estimates of differences in economic performance are dramatic. Output grew about 2.5 times faster in Japan than in the United States during 1960–79. Roughly 80% of this difference was due to differences in input growth. The Japanese capital stock grew nearly three times as fast as the U.S. capital stock; differences in labor growth were much smaller. The remaining 20% represents differences in total factor productivity growth. These large differences in output growth and small differences in labor growth imply large differences in the growth of labor productivity (output per worker). Differences in total factor productivity explain about one-quarter of the difference in labor productivity, while the remainder is attributable to differences in the growth of capital per worker and intermediate input per worker.

There are some anomalies in the results for the individual industries. Consider motor vehicles, for example. Output in this industry grew much faster in Japan than in the United States during the twenty-five-year period covered in this study. Tables 1.3–1.5 in the paper attribute all of the difference in output to differences in inputs; estimated productivity growth was lower in Japan than in the United States. This may be correct, but I doubt it; certainly, it is at odds with Japan's growing role in the world automobile and truck markets and the widespread belief that Japanese auto firms are the models of efficiency and productivity. A more plausible explanation is that the results for this industry are symptomatic of some of the well-known shortcomings of growth accounting. In that framework we measure productivity growth as a residual, and therefore our estimates are contaminated by all sorts of measurement errors inherent in the data. In the aggregate, over a long time period, these errors will hopefully cancel and our estimates of productivity growth will be sound. If we focus on any single industry, however, we may not be so fortunate.

The paper's analysis of various subperiods is provocative. In the version of the paper presented at the conference, the authors conclude that during the 1960–70 economic "boom," productivity growth was substantially higher in Japan that in the United States. In the later years, particularly after the oil crisis began in 1973, differences in productivity growth between the two countries were insignificant.

I have two comments on this conclusion. First, it is inconsistent with some earlier studies of Japanese and U.S. economic performance. For example, Norsworthy and Malmquist (*American Economic Review*, 1983) estimated that average annual productivity growth in Japan was about eight-tenths of a percentage point higher during 1973–78 than during 1965–73, when the U.S. average fell two-tenths of a point; thus according to the Norsworthy-Malmquist estimates, the gap between Japanese and U.S. productivity growth widened after the oil shock. There are a number of possible explanations of these divergent results. The time periods in other studies do not match exactly; the studies use different data sets; some studies focus on economic aggregates while this study looks at individual industries. Still, these differences are puzzling and deserve further attention.

Second, if Jorgenson and Kuroda are correct, we are left with the question of why productivity trends converged. Perhaps Japan was more vulnerable to the oil shock than was the United States. Certainly the Japanese economy was more dependent on foreign oil, though it is not clear that increases in foreign oil prices would have a larger impact on productivity than would increases in domestic oil prices. Perhaps U.S. price controls shielded U.S. industries from some of the short-run effects of the oil shock, or perhaps differences in the structure of production were important. Since there are problems with the oil price shock story, and since there is at least some evidence that differences in productivity had already begun to narrow during 1970–73, I suspect that we need to look at additional explanations in order to understand this result.

One such explanation would draw on the "catching up" hypothesis. Advocates of this hypothesis might argue that Japan was operating well inside the best-practices production possibilities frontier after the war. Thus two avenues of growth were available: the frontier would shift out over time, and Japan would move closer to the frontier. When Japan had fully adopted all of the existing technology, Japanese productivity growth from that point forward would be roughly the same as that of other countries. This explanation of course has a testable implication; if it is correct, we would expect to find that differences in productivity growth were associated with differences in the level of productivity. The paper offers some evidence that suggests that this was, in fact, the case in some industries, but by no means all. It would therefore seem that catching up is a very complex phenomenon and one that deserves a good deal of attention in the future.

In sum, Jorgenson and Kuroda have made an important contribution to the literature on international productivity comparisons. Their analysis is meticulous, wide ranging, and provocative. I am certain that this paper will become one of the standard references in this field.

2 Bilateral Models of Production for Japanese and U.S. Industries

Dale W. Jorgenson, Hikaru Sakuramoto, Kanji Yoshioka, and Masahiro Kuroda

2.1 Introduction

The purpose of this paper is to present bilateral models of production for 28 Japanese and U.S. industries for the period 1960–79. We treat data on production for the two countries as separate sets of observations. However, we assume that these observations are generated by an econometric model with common parameters. This model determines the distribution of the value of output among capital, labor, and intermediate inputs in each country. It also determines rates of technical change for both countries and the difference between the level of technology in the two countries.

Our methodology is based on the economic theory of production. The underlying model of production is the same as that employed in a companion paper by Jorgenson and Kuroda (this volume). We utilize this model in generating an econometric model of producer behavior for individual industries. Jorgenson and Kuroda employ the model to generate index numbers of productivity growth and differences in productivity between Japan and the United States. We use these indices as data, together with prices and quantities of output and inputs for each industry in modeling production.

Our models of production are based on the bilateral translog model introduced by Jorgenson and Nishimizu (1978). The point of departure for these models is a production function for each industry, giving output as a function of capital, labor, and intermediate inputs, a dummy variable equal to zero for the United States and one for Japan, and a time trend. The dummy variable allows for productivity differences between the two countries, while the time trend permits technology in each country to change from period to period.

Dale W. Jorgenson is a professor of economics at Harvard University. Hikaru Sakuramoto is a professor of economics, Faculty of Business and Commerce, Keio University. Kanji Yoshioka is a professor of economics, Keio Economic Observatory, Keio University. Masahiro Kuroda is a professor of economics, Faculty of Business and Commerce, Keio University.

In analyzing differences in each industry's production patterns between the two countries, we combine the production function with necessary conditions for producer equilibrium. We express these conditions as equalities between shares of input in the value of output and the elasticity of output with respect to that input. The elasticities depend on input levels, the dummy variables for each country, and time. For given input intensities and given levels of technology, we find that U.S. industries have higher rates of labor remuneration than the corresponding Japanese industries. Japanese industries have higher rate of remuneration for capital and intermediate inputs. Technical change is predominantly capital saving, labor saving, and intermediate input using in both countries.

An important focus for our bilateral models of production is the difference between rates of technical change in Japanese and U.S. industries. For six of the 28 industries, we find that rates of technical change are higher in the United States than in Japan at given relative input intensities. Rates of technical change are higher in Japan for the remaining 22 industries. An alternative and equivalent interpretation of these results can be given in terms of the difference in technology between the two countries or the "technology gap." The technology gap between Japan and the United States is increasing for 22 of the industries included in our study and decreasing for only six industries. For industries where the United States has an advantage, the gap is closing; for industries where Japan has an advantage, the gap is widening.

Our industry classification is based on that of Jorgenson and Kuroda (in this volume). The Japanese industries are classified among 31 industries, while the U.S. industries are classified among 35 industries. In estimating our bilateral production model, we have consolidated the two classifications to 28 industries. In section 2.2, we provide a theoretical framework for our bilateral models of production. Section 2.3 outlines the empirical results, and section 2.4 provides a brief summary and conclusion. We present additional details on the constraints that must be satisfied by the parameters of our econometric models in order to meet the requirements imposed by the theory of production presented below in appendix A. The detailed empirical results are presented in appendix B.

2.2   Theoretical Framework

We treat data on production patterns for Japan and the United States as separate sets of observations. We assume that these observations are generated by an econometric model with common parameters. We describe the implications of the theory of production in terms of a bilateral production function for each sector. These functions are homogeneous of degree one, nondecreasing, and concave in capital, labor, and intermediate inputs.

In representing our bilateral models of production we employ the same notation as Jorgenson and Kuroda (in this volume). To characterize producer behavior in greater detail we introduce *share elasticities with respect to quantity*,[1] defined as derivatives of the vectors of value shares (v^i) with respect to vectors of logarithms of the inputs ($\ln X_j$):

(1) $$\frac{\partial v_i}{\partial \ln X_i} = \frac{\partial^2 \ln Z_i}{\partial \ln X_i \partial \ln X_i'} = B_{XX}^i, \quad (i = 1, 2, \ldots, I),$$

where $\ln Z_i (i = 1, 2, \ldots, I)$ is the logarithm of output in the *i*th sector.

For the translog production functions the share elasticities $\{B_{XX}^i\}$ are constant. We can also characterize these production functions as constant share elasticity (CSE) production functions, indicating the role of fixed parameters.[2] If a share elasticity is positive, the value share increases with the input. If a share elasticity is negative, the value share decreases with the input. Finally, if a share elasticity is zero, the value share is independent of the input.

Continuing with a detailed characterization of producer behavior we define biases of technical change with respect to quantity as derivatives of the value shares with respect to time T:[3]

(2) $$\frac{\partial v_i}{\partial T} = \frac{\partial \ln Z_i}{\partial \ln X_i \partial T} = \beta_{XT}^i, \quad (i = 1, 2, \ldots, I),$$

Alternatively, we can define these biases as derivatives of the rates of technical change (v_T^i) with respect to logarithms of the inputs. These two definitions are equivalent. For translog production functions the biases of technical change (β_{XT}^i) are constant.

If a bias of technical change is positive, the corresponding value share increases with technology; we say that technical change is *input using*. If a bias is negative, the value share decreases with technology and technical change is *input saving*. Finally, if a bias is zero, the value share is independent of technology and we say that technical change is *neutral*. Alternatively, biases of technical change contain the implications of changes in inputs for the rate of technical change. If a bias is positive, the rate of technical change increases with the corresponding input. If a bias is negative, the rate of technical change decreases with the input. Finally, if a bias is zero, the rate is independent of the input.

Similarly, we define biases of the difference in technology with respect to quantity as derivatives of the value shares with respect to the dummy variable D,[4] equal to zero for the United States and one for Japan.

(3) $$\frac{\partial v_i}{\partial D} = \frac{\partial^2 \ln Z_i}{\partial \ln X_i \partial D} = \beta_{XD}^i, \quad (i = 1, 2, \ldots, I),$$

Alternatively, we can define these biases as derivatives of the differences in technology (v_D^i) between Japan and the United States with respect to logarithms of the inputs. These two definitions are equivalent. For the translog production functions the biases of differences in technology (β_{XD}^i) are constant.

If a bias of the difference in technology is positive, the corresponding value share increases between the United States and Japan and we say that the difference in technology is input using. If a bias is negative, the value share decreases between the United States and Japan and the difference in technology is input saving. Finally, if a bias is zero, the value share is the same in the United States and Japan and we say that the difference in technology is neutral. Alternatively, the vectors of biases of differences in technology contain the implications of changes in inputs for the difference in technology between the United States and Japan. If a bias of the difference in technology is positive, the difference in technology increases with the input. If a bias is negative, the difference in technology decreases with the input. Finally, if a bias is zero, the difference in technology is independent of the input.

Finally, we can define the biases of technical change with respect to the difference in technology between Japan and the United States as the derivatives of the rates of technical change (v_T^i) with respect to the dummy variable:[5]

$$(4) \qquad \frac{\partial v_D^i}{\partial T} = \frac{\partial^2 \ln Z_i}{\partial T \partial D} = \frac{\partial v_T^i}{\partial D} = \beta_{TD}^i, \quad (i = 1, 2, \ldots, I).$$

Alternatively, we can define these biases as the derivatives of the differences in technology (v_D^i) with respect to technology. The two definitions are equivalent.

For the translog production functions the biases (β_{TD}^i) are constant. If the bias is positive, the difference in technology increases with technology; correspondingly, the rate of technical change increases between the United States and Japan. If the bias is negative, the difference in technology decreases with technology; correspondingly, the rate of technical change decreases between the United States and Japan. Finally, if the bias is zero the difference in technology is independent of technology and the rate of technical change is the same for the United States and Japan.

To complete the description of technical change we can define the acceleration of technical change as the derivative of the rate of technical change with respect to technology:

$$(5) \qquad \frac{\partial v_T^i}{\partial T} = \frac{\partial^2 \ln Z_i}{\partial T^2} = \beta_{TT}^i, \quad (i = 1, 2, \ldots, I).$$

If the acceleration is positive, negative, or zero, the rate of technical change is increasing, decreasing, or independent of the level of technology.

Similarly, we can define the difference of the difference in technology as the derivative of the difference in technology between Japan and United States with respect to the dummy variable.[6]

$$(6) \qquad \frac{\partial v_D^i}{\partial D} = \frac{\partial^2 \ln Z_i}{\partial D^2} = \beta_{DD}^i, \quad (i = 1, 2, \ldots, I).$$

If this difference is positive, negative, or zero, the difference in technology is increasing, decreasing, or independent, respectively, of the dummy variable. For the translog production functions, both the accelerations (β_{TT}^i) and the differences (β_{DD}^i) are constant. This completes the detailed characterization of producer behavior in terms of the parameters of our bilateral translog models of production.

To estimate the unknown parameters of the bilateral translog production function we combine the first two equations for the average value shares in Japan and the United States, the equations for the average rates of technical change in the two countries, and the equation for the average difference in technology to obtain a complete econometric model of production. We estimate the parameters of the equations for the remaining average value shares in the two countries, using the restrictions on these parameters given below in appendix A. The complete model involves 14 unknown parameters. A total of 16 additional parameters can be estimated as functions of these parameters, given the restrictions. Our estimates of the unknown parameters of the econometric model of production is based on the nonlinear three-stage least squares estimator introduced by Jorgenson and Laffont (1974).

2.3   Empirical Results

To implement the bilateral econometric models of production developed in section 2.2, we employ a data base for 28 U.S. and Japanese industrial sectors compiled by Jorgenson, Kuroda and Nishimizu (1987). For each sector they have assembled data on the value shares of capital, labor, and intermediate inputs for both countries, annually, for the period 1960–79. They have also compiled quantity indices of output and all three inputs for both countries for the same period. Finally, they have developed translog indexes of technical change for both countries and a translog index of the difference in technology between the two countries. There are 19 observations for each country, since two-period averages of all data are employed.

The parameters (α_K^i, α_L^i, α_M^i) can be interpreted as average value shares of capital input, labor input, and intermediate input, respectively, for the corresponding industrial sector in Japan and the United States. Similarly, the parameters (α_T^i) are averages of rates of technical change and the parameters (α_D^i) are averages of differences in technology between the two countries. The parameters (β_{KK}^i, β_{KL}^i, β_{KM}^i, β_{LL}^i, β_{LM}^i, β_{MM}^i) can be interpreted as constant share elasticities with respect to quantity for the corresponding sector in Japan and the United States.

Similarly, the parameters (β_{KT}^i, β_{LT}^i, β_{MT}^i) are constant biases of technical change with respect to quantity for the corresponding sector in the two countries, and the parameters (β_{KD}^i, β_{LD}^i, β_{MD}^i) are constant biases of differences in technology between the two countries. Finally, the parameters (β_{TT}^i) are constant accelerations of technical change in Japan and the United States, the parameters (β_{TD}^i) are constant biases of technical change with respect to the difference in technology between the two countries, and the parameters (β_{DD}^i) are constant differences in the difference in technology.

In estimating the parameters of our bilateral models of production, we retain the average value shares, the average rate of technical change, and the average difference in technology between the two countries as parameters to be estimated for all 28 industrial sectors. Similarly, we estimate the biases of technical change, the biases of differences in technology, and the biases of technical change with respect to the difference in technology. Finally, we estimate the accelerations of technical change and the differences in the difference in technology for all 28 sectors.

Estimates of the share elasticities with respect to quantity are obtained under the restrictions implied by the necessary and sufficient conditions for concavity of the bilateral production function described in appendix A below. Under these restrictions the matrices of constant share elasticities must be nonpositive definite for all industries. To impose the concavity restrictions, we represent the matrices of constant share elasticities for all sectors in terms of their Cholesky factorizations. The necessary and sufficient conditions are that the diagonal elements (δ_1^i, δ_2^i) of the matrices (D^i) that appear in the Cholesky factorizations must be nonpositive. The estimates presented below in appendix B incorporate these restrictions for all 28 industries.

Our interpretation of the parameter estimates reported in appendix B begins with an analysis of the estimates of the parameters (α_K^i, α_L^i, α_M^i, α_T^i, α_D^i). The average value shares are nonnegative for all 28 industries included in our study. The estimated average rates of technical change are positive in 19 sectors and negative in 9 sectors. The estimated average differences in technology between the United States and Japan are positive in 17 sectors and negative in 11. For given input levels, differences in technology favor Japan in 17 of the 28 industries. The industries with positive and negative estimates of these parameters are listed in table 2.1.

The estimated share elasticities with respect to quantity (β_{KK}^i, β_{KL}^i, β_{KM}^i, β_{LL}^i, β_{LM}^i, β_{MM}^i) describe the implications of patterns of substitution among capital, labor, and intermediate inputs for the relative distribution of the value of output among these three inputs. Positive share elasticities imply that the value shares increase with the quantity of the corresponding input; negative share elasticities imply that the value shares decrease with the input; share elasticities equal to zero imply that the value shares are independent of the input. It is important to keep in mind that we have fitted these parameters subject to the restrictions implied by concavity of the bilateral production functions. These restrictions require that all share elasticities be set equal to zero for six of the 28 industries—construction, food processing, stone, clay, and glass, machinery, transportation equipment, and precision instruments.

Our interpretation of the parameter estimates given in appendix B continues with the estimated elasticities of the share of each input with respect to the

Table 2.1   Rates of Technical Change and Differences in Technology

Rates of Technical Change		Differences in Technology	
$\alpha_T > 0$	$\alpha_T < 0$	$\alpha_D > 0$	$\alpha_D < 0$
(1) Agriculture, Forestry & Fisheries	(2) Mining	(3) Construction	(1) Agriculture, Forestry & Fisheries
(4) Food & Kindred Products	(3) Construction	(4) Food & Kindred Products	(2) Mining
(5) Textile Mill Products	(7) Lumber and Wood Products (except furniture)	(5) Textile Mill Products	(6) Apparel & Other Fabricated Textiles
(6) Apparel & Other Fabricated Textile Products	(12) Petroleum Refinery	(7) Lumber & Wood Products	(9) Paper & Allied Products
(8) Furniture & Fixtures	(15) Stone, Clay, & Glass	(8) Furniture & Fixtures	(12) Petroleum Refinery
(9) Paper & Allied Products	(16) Iron & Steel	(10) Printing & Publishing	(14) Leather & Leather Products
(10) Printing & Publishing	(23) Miscellaneous Manufacturing	(11) Chemical & Allied Products	(15) Stone, Clay & Glass Products
(11) Chemical	(25) Electric Utility, Gas Supply & Water Supply	(13) Rubber & Miscellaneous Plastic Products	(16) Iron & Steel
(13) Rubber & Miscellaneous Plastic Products	(28) Service	(17) Faabricated Metal	(18) Machinery
(14) Leather		(20) Motor Vehicle & Equipment	(19) Electric Machinery
(17) Fabricated Metal Products		(21) Transportation Equipment (except motor)	(22) Precision Instruments
(18) Machinery		(23) Miscellaneous Manufacturing	
(19) Electric Machinery		(24) Transportation & Communication	
(20) Motor Vehicles & Equipment		(25) Electrical Utilities, Gas Supply & Water Supply	
(21) Transportation Equipment (except motor)		(26) Wholesale & Retail Trade	
(22) Precision Instruments		(27) Finance & Insurance	
(24) Transportation & Communication		(28) Service	
(26) Wholesale & Retail Trade			
(27) Finance & Insurance			

quantity of the input itself (β^i_{KK}, β^i_{LL}, β^i_{MM}). Under the necessary and sufficient conditions for concavity of the bilateral production functions, these share elasticities are nonpositive. The share of each input is nonincreasing in the quantity of the input itself. This condition together with the condition that the sum of all the share elasticities with respect to a given input is equal to zero implies that only one of the elasticities of the share of each input with respect to the quantities of the other two inputs (β^i_{KL}, β^i_{KM}, β^i_{LM}) can be negative. All three of these share elasticities can be nonnegative, and this condition holds for 17 of the 28 industries.

The share elasticity of capital with respect to the quantity of labor (β^i_{KL}) is nonnegative for all 28 industries. By symmetry this parameter can also be interpreted as the share elasticity of labor with respect to the quantity of capital. This share elasticity is positive for the 15 industries listed in table 2.2 and zero for the remaining 13 industries. The share elasticity of capital with respect to the quantity of intermediate input (β^i_{KM}) is negative for the five industries listed in table 2.2, zero for 13 industries and positive for 10 industries. This parameter can also be interpreted as the share elasticity of intermediate input with respect to the quantity of capital. Finally, the share elasticity of labor with respect to the quantity of intermediate input (β^i_{LM}) is negative for the 6 industries listed in table 2.2, zero for 6 industries, and positive for 16 industries. This last parameter can also be interpreted as the share elasticity of intermediate input with respect to the quantity of labor.

We continue the interpretation of parameter estimates given in Appendix B with the estimated biases of technical change with respect to the quantity of each input (β^i_{KT}, β^i_{LT}, β^i_{MT}). The estimated biases describe the implications of technical change for the relative distribution of the value of output among capital, labor, and intermediate inputs. Alternatively, they give the implications of patterns of substitution among these three inputs for the rate of technical change. Positive biases imply that the value shares increase with the level of technology; negative biases imply that the value shares decrease with technology. If a bias is positive, we say that technical change uses the corresponding input; if a bias is negative, we say that technical change saves the input. Input-using change implies that the rate of technical change increases with the quantity of the corresponding input, while input-saving change implies that this rate decreases with the input.

The sum of the three biases of technical change with respect to quantity is equal to zero, so that we can rule out the possibility that the three biases are either all negative or all positive. Of the six remaining logical possibilities, only capital-saving and intermediate input-saving and labor-using technical change fails to occur among the results for individual industries presented in table 2.3. The biases of technical change are not affected by the concavity restrictions on the bilateral production functions, so that all three parameters are fitted for each of the 28 industries included in our study.

We first consider the bias of technical change with respect to the quantity of capital input. If the estimated value of this parameter is positive, technical

Table 2.2   Share Elasticities

	Capital-Labor			Capital-Intermediate			Labor-Intermediate		
	$\beta_{KL} < 0$	$\beta_{KL} = 0$	$\beta_{KL} > 0$	$\beta_{KM} < 0$	$\beta_{KM} = 0$	$\beta_{KM} > 0$	$\beta_{LM} < 0$	$\beta_{LM} = 0$	$\beta_{LM} > 0$
	...	(3) Construction (4) Foods (5) Textiles (11) Chemical (14) Leather (15) Stone, Clay (16) Iron & Steel (18) Machinery (21) Transportation Equipment (22) Precision Instruments (23) Miscellaneous Manufacturing (25) Utilities (27) Finance	(1) Agriculture (2) Mining (6) Apparel (7) Lumber (8) Furniture (9) Paper (10) Printing (12) Petroleum (13) Rubber (17) Fabricated Metal (19) Electric Machinery (20) Motor Vehicles (24) Transportation & Communication (26) Trade (30) Other Services	(8) Furniture (13) Rubber (19) Electrical Machinery (24) Transportation & Communication (30) Other Services	(3) Construction (4) Foods (5) Textiles (11) Chemical (14) Leather (15) Stone, Clay (16) Iron & Steel (18) Machinery (21) Transportation Equipment (22) Precision Instruments (23) Miscellaneous Manufacturing (25) Utilities (27) Finance	(1) Agriculture (2) Mining (6) Apparel (7) Lumber (9) Paper (10) Printing (12) Petroleum (17) Fabricated Metal (20) Motor Vehicle (26) Trade	(1) Agriculture (2) Mining (6) Apparel (7) Lumber (20) Motor Vehicle (26) Trade	(3) Construction (4) Foods (15) Stone, Clay (18) Machinery (21) Transportation Equipment (22) Precision Instruments	(5) Textile (8) Furniture (9) Paper (10) Printing (11) Chemical (12) Petroleum (13) Rubber (14) Leather (16) Iron & Steel (17) Fabricated Metal (19) Electric Machinery (23) Miscellaneous Manufacturing (24) Transportation & Communication (25) Utilities (27) Finance (30) Other Services

Table 2.3   Biases of Technical Change

$\beta_{TK} > 0$	(3) Construction, (5) Textile, (26) Trade
$\beta_{TL} > 0$	. . .
$\beta_{TM} < 0$	. . .
$\beta_{TK} > 0$	(1) Agriculture, (8) Furniture, (10) Printing
$\beta_{TL} < 0$	(17) Fabricated Metal, (19) Electric Machinery, (21) Transportation Equipment
$\beta_{TM} > 0$	(24) Transportation & Communication
$\beta_{TK} > 0$	(6) Apparel, (7) Lumber
$\beta_{TL} < 0$	. . .
$\beta_{TM} < 0$	. . .
$\beta_{TK} < 0$	(4) Foods, (9) Paper, (16) Iron & Steel
$\beta_{TL} > 0$	(20) Motor Vehicles, (22) Precision Instruments, (27) Finance
$\beta_{TM} > 0$	(30) Other Services
$\beta_{TK} < 0$	. . .
$\beta_{TL} > 0$	. . .
$\beta_{TM} < 0$	. . .
$\beta_{TK} < 0$	(2) Mining, (11) Chemical, (12) Petroleum
$\beta_{TL} < 0$	(13) Rubber, (14) Leather, (15) Stone, Clay
$\beta_{TM} < 0$	(18) Machinery, (23) Miscellaneous Manufacturing, (25) Utilities

change is capital using. Alternatively, the rate of technical change increases with an increase in the quantity of capital input. If the estimated value is negative, technical change in capital saving and the rate of technical change decrease with the quantity of capital input. Technical change is capital using for 12 of the 28 industries included in our study and capital saving for the remaining 16.

The interpretation of biases of technical change with respect to the quantities of labor and intermediate inputs is analogous to the interpretation of the bias for capital input. Technical change is labor using for 10 of the 28 industries and laborsaving for the 18 remaining industries. Technical change is intermediate input using for 23 of the 28 industries and intermediate input saving for the remaining 5. We conclude that technical change is predominantly capital saving, laborsaving, and intermediate input using for Japanese and U.S. industries.

We next consider the interpretation of the estimated biases of the difference in technology with respect to the quantity of each input (β^i_{KD}, β^i_{LD}, β^i_{MD}). The estimated biases describe the implications of the difference in technology between the United States and Japan for the relative distribution of the value of output among capital, labor, and intermediate inputs. Alternatively, they give the implications of patterns of substitution among these three inputs for the difference in technology. Positive biases imply that the value shares increase from the United States and Japan; negative biases imply that the value shares decrease from the United States to Japan. If a bias is positive, we say that the difference in technology between the United States and Japan uses the corresponding input; if a bias is negative, we say that technical change saves the

Table 2.4   **Biases of the Differences in Technology**

$\beta_{DK} > 0$	(2) Mining, (11) Chemical, (12) Petroleum
$\beta_{DL} > 0$	(25) Utilities, (27) Finance
$\beta_{DM} < 0$	
$\beta_{DK} > 0$	(3) Construction, (5) Textile, (9) Paper (15) Stone, Clay
$\beta_{DL} < 0$	(16) Iron & Steel, (19) Machinery, (22) Transportation Equipment
$\beta_{DM} > 0$	(27) Trade
$\beta_{DK} > 0$	(1) Agriculture, (4) Foods, (14) Leather
$\beta_{DL} < 0$	. . .
$\beta_{DM} < 0$	. . .
$\beta_{DK} < 0$	(8) Furniture, (24) Miscellaneous Manufacturing, (30) Other Services
$\beta_{DL} > 0$	. . .
$\beta_{DM} > 0$	. . .
$\beta_{DK} < 0$	(10) Printing, (25) Transportation & Communication
$\beta_{DL} > 0$	. . .
$\beta_{DM} < 0$	. . .
$\beta_{DK} < 0$	(6) Apparel, (7) Lumber, (13) Rubber, (17) Fabricated Metal
$\beta_{DL} < 0$	(19) Electric Machinery, (20) Motor Vehicles, (22) Precision Instruments
$\beta_{DM} < 0$	. . .

input. An input using difference in technology implies that the difference in technology increases with the quantity of the corresponding input, while input-saving change implies that this rate decreases with the input.

The sum of the three biases of the difference in technology with respect to quantity is equal to zero, so that we can rule out the possibility that the three biases are either all negative or all positive. All six of the remaining logical possibilities occur among the results for individual industries presented in table 2.4. The biases of the difference in technology, like the biases of technical change, are not affected by the concavity restrictions on the bilateral production functions, so that all three parameters are fitted for each of the 28 industries included in our study.

We first consider the bias of the difference in technology between the United States and Japan with respect to the quantity of capital input. If the estimated value of this parameter is positive, the difference in technology is capital using. Alternatively, the difference in technology increases with an increase in the quantity of capital input. If the estimated value is negative, the difference in technology is capital saving and the difference in technology decreases with the quantity of capital input. The difference in technology is capital using for 16 of the 28 industries included in our study and capital saving for the remaining 12.

The interpretation of biases of the difference in technology with respect to the quantities of labor and intermediate inputs is analogous to the interpretation of the bias for capital input. The difference in technology between the United States and Japan is labor using for 10 of the 28 industries and laborsaving for the 18 remaining industries. The difference in technology is intermediate input using for 18 of the 28 industries and intermediate input saving for the remaining 10. We conclude that, for given input prices and a given level of technology, production is more capital intensive and intermediate input intensive in Japanese industries and more labor intensive in U.S. industries.

We continue with the interpretation of the estimated biases of technical change with respect to the difference in technology between the United States and Japan (β_{TD}). The estimated biases describe the implications of the difference in technology for the rate of technical change. Alternatively, they give the implications of the level of technology for the difference in technology. A positive bias implies that the rate of technical change increases from the United States to Japan; a negative bias implies that the rate of technical change decreases from the United States to Japan. Alternatively, a positive bias implies that the difference in technology between the United States and Japan increases with the level of technology, while a negative bias implies that the difference in technology between the two countries decreases with the level. The rate of technical change increases from the United States to Japan for 22 of the 28 industries included in our study; the rate of technical change decreases for only six of the 28 industries. More detailed results are given in table 2.5.

Our interpretation of the parameter estimates given in appendix B concludes with the accelerations of technical change (β_{TT}) and the differences in the difference in technology (β_{DD}^i). A positive acceleration corresponds to a rate of technical change that is increasing with the level of technology, while a negative acceleration implies that the rate of technical change is decreasing with the level of technology. The estimated accelerations given in table 2.6 are positive for 10 industries and negative for the 18 remaining industries. A positive difference in the difference in technology corresponds to a difference in technology that is increasing between the United States and Japan, while a negative difference implies that the estimated differences given in table 2.6 are positive for 11 industries and negative for the 17 remaining industries.

2.4 Conclusion

Our empirical results on bilateral models of production in Japan and the United States reveal some striking differences between the two countries. With identical relative quantities of all inputs, Japanese industries have higher rates of compensation for capital and intermediate inputs than their U.S. counterparts. By contrast U.S. industries have higher rates of labor compensation than the corresponding Japanese industries. It is important to emphasize that these differences in technology would prevail under identical input proportions in the two countries. The observed patterns of production also reflect differences in these proportions.

High rates of technical change in Japan relative to the United States have been revealed by the results of Jorgenson, Kuroda, and Nishimizu (1987). Our finding that rates of technical change increase from the United States to Japan

Table 2.5   **Biases of Technical Change with Respect to the Difference in Technology**

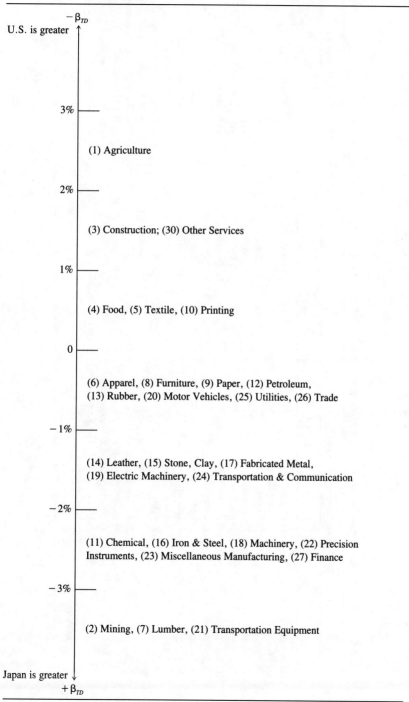

$-\beta_{TD}$

U.S. is greater

3% ——

(1) Agriculture

2% ——

(3) Construction; (30) Other Services

1% ——

(4) Food, (5) Textile, (10) Printing

0 ——

(6) Apparel, (8) Furniture, (9) Paper, (12) Petroleum,
(13) Rubber, (20) Motor Vehicles, (25) Utilities, (26) Trade

−1% ——

(14) Leather, (15) Stone, Clay, (17) Fabricated Metal,
(19) Electric Machinery, (24) Transportation & Communication

−2% ——

(11) Chemical, (16) Iron & Steel, (18) Machinery, (22) Precision
Instruments, (23) Miscellaneous Manufacturing, (27) Finance

−3% ——

(2) Mining, (7) Lumber, (21) Transportation Equipment

Japan is greater
$+\beta_{TD}$

Table 2.6   Accelerations of Technical Change and Differences in the Difference in Technology

Accelerations of Technical Change		Differences in the Difference in Technology	
$\beta_{TT} > 0$	$\beta_{TT} < 0$	$\beta_{DD} > 0$	$\beta_{DD} < 0$
(1) Agriculture	(2) Mining	(1) Agriculture	(3) Construction
(4) Food	(3) Construction	(2) Mining	(4) Food
(6) Apparel	(5) Textile	(6) Apparel	(5) Textile
(10) Printing	(7) Lumber	(9) Paper	(7) Lumber
(13) Rubber	(8) Furniture	(12) Petroleum	(8) Furniture
(16) Iron & Steel	(9) Paper	(14) Leather	(10) Printing
(18) Machinery	(11) Chemical	(15) Stone, Clay	(11) Chemical
(19) Electric Machinery	(12) Petroleum	(16) Iron & Steel	(13) Rubber
(20) Motor Vehicles	(14) Leather	(18) Machinery	(17) Fabricated Metals
(27) Finance	(15) Stone, Clay	(19) Electric Machinery	(20) Motor Vehicles
	(17) Fabricated Metal	(22) Precision	(21) Transportation Equipment
	(21) Transportation Equipment	Instruments	(23) Miscellaneous Manufacturing
	(22) Precision Instruments		(24) Transportation & Communication
	(23) Miscellaneous Manufacturing		(25) Electric Utilities
	(24) Transportation & Communication		(26) Wholesale & Retail Trade
	(25) Electric Utilities, Gas Supply & Water Supply		(27) Finance
	(26) Wholesale & Retail Trade		(28) Service
	(28) Service		

is, therefore, not surprising. This increase characterizes 22 of the 28 industries included in our study. An alternative and equivalent interpretation of these results is that the difference in technology between the United States and Japan increases with the level of technology. The technology gap between the two countries is closing for most industries at given relative quantities of all inputs. Observed changes in the technology gaps also reflect changes in input proportions.

Our bilateral models of production are based on strong simplifying assumptions. Although we allow for differences in the value shares of the three inputs—capital, labor, and intermediate inputs—the rate of technical change, and the difference in technology between the two countries, we require that share elasticities and the biases and accelerations of technical change are the same for each industry in the two countries. In addition, we have employed conditions for producer equilibrium under perfect competition, and we have assumed constant returns to scale at the industry level for both countries. These assumptions must be justified primarily by their usefulness in implementing production models that are uniform for all 28 industrial sectors in Japan and the United States.

Our important simplification of the theory of production is the imposition of concavity of the sectoral production function for Japan and the United States. By imposing concavity we have reduced the number of share elasticities to be fitted from 168, or six for each of our 28 industrial sectors, to 93, or somewhat more than three per sector on average. All share elasticities are constrained to be zero for six of the 28 industries. The concavity constraints have contributed to the precision of our estimates but require that the share of each input be nonincreasing in the quantity of the input itself.

Appendix A

Our objective is to describe restrictions on the parameters of our econometric models. If a system of equations, consisting of value shares, the rate of technical change, and the difference in technology can be generated from a production function, we say that the system is integrable. A complete set of conditions for integrability is given below.

1. *Homogeneity.*   The value shares, rate of technical change, and difference in technology are homogeneous of degree zero in the inputs.

We can write the value shares, the rate of technical change, and the difference in technology in the form

$$v^i = \alpha_X^i + B_{XX}^i \ln X_i + \beta_{XT}^i \cdot T + \beta_{XD}^i \cdot D,$$

(A1) $$v_T^i = \alpha_T^i + \beta_{XT}^{i\,\prime} \ln X_i + \beta_{TT}^i \cdot T + \beta_{TD}^i \cdot D,$$

$$v_D^i = \alpha_D^i + \beta_{XD}^{i\,\prime} \ln X_i + \beta_{TD}^i + T + \beta_{DD}^i \cdot D,$$

$$(i = 1, 2, \ldots, I).$$

where the parameters $(\alpha_X^i, \alpha_T^i, \alpha_D^i, B_{XX}^i, \beta_{XT}^i, \beta_{XD}^i, \beta_{TT}^i, \beta_{TD}^i, \beta_{DD}^i)$ are constant. Homogeneity implies that these parameters must satisfy

(A2)
$$
\begin{aligned}
B_{XX}^i i &= 0, \\
\beta_{XT}^{i\prime} i &= 0, \\
\beta_{XD}^{i\prime} i &= 0, \quad (i = 1, 2, \ldots, I),
\end{aligned}
$$

where i is a vector of ones. Five restrictions are implied by homogeneity for three inputs.

2. *Product exhaustion.* The sum of the value shares is equal to unity:

$$
v_i' i = 1, \quad (i = 1, 2, \ldots, I).
$$

The three inputs exhaust the value of the product. This implies that the parameters must satisfy the restrictions

(A3)
$$
\begin{aligned}
\alpha_X^{i\prime} i &= 1, \\
B_{XX}^{i\prime} i &= 0, \\
\beta_{XT}^{i\prime} i &= 0, \\
\beta_{XD}^{i\prime} i &= 0, \quad (i = 1, 2, \ldots, I).
\end{aligned}
$$

Six restrictions are implied by product exhaustion for three inputs.

3. *Symmetry.* The matrix of share elasticities, biases, acceleration, and the difference in the difference in technology must be symmetric.

Imposing homogeneity and product exhaustion restrictions, we can represent the system of value shares, the rate of technical change, and the difference in technology without imposing symmetry. A necessary and sufficient condition for symmetry is that the matrix of parameters must satisfy the restrictions:

(A4)
$$
\begin{bmatrix} B_{XX}^i & \beta_{XT}^i & \beta_{XD}^i \\ \beta_{XT}^{i\prime} & \beta_{TT}^i & \beta_{TD}^i \\ \beta_{XD}^{i\prime} & \beta_{TD}^i & \beta_{DD}^i \end{bmatrix} = \begin{bmatrix} B_{XX}^i & \beta_{XT}^i & \beta_{XD}^i \\ \beta_{XT}^{i\prime} & \beta_{TT}^i & \beta_{TD}^i \\ \beta_{XD}^{i\prime} & \beta_{TD}^i & \beta_{DD}^i \end{bmatrix}'.
$$

For three inputs the number of symmetry restrictions is 10.

4. *Nonnegativity.* The value shares must be nonnegative.

$$
v_i \geqq 0, \quad (i = 1, 2, \ldots, I).
$$

By product exhaustion the value shares sum to unity, so that we can write

$$
v_i \geq 0, \quad (i = 1, 2, \ldots, I),
$$

where $v_i \geq 0$ implies $v_i \geqq 0$ and $v_i \neq 0$.

Nonnegativity of the value shares is implied by monotonicity of the production functions.

$$\frac{\partial \ln Z_i}{\partial \ln X_i} \geqq 0, \quad (i = 1, 2, \ldots, I).$$

For the translog production functions, the conditions for monotonicity take the form

(A5) $\dfrac{\partial \ln Z_i}{\partial \ln X_i} = \alpha_X^i + B_{XX}^i \ln X_i + \beta_{XT}^i \cdot T + \beta_{XD}^i \cdot D, (i = 1, 2, \ldots, I).$

Since the production functions are quadratic in the logarithms of inputs $\ln X_i$ ($i = 1, 2, \ldots, I$), we can always choose inputs so that monotonicity is violated. Accordingly, there are no restrictions on the parameters that would imply nonnegativity of the value shares for all inputs. Instead we consider restrictions that imply concavity of the production functions for all nonnegative value shares.

5. *Monotonicity.* The matrix of share elasticities must be nonpositive definite.

Concavity of the production functions implies that Hessian matrices, say (H_i), are nonpositive definite, so that the matrices $(B_{XX}^i + v_i v_i' - V_i)$ are nonpositive definite:

(A6) $\dfrac{1}{Z_i} \cdot N_i \cdot H_i \cdot N_i = B_{XX}^i + v_i v_i' - V_i, \quad (i = 1, 2, \ldots, I),$

where

$$N_i = \begin{bmatrix} K_i & 0 & 0 \\ 0 & L_i & 0 \\ 0 & 0 & M_i \end{bmatrix}, V_i = \begin{bmatrix} v_k^i & 0 & 0 \\ 0 & v_L^i & 0 \\ 0 & 0 & v_M^i \end{bmatrix}, \quad (i = 1, 2, \ldots, I),$$

the production functions are positive, so that $Z_i > 0$, ($i = 1, 2, \ldots, I$), and (B_{XX}^i) are matrices of constant share elasticities defined above.

Without violating the product exhaustion and nonnegativity restrictions we can set the matrices $(v_i v_i' - V_i)$ equal to zero, for example, by choosing one of the value shares equal to unity and the others equal to zero. Necessary conditions for the matrices $(B_{XX}^i + v_i v_i' - V_i)$ to be nonpositive definite are that the matrices of constant share elasticities (B_{XX}^i) must be nonpositive definite. These conditions are also sufficient, since the matrices $(v_i v_i' - V_i)$ are nonpositive definite for all nonnegative value shares summing to unity. The sum of two nonpositive definite matrices is nonpositive definite.[7]

To impose concavity on the translog production functions, the matrices of constant share elasticities (B_{XX}^i) can be represented in terms of the Cholesky factorizations:

$$B_{xx}^i = T_i D_i T_i', \quad (i = 1, 2, \ldots, I),$$

where the matrices (T_i) are unit lower triangular and the matrices (D_i) are diagonal. For three inputs we can write the matrices (B_{xx}^i) in terms of their Cholesky factorizations as follows:

$$B = \begin{bmatrix} \delta_l^i & \lambda_{21}^i\delta_l^i & \lambda_{31}^i\delta_l^i \\ \lambda_{21}\delta_l^i & \lambda_{21}^i\lambda_{21}^i\delta_l^i + \delta_2^i & \lambda_{21}^i\lambda_{31}^i\delta_l^i + \lambda_{32}^i\delta_2^i \\ \lambda_{31}^i\delta_l^i & \lambda_{31}^i\lambda_{21}^i\delta_l^i + \lambda_{32}^i\delta_2^i & \lambda_{31}^i\lambda_{31}^i\delta_l^i + \lambda_{32}^i\lambda_{32}^i\delta_2^i + \delta_3^i \end{bmatrix},$$

$$(i = 1, 2, \ldots, I),$$

where

$$T_i = \begin{bmatrix} l & 0 & 0 \\ \lambda_{21}^i & l & 0 \\ \lambda_{31}^i & \lambda_{32}^i & l \end{bmatrix}, D_i = \begin{bmatrix} \delta_l^i & 0 & 0 \\ 0 & \delta_2^i & 0 \\ 0 & 0 & \delta_3^i \end{bmatrix}, \quad (i = 1, 2, \ldots, I).$$

The matrices of constant share elasticities (B_{xx}^i) must satisfy symmetry restrictions and restrictions implied by product exhaustion. These imply that the parameters of the Cholesky factorizations must satisfy the conditions:

$$1 + \lambda_{2l}^i + \lambda_{3l}^i = 0,$$
$$1 + \lambda_{32}^i = 0,$$
$$\delta_3^i = 0, \quad (i = 1, 2, \ldots, I).$$

Under these conditions there is a one-to-one transformation between the share elasticities (B_{xx}^i) and the parameters of the Cholesky factorizations (T_i, D_i). The matrices of share elasticities are nonpositive definite if and only if the diagonal elements of the matrices (D_i), the so-called Cholesky values, are nonpositive.

Our econometric models are generated from translog production functions for each industrial sector. To complete these models we add a stochastic component to the system of equations. We associate this component with unobservable random disturbances. Producers maximize profits for given prices of inputs, but the value shares, the rates of technical change, and the difference in technology are subject to random disturbances. These disturbances result from errors in implementation of production plans, random elements in technologies not reflected in the production functions, or errors of measurement. We assume that each equation has two additive components. The first is a nonrandom function of the inputs, time, and the dummy variable; the second is a random disturbance that is functionally independent of these variables.[8]

Appendix B

(Table 2B.1 follows on pages 78–81.)

Table 2B.1   Parameter Estimates for Bilateral Models of Production in Japan and the United States

Parameter	Agriculture, Forestry & Fisheries	Mining	Construction	Food & Kindred Products	Textile Mill Products	Apparel & Other Fabricated Textile Products	Lumber & Wood Products, Except Furniture	Furniture & Fixtures	Paper & Allied Products	Printing, Publishing & Allied Products	Chemical & Allied Products	Petroleum Refinery & Related Industries	Rubber & Miscellaneous Plastic Products	Leather & Leather Products
α_K	.124 (16.503)	.281 (36.681)	.064 (38.959)	.065 (26.212)	.085 (37.141)	.040 (15.397)	.145 (44.960)	.065 (33.621)	.129 (80.912)	.109 (52.086)	.159 (87.053)	.091 (16.958)	.982 (34.947)	.054 (21.223)
α_L	.296 (40.709)	.184 (79.135)	.391 (99.969)	.164 (54.226)	.268 (72.509)	.326 (105.669)	.341 (49.424)	.356 (49.171)	.255 (52.148)	.394 (96.059)	.202 (50.691)	.103 (22.254)	.370 (59.380)	.356 (69.442)
α_M	.580 (119.647)	.535 (84.111)	.545 (164.769)	.771 (442.898)	.646 (133.167)	.634 (192.393)	.514 (71.545)	.578 (73.132)	.616 (109.489)	.497 (96.991)	.639 (141.025)	.805 (158.978)	.532 (75.830)	.590 (92.986)
α_D	-3940.953 (-0.644)	-40714.641 (-1.588)	9865.922 (1.620)	1218.600 (.125)	10900.395 (.699)	-17440.969 (-1.923)	7526.488 (.802)	26555.227 (3.487)	-1779.908 (-.405)	9356.211 (.611)	1655.133 (.406)	-35802.32 (-1.633)	2931.092 (.178)	-9925.094 (-1.704)
α_T	.017 (1.868)	-.023 (-.649)	-.007 (-0.992)	.001 (.037)	.027 (1.228)	.010 (1.316)	-.012 (-.566)	.004 (.496)	.001 (.033)	.006 (.362)	.004 (.455)	-.044 (-1.109)	.014 (.416)	.004 (.145)
β_{KK}	⋮	⋮	⋮	⋮	⋮	-.102 (-11.373)	⋮	-.073 (-6.001)	-.010 (-1.639)	-.165 (-7.715)	⋮	⋮	-.016 (-2.169)	-.004 (-.988)
β_{LL}	⋮	⋮	⋮	⋮	-.004 (-.253)	-.018 (-2.745)	⋮	-.111 (-5.107)	-.0563 (-2.890)	-.182 (-8.618)	-.124 (-17.996)	⋮	-.115 (-5.818)	-.092 (-3.517)
β_{MM}	⋮	⋮	⋮	⋮	-.004 (-.253)	-.034 (-3.490)	⋮	-.004 (-.855)	-.027 (-1.033)	-.053 (-2.508)	-.124 (-17.996)	⋮	-.045 (-3.509)	-.056 (-1.914)
β_{DD}	7881.535 (.644)	81429.375 (1.588)	-19732.504 (-1.620)	-2437.716 (-0.125)	-21801.141 (-.699)	34881.598 (1.923)	-15053.172 (-.802)	-53111.727 (-3.487)	3559.253 (.404)	-18714.41 (-.611)	-3309.924 (-.406)	71604.250 (1.633)	-5862.695 (-.178)	19849.809 (1.704)

β_{TT} .001 (.729)	−.003 (−.464)	−.001 (−1.031)	.001 (.272)	−.001 (−.347)	.0002 (.181)	−.006 (−1.615)	−.002 (−1.368)	−.002 (−.738)	.0002 (.091)	−.301 (−1.827)	−.003 (−.450)	.001 (.128)	−.003 (−.569)
β_{LK} ⋮	⋮	⋮	⋮	⋮	.043 (5.159)	⋮	.901 (7.377)	.020 (2.010)	.147 (11.620)	⋮	⋮	.043 (3.561)	.020 (2.065)
β_{MK} ⋮	⋮	⋮	⋮	⋮	.059 (6.045)	⋮	−.017 (−1.826)	−.010 (−.913)	.018 (.973)	⋮	⋮	−.027 (−5.047)	−.016 (−2.803)
β_{ML} ⋮	⋮	⋮	⋮	.004 (.253)	−.025 (−10.367)	⋮	.021 (1.502)	.036 (1.814)	.034 (1.994)	.124 (17.996)	⋮	.072 (4.979)	.072 (2.565)
β_{DK} .216 (24.660)	.060 (3.458)	.070 (11.021)	.176 (18.730)	.106 (41.254)	.003 (.215)	−.077 (−12.093)	−.144 (−7.172)	−.006 (−.388)	−.234 (−11.604)	.012 (1.414)	.111 (6.796)	−.022 (−1.442)	.003 (.189)
β_{DL} −.035 (−4.223)	.080 (10.218)	−.165 (−24.873)	−.057 (−8.670)	−.168 (−6.149)	−.104 (−9.498)	−.155 (−11.236)	.098 (2.493)	−.060 (−1.859)	.216 (6.104)	.048 (5.017)	−.068 (−12.542)	−.025 (−1.056)	−.071 (−2.180)
β_{DM} −.181 (−39.107)	−.139 (−10.382)	.095 (22.882)	−.119 (−14.538)	.062 (2.241)	.101 (16.295)	.233 (20.756)	.046 (1.678)	.066 (1.911)	.018 (.601)	−.060 (−6.175)	−.042 (−2.894)	.047 (3.063)	.068 (1.964)
β_{TK} .003 (3.393)	−.001 (−1.518)	.001 (4.059)	−.002 (−6.429)	.001 (3.236)	.004 (9.256)	.0007 (1.781)	.002 (3.50)	.0002 (.621)	.003 (7.843)	−.004 (−12.956)	−.004 (−6.831)	−.0003 (−.602)	.001 (1.470)
β_{TL} −.004 (−6.082)	−.003 (−9.162)	.003 (11.479)	−.0002 (−1.373)	.001 (1.160)	.0002 (.410)	−.003 (−7.560)	−.005 (−4.068)	−.002 (−1.694)	−.004 (−6.568)	−.006 (−11.492)	−.001 (−8.951)	−.001 (−.700)	−.002 (−1.608)
β_{TM} −.064 (−4.064)	.004 (11.288)	−.004 (−13.935)	.002 (11.688)	−.002 (−2.258)	−.005 (−7.021)	.002 (6.928)	.003 (2.809)	.002 (1.506)	.001 (.985)	.010 (16.974)	.005 (9.426)	.001 (1.065)	.001 (.890)
β_{TD} −.023 (−11.723)	.060 (8.201)	−.012 (−4.577)	.0002 (.088)	−.015 (−3.172)	.006 (2.127)	.033 (12.214)	.012 (4.223)	.007 (3.495)	−.002 (−.503)	.024 (15.590)	.003 (.507)	.003 (.566)	.012 (5.844)

Table 2B.1   (continued)

Parameter	Stone, Clay & Glass Products	Iron & Steel	Fabricated Metal Products	Machinery	Electric Machinery	Motor Vehicle & Equipment	Transportation Equipment, Except Motor	Precision Instruments	Miscellaneous Manufacturing	Transportation & Communication	Electric Utility, Gas Supply & Water Supply	Wholesale & Retail Trade	Finance & Insurance	Service
α_K	.130 (48.845)	.092 (44.968)	.094 (33.979)	.120 (44.149)	.098 (23.830)	.112 (20.575)	.043 (10.994)	.149 (26.604)	.153 (46.026)	.171 (78.090)	.278 (76.882)	.149 (58.100)	.186 (59.765)	.430 (129.970)
α_L	.342 (96.358)	.239 (59.960)	.376 (126.698)	.380 (66.547)	.371 (105.181)	.206 (50.784)	.345 (50.987)	.498 (65.066)	.294 (61.543)	.319 (149.582)	.150 (44.945)	.520 (77.690)	.211 (51.148)	.250 (119.346)
α_M	.528 (139.675)	.669 (159.034)	.531 (182.333)	.500 (75.034)	.531 (134.562)	.682 (104.216)	.612 (70.859)	.353 (43.445)	.553 (84.550)	.510 (265.597)	.562 (112.380)	.331 (48.761)	.603 (130.635)	.320 (81.072)
α_D	-.167 (-.020)	-3754.465 (-.512)	5048.535 (1.033)	-10990.098 (-1.173)	-10809.703 (-1.665)	.0001 (.501)	.0003 (.016)	-5894.293 (-.856)	1729.229 (.212)	8332.473 (1.087)	18942.898 (2.081)	9951.582 (1.213)	44612.750 (3.295)	9306.051 (2.046)
α_T	-.004 (-.309)	-.002 (-.172)	.009 (.864)	.003 (.178)	.018 (2.119)	.00482 (.225)	.006 (.497)	.012 (.543)	-.003 (-.129)	.009 (1.310)	-.004 (-.344)	.010 (1.739)	.006 (1.487)	-.002 (-.367)
β_{KK}	...	...	-.011 (-.786)	...	...	-.080 (-4.960)	-.048 (-4.37)	-.020 (-1.841)	-.00494 (-1.036)	-.902 (-2.701)	...	-.081 (-3.472)	...	...
β_{LL}	...	-.008 (-1.401)	-.036 (-2.571)	...	-.019 (-1.000)	-.030 (-1.913)	-.002 (-.518)	-.020 (-1.034)	-.088 (-4.293)	-.119 (-3.922)	-.122 (-8.713)	-.022 (-1.531)	...	...
β_{MM}	...	-.008 (-1.401)	-.035 (-1.737)	...	-.019 (-1.000)	-.057 (-1.956)	-.069 (-2.989)	-.000002 (-.009)	-.052 (-2.181)	-.002 (-.188)	-.122 (-8.713)	-.019 (-1.172)	...	...
β_{DD}	333.760 (.020)	7508.832 (.512)	-10097.117 (-1.033)	21979.551 (1.172)	21618.820 (1.665)	-13130.848 (-.501)	-.002 (-.017)	11788.879 (.856)	-3458.634 (-.212)	-16665.172 (-1.087)	-37888.145 (-2.081)	-19903.762 (-1.213)	-89225.500 (-3.295)	-18612.191 (-2.046)

β_{TT}	-.002 (-.977)	.005 (2.178)	-.0003 (-.153)	.00103 (.396)	.0001 (.050)	.004 (1.101)	-.002 (-.969)	-.002 (-.576)	-.001 (-.357)	-.002 (-1.383)	-.001 (-.512)	-.0004 (-.430)	-.002 (2.929)	-.001 (-1.103)
β_{LK}	⋮	⋮	.006 (.592)	⋮	⋮	.027 (2.527)	-.010 (-1.057)	.020 (1.721)	.021 (2.088)	.104 (3.569)	⋮	.042 (2.675)	⋮	⋮
β_{MK}	⋮	⋮	.005 (.336)	⋮	⋮	.0535 (2.856)	.058 (4.267)	.0002 (.017)	-.016 (-2.901)	-.013 (-.801)	⋮	.039 (1.906)	⋮	⋮
β_{ML}	⋮	.008 (1.401)	.030 (2.481)	⋮	.0194 (1.000)	.0036 (.200)	.011 (.903)	-.0002 (-.017)	.068 (3.057)	.016 (1.194)	.122 (8.713)	-.020 (-3.387)	⋮	⋮
β_{DK}	.0212 (2.783)	.046 (10.845)	-.001 (-.076)	.020 (3.396)	.064 (12.958)	.024 (1.410)	.117 (8.341)	-.051 (-3.172)	-.094 (-6.266)	-.092 (-2.206)	.066 (4.991)	.071 (3.338)	.196 (27.958)	-.127 (-15.222)
β_{DL}	-.155 (-30.647)	-.165 (-16.727)	-.060 (-2.644)	-.169 (-13.343)	-.170 (-5.908)	-.030 (-1.190)	-.113 (-7.114)	-.257 (-9.358)	.012 (.456)	.280 (6.475)	.172 (9.670)	-.162 (-7.036)	.123 (17.046)	-.051 (-9.888)
β_{DM}	.134 (23.953)	.119 (11.360)	.061 (3.093)	.149 (13.741)	.105 (3.699)	.006 (.199)	-.005 (-.186)	.308 (13.231)	.081 (2.764)	-.188 (-10.091)	-.238 (-11.395)	.090 (5.770)	-.319 (-35.387)	.178 (22.825)
β_{TK}	-.003 (-6.632)	-.003 (-8.980)	.001 (1.477)	-.002 (-5.314)	-.001 (-1.616)	-.004 (-4.591)	-.001 (-1.368)	-.006 (-5.394)	.001 (1.435)	.003 (1.876)	-.006 (-10.327)	.002 (3.018)	-.004 (-9.536)	-.002 (-3.170)
β_{TL}	-.0001 (-1.543)	.0002 (.320)	-.002 (-3.201)	-.831 (-.516)	.0003 (.390)	.001 (.824)	-.001 (-2.689)	-.003 (-.139)	-.003 (-3.076)	-.003 (-2.339)	-.008 (-11.689)	.002 (2.400)	.002 (4.251)	-.003 (12.375)
β_{TM}	.003 (6.406)	.003 (5.074)	.001 (2.336)	.002 (4.983)	.001 (.767)	.003 (3.328)	.002 (2.381)	.006 (5.757)	.003 (2.058)	.001 (.682)	.014 (14.432)	-.004 (-8.196)	.003 (10.816)	-.002 (-4.236)
β_{TD}	.016 (6.500)	.018 (7.748)	.015 (9.390)	.022 (7.503)	.026 (10.492)	-.002 (-.537)	.029 (5.079)	.015 (5.238)	.019 (5.296)	.022 (6.976)	.014 (4.283)	-.003 (-1.053)	.027 (6.744)	-.011 (-6.290)

Notes

1. The share elasticity was introduced by Christensen, Jorgenson, and Lau (1971, 1973) and by Samuelson (1973).

2. Share elasticities were first employed as constant parameters of an econometric model of producer behavior by Christensen, Jorgenson, and Lau (1971, 1973). Constant share elasticities and biases of technical change are employed by Jorgenson and Fraumeni (1981); Jorgenson (1983, 1984), and Kuroda, Yoshioka, and Jorgenson (1984). Binswanger (1974a, 1974b, 1978a) uses a different definition of biases of technical change in parameterizing an econometric model with constant share elasticities.

3. Alternative definitions of biases of technical change are compared by Binswanger (1978b).

4. Biases of the difference in technology were introduced by Binswanger (1974a, 1974b, 1978a).

5. Biases of technical change with respect to the difference of technology were introduced by Jorgenson and Nishimizu (1978) in the context of a bilateral model of production for Japan and the United States at the aggregate level. This model was extended to the sectoral level by Jorgenson and Nishimizu (1981).

6. The difference of the difference of technology was introduced by Jorgenson and Nishimizu (1978, 1981).

7. This approach to global concavity was originated by Jorgenson and Fraumeni (1981). The Cholesky factorization was first employed in imposing local concavity restrictions by Lau (1978).

8. Alternative stochastic specifications for econometric models of production are discussed by Fuss, McFadden, and Mundlak (1978). Additional detail on econometric methods for modeling producer behavior is given by Jorgenson (1986).

References

Binswanger, H. P. 1974a. A cost-function approach to the measurement of elasticities of factor demand and elasticities of substitution. *American Journal of Agricultural Economics* 56, no. 2 (May):377–86.

———. 1974b. The measurement of technical change biases with many factors of production. *American Economic Review* 64, no. 5, (December):964–76.

———. 1978a. Induced technical change: Evolution of thought. In *Induced innovation,* ed. H. P. Binswanger and V. W. Ruttan, 13–43. Baltimore: Johns Hopkins University Press.

———. 1978b. Issues in modeling induced technical change. In *Induced innovation,* ed. H. P. Binswanger and V. W. Ruttan, 128–63. Baltimore: Johns Hopkins University Press.

Christensen, L. R., D. W. Jorgenson, and L. J. Lau. 1971. Conjugate duality and the transcendental logarithmic production function. *Econometrica* 39, no. 4 (July):255–56.

———. 1973. Transcendental logarithmic production frontiers. *Review of Economics and Statistics* 55, no. 1 (February):28–45.

Fuss, M., D. McFadden, and Y. Mundlak. 1978. A survey of functional forms in the economic analysis of production. In *Production Economics,* ed. M. Fuss and D. McFadden, 1:219–68. Amsterdam: North-Holland.

Jorgenson, D. W. 1983. Modeling production for general equilibrium analysis. *Scandinavian Journal of Economics* 85 (2):101–12.

———. 1984. The role of energy in productivity growth. In *International comparisons of productivity and causes of the slowdown,* ed. J. W. Kendrick, 279–323. Cambridge: Ballinger.

———. 1986. Econometric methods for modeling producer behavior. In *Handbook of econometrics,* ed. Z. Griliches and M. D. Intriligator, 3:1841–1915. Amsterdam: North-Holland.

Jorgenson, D. W., and B. M. Fraumeni. 1981. Relative prices and technical change. In *Modeling and measuring natural resource substitution,* ed. E. R. Berndt and B. C. Field, pp. 17–47. Cambridge, Mass.: MIT Press.

Jorgenson, D. W., M. Kuroda, and M. Nishimizu. 1987. Japan-U.S. industry-level productivity comparisons, 1960–1979. *Journal of the Japanese and International Economies* 1, no. 1 (March):1–30.

Jorgenson, D. W., and J.-J. Laffont. 1974. Efficient estimation of non-linear simultaneous equations with additive disturbances. *Annals of Social and Economic Measurement* 3, no. 4 (October):615–40.

Jorgenson, D. W., and M. Nishimizu. 1978. U.S. and Japanese economic growth, 1952–1974: An international comparison. *Economic Journal* 88, no. 352, (December):707–26.

———. 1981. International differences in levels of technology: A comparison between U.S. and Japanese industries. In *International roundtable conference proceedings.* Tokyo: Institute of Statistical Mathematics.

Kuroda, M., K. Yoshioka, and D. W. Jorgenson. 1984. Relative price changes and biases of technical change in Japan. *Economic Studies Quarterly* 35, no. 2, (August):116–38.

Lau, L. J. 1978. Testing and imposing monotonicity, convexity and quasi-convexity constraints, In *Production economics,* ed. M. Fuss and D. McFadden, 1:409–53. Amsterdam: North-Holland.

Samuelson, P. A. 1973. Relative shares and elasticities simplified: Comment. *American Economic Review* 63, no. 4 (September):770–71.

3 Productivity Growth in the Motor Vehicle Industry, 1970–1984: A Comparison of Canada, Japan, and the United States

Melvyn Fuss and Leonard Waverman

3.1 Introduction

The motor vehicle industry is perhaps the prime example of the Japanese competitive threat to U.S. manufacturing. Aided by the oil price shocks of the 1970s, Japanese imports developed into an important segment of the North American market for vehicles and have come to enjoy a reputation for low cost and high quality compared with domestic products. In response to these Japanese inroads, both Canada and the United States in 1981 placed quotas on Japanese imports (the Voluntary Export Restraints Agreements). The G.M.-Toyota joint venture in automobile stamping and assembly in Fremont, California was approved by the U.S. government in 1985, despite antitrust concerns, in the hope that this would accelerate the transfer of Japanese production methods to North America.

Changing circumstances in the international environment for production and trade in motor vehicles can be thoughtfully analyzed only if knowledge is available about the trends, over time, of cost and productivity differentials and the sources of these differences. It is important to determine whether different growth rates of cost are due to variations among nations in factor price growth rates or in changes in technological conditions such as economies of scale, capacity utilization, and the rate of technical progress.

In this study we utilize an econometric cost function and a decomposition

The authors wish to thank Michael Denny, Charles Hulten, and Raymond Kopp for helpful comments. They are also indebted to Jeremy Rudin, Richard Knabl, and Steven Murphy for invaluable research assistance. Financial support from the Ontario Economic Council, the National Science Foundation (grant SES-8420937), and the Canadian Donner Foundation is gratefully acknowledged.

Melvyn Fuss is the chairman of the Department of Economics, University of Toronto, and a research associate of the National Bureau of Economic Research. Leonard Waverman is a professor of economics at the University of Toronto.

analysis of that function to measure the growth in average cost and productivity in motor vehicle production in Canada, the United States, and Japan over the period 1970–84 and to determine the sources of growth. Unlike previous studies of this industry, we are particularly careful to take into account short-run disequilibrium effects. The major source of disequilibrium in the auto industry is the periodic underutilization of capacity. The auto industry is an industry characterized by quasi-fixed factors (capital and overhead labor) and product-specific manufacturing facilities. Swings in consumer tastes among different products can lead to variations in capacity utilization that affect measured cost and total factor productivity growth to a significant extent. The empirical results presented below indicate that, had capacity utilization effects not been accounted for, we would have overestimated long-run total factor productivity (TFP) growth during the 1970–84 period by 22% in the United States and 21% in Canada. This problem is much more severe for the two subperiods we consider: 1970–80 and 1980–84. We control for utilization effects by including a measure of capacity utilization as an argument of the cost function.

The Japanese productivity "miracle" is evident from our results for motor vehicle production. During the period 1970–84 total factor productivity in the Japanese industry grew at an average rate of 3.0% per annum. By way of contrast, the Canadian and U.S. automotive industries experienced average per annum utilization-corrected TFP growth rates of only 0.9% and 1.1% respectively, about one-third of the Japanese rates. The more rapid efficiency gain in Japan is a major reason why long-run average cost, as measured in each country's own currency, grew at only a 2.5% annual rate for Japanese vehicle production, whereas long-run average cost increased at a 7.1% rate in Canada and at a 6.6% rate in the United States.

As noted previously, these empirical results are obtained from an estimated econometric cost function and a decomposition analysis. In section 3.2 we present a nontechnical explanation of cost and efficiency measurement and decomposition. The specific empirical results are presented in sections 3.3 and 3.4. In section 3.5 we conclude the paper's main discussion with some summary remarks. Data are presented in appendix A, and a formal analysis of the underlying theory appears in the technical appendix (app. B).

3.2   The Cost Function Approach to the Analysis of Cost and TFP Growth Rates

We begin by assuming that the motor vehicle production process can be represented indirectly by the cost function

$$(1) \qquad C_{it} = G_{it}(w_{it}, Q_{it}, T_{it}),$$

where C_{it} is the total cost of production in country i at time t, w_{it} is a vector of factor prices, Q_{it} is the level of output, and T_{it} is a vector of technological conditions that could be viewed as the "characteristics" of the production process. Examples of characteristics to be used in this study are an index of research and development (R&D) expenditures (a proxy for technical change) and capacity utilization. Since capacity utilization (T_{1it}) is an explanatory variable in the cost function, Q_{it} will be defined as full (normal) capacity output. Actual output will be denoted q_{it}, where $q_{it} = Q_{it} \cdot T_{1it}$. Then Q_{it} is the output produced when the firm is operating at full utilization $(T_{1it} = 1)$.

The cost function (1) is the solution to the firm's problem of minimizing the cost of producing output conditional on the exogenous factor prices and the levels of characteristics. Given the assumption of cost-minimizing behavior, the theory of duality between cost and production insures that the cost function is as basic a tool of analysis as the production function and can be used to estimate any desired aspect of the production process, including TFP growth.[1] In this paper we measure TFP growth by the growth in cost efficiency (CE). This CE growth is defined as the reduction in average minimum *real* cost over time; that is, the reduction in average cost that occurs after the effects of intertemporal changes in factor prices have been accounted for. Hence, CE is dual to TFP, since TFP growth measures the improvement in the efficiency of the use of inputs over time. In the technical appendix (app. B) we demonstrate that the rate of TFP growth is equal to the rate of CE growth, so that either concept can be used to measure intertemporal efficiency improvements. The formula that we will use to measure CE growth is the translog (Törnqvist) index of cost efficiency growth between periods 0 and 1 (Denny, Fuss, and May 1981),

$$(2) \quad \log CE_{i1} - \log CE_{i0} = - [\log(C_{i1}/q_{i1}) - \log(C_{i0}/q_{i0})$$
$$- \frac{1}{2}\sum_{k=1}^{K}(s_{ki1} + s_{ki0})(\log w_{ki1} - \log w_{ki0})],$$

where s_{ki1} is the cost share of the kth input in country i in period 1. The minus sign in front of the right-hand side of (2) is to convert an efficiency gain that *lowers* average cost into a positive quantity. Following Denny and Fuss (1983), we call (2) a translog index if C_{i1}, C_{i0}, s_{ki1}, s_{ki0} are estimated from an econometric cost function, and a Törnqvist index if they are measured directly from the actual observed data. Equation (2) is derived in the technical appendix, and shown to be closely linked to the assumption that the motor vehicle production process can be represented by a translog cost function in which the zero- and first-order parameters differ across countries, but the second-order parameters are the same for each country.

3.2.1 Cost and Productivity Growth—a Decomposition Analysis

One of the purposes of this paper is to compare average cost and TFP growth rates for Canada, the United States, and Japan over the 1970–84 period. A second purpose is to decompose these growth rates into their sources.

In this section we present a graphical representation of the decomposition analysis. The equations corresponding to the graphs are contained in the technical appendix.

Suppose $(C_0, q_0, p_{L0}, p_{K0}, T_{10}, T_{20})$ and $C_1, q_1, p_{L1}, p_{K1}, T_{11}, T_{21})$ represent observed cost, actual output, prices of labor and capital services,[2] the capacity utilization rate, and an index of the state of technology in years 0 and 1, respectively.[3] As a first step, we wish to decompose the increase in average cost $(C_1/q_1 - C_0/q_0)$ into its sources. The graphical presentation is greatly simplified by changing the decomposition to one involving cost per unit of capacity output $(C_1/Q_1 - C_0/Q_0)$. This decomposition can easily be linked to the decomposition of actual average cost (as is done in the technical appendix) since $(C/q) = (C/T_1 \cdot Q)$. Equation (1) can be transformed into a per unit of capacity (or average) cost function by dividing both sides by Q_{it}:

(3) $$C_{it}/Q_{it} = H_{it}(w_{it}, Q_{it}, T_{it}).$$

Figure 3.1 contains a series of per unit capacity output cost curves, which can be used to represent the decomposition analysis. To simplify notation,

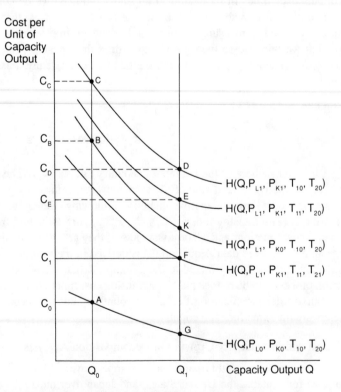

Fig. 3.1   **The decomposition of changes in average cost**

Table 3.1   **Average Production Cost Increase and Its Sources**

	Source of Increase				
Average Cost Increase (1)	Price of Labor (2)	Price of Capital (3)	Scale Economies (4)	Capacity Utilization (5)	Technical Change (6)
$C_1 - C_0$	$C_B - C_0$	$C_C - C_B$	$C_D - C_C$	$C_E - C_D$	$C_1 - C_E$

from this point on we will denote average cost by C rather than C/Q. All variables are assumed to increase between periods 0 and 1. An increase in the price of labor services from p_{L0} to p_{L1} shifts the average cost curve up and average cost increases from C_0 to C_B, ceteris paribus. Therefore the labor price increase could be said to be the source of $C_B - C_0$ of the average cost increase $C_1 - C_0$. In an analogous way we could decompose the average cost increase into the remainder of its sources as is represented in table 3.1. The movement from A to B to C in figure 3.1 represents the effect of factor price increases, and results in an average cost increase. Increases in capacity output (under increasing returns to scale), capacity utilization, and improvements in the state of technology ($T_{21} > T_{20}$) reduce average cost; hence the negative effects associated with the movement from C to D to E to F.

Recall that once the price effects are removed from the average cost increase, the remainder is the average cost change due to cost efficiency effects (eq. [2]). Therefore the CE change (ΔCE) can be measured in figure 3.1 as the (positive) movement from C to F, or

$$(4) \qquad \Delta CE = - \{C_1 - [C_0 + (C_B - C_0) + (C_C - C_B)]\}$$
$$= - \{C_1 - C_0 - [(C_B - C_0) + (C_C - C_B)]\},$$

which is the graphical representation of equation (2) (with Q_i replacing q_i),[4] in absolute rather than logarithmic differences. The expression $- \Delta CE$ is also {column (1) $-$ [column (2) $+$ column (3)]} in table 3.1.

From figure 3.1 it is obvious that ΔCE, the movement from C to F, can also be represented by

$$(5) \qquad \Delta CE = - [(C_D - C_C) + (C_E - C_D) + (C_1 - C_E)].$$

Thus $- \Delta CE$ is the sum of columns (4) $+$ (5) $+$ (6) in table 3.1. Cost efficiency (TFP) growth has as its sources: capacity output growth under increasing returns to scale, increased capacity utilization, and improvements in the state of technology (technical progress). Improvements in the state of technology are usually associated with shifts in the cost (or production) function. As the above discussion demonstrates, cost efficiency (or TFP) growth is identical to a shifting of the relevant function only if production is subject to constant returns to scale ($C_D - C_C = 0$) and capacity utilization is constant

Table 3.2   **Total Factor Productivity (TFP) Growth and Its Sources**

	Source of Growth		
TFP Growth (1)	Scale Economies (2)	Capacity Utilization (3)	Technical Change (4)
$-(C_1 - C_C)$	$-(C_D - C_C)$	$-(C_E - C_D)$	$-(C_1 - C_E)$

$(C_E - C_D = 0)$. If these assumptions are not satisfied, TFP growth can be decomposed into its sources as depicted in table 3.2.

The decomposition outlined above is not unique. For example, another possible decomposition of the change in average cost is: A to G (scale economies), G to K (price of labor), K to D (price of capital), D to E (capacity utilization), and E to F (technical change). The choice of decomposition is equivalent to the inevitable necessary choice of weights with which to weight the changes in the variables that are the sources of average cost or TFP growth. Corresponding to each aggregation formula will be a correct weighing procedure. For the translog (Törnqvist) model that underlies our empirical results, the correct weights are the average cost elasticities averaged over time periods 0 and 1. These weights are applied to the logarithms of the relative change in variables—that is, $\log (p_{L1}/p_{L0})$—to decompose the logarithm of relative average cost or relative TFP. Details are presented in the technical appendix.

3.3 Empirical Results: Cost Function Estimation

The analysis of the sources of TFP growth between 1970 and 1984 for the three countries' motor vehicle industries is based on an estimated translog cost function.[5] The cost function was estimated using annual pooled three-digit SIC motor vehicle production data (assembly + parts production) from Canada (1961–84), Japan (1968–84), and the United States (1961–84). The arguments of the cost function are prices of labor, capital, and materials (w_{it}), constant dollar average capacity production of vehicles and parts per plant (Q_{it}), capacity utilization rate (T_{1it}), and an index of the real stock of R&D expenditures (T_{2it}). C_{it} is total cost per plant. A more detailed description of the data is contained in the data appendix.

The translog cost function and the cost share equations (obtained by applying Shephard's lemma to the cost function) were used to form a system of equations, and the parameters of the system were estimated using the Zellner iterative technique to obtain maximum-likelihood estimates. Initial estimation implied the existence of positive serial correlation in the share equations and a violation of concavity at several data points. A first-order autocorrelation specification for share equations was adopted (see Berndt and Savin 1975), and the parameter constraints necessary to insure concavity over the sample were imposed.[6] The exact specification of the cost function and additional details of the estimation procedure are contained in Fuss and Waverman (1990). Also contained in an unpublished appendix to that reference is the list of parameter estimates, their asymptotic standard errors, and the usual diagnostic summary statistics. This appendix is available upon request from the authors.

Instead of attempting to digest the detailed regression results, it is more useful if the reader acquires some idea of the estimated structure of production, since this estimated structure underlies the decomposition results to be presented below. Tables 3.3 and 3.4 present estimates of factor own price elasticities, elasticities of substitution, and other elasticities of interest, calculated assuming full capacity utilization ($T_{1it} = 1$). These results provide a characterization of the long-run equilibrium structure. Table 3.3 demonstrates that all factors are inelastically demanded in the three countries, and all factors are substitutes for one another. From Table 3.4 it can be seen that production in the United States and Japan is subject to slightly increasing returns to scale at the mean data point, but the departure from constant returns is not statistically significant. For Canada, production is subject to statistically significant and economically important increasing returns to scale. Any increase in research and development expenditures appears to have more of a cost-reducing impact in Japan than in the United States. R&D has the least cost-reducing impact in Canada.

The input-capacity output elasticities suggest that the production processes in all three countries are nonhomothetic, with capacity expansion utilizing

Table 3.3   **Factor Own-Price Elasticities and Elasticities of Substitution**

Inputs	Canada	United States	Japan
Factor own-price elasticities:			
Capital	− .06	− .12	− .13
	(.04)	(.03)	(.01)
Materials	− .10	− .14	− .08
	(.03)	(.03)	(.03)
Labor	− .45	− .49	− .36
	(.13)	(.10)	(.17)
Elasticities of substitution (Allen-Uzawa):			
Capital-materials	.03	.05	.16
	(.05)	(.05)	(.01)
Capital-labor	.24	.46	.09
	(.05)	(.03)	(.03)
Labor-materials	.59	.65	.48
	(.18)	(.15)	(.23)

Note: Computed at the mean data point for each country. Approximate standard errors appear in parentheses.

Table 3.4   Capacity Output Elasticities, Scale Elasticities, and Technical Change
                   Elasticities

Elasticity	Canada	United States	Japan
Cost–capacity output	.87	.93	.93
	(.04)	(.05)	(.05)
Scale	1.16	1.07	1.07
	(.05)	(.05)	(.06)
Cost–technical change	− .08	− .23	− .33
	(.06)	(.04)	(.05)
Capital-output	.42	.53	.53
	(.09)	(.09)	(.09)
Materials-output	.99	1.07	1.05
	(.04)	(.05)	(.06)
Labor-output	.70	.80	.72
	(.07)	(.07)	(.09)
Capital–technical change	.40	.20	.10
	(.13)	(.11)	(.11)
Materials–technical change	− .17	− .33	− .42
	(.07)	(.05)	(.06)
Labor–technical change	− .09	− .24	− .34
	(.11)	(.08)	(.13)

Note: Computed at the mean data point for each country. Approximate standard errors in parentheses.

proportionately less capital than labor. As expected, materials use expands approximately proportionately with capacity output. Technical change is capital using and materials and labor saving in all three countries.

The estimated disequilibrium effects are as expected. As the capacity utilization rate is reduced below unity, average cost increases and TFP declines. For example, for the United States, the TFP difference between production at capacity output (Q) and noncapacity output (q), calculated at the U.S. mean data point, is given by the equation

(6) $\log \text{TFP}(Q) - \log \text{TFP}(q) = -0.07 \log T_1 + 0.41(\log T_1)^2,$

where T_1 is the capacity utilization rate. When capacity is underutilized, $q < Q$ and hence $T_1 < 1$. In this case, from (6), TFP $(q) <$ TFP(Q); that is, total factor productivity declines.

3.4 Empirical Results: Rates of Growth of Average Cost, Total Factor Productivity, and Their Decomposition

Tables 3.6–3.10 below present the empirical results on costs and productivity that are the focus of this paper. Table 3.6 below contains our analysis of average production cost increases over the 1970–84 period and the 1970–80 and 1980–84 subperiods. The average annual percentage cost increases in a common currency (Canadian dollars) is contained in column 1. In Canadian dollars, over the 1970–84 period, average cost increased by an annual rate of 6.9% in Canada, 7.9% in the United States, and 7.2% in Japan. Both Canada and Japan improved their cost-competitive positions relative to the United States, but those improvements were not particularly large. The pattern of cost increases in each country's own currency tells a dramatically different story. The Japanese cost increase is only 2.5% per year, compared with 6.3% for the United States and 6.9% for Canada. The difference in the results is due to a substantial appreciation of the Japanese yen relative to the U.S. and Canadian dollars and a smaller appreciation of the U.S. dollar relative to the Canadian dollar. Table 3.5 contains the time path of the relevant exchange rates that had such a large impact on intercountry differences in average cost growth rates. The significant appreciation of the yen over the 1970–84 period, along with the Voluntary Export Restraints Agreements of 1981, has meant that the North American industries remained viable despite relative productivity stagnation (see below). This phenomenon has been even more important over the 1984–88 period, since the Japanese yen appreciated from 237 yen/ $1U.S. to 130 yen/$1U.S.

The period 1970–80 was similar to 1970–84, with the above effects being even more pronounced. The 1980–84 period saw a narrowing of the rate of average cost increases, due to lower inflation rates in North America and, as we will see below, a narrowing of relative TFP growth rates.

Table 3.6 also contains our decomposition of the average cost increases. The decomposition in table 3.6 and subsequent tables is with respect to average costs as measured in the country's *own* currency. The formulas used to calculate the decomposition are developed in the technical appendix. The numbers in the "Sources of Increase" part of table 3.6 have the following interpretation. Consider the number 1.5 under the column labeled "Price of Labor" for Canada, 1970–84. If all variables affecting cost in Canada had remained constant at the geometric average of their 1970 and 1984 levels, *except for the price of labor,* unit production cost in Canada would have in-

Table 3.5   **Capacity Utilization Rates and Exchange Rates: Selected Years**

	Capacity Utilization Rate			Exchange Rate		
Year	Canada	United States	Japan	$CAN to $U.S.	Yen to $U.S.	Yen to $CAN
1970	.76	.74	1.00	.96	358	343
1972	.89	.96	1.00	1.01	303	306
1973	.94	1.04	1.03	1.00	271	271
1979	.77	.84	.98	.85	218	186
1980	.63	.62	1.01	.86	225	193
1982	.58	.58	.95	.81	248	201
1984	.85	.90	.95	.77	237	183

Table 3.6 Average Production Cost Increases and Their Sources[a]

Country/Time Period	Average Annual Unit Production Cost Increase (%)			Sources of Increase (%)					
	Canadian Dollars	U.S. Dollars	Yen	Price of Labor	Price of Capital	Price of Materials	Scale Economies	Technical Change	Capacity Utilization
Canada:									
1970–84	6.9			1.5	1.3	5.2	−.7	−.3	−.3
1970–80	8.2			1.7	1.4	5.3	−.8	−.4	.9
1980–84	3.6			1.2	1.4	4.3	−.4	−.1	−3.0
United States:									
1970–84	7.9	6.3		1.7	1.2	4.6	−.2	−.8	−.3
1970–80	10.1	8.9		2.4	1.8	5.1	−.2	−1.1	.7
1980–84	2.6	.0		.4	.4	2.4	−.4	−.2	−2.7
Japan:									
1970–84	7.2		2.5	1.3	.6	3.6	−.5	−2.5	.0
1970–80	9.4		3.3	1.5	.6	5.0	−.6	−3.1	.0
1980–84	1.8		.5	.7	.4	.5	−.2	−.9	.1

[a] Costs are estimated costs derived from the cost function.

creased by 1.5% per annum because of the increase in the price of labor between 1970 and 1984. Similarly, the number -0.3 under the column labeled "Technical Change" in the first row of table 3.6 implies that if all variables except the technical change variable (stock of R&D) had been constant, Canadian unit production cost would have fallen by 0.3% per annum over the 1970–84 period. From the above description, it can be seen that what we have calculated in the "Sources of Increase" portion of table 3.6 is a set of discrete comparative statics results for variations in the exogenous variables affecting average production costs.

The major determinant of average cost increases over the 1970–84 period in all three countries has been increases in materials prices. Technical change has been the major source of cost reduction in the United States and Japan, whereas for Canada the major source of cost reduction was the realization of economies of scale associated with larger plant size.

As noted in the introduction, capacity utilization rates have varied considerably from year-to-year in the North American automotive industry. Utilization rates for selected years of our sample are presented in table 3.5. For the United States, capacity utilization (CU) has varied from a high of 1.04 in 1973 to a low of 0.58 in 1982. A similar variation has occurred for Canada. The Japanese industry's utilization rate is relatively constant over the whole period at nearly full utilization. The effect on cost of variations in CU in North America is most pronounced in the subperiods 1970–80 and 1980–84. For example, in the United States, average production costs would have increased by 0.7% per year between 1970–80 and decreased by 2.7% per year between 1980–84 due to the CU effect alone. Between 1980 and 1984, the increase in CU from 0.62 to 0.90 was the major force reducing average cost increases in the U.S. industry.

In order to analyze cost increases on a long-run basis, we present in table 3.7 the long-run equilibrium results, calculated from the estimated cost function, assuming capacity utilization rates are constant at the normal rate (unity) for all years for all three countries. As expected, Canadian and U.S. cost growth rates become less variable over subperiods. The U.S. cost growth advantage over Japan during 1980–84, which appeared in table 3.6, is reversed since it was entirely a capacity utilization phenomenon.

Table 3.8 presents the long-run equilibrium decomposition in a slightly different way. The components of TFP growth are aggregated (using eq. [B15] of the technical appendix with $T_1 = 1$) and compared with the factor price effects. This table portrays in a graphic way the fact that the Japanese auto industry has used productivity growth to keep unit production cost increases to a minimum, compared to North American producers. This effect was particularly pronounced during the 1970–80 period, but seems to have slackened off between 1980 and 1984.

Tables 3.9 and 3.10 examine changes in total factor productivity in the three countries. From 1970 to 1984 TFP grew by only 1.2% per year in Canada and

Table 3.7 Unit Production Cost Increases and Their Sources: Long-Run Equilibrium

Country/Time Period	Average Annual Unit Production Cost Increase (%)			Sources of Increase (%)				
	Canadian Dollars	U.S. Dollars	Yen	Price of Labor	Price of Capital	Price of Materials	Scale Economies	Technical Change
Canada:								
1970–84	7.1			1.4	1.2	5.3	−.7	−.3
1970–80	7.4			1.5	1.2	5.7	−.8	−.4
1980–84	6.5			1.1	1.2	4.6	−.4	−.1
United States:								
1970–84	8.3	6.6		1.7	1.0	4.8	−.2	−.8
1970–80	9.5	8.2		2.3	1.4	5.6	−.2	−1.0
1980–84	5.4	2.7		.4	.3	2.6	−.4	−.2
Japan:								
1970–84	7.2		2.5	1.3	.6	3.6	−.5	−2.5
1970–80	9.5		3.3	1.5	.6	5.0	−.6	−3.1
1980–84	1.7		.4	.7	.4	.5	−.2	−.9

Table 3.8   Unit Production Cost Increase: Long-Run Equilibrium

Country	Average Annual Unit Production Cost Increase (%)			Sources of Increase (%)	
	Canadian Dollars	U.S. Dollars	Yen	Factor Prices	TFP Growth
Canada:					
1970–84	7.1			8.1	-.9
1970–80	7.4			8.6	-1.1
1980–84	6.5			7.0	-.4
United States:					
1970–84		6.6		7.7	-1.0
1970–80		8.2		9.5	-1.2
1980–84		2.7		3.3	-.5
Japan:					
1970–84			2.5	5.6	-3.0
1970–80			3.3	7.2	-3.8
1980–84			.4	1.5	-1.1

Table 3.9   **Total Factor Productivity (TFP) Growth**

Country	Average Annual TFP Growth Rate (%)	Percentage Contributions to Growth		
		Scale Economies	Capacity Utilization	Technical Change
Canada:				
1970–84	1.2	55	21	24
1970–80	.4	217	−241	124
1980–84	3.4	10	87	3
United States:				
1970–84	1.3	16	22	62
1970–80	.6	25	−115	190
1980–84	3.2	11	83	6
Japan:				
1970–84	3.0	17	−1	84
1970–80	3.8	17	0	83
1980–84	1.0	20	−8	88

Table 3.10   **Total-Factor Productivity (TFP) Growth: Long-Run Equilibrium**

Country	Average Annual TFP Growth Rate (%)	Percentage Contributions to Growth	
		Scale Economies	Technical Change
Canada:			
1970–84	.9	72	28
1970–80	1.1	69	31
1980–84	.4	84	16
United States:			
1970–84	1.0	21	79
1970–80	1.2	13	87
1980–84	.5	66	34
Japan:			
1970–84	3.0	17	83
1970–80	3.8	17	83
1980–84	1.1	18	82

1.3% in the United States, compared with a TFP growth rate of 3.0% for Japan. The difference is even more substantial during the 1970–80 period. On the other hand, TFP growth was considerably faster in the United States and Canada than in Japan during 1980–84. This latter result is quite misleading, since it is a phenomenon of variation in CU rates and points to the importance of accounting for variations in CU in a highly cyclical industry. In table 3.10, CU effects are removed and the underlying trends in efficiency are revealed. Over the 1970–84 period, North American long-run TFP growth rates were about 1% per annum, only about one-third of the TFP growth rate for Japan.

The contributions of the various sources of TFP growth over the 1970–84 period were very similar in the United States and Japan: approximately 80% of growth was due to technical change and 20% due to the growth of the average size of plant in the presence of increasing returns to scale. For Canada, 72% of TFP growth was due to scale economies and only 28% due to technical change.[7] The 1970–80 period was similar to the 1970–84 period. TFP grew somewhat more rapidly in all three countries with Japan maintaining a 3:1 edge. The 1980–84 period was quite different. TFP growth rates fell in all three countries, dramatically so in Japan. The 1980–84 results may not represent a long-run trend. First, the period is a fairly short one for calculations of this type. Second, this period saw very large modernization investments in all three countries, and during such periods the amount of productive capital stock tends to be overstated by perpetual inventory accumulation methods since obsolescence is not properly accounted for. On the other hand, if our 1980–84 results signal a long-run trend, the stagnation of productivity improvements will have far-reaching effects on the international motor vehicle industry.

Finally, it is of some interest to compare our TFP growth rate results with previous estimates. To our knowledge, there are no previous Canadian estimates. Previous estimates for the United States and Japan are presented in table 3.11. Conrad and Jorgenson (1985) and Jorgenson, Kuroda, and Nishimizu's (1987) TFP growth rates are below ours, and the difference for Japan is quite large. Part of the difference can be attributed to their adjustment of labor hours for educational attainment, which tends to increase the rate of growth of the labor input, thus lowering measured TFP growth. But this adjustment cannot account for the magnitude of the difference. Our results are

Table 3.11   **A Comparison of Estimates of Annual Average Total Factor Productivity Growth Rates (%)**

Time Period/ Country	Conrad and Jorgenson (1985)	Jorgenson, Kuroda, and Nishimizu (1987)	Griliches and Mairesse (1985)[a]	This Study[b]
1970–79:				
United States	.9			2.2
Japan	.6			3.5
1973–79:				
United States		− .2		1.2
Japan		1.4		3.6
1973–80:				
United States			− .7	− .4
Japan			4.4	3.9

[a] This paper examines transportation equipment industry only.
[b] Calculated using the Törnqvist index for purposes of comparison.

quite similar to those of Griliches and Mairesse (1985), who estimate TFP growth from a sample of individual firms drawn from the two-digit transportation equipment industry. Since 1973 was a peak and 1980 a trough in the North American automobile business cycle, the negative number for the United States is due to the effects on TFP of the decline in capacity utilization (from 1.04 to 0.62). Our estimates of the long-run underlying TFP growth rate over the period 1973–80 is +1.1% per annum.

3.5 Conclusions

In this paper we have calculated and analyzed the motor vehicle industry's cost and productivity experience during the period 1970–84 in Canada, the United States, and Japan. Percentage cost increases in a common currency (Canadian dollars) differed less significantly than the increases in each country's own currency due to currency realignments. The appreciation of the Japanese yen masked the superior performance of the Japanese auto industry relative to the North American industries during the period under consideration.

We have emphasized the importance of taking account of variations in capacity utilization when analyzing TFP growth rates for an industry as cyclical as the motor vehicle industry. Failure to do so would have resulted in a 21% overestimate of long-run TFP growth in Canada and a 22% overestimate for the United States during the 1970–84 period (see table 3.9). More extreme problems would have occurred in subperiods. For example, over the 1970–80 period, ignoring capacity utilization effects would have resulted in a 241% underestimate of long-run TFP growth in Canada and a 115% underestimate for the United States.

The rate of growth of total-factor productivity in Japan over the 1970–84 period was three times as rapid as that which occurred in North America, which meant that Japan improved its relative long-run efficiency position by approximately 30 percentage points from 1970 to 1984. According to our analysis of productivity levels (Fuss and Waverman 1990), by 1984 Japanese producers had an 18% efficiency advantage over U.S. producers (at normal capacity utilization rates). On the other hand, there is some tentative evidence of a substantial slowdown in Japanese TFP growth rates during the 1980s, which, along with the continuing appreciation of the yen, places the North American industry in a much more competitive position at the close of the decade than was the case in the early 1980s.

Appendix A
Data Appendix

In this data appendix we provide a brief description of the sources and construction of data used in the empirical analysis. Greater detail can be found in

Fuss and Waverman (1991). The general data sources are the Annual Surveys (or Census) of Manufactures in each country. One problem with these data is the omission of a number of automotive-related production statistics from the annual surveys undertaken by the specific country's statistical office. Several relevant four-digit SIC codes are not classified to the Motor Vehicles Industries in the United States and Canada (e.g., automotive products foundries are classified to SIC 294 [foundries] in Canada; in the United States, automotive stampings are included in All Metal Stampings). These omissions affect our results to the extent that some bias is imparted if the omitted subindustries are significantly different from those included.

Nominal gross actual output data were taken from the central statistical surveys and converted to real actual output in constant dollars by applying the appropriate price deflators (available in Canada from Statistics Canada, in the United States, from the Bureau of Industrial Economics [BIE] and in Japan from the Bank of Japan).

Capacity output is real actual output divided by the capacity utilization rate (CU) (see below for the construction of CU). Average output per plant was computed as a weighted average (weighted by proportion of total output) of the average output in seven size classes. The weighting procedure was used so that the large number of plants in the smallest size classes would not distort the data. The "effective" number of plants is total output divided by average output per plant, and this number is used to compute cost per plant. The size-class data are available in each year for Canada and Japan. For the United States, these data are available only for census years, and the average plant size for other years was obtained by interpolation.

The output price deflators are indices that are normalized to unity in a particular year for each country. The same normalization occurs for materials and capital services prices. Because the cost function contains only zero- and first-order country-specific coefficients, the estimated characterization of the production process in terms of elasticities is invariant to the choice of the benchmark data set that is used to bridge the intercountry price indices to obtain absolute level comparisons. This is also true for country-specific rates of growth of average cost and total factor productivity, which are the topics of this paper. However, the data are also being used to make intercountry cost and productivity level comparisons, and so great care was exercised in calculating the benchmark data. The interested reader can find the details in Fuss and Waverman (1990, 1991). Of course the country-specific zero- and first-order regression coefficients do depend on the specific benchmark data set used to bridge the country-specific data.

Three inputs are used—materials, labor and capital. Materials price deflators were available for all three countries. The total compensation (rather than just the money wage) of labor has been calculated and hours worked estimated for production plus nonproduction workers. Real capital stock data were available for Canada from Statistics Canada, and for the United States from Norsworthy and Zabala (1983) and the Office of Business Analysis. Capital stock data had to be estimated for Japan using investment from the annual census and the perpetual inventory method.

The appropriate price of capital services is the ex ante neoclassical user cost of capital services $PK = QK \cdot (r + d)(1 - uz)/(1 - u)$, where QK is the capital asset price, r is the ex ante rate of return, d is the depreciation rate, u is the corporate tax rate, and z is the present value of the depreciation allowances for tax purposes on an investment of one unit of currency. The motor-vehicle-industry-specific capital service price series that were available for the United States had been estimated by the residual method, which is an inappropriate ex ante measure for such a highly cyclical industry. We have instead constructed a user cost of capital series by combining the rate of return and tax effects for U.S. total manufacturing (which would not be subject to such cyclical variations), which can be calculated from Norsworthy and Malmquist (1983), with the motor-vehicle-industry-specific capital asset price index, that is, PK (motor vehicles) $= PK$ (manufacturing) $\cdot QK$ (motor vehicles) / QK (manufacturing). This construction implies that we are assuming that ex ante rates of return, depreciation rates, and tax effects for motor vehicles and manufacturing are equal in a particular year. We believe this assumption is preferred to the only other ones available to us—that ex ante and ex post rates of return are equal or tax effects are the same across countries. The Norsworthy Malmquist (NM) data are published only to 1977 and were updated to 1980 using internal U.S. Bureau of the Census data. The U.S. capital service price series was extrapolated to 1984, assuming no change in tax parameters. The capital service price for Japan is constructed in the same way as for the United States, except that the NM data are available only to 1978, and hence the extrapolation method is used for the period 1979–84. The motor vehicles asset price deflator was kindly provided by Masahiro Kuroda from his unpublished data base. For Canada, the method of combining the asset price for motor vehicles with manufacturing tax, rate of return, and depreciation data was utilized over the complete sample. Unpublished estimates of manufacturing user costs for 1961–81 were kindly provided to us by Michael Denny. These data were updated to 1984 using a Törnqvist aggregation of unpublished Economic Council of Canada estimates for durable and nondurable manufacturing sectors.

Capacity utilization (CU) rates were calculated from data for total vehicle assembly. For Japan, the count of motorcycles and other vehicles were value weighted so that fluctuations in motorcycle production would not distort the comparative data. Maximum (potential) output was measured in the United States and Canada from individual plant data as the maximum weekly nameplate output, and in Japan from more aggregate data as the maximum monthly output.

The "normal," or full CU rate was defined as the average utilization rate (ratio of actual to maximum output) for Japan 1969–80, since yearly CU rates were reasonably constant over that period. Actual CU rates were normalized so that this average rate was equal to unity.

For each country we have estimated a technological change indicator—the "capital stock" of R&D. This stock is constructed by converting annual R&D expenditures to a real capital stock utilizing the perpetual inventory method, the country-specific consumer price index (CPI), and a depreciation rate of 15%. Our data on R&D expenditures for Japan began in 1967. Therefore, we needed a benchmark R&D stock. We assumed that in 1967 the technology available to Japan could be represented by the R&D stock in North America, and we normalized the Canada, U.S., and Japan stock to unity in each country in 1967. By this construction we are estimating the effect of the change in the R&D stock on the change in costs, which is appropriate for an analysis of the growth rate of average cost and TFP. From another perspective, our R&D variable can be viewed as a method of tracing the country-specific, unexplained technical change. From this point of view, the variable is similar to a time trend, although it consistently outperformed a time trend in the regression analysis.

Technical Appendix

Equality of Total Factor Productivity and Cost Efficiency Growth Rates

(B1)
$$C = \sum_{k=1}^{K} w_k \cdot X_k,$$

where C is total cost, and X_k and w_k are quantities and prices of the kth input, respectively. Differentiating (B1) we obtain

(B2)
$$dC = \sum_k w_k dX_k + \sum_k X_k dw_k,$$

or

(B3)
$$\frac{dC}{C} = \sum_k \left(\frac{w_k X_k}{C}\right)\frac{dX_k}{X_k} + \sum_k \left(\frac{w_k X_k}{C}\right)\frac{dw_k}{w_k}.$$

Subtracting dq/q (proportionate change in actual output) from both sides of (B3) and rearranging yields

(B4)
$$\frac{dC}{C} - \frac{dq}{q} - \sum_k s_k \frac{dw_k}{w_k} = -\left(\frac{dq}{q} - \sum_k s_k \frac{dX_k}{X_k}\right),$$

where s_k is the cost share of the kth input in total cost.
   Equation (B4) can be rewritten as

(B5)
$$-[d\log C/q - \sum s_k d\log w_k] = d\log q - \sum s_k d\log X.$$

The left-hand side of (B5) is the Divisia index of cost efficiency growth and the right-hand side is the Divisia index of total factor productivity (TFP) growth.

The Törnqvist Index of Cost Efficiency and the Translog Cost Function

The Törnqvist discrete approximation to the left-hand side of (B5) for the ith country is

$$(B6) \qquad \Delta \log CE_i = -[\Delta \log C_i/q_i - \sum_k \tfrac{1}{2}(s_{ki1} + s_{ki0}) \Delta \log w_{ki}],$$

or

$$\log CE_{i1} - \log CE_{i0} = -[(\log C_{i1}/q_{i1} - \log C_{i0}/q_{i0})$$
$$- \tfrac{1}{2} \sum_k (s_{ki1} + s_{ki0})(\log w_{ki1} - \log w_{ki0})],$$

which is equation (2) in the text.

We can link the above index to the translog cost function in the following way. Suppose the cost function (1) is approximated by a translog cost function (a quadratic function in the logarithms of w_{it}, Q_{it}, and T_{it}) in which the zero- and first-order parameters differ across countries, but the second-order parameters are the same for each country. In that case the translog cost function will be of the form

$$(B7) \qquad \log C_{it} = G(\log w_{it}, \log Q_{it}, \log T_{it}, D)$$

where G is a quadratic function and D is a vector of country-specific dummy variables. Following Denny and Fuss (1983), we can apply the quadratic lemma to (B7) for the ith country and time periods 1 and 0 to obtain

$$\Delta \log C = \log C_{i1} - \log C_{i0}$$

$$= \tfrac{1}{2} \left(\frac{\partial G}{\partial D_i}\Big|_i + \frac{\partial G}{\partial D_i}\Big|_i \right) \left(D_i - D_i \right)$$

$$(B8) \qquad + \tfrac{1}{2} \sum_k \left(\frac{\partial G}{\partial \log w_k}\Big|_{w_k = w_{ki1}} + \frac{\partial G}{\partial \log w_k}\Big|_{w_k = w_{ki0}} \right) \cdot$$

$$\left[\log w_{ki1} - \log w_{ki0} \right]$$

$$+ \tfrac{1}{2} \left(\frac{\partial G}{\partial \log Q}\Big|_{Q = Q_{i1}} + \frac{\partial G}{\partial \log Q}\Big|_{Q = Q_{i0}} \right) \cdot$$

$$\left(\log Q_{i1} - \log Q_{i0} \right)$$

$$+ \tfrac{1}{2} \sum_j \left(\frac{\partial G}{\partial \log T_j}\Big|_{T_j = T_{ji1}} + \frac{\partial G}{\partial \log T_j}\Big|_{T_j = T_{ji0}} \right) \cdot$$

$$\left(\log T_{ji1} - \log T_{ji0} \right).$$

Assuming price-taking behavior in factor markets and utilizing Shephard's lemma, (B8) can be written as

(B9)

$$\Delta \log C = \frac{1}{2} \sum_k \left(s_{ki1} + s_{ki0} \right) \left(\log w_{ki1} - \log w_{ki0} \right)$$
$$+ \frac{1}{2} \left(ECQ_{i1} + ECQ_{i0} \right) \left(\log Q_{i1} - \log Q_{i0} \right)$$
$$+ \frac{1}{2} \sum_j \left(ECT_{ji1} + ECT_{ji0} \right) \left(\log T_{ji1} - \log T_{ji0} \right)$$
$$+ \Theta_{ii},$$

where

(B10)

$$\Theta_{ii} = \frac{1}{2} \left(\frac{\partial G}{\partial D_i} \bigg| i + \frac{\partial G}{\partial D_i} \bigg| i \right) \cdot \left(D_i - D_i \right) = 0,$$

where ECQ = elasticity of cost with respect to capacity output and
ECT_j = elasticity of cost with respect to the jth technological characteristic.

If we subtract $(\log Q_{i1} - \log Q_{i0})$ from both sides of equation (B9) we obtain the decomposition of cost per unit capacity output growth used in the graphical analysis:

(B11)

$$\Delta \log (C/Q) = \frac{1}{2} \sum_k \left(s_{ki1} + s_{ki0} \right) \left(\log w_{ki1} - \log w_{ki0} \right)$$
$$+ \frac{1}{2} \left(ECQ_{i1} + ECQ_{i0} - 2 \right) \left(\log Q_{i1} - \log Q_{i0} \right)$$
$$+ \frac{1}{2} \sum_j \left(ECT_{ji1} + ECT_{ji0} \right) \left(\log T_{ji1} - \log T_{ji0} \right).$$

The decomposition (B11) is the translog specification corresponding to table 3.1 in the text. The correspondence is presented in table 3.B1.

TFP growth and its decomposition corresponding to table 3.2 can be obtained by subtracting the factor price effect from both sides of (B11) and mul-

Table 3B.1   **Decomposition of Cost per Unit Capacity Output Growth**

Effect	Translog Specification	Table 3.1 Representation
Factor price k	$\frac{1}{2}(s_{ki1} + s_{ki0})(\log w_{ki1} - \log w_{ki0})$	$C_B - C_O$ and $C_C - C_B$
Scale economies	$\frac{1}{2}(ECQ_{i1} + ECQ_{i0} - 2)(\log Q_{i1} - \log Q_{i0})$	$C_D - C_C$
Capacity utilization	$\frac{1}{2}(ECT_{1i1} + ECT_{1i0})(\log T_{1i1} - \log T_{1i0})$	$C_E - C_D$
Technical change	$\frac{1}{2}(ECT_{2i1} + ECT_{2i0})(\log T_{2i1} - \log T_{2i0})$	$C_I - C_E$

Table 3B.2   TFP Growth and Its Decomposition

	Translog Specification	Table 3.2 Representation
TFP growth (in terms of capacity output)	$-\{\Delta\log (C/Q) - \frac{1}{2}\sum_k [s_{ki1} + s_{ki0}][\log w_{ki1} - \log w_{ki0}]\}$	$-(C_1 - C_C)$
Effect:		
Scale economies	$-\frac{1}{2}(ECQ_{i1} + ECQ_{i0} - 2)(\log Q_{i1} - \log Q_{i0})$	$-(C_D - C_C)$
Capacity utilization	$-\frac{1}{2}(ECT_{1i1} + ECT_{1i0})(\log T_{1i1} - \log T_{1i0})$	$-(C_E - C_C)$
Technical change	$-\frac{1}{2}(ECT_{2i1} + ECT_{2i0})(\log T_{2i1} - \log T_{2i0})$	$-(C_1 - C_E)$

tiplying both sides by minus one. The correspondence is presented in table 3.B2.

If instead of subtracting $\Delta\log Q_i$ we subtract $(\log q_{i1} - \log q_{i0})$ from both sides of equation (B9) and recall that $q_{it} = Q_{it} \cdot T_{1it}$, $t = 0,1$, then (B9) provides a decomposition of the actual average cost increase between periods 1 and 0 for country i

(B12)
$$\Delta\log (C/q) = \frac{1}{2}\sum_k \left(s_{ki1} + s_{ki0}\right)\left(\log w_{ki1} - \log w_{ki0}\right)$$
$$+ \frac{1}{2}\left(ECQ_{i1} + ECQ_{i0} - 2\right)\left(\log Q_{i1} - \log Q_{i0}\right)$$
$$+ \frac{1}{2}\left(ECT_{1i1} + ECT_{1i0} - 2\right)\left(\log T_{1i1} - \log T_{1i0}\right)$$
$$+ \frac{1}{2}\left(ECT_{2i1} + ECT_{2i0}\right)\left(\log T_{2i1} - \log T_{2i0}\right).$$

The decomposition (B12) is the formula used to obtain the average cost results contained in tables 3.6 and 3.7. For example, the scale-economies effect over the period 1970–84 is calculated as $\{[\exp(x)]^{1/14} - 1\} \cdot 100$ where

(B13) $x = \frac{1}{2} (ECQ_{i,1984} + ECQ_{i,1970} - 2)(\log Q_{i,1984} - \log Q_{i,1970}).$

The translog (Törnqvist) index of the growth in cost efficiency or total factor productivity between periods 0 and 1 for country i is obtained from (B12) by subtracting the factor price effects from both sides of the equation and multiplying the result by -1:

(B14) $\log CE_{i1} - \log CE_{i0} = \log TFP_{i1} - \log TFP_{i0} = -[\Delta\log(C/q)$
$$- \frac{1}{2} \sum_k (s_{ki1} + s_{ki0})(\log w_{ki1} - \log w_{ki0}),$$

and

$$\log CE_{i1} - \log CE_{i0} = -\frac{1}{2}(ECQ_{i1} + ECQ_{i0} - 2)(\log Q_{i1} - \log Q_{i0})$$
$$- \frac{1}{2} (ECT_{1i1} + ECT_{1i0} - 2)(\log T_{1i1} - \log T_{1i0})$$
$$- \frac{1}{2} (ECT_{2i1} + ECT_{2i0})(\log T_{2i1} - \log T_{2i0}).$$

Equation (B14) is just equation (2) in the text. Equation (B15) provides the decomposition of the translog index of efficiency growth into its sources. This formula underlies the results presented in tables 3.9 and 3.10. For example, the average annual growth rate of TFP for country i over the period 1970–84 is given by $\{[\exp(\Delta\log \mathrm{CE}_i)]^{1/14} - 1\} \cdot 100$. The percentage contribution of scale economies is calculated as $(x/y) \cdot 100$ where

$$x = -\tfrac{1}{2}(\mathrm{ECQ}_{i1} + \mathrm{ECQ}_{i0} - 2)(\log Q_{i1} - \log Q_{i0}),$$

and

$$y = \Delta\log \mathrm{CE}_i.$$

Notes

1. Reasonably accessible (nontechnical) discussions of the cost function approach to production analysis can be found in Baumol (1977), Varian (1984) and Fuss (1987). Fuss and McFadden (1978) provide a more technically difficult and detailed treatment. The rationale for including the capacity utilization rate as an argument in the cost function is developed in Fuss and Waverman (1991).
2. In the empirical analysis, materials constitutes a third factor of production. For simplicity it is not considered explicitly at this stage of the exposition.
3. The most common index of the state of technology is a time trend. In this paper we use the real net stock of R&D expenditures to index the state of technology.
4. The cost efficiency expression can be calculated from (2) by noting that $\log (C_i/Q_i) = \log (C_i/q_i) + \log T_{1i}$.
5. The cost function that was actually estimated is not quite the standard translog function since it contains several third-order terms. These terms were necessary in order to insure that the short-run, long-run effects generated by including capacity utilization as an argument of the cost function satisfied the Viner-Wong envelope theorem (Viner 1952). See Fuss and Waverman (1990, 1991) for details.
6. An output mix variable (the average weight of automobiles produced in a particular country in a specific year) was added to the list of explanatory variables to control for the bias in the calculation of real output, which occurs when the price = marginal cost assumption is violated (as it is in this industry) and the mix of vehicles (by size class) is changing over time. Between 1970 and 1984 there was a trend to the production of smaller vehicles in North America and larger vehicles in Japan. The average cost and TFP growth rates presented below have been corrected for the bias using the results of the cost function estimation. For further details see Fuss and Waverman (1990).
7. The sources of growth columns in tables 3.9 and 3.10 are organized according to conventional growth accounting procedures, in contrast with tables 3.6–3.8. They measure the proportions of TFP growth that can be attributed to the various effects.

References

Baumol, W. J. 1977. *Economic theory and operations analysis,* 4th ed. Englewood Cliffs, N.J.: Prentice-Hall.
Berndt, E., and N. Savin. 1975. Estimation and hypothesis testing in singular equation

systems with autoregressive disturbances. *Econometrica* 45 (September–November): 937–57.

Conrad, K., and D. Jorgenson. 1985. Sectoral productivity gaps between the United States, Japan and Germany, 1960–1979. In *Vereins für Socialpolitik, Probleme und Perspektiven der weltwirtschaftlichen Entwicklung,* 335–46. Berlin: Duncker and Humbolt.

Denny, M., and M. Fuss. 1983. A general approach to intertemporal and interspatial productivity comparisons. *Journal of Econometrics* 23 (December): 315–30.

Denny, M., M. Fuss, and J. D. May. 1981. Intertemporal changes in regional productivity in Canadian manufacturing. *Canadian Journal of Economics* 15 (August): 390–408.

Fuss, M. 1987. Cost and production functions. In *The new Palgrave: A dictionary of economic theory and doctrine,* ed. J. Eatwell, M. Milgate, and P. Newman, 3:995–1000. New York: Stockton.

Fuss, M., and D. McFadden, eds. 1978. *Production economics: A dual approach to theory and applications.* 2 vols. Amsterdam: North-Holland.

Fuss, M., and L. Waverman. 1990. The extent and sources of cost and efficiency differences between U.S. and Japanese motor vehicle producers. *Journal of the Japanese and International Economies,* vol. 4 (September).

———. 1991. *Costs and productivity in automobile production: A comparison of Canada, Germany, Japan and the United States.* Cambridge: Cambridge University Press (in press).

Griliches, Z., and J. Mairesse. 1985. R&D and productivity growth: Comparing Japanese and U.S. manufacturing firms. National Bureau of Economic Research Working Paper no. 1778. Cambridge, Mass., December.

Jorgenson, D., M. Kuroda, and M. Nishimizu. 1987. Japan-U.S. industry-level productivity comparisons, 1960–1979. *Journal of the Japanese and International Economies* 1 (March):1–30.

Norsworthy, J. R., and D. H. Malmquist. 1983. Input measurement and productivity growth in Japanese and U.S. manufacturing. *American Economic Review* 73 (December):947–67.

Norsworthy, J. R., and C. A. Zabala. 1983. Output measurement and productivity growth in the U.S. auto industry. Unpublished background paper. Bureau of the Census, Washington, D.C., April.

Varian, H. 1984. *Microeconomic analysis,* 2d ed. New York: Norton.

Viner, J. 1952. Cost curves and supply curves. In *AEA readings in price theory,* ed. G. J. Stigler and K. E. Boulding. Homewood, IL: Irwin.

4 Comparison and Analysis of Productivity Growth and R&D Investment in the Electrical Machinery Industries of the United States and Japan

M. Ishaq Nadiri and Ingmar R. Prucha

4.1 Introduction

During the 1970s the growth rates of labor productivity in the Japanese manufacturing sector dramatically exceeded those of the United States, particularly in such key industries as primary metals, chemicals, electrical machinery, and transportation equipment. This enabled the Japanese to reach and eventually surpass levels of U.S. labor productivity in these industries (Grossman 1985). Although each of these Japanese industries is a key competitor to the U.S. high-technology industries in both the domestic and in the world market, the electrical machinery industry stands out in certain respects. It has experienced very rapid growth in output and productivity and high rates of capital formation both in the United States and Japan. Also, a substantial amount of research and development (R&D) resources—over 20% of total R&D expenditures in total manufacturing—is concentrated in this industry in both countries. Furthermore, Japan has increased its share of free world exports in electrical machinery from 22% in 1971 to 48% in 1981 and has also dramatically increased its share of U.S. imports of electrical machinery products over the same period (Grossman 1985).

M. Ishaq Nadiri is the Jay Gould Professor of Economics at New York University and a research associate of the National Bureau of Economic Research. Ingmar R. Prucha is an associate professor of economics at the University of Maryland and a research associate of the National Bureau of Economic Research.

The authors would like to thank Jack Triplett, Ernie Zampelli, and the participants of the NBER Conference on Research in Income and Wealth for valuable comments. Yuzu Kumasaka and Yoichi Nakamura were extremely helpful in the preparation of the Japanese data. The authors would further like to thank Elliot Grossman for providing them with his data set and Jennifer Bond, Milo Peterson, and Ken Rogers for their help with the U.S. data. Nancy Lemrow provided very able research assistance. The research was supported in part by NSF grant PRA-8108635 and by the C. V. Starr Center's Focus Program for Capital Formation, Technological Change, Financial Structure, and Tax Policy. The authors would also like to acknowledge the support with computer time from the Computer Science Center of the University of Maryland.

Because of these characteristics, we have chosen to examine the productivity performance of this industry in the United States and Japan. The analysis is based on a dynamic factor demand model. The model links intertemporal production decisions by explicitly recognizing that the level of certain factors of production cannot be changed without incurring some costs. These costs are often referred to as "adjustment costs" and are defined here in terms of forgone output from current production. Not all inputs are subject to adjustment costs; some inputs, like materials, which can be adjusted very easily, are called variable factors while others, like capital and R&D, which are subject to adjustment cost (and only adjust partially in the first period), are referred to as quasi-fixed inputs. Since output growth has been fairly high in the electrical machinery industry both in the United States and Japan, we have not imposed a priori constant returns to scale. Rather, returns to scale are estimated from the data. Since the rate of R&D investment in the electrical machinery industry has been very rapid, we have also incorporated R&D explicitly as one of the inputs. The stocks of physical capital and R&D are considered to be quasi-fixed inputs, while labor (hours worked) and materials are considered to be variable factors in the production process. Using the structural parameter estimates, we analyze the sources of growth in output, labor productivity, and total factor productivity.

The paper is organized as follows. In section 4.2 we provide a brief description of the behavior of productivity growth as well as input and output growth in the electrical machinery industries of the United States and Japan. Section 4.3 describes the basic features of the analytical model. In section 4.4 we describe the results obtained by estimating the model using annual data. We report output and price elasticities of the variable and quasi-fixed factors of production in the short run, the intermediate run, and the long run, and we calculate the speeds of adjustment of the quasi-fixed factors—physical and R&D capital. Section 4.5 is devoted to examining the sources of output and factor productivity growth rates. Summary and conclusions are offered in section 4.6. Mathematical details of the analytic model are given in appendix A. Appendix B contains the data description. Explicit formulas for expressions used in the decomposition of total factor productivity growth are given in appendix C.

4.2 Some Descriptive Characteristics

In this section, we provide a brief description of total and partial factor productivity growth and the growth of gross output, labor, materials, capital, and R&D in the electrical machinery industry for the periods 1968–73 and 1974–79. We refer to these periods as the pre-OPEC and the post-OPEC periods, respectively.

Average growth rates for gross output and factor inputs for the two periods are given in table 4.1. For the pre-Opec period, the growth rates were extremely high for Japan in comparison to the United States. However, in the

Table 4.1   Growth of Output and Inputs and Input Shares in the U.S. and Japanese Electrical Machinery Industries, 1968–73 and 1974–79.

Period	Output		Labor		Materials		Capital		R&D	
	United States	Japan	United States	Japan	United States	Japan	United States	Japan	United States	Japan
Average annual rates of growth (%):										
1968–73	4.2	16.9	−0.5	4.3	3.3	14.8	5.4	11.4	5.3	19.2
1974–79	4.9	6.4	1.4	−2.5	2.1	2.5	4.3	6.5	1.7	11.4
Input shares in total cost:										
1968–73			.35	.16	.47	.74	.07	.08	.11	.02
1974–79			.33	.20	.48	.68	.08	.09	.11	.03

post-OPEC period, the Japanese electrical machinery industry experienced a substantial drop in rates of growth of output and of most inputs. For example, the average output growth rate declined from 16.9% to 6.4% for Japan while increasing from 4.2% to 4.9% in the United States. Still, the level of output growth rates for the Japanese industry remained high compared to the U.S. industry. The average growth rate of capital over the period 1968–73 was twice as high in Japan as in the United States even though the U.S. industry experienced a healthy 5.4% per annum growth rate over this period. However, Japan's rate of growth in capital formation decelerated by more than 40% after 1973. Materials inputs grew much faster in Japan than in the United States in the pre-OPEC period, but again Japan experienced a dramatic slowdown in the growth rate of this input during the second period.

As indicated in table 4.1 the R&D stock grew at a much more rapid rate in Japan than in the United States in both periods, reflecting the very high rate of growth in R&D investment in Japan. In both the U.S. and Japanese electrical machinery industries the growth in the stock of R&D slowed down in the 1974–79 period. The input shares in total cost shown in the lower panel of table 4.1 indicate, for Japan, a tendency toward increase in the labor share and a decline in the share of materials in the two periods. The cost shares in the United States are generally very stable in this industry over the two periods.

The growth rate of labor measured in hours worked shows a dramatically different pattern in the two countries. It increased from -0.5% in 1968–73 to 1.4% in 1974–79 in the United States, while in Japan the growth in this input declined from 4.3% to an actual reduction of -2.5%. This phenomenon is consistent with the general pattern of employment in the two countries: Japan experienced declines in employment in several industries while the United States experienced increases in employment in most industries (Griliches and Mairesse, in this volume; Norsworthy and Malmquist 1983).

As demonstrated by table 4.2, an important characteristic of the electrical machinery industry in both countries is the high ratio of R&D investment in output. While the ratio of capital investment in value added or gross output in this industry is generally lower than in total manufacturing, the opposite is true for R&D cnvestment. The R&D ratios in the electrical machinery industry are two to three times as large as those in total manufacturing. It is also important to note that in the U.S. electrical machinery industry the R&D investment ratios are considerably higher than the capital investment ratios, while the opposite is true in Japan.

Total and partial productivity growth rates based on a gross output measurement framework are shown in table 4.3. Both total and labor-productivity growth rates were much higher in the Japanese electrical machinery industry than in the United States.[1] This was particularly true in the pre-OPEC period. Unlike the aggregate manufacturing sector (Norsworthy and Malmquist 1983), total factor productivity growth was rising in this industry in the two countries over the two periods. The differences in the growth of labor productivity in the industries of the two countries are substantial. In the United

Table 4.2   **Ratio of Investment Expenditures in Capital and Total R&D to Gross Output and Value Added in the U.S. and Japanese Total Manufacturing Sectors and Electrical Machinery Industries, 1970 and 1980 (in percentages)**

| | Investment Expenditures in Value Added | | | | Investment Expenditures in Gross Output | | | |
| | Capital | | R&D | | Capital | | R&D | |
	United States	Japan	United States	Japan	United States	Japan	United States	Japan
Total manufacturing:								
1970	7.4	30.0	5.8	2.9	3.5	9.8	2.7	.9
1980	9.4	18.5	5.7	4.0	3.8	5.6	2.3	1.2
Electrical machinery industry:								
1970	5.5	21.1	16.9	8.0	3.1	7.4	7.5	2.8
1980	8.6	18.0	12.8	9.4	4.8	6.9	7.1	3.6

Table 4.3   **Average Annual Rates of Growth of Total and Partial Factor Productivity in the U.S. and Japanese Electrical Machinery Industries (in percentages)**

| | Total Factor Productivity | | Labor Productivity | | Materials Productivity | | Capital Productivity | | R&D Productivity | |
	United States	Japan	United States	Japan	United States	Japan	United States	Japan	United States	Japan
1968–73	1.8	4.1	4.7	12.6	.9	2.1	−1.2	5.5	−1.1	−2.3
1974–79	2.9	4.5	3.6	8.9	2.8	3.9	.6	−.1	3.2	−7.0

States, labor productivity grew about 4.7% in 1968–73 and declined to 3.6% in 1974–79; in Japan, the corresponding growth rates are 12.6% and 8.9%, respectively. Substantial improvements in materials productivity in this industry in both countries in the post-OPEC period are also noted.

Thus, the elements of the Japanese productivity "miracle" can also be observed in the electrical machinery industry: high rates of labor-productivity growth accompanied by rapid growth rates of output and other inputs such as materials, capital, and R&D before 1973 and diminishing but still very high rates of labor-productivity growth after 1973 accompanied by a substantial falloff in the growth rates of output and other inputs. To explore the reasons for these productivity patterns, we proceed to estimate the production structure of the electrical machinery industry of the two countries.

4.3 Model Specification

The model specified below generates a set of factor demand equations for both variable inputs (materials and labor) and the quasi-fixed inputs (capital and R&D). Each demand equation allows for the effect of changes in output, changes in relative prices, and technological change. Also, the model allows for the interaction (i.e., nonseparability) of the quasi-fixed inputs, capital and R&D, during the adjustment process. From the structural parameters various underlying features of the technology, such as the degree of economies of scale and the output and price elasticities of the inputs in the current and subsequent periods, can be measured. Finally, these parameters can be used to decompose the factors that affect total and labor-productivity growth rates in the Japanese and U.S. electrical machinery industries.

Consider a firm that employs two variable inputs and two quasi-fixed inputs in producing a single output from a technology with internal adjustment costs. Specifically, assume the firm's production function takes the form:

(1) $$Y_t = F(V_t, X_{t-1}, \Delta X_t, T_t),$$

where Y_t denotes gross output, $V_t = [V_{1t}, V_{2t}]'$ is the vector of variable inputs, $X_t = [X_{1t}, X_{2t}]'$ is the vector of end-of-period stocks of the quasi-fixed inputs, and T_t is an exogenous technology index. The vector $\Delta X_t = X_t - X_{t-1}$ represents the internal adjustment costs in terms of foregone output.

The firm's input markets are assumed to be perfectly competitive. It proves convenient to describe the firm's technology in terms of the normalized restricted cost function defined as $G(W_t, X_{t-1}, \Delta X_t, Y_t, T_t) = \hat{V}_{1t} + W_t \hat{V}_{2t}$. Here $\hat{V}_{1t}$ and $\hat{V}_{2t}$ represent the cost-minimizing amounts of variable inputs needed to produce the output Y_t conditional on X_{t-1} and ΔX_t, and W_t denotes the price of V_{2t} normalized by the price of V_{1t}. We assume that the normalized restricted cost function satisfies standard properties. In particular $G(\cdot)$ is assumed to be convex in X_{t-1} and ΔX_t and concave in W_t; compare, for example, Lau (1976).[2]

Given the presence of large firms in the electrical machinery industries of both the United States and Japan, we do not impose a priori constant returns to scale. Rather, we allow the technology to be homogeneous of (constant) degree and determine the returns to scale parameter ρ from the data.[3] Given that $F(\cdot)$ is homogeneous of degree ρ, the corresponding normalized restricted cost function is of the following general form:[4]

(2) $$G(W_t, X_{t-1}, \Delta X_t, T_t) = G(W_t, X_{t-1}/Y_t^{1/\rho}, \Delta X_t/Y_t^{1/\rho}, T_t) Y_t^{1/\rho}.$$

In the empirical analysis we take materials, M, and labor (hours worked), L, as the variable factors and the stocks of capital, K, and research and development, R, as the quasi-fixed factors. We adopt the convention $V_1 = M$, $V_2 = L$, $X_1 = K$, $X_2 = R$; W is the real wage rate; the price of materials is the numeraire. In the empirical analysis, we further take $T_t = t$, that is, technical change, other than that reflected by the stock of R&D, is represented by a simple time trend. We specify the following functional form for the normalized restricted cost function:

$$G(W_t, X_{t-1}, \Delta X_t, Y_t, T_t) = (\alpha_0 + \alpha_W W_t + \alpha_{WT} W_t T_t + \alpha_{WW} W_t^2/2) Y_t^{1/\rho}$$

(3)
$$+ a' X_{t-1} + b' X_{t-1} W_t + c' X_{t-1} T_t$$

$$+ X'_{t-1} A X_{t-1} / (2Y_t^{1/\rho}) + \Delta X'_t B \Delta X_t / (2Y_t^{1/\rho})$$

where

$$a = \begin{bmatrix} \alpha_K \\ \alpha_R \end{bmatrix}, \ b = \begin{bmatrix} \alpha_{KW} \\ \alpha_{RW} \end{bmatrix}, \ c = \begin{bmatrix} \alpha_{KT} \\ \alpha_{RT} \end{bmatrix}, \ A = \begin{bmatrix} \alpha_{KK} & \alpha_{KR} \\ \alpha_{KR} & \alpha_{RR} \end{bmatrix}, \ B = \begin{bmatrix} \alpha_{\dot{K}\dot{K}} & 0 \\ 0 & \alpha_{\dot{R}\dot{R}} \end{bmatrix}.$$

In light of the above discussion, we can view (3) as a second-order approximation to a generalized normalized restricted cost function that corresponds to a homogeneous technology of degree ρ. Expression (3) is a generalization of the normalized restricted cost function introduced by Denny, Fuss, and Waverman (1981) and Morrison and Berndt (1981) for linear homogeneous technologies.[5] As in these references we impose parameter restrictions such that the marginal adjustment costs at $\Delta X_t = 0$ are zero. The convexity of $G(\cdot)$ in X_{t-1} and ΔX_t and concavity in W_t implies the following inequality parameter restrictions: $\alpha_{KK} > 0$, $\alpha_{RR} > 0$, $\alpha_{KK} \alpha_{RR} - \alpha^2_{KR} > 0$, $\alpha_{\dot{K}\dot{K}} > 0$, $\alpha_{\dot{R}\dot{R}} > 0$, $\alpha_{WW} < 0$.

We assume that in each period t (for given initial stocks X_{t-1} and static expectations on relative factor prices, output, and the technology) the firm derives an optimal plan for inputs in period $t, t + 1, \ldots$ such that the present value of the future cost stream is minimized, and that the firm chooses its inputs in period t accordingly. In each period, the firm revises its expectations and the optimal plan for its inputs, based on new information.

A mathematical formulation and analysis of the firm's optimization problem is given in appendix A. It is shown there that the implied demand equations for the quasi-fixed factors, capital and R&D, are in the form of an accelerator model. We denote the accelerator matrix with $M = (m_{i,j})_{i,j = K,R}$. The firm's demand equations for the variable factors, labor and materials, can be derived from the restricted cost function via Shephard's lemma. Instead of estimating the parameter matrices A and B, it proves advantageous to estimate the matrices $C = (c_{ij})_{i,j=K,R} = -BM$ and B (and to express A as a function of C and B). The matrix C is found to be symmetric and negative definite. Explicit expressions for the resulting demand equations for labor, materials, capital, and R&D are given in equations (A4) and (A5) of appendix A.

4.4   Empirical Results

In this section, we report the structural parameter estimates for the U.S. and Japanese electrical machinery industries as well as implied estimates for short-run, intermediate-run, and long-run price and output elasticities.

A detailed description of the data sources and the variables of the model is given in the appendix B. The data on gross output, materials, labor, capital and R&D are in constant 1972 dollars and yen and have been normalized by their respective sample means. Prices were constructed conformably. The model parameters were estimated by full-information maximum likelihood from the demand equations (A4) and (A5); for further details see appendix A.

4.4.1   Parameter Estimates

The structural parameter estimates are given in table 4.4. As indicated by the squared correlation coefficients between actual and fitted data, the estimated factor demand equations seem to fit the data quite well. (Fitted values are calculated from the reduced form). The parameter estimates are, in general, statistically significant. For both the United States and Japan, the parameter estimates satisfy the theoretical restrictions. In particular, the estimates for c_{KK}, c_{RR}, and α_{WW} are negative, and those for $\alpha_{\dot{K}\dot{K}}$, and $\alpha_{\dot{R}\dot{R}}$, and $(c_{KK}c_{RR} - c^2_{KR})$ are positive. The variables underlying the estimates for the U.S. and Japanese electrical machinery industries are, as explained above, measured in

Table 4.4   **Full Information Maximum-Likelihood Estimates of the Parameters of the Dynamic Factor Demand Model for the U.S. and Japanese Electrical Machinery Industries**

Parameters	United States		Japan	
α_0	1.83	(7.40)	1.45	(18.14)
ρ	1.21	(17.23)	1.39	(13.20)
α_K	−.95	(3.13)	−.47	(2.89)
α_R	−.65	(1.85)	−.67	(7.82)
α_{KT}	−.19	(4.47)	−.05	(.75)
α_{RT}	.22	(3.03)	−.02	(5.66)
c_{KK}	−2.05	(3.07)	−.58	(8.77)
c_{RR}	−2.10	(1.90)	−.14	(7.99)
c_{RK}	.15	(.74)	.01	(1.54)
$\alpha_{\dot{K}\dot{K}}$	8.70	(3.06)	2.57	(4.92)
$\alpha_{\dot{R}\dot{R}}$	13.80	(1.63)	1.11	(5.15)
α_W	1.91	(25.41)	1.33	(10.01)
α_{WW}	−.48	(3.66)	−.81	(3.13)
α_{WK}	.29	(2.59)	.39	(4.65)
α_{WR}	−.52	(4.62)	.02	(1.47)
α_{WT}	−.28	(6.89)	−.42	(4.43)
Sample Period	1960–80		1968–80	
Log of Likelihood	222.1		147.4	
M-equation: R^2	.87		.94	
L-equation: R^2	.65		.75	
K-equation: R^2	.99		.99	
R-equation: R^2	.99		.99	

Note: Absolute values of the asymptotic t-ratios are given in parentheses. The R^2 values correspond to the squared correlation coefficients between the actual M, L, K, R variables and their fitted values calculated from the reduced form.

Table 4.5   **Full Information Maximum-Likelihood Estimates of the Accelerator Coefficients for Capital and R&D in the U.S. and Japanese Electrical Machinery Industries**

	Accelerator Coefficient			
	m_{KK}	m_{KR}	m_{RK}	m_{RR}
United States	.236	−.017	−.011	.152
	(8.55)	(.66)	(.68)	(6.82)
Japan	.227	.003	−.006	.125
	(4.41)	(1.47)	(1.47)	(7.47)

Note: Absolute values of the asymptotic *t*-ratios are given in parentheses.

different units. Hence, a direct comparison of individual parameter estimates is difficult. However, we do calculate various unit-free characteristics that allow a meaningful comparison.

In general the adjustment cost coefficients $\alpha_{\dot{K}\dot{K}}$ and $\alpha_{\dot{R}\dot{R}}$ are significantly different from zero. They are crucial in determining the investment patterns of the quasi-fixed factors via the accelerator coefficients. Omitting those terms would not only have resulted in a misspecification of the investment patterns but also (in general) in inconsistent estimates of the other technology parameters.

Table 4.5 shows the estimates for the accelerator coefficients m_{KK}, m_{KR}, m_{RK}, and m_{RR}.[6] For both the U.S. and Japanese electrical machinery industries we find that the cross-adjustment coefficients m_{KR} and m_{RK} (as well as c_{KR}) are very small in absolute magnitude and are not significantly different from zero at the 95% level. In describing the adjustment speed, we can therefore concentrate on the own-adjustment coefficients m_{KK} and m_{RR}. As a first observation, we note that the obtained estimates are quite similar across countries. For both the United States and Japan, capital adjusts faster than R&D. While capital closes approximately one-fourth of the gap between the initial and the desired stock in the first period, R&D only closes approximately one-seventh of its gap.[7]

As remarked earlier, our specification does not impose a priori constant returns to scale. Rather, we estimate the scale elasticity (represented by ρ) from the data. For both countries, we find substantial and significant scale effects in the industry. For the United States, our estimate for the scale elasticity is 1.21; for Japan we obtained a considerably higher estimate of 1.39. As we explain in more detail in section 4.5, this difference in scale elasticities will translate into substantial differences in productivity growth. It is also interesting to note that, contrary to our finding of increasing returns to scale at the industry level, Griliches and Mairesse (in this volume) find decreasing returns to scale in the U.S. and Japanese total manufacturing sectors at the firm level.

4.4.2 Price and Output Elasticities

The own- and cross-price elasticities of labor, materials, capital, and R&D for 1976 are reported in table 4.6. The elasticities are calculated for the short run (SR), intermediate run (IR), and long run (LR) for each input for the electrical machinery industry in both the United States and Japan.[8] All of the own-price elasticities have the expected negative sign. The magnitudes of the elasticities are fairly similar between the two countries. In the United States, the own-price elasticity of labor is the largest among the inputs followed by materials, R&D stock, and capital stock. In Japan, with minor exceptions, the same pattern holds; the quasi-fixed inputs, capital and R&D, seem to have a higher own-price elasticity in the Japanese than in the U.S. electrical machinery industry. These results are similar to those reported for the total manufacturing sectors of the United States and Japan in Mohnen, Nadiri, and Prucha (1986).

Although the cross-price elasticities are generally small in comparison to own-price elasticities, some of the elasticities are sizable. The elasticities of materials and R&D with respect to the wage rate, and the elasticities of labor, R&D, and capital inputs with respect to the price of materials, are quite large

Table 4.6   Short-Run (SR), Intermediate-Run (IR), and Long-Run (LR) Price Elasticities in the U.S. and Japanese Electrical Machinery Industries, 1976

	United States			Japan		
Elasticity	SR	IR	LR	SR	IR	LR
ε_{M_wM}	−.32	−.40	−.64	−.04	−.18	−.64
ε_{M_wL}	.36	.41	.65	.09	.15	.36
ε_{M_cK}	−.01	.02	.09	−.02	.04	.20
ε_{M_cR}	−.01	−.02	−.08	−.03	−.01	.09
ε_{L_wM}	.47	.55	.90	.37	.51	.85
ε_{L_wL}	−.48	−.58	−1.12	−.38	−.44	−.57
ε_{L_cK}		−.02	−.06		−.06	−.23
ε_{L_cR}		.04	.27		−.01	−.05
ε_{K_wM}	.10	.17	.38	.27	.46	.99
ε_{K_wL}	−.05	−.09	−.17	−.13	−.23	−.48
ε_{K_cK}	−.04	−.08	−.18	−.14	−.24	−.49
ε_{K_cR}	−.01	−.01	−.04	−.01	−.01	−.02
ε_{R_wM}	−.05	−.09	−.27	.19	.33	.91
ε_{R_wL}	.11	.20	.65	−.05	−.08	−.23
ε_{R_cK}	−.01	−.01	−.03	−.01	−.01	−.04
ε_{R_cR}	−.06	−.10	−.34	−.14	−.24	−.65

Note: ε_{Zs} is the elasticity of factor Z = materials (M), labor (L), capital (K), and R&D (R) with respect to s = price of materials (w^M), labor (w^L), capital (c^K), and R&D (c^R).

Table 4.7   **Short-Run (SR), Intermediate-Run (IR), and Long-Run (LR) Output Elasticities in the U.S. and Japanese Electrical Machinery Industries, 1976**

	United States			Japan		
Elasticity	SR	IR	LR	SR	IR	LR
ε_{MY}	1.19	1.07	.82	1.06	.99	.72
ε_{LY}	1.07	1.06	.82	.39	.45	.72
ε_{KY}	.20	.34	.82	.20	.34	.72
ε_{RY}	.14	.24	.82	.15	.26	.72

Note: ε_{ZY} is the elasticity of factor Z = materials (M), labor (L), capital (K), and R&D (R) with respect to output (Y).

in both countries. Materials are substitutes for other inputs, except for R&D in the United States. Labor and R&D are substitutes in the United States and weak complements in the Japanese electrical machinery industry. Labor and capital and R&D and capital are complements in both countries.

The output elasticities of the inputs for 1976 are shown in table 4.7. The long-run elasticities of the inputs are .8 and .7, respectively, for the United States and Japan, reflecting fairly sizable economies of scale. The results are consistent with Fuss and Waverman (in this volume), Nadiri and Prucha (1983, 1990) and Nadiri and Schankerman (1981). The patterns of the output elasticities, particularly in the United States, indicate that the variable factors of production, labor and materials, respond strongly in the short run to changes in output. This is because both labor and materials in the United States and materials in Japan overshoot their long-run equilibrium values in the short-run to compensate for the sluggish adjustment of the quasi-fixed factors. They slowly adjust toward their long-run equilibrium values as capital and R&D adjust. The output elasticities of capital and R&D are small in the short-run but increase over time and are quite similar. At least in the short-run and intermediate-run, the output elasticities of both the variable and quasi-fixed factors substantially exceed their own-price elasticities. It is surprising that, except for the labor input, the patterns of input responses are similar in both countries.

Thus, the production structure of the electrical machinery industry in the two countries, characterized by the patterns of factor input substitution and complementarity as well as the degree of scale, is qualitatively similar. Quantitatively, there are some differences in scale and in the responses of inputs to changes in prices and output in the two industries. Both industries are characterized by increasing returns to scale. However, the Japanese industry has a higher scale, which substantially influences its productivity growth and is a major source of divergence between the productivity growth rates in this industry in the two countries.

4.5 Productivity Analysis

Using the estimates of the production structure, we can quantitatively examine the sources of output and productivity growth. The contributions of the factor inputs, technical change, and adjustment costs to output growth are shown in table 4.8. This decomposition is based on the approximation:

$$(4) \quad \Delta \ln Y_t = \tfrac{1}{2} \sum_{i=1}^{6} [\varepsilon_{YZ_i}(t) + \varepsilon_{YZ_i}(t-1)] \Delta \ln Z_{it} + \tfrac{1}{2} [\lambda_Y(t) + \lambda_Y(t-1)],$$

with $Z_1 = L$, $Z_2 = M$, $Z_3 = K_{-1}$, $Z_4 = R_{-1}$, $Z_5 = \Delta K$, and $Z_6 = \Delta R$. The ε_{YZ_i}'s denote respective output elasticities and $\lambda_Y(t) = (1/Y_t)(\partial Y_t / \partial t)$ denotes technical change.[9]

The average growth of gross output was very rapid in Japan in the period 1968–73, but growth decelerated substantially in the period 1974–79. For the United States, output growth rates were similar in the two periods. The contributions of various inputs to the growth of output differ considerably between the two periods and the two industries. The most significant source of gross output growth is materials growth, particularly in Japan. The contribution of capital is larger in Japan than in the United States, but falls in both countries over the post-OPEC period. The R&D stock contributes significantly to the growth of output in both industries. In the post-OPEC period its contribution falls in the United States but remains the same for Japan. The large contribution of R&D to the output growth may come as a surprise but can be explained by two factors. First, the share of R&D investment in gross output, as noted earlier, is very high in the electrical machinery industries of both countries; second, the marginal product of R&D, because of the relatively large adjustment costs and the considerable degree of scale, is fairly large in the two industries. The direct contributions of the adjustment costs are fairly small, as one would expect. The contribution of technical change is clearly important in explaining the growth of output in both industries. Its contribution is twice as large in Japan as in the United States.

In table 4.9 we provide a decomposition of labor-productivity growth. This decomposition is based on the approximation:

$$(5) \quad \Delta \ln(Y_t / L_t) = \tfrac{1}{2} \sum_{i=2}^{6} [\varepsilon_{YZ_i}(t) + \varepsilon_{YZ_i}(t-1)] \Delta \ln(Z_{it} / L_t)$$
$$+ \tfrac{1}{2} [\lambda_Y(t) + \lambda_Y(t-1)] + (\rho - 1) \Delta \ln L_t,$$

where ρ is the scale elasticity.[10] The most significant contribution again stems from the growth of materials, particularly in Japan, although the contribution of physical capital is also important. In comparison to the results reported by Norsworthy and Malmquist (1983) for the total manufacturing sector, the contribution of physical capital is somewhat larger for the United States but

Table 4.8 Sources of Output Growth for the U.S. and Japanese Electrical Machinery Industries: Average Annual Rates of Growth (in %)

	Gross Output	Labor Effect[a]	Materials Effect[a]	Capital Effect[a]	R&D Effect[a]	Adjustment Cost		Technical Change	Residual
						Capital	R&D		
United States:									
1968–73	4.2	−.24	1.83	.87	1.18	.06	.12	.73	−.32
1974–79	4.9	.39	1.06	.69	.31	−.09	.04	.86	1.67
Japan:									
1968–73	16.9	.94	14.32	2.12	.7	−.26	−.34	1.55	−2.11
1974–79	6.4	−.66	2.08	1.10	.72	.09	−.12	2.55	.69

[a]Growth rate of input weighted by average output elasticity.

Table 4.9 Decomposition of Labor Productivity Growth in the U.S. and Japanese Electrical Machinery Industries. Average Annual Rates of Growth (in %)

	Labor Productivity	Labor Effect	Materials Effect[a]	Capital Effect[a]	R&D Effect[a]	Adjustment Cost Capital	Adjustment Cost R&D	Technical Change	Residual
United States:									
1968–73	4.68	−.04	2.07	.91	1.28	.06	.12	.73	−.44
1974–79	3.56	.15	.43	.37	.12	−.07	.04	.86	1.66
Japan:									
1968–73	12.63	.81	10.24	1.33	.56	−.13	−.26	1.55	−1.48
1974–79	8.95	−.47	4.48	1.54	.86	.05	−.16	2.55	.10

[a]Growth rate of input per unit of labor, weighted by average output elasticity.

smaller for Japan. The contribution of R&D is somewhat smaller and rising for Japan. For the United States, the contribution of R&D is very substantial in the pre-OPEC period but only marginal in the post-OPEC period. The direct contribution of adjustment costs is again small. The contribution of technical change is very substantial (particularly in Japan) and rising in both countries.

The labor effect (given by the last term on the right-hand side of [5]) follows from the fact that scale is not equal to one. The contribution of this term to labor-productivity growth is shown in the second column of table 4.9. Its effect is positive in Japan in the pre-OPEC period and negative in the post-OPEC period. The opposite is the case for the United States. This reflects the growth pattern of the labor input in the two industries over the two periods.

Denny, Fuss, and Waverman (1981) have shown that if all factors are variable, then the traditional measure of total factor productivity (using cost shares) can be decomposed into two components, one attributable to scale and one to technical change. Nadiri and Prucha (1983, 1990) extend this decomposition to technologies with adjustment costs. More specifically, consider the Törnqvist approximation of the growth rate of total factor productivity, ΔTFP_t, defined implicitly by:

$$(6) \qquad \Delta \ln Y_t = \frac{1}{2} \sum_{i=1}^{4} [s_{Z_i}(t) + s_{Z_i}(t-1)] \Delta \ln Z_{it} + \Delta TFP_t,$$

with $Z_1 = L, Z_2 = M, Z_3 = K_{-1}, Z_4 = R_{-1}$ and where the s_{Z_i}'s denote respective long-run cost shares. Given increasing returns to scale and adjustment costs we find that the output elasticities ε_{YZ_i} exceed the cost shares s_{Z_i}. As a consequence, as is evident from a comparison of equations (4) and (6), total factor productivity will not equal technical change.[11] Prucha and Nadiri (1983, 1990) shows that total factor productivity growth can be decomposed as follows:

$$(7) \qquad \Delta TFP_t = (1 - \rho^{-1}) \Delta \ln Y_t + \phi_{1t} + \phi_{2t} + \frac{1}{2} [\lambda_x(t) + \lambda_x(t-1)],$$

where $\lambda_X = (1/\rho)\lambda_Y$. The first term on the right-hand side of (7) represents the scale effect and the last term the pure effect of technical change on the growth of total factor productivity. The terms ϕ_1 is attributable to the fact that, in short-run temporary equilibrium, the rate of technical substitution between the quasi-fixed and variable factors differs from the long-run price ratios. We will refer to ϕ_1 as the temporary equilibrium effect. The terms ϕ_2 reflects the direct adjustment-cost effect in terms of forgone output due to the presence of ΔK and ΔR in the production function. We will refer to ϕ_2 as the direct adjustment-cost effect. Explicit expressions for the terms ϕ_1 and ϕ_2 (and a further discussion of those terms) are given in appendix C.

Table 4.10 presents the decomposition of total factor productivity based on

Table 4.10   Decomposition of Total Factor Productivity Growth in the U.S. and Japanese Electrical Machinery Industries for Respective Sample Periods (in %)

	United States, 1960–80	Japan, 1968–80
Scale effect +	1.04	3.38
Temporary equilibrium effect +	.28	.16
Direct adjustment-cost effect +	.03	−.04
Technical change +	.60	1.49
Unexplained residual =	.10	−.24
Total factor productivity	2.04	4.74

(7) for the sample periods used in estimating the production technology of the U.S. and Japanese electrical machinery industries.[12] The scale effect is, by far, the most important contributor to total factor productivity growth. This is particularly the case in the Japanese industry where the output growth was very rapid and the estimated degree of scale larger than in the U.S. industry. The temporary equilibrium effect, ϕ_1, is fairly large in the United States and about twice as big as in the Japanese electrical machinery industry. The direct effect of the adjustment costs, ϕ_2, is negligible. The combined effect of ϕ_1 and ϕ_2 due to the adjustment costs is 15% and 4% of the measured total factor productivity growth for the United States and Japan, respectively, and hence not negligible, particularly for the United States. Consequently, if zero adjustment costs would have been imposed, a nonnegligible portion of measured total factor productivity growth would have been misclassified. In addition, inconsistency of the estimates of the underlying technology parameters would have distorted the decomposition of total factor productivity growth. The contribution of technical change to the growth of total factor productivity is second only to the scale effect. For each of the sample periods, the unexplained residual is small.

4.6   Conclusion and Summary

In this paper, we have modeled the production structure and the behavior of factor inputs and have analyzed the determinants of productivity growth in the U.S. and Japanese electrical machinery industries. These industries have experienced a very high rate of output growth, are technologically very progressive (measured by the rate of expenditures on R&D), and are highly competitive in the domestic U.S. and world markets. Our model allows for scale effects and the quasi fixity of some of the input factors. It also incorporated R&D to capture the high-technology feature of the industry. Other inputs considered are labor, materials, and physical capital. We have also allowed for exogenous technical change using a time trend. The model was estimated using annual data from 1960–80 and 1968–80 for the United States and Japan, respectively.

The main results of this paper can be summarized as follows:

(i) The production structure of the electrical machinery industry in both countries is characterized by increasing returns to scale; the Japanese electrical machinery industry exhibits higher returns to the scale than the US industry. The responses of the factors of production to changes in factor prices and output in the short run, intermediate run and long run are similar in the two industries. Materials are generally found to be substitutes for other inputs. Other inputs are generally complements except for labor and R&D in the U.S. industry. Capital and R&D are found to be quasi fixed, and their adjustment speeds are found to be similar across countries. The stock of capital adjusts much faster than the stock of R&D.

(ii) The elements of the so-called Japanese productivity miracle noted by others are, to a large extent, present in the electrical machinery industry: high rates of labor-productivity growth accompanied by rapid output growth and input growth before 1973 and diminishing but still high rates of labor productivity growth after 1973 accompanied by a substantial slowdown in the growth rates of outputs and factor inputs.

(iii) Based on the structural estimates of our model, we identify the following sources of growth of output and labor productivity: (a) The most important source of output and labor-productivity growth is the growth of materials for both pre- and post-OPEC periods in both countries. Technical change and capital were found to be the next most important factors. For the United States, capital's contribution exceeds that found at the total manufacturing level; the reverse is true for Japan. (b) Consistent with the high ratio of R&D expenditures to gross output in the electrical machinery industry, we find significant contributions of R&D to both output and labor-productivity growth. However, the R&D contribution to both has significantly declined in the United States from the pre-OPEC to the post-OPEC period.

(iv) The most important source of growth in total factor productivity for both countries is the scale effect. This is particularly true in Japan due to the higher scale elasticity and higher rate of growth of output. A significant portion of the differential of total factor productivity in the electrical machinery industry in the United States and Japan is due to the greater contribution of economies of scale to the growth of total factor productivity in Japan. Technical change is the second most important contributor. In the context of our dynamic model the rate of technical substitution for the quasi-fixed factors deviates in the short run from the long-run relative price ratios. This source also explains part of the traditional measure of total factor productivity growth.

Our model provides a richer framework for the analysis of productivity growth than some of the conventional approaches by incorporating dynamic aspects, nonconstant returns to scale, and R&D. The omission of dynamic aspects will typically result in inconsistent estimates of the technology parameters and a misallocation in the decomposition of measured total factor productivity growth. However, a number of issues remain unresolved.

(i) Given the rapid expansion of the electrical machinery industries in the United States and Japan, it seems important to explore the effect of nonstatic expectations on the input behavior and its implications for the productivity growth analysis.

(ii) It may also be of interest to explore a more general lag structure for the quasi-fixed factors and to adopt a more general formulation of the model that allows for scale to vary over the sample period.

(iii) A further area of research is the decomposition of labor into white- and blue-collar workers and the modeling of white-collar workers as potentially quasi-fixed. The quasi-fixity of labor may be particularly important in Japan where employment is considered fairly long term.

(iv) Finally, an important extension of the model would be to incorporate explicitly the role of demand and thereby analyze the role of the utilization rate on productivity growth.

Appendix A
Estimated System of Factor Demand Equations

Given the assumptions of section 4.3, the firm's optimum problem in period t can be written as

$$\text{(A1)} \quad \min_{\{K_{t+\tau}, R_{t+\tau}\}_{\tau=0}^{\infty}} \text{PVC}_t = \sum_{\tau=0}^{\infty} \{[G_{t,\tau} + \hat{Q}_t^R(\Delta R_{t+\tau} + \delta_R R_{t+\tau-1})](1 - u_t) + \hat{Q}_t^K(\Delta K_{t+\tau} + \delta_K K_{t+\tau-1})\}(1 + r)^{-\tau},$$

where the restricted cost function $G_{t,\tau} = G(\hat{W}_t, K_{t+\tau-1}, R_{t+\tau-1}, \Delta K_{t+\tau}, \Delta R_{t+\tau}, \hat{Y}_t, T_t)$ is defined by (3). With Q_t^K and Q_t^R we denote the acquisition price of capital and R&D normalized by the price of materials, respectively, δ_K and δ_R denote the depreciation rates of capital and R&D, respectively, u_t is the corporate tax rate, and r is the constant (real) discount rate. Expectations are characterized with a carat ($\hat{\ }$). We maintain $\hat{W}_t = W_t$, $\hat{Q}_t^K = Q_t^K$, and $\hat{Q}_t^R = Q_t^R$. R&D expenditures are assumed to be expended immediately. The minimization problem (A1) represents a standard optimal control problem. Its solution is well known and implies the following system of quasi-fixed factor demand equations in accelerator form:[13]

(A2)
$$\Delta K_t = m_{KK}(K_t^* - K_{t-1}) + m_{KR}(R_t^* - R_{t-1}),$$
$$\Delta R_t = m_{RK}(K_t^* - K_{t-1}) + m_{RR}(R_t^* - R_{t-1}),$$

where

$$\begin{bmatrix} K_t^* \\ R_t^* \end{bmatrix} = - \begin{bmatrix} \alpha_{KK} & \alpha_{KR} \\ \alpha_{KR} & \alpha_{RR} \end{bmatrix}^{-1} \begin{bmatrix} \alpha_K + \alpha_{KW}W_t + \alpha_{KT}T_t + C_t^K \\ \alpha_R + \alpha_{RW}W_t + \alpha_{RT}T_t + C_t^R \end{bmatrix} \hat{Y}_t^{1/\rho},$$

with $C_t^K = Q_t^K(r + \delta_K)/(1 - u_t)$ and $C_t^R = Q_t^R(r + \delta_R)$. The matrix of accelerator coefficients $M = (m_{ij})_{i,j=K,R}$ has to satisfy the following matrix equation:

(A3)
$$BM^2 + (A + rB)M - A = 0;$$

furthermore, the matrix $C = (c_{ij})_{i,j=K,R} = -BM$ is symmetric and negative definite. Unless we impose separability in the quasi-fixed factors, that is, $\alpha_{KR} = 0$, which implies $m_{KR} = 0$, (A3) cannot generally be solved for M in terms of A and B. We can, however solve (A3) for A in terms of M and B: $A = BM(M + rI)(I - M)^{-1}$. Since the real discount rate r was assumed to be constant, M is constant over the sample. Hence, instead of estimating the elements of A and B, we may estimate those of M and B.[14] To impose the symmetry of C we can also estimate B and C instead of B and M. Let $D = (d_{ij})_{i,j=K,R} = -MA^{-1}$, and we observe that $A = C - (1+r)[B - B(C+B)^{-1}B]$ and that $D = B^{-1} + (1+r)(C-rB)^{-1}$ are symmetric. It is then readily seen that we can write (A2) equivalently as:

$$\Delta K_t = d_{KK}[\alpha_K + \alpha_{KW}W_t + \alpha_{KT}T_t + C_t^K]\hat{Y}_t^{1/\rho}$$
$$+ d_{KR}[\alpha_R + \alpha_{RW}W_t + \alpha_{RT}T_t + C_t^R]\hat{Y}_t^{1/\rho}$$

(A4)
$$+ [c_{KK}/\alpha_{K\dot{K}}]K_{t-1} + [c_{KR}/\alpha_{K\dot{K}}]R_{t-1},$$

$$\Delta R_t = d_{KR}[\alpha_K + \alpha_{KW}W_t + \alpha_{KT}T_t + C_t^K]\hat{Y}_t^{1/\rho}$$
$$+ d_{RR}[\alpha_R + \alpha_{RW}W_t + \alpha_{RT}T_t + C_t^R]\hat{Y}_t^{1/\rho}$$

$$+ [c_{KR}/\alpha_{\dot{R}\dot{R}}]K_{t-1} + [c_{RR}/\alpha_{\dot{R}\dot{R}}]R_{t-1},$$

where

$$d_{KK} = 1/\alpha_{K\dot{K}} + (1 + r)[c_{RR} - r\alpha_{\dot{R}\dot{R}}]/e,$$
$$d_{RR} = 1/\alpha_{\dot{R}\dot{R}} + (1 + r)[c_{KK} - r\alpha_{K\dot{K}}]/e,$$
$$d_{KR} = -(1 + r)c_{KR}/e,$$

and

$$e = (c_{KK} - r\alpha_{K\dot{K}})(c_{RR} - r\alpha_{\dot{R}\dot{R}}) - c_{KR}^2.$$

The firm's demand equations for the variable factors can be derived from the normalized restricted cost function via Shephard's lemma, as $L_t = \partial G_{t,0}/\partial W_t$ and $M_t = G_{t,0} - W_t L_t$:

$$
\begin{aligned}
(A.5) \quad L_t &= [\alpha_W + \alpha_{WW}W_t + \alpha_{WT}T_t]\hat{Y}_t^{1/\rho} + \alpha_{KW}K_{t-1} + \alpha_{RW}R_{t-1}, \\
M_t &= [\alpha_0 - \tfrac{1}{2}\alpha_{WW}W_t^2]\hat{Y}_t^{1/\rho} + \alpha_K K_{t-1} + \alpha_R R_{t-1} + \alpha_{KT}K_{t-1}T_t \\
&\quad + \alpha_{RT}R_{t-1}T_t + [\tfrac{1}{2}\alpha_{KK}K_{t-1}^2 + \alpha_{KR}K_{t-1}R_{t-1} + \tfrac{1}{2}\alpha_{RR}R_{t-1}^2 \\
&\quad + \tfrac{1}{2}\alpha_{\dot{K}\dot{K}}\Delta K_t^2 + \tfrac{1}{2}\alpha_{\dot{R}\dot{R}}\Delta R_t^2]/\hat{Y}_t^{1/\rho},
\end{aligned}
$$

where

$$
\alpha_{KK} = c_{KK} - (1 + r)[\alpha_{\dot{K}\dot{K}} - (\alpha_{\dot{K}\dot{K}})^2(\alpha_{\dot{R}\dot{R}} + c_{RR})/f],
$$

$$
\alpha_{RR} = c_{RR} - (1 + r)[\alpha_{\dot{R}\dot{R}} - (\alpha_{\dot{R}\dot{R}})^2(\alpha_{\dot{K}\dot{K}} + c_{KK})/f],
$$

$$
\alpha_{KR} = c_{KR} - (1 + r)(\alpha_{\dot{K}\dot{K}}\alpha_{\dot{R}\dot{R}}c_{KR})/f,
$$

and

$$
f = (\alpha_{\dot{K}\dot{K}} + c_{KK})(\alpha_{\dot{R}\dot{R}} + c_{RR}) - c_{KR}^2.
$$

The complete system of factor demand equations consists of (A4) for the quasi-fixed factors and (A5) for the variable factors. This system is nonlinear in parameters and variables. For the empirical estimation, we have added stochastic disturbance terms to each of the factor demand equations. When necessary, we have corrected for first-order autocorrelation of the disturbances. Expectations on gross output were calculated as follows. We first estimated a first-order autoregressive model for output that was then used to predict Y_t rationally.

Appendix B
Data Sources and Construction of Variables

U.S. Electrical Machinery Industry

Gross Output: Data on gross output in current and constant 1972 dollars were obtained from the U.S. Department of Commerce, Office of Business Analysis (OBA) data base and correspond to the gross output series of the U.S. Department of Commerce, Bureau of Industrial Economics (BIE). Gross output is defined as total shipments plus the net change in work in process inventories and finished goods inventories.

Labor: Total hours worked were derived as the sum of hours worked by production workers and nonproduction workers. Hours worked by production workers were obtained directly from the OBA data base. Hours worked by nonproduction workers were calculated as the number of nonproduction workers times hours worked per week times 52. The number of nonproduction workers was obtained from the OBA data base. Weekly hours worked by nonproduction workers were taken to be 39.7. A series of total compensation in current dollars was calculated by multiplying the total payroll series from the OBA data base with the ratio of compensation of employees to wages and salaries from the U.S. Department of Commerce, Bureau of Economic Analysis (1981, 1984).

Materials: Materials in current dollars were obtained from the OBA data base. Materials in constant 1972 dollars were calculated using deflators provided by the U.S. Department of Commerce, Bureau of Economic Analysis.

Value Added: Value added in current and constant 1972 dollars was calculated by subtracting materials from gross output.

Capital: The net capital stock series in 1972 dollars and the current and constant 1972 dollar gross investment series were taken from the OBA data base. The method by which the capital stock series is constructed is described in the U.S. Department of Labor, Bureau of Labor Statistics (1979). The user cost of capital was constructed as $c_K = q^K(r + \delta_K)/(1 - u)$, where $q^K =$ investment deflator, $\delta_K =$ depreciation rate of the capital stock, $u =$ corporate tax rate, and $r = 0.05$.

R&D: The stock of total R&D is constructed by the perpetual inventory method with a depreciation rate $\delta_R = 0.1$. The benchmark in 1958 is obtained by dividing total R&D expenditures by the depreciation rate and the growth rate in real value added. The nominal R&D expenditures are taken from the National Science Foundation (1984) and earlier issues. To avoid double counting we have subtracted the labor and material components of R&D from the labor and material inputs. The gross domestic product (GDP) deflator for total manufacturing is used as a deflator for R&D.

All constant dollar variables were normalized by respective sample means. Prices were constructed conformably.

Japanese Electrical Machinery Industry

Gross Output: For the period 1970–80, the data series on gross output in current and constant 1975 yen were obtained from Economic Planning Agency (1984). The data for the period before 1970 were constructed by connecting these series with the corresponding series reported in Economic Planning Agency (1980) via identical growth rates.

Labor: Total hours worked were calculated as total numbers of employees times monthly hours worked times 12. For the period 1970–80, the number of employees was taken from Economic Planning Agency (1984). For the period before 1970 the number of employees was calculated by connecting this series with the employment index provided by the Economic Planning Agency (EPA). Monthly hours worked for the period 1977–80 were obtained from the Statistics Bureau (1985). For previous years, monthly hours worked were calculated by using the monthly hours work index provided by the EPA. For the period 1970–80, total compensation is reported in the EPA (1984). For the period before 1970, total compensation was calculated by connecting this series with an index on cash earnings provided by EPA.

Value Added: For the period 1970–80, data on value added in current and constant 1975 yen were obtained from the EPA (1984). The data for the period before 1970 were obtained by connecting these series with the corresponding series reported in the EPA (1975) via identical growth rates.

Materials: Materials in current and constant 1975 yen were calculated as the differences between gross output and value added.

Capital Stock: Data for the stock of capital and gross investment in 1975 yen were taken from the EPA (1985). A series for current dollar gross investment was obtained from the Japanese Ministry of Finance. This series was adjusted in such a way that it coincided with the constant yen EPA series in 1975. The user cost of capital was constructed analogously to that for the United States.

R&D: Current yen R&D expenditures are taken from Organization for Economic Cooperation and Development (1983 and earlier issues). To avoid double counting we have subtracted the labor and material component of R&D from the labor and material inputs. The GDP deflator for total manufacturing is used as the deflator for R&D. The stock of R&D is constructed analogously to that for the United States with 1965 as the benchmark year.

All constant yen variables were transformed to a 1972 base and then normalized by respective sample means. Prices were constructed conformably.

Appendix C
Expressions in TFP Growth Decomposition

In the following we give explicit expressions for the temporary equilibrium effect and the direct adjustment-cost effect in the decomposition (7) of total factor productivity growth. We make use of the cost-share weighted index of aggregate inputs F defined as

$$\Delta \ln F_t := \tfrac{1}{2}[\Delta \ln F_t^t + \Delta \ln F_t^{t-1}],$$
$$\Delta \ln F_t^\tau = s_M(\tau)\Delta \ln M_t + s_L(\tau)\Delta \ln L_t + s_{K_{-1}}(\tau)\Delta \ln K_{t-1}$$
$$+ s_{R_{-1}}(\tau)\Delta \ln R_{t-1},$$

where $\tau = t, t-1$. The cost shares are defined as $s_M(t) = M_t/TC_t$, $s_L(t) = W_tL_t/TC_t$, $s_{K_{-t}}(t) = C_t^KK_{t-1}/TC_t$, $s_{R_{-1}}(t) = C_{t-1}^RR_{t-1}/TC_t$, with $TC_t = M_t + W_tL_t + C_t^KK_{t-1} + C_t^RR_{t-1}$. Here C_t^K and C_t^R denote, respectively, the rental price of capital and R&D normalized by the price of materials; compare appendix A. The following expressions for the temporary equilibrium effect ϕ_1 and the direct adjustment cost effect ϕ_2 are taken from Nadiri and Prucha (1983, 1990) and can be derived by comparing equations (4) and (6):

$$\phi_{1t} = \frac{1}{2\rho}\Sigma_{\tau=t,\ t-1}\left\{\frac{(-\partial G_\tau/\partial K_{\tau-1}-C_\tau^K)K_{\tau-1}}{(\partial G_\tau/\partial Y_\tau)Y_\tau}\ [\Delta\ln K_{t-1} - \Delta\ln F_t^\tau]\right.$$

$$+ \frac{1}{2\rho}\Sigma_{\tau=t,\ t-1}\left\{\frac{(-\partial G_\tau/\partial R_{\tau-1}-C_\tau^R)R_{\tau-1}}{(\partial G_\tau/\partial Y_\tau)Y_\tau}\ [\Delta\ln R_{t-1} - \Delta\ln F_t^\tau],\right.$$

$$\phi_{2t} = \frac{1}{2\rho}\Sigma_{\tau=t,\ t-1}\left\{\frac{(-\partial G_\tau/\partial\Delta K_\tau)\Delta K_\tau}{(\partial G_\tau/\partial Y_\tau)Y_\tau}\ [\Delta\ln\Delta K_t - \Delta\ln F_t^\tau]\right.$$

$$+ \frac{1}{2\rho}\Sigma_{\tau=t,\ t-1}\left\{\frac{(-\partial G_\tau/\partial\Delta R_\tau)\Delta R_\tau}{(\partial G_\tau/\partial Y_\tau)Y_\tau}\ [\Delta\ln\Delta R_t - \Delta\ln F_t^\tau]\right.$$

where $(\tau = t, t-1)$. In long-run equilibrium both the temporary equilibrium effect and the direct adjustment-cost effect are zero since $\partial G/\partial K + C^K = \partial G/\partial R + C^R = \partial G/\Delta K = \partial G/\Delta R = 0$. Furthermore both effects are zero if all factors (and hence the aggregate input index) grow at the same rate.

Notes

1. The total factor productivity growth rates are calculated from the Törnqvist approximation formula (using long-run cost shares). The divergence in total factor productivity growth rates is much more pronounced in a value-added measurement framework. However, Norsworthy and Malmquist (1983) found that such a framework is inappropriate—at least at the total manufacturing level.

2. The restricted cost function $G(\cdot)$ is furthermore assumed to satisfy

$$G_{X_i} < 0,\ G_{|\Delta x_i|} > 0,\ G_Y > 0,\ G_W > 0.$$

3. Clearly the scale elasticity depends for general $F(\cdot)$ on the various factor inputs. However, to keep the model specification reasonably parsimonious, we have assumed that $F(\cdot)$ is homogeneous of constant degree ρ.

4. Compare, e.g., Nadiri and Prucha (1983, 1990).

5. For a generalization to homothetic technologies see Nadiri and Prucha (1983, 1990).

6. These coefficients have been calculated from the estimates in table 4 observing that $M = -B^{-1}C$.

7. We note that those adjustment speeds are consistent with earlier results obtained by Mohnen, Nadiri, and Prucha (1986) for the total manufacturing sectors of the two countries.

8. Let $\{X_{t,\tau}, V_{t,\tau}\}_{\tau=0}^{\infty}$ denote the optimal plan values of the inputs in periods t, $t+1$, . . . , corresponding to the firm's optimization problem in period t. Short-run, intermediate-run, and long-run elasticities then refer to the elasticities of $X_{t,\tau}$ and $V_{t,\tau}$ in periods $\tau = 0, 1,$ and ∞, respectively ($X_t^* = X_{t,\infty}$).

9. The contribution of each of the variables is calculated by multiplying the respective (average) elasticities with the growth rate of the corresponding variable. The output elasticities are computed from the estimated restricted cost function using standard duality theory. For both variable and quasi-fixed factors, those output elasticities exceed long-run cost shares because of increasing returns to scale. For the quasi-fixed factors the output elasticities also differ from long-run cost shares because of adjustment costs.

10. This approximation is readily obtained from the decomposition of output growth by noting that the sum of the output elasticities must equal scale.

11. For an excellent discussion of problems in measuring technical change see Griliches (1988).

12. Note that in this table technical change corresponds to $\lambda_x = \lambda^y/\rho$ while in tables 4.8 and 4.9 technical change corresponds to λ_Y. Furthermore, note that the decomposition of output growth and labor productivity growth in tables 8 and 9 only gives the direct effect of adjustment costs. The "indirect" temporary equilibrium effect in those decompositions is accounted for by using (estimated) output elasticities rather than cost shares as weights.

13. Compare, e.g., Epstein and Yatchew (1985), Madan and Prucha (1989), and Prucha and Nadiri (1986).

14. Such a reparametrization was first suggested by Epstein and Yatchew (1985) for a somewhat different model with a similar algebra. Mohnen, Nadiri, and Prucha (1986) used such a reparametrization within the context of a constant returns to scale model. Recently Madan and Prucha (1989) generalized this approach to the case where B may be nonsymmetric.

References

Denny, M., M. A. Fuss, and L. Waverman. 1981. Substitution possibilities for energy: Evidence from U.S. and Canadian manufacturing industries. In *Modeling and measuring national resource substitution,* ed. E. R. Berndt and B. C. Field. Cambridge, Mass.: MIT Press.

Economic Planning Agency. 1975. *Economic analysis.* Tokyo: Government of Japan (August).

———. 1980. *Supply and disposition of commodities.* Tokyo: Government of Japan.

———. 1984 (and earlier issues). *Annual report on national accounts.* Tokyo: Government of Japan.

———. 1985. *Private industrial capital stock.* Tokyo: Government of Japan (February).

Epstein, L., and A. Yatchew. 1985. The empirical determination of technology and expectations: A simplified procedure. *Journal of Econometrics* 27:235–58.

Griliches, Z. 1988. Productivity: Measurement problems. In *The new Palgrave: A dictionary of economics,* ed. J. Eatwell, M. Milgate, and P. Newman. New York: Stockton Press.

Grossman, E. S. 1985. Productivity and international competition: United States and

Japanese industries. In *Interindustry differences in productivity growth,* ed. J. Kendrick. Washington, D.C.: American Enterprise Institute.

Lau, L. J. 1976. A characterization of the normalized restricted profit function. *Journal of Economic Theory* 12:131–63.

Madan, D. B., and I. R. Prucha. 1989. A note on the estimation of non-symmetric dynamic factor demand models. *Journal of Econometrics,* 42:275–83.

Mohnen, P. A., M. I. Nadiri, and I. R. Prucha. 1986. R&D, production structure, and rate of return in the U.S., Japanese and German manufacturing sectors: A nonseparable dynamic factor demand model. *European Economic Review* 30:749–71.

Morrison, C. J., and E. R. Berndt. 1981. Short-run labor productivity in a dynamic model. *Journal of Econometrics* 15:339–65.

Nadiri, M. I., and I. R. Prucha. 1983. Nonstatic expectations, adjustment costs and the production structure and dynamic factor demand for AT&T. Mimeograph of paper presented at the 1983 NBER Summer Institute Workshop on Investment and Productivity, Cambridge, Mass.

———. 1990. Dynamic factor demand models, productivity measurement, and rates of return: Theory and an empirical application to the U.S. Bell system. *Structural Change and Economic Dynamics* (in press).

Nadiri, M. I., and M. Schankerman. 1981. The structure of production, technological change and the rate of growth of total factor productivity in the U.S. Bell system. In *Productivity measurement in regulated industries,* ed. T. Cowing and R. Stevenson, 219–47. New York: Academic Press.

National Science Foundation. 1984. *Research and development in industry, 1982.* Washington, D.C.: Government Printing Office.

Norsworthy, J. R., and D. H. Malmquist. 1983. Input measurement and productivity growth in Japanese and U.S. manufacturing. *American Economic Review* 73:947–67.

Organization for Economic Cooperation and Development. 1983. *International Statistical Year (1981), Japan.* Mimeograph. Paris.

Prucha, I. R., and M. I. Nadiri. 1986. A comparison of alternative methods for the estimation of dynamic factor demand models under nonstatic expectations. *Journal of Econometrics* 33:187–211.

Statistics Bureau, Management and Coordination Agency. 1985. *Monthly Statistics of Japan.* Tokyo (January).

U.S. Department of Commerce, Bureau of Economic Analysis. 1981. *The national income and product accounts of the United States, 1928–76, statistical tables.* Washington, D.C.: Government Printing Office.

———. 1984 (and earlier issues). *Survey of Current Business.* Washington, D.C.: Government Printing Office.

U.S. Department of Labor, Bureau of Labor Statistics. 1979. *Capital stock estimates for input-output industries: Methods and data.* Bulletin 2034. Washington, D.C.: U.S. Government Printing Office.

5   Decisions of Firms and Productivity Growth with Fixed Input Constraints: An Empirical Comparison of U.S. and Japanese Manufacturing

Catherine Morrison

5.1   The Background

In the last few years a substantial body of literature has developed on comparing labor and multifactor productivity growth in the United States and Japan.[1] These studies indicate that a productivity gap still exists in favor of the United States for most industries in terms of productivity levels. However, the recent strong productivity growth experience of Japan as compared to the United States has caused productivity in some industries, such as steel, to overtake the corresponding U.S. industries, and in others this growth has caused a significant narrowing of the productivity gap. This trend has been particularly evident in the United States since the 1973 energy shocks, when Japan appeared to respond much more quickly to the constraints imposed by more expensive energy. Thus, although the energy price shocks of the 1970s likely contributed to depressed conditions in all industrial nations, the common belief is that the "snapback" response of the Japanese industries, as well as their investment and labor practices, enabled them to exploit further their productivity growth advantage.

Sato and Suzawa (1983) attribute the observed greater productivity growth in Japan to the responsiveness of its production process. They postulate that both workers and capital exhibit more flexibility in Japan than in the United States, facilitating higher productivity growth in Japan after major exogenous shocks. This was evident, they argue, after the energy price shocks of 1973–74, when Americans tended to react in disbelief while the Japanese reacted to

Catherine Morrison is an associate professor of economics at Tufts University and a research associate of the National Bureau of Economic Research.

Support from the National Science Foundation, grant SES-8309352, is gratefully acknowledged. The author is also indebted to Ernst R. Berndt and David O. Wood of MIT for providing the U.S. data and to Takamitsu Sawa of Kyoto University for the Japanese data.

a "national emergency" (p. 156). According to Sato and Suzawa, these very different responses stimulated U.S. workers to attempt to retain the same standard of living by demanding higher wage increases for the same level of work effort and U.S. firms to attempt to substitute relatively less expensive capital and labor for energy. This substitution away from energy was difficult, however, since this necessity was not anticipated when the existing energy-using technology was originally acquired. By contrast, the Japanese took stronger measures, including increased saving and investment and greater work effort, both contributing to a strong responsiveness to the energy price shocks and thus a productivity snapback.

In Sato and Suzawa's view the greater responsiveness in Japan may have stemmed at least in part from the Japanese "forcing the energy-capital relationship into a substitutable relationship" by recognizing that saving energy required augmenting labor input by increased work effort. The Sato-Suzawa arguments imply that capital and energy tended to be complements in the United States as contrasted to substitutes in Japan, and that labor was more substitutable with energy in Japan; thus even in the short run, energy responsiveness to its own price was higher in Japan.[2] This argument specifically recognizes the importance of the short-run-versus-long-run nature of both the energy-capital relationship and the interrelationship of these inputs with labor.

Several researchers have attempted to assess the validity of the assertions about relative flexibility in Japan and its impact on productivity trends. One way to approach this is to model explicitly substitution possibilities and the resulting input mixes in the two countries. A major example of this approach is Norsworthy and Malmquist (1983). In that study the authors employed a specification of the production structure including capital (K), labor (L), energy (E), and materials (M) inputs, whereas earlier productivity measurement approaches often were based on more restrictive assumptions. Norsworthy and Malmquist determined their richer structure could be used constructively to assess productivity growth trends, since it was more capable of capturing important characteristics of Japanese as compared to U.S. production. One of the most important of these characteristics in their view is the capital-energy interaction noted by Sato and Suzawa, which cannot be assessed in the common value-added framework. According to Norsworthy and Malmquist, energy-capital complementarity reflects "vulnerability" of a country to exogenous shocks since greater substitutability would allow industries to respond more effectively and therefore to snap back more easily after exogenous shocks. The Norsworthy-Malmquist results of energy-capital complementarity in the United States and substitutability in Japan, however, still depend on data only up to 1978. These results also are based on strong assumptions about instantaneous adjustment, assumptions that bypass the issue of short-run as compared to long-run responses, recognized as being so important by Sato and Suzawa.

This distinction between short- and long-run responsiveness clearly has important consequences for productivity growth since short-run adjustment may differ dramatically from the final long-run responses to a shock. Fixity of inputs, which causes the short run to differ from the long run, will tend to vary across countries since the capability of firms to adjust inputs will depend on the production structure. Empirical assessment of the data is necessary, therefore, to assess these relationships and their impact on the alleged responsiveness of U.S. and Japanese firms.

It is evident, for example, that the capital-adjustment responses of many industries to the 1973–74 and 1979–80 energy price shocks were torturously slow, even though it was immediately clear that current energy-capital configurations were no longer optimal. Such a tendency was possibly even stronger in the United States than Japan, but this is not clear. The available evidence also suggests that capital accumulation proceeded at a prodigious rate in Japan during the last two decades, slowing only slightly after 1973 and 1979. However, it is not clear whether this reflects extra flexibility of the Japanese production structure, perhaps because the Japanese are simply more rapid in replacing obsolescent capital stock, or instead implies that the existing small stock of capital was so greatly overutilized in Japan compared to the United States that a large investment rate was required to close the "gap."

Other inputs may also exhibit fixity. For example, it is often postulated that because of labor-hiring practices in Japan, the labor input has an important "permanent" and therefore fixed component that has no counterpart in the United States. However, it has also been asserted by, for example, Sato and Suzawa (1983), that the Japanese labor force is in some sense very flexible. The short-run fixed or flexible nature of both the capital and labor inputs crucially affects production and thus productivity, and the differential impact of the labor structure on the United States as compared to Japan is not clear a priori.

Although the effect of short-run fixities or flexibility on production responsiveness is crucial to incorporate into analyses of the production process and productivity growth trends, the extent of the impacts is inherently difficult to quantify. One way to approach this issue is to develop and empirically implement a framework in which the production decisions of firms are explicitly formulated to depend on short-run input stock rigidities. This type of model can then be used to construct economic measures of capacity utilization, shadow values of fixed factors, and short- and long-run demand elasticities. The resulting measures depend explicitly on the fixity of such inputs as capital and labor in production, and can be used to determine the relative flexibility of the production processes and the resulting impact on productivity growth. This type of framework, applied to recent U.S. and Japanese data series, could provide a basis for assessing the differential responsiveness of the United States and Japan to events of the 1970s.

In this paper I employ a cost-based framework proposed by Morrison (1986b) to estimate and analyze the impacts of quasi-fixed inputs on firm behavior and thus observed demand behavior, capacity utilization and productivity growth in the manufacturing sectors of the United States and Japan. This procedure allows a direct adjustment of standard productivity growth measures to take fixity of inputs into account. This provides some insights about the extent of deviations in productivity growth that are generated simply from limitations on firm behavior in the short run. I proceed as follows. In section 5.2 I first briefly develop the short run or restricted generalized Leontief (GL) cost function and its use for calculation of shadow values and capacity utilization measures employed for adjusting the productivity growth measures. I then carry out empirical implementation of this framework using a model allowing for fixity of both capital (K) and labor (L) to incorporate both fixed plant and equipment and labor hoarding or implicit contractual obligations with workers. Then, in section 5.3, I discuss empirical results, focusing on indexes of productivity and capacity utilization, and measures of short- and long-run demand elasticities in the manufacturing industries of the United States and Japan through 1981. In section 5.4 I provide brief concluding remarks.

5.2   The Theoretical Structure

Most current studies of short-run behavior are based on restricted cost functions such as the translog or quadratic function. Morrison (1986b) has developed an alternative GL restricted cost function that avoids the inability to obtain closed-form solutions for long-run values and the lack of invariance to normalization, problems that plague the translog and the quadratic forms, respectively.

The GL restricted cost function with long-run constant returns to scale (CRTS) imposed can be written as

$$
\begin{aligned}
G = Y^{.5} \cdot [& (\Sigma_i \Sigma_j \beta_{ij} p_i^{.5} \cdot p_j^{.5} + \Sigma_i \alpha_{it} p_i \cdot t^{.5}) \cdot Y^{.5} \\
& + \Sigma_i \Sigma_k \delta_{ik} p_i \cdot x_k^{.5} + 2 \cdot \Sigma_i p_i \cdot \Sigma_k \alpha_{kt} x_k^{.5} \cdot t^{.5}] \\
& + \Sigma_i p_i \cdot \Sigma_k \Sigma_l \gamma_{kl} x_k^{.5} \cdot x_l^{.5},
\end{aligned}
$$

(1)

where x_k and x_l refer to quasi-fixed inputs k and l, p_i and p_j denote the prices of variable inputs i and j, respectively, Y is output, and t represents the state of technology.[3]

The above form is quite general. In particular, it can be used to represent a model with only capital fixed and all other inputs variable, it can also include fixed labor as an x_k variable, and it can even capture costs of adjustment for capital (and/or for labor) by including investment in x_k, $\dot{x}_k$, as an argument of the function.

For econometric implementation, greater efficiency in estimation can be attained by adding to (1) the optimal input-output equations for variable inputs derived from Shephard's lemma. Here such equations are of the form

(2)
$$\frac{\partial G}{\partial p_i}\frac{1}{Y} = \frac{v_i}{Y} = \sum_j \beta_{ij}\cdot(p_j/p_i)^{.5} + \alpha_{it}\cdot t^{.5}$$
$$+ Y^{-.5}\cdot(\Sigma_k \delta_{ik} x_k^{.5} + 2\cdot\Sigma_k \alpha_{kt}\cdot x_k^{.5}t^{.5})$$
$$+ \Sigma_k\Sigma_l \gamma_{kl} x_k^{.5}x_i^{.5}/Y,$$

where v_i denotes variable input i.

In addition, this function provides information on the shadow values of the quasi-fixed inputs, since

(3)
$$-\frac{\partial G}{\partial x_k} \equiv Z_k \,,$$

where Z_k is the shadow value of quasi-fixed input x_k—the potential reduction in variable costs from having an additional unit of x_k. For example, for quasi-fixed input x_k, this shadow value is

(4) $$Z_k = -.5\cdot\{\Sigma_i p_i\cdot\gamma_{kk} + x_k^{-.5}\cdot[Y^{.5}\cdot(\Sigma_i\delta_{ik}\cdot p_i + 2\cdot\Sigma_i p_i\,\alpha_{kt}\cdot t^{.5})$$
$$+ \Sigma_i p_i\Sigma_l\gamma_{kl(k\neq l)}\cdot x_i^{.5}]\}.$$

Note that the shadow valuation depends on all price levels, stocks of all quasi-fixed inputs, cyclical variations in output, and the state of technology.

The shadow value expressions can also be used as equations for estimation. It is possible to determine the ex post return to the fixed inputs as the gross operating surplus, $P\cdot Y - G = R_{net}$, where P is the price of output and R represents revenue. Under long-run constant returns to scale, with the competitive price equal to marginal cost and with only one quasi-fixed factor, x_k, Z_k can be calculated as $Z_k = R_{net}/x_k$ for the dependent variable for equation (4). If more quasi-fixed inputs exist—although there is no way independently to identify the returns to each of the different quasi-fixed inputs—it is possible to estimate a "sum-of-the-shadow-value" equation $\Sigma_k Z_k\cdot x_k = -\Sigma_k(\partial G/\partial x_k)\cdot x_k$ where the dependent variable is R_{net} and the right-hand side is the sum of the expressions in (4), each weighted by the given input levels.

Alternatively, the output price equation $P = MC$ proposed by Mork (1978) may be used for estimation, where MC is marginal cost, or $\partial G/\partial Y$ in the short run, and P is output price:

(5)
$$P = \frac{\partial G}{\partial Y} = \Sigma_i \Sigma_j \beta_{ij} p_i^{.5}\cdot p_j^{.5} + \Sigma_i \alpha_{it} p_i\cdot t^{.5}$$
$$+ .5\cdot Y^{-.5}\cdot(\Sigma_i \Sigma_k \delta_{ik} p_i\cdot x_k^{.5} + 2\cdot\Sigma_i p_i\cdot\Sigma_k \alpha_{kt} x_k^{.5}\cdot t^{.5}).$$

The output price equation should not be estimated along with the shadow value equation, however. Rather, because of their interdependence with constant returns to scale, they should be considered alternatives. Specifically, with CRTS, as shown by Lau (1978),[4]

(6)
$$1 = \frac{\partial \ln G}{\partial \ln Y} + \Sigma_k \frac{\partial \ln G}{\partial \ln x_k} = \varepsilon_{GY} + \Sigma_k \varepsilon_{Gk}.$$

Thus the ε_{GY} and ε_{GK} elasticities are not independently identifiable for estimation; they must always sum to one.

The variable cost derivatives $\partial G/\partial p_i$, $\partial G/\partial x_k$, and $\partial G/\partial Y$ are not only the basis for constructing estimating equations, but they also contain useful information about short- and long-run input demands. Traditional price elasticities and elasticities of demand for v_i with respect to changes in output, or potential relaxation of the fixed input constraint, may be computed from the expression for $\partial G/\partial p_i$ based on (2). For example, since this expression represents v_i, short-run (SR) price elasticities are computed directly as

$$\varepsilon_{ij}^{SR} = \partial \ln v_i/\partial \ln p_j \mid x_k = \bar{x}_k.$$

Calculation of the corresponding long-run (LR) elasticities requires appending the adjustment to the desired long-run level of the quasi-fixed inputs x_k^* from (7) below as

$$\varepsilon_{ijLR} = (p_j/v_i) \cdot [\partial v_i/\partial p_j \mid x_k = \bar{x}_k + \Sigma_k(\partial v_i/\partial x_k^*) \cdot (dx_k^*/dp_j)].$$

In addition, the variable cost derivatives include information on the shadow values of quasi-fixed inputs and therefore the extent to which a deviation exists between temporary and long-run equilibrium—the extent of "subequilibrium." This deviation can be expressed in terms of the costs of being away from full equilibrium, measured by the difference between the shadow values $(-G_k = Z_k)$ and the ex ante rental or current market transaction values (p_k) of the individual quasi-fixed inputs. The extent of subequilibrium is even more directly measured by considering the difference between the given and "desired" (steady-state) levels of each the quasi-fixed inputs x_k and x_k^*, where x_k^* is the level of x_k implied by the steady-state equality $Z_k = p_k$.

Alternatively, subequilibrium indicators can be computed as scalar values combining all quasi-fixed inputs. Both cost and "primal" (quantity) perspectives can be represented in this scalar context analogous to the value and level or quantity measures for each individual input. Construction of such measures requires comparing the shadow and total cost function or the capacity and actual output levels, respectively. More specifically, the cost-capacity utilization index depends on the comparison of shadow costs defined as total costs with quasi-fixed inputs evaluated at their shadow values, SHCOST $= C^* = G + \Sigma_k Z_k x_k$, and total costs defined as $C = G + \Sigma_k p_k x_k$. On the primal side, capacity output is defined as the steady-state level of output, Y^*, calculated by solving for Y^* from the steady-state equality $C^* = C$ given quantities of all quasi-fixed inputs. Representation of the primal capacity-utilization measure then requires comparison of Y^* with the given output level Y.

Each of these measures of subequilibrium impacts is based on the difference between the Z_k and p_k and thus can be computed parametrically from the expression for Z_k in (4), even if this equation is not directly estimated. The resulting measures for x_k^* and Y^* may then be computed in a straightforward manner as closed-form solutions, given the GL framework.

More specifically, solving for x_k^* from the steady-state relationship $p_k = Z_k$ using (4) results in

$$(7) \quad x_k^* = \left[\frac{-Y^{.5} \cdot (\Sigma_i \delta_{ik} \cdot p_k + 2 \cdot \Sigma_i p_i \, \alpha_{kt} \cdot t^{.5}) - \Sigma_i p_i \Sigma_{l \, (l \neq k)} \, \gamma_{kl} x_l^5}{p_k + \Sigma_i p_i \cdot \gamma_{kk}} \right]^2.$$

An important point to note about this expression is that, although calculation of x_k^* is straightforward for the one quasi-fixed input case, with multiple quasi-fixed inputs the long run depends on the movement of all quasi-fixed inputs. Thus, as long as $\gamma_{kl} \neq 0$, all the x_k^* expressions represented by (7) must be solved simultaneously to compute long-run values.

Capacity output can also be imputed given this ex ante price equals shadow value relationship, in which C^* equals C. Solving for the implied level of Y results in a steady-state value given variable input prices and the available stocks of quasi-fixed inputs or "capacity":[5]

$$(8) \quad Y^* = \left[\frac{-(\Sigma_k p_k \cdot x_k + \Sigma_i p_i \Sigma_k \gamma_{kk} \cdot x_k + \Sigma_i p_i \Sigma_k \Sigma_{l \, (l \neq k)} \, \gamma_{kl} x_k^5 x_l^5)}{\Sigma_i \Sigma_k \delta_{ik} \cdot p_{ik} x_k^5 + 2 \cdot \Sigma_i p_i \Sigma_k \, \alpha_{kt} \cdot x_k^5 \cdot t^{.5}} \right]^2.$$

The comparison of these shadow value and quantity measures with their measured values is generally carried out in terms of ratios. Ratios in the scalar case in either form represent capacity utilization (CU). For example, on the primal side the ratio Y/Y^* is defined as capacity utilization, since it compares actual with capacity output. From (8), this measure is

$$(9) \quad CU_y = Y/Y^* = Y \left[\frac{-(\Sigma_i \Sigma_k \delta_{ik} \cdot p_{ik} x_k^5 + 2 \cdot \Sigma_i p_i \Sigma_k \, \alpha_{kt} \cdot x_k^5 \cdot t^{.5})}{\Sigma_k p_k \cdot x_k + \Sigma_i p_i \Sigma_k \gamma_{kk} \cdot x_k + \Sigma_i p_i \Sigma_k \Sigma_{l \, (l \neq k)} \, \gamma_{kl} x_k^5 x_i^5} \right]^2.$$

With only one quasi-fixed input, CU_y is also equal to x_k^*/x_k from (7), reflecting the CRTS assumption. Thus, in this case x_k^*/x_k, a measure of *capital* utilization, is also a measure of *capacity* utilization; there are no cross-effects due to multiple fixed inputs.

The ratio of the desired to actual level of each quasi-fixed input, if $x_k^* > x_k$, reveals the proportional additional x_k required to reach a steady state, and therefore represents the amount the given stock of x_k is overutilized in terms of the short-run application of variable inputs. The converse—if $x_k^* < x_k$—is interpreted analogously. Similarly, if $Y > Y^*$, the CU_y ratio indicates the extent to which fixed inputs in general are overutilized—the shortage of available economic capacity. In reverse, if $Y < Y^*$, the fixed inputs are underutilized, and excess capacity exists.

The cost-side capacity-utilization measure CU_c, dual to $Y/Y^* = CU_y$, can be calculated as C^*/C, where Z_k is evaluated at the given levels of x_k. This measure traces fluctuations similarly to CU_y, since both are based on a comparison of Z_k and p_k. However, CU may indicate larger or smaller variations, depending on the flatness of the short-run average cost (SRAC) curves. This CU_c measure is written as

$$
(10) \qquad CU_c \equiv \frac{C^*}{C} = \frac{G + \Sigma_k Z_k x_k}{G + \Sigma_k p_k x_k}
$$

$$
= 1 - \frac{\Sigma_k (p_k x_k - Z_k x_k)}{C} = 1 - \Sigma_k \varepsilon_{Ck},
$$

where $\varepsilon_{Ck} \equiv \partial \ln C / \partial \ln x_k$.

For a single fixed input, a similar indicator can be constructed as Z_k/p_k, which differs from CU_c because of the smoothing result of having G in both the numerator and denominator in the latter measure. Z_k/p_k represents the amount the particular input is over- (under-) valued relative to its market transaction cost to the firm and, therefore, indicates how much the firm will over (under) use input k by applying excess (insufficient) variable inputs to its use. Clearly this is also an indicator of investment incentives and, in fact, underlies the notion of Tobin's q, as has been shown by Abel (1979). CU_c reflects the same relationship for all fixed inputs in the aggregate.

Since these subequilibrium indicators reflect utilization that deviates from optimal levels, they can be used to compute the effects on productivity measures of misutilization of capacity. In the context of the cost framework in this study, this is equivalent to carrying out value adjustments for the quasi-fixed inputs to adjust for the impact of subequilibrium on observed productivity.

More specifically, Berndt and Fuss (1986) have demonstrated that a subequilibrium adjustment to productivity measures can be obtained by multiplying the prices of quasi-fixed inputs by a Tobin's q-type measure to revalue the quasi-fixed inputs at their shadow, instead of observed, prices. Alternatively, Morrison (1985b, 1986a) has used (10) as the motivation for a corresponding scalar CU adjustment of productivity for the effects of fixed inputs; her adjustment simply involves dividing the usual productivity growth measure by $CU_c = 1 - \Sigma_k \varepsilon_{Ck}$.

To see this, say that total potential productivity growth measures from the cost side can be represented by $-\partial \ln C / \partial t = \varepsilon_{Ct}$. With quasi-fixed inputs, this becomes

$$
(11) \qquad \varepsilon_{Ct} = (1 - \Sigma_k \varepsilon_{Ck}) \cdot \frac{\dot{Y}}{Y} - \Sigma_k \frac{Z_k x_k}{C} \cdot \frac{\dot{x}_k}{x_k} - \Sigma_j \frac{p_j v_j}{C} \cdot \frac{\dot{v}_j}{v_j}.
$$

If one wishes to determine potential productivity, or true productivity with the effects of disequilibrium purged, it is necessary to calculate

$$
(12) \qquad \varepsilon'_{Ct} = \frac{\varepsilon_{Ct}}{(1 - \Sigma_k \varepsilon_{Ck})} = \frac{\dot{Y}}{Y} - \Sigma_k \frac{Z_k x_k}{C^*} \cdot \frac{\dot{x}_k}{x_k} - \Sigma_j \frac{p_j v_j}{C^*} \cdot \frac{\dot{v}_j}{v_j},
$$

where C^* represents shadow costs. Thus, to determine true productivity growth, it is sufficient simply to divide the observed productivity change by $(1 - \Sigma_k \varepsilon_{Ck}) = CU_c$.[6]

The shadow value, CU, and productivity measures discussed above provide one set of indicators that reflect the effects of subequilibrium. In addition, elasticities may be specified to determine the impacts of changes in exogenous variables on subequilibrium. For example, given the analytical representations of x_k^* in (7) and Y^* in (8), elasticities with respect to these values (and therefore with respect to the corresponding subequilibrium indicators such as CU_y) may be computed. In addition, although the expression is slightly more complex, (1) implies that CU_c may also be written analytically so elasticities of cost CU (CU_c) with respect to an exogenous change may also be computed.

For example, the desired fixed input and capacity output elasticities are

(13a)
$$\varepsilon_{kj}^* = \frac{\partial \ln x_k^*}{\partial \ln p_j} = \frac{p_j}{x_k^*} \cdot \frac{\partial x_k^*}{\partial p_j}$$

and

(13b)
$$\varepsilon_{Yj}^* = \frac{\partial \ln Y^*}{\partial \ln p_j} = \frac{p_j}{Y^*} \cdot \frac{\partial Y^*}{\partial p_j} ,$$

where x_k^* and Y^* are given by (7) and (8) above and where ε_{kj}^* is inversely related to ε_{Yj}^* if only one quasi-fixed input exists. ε_{kj}^* has the same sign as the elasticity of $CU_y = Y/Y^*$ with respect to p_j. With multiple quasi-fixed inputs, the direct relationship between ε_{Yj}^* and the ε_{kj}^* is lost and the full relationship between changes in x_k^* and x_l^* must be recognized.[7] For example, the long-run desired level of each quasi-fixed input depends on the long-run level of the other inputs; not only the x_k^* but also all other long-run elasticities must be computed simultaneously.

To clarify this notion, consider the following, which is based on the CRTS assumption. CRTS conditions imply that the long-run output elasticity $d \ln x_k / d \ln Y$ is equal to one, or, equivalently, dx_k/dY is equal to x_k/Y. If this is not the case, some intermediate output elasticity of the quasi-fixed input with respect to Y is incorporated into this elasticity. For this condition to hold, the full long run must be captured by dx_k/dY, or, if the implications of this constraint from CRTS are derived from the expression for x_k^*, it must be the case that

(14)
$$\frac{dx_k}{dY} = \frac{\partial x_k}{\partial Y} + \Sigma_l \frac{\partial x_k}{\partial x_l} \frac{dx_l}{dY}.$$

Clearly, since dx_k/dY and dx_l/dY are interdependent, they must be solved simultaneously. Note that this also has implications for construction of the long-run demand elasticities mentioned above since the long-run adjustment component is made up of the individual x_k^* elasticities.

The ε^*_{kj} and ε^*_{Yj} elasticities can be interpreted as utilization elasticities because they indicate whether an increase in the price of a variable input j causes further over- (under-) utilization, or whether the existing over- or underutilization is attenuated. If the existing stock of x_k is too low, for example, and an increase is p_j causes x^*_k to increase further relatively to x_k, this implies further overutilization of x_k relative to the optimum because optimally the firm wants to cut back on input j; inputs k and j are substitutes in the long run. Another way to interpret this is that, if an increase in input price p_j causes the desired capital level to increase, it is equivalent to an increase in x_k being input j saving. Thus when the stock of x_k is too low there is overutilization of x_k via extra use of input j in the short run, also indicating that x_k and v_j are substitutes.

The elasticity of Z_k with respect to p_j may also be computed. This elasticity, $\partial \ln Z_k / \partial \ln p_j$, is a valuation-utilization measure; if the price of a variable input increases, for example, and Z_k increases, the value of x_k on the margin has increased, implying additional overutilization of the existing x_k.

By definition, the total fixed input valuation elasticity $\partial \ln CU_c / \partial \ln p_j$ will be a function of the individual $\partial \ln Z_k / \partial \ln p_j$ elasticities with the form

$$(15) \qquad \frac{\partial \ln CU_c}{\partial \ln p_j} = S^*_j \cdot (1 - CU_c) + \Sigma_k \frac{\partial \ln Z_k}{\partial \ln p_j} \cdot S^*_k = \varepsilon^*_{CUj},$$

Where S^*_j is defined as $p_j v_j / C^*$ and S^*_k is $Z_k x_k / C^*$. These value or cost-side elasticities are closely related to the primal elasticities ε^*_{kj} and ε^*_{Yj}. In particular, ε^*_{CUj} and ε_{Zkj} will have the same sign with one quasi-fixed input, as will ε^*_{kj}, although ε^*_{Yj} will be inversely related as mentioned above because it represents capacity output rather than utilization. If multiple quasi-fixed inputs exist, however, the individual shadow value and desired input elasticities ε_{Zkj} and ε^*_{kj} will be the same sign since an increased valuation of input x_j implies a greater desired level of the input, and the full capacity output elasticity that will depend on the overall pattern of all the fixed inputs will be the opposite sign of the utilization elasticity ε^*_{CUj}.

5.3   Comparing the United States and Japan: Empirical Results

5.3.1   Introduction

For empirical implementation of the framework discussed above, the relevant variable and fixed inputs and the estimating methods must be determined. The model used for the empirical results below includes four inputs: capital (K), labor (L), energy (E) and nonenergy intermediate materials (M), where both K and L are fixed in the short run. The cost function for this specification is therefore $G(K, L, p_E, p_M, t, Y)$. A priori information about quasi-permanent hiring of labor in Japan, as well as important rigidities in the United States from labor contracts, imply that this specification with fixed labor as well as fixed capital may provide useful insights.

Alternative specifications including a one quasi-fixed input model and also a dynamic specification were attempted, but the fixity of labor appeared important for reasonable computation of CU measures, and the dynamic specification generated less significant estimates and therefore less robust results. Thus the two quasi-fixed static specification was chosen as the preferred model for presentation. The overall patterns of the results for the alternative models were close to those generated by the specification reported here. In addition, previous estimation was also carried out using data from Norsworthy and Malmquist (1983). As will be noted, however, the results for the Japanese data including post-1978 information differ, in some cases substantially, from results based on the Norsworthy-Malmquist data omitting the second OPEC price shock.

The base estimating equations are the input-output equations for E and M. In addition, the shadow-share or output-price equation may be appended to this system. For the empirical results below the output-price equation was used as the additional estimating equation, although empirical results were quite robust when the alternative shadow-value equation was estimated instead. When neither the shadow-value nor output-price equation was employed, the γ_{KK} parameter—critical in determining the sign and size of Z_K— tended to be statistically insignificant, although close in magnitude to the other specifications.

The U.S. and Japanese data used to generate the results for U.S. manufacturing 1952–81 are from Berndt and Wood (1984) and for Japanese manufacturing 1955–81 are from Takamitsu Sawa (1986). The Sawa data were constructed using the same principles as the Berndt and Wood data, but from Japanese sources.

The pooling method used in this paper is a structural approach; different first-order terms are added to the cost function so that the derived input demand equations have country-specific intercepts. An additive disturbance term was appended to each of the demand and output-price equations, and the resulting vector was assumed to be independently and identically normally distributed with mean vector zero and constant nonsingular covariance matrix. Estimation of the equation system was carried out using the method of maximum likelihood.

The remaining subsections in section 5.3 provide empirical estimates of the different types of measures discussed in the previous section. Section 5.3.2 briefly summarizes the parameter estimates of the model. Section 5.3.3 outlines the unadjusted productivity growth estimates from the data, focusing on the similarities and differences of the trends in the United States and Japan. Section 5.3.4 includes measures of capacity utilization and their components—the desired to actual quasi-fixed input and shadow to market value ratios—to reflect the impacts of short-run rigidities. Section 5.3.5 returns to productivity measurement and discusses the adjustment of productivity indexes to take capacity-utilization fluctuations into account. Section 5.3.6 moves into an overview of substitution elasticities and the flexibility implied by these measures. Finally, based on CU elasticities, Section 5.3.7 provides evidence concerning the impacts of exogenous changes on capacity utilization.

5.3.2   Parameter Estimates

The first estimates to consider briefly are the parameter estimates presented in table 5.1. Differences in the first-order terms of the cost function between Japan and the United States are measured by the parameters α_{MJ}, α_{EJ}, γ_{KJ}, γ_{LJ}, and γ_{KLJ}. Note that, except for these country-specific parameters, most of the parameter estimates are statistically significant; the only country-specific parameter that is significant is α_{MJ}. This suggests that the determinants of manufacturing firms' demand for intermediate materials differs in the two countries, although in other dimensions production processes are quite similar in the two countries. For example, the statistical insignificance of γ_{LJ} and γ_{KLJ} indicate a lack of important deviations in Japanese labor practices from those in the United States. The above results suggest, therefore, that the structure of

Table 5.1   **General Leontief Restricted Cost Function Maximum-Likelihood Parameter Estimates for U.S. and Japanese Manufacturing**

Parameter	Estimate and Asymptotic t-Statistic	Parameter	Estimate and Asymptotic t-Statistic
β_{EM}	.0190 (6.366)	γ_{KJ}	-2.2303 (1.7225)
β_{EE}	.2635 (9.224)	δ_{EK}	$-.4058$ (3.206)
β_{MM}	1.7542 (46.091)	δ_{MK}	-2.0491 (14.659)
α_{Et}	$-.0141$ (5.384)	γ_{LL}	.8804 (2.182)
α_{Mt}	$-.0569$ (11.671)	γ_{LJ}	$-.2550$ (.700)
α_{EJ}	.0076 (1.595)	δ_{EL}	$-.5881$ (11.480)
α_{MJ}	.1526 (15.597)	δ_{ML}	-1.1272 (17.575)
γ_{KK}	3.6858 (2.808)	γ_{KL}	$-.4650$ (.6124)
α_{Kt}	$-.0356$ (5.397)	γ_{KLJ}	.7486 (1.080)
α_{Lt}	.0385 (2.664)		

Note: Absolute values of asymptotic t-statistics are in parentheses.

the labor market in manufacturing, as well as that for energy and capital, does not differ fundamentally between the United States and Japan.

By themselves, the parameter estimates do not provide very much inter-pretable information. To assess the differential economic performance in U.S. and Japanese manufacturing, productivity growth must be computed along with measures of capacity utilization and demand responses to events in the 1970s. Further, their impact on productivity growth must also be assessed based on these parameter estimates.

5.3.3 Productivity Growth

Productivity growth estimates for the United States and Japan appear in table 5.2, in terms of percentage growth indexes of multifactor productivity by year and averages for selected periods. I first consider the unadjusted or traditional productivity growth measures.

An overview of table 5.2 suggests that trends in productivity growth were surprisingly similar for the two countries, although at different levels. At least three dominant differences draw attention, however.[8] First, when Japanese productivity increased, it often did so more dramatically than did U.S. pro-ductivity. This can be seen particularly clearly in 1958, 1960, and 1981. Not surprisingly, therefore, on average Japanese productivity growth was greater than for the United States. Second, the mid to late 1960s were years of partic-ularly strong productivity growth for Japan but not for the United States. Fi-nally, the downturn in 1974–75 was experienced even more dramatically by Japan (especially in 1974) than by the United States, although the subsequent upturn is better maintained in Japan.

One important implication of these traditional measures is that, although Japanese productivity growth is generally better than in the United States, it did not clearly snap back after 1975, leaving the United States behind; 1976 and 1977 were years of very similar productivity growth in both countries. In addition, these numbers imply that the Japanese manufacturing sector really did have a more critical post-1973 crisis. Although U.S. productivity took a sudden downturn, Japanese productivity fell even more abruptly at a negative growth rate of over 5%. While this downward productivity shock was severe, the overall trend is not strongly downward from that point onward in either country.

This last conclusion is not directly obvious from the productivity growth averages presented at the bottom of table 5.2. The post-1973 traditional pro-ductivity growth rates for both the United States and Japan are substantially below the average for the entire sample and, in fact, are very similar for both countries at approximately .5% per year. However, from the 1973–76 and 1973–78 averages it is evident that this result is due to the terrible productivity growth performance in 1974–75. In fact the averages after 1975 are very high, especially for Japan; they are much higher than the average over the entire time period and are nearly as high as they were in the United States during

Table 5.2   **Primal Output and Dual Cost Productivity Growth (%) Indexes and Productivity Growth Average for U.S. and Japanese Manufacturing**

Year	U.S. Traditional		U.S. Adjusted		Japanese Traditional		Japanese Adjusted	
	Cost	Quantity	Cost	Quantity	Cost	Quantity	Cost	Quantity
Growth by years:								
1952	.334	.362	.317	.319				
1953	1.320	1.320	1.259	1.117				
1954	-.664	-.664	-.642	-.615				
1955	3.035	3.035	2.908	2.733				
1956	-.880	-.881	-.859	-.830				
1957	-.692	-.692	-.680	-.663	.645	.646	.574	.523
1958	1.622	1.623	1.585	1.540	4.596	4.592	4.212	3.932
1959	.716	.716	.705	.690	.325	.325	.291	.263
1960	2.071	2.073	2.009	1.925	4.414	4.414	3.837	3.264
1961	.331	.331	.322	.310	1.153	1.154	.995	.824
1962	2.679	2.679	2.601	2.488	1.843	1.841	1.614	1.366
1963	-.188	-.188	-.183	-.175	.726	.725	.641	.554
1964	2.431	2.431	2.364	2.260	.302	.302	.266	.226
1965	.800	.800	.776	.736	.132	.132	.118	.102
1966	-.957	-.957	-.937	-.905	1.525	1.525	1.336	1.118
1967	-.184	-.184	-.182	-.179	3.164	3.164	2.734	2.161

1968	1.051	1.051	1.049	1.045	2.935	2.935	2.526	1.935
1969	.430	.430	.431	.432	2.294	2.294	1.988	1.514
1970	−1.198	−1.198	−1.229	−1.276	2.658	2.658	2.310	1.749
1971	1.494	1.494	1.525	1.572	−.346	−.345	−.309	−.256
1972	2.266	2.266	2.268	2.272	1.161	1.161	1.045	.871
1973	2.636	2.636	2.586	2.505	1.269	1.269	1.132	.922
1974	−1.124	−1.156	−1.110	−1.124	−5.438	−5.438	−5.269	−5.174
1975	−1.107	−1.109	−1.111	−1.117	−1.253	−1.255	−1.279	−1.302
1976	1.838	1.844	1.797	1.755	1.627	1.627	1.615	1.605
1977	1.491	1.491	1.448	1.398	1.030	1.030	1.007	.988
1978	.648	.647	.633	.615	2.423	2.423	2.445	2.468
1979	.642	.640	.628	.613	1.999	1.999	2.007	2.015
1980	.204	.197	.207	.202	.328	.316	.334	.326
1981	1.505	1.506	1.552	1.582	2.954	2.954	3.000	3.027

Average annual
growth rate:

1956–81	.7746	.7762	.7622	.7400	1.2987	1.2979	1.1668	1.0008
1956–65	1.0859	1.0855	1.0554	1.0123	1.5707	1.5701	1.3942	1.2282
1965–73	.6922	.6922	.6889	.6832	1.8326	1.8325	1.5952	1.2518
1973–76	−.1403	−.1310	−.1413	−.1620	−1.6880	−1.6887	−1.6443	−1.6237
1973–78	.3434	.3492	.3314	.3054	−.3222	−.3226	−.2962	−.2830
1973–81	.5075	.5121	.5055	.4905	.4588	.4570	.4825	.4942
1975–81	1.0541	1.0547	1.0442	1.0275	1.7268	1.7248	1.7347	1.7382

1956–65 and in Japan during 1965–73, the previous maxima. This is the case even with the decrease to a .33% growth rate in 1980 in Japan following the 1979 energy price shocks. The impact was not nearly as severe as it was after 1973 and was accommodated quickly, particularly in Japan. Assertions about a substantial post-1973 productivity slowdown in the United States, therefore, as well as those postulating much stronger and faster recovery in Japan, appear from this data to have less basis than casual empiricism would suggest.[9]

The average growth rates also highlight other earlier similarities and differences between U.S. and Japanese productivity patterns. For example, both countries exhibited high growth rates in the 1956–65 time period, with Japanese productivity in manufacturing almost .5% higher per year than in the United States. It is significant that the 1965–73 period for the United States is the beginning of a downturn, whereas this period for Japan is one of even higher productivity growth.

One interpretation of the strong decrease in productivity growth in 1974–75 is that the decrease can be attributed to the energy price shocks of 1973–74, as can the smaller drop in 1980 after the 1979 shock. Assuming this is the case, the response to and recovery from the first energy price increase appears relatively slow for both countries, contrary to the postulated comparative productivity patterns suggested from the literature. The response to the 1979 price shock, however was relatively rapid in Japan.

These productivity measures suggest that the difference between countries does not seem nearly as strong as is often suggested. It is, however, true that Japan recovered from a far worse crisis in 1974 and retained its larger productivity growth for a more complete recovery, including even the 1979 experience with further price increases. This recovery may have been a result of numerous characteristics of the production process, many of which were postulated in the introduction to this paper, such as differences in capacity utilization and overall flexibility of the substitution process in Japanese as compared to U.S. manufacturing. Such issues can be addressed by considering (i) capacity utilization indexes and their impact on productivity measures, (ii) shadow values (and implied desired levels) of the fixed inputs, and (iii) elasticities of both demand and capacity with respect to exogenous shocks.

5.3.4 Capacity Utilization

Greater overall flexibility has been postulated to be an important determinant of relative productivity trends in the United States and Japan. This may manifest itself as stronger short-run responses and therefore more optimal short-run capacity utilization performance in Japan as compared to the United States. The empirical issue is, therefore, how much impact fixity has on shadow values and utilization and thus on productivity and demand responses. Measures of capacity utilization and elasticities developed in the previous section can be used to assess this impact.

First consider the estimated CU indexes presented in table 5.3. Recall that

Table 5.3 Cost and Quantity CU indexes, CU_c and CU_y

Year	United States		Japan	
	CU_c	CU_y	CU_c	CU_y
1952	1.0535	1.1328		
1953	1.0485	1.1247		
1954	1.0340	1.0802		
1955	1.0436	1.1103		
1956	1.0253	1.0619	1.0997	1.1707
1957	1.0186	1.0440	1.1235	1.2358
1958	1.0235	1.0540	1.0912	1.1679
1959	1.0158	1.0381	1.1178	1.2364
1960	1.0310	1.0767	1.1502	1.3524
1961	1.0270	1.0662	1.1592	1.4002
1962	1.0300	1.0768	1.1414	1.3484
1963	1.0276	1.0725	1.1318	1.3101
1964	1.0282	1.0754	1.1355	1.3364
1965	1.0312	1.0872	1.1228	1.2956
1966	1.0208	1.0567	1.1415	1.3642
1967	1.0109	1.0288	1.1573	1.4638
1968	1.0021	1.0056	1.1619	1.5170
1969	.9986	.9964	1.1540	1.5153
1970	.9748	.9394	1.1505	1.5202
1971	.9797	.9507	1.1168	1.3536
1972	.9990	.9975	1.1117	1.3324
1973	1.0191	1.0520	1.1204	1.3759
1974	1.0125	1.0293	1.0321	1.0680
1975	.9966	.9930	.9800	.9641
1976	1.0229	1.0504	1.0076	1.0139
1977	1.0294	1.0663	1.0227	1.0428
1978	1.0232	1.0527	.9908	.9816
1979	1.0212	1.0445	.9960	.9922
1980	.9860	.9757	.9820	.9706
1981	.9696	.9520	.9784	.9761

CU indexes are defined to exceed unity when the valuation of the fixed inputs on the margin exceeds their ex ante market value, that is, when there is a shortage of existing capital and/or labor and thus these stocks are overutilized in terms of the application of variable inputs. These indexes summarize information, therefore, on the measured shadow values and K^* and L^*; $CU > 1$ if $Z_K > p_K$ and $Z_L > p_L$, which implies that $K^* > K$ and $L^* > L$. If, however, one fixed input is over- and one underutilized, the combined effect will depend on which impact is dominant.

The first comparison is that between the output or primal CU measure, CU_y, and the cost CU measure, CY_c. CU_c is always closer to 1.0, which implies that costs change less than output in response to shocks and that the corresponding short-run average total cost curves are somewhat "flat." This is particularly true for Japan, where the primal measure is in some cases quite large (around 1.5 in the late 1960s), indicating substantial shortage of capacity until 1978. Note also that the CU values tend to exceed one in most years, consistent with previous economic CU measures computed by, for example, Morrison and Berndt (1981).

The most important comparison of the CU measures is, however, across countries. As with the productivity measures, one surprising and dominant tendency is that the capacity utilization measures exhibit similar trends for both countries. In particular, both 1975 and 1980–81 were periods of substantial drops in capacity utilization, particularly for Japan. In addition, there is a general downward trend in utilization of capacity in both countries. Differences are also evident, however, including an increase in capacity utilization (overutilization) in Japan in 1970, whereas CU decreased substantially in the United States from 1969–72. Also, both the downward trend over time, and the drops in CU in 1975 and the late 1970s to early 1980s are more dramatic in Japan than for the United States.

Note also that the difference between pre- and post-1973 capacity utilization was more substantial in Japan than in the United States. Japan, in fact, appears to have adjusted further from events in 1973 than did the United States, at least in terms of capacity utilization. Although before 1973 a shortage of capacity of nearly 50% (or 14% in terms of costs) was evident, after 1973 the existing capacity was sufficient and, in fact, in many cases excessive. In 1980, after the 1979 energy price shocks, utilization remained below one, and was lower than for the United States except for 1981.

One important tendency to recognize is that the Japanese capacity utilization indexes suggest greater deviations from optimal capacity utilization over time, at least before 1973. This may imply that the production process is not as flexible as is sometimes postulated. If great flexibility existed, adjustment of the quasi-fixed inputs would be carried out to a more optimal level—CU would more closely approximate one. Alternatively, it more likely reflects the very large capacity gap existing early in this time period from a very low postwar level of capital stock and high and increasing demand for products, so that even with rapid adjustment Japan was not able to close the gap quickly.

The patterns noted in the CU measures could result from adjustment trends of either labor or capital. The resulting implications, therefore, could differ substantially depending on which of these inputs is imposing the constraints. From the raw data, for example, it appears that in Japan capital has adjusted amazingly quickly; capital accumulation has been extremely rapid during most of the time period under discussion. Note that the difference between the U.S. and Japanese investment to capital rates declined but was still evident after 1974. By contrast, labor input has remained fairly steady throughout the period. This is reflected in the trends of the shadow value to market rental price ratios for capital and labor, and the ratios of the desired to existing levels of these fixed inputs, presented in table 5.4. These ratios suggest that the shortage of capacity appearing in table 5.3 results primarily from a shortage in the capital input for both countries. Labor does not have much of an impact, and, particularly in the United States, actually tends to temper the evidence of a shortage of capacity.

In particular, note that these ratios reflect a strong incentive for investment in capital in both countries. In some years the capital quantity ratio suggests that more than twice as much capital as was available would have been desired by Japanese manufacturing firms. This ratio peaks in the late 1960s, when productivity was very high in Japan. Its lowest value is in the 1980–81 period, a level which, it should be noted, appears to result not only from energy price increases but at least partly from a substantial increase in the ex ante market rental price, p_K, as well.

At the same time, some incentives to expand employment existed in Japan, although this pressure was relatively negligible. At its peak in 1961, less than a 20% expansion would have been desired, and after 1971 lower employment than was actually hired would have been desired. For the United States the labor stock seems always to have been too high; excess labor is evident for all years in the sample, although the difference is rather small in 1980–81.

These patterns provide limited evidence of more flexibility in Japanese than U.S. production, especially with respect to capital. Although the desired to actual capital stock ratio in Japan is higher than for the United States, a larger percentage of the "gap" is closed each period;[10] for similar differences in levels a much larger investment rate is reflected in the Japanese data. This flexibility is also somewhat evident for labor, not due to more substantial employment expansion but because the ratios more closely approximate one in Japan than in the United States. Therefore, although the overall capacity-utilization ratios suggest that Japan is further from optimality, these individual input ratios suggest more adjustment toward the optimum, especially for capital, which is the main factor behind the deviation from one in the CU ratio. The reason that the United States appears closer to the optimum in total is at least partly because of the tempering effect of the low levels of desired labor stock.

Although the investment incentive for capital was smaller in the United States than Japan, peaking at an extra 75% of the existing capital stock desired in 1965, the strength of this investment incentive is surprising given the much lower investment rate in the United States as compared to Japan. This may arise, however, because of obsolescence. Specifically, one interpretation of this result is that, on the margin, investment in capital is desirable in the United States, but the manufacturing sector is weighted down by excessive capacity from previous years, so the average valuation of the existing capital is very low. This may cause sluggish responses by firms "stuck" with this inefficient capital. By contrast, in Japan most capital is relatively new given the recent history of rapid investment, so the marginal and average valuations of the capital stock may be more closely related.

One other interesting feature of the fixed input and shadow-value ratios

Table 5.4 **Shadow Value and Fixed Input Ratios**

Year	United States				Japan			
	Z_K/p_K	Z_L/p_L	K^*/K	L^*/L	Z_K/p_K	Z_L/p_L	K^*/K	L^*/L
1952	2.217	.910	1.451	.926				
1953	2.322	.871	1.514	.893				
1954	2.210	.843	1.416	.870				
1955	2.104	.870	1.445	.891				
1956	1.856	.833	1.382	.860	1.626	1.057	1.544	1.023
1957	1.957	.800	1.390	.831	1.767	1.160	1.701	1.069
1958	2.107	.808	1.378	.836	1.568	1.040	1.509	1.019
1959	2.068	.772	1.429	.801	1.698	1.134	1.650	1.066
1960	2.554	.762	1.565	.792	1.904	1.282	1.883	1.154
1961	2.532	.751	1.553	.781	1.934	1.306	1.913	1.191
1962	2.638	.738	1.637	.767	1.792	1.215	1.749	1.149
1963	2.689	.724	1.674	.750	1.761	1.118	1.693	1.087
1964	2.689	.718	1.702	.744	1.752	1.137	1.694	1.110

1965	2.651	.717	1.756	.738	1.681	1.069	1.613	1.059
1966	2.575	.687	1.746	.711	1.820	1.100	1.746	1.081
1967	2.455	.674	1.672	.696	1.953	1.141	1.911	1.136
1968	2.331	.661	1.631	.677	2.080	1.112	2.040	1.116
1969	2.336	.649	1.633	.664	2.038	1.067	2.032	1.074
1970	2.026	.631	1.470	.646	1.994	1.045	2.006	1.053
1971	1.957	.652	1.433	.664	1.780	.916	1.736	.899
1972	2.113	.670	1.532	.680	1.810	.851	1.750	.818
1973	2.194	.705	1.587	.719	1.810	.875	1.785	.842
1974	1.575	.812	1.251	.844	1.230	.862	1.174	.846
1975	1.417	.824	1.145	.857	1.071	.759	1.047	.737
1976	1.873	.819	1.270	.851	1.176	.786	1.114	.766
1977	1.925	.827	1.292	.858	1.263	.775	1.168	.748
1978	1.821	.814	1.280	.847	1.119	.738	1.090	.693
1979	1.653	.854	1.201	.888	1.099	.792	1.073	.760
1980	1.046	.923	1.011	.947	.969	.917	.981	.914
1981	.841	.959	.952	.973	.985	.906	.992	.903

worth noting is that Japan's decrease in overall capacity utilization over time results from a decrease in the desired levels of both capital and labor stocks, even though pressure in the capital market is the dominant force. By contrast, in the United States the downward trend in capacity utilization stems primarily from capital utilization; the desired labor stock relative to its existing level drops to its lowest value in the late 1960s and then recovers to above its original levels.

Finally, it should be noted that changes in the production structure that apparently resulted from the dramatic increases in energy prices in 1973, and the correspondingly smaller adaptations due to the 1979 price increases, had a very strong impact on the desired to actual capital ratio for both countries. In particular, in 1974 the desired capital ratio in the United States dropped 21% from 1.587 to 1.251, and in Japan it decreased 34% from 1.785 to 1.174, indicating a strong difference in the production structure. Similarly, in 1980 the ratios dropped 17% from 1.201 to 1.001 (and then 5% more to .952 in 1981) for the United States and 1.073 to .981 (a 9% drop followed by a 1% increase to .992 in 1981) for Japan. One important point to note here is that although the implied "gap" between desired and actual levels of capital therefore decreased more substantially in Japan than in the United States, the investment response was different in the two countries; Japanese investment remained relatively strong.

By contrast, the desired to actual labor ratio in 1974 and 1980 increased in the United States from .719 to .844, and .888 to .947, respectively, and, during those same time periods, in Japan from .842 to .846 and .760 to .914. Although this is not nearly as strong an effect, it suggests that the energy price increases stimulated relative labor as compared to capital efficiency as seen by manufacturing firms.

5.3.5   Adjusting Multifactor Productivity for Capacity Utilization

The impact of capacity utilization, as reflected in the CU measures in table 5.3, may be used to adapt measured productivity growth, as presented in table 5.2, to take into account the impacts of short-run fixity. This results in the adjusted indexes presented in table 5.2. Since the CU measures fluctuate much less than the productivity measures, the impact of this adjustment is not large on either the indexes or the averages.

For example, for the United States, over the 1956–81 time period the traditionally measured average annual productivity growth rate is approximately .77%, while the adjusted rate is .74% to .76%, depending on whether the adjustment is carried out on the primal or dual cost side. The larger pre-1975 than post-1965 productivity growth and short 1973–76 productivity slowdown remains almost unaffected in the adjusted averages; the 1965–73 growth rate is .69% and the 1973–76 rate is − .13% for the traditional numbers (cost side), and approximately .68% and − .14% to − .16% respectively, once adjusted. Similarly, the 1973–81 rates and 1975–81 rates, traditionally measured averages of .51% and 1.05%, correspond to adjusted averages of .49% to .50% and 1.03% to 1.04%. Therefore, although the trends in CU in the United States are substantive, their impact on productivity fluctuations is modest at best and the traditionally measured productivity growth trends remain.

The implications from the capacity-utilization adjustments to productivity trends for Japan are similar, although the adjustments are slightly larger. For example, the traditionally measured overall average is 1.3% per year, which corresponds to the CU-adjusted average of between 1.0% and 1.2%. This average is made up of a 1.57% traditional—or 1.23% to 1.39% adjusted—average growth rate in the first part of the time period, increasing to a 1.83% traditional—1.25% to 1.6% adjusted—annual increase in the 1965–73 time period. The drop to a 1.67% (1.62% to 1.64% adjusted) *decline* in productivity during the 1973–76 period remains in the adjusted numbers as a 1.62% to 1.64% decrease on average, still driven by the extreme value in 1974 even though it is tempered somewhat by a corresponding decrease in CU. This average increases to a .46% (.48% to .49%) rate of growth in the 1973–81 period or 1.73% (1.74% adjusted) productivity growth after 1975.

One point worth noting about these values in Japan is that the adjusted 1975–81 average yearly growth in productivity appears even stronger than the maximum traditionally measured productivity growth average from the 1965–73 time period. This again emphasizes that productivity growth does not appear to be on a general downward trend following the 1974–75 fiasco.

In summary, the measured post-1973 productivity growth indexes for Japan slightly underestimate average productivity growth, whereas for pre-1973 they overestimate productivity. That is, the shortage of capacity in earlier years caused the marginal productivity of the quasi-fixed inputs to be higher than traditionally measured, implying that "true" productivity must be revalued downward. Thus only a small part of the alleged decrease in Japanese productivity growth may be attributed to changes in capacity utilization. This trend also appears very weakly in the U.S. indexes; it is not as powerful because the downward trend in capacity utilization is not as evident. The overall effect of fixity for both countries, however, is small compared to the extreme variations in productivity.

5.3.6   Substitution Elasticities

Another way to assess the flexibility of the production processes in the U.S. and Japan is in terms of substitutability patterns among inputs. The relevant elasticities necessary for consideration of relative substitutability in the short and long run are presented in table 5.5.

One striking implication of these elasticities is the similarities among them for the two countries. At first glance it may appear that this is simply the result of the structural pooling process with different first-order terms but equal second-order effects. However, preliminary work presented in Morrison (1985c) using the same procedures but data only through 1978 did not find

Table 5.5   **Selected Elasticities (reported for 1980)**

Parameter	United States		Japan	
	A. Variable Input Price Elasticities			
	SR	LR	SR	LR
ε_{EE}	−.1586	−.5906	−.1577	−.4776
ε_{EM}	.1586	.5584	.1577	.7311
ε_{EL}		.2914		.3739
ε_{EK}		−.2592		−.6274
ε_{EY}	.4506	1.0000	.3326	1.0000
ε_{ME}	.0285	.1005	.0309	.1316
ε_{MM}	−.0285	−.4511	−.0309	−.5972
ε_{ML}		.2445		.1138
ε_{MK}		.1061		.3517
ε_{MY}	1.6354	1.0000	1.7804	1.0000
	B. Long-Run Fixed Input Elasticities			
ε_{LE}	.1376		.3254	
ε_{LM}	.6416		.5506	
ε_{LL}	−.7259		−1.0840	
ε_{LK}	−.0533		.2080	
ε_{LY}	1.0000		1.0000	
ε_{KE}	−.3001		−.2482	
ε_{KM}	.6824		.7732	
ε_{KL}	−.1306		.0945	
ε_{KK}	−.2516		−.6195	
ε_{KY}	1.0000		1.0000	
	C. Shadow-Value Elasticities			
$\varepsilon_{ZL,E}$	.2633		.2376	
$\varepsilon_{ZL,M}$	.7367		.7624	
$\varepsilon_{ZL,L}$	−1.5106		−.9898	
$\varepsilon_{ZL,K}$	.3197		−.3491	
$\varepsilon_{ZL,Y}$	1.1908		1.3389	
$\varepsilon_{ZK,E}$	−1.2515		−.4367	
$\varepsilon_{ZK,M}$	2.2515		1.4367	
$\varepsilon_{ZK,L}$	.7309		−.1666	
$\varepsilon_{ZK,K}$	−3.9712		−1.8430	
$\varepsilon_{ZK,Y}$	.0036		.0020	
	D. Capacity-Utilization Elasticities			
$\varepsilon_{CU,E}$	−.0609		−.0758	
$\varepsilon_{CU,M}$	.3856		.4394	
$\varepsilon_{CU,L}$	−.2581		−.1512	
$\varepsilon_{CU,K}$	−.3095		−.4776	
$\varepsilon_{CU,Y}$	.2819		.1770	

Table 5.5 (*continued*)

Parameter	United States	Japan
	E. Shadow-value and Utilization Elasticities with Respect to t	
$\varepsilon_{ZK,t}$	.0205	.0127
$\varepsilon_{ZL,t}$	$-.0162$	$-.0183$
$\varepsilon_{CU,t}$	.0188	.0245

Note: SR = short run; LR = long run.

this to be the case. In particular, using this shorter data set it was found that each of the pooling parameters except α_{EJ} was significantly different from zero, and, as a result, Japan's responses to exogenous shocks as measured by the estimated elasticities were significantly larger. With the more recent data, however, this pattern is not evident, even when only data to 1978 is used for estimation.

As seen in table 5.5, the price elasticity estimates provide ambiguous evidence about the hypothesis of greater Japanese than U.S. flexibility with respect to price shocks.[11] For example, the short-run own-price elasticity for materials is slightly larger in Japan ($-.031$) than in the United States (-0.28), as is the implied substitutability between materials and energy in the short run. However, the own-price elasticity for energy is slightly smaller in Japan ($-.158$) than in the United States ($-.159$). Since this elasticity is very important for assessment of responses to the energy price shocks, this is particularly surprising. In addition, the small energy-output elasticity suggests that energy use does not respond quickly to output changes, and this response is even smaller in Japan than in the United States; this suggests that "overhead" use of energy may be very important in manufacturing. Materials usage, by contrast, adjusts quickly in response to output fluctuations, more in Japan than in the United States. This result, along with the larger materials elasticity in Japan and the earlier finding of significant difference between materials demand in the United States and Japan, suggests that materials demand responses may be important for facilitating flexibility in Japan.

The long-run elasticities provide important implications about the relationships of capital and labor demand with energy and materials. First, note that the difference between the short- and long-run elasticities is quite large; long-run own-price elasticities for energy and for materials are about four and fifteen times the size of the short-run elasticities, respectively. This does not cause a significant difference between U.S. and Japanese responses, however. In fact the long-run demand elasticities for energy and materials exhibit the same relative patterns between the United States and Japan as do the short-run elasticities, and energy and capital appear to be even stronger complements and labor and energy less substitutable in Japan than in the United States.

There seems to be little reason, therefore, to think that there is more difficulty substituting capital and labor for energy in the United States as compared with Japan. By contrast, capital and labor are both substitutes with materials, and K–M substitutability is quite large in Japan. This substitutability may imply that adjustment with respect to materials is an important response by manufacturing firms to exogenous shocks.

Although long-run responses of Japanese as compared to U.S. firms appear quite comparable, the more rapid adjustment of capital and labor input stocks suggested by the raw data may imply greater differences than are immediately apparent. Reaching the long run may simply take longer for the United States as compared to Japan, particularly when the exogenous shock stimulating the response is not as strong in the United States, which was true of the productivity crisis in 1974.

The fixed input elasticities presented in table 5.5 reflect the impact on the desired values of labor or capital when an exogenous variable changes. These provide similar information about relationships between the fixed and variable inputs. That is, the negative elasticity value for the capital-energy elasticity suggests that the desired capital stock decreases with an energy price increase—K and E are complements for both countries. Again, this is inconsistent with the hypothesis of greater vulnerability of the U.S. production process to energy price changes because of energy-capital complementarity suggested by Norsworthy and Malmquist (1983) and alluded to by Sato and Suzawa (1983). It is consistent, however, with the evidence from the productivity indexes that the 1973 energy price shock had a large, if short, impact on Japanese manufacturing, and from the capacity indexes that the effect on the desired capital ratio was strong.

These elasticities, however, also provide information about the relationship between the capital and labor inputs. In particular, one difference evident from the elasticities is the complementarity of labor and capital in the United States whereas substutability exists in Japan, suggesting one area where additional flexibility may exist in Japanese production. Desired capital decreases with an increase in the price of labor in the United States but increases in Japan. Also, the own-price responsiveness of both capital and labor is larger in Japan than in the United States, implying that not only is capital accumulation responsive, as would be found from casual empiricism due to the enormous observed investment rate in Japan, but also that labor is quite flexible which may not be expected a priori.

Perhaps the most significant finding from the fixed input elasticities is that more substitutability is evident in Japan than in the United States. In particular, when variable inputs are substitutable with the fixed capital and labor inputs, as with ε_{LE}, the larger value for Japan reflects a larger increase in the desired amount of labor with an upward price shock for energy than found for the United States. Similarly, when inputs are complements, such as for capital and energy, the complementarity appears less in Japan; if energy prices increase, the desired capital stock decreases less than for the United States. The own-price elasticities for both labor and capital are also larger in Japan; for both inputs, if the price increases the responsiveness is greater in Japan. These results strongly suggest more flexibility in the production technology for Japan relative to the United States, even if the adjustment proportion is the same for both countries given a gap between the desired and actual levels of the stock input; the gap itself changes more for Japan. With a larger proportion of the gap also closed with more rapid investment in Japan, as was conjectured above, the larger adjustment implied by the desired fixed input response is augmented.

5.3.7 Shadow Value and CU Elasticities

Next, consider the shadow value and capacity-utilization elasticities reported in table 5.5. The shadow value elasticities represent information reflected by the quasi-fixed input elasticities; increases in the desired capital (labor) stock with an exogenous change correspond to increases in the shadow value of the stock. The Z_k elasticities, however, provide information on the valuation rather than quantity changes, and the capacity utilization measures summarize the total impact.

Again it is evident from the Z_L elasticities that all inputs are substitutes with labor for Japan but labor and capital are complements for the United States; increases in the price of energy, materials, or the capital stock (this is not a price elasticity but a stock level elasticity) cause an increase in the shadow value of labor in the United States, although an increase in K implies a decrease in Z_L for Japan. A similar relationship holds for output; output increases imply a large increase in the shadow value for both countries. The own elasticity is also substantial, indicating a strong response of the shadow value of labor to changes in its own stock, particularly for the United States.

For capital the own elasticity of Z_K with respect to K is very large, and larger in the United States than in Japan. This suggests that responsiveness is lower in the United States, since any augmentation of the capital stock substantially decreases further incentives for investment, consistent both with the ε_{KK} elasticity results and with the larger investment rate in Japan as compared to the United States for a given gap between the desired and actual capital stock. The responsiveness to energy and material prices is also substantial, although for energy it is negative (complements) and for materials it is positive (substitutes).

The capacity-utilization elasticities imply that increases in energy prices cause decreases in overall capacity utilization. Similarly, additions to labor or capital stocks result in more capacity to utilize and therefore a decline in CU. An increase in the price of materials, however, increases capacity utilization, since labor and capital are substituted for the previously used partly finished goods. These results imply that a strong energy price shock or increase in capital or labor stocks, and resulting decrease in capacity utilization, bias the observed productivity level downward. This was found above for Japan, although, as noted, the effect was weak compared to the large fluctuations in productivity growth.

Finally, it may be useful to consider the elasticities of the shadow values and capacity utilization with respect to changes in technology, or technical progress. This can be interpreted as the reverse of assessing how productivity is affected by fixed inputs; a change in technology may affect the various fixed inputs differently. As can be seen from the last set of elasticities presented in table 5.5, an increase in technology increases overall CU in both countries. This change is composed of two components, an increase in the shadow value of capital and decrease in the shadow value of labor for both countries, although these elasticities do vary over time. The capital effect dominates, therefore, generating the overall increase in efficiency reflected in the CU elasticities. These results imply that technical change has a tendency to cause capital to be noticeably more efficient and labor to be slightly less efficient, implying that technology is capital using and labor saving. This suggests an interpretation for the small desired labor ratio relative to that for capital found above, which reflects pressure for increasing capital intensity over time. This may, therefore, provide some support for the idea that the greater capital accumulation rate observed in Japan is consistent with a greater increase in efficiency of the capital stock, and therefore increases in overall productivity in Japan as compared to the United States.

5.4. Summing Up

It is clear that short-run fixities and the resulting short- and long-run substitution possibilities are important elements in the response of U.S. and Japanese firms to exogenous shocks. These possibilities are particularly important for comparisons across countries, since different patterns of industrial structure and rigidities may have a decisive impact on observed economic indicators. In this study, a framework has been developed capable of capturing underlying relationships among variable and quasi-fixed inputs, and has been used for an empirical comparison of the manufacturing industries of the United States and Japan. This framework provides a rich basis for analysis of input substitutability, CU, and productivity trends because it is capable of quantifying differences in short-run utilization and long-run input adjustment responses to exogenous shocks, differences which may cause important variations in economic performance.

More specifically, most hypotheses about the relative production structures and resulting productivity growth trends in the United States and Japan have focused on the alleged greater flexibility of Japan in response to exogenous shocks and the resulting potential for greater productivity growth. Flexibility appeared evident from the decrease in energy intensity of production in Japan after 1973, whereas in the U.S. little responsiveness was directly evident before the second energy price shock in 1979.

The data and econometric analysis of the problem presented in this study, however, suggests that the differences between U.S. and Japanese production structures in manufacturing may not be as large as alleged. The findings can be summarized as follows.

1. Productivity growth has been larger in Japan by 30% to 50% on average over the 1956–81 period, although the magnitude of the differences varies over time and appears slightly smaller since 1975. Important characteristics of the productivity growth profile that stand out are: (a) there is a larger drop in productivity growth in 1974 in Japan than the United States, supporting the idea of a "crisis" mentality in Japan as compared to the United States; (b) 1975 was a comparably low productivity growth year and 1976 and 1977 strong productivity growth years for both countries; and (c) Japan better managed to sustain this post-1974 growth even with a drop in 1980 after the 1979 energy price increases, whereas the United States experienced another less severe decline in productivity growth. Japan was able, therefore, to recover from a more severe decline in productivity growth and maintain it more effectively than U.S. manufacturing, but the differences were not as substantial as have sometimes been suggested.

2. Short- and long-run energy demand responsiveness in the two countries appears quite similar. There are insignificant differences in pooling parameters for the energy demand relationship in the two countries and elasticities are comparable. Short-run elasticities are small, and long-run own elasticities are quite large for both countries (yet still price inelastic); energy and labor are long-run substitutes, and energy and capital are long-run complements.

3. The labor structure in the two countries also does not appear to be different. The pooling parameters for labor are insignificant and the energy-labor and materials-labor relationships appear quite similar. The major difference is slight capital-labor complementarity in the United States contrasted to substitutability in Japan. In addition, more flexibility of labor in Japan may be implied by the $L*/L$ ratios presented in table 5.4, which are closer to one in Japan than in the United States.

4. Capacity-utilization ratios are not substantially different in the two countries in terms of trends, although those for Japan exhibit a stronger decreasing trend over time as capital and labor adjustment takes place in response to overutilization of both fixed inputs in the beginning of the sample. The fixity represented by these indexes, however, does not provide much information about productivity growth trends, because productivity growth fluctuates much more dramatically than do the impacts of fixity. The capacity utilization adjustment of productivity growth therefore has a relatively modest impact.

5. One important difference appears to involve substitution with intermediate materials. The country-specific intercept parameter in the materials equa-

tion is the only one that is significantly different from zero, indicating a different embedded technology and demand structure in Japan as compared to the United States. Also, firms in Japanese manufacturing appear to carry out a substantial part of their adjustment following exogenous changes by substituting intermediate materials; the substitution possibilities as exhibited by the demand elasticities are larger in Japan than in the United States. This may result in faster response time because adjustment of this relatively variable input may be accomplished more quickly than that for the more fixed inputs.

6. Overall the most important difference between these two countries may be capital accumulation in response to investment incentives. Capital accumulation has been much stronger in Japan than in the United States, although the investment incentives, as measured by the ratio of desired to actual capital stock or the shadow value as compared to market value of capital is not correspondingly large. The small own-capital elasticities found in the United States as compared to Japan also highlight this difference.

It is difficult, based on these observations, to reach a final conclusion about the reasons underlying differences in Japanese and U.S. manufacturing productivity growth, because greater overall flexibility is not strongly evident from the data. It does appear, however, that there were many determinants, including a very high investment rate in Japan, which may have contributed to more observed flexibility of the Japanese production process, especially in response to the energy price shocks of the 1970s.

In particular, the greater dependence of Japanese manufacturing on imported energy resulted in a severe impact of energy prices on productivity growth in 1974. The response to this by the Japanese as compared to U.S. manufacturing firms may partly be a result of this greater "crisis," but also is likely due to more rapid capital adjustment resulting in newer more energy-efficient capital in place. This is consistent with evidence of an enormous amount of competition in Japanese industry both to produce and use energy efficient technology after the price increases in 1973 and 1979; see, for example, Uchida and Fujii (1986). The post-1973 rapid investment to expand new technology developed sufficiently by 1979 to make the 1980 impact small and short compared to that in 1974 for Japan. The Japanese response to the second energy price shock was also smaller than that in the United States, which did not experience a correspondingly strong post-1974 capital accumulation response.

In addition, greater flexibility of workers, in the sense of their ability to accept and use new technology and readjust working patterns, has been suggested by researchers such as Sato and Suzawa. This could be reflected in the higher capital/labor ratio and capital replacement patterns found for Japanese manufacturing and the greater substitutability that appears to exist with respect to labor and capital in Japan.

Thus, although long-run variable input elasticities are roughly equal in the United States and Japan, the fixed input elasticities indicate greater long-run substitutability. This, along with faster capital and labor adjustment may have caused Japanese manufacturing to move toward the long run more quickly, resulting in better productivity performance in the late 1970s.

Notes

1. See, e.g., Jorgenson and Nishimizu (1978), Norsworthy and Malmquist (1983), Conrad and Jorgenson (1984), Sato and Suzawa (1983), and Jorgenson and Kuroda (in this volume).

2. Higher investment in new capital and increasing work effort (and possibly quality—investment in human capital) may also result from these interrelationships, providing Japan with an increasingly efficient capital and labor stock. This component of the substitutability or flexibility hypothesis cannot be assessed directly in the kind of econometric model used here; for explicit consideration of these potential forces see Isamura (in this volume), Tan (in this volume), and Dean, Darrough, and Neef (in this volume).

3. See Morrison (1986b) for further development of this function and a corresponding nonconstant returns to scale generalization.

4. See Morrison (1986a) for further development of this interdependence.

5. Note that this measure, since it is based on static optimization, does not require that nonstatic expectations assumptions be specified. If dynamic aspects were incorporated, however, this measure as well as the K^* measure must be adapted to take present value optimization into account as in Morrison (1985a).

6. See Morrison (1985b, 1985c, 1986a) for further elaboration and for an alternative, more rigorous proof proposed by Ingmar Prucha.

7. Note that it also appears possible and potentially useful similarly to define elasticities of the change in Y^* with respect to a relaxation of the constraint on x_k or the change in x_k^* with a change in output demand—$\partial \ln Y^*/\partial \ln x_k$ and $\partial \ln x_k^*/\partial \ln Y$. However, if these are long-run elasticities, these are trivially equal to one.

8. With previous data these trends appeared very different. In particular, using the Norsworthy and Malmquist (1983) Japanese data, 1971 and especially 1973 were catastrophic years for productivity growth, but productivity recovered substantially after 1973, particularly during 1974 and 1975. The numbers presented in the current study are much more consistent with a priori information about the trends in Japan.

9. Note that previous studies using the data set by Norsworthy and Malmquist generate a different type of pattern inconsistent with the well-documented decline in Japanese economic performance following the OPEC price shocks. See, e.g., Norsworthy and Malmquist (1983) or Morrison (1985c).

10. To assess directly the speed of adjustment, a dynamic model explicitly representing the adjustment process, such as Morrison and Berndt (1981), must be utilized. A recent study by Ingmar Prucha and M. I. Nadiri (1986), however, has suggested that different methods of dealing with dynamic models may yield very different results. For this study, therefore, use of a dynamic model was rejected in favor of using a model based on static optimization and imputing an adjustment speed based on the implied gap between desired and actual stocks and the rate of change of the stock. Moreover, capital markets may be different in the United States and Japan, implying different external costs of adjustment.

11. Morrison (1985c) found much larger elasticities, for example for the own-price response to energy, in Japan as compared to the United States using the data from

Norsworthy and Malmquist (1983) that only included information to 1978. The data used here differs somewhat for Norsworthy and Malmquist up to 1978, and includes the second OPEC price shock years of 1979–81.

References

Abel, A. B. 1979. *Investment and the value of capital.* New York: Garland.

Berndt, E. R., and M. Fuss. 1986. Productivity measurement with adjustments for variations in capacity utilization and other forms of temporary equilibrium. *Journal of Econometrics* 33:7–29.

Berndt, Ernst R., and David O. Wood. 1984. Energy price changes and the induced revaluation of durable capital in U.S. manufacturing during the OPEC decade. MIT Energy Laboratory Report no. 84-003. Cambridge, Mass. (March).

Conrad, Klaus, and D. W. Jorgenson. 1984. Sectoral productivity gaps between the United States, Japan and Germany, 1960–1979. Discussion Paper no. 298/84. University of Mannheim, Institut für Volkswirtschaftslehre und Statistik.

Jorgenson, Dale W., and Mieko Nishimizu. 1978. U.S. and Japanese economic growth, 1952–74: An international comparison. *Economic Journal* 88 (December): 707–726.

Lau, Lawrence J. 1978. Applications of profit functions. In *Production economics: A dual approach to theory and applications,* ed. M. Fuss and D. McFadden. Amsterdam: North-Holland.

Mork, Knut A. 1978. The aggregate demand for primary energy in the short and long run for the U.S., 1949–75. MIT Energy Laboratory Report no. MIT-EL 7809-007WP. Cambridge, Mass. (May).

Morrison, Catherine J. 1985a. On the economic interpretation and measurement of optimal capacity utilization with anticipatory expectations. *Review of Economic Studies* 52(169):295–310.

———. 1985b. Primal and dual measures on economic capacity utilization: An application to productivity measurement in the U.S. automobile industry. *Journal of Business and Economic Statistics* 3, no. 4 (October):163–94.

———. 1985c. The impacts of fixed inputs on firm behavior and productivity: An empirical comparison of the U.S. and Japanese manufacturing industries. Original manuscript presented at the U.S. Japan Productivity Conference on Research in Income and Wealth, National Bureau of Economic Research (August).

———. 1986a. Productivity measurement with nonstatic expectations and varying capacity utilization: An integrated approach. *Journal of Econometrics* 33, nos. 1/2 (October/November): 51–74.

———. 1986b. The impact of quasi-fixed inputs in U.S. and Japanese manufacturing: An application of the generalized Leontief restricted cost function. *Review of Economics and Statistics* 70, no. 2 (May): 275–87.

Morrison, Catherine J., and Ernst R. Berndt. 1981. Short run labor productivity in a dynamic model. *Journal of Econometrics* 16:339–65.

Norsworthy, J. R., and David H. Malmquist. 1983. Input measurement and productivity growth in Japanese and U.S. manufacturing. *American Economic Review* 73 (December): 947–67.

Prucha, Ingmar R., and M. I. Nadiri. 1986. A comparison of alternative methods for the estimation of dynamic factor demand models under nonstatic expectations. *Journal of Econometrics* 33(1/2):187–212.

Sato, Ryuzo, and Gilbert S. Suzawa. 1983. *Research and productivity.* Boston: Auburn House.
Sawa, Takamitsu. 1986. Japanese data provided through correspondence via MIT Energy Laboratory, Cambridge, Mass.
Uchida, Mitsuho, and Yoshifumi Fujii. 1986. Historical change in energy use in Japan. Paper presented at the International Roundtable on Energy, Technology and the Economy, International Institute for Applied Systems Analysis. Laxenburg, Austria (October).

Comment   Ingmar R. Prucha

Overview

Catherine Morrison's paper represents an interesting new analysis and comparison of the production structure of the U.S. and Japanese manufacturing sector. The paper pays particular attention to the quasi fixity of some of the inputs and finds that the differences between the production structure of the U.S. and Japanese manufacturing sector may not be as large as has often been suggested in the literature.

The paper consists essentially of two parts: one theoretical, the other empirical. In the theoretical part Morrison introduces a new restricted cost function as the basic modeling device for the quasi fixity of some of the inputs. This restricted cost function represents an extension of the generalized Leontief cost function introduced by Diewert (1971). The paper further derives corresponding measures of productivity, capacity utilization, and various short- and long-run elasticities.

In the empirical part Morrison applies the modeling framework to U.S. and Japanese total manufacturing data. The empirical specification includes four inputs: capital, labor, energy and nonenergy material inputs. Both capital and labor are allowed to be quasi fixed. Expectations are taken to be static and returns to scale are assumed to be constant. The U.S. data are from Berndt and Wood (1984) and cover the period 1952–81. The Japanese data set has been provided by Takamitsu Sawa and covers the period 1955–81. The estimating equations consist of the demand equations for energy and material inputs, and an output price equation. Those equations are estimated by pooling the U.S. and Japanese data and allowing for country-specific first-order terms in the restricted cost function. Based on the parameter estimates the paper reports estimates for productivity growth, capacity utilization, and short- and long-run elasticities of substitution for the U.S. and Japanese total manufacturing sector. The most striking finding (among the wealth of information provided by those estimates) is that the results indicate much smaller

Ingmar R. Prucha is associate professor of economics at the University of Maryland and a research associate of the National Bureau of Economic Research

differences between the U.S. and Japanese production structures in manufacturing than typically found in the literature.[1] One explanation for Morrison's
novel findings may be that her study is based on a new Japanese data set that
includes post-1978 information. Still, it seems of interest to explore in future
work the robustness of those findings, in particular, against alternative functional specifications.

In motivating her restricted cost function Morrison points out some of the
shortcomings of existing functional forms. She notes, in particular, that the
linear-quadratic restricted cost function is not invariant to normalization.
Morrison's choice of taking the Generalized Leontief cost function as a starting point for a new restricted cost function is a good one. However, such an
extension of the Generalized Leontief cost function may take different forms.
In the following remarks, I point out some properties of Morrison's extension
that seem restrictive. Furthermore, I introduce alternative extensions of the
Generalized Leontief cost function that may be useful for empirical research
and can be used to check the robustness of Morrison's findings. One of those
restricted cost functions is shown to have the property that the corresponding
long-run cost function is again of the form of a Generalized Leontief cost
function.

Extensions of the Generalized Leontief Cost Function

Consider a firm that produces a single output good, Y, from m variable
inputs, $v = [v_1, \ldots, v_m]^T$, and n (possibly) quasi-fixed inputs, $x =
[x_1, \ldots, x_n]^T$. Let $p = [p_1, \ldots, p_m]^T$ be the corresponding vector of prices
for the variable inputs and $r = [r_1, \ldots, r_n]^T$ the corresponding vector of ex
ante rental prices for the quasi-fixed inputs. We adopt the following convention: If z is a vector (matrix), then $z^{.5}$ denotes the vector (matrix) whose elements are the square roots of those of z. Using matrix notation, Morrison's
extensions of the Generalized Leontief cost function with long-run constant
returns to scale can then be written as:[2]

(1) $\quad G(p,x,Y) = Yg(p,x/Y)$

$$= Y\left[(p^{.5})^T Bp^{.5} + p^T D\left(\frac{x}{Y}\right)^{.5} + \left(\sum_{i=1}^{m} p_i\right)\left(\frac{x^T}{Y}\right)^{.5} C\left(\frac{x}{Y}\right)^{.5}\right],$$

where $B = B^T = (b_{ij})$, $C = C^T = (c_{ij})$, $D = (d_{ij})$ are matrices of parameters
of dimension $m \times m$, $n \times n$, and $m \times n$, respectively. The term $\sum_{i=1}^{m} p_i$ in (1) needs
to be interpreted with care. Clearly, we can only sum over variables that are
measured in equal units. Hence, if the p_i are measured in, say, dollars per unit
of the input v_i then $\sum_{i=1}^{m} p_i$ could be interpreted as $\sum_{i=1}^{m} p_i a_i$ where $a_i = 1$
denotes one unit of v_i. Given this interpretation we sum over variables mea-
sured in equal units. While this observation is trivial it is nevertheless important if we change the units of measurement for p_i and v_i, as discussed in more
detail below.

Morrison assumes that $G(\cdot)$ satisfies standard properties. The function $G(\cdot)$ is clearly linear homogeneous in p and invariant to normalization by a particular variable input. It follows immediately from Diewert (1971) that a sufficient condition for $G(\cdot)$ to be concave in p is that the b_{ij} are nonnegative. The demand equations for the variable inputs can be readily obtained via Shephard's lemma, that is, $v_i = \partial G / \partial p_i$.

To discuss the specification issues stemming from the term $\Sigma_{i=1}^{m} p_i$ in more detail, it is useful to consider the case of two variable factors, $m = 2$, and one quasi-fixed factor, $n = 1$. In this case the demand equations for the variable factors derived from (1) are given by

(2a) $v_1 = Y[b_{11} + b_{12}(p_2/p_1)^{.5}] + d_{11}(x_1 Y)^{.5} + c_{11} x_1,$

(2b) $v_2 = Y[b_{22} + b_{12}(p_1/p_2)^{.5}] + d_{21}(x_1 Y)^{.5} +$

Inspection of (2) shows that the coefficient corresponding to x_1 (by itself) is the same in both demand equations. Now suppose we change the units of measurement of the first variable input. Let $v_1^{\circ} = s v_1$ and $p_1^{\circ} = s^{-1} p_1$ denote, respectively, the quantity and price of the first variable factor in new units where s is the scale factor. Upon interpreting $\Sigma_{i=1}^{m} p_i$ as $\Sigma_{i=1}^{m} p_i a_i$ the demand system (2) then becomes

(2°a) $v_1^{\circ} = Y[b_{11}^{\circ} + b_{12}^{\circ}(p_2/p_1^{\circ})^{.5}] + d_{11}^{\circ}(x_1 Y)^{.5} + c_{11}^{\circ} x_1,$

(2°b) $v_2 = Y[b_{22} + b_{12}^{\circ}(p_1^{\circ}/p_2)^{.5}] + d_{21}(x_1 Y)^{.5} + c_{11} x_1,$

where $b_{11}^{\circ} = s b_{11}$, $b_{12}^{\circ} = s^{.5} b_{12}$, $d_{11}^{\circ} = s d_{11}$, and, in particular, $c_{11}^{\circ} = s c_{11} \neq c_{11}$. This suggests that the restricted cost function (1) may be restrictive in that it imposes, a priori, the same coefficient for the quasi-fixed factors across the demand equations for the variable inputs. This problem can be readily alleviated if $\Sigma_{i=1}^{m} p_i$ is replaced by $\Sigma_{i=1}^{m} p_i c_i$ where the c_i (with $c_1 = 1$ for reasons of identifiability) are parameters that are estimated from the data. The demand equations corresponding to (2) are then given by

(3a) $v_1 = Y[b_{11} + b_{12}(p_2/p_1)^{.5}] + d_{11}(x_1 Y)^{.5} + c_1 c_{11} x_1,$

(3b) $v_2 = Y[b_{22} + b_{12}(p_1/p_2)^{.5}] + d_{21}(x_1 Y)^{.5} + c_2 c_{11} x_1.$

It seems of interest to check if Morrison's empirical results are robust against the above-described generalization of the functional form of the restricted cost function. Of course, one may also define and consider various alternative forms of restricted cost functions that extend the Generalized Leontief cost function, for example,

(4) $G(p,x,Y) = Y g(p,x/Y)$

$$= Y\left[(p^{.5})^T B p^{.5} + p^T D\left(\frac{x}{Y}\right) + \left(\sum_{i=1}^{m} p_i c_i\right)\left(\frac{x^T}{Y}\right) C\left(\frac{x}{Y}\right)\right].$$

The appealing feature of the above linear quadratic specification is that it allows for explicit solutions for the quasi-fixed factors even in the dynamic case with explicitly modeled adjustment costs; for corresponding estimation procedures see, for example, Epstein and Yatchew (1985) and Madan and Prucha (1989).

The long-run cost function is given by $C(p,r,Y) = G(p,x^*,Y) + r^Tx^*$ where x^* denotes the long-run optimal quasi-fixed inputs. None of the above restricted cost functions has the property that the corresponding long-run cost function is of the form of the Generalized Leontief cost function, that is,

$$(5) \qquad C(p,r,Y) = Y\left[(p^{.5})^TBp^{.5} + 2(r^{.5})^TEp^{.5} + (r^{.5})^TFr^{.5}\right],$$

where $B = B^T = (b_{ij})$, $E = (e_{ij})$ and $F = F^T = (f_{ij})$ are matrices of parameters of dimensions $m \times m$, $n \times m$, and $n \times n$, respectively. We assume that the elements of B, E, and F are nonnegative. This condition is sufficient for $C(p,r,Y)$ to satisfy standard properties, that is, to be nondecreasing, concave, and homogeneous of degree one in (p,r) and nondecreasing in Y; compare Diewert (1971). We introduce the following alternative restricted cost function with constant return to scale:[3]

$$(6) \qquad \underline{G}(p,x,Y) = Y(p^{.5})^T[B + E^T(X-F)^{-1}E]p^{.5},$$
$$X = \text{diag}(x_1/Y_1 \ldots, x_n/Y),$$

where we take $\underline{G}(\cdot)$ to be a real valued function defined on $R_+^m \times \Theta$, $\Theta \subseteq R_+^{n+1}$. Here R_+^m and R_+^{n+1} denote the interior of the nonnegative orthants of R^m and R^{n+1}. Θ is taken to be an open convex subset of R_+^{n+1} such that for each element of Θ the matrix $X - F$ is positive definite and the elements of the matrix $(X-F)^{-1}$ are nonnegative. In the appendix we show that $\underline{G}(\cdot)$ has the usual properties of a restricted cost function, that is, it is nondecreasing, concave, and homogeneous of degree one in p, nonincreasing and convex in x, and nondecreasing in Y. Let $B^* = (b_{ij}^*) = B + E^T(X-F)^{-1}E$, then the demand equations for the variable inputs are given by

$$(7) \qquad v_i^* = Y\sum_{j=1}^m b_{ij}^* p_j^{.5} / p_i^{.5}, \quad i = 1, \ldots, m.$$

The long-run cost function is obtained by minimizing $\underline{G}(p,x,Y) + r^Tx$. Given r is such that an interior solution exists we show in the appendix that the optimal long-run quasi-fixed inputs x^* satisfy:

$$(8) \qquad (X^*-F)^{-1}Ep^{.5} = r^{.5}, \quad X^* = \text{diag}(x_1^*/Y, \ldots, x_n^*/Y),$$

or, equivalently,

$$(9) \qquad x_i^* = Y\left(\sum_{j=1}^m e_{ij}p_j^{.5}/r_i^{.5} + \sum_{j=1}^n f_{ij}r_j^{.5}/r_i^{.5}\right), \quad i = 1, \ldots, n.$$

Because of (8) we have $(p^{.5})^TE^T(X^*-F)^{-1}Ep^{.5} = (p^{.5})^TE^Tr^{.5}$, and $r^Tx^* = Y(r^{.5})^TX^*r^{.5} = Y[(r^{.5})^TEp^{.5} + (r^{.5})^TFr^{.5}]$. Substitution of those expressions into

$\underline{G}(p,x^*,Y) + r^T x^*$ yields (5). That is, the restricted cost function $\underline{G}(p,x,Y)$ has the property that the corresponding long-run cost function is the Generalized Leontief cost function $C(r,p,Y)$.

Appendix

In the following we verify the claims made with respect the restricted cost function $\underline{G}(p,x,Y)$. We make use of the following matrix differentiation formulae: Let α and β be two $n \times 1$ vectors of constants and let x/Y be such that $\Phi = X - F$ is nonsingular, then

(A1) $\partial(\alpha'\Phi^{-1}\beta)/\partial x = -Y^{-1}[\alpha^T\phi^1\beta^T\phi^1, \ldots \alpha^T\phi^n\beta^T\phi^n]^T$

(A2) $\partial(\alpha'\Phi^{-1}\alpha)/\partial x\partial x^T = Y^{-2}\mathrm{diag}(\alpha^T\phi^1, \ldots, \alpha^T\phi^n) \cdot$
$\Phi^{-1}\mathrm{diag}(\alpha^T\phi^1, \ldots, \alpha^T\phi^n),$

where ϕ^i denotes the ith column of Φ^{-1}. Formula (A1) can be readily obtained by using propositions 98 and 105 and corollary 22 in the appendix of Dhrymes (1978). Formula (A2) is obtained by using (A1) and observing that $\alpha^T\phi^i = \alpha^T\Phi^{-1}e_i$, where e_i is the ith column of the $n \times n$ identity matrix.

Since the element of $B + E^T(X-F)^{-1}E$ are nonnegative, it follows immediately that $\underline{G}$ is nondecreasing, concave, and homogeneous of degree one in p; compare Diewert (1971). Applying (A1) and (A2) we get

(A3) $\partial\underline{G}/\partial x = - \{[(\phi^1)^T Ep^{.5}]^2, \ldots ,[(\phi^n)^T Ep^{.5}]^2\}^T < 0,$

(A4) $\partial^2\underline{G}/\partial x\partial x^T = 2Y^{-1}\Psi\Phi^{-1}\Psi, \quad \Psi = \mathrm{diag}\{(\phi^1)^T Ep^{.5}, \ldots ,(\phi^n)^T Ep^{.5}\},$

thus verifying that $\underline{G}$ is nonincreasing in x and convex in x (upon observing that Φ is positive definite). Similarly we find that $\partial\underline{G}/\partial Y > 0$. Equation (8) follows by observing that $\partial\underline{G}/\partial x + r = 0$ implies $(\phi^i)^T Ep^{.5} = r_i^{.5}$ for $i = 1, \ldots, n,$ or equivalently $\Phi^{-1}Ep^{.5} = r^{.5}$. (Note that $(\phi^i)^T Ep^{.5}$ is positive.)

Notes

1. Compare, e.g., Norsworthy and Malmquist (1983), Mohnen, Nadiri, and Prucha (1986).

2. To keep the notation simple I have dropped the technology index from Morrison's specification. Note that the subsequent discussion also applies with obvious modifications to the case where a technology index is included. Note further that all of the subsequent discussion can be readily generalized to the case of a homothetic technology by replacing in the respective formulas Y by $h(Y)$, h nondecreasing. In this case the scale elasticity is given by $h(Y)/[Yh'(Y)]$.

3. The functional form was found by considering the problem $\sup_r[C(p,r,Y) - x^T r]$. This restricted cost function can be readily generalized to the homothetic case by replacing Y by $h(Y)$; cf. n. 2 above.

References

Berndt, E. R., and D. O. Wood. 1984. Energy price changes and the induced revaluation of durable capital in U.S. manufacturing during the OPEC decade. Typescript. MIT Center for Energy Policy Research, Cambridge, Mass. (January).

Dhrymes, P. J. 1978. *Introductory econometrics*. New York: Springer Verlag.

Diewert, E. 1971. An application of the Shephard duality theorem: A Generalized Leontief production function. *Journal of Political Economy* 79:481–507.

Epstein, L. G., and A. J. Yatchew. 1985. The empirical determination of technology and expectations: A simplified procedure. *Journal of Econometrics* 27:235–58.

Madan, D. B., and I. R. Prucha. 1989. A note on the estimation of non-symmetric dynamic factor demand models. *Journal of Econometrics* 42: 275–83.

Mohnen, P. A., M. I. Nadiri, and I. R. Prucha. 1986. R&D, production structure, and productivity growth in the U.S., Japanese and German manufacturing sectors. *European Economic Review* 30:749–71.

Norsworthy, J. R., and D. H. Malmquist. 1983. Input measurement and productivity growth in Japanese and U.S. manufacturing. *American Economic Review* 73:947–67.

6   Energy Price Shocks and Productivity Growth in the Japanese and U.S. Manufacturing Industries

Ernst R. Berndt, Shunseke Mori, Takamitsu Sawa, and David O. Wood

6.1   Introduction

The coincidence of the energy price shocks in the 1970s and the sharp changes in productivity growth rates in industrialized economies have presented a puzzle for productivity growth analysts. Traditional productivity accounting procedures, measuring multifactor productivity growth as output growth minus the value share weighted growth in factor inputs, have been unable to attribute much significance to the coincidence of the energy price shocks and sharp changes in multifactor productivity growth. For example, Edward Denison, a distinguished productivity analyst, concludes that "I do not think that much of the productivity slowdown can be ascribed to energy prices" (1979, p. 138).[1]

Yet the apparent simultaneity is striking; between 1973 and 1975, real energy prices faced by Japan and U.S. manufacturing establishments roughly doubled, while multifactor productivity growth fell at the rate of 2.43% and 0.70% per year in Japan and the United States, respectively.[2] More generally, multifactor productivity growth rates decreased sharply for both countries in the postembargo period while the pattern of real energy prices shifted from being relatively stable to increasing dramatically. In Japan (the United States), productivity growth rates fell from 1.58% (1.11%) per year to 0.42% (0.52%)

Ernst R. Berndt is professor of applied economics at the MIT Sloan School of Management, Shunseke Mori is professor of industrial administration at the Science University of Tokyo, Takamitsu Sawa is professor of economics at Kyoto University, and David O. Wood is senior lecturer at the MIT Sloan School of Management and director of the MIT Center for Energy Policy Research.

An earlier version of this paper was presented at the NBER Conference on Productivity Growth in Japan and the United States, held 26–28 August 1985 in Cambridge, Massachusetts. We have benefited greatly from the comments of Charles Hulten and Kanji Yoshioka. Berndt and Wood gratefully acknowledge financial support from the MIT Center for Energy Policy Research.

per year between 1958 and 1973 and 1973 and 1981, while real energy price changes grew at a rate of -1.43% (0.14%) to 19.9% (17.2%) per year for the comparable periods. Although these numbers are striking, traditional growth accounting methods have only been able to locate coincidence, not causality, in the arithmetic drama.

The basic problem faced by productivity growth analysts involves the following structural issue: By what mechanism could unexpected energy price changes have been related to sharp changes in multifactor productivity growth? Whatever the mechanism is, it must be consistent with two important facts. First, the average energy efficiency of durable capital goods changes only gradually, depending upon replacement investment in fully depreciated capital, new additions to the capital stock, and the change in average energy efficiency of capital goods between the pre- and post–price shock periods. Since the deterioration rate for equipment goods is about 13.5% per year in both Japanese and U.S. manufacturing, it would seem that nearly simultaneous reductions in energy input growth and energy price increases are ruled out by the more gradual adjustment of the average energy efficiency of durable goods.

The second fact that the energy price shock/productivity growth mechanism must account for is the relatively small value share of energy inputs in total production costs (only about 10% in both Japanese and U.S. manufacturing in 1981, up from about 4% in 1973). This implies that even large energy price changes translate into only relatively small changes in total costs and energy value shares, the latter being the weights employed in computing the energy input contribution to multifactor productivity growth.[3]

The combined effect of these two "facts"—that (1) large energy price changes have a modest effect upon total production costs and energy value shares and (2) energy input growth rates depend critically upon the slowly adjusting average efficiency of the energy using durable goods—suggests that sharp changes in traditionally measured multifactor productivity growth cannot be attributed to unexpected energy price shocks.

Recent research by Berndt and Wood (1984, 1987a, 1987b), Mori and Sawa (1985), and McRae (1985) has focused on the possibility that an important adjustment mechanism for the effects of unexpected energy price changes has been overlooked in traditional productivity measurement. Specifically, firms are able to adjust utilization rates for capital vintages embodying different energy efficiencies, thereby partially mitigating the effects of the unexpected energy price changes. If this utilization effect could be measured and properly incorporated into multifactor productivity accounting procedures, then energy price shocks could conceivably have a more substantial impact on productivity and still be consistent with the two facts noted above.

The empirical significance of this utilization adjustment mechanism in accounting for changes in productivity growth coincident with unexpected energy price changes will depend of course on technical possibilities for adjusting the energy efficiency of capital, and the vintage structure and the energy efficiency embodied in long-lived capital, the latter depending on the history of expectations about relative energy/capital prices. One major problem in evaluating the potential importance of the energy-price induced aggregate capital utilization effect upon productivity growth, however, is that both capital vintage energy efficiency and utilization rates are generally unobserved variables; hence evaluation requires measurement models based on economic theory and plausible assumptions regarding firm behavior.

In this paper we examine utilization responses to energy price shocks in the manufacturing sectors of the United States and Japan. We employ a consistent data base of output and input factor accounts for Japan and U.S. manufacturing, 1958–81, and then evaluate the potential importance of the utilization adjustment mechanism in aggregate capital stock and multifactor productivity measurement. The study employs simulation methods based on historical data on real investment and relative energy/capital prices, together with a range of values for the key parameter of the model—the *ex ante* energy-capital substitution elasticity—in calculating utilization adjusted measures of aggregate capital stock and of multifactor productivity growth. We find that even for relatively low values of this parameter, utilization adjustment effects make an important contribution in accounting for the productivity slowdown in the Japanese and U.S. manufacturing industries beginning in 1973, especially for Japan in the 1973–75 period.

The outline of the paper is as follows. In section 6.2 we present and compare real energy prices, investment patterns, and multifactor productivity growth in Japanese and U.S. manufacturing, with special attention to the post-1973 period. Section 6.3 presents a model by which energy price shocks affect productivity growth through their impact on the economic measure of aggregate utilized capital services, and section 6.4 presents and interprets the simulation results. We then conclude with remarks on directions for future econometric research and data development.

6.2   Energy Prices, Investment, and Productivity Growth in the Japanese and U.S. Manufacturing Industries

We begin by comparing basic information on energy prices, investment, and multifactor productivity performance for Japanese and U.S. manufacturing. Overall, the data suggest that Japan and U.S. manufacturing industries (*a*) sustained similar real energy price patterns for the first price shock, with Japan experiencing a much smaller real price increase in the second shock; (*b*) had quite different investment levels and patterns throughout the 1947–81 period; and (*c*) had dissimilar, traditionally measured multifactor productivity growth rates, with Japan generally having higher growth rates and experiencing a much greater productivity growth reduction coincident with the first price shock, and a much smaller reduction coincident with the second shock.

We first consider two measures of energy prices: nominal energy prices deflated by the manufacturing output price (an indicator of the overall rate of inflation), and the nominal energy price relative to the price of investment goods—a measure reflecting the operating versus fixed costs faced by the firm in choosing energy efficiency characteristics of new capital goods. Table 6.1 presents growth rates for these two energy-price measures for selected periods. Several features should be noted. First, for the preembargo period 1947–73, nominal energy prices, deflated by the gross output price deflator, decreased 1.3% per year in Japan and increased 0.7% per year in the United States, indicating that for this measure of real energy prices, Japanese and U.S. manufacturing firms faced quite different real energy prices. The second real energy price measure—equipment price-deflated energy prices—indicates, however, that real energy prices on average decreased more in the United States than in Japan in that period (-0.6% per year vs. -0.2% per year). Choice of end points matters most for the first real energy price measure; if we ignore the post–World War II and post–Korean War adjustments, for the period 1952–73 average output price-deflated energy prices increased 0.8% per year in Japan and 0.3% per year in the United States, while the corresponding equipment price-deflated energy prices increased 0.6% per year in the United States. This change in end points reduces the country disparity in the output price deflated measure and increases it for the investment price deflated measure.

Second, the average percentage increase was greatest in Japan for both measures of real energy prices for the period 1973–81, with the equipment price deflated energy price increasing more than the output price-detailed measure. This suggests that Japanese firms have had a somewhat greater relative incentive than U.S. firms to increase the energy efficiency of their equipment capital during the postembargo period

Table 6.1   **Japanese and U.S. Manufacturing Industries' Real Energy Price Growth Rates for Selected Periods**

	Deflator			
	Output Price		Equipment Price	
Period	Japan	United States	Japan	United States
1947–81	3.7	4.6	5.6	4.5
1947–73	− 1.3	.7	− .2	− .6
1952–73	.9	.3	.6	− .6
1958–73	− 1.4	.1	− .6	− .2
1973–81	19.9	17.2	24.7	20.8
1973–78	25.2	18.5	29.9	21.1
1978–81	14.7	16.0	19.4	20.6

Finally, it should be noted that for both deflation methods, although the two energy price shocks were roughly of equal magnitude in the United States, the second price shock in Japan was much less severe than the first.

Next, we consider the data on Japanese and U.S. manufacturing industry investment in equipment and structures. Figures 6.1 and 6.2 present real total and equipment investment divided by real gross output (constant 1975 yen and dollars) for the Japanese and U.S. manufacturing industries, respectively, while figure 3 presents the equipment investment/gross output ratios for both countries. Dividing by real gross output is intended, in part, to adjust for cyclical effects and for increases in scale.

A striking feature of these graphs is the consistently higher and more volatile investment/gross output ratios in Japan relative to those in the United States. Further, as can best be seen in figure 6.3, from 1955–78 the pattern of change in investment/gross output ratios in the two countries moves in opposite directions; that is, the peak-to-peak periods for Japan correspond almost exactly to a trough-to-trough period for the United States, a relation that appears to be coincidental. This pattern changes for the 1978–81 period when the investment/gross output ratios move in the same direction, with the United States ratios finally beginning to approach those of Japan.

Two additional points should be noted. First, the average overall investment/gross output ratios for the two countries move differently for the period 1947–73 versus 1974–81, with the ratio dropping slightly in Japan (.072 to .068) and rising in the United States (0.36 to .042). Within these periods, there is considerable volatility; for example, for the subperiods 1947–55 (1974–77) and 1956–73 (1978–81), the ratios increase 35.3% (decrease 8.8%) and decrease 9.2% (increase 23.7%) in Japan and the United States,

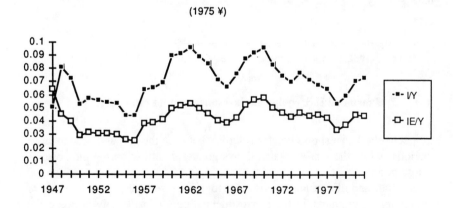

(1975 ¥)

Note: I= Total Investment; IE= Equipment Investment; Y = Output

Fig. 6.1   Japan investment/output ratios

(1975 $)

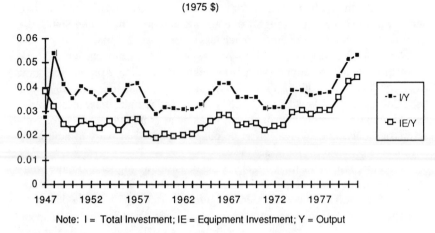

Note: I = Total Investment; IE = Equipment Investment; Y = Output

Fig. 6.2   U.S. investment/output ratio

(1975 ¥ and $)

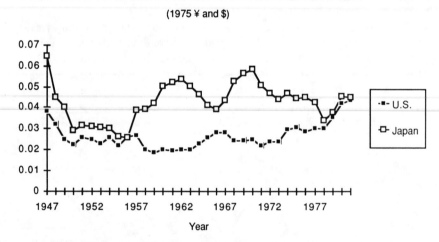

Year

Fig. 6.3   Japan and U.S. equipment investment/output ratio

respectively. Japan shows greater volatility between the pre- and postembargo periods, while the United States shows greater volatility during the postembargo period.

Second, and of considerable interest for our present purposes, the share of equipment investment in total investment differs considerably between the two countries for the pre- and postembargo periods. For Japan, the equipment investment share in total investment increases slightly between 1947–73 and 1974–81 (61% to 64%), with the share relatively constant over the postembargo period. In contrast, the equipment investments share in total investment for the United States increases from 68% to 80% between the pre- and postembargo periods. Similar to Japan, however, U.S. equipment investment is a relatively constant share of total investment over the postembargo period.

We conclude this brief survey of significant pre- and postembargo developments in the Japanese and U.S. manufacturing industries with a comparison of multifactor productivity (MFP) growth in the two countries. MFP growth rates for selected periods are presented in table 6.2.[4] Several features should be noted. First, while there is some year-to-year variability, on average Japanese MFP growth rates have exceeded U.S. rates for all periods except 1973–75. The average Japanese and U.S. MFP growth rates for the period 1958–73 (1975–81) are 1.58% (1.39%) and 1.11% (0.92%), respectively.

Second, comparison of 1958–73 and 1973–81 periods suggests that there has been a slowdown in MFP growth rates in both the Japanese and U.S. manufacturing industries. The slowdown has been greater in Japan (1.58% vs. 0.42%) than in the United States (1.11% vs. 0.52%).

Third, the greatest contribution to the slowdown in productivity growth rates occurs in the period 1973–75—coincident with the first OPEC-induced energy price shock (OPEC-1)—in both Japan and the United States. The decrease in MFP growth rates in that period is much greater in Japan (-2.43%) than in the United States (-0.69%).

Finally, a comparison of the 1975–78 and 1978–81 periods indicates virtually no change in the Japanese MFP growth rate (1.42% vs. 1.37%) and a significant reduction for the United States (1.16% versus 0.70%). Hence, the second OPEC-induced energy price shock is again coincident with some slowdown in U.S. productivity growth—although not nearly as large as the first price shock—but it does not coincide with any change in Japanese MFP growth experiences.

6.3 Energy Price Shocks, Induced Variations in Capital Utilization, and the Measurement of Productivity

We now develop more formally the notion of how energy price changes may affect the relationship between aggregate utilized capital services and

Table 6.2   **Japanese and U.S. Manufacturing Industries' Multifactor Productivity Growth Rates for Selected Periods**

Period	Japan	United States
1958–81	1.172	.900
1958–73	1.575	1.105
1973–81	.419	.516
1973–75	-2.430	$-.702$
1975–81	1.387	.924
1975–78	1.415	1.120
1978–81	1.358	.681

aggregate capital stock, which in turn may have important implications for productivity measurement. As noted above, the analysis of the influence of energy price changes on productivity is greatly complicated by the fact that vintage specific utilization and energy efficiency information are not generally observed for most assets comprising the manufacturing industry investment and capital stock data.

Following the ancient econometric proverb, "If you don't have data, think," we will make use of two plausible assumptions.

1. Firms choose the energy efficiency characteristics of new capital goods consistent with minimizing expected life-cycle costs.
2. Firms choose relative utilization rates between old and new capital so as to minimize current period variable costs.

We now appeal to economic theory regarding firm behavior in order to develop the economic structure necessary to identify and evaluate the potential significance of a "utilization adjustment" effect for such economic measures as multifactor productivity.

We begin by noting that in virtually all research involving capital input in production or cost functions, it is assumed that the flow of capital services is proportional to the capital stock and that this factor of proportionality is constant over time. With traditional capital stock aggregation over vintages, it is assumed that capital physically deteriorates or "evaporates" at the constant rate δ. The significance of this assumption is that the relative marginal product at time t of a \$1 investment in each of the two periods $t-\tau$ and $t-\tau-v$ equals $(1 - \tau)^v$. More specifically, the marginal products at time t of period t, $t-\tau$, and $t-\tau-v$ investments of \$1 are 1, $(1-\delta)^\tau$, and $(1-\delta)^{\tau+v}$. In such a case of constant geometric deterioration, and only in such a case, the rate of economic depreciation is also constant and equal to δ.[5]

Since relative prices equal relative marginal products, the implication of the "constant deterioration" assumption is that the relative prices of any surviving vintages of capital are constant over time. Further, using the fact that relative prices are fixed, one can employ the Hicksian aggregation condition to form an aggregate capital stock over vintages defined as:[6]

$$(1) \qquad K_t \equiv \sum_{\tau=0}^{T} S_\tau I_{t-\tau} \equiv \sum_{\tau=0}^{E} K_{t,t-\tau},$$

where S_τ is the physical survival rate, $S_\tau \equiv (1-\delta)^\tau$, T is the physical lifetime of equipment, $I_{t-\tau}$ is the amount of real investment put in place at time $t-\tau$, and $K_{t,t-\tau}$ is the amount of $t-\tau$ investment physically surviving to period t. Note that the S_τ are precisely the proportionality factors that reflect relative marginal products.

It is useful to generalize this traditional treatment of capital aggregation over vintages to account for energy-price-induced changes in vintage-specific rates of utilization. We now present a framework that permits us to construct an aggregate measure of utilized capital, denoted K_t^*, computed as,

$$(2) \qquad K_t^* = \sum_{\tau=0}^{T} e_{t,t-\tau} S_\tau I_{t-\tau} = \sum_{\tau=0}^{T} e_{t,t-\tau} K_{t,t-\tau},$$

where the $e_{t,t-\tau}$ are relative vintage-specific utilization rates of the physically surviving $t-\tau$ investment at time t. Notice that if $e_{t,t-\tau} = 1$ for all t, τ, then traditional (K) and "utilization-adjusted" (K^*) measures of capital coincide.

Our use of the term "utilization-adjusted" is very suggestive but obviously needs to be made more precise. When firms make investment decisions for new equipment, they recognize that equipment is durable, and thus they examine the present value of the life-cycle costs. Suppose firms first decide the amount of funds to be devoted to the sum of the capital and energy operating costs; this decision could be based on, for example, expectations concerning output demand, materials costs, wage rates, and operating rates. Second, having decided this, firms then choose the optimal split between capital and energy costs. Once the optimal energy efficiency is chosen in this second step, the capital utilization energy use relation is fixed in "clay"; hence, while flexible and "putty" *ex ante,* the amount of energy consumed per unit of capital service utilized is immutable *ex post.* Note that, in this framework, while the *ex post* energy-capital service utilization relationship is clay, *ex post* substitutability may still occur between the capital-energy bundle and labor or material inputs.

Assume further that, with the second decision noted above, the relevant production function is the familiar constant elasticity of substitution (CES) function with Hicks-neutral disembodied technical change and constant returns to scale. Using the first-order conditions for life-cycle costing, this CES production function yields the optimal *ex ante* energy intensity at time t, denoted F_t, as

$$(3) \qquad \ln F_t = \ln \left[\frac{E}{K} \right]_t = \ln a - \sigma \ln \left[\frac{P_E^*}{P_K^*} \right]_t,$$

where $\ln a$ is a constant, σ is the *ex ante* substitution elasticity between energy and capital equipment, and P_E^* and P_K^* are values of discounted expected prices for energy and capital equipment, respectively, over the expected lifetime of the new equipment. A discussion of how price expectations are computed is deferred to later in this section.

If firms followed this decision criterion at all points in time—at t and $t-\tau$ for all t, τ—and if relative energy prices suddenly changed, the optimal relative utilization rates for the surviving $t-\tau$ vintages could differ significantly from those originally chosen. Specifically, denote by $u_{t,t-\tau}$ the vintage-specific utilization rates at time t for $t-\tau$ vintage surviving to time t, and then note that the total energy costs at time t equal the sum of vintage-specific energy costs. Exponentiating equation (3) over all vintages yields variable costs at time $t (VC_t)$ as

$$(4) \quad VC_t \equiv P_{E,t} \sum_{\tau=0}^{T} F_{t-\tau} u_{t,t-\tau} K_{t,t-\tau} = P_{E,t} \sum_{\tau=0}^{T} a \left[\frac{P_E^*}{P_K^*} \right]_{t-\tau}^{-\sigma} u_{t,t-\tau} K_{t,t-\tau}.$$

Note that the first equality of equation (4) is an identity, relating total energy costs to the current price of energy $(P_{E,t})$, the vintage-specific energy efficiency of surviving vintages of capital $(F_{t-\tau})$, vintage-specific utilization rate $(u_{t,t-\tau})$, and the surviving amount of each vintage $(K_{t,t-\tau})$.

The shadow values of these surviving vintages, that is, their ability to reduce variable (energy) costs given their embodied energy efficiency and energy prices prevailing at time t, is given by

$$(5) \quad -\frac{\partial VC_t}{\partial K_{t,t}} = -P_{E,t} a \left[\frac{P_E^*}{P_K^*} \right]_t^{-\sigma} u_{t,t},$$

for the most recent (period t) surviving capital, and by

$$(6) \quad -\frac{\partial VC_t}{\partial K_{t,t-\tau}} = -P_{E,t} a \left[\frac{P_E^*}{P_K^*} \right]_{t-\tau}^{-\sigma} u_{t,t-\tau},$$

for surviving vintage $t-\tau$ capital.

Assume that the efficient firm utilizes these various surviving vintages of capital so that their shadow values in production are equal. Equating the shadow values in (5) and (6) for all t,τ and rearranging, we obtain

$$(7) \quad \frac{u_{t,t-\tau}}{u_{t,t}} = \left[\frac{P_{EK,t}^*}{P_{EK,t-\tau}^*} \right]^{-\sigma},$$

where $P_{EK,t}^*$ and $P_{EK,t-\tau}^*$ are the relative price terms in square brackets in equations (5) and (6), respectively.

At the level of the individual manufacturing establishment, a merit ranking of utilization rates by energy efficiency could indicate that some vintages would be utilized completely and others not at all.[7] While it might be desirable to incorporate such establishment-specific utilization constraints into our framework, it appears to be exceedingly difficulty to do so. Moreover, our data is at the aggregate manufacturing level, not at that of the individual establishment. As we shall see in the empirical implementation, the values of u_t predicted by the simple model all fall within reasonable ranges, and corner solutions do not emerge at the aggregate level.

One implication of (7) is that when these shadow values are equalized, vintage-specific utilization rates will adjust, with the magnitude of the adjustment depending on the size of the *ex ante* substitution elasticity σ and the change between time $t - \tau$ and t in the relative energy prices P_{EK}^*. In particular, if relative energy prices increase between $t - \tau$ and t, and if the *ex ante* energy-capital substitution elasticity equals zero (no *ex ante* substitution possibilities available), then by (3) the optimal *ex ante* energy intensities at t and $t - \tau$ would be identical in spite of energy price increases, and thus no utilization adjustment would occur among the surviving vintages. However, if σ were substantial, that is, if significant energy-capital substitution possibilities were available *ex ante*, then according to (7) the relatively energy-inefficient $t - \tau$ vintages would be utilized less in production. On the other hand, if relative energy prices fell unexpectedly and if $\sigma > 0$, then the relatively energy-inefficient vintages would be used more in production; the ratio in (7) can be on either side of unity. In our view, this utilization adjustment response to energy price shocks is eminently plausible.

Having derived vintage-specific rates of utilization that depend on relative energy prices and the *ex ante* substitution elasticity, we now employ them in constructing an aggregate measure of utilized capital over vintages. Since equating shadow values preserves relative service prices of capital vintages, the Hicksian aggregation condition can again be employed in aggregating these vintages. Specifically, we set the relative vintage-specific utilization rates $e_{t,t-\tau}$ equal to the left-hand side of (7), that is, set

$$(8) \qquad e_{t,t-\tau} = \frac{u_{t,t-\tau}}{u_{t,t}},$$

normalize by setting $u_{t,t} = 1$ for all t. Using (7) and (8) and substituting into (2) yields,

$$(9) \qquad K_t^* = \sum_{\tau=0}^{T} \left[\frac{P_{EK,t}^*}{P_{EK,t-\tau}^*} \right]^{-\sigma} S_\tau I_{-\tau}.$$

As noted above, the expression for $e_{t,t-\tau}$ provides constant valuation weights for aggregating surviving capital vintages, given relative price expectations, precisely the condition required for Hicksian aggregation of the surviving vintages.

We interpret the result of equation (9) as the utilization-adjusted aggregate capital stock, and the ratio of this measure to the traditional capital stock measure of (1),

$$(10) \qquad\qquad B_{K,t} = \frac{K_t^*}{K_t},$$

as the aggregate capital utilization adjustment coefficient. Note that this coefficient, $B_{K,t}$, can be less than, equal to, or greater than unity.

The aggregate utilization adjustment coefficient, $B_{K,t}$, should obviously be affected by energy price shocks. From equations (9) and (10) we can derive an elasticity relation between the aggregate capital utilization adjustment coefficient, $B_{K,t}$, and the relative expected life-cycle price, $P_{EK,t}^*$, as,

$$(11) \qquad\qquad \frac{\partial \ln K_t^*}{\partial \ln P_{EK,t}^*} = \frac{\partial \ln B_{K,t}}{\partial \ln P_{EK,t}^*} = -\sigma.$$

Equation (11) reflects the intuition that the extent to which the aggregate capital stock is adjusted downward for an unexpected increase in relative expected life-cycle costs depends upon the extent to which the firm has opportunities to choose increased energy efficiency in new capital goods, relative to the efficiency decisions it made prior to the change in energy prices.

Finally, we must consider how the expected life-cycle–relative price function, $P_{EK,t}^*$, is evaluated by the firm. We assume that in making energy efficiency choices, firms discount expected future prices, $\hat{P}_{E,t+1}$ and $\hat{P}_{K,t+1}$, by a real discount rate, r. Recalling that equipment put in place at the beginning of a period deteriorates at the constant geometric rate δ, we define the expected relative life-cycle price as

$$(12) \qquad\qquad P_{EK,t}^* = \sum_{l=0}^{T} \hat{P}_{EK,t+l+1} \left(\frac{(1-\delta)^l}{(1+r)^{l+1}} \right),$$

where now $\hat{P}_{EK,t+l+1}$ is the expected future price of energy relative to capital, and T is the physical service life of a new capital good.

But how do firms form expectations regarding future energy/capital relative prices? We consider the following two plausible possibilities: (1) relative energy/capital prices are expected to change at a constant rate of growth, g; (2) expected energy/capital prices are based on time-dependent forecasts, which are updated as new information becomes available to the firm.

In the first case, we can represent the expected relative price as

$$(13) \qquad\qquad P_{EK,t+l} = (1+g)^l \, P_{EK,t},$$

where g is the constant rate of growth. Substituting equation (13) into (11) gives

$$(14) \qquad\qquad P_{EK,t}^* = \Gamma \, P_{EK,t},$$

where, after some tedious algebra, it can be shown that $\Gamma = (1 - \lambda^T)$ and $\lambda = (1-\delta)(1+g)/(1+r)$. Note, however, that substituting (14) into (3) involves only an adjustment to the intercept term, $\ln a^* = \ln a - \sigma \ln \Gamma$. Since this term cancels out in evaluating $e_{t,t-\tau}$, the use of current prices as estimates of expected relative life-cycle prices is appropriate if we believe that a constant growth rate satisfactorily represents the firm's expectations about future relative energy/capital prices.

An alternative approach as to how firms form expected energy/capital prices is to assume that they employ historical information in making time-dependent forecasts that are then updated as new information becomes available. Such forecasts could be based on time-series techniques and may seem preferable to estimates based on constant growth rate assumptions. We are sympathetic with this view, but note that a constant growth rate can, in part, be justified by appeal to Hotelling's Law in resource economics, where g is interpreted as the real rate of interest minus the rate of technical progress in the discovery, extraction, and processing of energy resources. Then, according to Hotelling's Law, g is equivalent to the real rate of change in the energy resource price. We will examine time-series and rational expectation formulations of energy/capital price expectations in future research.

In the previous paragraphs we have developed a utilization-adjusted measure of capital input and compared it to the traditional measure. We now consider the implications of vintage utilization adjustment for multifactor productivity measurement. Growth accountants and productivity analysts typically measure the rate of multifactor productivity growth (r_{MFP}) as the growth rate in output (r_y) minus the growth rate of aggregate input (r_x), where the latter is computed as cost-share weighted growth in each of the N component inputs, that is

$$(15) \qquad r_{\text{MFP}_t} = r_{y,t} - r_{x,t} = r_{y,t} - \sum_{i=1}^{N} w_{i,t}\, r_{x_i,t},$$

and where $w_{i,t}$ is the arithmetic mean of the cost share of the ith input in the total costs of all N inputs for periods t and $t-1$.[8] Since (15) is the basic relation employed in most growth accounting analyses, improvements in data construction, as well as controversies among researchers, can often be described in terms of measurement issues involving output and input quantities (affecting the r_i), or involving value measurements (affecting the w_i).[9]

To highlight the effect on MFP measurement of accounting for energy-price-induced changes in capital utilization, we note first that any two measures of a given input may be related by a scalar, that is

$$(16) \qquad \beta_{i,t} \equiv \frac{x_{i,t}^*}{x_{i,t}}.$$

The growth rate in one measure of an input may be written as the sum of the growth rates of the other measure and the ratio of the two measures, that is,

$$(17) \qquad r_{x_{i,t}}^* = r_{\beta_{i,t}} + r_{x_{i,t}}.$$

Substituting (17) into (15) and denoting the alternative measure of MFP growth as MFP*, we have

$$(18) \qquad r^*_{\text{MFP}_t} = r_{y,t} - \sum_{i=1}^{N} w_{i,t}(r_{\beta_{i,t}} + r_{x_{i,t}}).$$

Subtracting equation (15) from (18), we obtain the difference in MFP measures associated with the difference in input measures:

$$(19) \qquad r^*_{\text{MFP}_t} - r_{\text{MFP}_t} = - \sum_{i=1}^{N} w_{i,t}\, r_{\beta_{i,t}}.$$

As is seen in (19), the effect on the multifactor productivity growth rate of the alternative measure is given by the negative of the sum of the cost-share weighted differences in growth rates of the scalar relating the alternative measures. Note that this interpretation applies regardless of the source of the differences in the two input measures.

In our case, however, there is ample reason to believe that the utilization-adjusted measure of capital input is preferable to the conventional measure, which takes no account of changes in the relationship between capital service flows and capital stock. The consequences for MFP measurement of incorrectly measuring capital input flows are clear from (19). If vintage-specific utilization rates fell after OPEC-1, then the $r_{\beta_{i,t}}$ term in (19) would be negative, and the difference between the conventional and the new utilization-adjusted measure of MFP growth would be positive, that is, growth in MFP* would be understated using the conventional accounting procedures.

In summary, equations (9) and (12), together with a specification of expected energy/capital prices, provide a model for vintage capital aggregation that explicitly accounts for a firm's decisions regarding the (unobserved) energy efficiency of new capital vintages, as well as its decisions regarding (unobserved) relative vintage utilization rates, given realized energy prices. The model retains the Hicksian aggregation condition, namely that relative vintage-specific valuation weights are constant given relative price expectations. Hence, even though two critical data series are unobserved, we are still able to introduce the effects of energy price shocks into an economic measure of aggregate capital stock. This is accomplished by the judicious use of economic theory and by several plausible assumptions regarding the optimizing behavior of the firm. In contrast to Koopman's worries concerning measurement without theory, measurement here is possible only because of our use of theory.

It remains to consider whether the ability to introduce energy price changes into the capital aggregation procedure is of any practical empirical importance. In particular, does the conceptual possibility of such a channel linking operating cost shocks to economic measures of durable assets have any empirical significance for such derived economic measures as multifactor productivity growth? Equation (19) provides the framework for addressing this question of significance, a question we now consider for Japanese and U.S. manufacturing.

6.4 Empirical Results

Our approach to evaluating the potential empirical importance of the vintage utilization adjustment effect is based on simulation methods. Rather than embedding the capital measurement model of section 6.3 within an econometric model of production and cost involving all factors of production, at this stage of our research we concentrate on evaluating the implications of plausible values of the energy-capital *ex ante* substitution elasticity on MFP growth and on the productivity slowdown for Japan and United States manufacturing industry.[10]

More specifically, we employ equations (1), (9), and (10) together with expected relative life-cycle prices and real investment, to calculate the aggregate capital utilization adjustment coefficient, $B_{K,t}$, for three assumed values of the *ex ante* energy-capital substitution elasticity, $\sigma = (1.0, .667, .333)$.[11] We then employ the three estimates of $B_{K,t}$ for each country in evaluating the capital utilization effect upon traditional measures of productivity growth and upon the productivity slowdown that began in Japanese and U.S. manufacturing industries in 1973.

One other issue requires further discussion, namely the relation between equipment and structures in accounting for vintage utilization effects. Clearly our motivation of utilization-adjusted aggregate capital stock measures seems particularly plausible with respect to equipment capital, for firms have considerable scope in adjusting utilization between machines and other equipment within a single plant and between plants. For structures, the notion of utilization adjustment, while still meaningful, seems more problematic. Of course, the firm may reduce or increase the number of shifts being worked in a particular plant (structure) depending upon the thermal integrity of the buildings, but it seems likely that the *ex ante* substitution elasticity for structures will be significantly smaller than that for equipment.

Rather than complicate our simulations by creating a grid of *ex ante* substitution elasticities for both equipment and structures, we instead adopt the assumption that the *ex ante* substitution elasticity between structures and energy equals zero. Further we assume a Cobb-Douglas relation between equipment and structures capital goods. With these assumptions the measure of aggregate utilization-adjusted capital stock becomes

$$(20) \qquad K_t^* = K_{E,t}^{*\alpha} K_{S,t}^{*(1-\alpha)} = (B_{E,t}^{\alpha} K_{E,t}^{\alpha} B_{S,t}^{1-\alpha} K_{S,t}^{(1-\alpha)}$$
$$= B_{E,t}^{\alpha} B_{S,t}^{1-\alpha} K_{E,t}^{\alpha} B_{S,t}^{1-\alpha} K_{S,t}^{(1-\alpha)} = B_{E,t}^{\alpha} K_t ,$$

since $B_{S,t} = 1$. In the subsequent empirical simulations, we calculate α as the average value share of equipment services in total capital services in 1974–75.

Note that this assumption of different values for the equipment and structures *ex ante* energy-capital substitution elasticity implies a slight modification to the expression for the utilization adjustment elasticity (eq. [11]). In particular, we now have

(21)
$$\frac{\partial \ln B_{K,t}}{\partial \ln P_{EK,t}^*} = \frac{\partial \ln K_t^*}{\partial \ln P_{EK,t}^*} = -\alpha\sigma.$$

Thus, the extent of the aggregate capital utilization adjustment to an unexpected energy price change depends upon the extent to which new capital equipment embodies differing energy efficiency compared with older equipment vintages, and the cost share of equipment services in total capital services.

Next we consider the formation of expected relative life-cycle costs. As was noted above, $P_{EK,t}^*$ is the value of an expected life-cycle relative price function affecting the optimal energy efficiency embodied in new equipment investment. In choosing such optimal energy efficiency, firms are assumed to discount expected energy/capital prices $\hat{P}_{EK,t+s}$ by the real discount rate r, recognizing that equipment put in place at the beginning of the next time period physically deteriorates at the annual rate δ until it is physically scrapped in T years. We therefore define $P_{EK,t}^*$ as the life-cycle discounted forecast made at time t (eq. [12]), which in turn equals the weighted sum of the expected or predicted relative future prices, say $\hat{P}_{EK,t+s}$.

We now turn to an analysis of the implications of energy price changes for measuring utilization-adjusted aggregate capital stock. As noted above, we employ equations (9) and (20)—together with historical real investment, expected relative life-cycle costs based on the constant growth assumption, and the three assumed values of the *ex ante* energy-capital substitution elasticity ($\sigma = 1.0, .667, .333$)—to calculate the traditional and utilization-adjusted aggregate capital stocks, which in turn determine three estimates of the aggregate capital utilization adjustment coefficient, $B_{K,t}$.[12] Table 6.3 and figures 6.4 and 6.5 below report the estimates of $B_{K,t}$ for the period 1958–81 for Japanese and U.S. manufacturing sectors. For Japan (fig. 6.4), the aggregate capital utilization adjustment coefficients (B_K) are slightly above 1.0 for the period 1958–71, reflecting the fact that expected relative life-cycle costs were generally falling since 1929 (see fig. 6.2). For the period 1972–73, the B_K values drop slightly below 1.0 due to energy price increases in those years, two full years before the sharp increase of the first energy price shock. The first OPEC price shock, then, significantly reduced B_K from 0.91 ($\sigma = .33$) to 0.77 ($\sigma = 1.0$) in 1974 with a slight further decline in 1975 followed by rapid improvement through 1978.

Japanese B_K values in 1978 are, however, still some .04 to .09 below their 1973 levels. The second energy price shock in 1979–80 had a smaller percentage effect upon B_K in Japan than did the earlier price shock, with the absolute affect being only slightly greater, for example, $B_K = 0.75$ ($\sigma = 1.0$) in

Table 6.3 **Japanese and U.S. Manufacturing Industry Aggregate Capital Utilization Adjustment Coefficients for Selected Values of _s_**

Period	United States			Japan		
	$B_K(1.0)$	$B_K(.67)$	$B_K(.33)$	$B_K(1.0)$	$B_K(.67)$	$B_K(.33)$
1958	1.045	1.029	1.014	1.014	1.008	1.004
1959	1.070	1.046	1.022	1.024	1.016	1.007
1960	1.068	1.044	1.021	1.022	1.014	1.007
1961	1.058	1.038	1.018	1.022	1.015	1.007
1962	1.053	1.034	1.017	1.015	1.010	1.005
1963	1.052	1.034	1.016	1.004	1.002	1.001
1964	1.050	1.032	1.015	1.011	1.007	1.003
1965	1.054	1.035	1.017	1.010	1.007	1.003
1966	1.055	1.036	1.017	1.016	1.011	1.005
1967	1.055	1.036	1.017	1.023	1.015	1.007
1968	1.050	1.032	1.016	1.018	1.012	1.006
1969	1.046	1.030	1.014	1.035	1.023	1.011
1970	1.027	1.018	1.008	1.027	1.018	1.009
1971	1.010	1.006	1.003	.980	.986	.993
1972	1.003	1.002	1.000	.985	.990	.995
1973	.953	.968	.983	.995	.996	.998
1974	.751	.822	.904	.766	.833	.910
1975	.791	.849	.918	.762	.827	.905
1976	.827	.874	.931	.785	.842	.913
1977	.839	.883	.936	.824	.870	.928
1978	.868	.904	.947	.907	.929	.959
1979	.811	.863	.925	.857	.894	.941
1980	.738	.807	.892	.747	.813	.896
1981	.749	.813	.894	.770	.828	.903

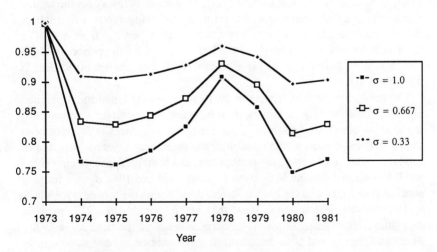

Fig. 6.4 Japan utilization adjustment coefficients B_{kt}

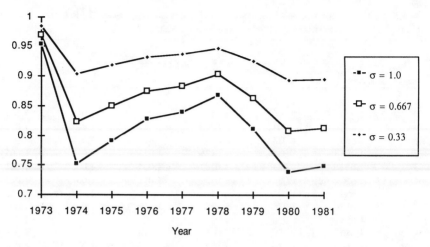

Fig. 6.5   U.S. utilization adjustment coefficients B_{kt}

1980. This is due, in part, to the smaller energy/capital price increase in the second shock in Japan (see table 6.1). Some recovery is indicated in 1981, the last year for which we are able to assemble consistent input accounts for the two countries.

A similar pattern of B_K values is obtained for United States manufacturing industry (fig. 6.5). The primary differences from the results for Japan are (a) a falling B_K from 1970–73 due to the fact that energy/capital prices reached their lowest sample point in 1969 and then began to rise in 1970; (b) slightly higher B_Ks prior to 1971, due primarily to the United States having a relatively older, more efficient, capital stock; (c) a quicker initial recovery for the United States from the first price shock, due primarily to having a more efficient capital stock and to a higher rate of investment in 1974 (see fig. 6.3); and (d) a somewhat lower recovery of B_K in the United States for the period 1973–78 due mostly, we believe, to the lower overall level of equipment investment in the United States.

The similarities and differences in the B_K measures for Japan and the United States are more clearly seen in figure 6.6, where the coefficients corresponding to $\sigma = 0.667$ are presented. Recall that the differences in B_K have been shown to depend upon a combination of the preembargo vintage structure of capital goods, relative energy/capital prices, and post-1973 investment behavior. Perhaps most striking in figure 6.6 is that 1974 and 1980 B_Ks are roughly equal in both Japan and the United States, even though the second price shock was significantly less severe in Japan than in the United States. This suggests the critical importance of the post-embargo investment, particularly in 1978–81. Both Japanese and U.S. manufacturing firms appear to have made significant progress in "insulating" themselves from advance energy price shocks.

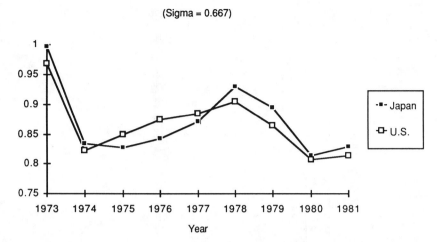

Fig. 6.6   Japan and U.S. utilization adjustment coefficient

Finally, we consider the effects of aggregate capital utilization adjustment upon MFP growth in Japan and U.S. manufacturing. In section 6.2 we noted three factors relating to the traditional MFP measures. In particular, (*a*) there was evidence of a productivity slowdown in both countries between the 1958–73 and 1973–81 periods; (*b*) the period 1973–75 made the greatest contribution to the productivity slowdown, especially in Japan; and (*c*) the second price shock is coincident with a much smaller reduction in MFP than the first price shock. We now ask, to what extent are these patterns of coincidence between price shocks and MFP growth affected by employing our new measure of utilization-adjusted aggregate capital?

Table 6.4 presents MFP indices based on the traditional measure of aggregate capital, and for the three measures of the utilization-adjusted aggregate capital for the Japanese and U.S. manufacturing sectors. Several important features are worth noting. First, it is instructive to employ equation (19) in examining the bias introduced in traditional MFP measures by ignoring the vintage utilization adjustment effect. In general, traditional MFP measures will understate (overstate) productivity growth depending on whether MFP* − MFP is positive (negative). Inspection of table 6.4, part A, reveals that MFP* − MFP is usually positive in *both* pre- and postembargo years, and that, as expected, the extent of the bias depends directly upon the size of the *ex ante* energy-capital substitution elasticity. Apparently, the traditional MFP measure has been underestimating productivity growth for quite some time, not just since 1973.

Second, while productivity growth in both the Japanese and U.S. manufacturing industries has been underestimated for some time, the extent of the bias differs between the pre- and postembargo periods. Values of the bias in per-

Table 6.4   Japanese and U.S. Manufacturing Industries' Traditional and Utilization-Adjusted Multifactor Productivity Indices

A. Multifactor productivity indices:

Year	Japan				United States			
	σ = .000	σ = 1.000	σ = .667	σ = .333	σ = .000	σ = 1.000	σ = .667	σ = .333
1958	.791	.782	.783	.783	.848	.841	.842	.844
1959	.794	.784	.785	.786	.856	.847	.849	.851
1960	.836	.828	.829	.830	.870	.862	.864	.866
1961	.847	.839	.840	.841	.875	.867	.869	.871
1962	.862	.856	.856	.857	.893	.886	.888	.890
1963	.869	.863	.864	.864	.910	.903	.905	.906
1964	.871	.865	.866	.866	.938	.932	.933	.935
1965	.872	.866	.867	.867	.946	.939	.941	.943
1966	.885	.879	.880	.881	.953	.947	.949	.951
1967	.913	.907	.908	.909	.941	.935	.937	.939
1968	.939	.934	.935	.936	.951	.945	.947	.949
1969	.960	.954	.955	.957	.955	.949	.951	.952
1970	.983	.978	.980	.981	.946	.941	.942	.943
1971	.980	.981	.981	.980	.958	.954	.955	.956

1972	.990	.991	.990	.990	.978	.974	.975	.976
1973	1.000	1.000	1.000	1.000	1.000	1.000	1.000	1.000
1974	.961	.999	.988	.975	.992	1.005	1.001	.997
1975	.952	.991	.980	.966	.986	.995	.993	.990
1976	.965	.999	.990	.979	1.002	1.009	1.008	1.006
1977	.973	1.000	.993	.984	1.015	1.021	1.020	1.018
1978	.993	1.001	1.001	.999	1.021	1.025	1.025	1.023
1979	1.009	1.028	1.024	1.018	1.027	1.035	1.034	1.031
1980	1.011	1.056	1.045	1.030	1.033	1.047	1.044	1.039
1981	1.034	1.074	1.065	1.053	1.042	1.056	1.053	1.049
B. Multifactor productivity growth rates, selected periods:								
1958–81	1.172	1.389	1.346	1.296	.900	.995	.997	.950
1958–73	1.575	1.653	1.644	1.640	1.105	1.161	1.153	1.137
1973–81	.419	.896	.790	.648	.516	.683	.648	.600
1973–75	−2.430	−.451	−1.005	−1.715	−.702	−.250	−.351	−.501
1975–78	1.414	.335	.709	1.126	1.120	.995	1.063	1.099
1978–81	1.358	2.374	2.087	1.770	.681	.998	.902	.840
C. Estimated bias in traditionally measured MFP slowdown (in %):								
1958–73	.078	.078	.069	.065		.056	.048	.032
1973–81	.477	.477	.371	.229		.167	.132	.084

centage points for the periods 1958–73 and 1973–81, and for each assumed value of σ, are presented in table 6.4, part C. These bias estimates are calculated as the difference between traditional and utilization-adjusted MFP growth rate estimates. Note that in both countries the bias associated with the earlier period is some three to four times smaller than that associated with the postembargo period for all three values of σ. Further, the bias associated with the U.S. manufacturing industry is consistently less than that for Japan by a factor of more than three. Hence, accounting for vintage utilization adjustment effects would seem to be significantly more important in measuring postembargo Japanese manufacturing industry productivity growth than it is for the United States.

Third, and closely related to the above, it appears that traditional productivity measures have overstated the productivity growth slowdown in both the Japanese and U.S. manufacturing sectors. Recall that the slowdown is measured as the difference between per annum growth rates in 1958–73 and 1973–81. Hence the bias in the traditional estimates of the slowdown would be the difference between the traditional and vintage utilization-adjusted estimates of the slowdown. Positive (negative) values calculated in this way indicate overstatement (understatement) of the productivity slowdown. Based on the data in table 6.4, part B, we find that the bias estimates for all values of σ for both Japan and the United States are negative, with values of 0.399%, 0.302%, and 0.164% per year for Japan and 0.111%, 0.084%, and 0.052% per year for the United States as σ = (1.0, .667, .333), respectively. Thus, ignoring the utilization adjustment effect leads to a consistent overstatement of the productivity growth slowdown, with the bias some 3.2–3.6 times greater in Japan than for the United States. Thus, not only is the vintage utilization adjustment more important in measuring productivity growth in Japan, it is also more important in measuring the extent of the productivity growth slowdown since 1973.

Fourth, the pattern of traditional and utilization-adjusted productivity growth within the 1973–81 period varies considerably, with both similarities and significant differences between the two countries. For the three subperiods—1973–75, 1975–78, and 1978–81—traditional MFP estimates understate, overstate, and understate utilization-adjusted MFP, respectively, in both Japan and the United States. Most striking is the effect of the utilization adjustment on traditional MFP measures for the period 1973–75, the period including the first energy price shock. While the traditional MFP measure decreased 2.43% per year (0.702% per year) for Japan (the United States) in that period, allowing for utilization adjustment mitigates the decrease by 81.4%, 58.6%, and 29.4% in Japan and 64.4%, 50.0%, and 28.6% in the United States for σ = (1.0, .667, .333), respectively. Hence, even for the low estimate of σ = .333, the utilization adjustment effect in both Japan and the United States accounts for almost 30% of the reduction in productivity growth rates coincident with the first energy price shock.

For the middle subperiod, 1975–78, the traditional measure overstates productivity growth in both countries, due to a combination of flat, even falling energy/capital prices plus new, more energy-efficient investment.

For the period 1978–81, which includes the second energy price shock, traditional measures again understate MFP growth in both countries. Moreover, while traditional measures decrease only slightly from 1975–78 for Japan (1.415 to 1.358), the decrease is some 64% (1.12 to 0.681) for the United States. Hence, for traditional MFP measures, it appears that the second price shock was coincident with a much greater reduction in U.S. productivity growth than in Japan.

However, a very different picture emerges when we compare the utilization-adjusted MFP. In particular, the Japan utilization-adjusted productivity growth rates increase between 1975–78 and 1978–81 by 608.7%, 194.4%, and 57.2%, while U.S. MFP growth changes by 0.3%, -15.1%, and -23.6%, for $\sigma = (1.0, .667, .333)$, respectively. For Japan, the energy/capital price reduction in the earlier period, coupled with the dramatic increase in investment/output ratios beginning in 1978, leads to very different MFP estimates when these economic conditions are expressed via the firm's efficiency choice and vintage utilization decisions. The effects are perhaps less dramatic for the United States, given its particular energy/capital price history and the fact that increasing investment/output ratios began earlier in 1974.

In summary, we find that our simple model accounting for the unobservable effects of efficiency choice and vintage utilization decisions has significant implications for productivity growth measurement. Our simulation results suggest that these effects differ substantially for the two countries considered here, depending critically upon the history of energy/capital prices, the vintage structure of surviving capital goods, and historical investment patterns, particularly in the postembargo period. Variation is also a function of the value assumed for a critical parameter in the model, the *ex ante* energy-capital substitution elasticity. Most important, we find that even for low values of σ, vintage utilization adjustment is an important factor in measuring both productivity growth and the so-called productivity growth slowdown in the Japanese and U.S. manufacturing sectors. These simulation results suggest the importance of further econometric research focused on estimation of this key parameter.

6.5 Concluding Remarks

Our purpose in this paper has been to employ a model accounting for the unobserved effects of vintage efficiency and utilization choice in measuring aggregate utilized capital services and multifactor productivity growth in Japanese and U.S. manufacturing. The approach has been exploratory, employing simulations in which historical data are combined with assumptions about expected energy/capital prices and the *ex ante* energy-capital substitution elasticity to estimate ranges for aggregate capital utilization adjustment effects on capital and MFP growth measures. The results suggest that accounting for these unobserved effects is in fact important; even low values of σ result in nontrivial impacts upon capital and productivity measures, especially in the Japanese manufacturing sector. Clearly, more systematic econometric research is warranted on this important issue.

Several modeling and measurement issues must also be considered in future research. These include (i) the formation of expected relative life-cycle prices; (ii) the possibility of alternative adjustment mechanisms that account for changing expected utilization over the remaining life of the asset, not just the current period utilization adjustments considered in this paper; and (iii) consideration of nonenergy factors contributing to utilization effects, in particular environmental regulations.

With respect to (ii), it is worth noting that utilization adjustments should affect expected present values of quasi rents, and thus should ultimately affect depreciation patterns of durable assets. In this context, it is of interest to note that the study by Hulten, Robertson, and Wykoff (1987) suggests that large energy-price-shock-induced depreciation effects did not occur. Research that reconciles these findings should receive high priority.

Finally, this paper highlights the fact that energy-price-induced productivity growth effects vary significantly between the Japanese and U.S. manufacturing industries. It is likely that adding other countries to the data set would increase the diversity of results and would provide a richer collection of analyses and evidence for obtaining better understanding of the economic consequences of the key economic event of the 1970s—the OPEC-induced energy price shocks.

Notes

1. Other leading students of productivity growth analysis also arrive at this conclusion. See, e.g., Kendrick (1983).

2. The pattern of annual energy price and productivity changes for the years 1947–81 in Japanese and U.S. manufacturing are discussed below; see tables 6.1–6.3 for details.

3. In addition to these two facts, Denison (1979) has pointed out that at the level of the aggregate economy, energy is both an input and an output, and thus energy effects tend to cancel out. In our context of the manufacturing sector, this point is, of course, irrelevant.

4. These measures are calculated as growth in output minus the sum of value-share weighted growth in capital, labor, energy, and nonenergy intermediate material inputs.

5. While economists are attracted to the geometric decay assumption, in part because of its analytical convenience, economic statisticians have often tended to employ other assumptions about deterioration profiles. Empirical evidence is mixed, but the

important recent study of Hulten and Wykoff (1981) tends to support the geometric decay form for a wide variety of durable goods.

6. See Diewert (1978) for a discussion of Hicksian aggregation.

7. Incidentally, the most recent vintage would not necessarily be used the most intensively.

8. Because r_{MFP} is computed as a residual, it can capture the effects of all types of errors and omissions. This has led Abramovitz (1956, p. 11) to call it a "measure of our ignorance."

9. See, e.g., the debate among Jorgenson-Griliches (1967, 1972) and Denison (1969).

10. The simulation approach adopted here is similar to that of Mori and Sawa (1985) for the total Japanese manufacturing industry, and to Berndt and Wood (1987) for two-digit SIC U.S. manufacturing industries.

11. Berndt and Wood (1984) have estimated this elasticity for U.S. manufacturing industries employing four alternative specifications of expected life-cycle costs and measurement error. Their estimates range from 0.390 to 0.935, and so are contained in the [0,1] interval. Recall that $\sigma = 0.0$ is equivalent to $B_{K,t} = 1.0$.

12. As will become clear, we require a series on energy/equipment prices roughly one investment cycle prior to the first year of analysis. Since our estimates of equipment depreciation rates are .133 and .135 for Japan and the United States, respectively, and since the starting year for analysis is 1958, the 29-year interval from 1929 to 1958 implies that, in 1958, approximately 1.6% of Japanese and 1.5% of U.S. manufacturing sector equipment investment made in 1929 is still surviving in 1958.

References

Abramovitz, Moses. 1956. Resource and output trends in the United States since 1870. *American Economic Review* 46, no. 2 (May):5–23.

Berndt, Ernst R., and David O. Wood. 1984. Energy price changes and the induced revaluation of durable capital in U.S. manufacturing during the OPEC decade. MIT Energy Laboratory Working Paper No. 84-003. Cambridge, Mass., March.

———. 1987a. Energy price shocks and productivity growth: A survey. In *Energy: Markets and regulation—essays in honor of M. A. Adelman*, ed. R. L. Gordon, H. D. Jacoby, and M. B. Zimmerman. Cambridge, Mass.: MIT Press.

———. 1987b. Interindustry differences in the effects of energy price-induced capital utilization changes on multifactor productivity measurement. In *Advances in the economics of energy and resources*, ed. John R. Moroney, 6:87–123. Greenwich, Conn.: JAI Press.

Denison, Edward F. 1969. Some major issues in productivity analysis: An examination of estimates by Jorgenson and Griliches. *Survey of Current Business* 49, pt. 2 (May): 1–27. (Reprinted in The measurement of productivity, *Survey of Current Business* 52, no. 5, pt. 2 (1972): 37–63.)

———. 1979. *Accounting for slower economic growth*. Washington, D.C.: Brookings Institution.

———. 1985. *Trends in American economic growth*, 1929–1982. Washington D.C.: Brookings Institution.

Diewert, W. Erwin. 1978. Hicks' aggregation theorem and the existence of a real value-added function. In *Production economics: A dual approach to theory and ap-*

plications, ed. Melvyn Fuss and Daniel McFadden, 2:17–51. Amsterdam: North-Holland.

Hulten, Charles R. 1986. Productivity change, capacity utilization, and the sources of efficiency growth. *Journal of Econometrics* 33, no. 1/2 (November):31–50.

Hulten, Charles R., James W. Robertson, and Frank C. Wykoff. 1987. Energy, obsolescence, and the productivity slowdown. In *Technology and capital formation,* ed. Dale W. Jorgenson and Ralph Landau pp. 225–58. Cambridge, Mass.: MIT Press.

Hulten, Charles R., and Frank C. Wykoff. 1981. The measurement of economic depreciation. In *Depreciation, inflation & the taxation of income from capital,* ed. Charles Hulten, 81–125. Washington, DC: Urban Institute Press.

Jorgenson, Dale W., and Zvi Griliches. 1967. The explanation of productivity change. *Review of Economic Studies* 34(3), no. 99 (July):249–82. (Reprinted in The measurement of productivity, *Survey of Current Business* 52, no. 5, pt. 2 (1972): 3–36.)

———. 1972. Issues in growth accounting: A reply to Edward F. Denison. *Survey of Current Business.* Special issue on the measurement of productivity. 52 (5), pt. 2, 65–94.

Kendrick, John W. 1983. *Interindustry differences in productivity growth.* Washington, D.C.: American Enterprise Institute.

McRae, Robert. 1985. The implications of capital revaluation to the demand for energy in Canadian manufacturing. *Papers and Proceedings,* Seventh Annual International Conference of the International Association of Energy Economists, 3–5 June 1985, Bonn.

Mori, Shunseke, and Takamitsu Sawa. 1985. Revaluation of durable capital stock in Japanese manufacturing during the OPEC decade. *Papers and Proceedings,* Seventh Annual International Conference of the International Association of Energy Economists, 3–5 June 1985, Bonn.

Comment
Kanji Yoshioka

Berndt, Mori, Sawa, and Wood present a simple but useful ex ante, ex post model of production in which the vintage-specific utilization rate of production equipment is endogenized. It then analyzes the slowdown in productivity observed in Japan and the United States in light of two important facts. First, it is known that investment in new, energy-efficient plants and equipment tends to be gradual and does not occur instantaneously. Second, it is also well-known that the cost share of energy is rather small.

Although their method is pioneering and suggestive, I believe that more development is needed before it is applicable to the measurement of multifactor productivity during the productivity slowdown. First, before 1973 the energy-relative price had decreased in the United States and had slightly decreased or fluctuated in Japan. Therefore, just after the oil embargo, we would expect to find that the utilization rate of relatively new equipment invested in

Kanji Yoshioka is an associate professor of economics, Keio Economic Observatory, Keio University.

the early 1970s was less than that of old equipment invested in the early 1960s. This does not seem to have happened. Also, it has been said that firms in Japan tried to adapt to the embargo by adding energy-saving investment or by changing only the parts of equipment, and that the utilization rate of new capital equipment was greater than that of the old. If this is so, disaggregation of the assets by energy intensity might be desirable.

As an alternative approach, a model of technical progress with an energy-saving bias in the ex ante aggregator function of energy and capital might be able to explain this "reverse utilization" problem. According to the Japanese experience, the input coefficient of the energy in the energy-using manufacturing industries (like aluminum, pig iron, and flat glass) has been almost constantly decreasing even before 1973, while the input coefficient of the capital input has been increasing (see Economic Planning Agency's *White Book of Economy* [Keizai Hakusho, 1979]).

Although these facts are not conclusive, they suggest that technical progress (including energy-saving bias or capital-embodied technical change) might have been dominant in these industries. To insert this technical progress term into the ex ante aggregator function would be one solution to the above-mentioned problem.

As a second general point, it should be noted that the authors' definition of utilization rate is somewhat ambiguous. The key equation for endogenizing the utilization rate is the short-run variable cost expressed in equation (4). In this equation, the utilization rates are the only variables, and cost is linear in them. Therefore, if utilization rates fall sufficiently, the most efficient vintage-specific capital equipment alone will be used, and if they are defined to have an upper bound like 1, the short-run cost minimization is in the corner equilibrium. This will be an undesirable property of their model.

7 Productivity Growth and Changes in the Terms of Trade in Japan and the United States

Catherine Morrison and W. Erwin Diewert

7.1 Introduction

The productivity change in a closed economy going from year $t - 1$ to year t is usually defined as an index of outputs divided by an index of primary inputs. Under certain assumptions, a productivity improvement in an economy can be identified with an outward shift in the economy's production possibilities set.

In a small open economy, the domestic production possibilities set is augmented by the possibility of exchanging exports for imports at constant world prices. Over time, this augmented production possibilities set can shift outwards for at least two different reasons: (i) improvements in efficiency or productivity (as in a closed economy) and (ii) improvements in the economy's terms of trade; that is, the prices of imported goods fall relative to the prices of exported goods. A third source of outward shift in an open economy can also be distinguished: namely, the economy can increase its merchandise trade deficit. This will allow domestic consumption and investment (which we shall call domestic sales below) to increase in the short run. However, this third source of outward shift will generally be temporary in nature (unless the trade deficit is financed by gifts or increased foreign aid) since the deficit in the current period will have to be repaid in future periods.

A framework for measuring these three types of outward shift in the context of production theory was developed recently by Diewert and Morrison (1986). We shall use this framework in the present paper to measure Japa-

Catherine Morrison is an associate professor of economics at Tufts University and a research associate of the National Bureau of Economic Research. W. Erwin Diewert is a professor of economics at the University of British Columbia and a research associate of the National Bureau of Economic Research.

Research support from the National Foundation, grant SES-8420937, is gratefully acknowledged.

nese and U.S. productivity and changes in the terms of trade for the years 1968–82.

In order to give the reader an intuitive, nonalgebraic explanation of the three types of outward shift mentioned above, we devote two sections of the paper to geometric exposition. In section 7.2 below, we illustrate the shifts using the traditional general equilibrium approach to (static) trade theory.[1] The problem with empirically implementing this traditional approach is that the informational requirements are very high: detailed price and quantity information on the allocations of producers, consumers, and governments is required.

Thus, in section 7.3 below, we illustrate the production theory approach that requires only producer information. In this approach, pioneered by Kohli (1978), all merchandise imports are channeled through the domestic production sector before being transformed into domestic goods. Also, exported goods are not regarded as domestic goods (but they can be highly substitutable with domestic goods).

In sections 7.4–7.7, we present the algebra of the production theory approach. The empirically oriented reader can skim over these sections and proceed to the empirical results.

In section 7.4, we define the sales function, which gives the maximum value of domestic sales a small, open, competitive economy can achieve, given the period t domestic technology and given domestic prices, export prices, import prices, domestic primary inputs, and the maximum merchandise trade deficit that the economy is allowed to run. In section 7.5, we use the sales function in order to define various theoretical productivity and terms-of-trade indexes.

In order to be able to evaluate these theoretical indexes using observable data, it is necessary to make some further assumptions. Thus, in section 7.6, we assume that the sales function in each period has a translog representation, and this assumption enables us to evaluate exactly the various theoretical indexes.

In section 7.7, we use a somewhat different approach in order to evaluate our theoretical indexes: a first- and second-order approximation approach. This approach and the previous translog approach were developed by Diewert and Morrison (1986).

In section 7.8, we turn to a description of the Japanese data, and we use this data in section 7.9 to calculate Japanese indexes of productivity, terms of trade, and "welfare" change. A similar program using U.S. data is followed in sections 7.10 and 7.11. Finally, section 7.12 offers some comparisons between the recent U.S. and Japanese productivity experience.

7.2   The Geometry of the Traditional General Equilibrium Approach

Consider an economy that produces two finally demanded goods, y_1 and y_2, using M primary inputs, $v_1, v_2, \ldots, v_M$, during two periods. For simplicity, we shall hold the utilization of primary inputs constant during the two periods. The general equilibrium of the economy during the two periods is represented in figure 7.1.

The domestic production possibilities set for the economy in period 1 is the region enclosed by OT_1T_1'. The international trading line that the economy faces is P_1P_1' (which has slope $-p_1^1/p_2^1$, where p_i^1 is the internationally fixed price for good i in period 1, $i = 1,2$). Note that this price line is just tangent to the frontier of the domestic production possibilities set T_1T_1'. The trade-augmented production possibilities set is the region bounded by OP_1P_1'.

For simplicity, assume that there is only one consumer in the economy. The highest indifference curve that is just tangent to the trade-augmented production possibilities set is U_1U_1' and the point of tangency occurs at C in figure 7.1. Thus, in period 1, the economy will export AB units of y_2 in exchange for BC units of the imported good, y_1. We are assuming that there is no merchandise trade surplus or deficit in period 1.

We turn now to an analysis of the equilibrium in period 2. We assume that the economy's domestic production possibilities set shifts outward in period 2 (due to technical progress) to the frontier T_2T_2'. A measure of productivity gain in this economy might be $OT_2/OT_1 > 1$ (measured in terms of good 1) or $OT_2'/OT_1' > 1$ (measured in terms of good 2).

Instead of having balanced trade in period 2, let us assume that the economy is able to run a balance of trade deficit of size T_2T_3 in period 2; that is, we assume that these imports do not have to be paid for by exports in period 2. The effect of this assumption is to shift the domestic production possibilities frontier T_2T_2' to the right by T_2T_3 units, which results in a period-2 effective frontier T_3T_2'.

If the international prices of y_1 and y_2 remained unchanged in period 2, the economy's period-2 trade-augmented technology set would be OP_2P_2' and the

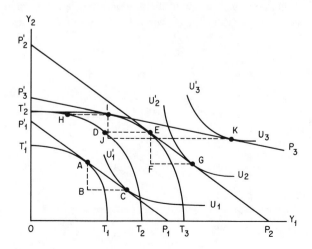

Fig. 7.1   The general equilibrium approach

highest indifference curve tangent to this set is U_2U_2' with the point of tangency at G. The point of domestic producer equilibrium would be D, the balance of trade deficit effect would be DE, and EF units of y_2 would be exported in exchange for FG units of imports.

However, the international prices are unlikely to remain constant. Suppose that the new period-2 international prices are p_i^2 for $i = 1,2$. The price line P_3P_3' has slope $-p_1^2/p_2^2$ and is tangent to the deficit-augmented domestic technology set OT_3T_2'. The highest indifference curve tangent to P_3P_3' is U_3U_3', and the point of tangency is at K. The terms-of-trade effect is some measure of the distance between the indifference curves U_2U_2' and U_3U_3'. In this case, the price of exports has increased relative to imports (i.e., $p_1^2/p_2^2 < p_1^1/p_2^1$), and so the terms-of-trade effect is positive and analogous to a domestic technology productivity improvement. Thus the final point of producer equilibrium in period 2 is at H, the distance HI represents the balance of trade deficit effect, and IJ units of exports are exchanged for JK units of imports.

We turn now to an alternative paradigm based on producer theory that will allow us to define counterparts to the above productivity, deficit, and terms-of-trade effects.

7.3 The Geometry of the Production Theory Approach

As in the previous section, we shall, for simplicity, hold the economy's primary inputs constant during the two periods. There are three additional goods in the economy: (i) a domestic consumption good, y_d, (ii) an exported good, y_x, and (iii) an imported good, y_m.

The frontier of the period-1 production possibilities set can be represented by a surface in y_d, y_x, and y_m space. We can represent this surface in a two-dimensional diagram by a family of domestic isoproduct curves. Thus, in figure 7.2, the curve T_1T_1' represents combinations of exports produced and imports utilized that are consistent with the production of a fixed amount of the domestic good, say $y_d = 95$. The curves T_2T_2', T_3T_3', and T_4T_4' represent com-

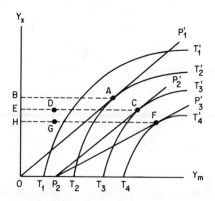

Fig. 7.2 The production theory approach

binations of exports and imports that are consistent with *higher* levels of domestic production in period 1, say y_d = 100, 105, and 110, respectively. Thus, for a fixed amount of imports, the economy's exports can increase only at the cost of diminishing domestic production.

In period 1, the rest of the world offers our small economy the trading line OP'_1, which has slope p^1_m/p^1_x, where $p^1_m > 0$ is the world price for a unit of the imported good and $p^1_x > 0$ is the world price for a unit of the exported good. The highest domestic isoproduct curve tangent to the trading line OP'_1 is $T_2T'_2$ and the point of tangency is at A. Thus, in period 1, the economy imports AB units of y_m in exchange for OB units of y_x. Note that for simplicity we are assuming balanced trade in period 1.

In period 2, the frontier of the production possibilities set will be a new surface in y_d, y_x, y_m space. Thus surface can be represented by a new family of domestic isoproduct curves in y_x, y_m space. For simplicity, we shall assume that this new family of curves coincides with the old period-1 family, except that, due to technical progress, the old curves represent higher levels of domestic output; for example, the curve $T_1T'_1$ now represents, say, y_d = 100 instead of 105, while $T_2T'_2$, $T_3T'_3$, and $T_4T'_4$ now represent domestic output levels of, say, 105, 110, 115. This relabeling (or shifting in the general case) of the curves $T_iT'_i$ represents the productivity effect in our new paradigm.

Suppose that in period 2, the economy is allowed to run a merchandise trade deficit of size OP_2. If the world prices of exports and imports remain constant, the new period-2 trading line would be $P_2P'_2$; the highest isoproduct curve tangent to this line is $T_3T'_3$, and the point of tangency is C. The economy would trade CD units of imports for OE units of exports and receive an additional $ED = OP_2$ units of imports by running a trade deficit. In this paradigm, the deficit effect is OP_2.

However, it is unlikely that the prices of exports and imports will remain constant. Thus, suppose that p^2_x and p^2_m are the prices of exports and imports in period 2 and the price line $P_2P'_3$ has slope equal to $p^2_m/p^2_x < p^1_m/p^1_x$. The highest domestic isoproduct curve tangent to $P_2P'_3$ is $T_4T'_4$, and the point of tangency occurs at F. Note that the economy's improved terms of trade have allowed it to move from C to F; that is, to a higher level of domestic output. This increase in domestic output is the terms-of-trade effect. Thus, in period 2, the economy will exchange FG units of the imported good for OH units of the exported good, and the balance of trade deficit effect is HG equal to OP_2.

We now turn to the derivation of general analytical techniques that will allow us to quantify the above three effects in the case where we have many domestic, import, export and primary goods and the utilization of primary factors of production is not held constant.

7.4 The Sales Function and Price and Quantity Effects

All of our theoretical indexes and effects may be defined in terms of the economy's period $t - 1$ and period t sales functions. The period t *sales func-*

tion S^t for the economy's period t technology set Γ^t (or production function) may be defined as follows:[2]

(1)
$$S^t(p_d, p_x, p_m, v, v_0)$$
$$\equiv \max_{y_d, y_x, y_m}\{p_d \cdot y_d : (y_d, y_x, y_m, v) \quad \text{belongs to } \Gamma^t;$$
$$p_x y_x - p_m \cdot y_m + v_0 \geq 0\}.$$

The sales function S depends on six sets of variables: (i) t indexes the technology set Γ^t, which corresponds to the period t domestic technology set that the economy can utilize; (ii) $p_d \equiv (p_{d1}, p_{d2}, \ldots, p_{dN_d})$, a vector of positive prices of the N_d domestic goods in the economy; (iii) $p_x \equiv (p_{x1}, p_{x2}, \ldots, p_{xNx})$, a vector of positive prices of the N_d export goods that the economy can produce, denominated in units of domestic currency; (iv) $p_m \equiv (p_{m1}, p_{m2}, \ldots, p_{mNm})$, a vector of positive prices of the N_m imported goods that the economy utilizes, denominated in units of domestic currency; (v) $v \equiv (v_1, v_2, \ldots, v_M)$, a vector of M positive amounts of primary inputs that the economy is utilizing; and (vi) v_0 is the balance of trade deficit (denominated in domestic currency) that the economy is allowed to run (if v_0 is negative, then $-v_0 > 0$ is the surplus that the economy is accumulating).

The nonnegative vectors y_d, y_x, and y_m of dimension N_d, N_x, and N_M, respectively, are vectors of domestic production, exports, and imports respectively. The notation $p_d \cdot y_d$ stands for the inner product of the vectors p_d and y_d; that is, $p_d \cdot y_d \equiv \sum_{i=1}^{Nd} p_{di} y_{di}$.

The sales function $S^t (p_d, p_x, p_m, v, v_0)$ tells us how much domestic output the period t economy can produce (valued at the reference prices p_d) given that the vector of primary inputs v is available, exports may be sold at prices p_x, imports may be purchased at prices p_m, and the private production sector is allowed to utilize a balance of trade deficit of size v_0. The sales function is the producer theory counterpart to Woodland's (1980) indirect trade utility function.

Define the private production sector's period t (net) deficit (surplus if negative) on merchandise trade by

(2) $v_0^t = p_m^t \cdot y_m^t - p_x^t \cdot y_x^t = $ value of imports $-$ value of exports.

When we evaluate the sales function S^t at the observed period t arguments, using the assumption of competitive profit maximizing behavior and a constant-returns-to-scale assumption on the technology set Γ^t, we find that

(3) $S^t (p_d^t, p_x^t, p_m^t, v^t, v_0^t) = p_d^t \cdot y_d^t = w^t \cdot v^t + v_0^t.$

In addition to the above assumptions, we assume that S^t is differentiable with respect to its arguments when evaluated at p^t, v^t, v_0^t. Then, adapting the arguments in Diewert (1983, 1092–94), we find that the first-order partial derivatives of S^t are equal to the following observable vectors:

$$\nabla_{p_d} S^t(p_d^t, p_x^t, p_m^t, v^t, v_0^t) = y_d^t,$$

(4)
$$\nabla_{p_x} S^t(p_d^t, p_x^t, p_m^t, v^t, v_0^t) = y_x^t,$$

$$\nabla_{p_m} S^t(p_d^t, p_x^t, p_m^t, v^t, v_0^t) = -y_m^t,$$

$$\nabla_v S^t(p_d^t, p_x^t, p_m^t, v^t, v_0^t) = w^t,$$

and
$$\frac{\partial S^t}{\partial v_0}(p_d^t, p_x^t, p_m^t, v^t, v_0^t) = 1.$$

The notion $\nabla_v S^t(p_d^t, p_x^t, p_m^t, v^t, v_0^t) \equiv [\partial S^t/\partial v_1, \partial S^t/\partial v_2, \ldots, \partial S^t/\partial v_M]$ stands for the vector of first-order partial derivatives of S^t with respect to the M components of $v \equiv [v_1, v_2, \ldots, v_M]$. We note also that $w^t \equiv [w_1^t, w_2^t, \ldots, w_M^t]$ is the vector of wage rates and rental prices that the primary factors charge to producers in period t.

It is evident from (3) and (4) that the deficit v_0 plays a role that is similar to the role of a primary input: a bigger deficit (holding other things constant) will lead to a bigger equilibrium value of domestic sales.

A last bit of notation will be required, on occasion, in what follows. Define $N \equiv N_d + N_x + N_m$ as the total number of nonprimary input goods in the economy, and define the following N dimensional vectors of prices and quantities: $p \equiv (p_d, p_x, p_m) = (p_1, p_2, \ldots, p_N)$ and $y \equiv (y_d, y_x, -y_m) \equiv (y_1, y_2, \ldots, y_N)$.

We shall conclude this section by utilizing the sales function in order to define various price and quantity effects. These effects will be useful in subsequent sections.

For each nonprimary input good n, define the period t theoretical Paasche and Laspeyres price effects, P_{Pn}^t and P_{Ln}^t and their geometric mean by:

(5) $$P_{Pn}^t \equiv S^t(p^t, v^t, v_0^t) /$$
$$S^t(p_1^t, \ldots, p_{n-1}^t, p_n^{t-1}, p_{n+1}^t, \ldots, p_N^t, v^t, v_0^t);$$

(6) $$P_{Ln}^t \equiv S^{t-1}(p_1^{t-1}, \ldots, p_{n-1}^{t-1}, p_n^t, p_{n+1}^{t-1}, \ldots, p_N^{t-1}, v^{t-1}, v_0^{t-1}) /$$
$$S^t(p^{t-1}, v^{t-1}, v_0^{t-1});$$

(7) $$P_n^t \equiv (P_{Ln}^t P_{Pn}^t)^{1/2}; \quad n = 1, 2, \ldots, N.$$

The indexes P_{Ln}^t and P_{Pn}^t provide answers to the following hypothetical global comparative-statistics-type question: What is the proportional change in domestic sales that can be attributed to the change in the nth output price going from period $t-1$ to t, p_n^{t-1}, to p_n^t, holding constant other prices and primary input availabilities, holding the technology constant at the period $t-1$ or period t level, and holding the economy's balance of trade deficit (or surplus) constant at the period $t-1$ level, v_0^{t-1}, or at the period t level v_0^t? We call P_{Pn}^t a Paasche-type index because the constant reference prices and quantities are current period or period t variables, while the reference variables being held constant in the Laspeyres-type index P_{Ln}^t are the base period or period $t-1$ variables.

We turn now to the input side and for each primary input m, we define the period t theoretical Paasche and Laspeyres quantity effects, Q_{Pm}^t and Q_{Lm}^t, and their geometric mean as follows:

$$(8) \qquad Q_{Pm}^t \equiv S^t(p^t, v^t, v_0^t)/S^t(p^t, v_1^t, \ldots, v_{m-1}^t, v_m^{t-1}, v_{m+1}^t, \ldots, v_M^t, v_0^t);$$

$$(9) \qquad Q_{Lm}^t \equiv S^{t-1}(p^{t-1}, v_1^{t-1}, \ldots v_{m-1}^{t-1}, v_m^t, v_{m+1}^{t-1}, \ldots, v_M^{t-1}, v_0^{t-1})/$$
$$S^{t-1}(p^{t-1}, v^{t-1}, v_0^{t-1});$$

$$(10) \qquad Q_m^t \equiv (Q_{Lm}^t Q_{Pm}^t)^{1/2}; \quad m = 1, 2, \ldots, M.$$

The indexes Q_{Lm}^t and Q_{Pm}^t provide answers to the following hypothetical questions: What is the proportional change in domestic sales that can be attributed to the change in the mth primary input going from period $t-1$ to period t, v_m^{t-1} to v_m^t, holding constant output prices and other primary input availabilities and also holding the technology and the balance of trade deficit constant?

Finally, we define the Paasche and Laspeyres theoretical deficit effects, Q_{P0}^t and Q_{L0}^t, and their geometric mean as follows:

$$(11) \qquad Q_{P0}^t \equiv S^t(p^t, v^t, v_0^t)/S^t(p^t, v^t, v_0^{t-1});$$

$$(12) \qquad Q_{L0}^t \equiv S^{t-1}(p^{t-1}, v^{t-1}, v_0^t)/S^{t-1}(p^{t-1}, v^{t-1}, v_0^{t-1});$$

$$(13) \qquad Q_0^t \equiv (Q_{L0}^t Q_{P0}^t)^{1/2}.$$

The indexes Q_{L0}^t and Q_{P0}^t provide answers to the following hypothetical question: What is the proportional change in private domestic sales that can be attributed to a change in the private sector's balance of trade deficit from v_0^{t-1} to v_0^t holding constant output, export, and import prices, and holding constant the technology set and primary input availabilities?

The indexes or effects defined above by (5)–(13) have been called theoretical effects because, in general, they cannot be evaluated using only observable price and quantity data. However, in section 7.6 below, we shall show that the above geometric mean effects can be evaluated if we assume that the technology can be represented by translog sales functions. In the following section, we shall define some additional theoretical indexes where we vary more than one variable at a time.

7.5   Theoretical Productivity, Terms of Trade, and Welfare Indexes

We define the period t theoretical Paasche and Laspeyres productivity indexes, R_P^t and R_L^t, and their geometric mean as follows:

$$(14) \qquad R_P^t \equiv S^t(p^t, v^t, v_0^t)/S^{t-1}(p^t, v^t, v_0^t);$$

$$(15) \qquad R_L^t \equiv S^t(p^{t-1}, v^{t-1}, v_0^{t-1})/S^{t-1};(p^{t-1}, v^{t-1}, v_0^{t-1});$$

$$(16) \qquad R^t \equiv (R_L^t R_P^t)^{1/2}.$$

The productivity index R^t_p calculates a hypothetical rate of increase in private domestic product going from the period $t-1$ technology to the period t technology but holding constant prices, primary inputs, and the trade deficit at their period t levels. The Laspeyres theoretical productivity index R^t_L undertakes the same type of computation except that output prices, primary input quantities, and the trade deficit are held constant at their period $t-1$ levels.

The period t theoretical Paasche and Laspeyres terms-of-trade adjustment indexes, A^t_p and A^t_L, and their geometric mean may be defined as follows:

(17) $A^t_p \equiv S^t(p^t_d, p^t_x, p^t_m, v^t, v^t_0)/S^t(p^t_d, p^{t-1}_x, p^{t-1}_m, v^t, v^t_0);$

(18) $A^t_L \equiv S^{t-1}(p^{t-1}_d, p^t_x, p^t_m, v^{t-1}, v^{t-1}_0)/S^{t-1}(p^{t-1}_d, p^{t-1}_x, p^{t-1}_m, v^{t-1}, v^{t-1}_0);$

(19) $A^t \equiv (A^t_L A^t_p)^{1/2}.$

The theoretical terms of trade adjustment index A^t_p calculates a hypothetical rate of increase in domestic product due to a change in export and import prices from the period $t-1$ values, p^{t-1}_x, p^{t-1}_m, to the period t values, p^t_x, p^t_m, holding constant the technology, domestic prices, primary inputs, and the trade deficit at their period t levels. The theoretical Laspeyres index A^t_L is similar, except that the constant variables are fixed at their period $t-1$ levels.

The combined effects of productivity improvements and changes in the terms of trade are exhibited in the following theoretical Paasche and Laspeyres "welfare" change indexes,[3] W^t_p and W^t_L, and their geometric mean:

(20) $W^t_p \equiv S^t(p^t_d, p^t_x, p^t_m, v^t, v^t_0)/S^{t-1}(p^t_d, p^{t-1}_x, p^{t-1}_m, v^t, v^t_0),$

(21) $W^t_L \equiv S^t(p^{t-1}_d, p^t_x, p^t_m, v^{t-1}, v^{t-1}_0)/S^{t-1}(p^{t-1}_d, p^{t-1}_x, p^{t-1}_m, v^{t-1}_0),$

(22) $W^t \equiv (W^t_L W^t_p)^{1/2}.$

Finally, the combined short-run effects of productivity improvements, changes in the terms of trade, and changes in the allowed merchandise trade deficit are contained in the following theoretical Paasche and Laspeyres "total welfare" change indexes, T^t_p and T^t_L, and their geometric mean:

(23) $T^t_p \equiv S^t(p^t_d, p^t_x, p^t_m, v^t, v^t_0)/S^{t-1}(p^t_d, p^{t-1}_x, p^{t-1}_{w6m}, v^t, v^{t-1}_0);$

(24) $T^t_L \equiv S^t(p^{t-1}_d, p^t_x, p^t_m, v^{t-1}, v^{t-1}_0)/S^{t-1}(p^{t-1}_d, p^{t-1}_x, p^{t-1}_m, v^{t-1}, v^{t-1}_0);$

(25) $T^t \equiv (T^t_L T^t_p)^{1/2}.$

In the following two sections, we show how the various theoretical indexes and effects defined in this section and the previous section can be evaluated using observable data.

7.6   Exact Indexes: The Translog Approach

Suppose that the sales function in period t, S^t, has the following translog functional form:

$$\ln S^t(p, v, v_0) \equiv \alpha_0^t + \sum_{n=1}^{N} \alpha_n^t \ln p_n + (\tfrac{1}{2}) \sum_{i=1}^{N} \sum_{j=1}^{N} \alpha_{ij} \ln p_i \ln p_j$$

(26)
$$+ \sum_{m=0}^{M} \beta_m^t \ln v_m^t + (\tfrac{1}{2}) \sum_{i=0}^{M} \sum_{j=0}^{M} \beta_{ij} \ln v_i \ln v_j$$

$$+ \sum_{n=1}^{N} \sum_{m=0}^{M} \gamma_{nm} \ln p_n \ln v_m$$

where $\alpha_{ij} = \alpha_{ji}$, $\beta_{ij} = \beta_{ji}$ for all i and j, and the parameters satisfy various other restrictions that ensure that $S^t (p_d, p_x, p_m, v, v_0)$ is (i) linearly homogeneous nondecreasing and concave in v_0, v for fixed $p \equiv (p_d, p_x, p_m)$, (ii) linearly homogeneous convex and nondecreasing in p_d for fixed p_x, p_m, v, v_0, and (iii) homogeneous of degree zero and quasi convex in $p_x, p_m,$ and v_0 for fixed p_d and v. The definition (26) requires that all prices and quantities be positive. In particular, we require $v_0 > 0$. If $v_0 < 0$, then we replace v_0 in (26) by $-v_0$.

Note that the coefficients corresponding to the quadratic terms in (26) do not depend on time t but that the other coefficients (α_0^t, α_n^t, and β_m^t) are allowed to be different in each time period. Also, the quadratic nature of (26) means that the translog sales function can provide a second-order approximation to an arbitrary twice continuously differentiable sales function $S(p, v, v_0)$; that is, the translog sales function is a flexible functional form.

Suppose that S^{t-1} and S^t are translog sales functions defined by (26) with $v_0^{t-1} v_0^t > 0$ (so that the trade deficit has the same sign in periods $t-1$ and t).[4] Then Diewert and Morrison (1986, 671–74) showed that the following theoretical indexes (defined in the previous two sections) may be *exactly* computed using observable price and quantity data as follows: the price effects P_n^t defined by (7) for $n = 1, \ldots, N$ may be computed using

(27) $\ln P_n^t = (1/2)[(p_n^t y_n^t / p_d^t \cdot y_d^t) + (p_n^{t-1} y_n^{t-1} / p_d^{t-1} \cdot y_d^{t-1})] \ln (p_n^t / p_n^{t-1})$;

the quantity effects Q_m^t defined by (10) for $m = 1, \ldots, M$ may be computed using

(28) $\ln Q_m^t = (\tfrac{1}{2})[w_m^t v_m^t / p_d^t \cdot y_d^t) + (w_m^{t-1} v_m^{t-1} / p_d^{t-1} y_d^{t-1})] \ln (v_m^t / v_m^{t-1})$;

the deficit effect Q_0^t defined by (13) may be computed using

(29) $\ln Q_0^t = (\tfrac{1}{2})[(v_0^t / p_d^t \cdot y_d^t) + (v_0^{t-1} / p_d^{t-1}) \cdot y_d^{t-1})] \ln (v_0^t / v_0^{t-1})$;

the productivity index R^t defined by (16) may be computed using

(30) $$R^t = p_d^t \cdot y_d^t / p_d^{t-1} \cdot y_d^{t-1} \left[\prod_{n=1}^{N} P_n^t \right] \left[\prod_{m=0}^{M} Q_m^t \right],$$

where the P_n^t are defined by (27) and the Q_m^t are defined by (28) and (29); the terms-of-trade adjustment index, A^t, defined by (19), may be computed using

$$
\ln A^t = \sum_{i=1}^{N_x} (\tfrac{1}{2})[(p_{xi}^t y_{xi}^t / p_d^t \cdot y_d^t)
$$

(31)
$$
+ (p_{xi}^{t-1} y_{xi}^{t-1} / p_d^{t-1} \cdot y_d^{t-1})] \ln (p_{xi}^t / p_{xi}^{t-1}) - \sum_{j=1}^{N_m} (\tfrac{1}{2})[(p_{mj}^t y_{mj}^t / p_d^t \cdot y_d^t)
$$

$$
+ (p_{mj}^{t-1} y_{mj}^{t-1} / p_d^{t-1} \cdot y_d^{t-1})] \ln (p_{mj}^t / p_{mj}^{t-1}),
$$

and the welfare change index, W^t, defined by (22), may be computed as follows:

(32)
$$
W^t = R^t A^t,
$$

where R^t and A^t are defined by (30) and (31). Thus the welfare change index decomposes nicely into the product of a productivity index times a terms-of-trade adjustment index.

Finally, under our translog assumptions, the theoretical total welfare change index, T^t, defined by (25), may be computed as follows:

(33)
$$
T^t = W^t Q_0^t = R^t A^t Q_0^t,
$$

where R^t, A^t, and Q_0^t are defined by (30), (31), and (29), respectively.

In subsequent sections of this paper, we shall evaluate the indexes defined in this section using Japanese and U.S. data. However, there is a problem with the exact translog approach outlined in this section: in order to theoretically justify our results, we must have the trade deficit retaining the same sign in the two periods under consideration. Since this assumption is not always satisfied (for either the Japanese or U.S. data), we need to utilize another approach to evaluate our theoretical indexes when the trade deficit changes sign. This alternative approach (due to Diewert and Morrison [1986, 674–77]) will be explained in the following section.

7.7   A Nonparametric First-Order Approximation Approach

Recall equations (4), which enable us to evaluate the first-order partial derivatives of the sales function S^t, evaluated at the period t prices and quantities p^t, v^t, v_0^t. If we replace t by $t-1$, then we may also use equations (4) to evaluate the first order partial derivatives $S^{t-1}(p^{t-1}, v^{t-1}, v_0^{t-1})$. We can use equations (4) to form first-order Taylor series approximations to the theoretical indexes, defined in sections 7.4 and 7.5, that can be evaluated numerically using observable data. Thus we define the following first-order approximations $\tilde{R}_P^t$ and $\tilde{R}_L^t$ to the theoretical productivity indexes R_P^t and R_L^t defined by (14) and (15) as follows:

(34)
$$
\tilde{R}_P^t \equiv S^t(p^t, v^t, v_0^t)/[S^{t-1}(p^{t-1}, v^{t-1}, v_0^{t-1})
$$

$$
+ \nabla_p S^{t-1}(p^{t-1}, v^{t-1}, v_0^{t-1}) \cdot (p^t - p^{t-1})
$$

$$
+ \nabla_v S^{t-1}(p^{t-1}, v^{t-1}, v_0^{t-1}) \cdot (v^t - v^{t-1})
$$

$$
+ \nabla_{v_0} S^{t-1}(p^{t-1}, v^{t-1}, v_0^{t-1}) \cdot (v_0^t - v_0^{t-1})]
$$

$$(35) \qquad = p_d^t \cdot y_d^t / [p_d^{t-1} \cdot y_d^{t-1} + y^{t-1} \cdot (p^t - p^{t-1})$$
$$+ w^{t-1} \cdot (v^t - v^{t-1}) + v_0^t - v_0^{t-1}],$$

where we have used (3) and (4) to derive (35) from (34). Similarly, we define the Laspeyres approximate productivity index $\tilde{R}_L^t$ by (36) and derive (37) using (3) and (4):

$$(36) \ \tilde{R}_L^t \equiv [S^t(p^t, v^t, v_0^t) + \nabla_p S^t(p^t, v^t, v_0^t) \cdot (p^{t-1} - p^t)$$
$$+ \nabla_v S^t(p^t, v^t, v_0^t) \cdot (v^t - v^{t-1})$$
$$+ \nabla_{v_0} S^t(p^t, v^t, v_0^t)(v_0^{t-1} - v_0^t)] / S^{t-1}(p^{t-1}, v^{t-1}, v_0^{t-1})$$

$$(37) \qquad = [p_d^t \cdot y_d^t + y^t \cdot (p^{t-1} - p^t) + w^t \cdot (v^{t-1} - v^t) + v_0^{t-1} - v_0^t] / p_d^{t-1} \cdot y_d^{t-1}.$$

Now define the geometric mean of the above two approximate productivity indexes by

$$(38) \qquad\qquad \tilde{R}^t \equiv (\tilde{R}_L^t \tilde{R}_P^t)^{1/2} ,$$

where $\tilde{R}_P^t$ and $\tilde{R}_L^t$ are defined by (35) and (37), respectively.

The quadratic approximation lemma of Denny and Fuss (1983a, 1983b) leads us to believe that the index $\tilde{R}^t$, defined by (38), will approximate the true index R^t, defined by (16), to the second order.

Analogous first-order approximations to the theoretical deficit effects Q_{P0}^t and Q_{L0}^t defined above by (11) and (12) are given by (39) and (40) below, and their geometric average is defined by (41):

$$(39) \ \tilde{Q}_{P0}^t \equiv S^t(p^t, v^t, v_0^t) / \{S^t(p^t, v^t, v_0^t) + [\partial S^t(p^t, v^t, v_0^t) / \partial v_0](v_0^{t-1} - v_0^t)\}$$
$$= [1 - (v_0^t - v_0^{t-1})(p_d^t \cdot y_d^t)^{-1}]^{-1};$$

$$(40) \ \tilde{Q}_{L0}^t \equiv \{S^{t-1}(p^{t-1}, v^{t-1}, v_0^{t-1}) + [\partial S^{t-1}(p^{t-1}, v^{t-1}, v_0^{t-1}) / \partial v_0](v_0^t - v_0^{t-1})\}$$
$$/ S^{t-1}(p^{t-1}, v^{t-1}, v_0^{t-1})$$
$$= 1 + (v_0^t - v_0^{t-1})(p_d^{t-1} \cdot y_d^{t-1})^{-1};$$

$$(41) \ \tilde{Q}_0^t \equiv (\tilde{Q}_{L0}^t \tilde{Q}_{P0}^t)^{1/2}.$$

First-order approximations to the theoretical terms-of-trade sales adjustment indexes defined by (17) and (18) and their geometric mean are defined by:

$$(42) \ \tilde{A}_L^t \equiv [p_d^{t-1} \cdot y_d^{t-1} + y_x^{t-1} \cdot (p_x^{t-1} - p_x^{t-1}) - y_m^{t-1} \cdot (p_m^{t-1} - p_m^{t-1})] / p_d^{t-1} \cdot y_d^{t-1},$$

$$(43) \ \tilde{A}_P^t \equiv p_d^t \cdot y_d^t / [p_d^t \cdot y_d^t + y_x^t \cdot (p_x^{t-1} - p_x^t) - y_m^t \cdot (p_m^{t-1} - p_m^t)],$$

$$(44) \ \tilde{A}^t \equiv (\tilde{A}_L^t \tilde{A}_P^t)^{1/2}.$$

Similar first-order approximations to the theoretical welfare indexes defined by (20) and (21) are defined by (45) and (46) (these indexes incorporate changes in productivity and changes in the terms of trade but hold the balance-of-trade deficit constant):

(45) $\tilde{W}_L^t \equiv [p_d^t \cdot y_d^t + y_d^t \cdot (p_d^{t-1} - p_d^t) + w^t \cdot (v^{t-1} - v^t)$
$+ (v_0^{t-1} - v_0^t)] / p_d^{t-1} \cdot y_d^{t-1},$

(46) $\tilde{W}_P^t \equiv p_d^t . y_d^t / [p_d^{t-1} \cdot y_d^{t-1} + y_d^{t-1} \cdot (p_d^t - p_d^{t-1})$
$+ w^{t-1} \cdot (v^t - v^{t-1}) + (v_0^t - v_0^{t-1})],$

(47) $\tilde{W}^t \equiv (\tilde{W}_L^t \tilde{W}_P^t)^{1/2}.$

Finally, first-order approximations to the theoretical total welfare change indexes defined by (23) and (24) are defined by (48) and (49) (these indexes are like the welfare indexes except that they also incorporate changes in the balance of trade deficit):

(48) $\tilde{T}_L^t \equiv p_d^t \cdot y_d^t + y_d^t \cdot (p_d^{t-1} - p_d^t) + w^t \cdot (v^{t-1} - v^t)] / p_d^{t-1} \cdot y_d^{t-1},$

(49) $\tilde{T}_p^t \equiv p_d^t . y_d^t / p_d^{t-1} \cdot y_d^{t-1} + y_d^{t-1} \cdot (p_d^t - p_d^{t-1}) + w^{t-1} \cdot (v^t - v^{t-1})],$

(50) $\tilde{T}^t \equiv (\tilde{T}_L^t \tilde{T}_p^t)^{1/2}.$

Since our new geometric mean indexes $\tilde{R}^t$, $\tilde{Q}_0^t$, $\tilde{A}^t$, $\tilde{W}^t$, and $\tilde{T}^t$ do not depend on any functional form assumptions, we call them nonparametric indexes.

Our new nonparametric indexes do not have the nice multiplicative properties that the translog indexes defined in the previous section had: recall (32), $W^t = R^t A^t$, and (33), $T^t = R^t A^t Q_0^t = W^t Q_0^t$. However, in our empirical work, we shall find that our new indexes had the above multiplicative properties to a high degree of approximation. We turn now to the empirical implementation of the indexes defined in this section and the previous section.

7.8   The Japanese Data

The Japanese data used for this study were developed from the *Economic Statistics Annual* (Bank of Japan 1986) from the Research and Statistics Department of the Bank of Japan. The data required are the prices and quantities of output (value added), labor, capital, exports, and imports for each calendar year. The capital and labor series were generated from data on gross fixed capital formation, operating surplus, consumption of fixed capital, compensation of employees, and number of employees. Value added was then computed as the sum of the values of capital and labor. The export and import data were generated from more detailed value and "quantum" data for six different types of exports and seven imports. This will allow us to assess the impact of the energy price shock in the early 1970s.

More specifically, the data on capital was constructed by using a benchmark capital level (for 1966), supplied by John Helliwell and his associates at the University of British Columbia and based on Organization for Economic Cooperation and Development (OECD) data, and then using the investment data from the Bank of Japan series on gross fixed capital formation, along with a

12.5% rate of depreciation, to construct the capital quantity series. The total value of capital ($w_K \cdot v_K = V_K$) was assumed to be the sum of the operating surplus plus the consumption of fixed capital. The price of capital was then computed as V_K/v_K. Bank of Japan series were also available for total compensation of employees ($w_L \cdot v_L = V_L$) and the number of employees (v_L), which were used to compute a price of labor as $w_L = V_L/v_L$.[5]

The export and import data, as mentioned above, included the value of six exports and eight imports plus totals. The export data encompassed separate information on food, textiles, chemicals, nonmetallic minerals, metal and metal products, and machinery and equipment. The import data included food, textiles, metals, mineral fuels, other raw materials, chemicals, and machinery and equipment. The prices of each component were computed by dividing each value by the "quantum" indicator, which is described by the Bank of Japan as the total value divided by the unit value. The resulting prices were used to calculate aggregate prices for exports and imports by using a translog aggregation procedure. The resulting total values for exports and imports did not exactly coincide with the full totals due to a small miscellaneous component that was not provided with a quantum index. The quantities (or quantum values) were therefore regenerated by using the aggregated prices (p_x and p_m) along with the full total values of exports and imports (V_x and V_m) to compute the constant dollar quantity indexes y_x and y_m.[6]

Finally, value added ($p \cdot y$) was calculated as $V_y = V_L + V_K$, and the corresponding price (p) was assumed to be equal to the implicit gross domestic product (GDP) deflator provided by the Bank of Japan. The value of domestic sales could then be calculated as $V_s = V_y - V_x + V_m$ and the price calculated implicitly as a translog index of the prices of these components of absorption. These data may be found in table 7.1.

Looking at the data in table 7.1, a number of trends emerge. For example, the price of labor increased dramatically, while the number of employees stayed relatively constant. Compensation per employee increased by at least a factor of seven during this time period, while the number of employees increased by only 20%. By contrast, the data indicate that the capital rental price increased by approximately two times and the stock level by close to three times.[7] During the same time span, output increased substantially; value added in constant dollars increased by a factor of almost three. The corresponding price of output also increased to approximately 275% of its value in the beginning of the sample.

The pattern of prices of traded goods is particularly interesting. The unit price of exported goods from Japan only doubled during this time period. The price of imported goods, however, provides a strong contrast to this. Although the price of some imported goods was actually falling slightly in the early 1970s, from 1972 to 1982—in response to dramatic increases in costs of raw materials and especially fuel—the price of imported goods increased by a factor of four. Since these price trends are so different and international trade is fairly substantial in Japan, explicit consideration of terms of trade adjust-

Table 7.1   Japanese Price and Quantity Data

Year	K	P_K	L	P_L	Y	P_Y	X	P_X	M	P_M	S	P_S
1967	29,024.2	.78710	41,305.5	.45343	54,194.4	.76405	3,940.108	.96745	3,836.849	.95994	57,191.9	.72517
1968	30,654.1	.87577	41,994.0	.52581	61,100.4	.80350	4,954.146	.96083	4,355.298	.96187	62,222.5	.77682
1969	33,070.7	.96136	42,313.0	.60483	68,797.4	.84201	5,882.085	.99749	4,992.975	.96506	68,738.2	.82042
1970	36,316.2	1.03890	42,766.3	.73013	75,335.9	.90373	6,821.044	1.04710	5,981.378	1.01768	76,251.3	.89196
1971	40,369.7	.95311	42,993.0	.86284	78,818.1	.95054	8,266.639	1.03638	5,989.071	1.07381	77,216.8	.95025
1972	44,320.0	1.00000	43,035.0	1.00000	85,815.0	1.00000	8,928.027	1.00000	6,597.156	1.00000	85,221.0	1.00000
1973	48,708.2	1.08639	44,151.6	1.22489	93,380.8	1.11940	9,512.114	1.09361	7,953.468	1.18050	95,460.4	1.12054
1974	53,883.1	1.08656	43,966.9	1.55597	92,531.9	1.34997	11,192.440	1.50515	7,869.874	2.15937	95,156.1	1.34471
1975	57,530.7	1.04612	43,849.4	1.81640	95,026.3	1.45533	11,278.783	1.55822	7,040.110	2.43634	97,603.6	1.43201
1976	60,671.8	1.10302	44,252.4	2.04039	100,089.4	1.54842	13,820.367	1.52077	7,706.426	2.47283	103,938.5	1.49972
1977	63,747.6	1.12564	44,848.4	2.24906	104,862.2	1.63615	15,047.310	1.50203	7,920.279	2.40759	109,137.5	1.55385
1978	66,957.2	1.21046	45,402.5	2.39676	110,281.2	1.71132	15,200.701	1.39419	8,242.751	2.00481	117,282.7	1.58858
1979	70,777.9	1.22444	45,998.6	2.55838	115,269.0	1.75614	15,027.924	1.57770	9,095.688	2.61892	126,517.7	1.63097
1980	74,882.9	1.25878	46,477.1	2.75886	120,847.1	1.80579	17,555.877	1.72185	8,724.714	3.55662	132,832.1	1.69111
1981	78,665.4	1.23931	46,854.9	2.94883	125,788.3	1.85284	19,466.441	1.80288	8,275.875	3.79426	135,839.3	1.71974
1982	82,516.0	1.25230	47,333.5	3.12253	129,723.4	1.88582	18,882.223	1.96821	8,153.281	4.03833	143,399.4	1.73282

Note: K is the quantity of capital services, L is the quantity of labor, Y is the real value added, X is the quantity of exports, M is the quantity of imports, and S is the quantity of domestic sales. P_K, P_L, P_Y, P_X, P_M and P_S are the corresponding price indices.

ments should have a relatively large impact on indexes for Japan. In addition, the balance of payments, $V_m - V_x$, is increasingly negative over this period; the value of exports becomes larger over time. We turn now to an evaluation of the indexes defined in sections 7.6 and 7.7.

7.9   Japanese Indexes of Productivity and Welfare Change

We need to reconcile the notation used in the previous section with the notation we used earlier in the theoretical sections. We are now assuming that N_d, N_x, and N_m (the number of domestic goods, exported goods, and imported goods respectively) all equal one, so that $N = N_d + N_x + N_m = 3$. The price vector $p^t \equiv (p_d^t, p_x^t, p_m^t) \equiv (p_1^t, p_2^t, p_3^t) = (P_S^t, P_X^t, P_M^t)$ where P_S^t is the price of sales in period t, P_X^t is the price of exports in period t, and P_M^t is the price of imports in period t. These three price series may be found in table 7.1. The quantity vectors y_d^t, y_x^t, and y_m^t, which occur in sections 7.6 and 7.7, are actually scalars in our present application and are equal to the quantity series S^t, X^t, and M^t which are listed in table 7.1. The period t quantity vector y^t, which occurs in sections 7.6 and 7.7 is defined to be the following three dimensional vector: $y^t \equiv (y_1^t, y_2^t, y_3^t) \equiv (S^t, X^t, -M^t)$. Note that the first two components of y^t are positive, while the third component is negative. The period t balance of trade deficit is defined as $v_0^t \equiv P_M^t M^t - P_X^t X^t$. Finally, the primary input vector $v^t \equiv (v_1^t, v_2^t)$ is defined to be (L^t, K^t) and the corresponding period t price vector $w^t \equiv (w_1^t, w_2^t)$ is defined to be (P_L^t, P_K^t), where L^t, K^t, P_L^t, P_K^t are listed in table 7.1.

The three *price effects*, P_1^t, P_2^t, and P_3^t, defined by (27), the two *quantity effects*, Q_1^t and Q_2^t, defined by (28), and the *deficit effect* Q_0^t defined by (29) are evaluated using the Japanese data listed in table 7.1 and are listed in table 7.2. Recall that P_i^t is a measure of the proportional increase in the value of domestic sales due to the change in the ith price from its actual period $t-1$ value to its period t value, holding constant the trade deficit, the technology, and other prices and quantities. Similarly, Q_j^t is a measure of the proportional increase in the value of domestic sales due to the change in the jth primary input from its period $t-1$ value to its period t value, holding constant the trade deficit, the technology, other primary input utilization, and the prices of domestic output, exports, and imports. Finally, Q_0^t is a measure of the proportional increase in the value of domestic sales due to the change in the country's balance of trade deficit holding constant the technology, the prices of domestic goods, exports and imports, and the utilization of primary inputs.

Information on single determinants of production trends is evident from the individual comparative statics indexes in table 7.2. For example, Q_1^t in table 7.2 shows the impact on the change in domestic product from increasing the use of labor. This index indicates that increases in the labor input have contributed to a greater product in all but two years—1974 and 1975, when labor growth was negative—but the effect is negligible. By contrast, the contribu-

Table 7.2   **Translog Price and Quantity Effects for Japan**

Year	P_1^t	P_2^t	P_3^t	Q_1^t	Q_2^t	Q_0^t
1967	1.077	1.003	1.000	1.008	1.019	1.017
1968	1.071	.999	.999	1.007	1.030	.987
1969	1.056	1.003	.999	1.003	1.043	.992
1970	1.087	1.005	.995	1.004	1.053	1.000
1971	1.065	.998	.995	1.002	1.058	.981
1972	1.052	.996	1.005	1.000	1.049	1.000
1973	1.120	1.009	.986	1.013	1.049	1.055
1974	1.200	1.037	.933	.997	1.049	
1975	1.064	1.004	.984	.998	1.029	
1976	1.047	.996	.998	1.005	1.023	.986
1977	1.036	.998	1.003	1.007	1.021	.989
1978	1.022	.990	1.018	1.007	1.021	.997
1979	1.026	1.014	.973	1.007	1.024	
1980	1.036	1.010	.961	1.005	1.023	1.000
1981	1.016	1.006	.991	1.004	1.020	
1982	1.007	1.013	.991	1.006	1.020	.997
Mean	1.061	1.005	.989	1.005	1.034	1.000

Note: P_1^t is the domestic sales price effect, P_2^t is the price of exports effect, P_3^t is the price of imports effect, Q_1^t is the quantity of labor effect, Q_2^t is the quantity of capital effect, and Q_0^t is the deficit effect.

tion of increases in the capital stock represented by Q_2^t is quite high; in 1970–74 in particular, around 5% of product growth can be attributed to an increase in capital.

The impact of changes in prices in domestic product can also be determined from table 7.2. For example, P_1^t indicates the year t increase in the value of domestic product attributable purely to domestic sales price increases. This index increased by a positive but decreasing proportion from about 7.8% in 1967 to .8% in 1982.

Looking at the price effects P_2^t, the changes in the price of exports caused increased total value of product for most years. However, in some years— 1968, 1971, 1972, 1976, 1977, and 1978—changes in the price of exports contributed to a very small decrease in product value.

The impacts of import price changes on domestic sales, the P_3^t, are particularly interesting. The substantial increase in import prices during the two energy crises leads to decreases in output for many years. This is particularly true for 1974, where the increase in the import price alone would have caused a 7% decrease in sales if not attenuated by changes in other determinants of the sales level. Note, however, that later—in 1977 and 1978—a slight increase in sales could be attributed to import price changes; the aggregate price of imported goods actually declined in this period due partly to a drop in total fuels imported.

The translog productivity indexes, R^t, defined by (30), the translog terms of trade adjustment indexes, A^t, defined by (31), the translog welfare change indexes, W^t, defined by (32), and the translog total welfare change indexes, T^t, defined by (33), are shown in table 7.3 using the Japanese data in table 7.1. The corresponding nonparametric indexes, $\tilde{R}^t$, defined by (38), $\tilde{A}^t$, defined by (44), $\tilde{W}^t$, defined by (47), and $\tilde{T}^t$, defined by (50), are also listed in table 7.3.

Note that the translog indexes R^t, W^t, and T^t are not defined for years when the merchandise trade deficit changes sign. The nonparametric indexes $\tilde{R}^t$, $\tilde{A}^t$, $\tilde{W}^t$, and $\tilde{T}^t$ are always well defined. Note that in years when the translog and nonparametric indexes are both defined, they approximate each other rather closely.

The productivity indexes R^t and $\tilde{R}^t$ show a substantial decrease in productivity growth in the 1970–71 period and an even stronger impact in 1973–74, when the rates of growth actually became negative. The post-1975 years were characterized by very healthy productivity growth rates, although not quite as high as in the earlier years of the sample, particularly for 1981, which exhibited growth of only .2%. The largest percentage growth in the post–energy crisis years was the "snapback" in 1976, when growth jumped back up to 4.9%; this is closely followed by a 4.7% increase in 1980.

The terms-of-trade adjustment indexes, A^t and $\tilde{A}^t$, which show the effects on domestic sales of combined changes in export and import prices, are rather close to one for most years. However, in three years, the terms-of-trade adjustment factor was significantly below one, which indicates an increase in import prices relative to export prices. These three years corresponded to the OPEC price shock years, and the combined effect of changes in export and import prices in these years was a *decrease* in growth of over 3% in 1974, 1.3% in 1979, and almost 3% in 1980. Thus, we are able to measure rather precisely the effects on growth of the adverse changes in Japan's terms of trade during these years.

Adjusting the productivity growth measures by these terms-of-trade indexes results in the welfare measures W^t and $\tilde{W}^t$, which are closely comparable and closely related to the productivity indexes since the A^t are close to 1.0. The impacts of the energy "crisis" are, of course, more evident in these "welfare" indexes; welfare growth in 1971 and 1974 was negative: about -3% and -5.7% respectively.

Finally, for the sales and first-order approximation approaches, the combined indexes incorporating productivity, terms-of-trade changes and the impact of the deficit are represented by the translog index T^t and the nonparametric index $\tilde{T}^t$, defined by (33) and (50), respectively. These indexes are nearly identical for those years where the translog index is defined. Years where the merchandise trade deficit grew significantly, thus causing $\tilde{T}^t$ to exceed $\tilde{W}^t$ by more than about 1%, were 1967, 1973, and 1979. Years where the trade deficit declined significantly were 1968, 1971, 1977, and 1981.

Table 7.3   **Japanese Productivity, Terms-of-Trade Adjustment, and Welfare Change Indexes**

Year	R^t	$\bar{R}^t$	A^t	$\bar{A}^t$	W^t	$\bar{W}^t$	T^t	$\bar{T}^t$
1967	1.059	1.064	1.004	1.004	1.064	1.068	1.082	1.082
1968	1.062	1.060	.999	.999	1.061	1.059	1.047	1.047
1969	1.059	1.059	1.003	1.003	1.063	1.063	1.055	1.055
1970	1.046	1.046	1.000	1.000	1.046	1.046	1.047	1.047
1971	.977	.976	.994	.994	.971	.971	.954	.953
1972	1.047	1.047	1.001	1.001	1.049	1.049	1.050	1.050
1973	1.003	1.035	.995	.995	.998	1.030	1.054	1.053
1974		.971	.968	.970		.943		.951
1975		1.016	.989	.988		1.005		.997
1976	1.054	1.049	.995	.995	1.049	1.044	1.035	1.035
1977	1.029	1.029	1.001	1.001	1.031	1.030	1.020	1.020
1978	1.038	1.038	1.009	1.009	1.047	1.047	1.044	1.044
1979		1.029	1.986	1.987		1.016		1.045
1980	1.047	1.047	.972	.972	1.018	1.018	1.019	1.019
1981		1.017	.997	.997		1.015		.997
1982	1.026	1.026	1.004	1.004	1.031	1.031	1.028	1.028
Mean	1.037	1.032	.995	.995	1.036	1.027	1.036	1.026

Note: The productivity indexes, R^t and $\bar{R}^t$, are defined by (30) and (38), the terms of trade adjustment indexes, A^t and $\bar{A}^t$, are defined by (31) and (44), the welfare change indexes, W^t and $\bar{W}^t$, are defined by (32) and (47), and the total welfare change indexes, which incorporate changes in productivity, in the terms of trade and in the trade deficit, T^t and $\bar{T}^t$, are defined by (33) and (50).

7.10 The U.S. Data

The data required to calculate the indexes include price and quantity information on national output, capital and labor inputs, exports, and imports. We have developed the output, import, and export data for 1967–82 from the National Income and Product Accounts (U.S. Department of Commerce 1981, 1982, 1983) and have used real capital stock data constructed by the Bureau of Labor Statistics (U.S. Department of Labor 1983) and real labor data updated from Jorgenson and Fraumeni (1981), since these series closely approximate our theoretically ideal indexes.

More specifically, we have calculated the value of output $(P_Y^t Y^t)$ as the gross domestic business product including tenant-occupied housing output, property taxes, and federal subsidies to businesses, but excluding federal, state, and local indirect taxes and owner-occupied housing. The corresponding price index (P_Y^t), was computed by cumulating the Business Gross Domestic Product Chain Price index. Note that our output series for the United States is conceptually somewhat different from our value-added output series for Japan. The Y^t and P_Y^t series for the United States may be found in table 7.4.

The values of merchandise exports $(p_x^t \cdot y_x^t)$ and imports $(p_m^t \cdot y_m^t)$ were deter-

Table 7.4   U.S. Prices and Quantities

Year	K	P_K	L	P_L	Y	P_Y	X	P_X	M	P_M	S	P_S
1967	254.516	.92252	543.092	.72204	788.585	.79501	36.0953	.84947	35.6903	.80249	779.516	.80182
1968	266.369	.95383	556.789	.77277	838.986	.81567	38.9682	.86270	43.2146	.81339	830.649	.82588
1969	278.533	.94054	576.440	.82668	872.243	.84667	40.8635	.89104	45.5838	.83500	860.247	.86056
1970	290.697	.90078	570.485	.88226	863.168	.88646	45.2778	.93788	47.4815	.88906	846.679	.90359
1971	300.990	.95611	573.463	.93318	888.341	.92636	44.6520	.96959	51.5564	.94030	869.694	.95239
1972	311.907	1.00000	595.496	1.00000	938.255	.96712	49.3530	1.00000	58.6285	1.00000	916.821	1.00000
1973	326.255	1.09631	625.866	1.06135	1,021.939	1.00000	61.2051	1.16592	62.7543	1.17375	981.204	1.04900
1974	340.914	1.08115	630.035	1.15423	1,037.676	1.05601	65.9362	1.48958	60.7473	1.76037	996.297	1.10873
1975	350.272	1.21930	611.574	1.22917	1,019.453	1.15632	63.9734	1.66677	53.1780	1.94587	960.740	1.22404
1976	356.822	1.32665	635.394	1.32006	1,038.203	1.26385	66.5975	1.71765	65.1605	1.96222	994.593	1.33298
1977	366.179	1.48218	666.360	1.40568	1,086.373	1.33211	66.9110	1.78929	72.8799	2.13216	1,076.490	1.40762
1978	379.279	1.57942	705.067	1.53092	1,188.673	1.41203	74.1455	1.90020	78.9832	2.29565	1,146.755	1.49912
1979	393.627	1.64533	736.629	1.66222	1,229.876	1.52217	82.6177	2.16876	80.0676	2.70617	1,182.880	1.61455
1980	407.663	1.70086	743.179	1.78329	1,214.455	1.66221	91.4960	2.40338	73.4325	3.41670	1,160.537	1.76632
1981	419.203	1.93726	759.257	1.93094	1,257.408	1.81181	88.0600	2.63230	74.0626	3.62441	1,185.064	1.95356
1982	435.110	1.86782	738.415	2.06104	1,177.835	1.98212	79.7703	2.62128	71.8893	3.53622	1,116.955	2.12937

Note: K is the quantity of capital services, L is the quantity of labor, Y is real value added, X is the quantity of exports, M is the quantity of imports, and S is the quantity of domestic sales. P_K, P_L, P_Y, P_X, P_M, and P_S are the corresponding price indexes.

mined by adding the durable and nondurable export and import values, respectively, reported in the national accounts (U.S. Department of Commerce 1981, 1982, 1983). Tariff revenues were added to the value of imports. Corresponding prices (P_X^t and P_M^t) were calculated as translog indexes of the components of each measure, and quantities (X^t and M^t) were determined implicitly. For 1967–82, value and price data for nine different types of exports and 10 types of imports were available, which were used to compute chain price indexes.

Using the values of imports and exports, $P_M^t \cdot M^t = p_m^t \cdot y_m^t$ and $P_X^t X^t = p_x^t \cdot y_x^t$, tax-adjusted gross domestic private business sales to domestic purchasers, or sales, was calculated as $P_S^t S^t = P_Y^t Y^t - P_X^t X^t + P_M^t M^t$. The corresponding price (P_S^t) was determined by cumulating the gross domestic purchases chain price index from the national accounts, and the constant dollar quantity S^t was calculated by division.

For our labor quantity series, L^t, we used the series constructed by Jorgenson and Fraumeni (1981), which is conveniently shown in a table elsewhere (U.S. Department of Labor 1983, 77). Our total private labor compensation series, $P_L^t L^t$, was taken from the same publication. The price of labor, P_L^t, was determined by division.[8]

For our capital services quantity series, K^t, we used the private business sector (excluding government enterprises) constant dollar capital services input as displayed by the U.S. Department of Labor (1983, 77). In order to ensure that the value of privately produced outputs equals the value of privately utilized inputs, we determined the price of capital services, P_K^t, residually, that is, $P_K^t \equiv (P_Y^t Y^t - P_L^t L^t)/K^t$. All of these U.S. series are presented in table 7.4.

The patterns in the data for the United States vary considerably from those seen for Japan. For example, the price of labor did not increase nearly as substantially as it did in Japan, and the corresponding change in labor quantity is much higher. Total compensation to labor, therefore, increased similarly to Japan, but, for the United States, this was a result of increased levels of labor input whereas for Japan the price adjustment was more important. The capital trends are more similar; the U.S. price of capital increased slightly more than for Japan and the quantity increased a bit less, but the magnitudes are closely comparable. The output trend is analogous to that for capital; the volume of output increased more in Japan and price increased less than that for the United States. The import and export price and quantity trends also follow expected patterns. Import prices increased substantially in the United States, particularly after 1973, but the price increase is greater for Japan, and the increase in quantity of imports is similar for the two countries. By contrast, export price increases are more substantial for the United States, and the corresponding increase in exports is much lower than for Japan. We turn now to the evaluation of the indexes defined in sections 7.6 and 7.7 for the U.S.

7.11   U.S. Indexes of Productivity and Welfare Change

We make exactly the same notational conventions with the U.S. data as we did with the Japanese data at the beginning of section 7.9.

The three translog *price effects*, P_1^t, P_2^t, P_3^t, defined by (27), the two translog *quantity effects*, Q_1^t, Q_2^t, defined by (28), and the translog *deficit effect* Q_0^t defined by (29) are listed in table 7.5 using the U.S. data listed in table 7.4.

The U.S. labor effect, Q_1^t, in table 7.5 is different from Japan's, as would be expected from the differing labor trends; increases in the labor input in the United States have contributed to greater product except in the worst recession years, including 1970, 1975, 1982. Overall, the contribution is strongly positive (and more so than in Japan, a circumstance that can be seen by comparing the respective Q_1^t indexes).

Q_2^t shows the impact on domestic sales' growth of growth in the capital stock. A comparison of the U.S. Q_2^t in table 7.5 with the Japanese Q_2^t in table 7.2 shows that the average U.S. capital effect of 1.2% is much smaller than the corresponding Japanese average capital effect of 3.4%. The smaller U.S. effect reflects its smaller rate of growth of the capital stock.

The individual price effects are particularly interesting for the United States; although the export price effects, P_2^t, induced increased product value in the United States in every year except 1982, changes in the price of imports reflected in the price effects P_3^t caused decreased product value except in 1982. The overall impacts are, however, especially for the earlier years, very small

Table 7.5   **Translog Price and Quantity Effects for the United States**

Year	P_1^t	P_2^t	P_3^t	Q_1^t	Q_2^t	Q_0^t
1968	1.030	1.000	.999	1.015	1.017	
1969	1.042	1.001	.998	1.002	1.016	1.000
1970	1.050	1.002	.996	.993	1.014	
1971	1.054	1.001	.997	1.003	1.012	
1972	1.050	1.001	.996	1.024	1.012	1.004
1973	1.044	1.009	.989	1.032	1.015	.991
1974	1.062	1.019	.966	1.004	1.015	1.006
1975	1.104	1.010	.991	.980	1.009	
1976	1.089	1.002	.999	1.024	1.006	
1977	1.056	1.003	.992	1.030	1.009	1.016
1978	1.065	1.004	.992	1.035	1.012	1.002
1979	1.077	1.011	.982	1.028	1.012	.998
1980	1.094	1.010	.973	1.005	1.011	.996
1981	1.106	1.009	.993	1.013	1.009	1.002
1982	1.090	.999	1.002	.982	1.012	1.002
Mean	1.067	1.005	.991	1.011	1.012	1.002

Note: P_1^t is the domestic sales price effect, P_2^t is the price of exports effect, P_3^t is the price of imports effect, Q_1^t is the quantity of labor effect, Q_2^t is the quantity of capital effect and Q_0^t is the deficit effect.

in magnitude. By contrast, the increase in product value from domestic price increases, P_1^t, is positive and quite large throughout; it does not show the declining effect over time that is found for Japan.

The translog productivity indexes, R^t, defined by (30), the translog terms of trade adjustment indexes, A^t, defined by (31), the translog welfare change indexes W^t, defined by (32), and the translog total welfare change indexes, T^t, defined by (33) are listed in table 7.6 using the U.S. data in table 7.4. The corresponding U.S. nonparametric indexes, $\tilde{R}^t$, defined by (38), $\tilde{A}^t$, defined by (44), $\tilde{W}^t$, defined by (47), and $\tilde{T}^t$, defined by (50) are also listed in table 7.6.

The translog productivity growth measure, R^t, and the nonparametric measure, $\tilde{R}^t$, are represented in columns 2 and 3 of table 7.6. Note that these multifactor productivity indexes are quite similar for the years when the U.S. trade deficit did not change sign. There were large drops in productivity in 1970, 1975, 1979–80, and especially 1982. The year 1975 was a poor productivity year—there was a 2% decrease in productivity—which caused concern in the late 1970s about the observed "productivity slowdown." The late 1960s were also disappointing, but 1977 appeared very strong in terms of productivity growth. In addition, 1980 exhibited a 2% productivity decline, and 1982 was catastrophic with a 6% drop in productivity. These patterns suggest that productivity trends cannot be characterized by a unique productivity downturn in 1973, although there does appear to be a trend toward deterioration of productivity growth over time.

The U.S. terms-of-trade adjustment indexes, A^t and $\tilde{A}^t$, are generally very close to 1.0, since internationally traded goods are such a small proportion of total output for the United States, even in the most recent years of the sample. However, in 1974 and 1980 (two energy shock years), increases in the prices of imported goods relative to exported goods were responsible for declines in real output of about 1½% in each year.

With the exception of these two years, the translog "welfare" index, W^t, (obtained by multiplying R^t and A^t together) and the nonparametric "welfare" index, $\tilde{W}^t$, do not vary significantly from R^t; for a relatively closed economy like the United States, improvements in the terms of trade have a relatively small effect on economic welfare defined in this manner.

Since the U.S. merchandise trade deficits and surpluses were relatively small over the years 1967–82, the total welfare change indexes T^t and $\tilde{T}^t$ do not differ much from the welfare change indexes W^t and $\tilde{W}^t$. The exception to this is 1977, where the increase in the trade deficit relative to 1976 was large enough to account for an approximate 1.6% gain in the real domestic output.

7.12 Conclusion

Comparing the U.S. and Japanese productivity performance over the years 1967–82, the Japanese indexes $\tilde{R}^t$ show only two years of decline throughout

Table 7.6   U.S. Productivity, Terms-of-Trade Adjustment, and Welfare Change
                     Indexes

Year	R^t	$\bar{R}^t$	A^t	$\bar{A}^t$	W^t	$\bar{W}^t$	T^t	$\bar{T}^t$
1968		1.025	1.000	1.000		1.025		1.031
1969	.996	.996	1.000	1.000	.996	.996	.996	.996
1970		.979	.999	.999		.978		.976
1971		1.005	.998	.998		1.004		1.011
1972	1.013	1.013	.998	.997	1.011	1.011	1.016	1.016
1973	1.029	1.029	.999	.998	1.029	1.027	1.020	1.020
1974	1.003	1.004	.985	.985	.989	.989	.995	.995
1975		.983	1.001	1.000		.984		.973
1976		.988	1.001	1.001		.990		1.003
1977	1.028	1.029	.995	.995	1.023	1.024	1.040	1.040
1978	1.015	1.015	.997	.997	1.012	1.012	1.015	1.015
1979	.997	.998	.994	.993	.992	.991	.990	.990
1980	.983	.984	.983	.982	.967	.967	.964	.963
1981	.992	.992	1.002	1.002	.995	.994	.997	.997
1982	.942	.942	1.002	1.002	.944	.944	.947	.947
Mean	1.000	.999	.997	.997	.996	.996	.998	.998

Note: The productivity indexes, R^t and $\bar{R}^t$, are defined by (30) and (38), the terms of trade adjustment indexes, A^t and $\bar{A}^t$, are defined by (31) and (44), the welfare change indexes, W^t and $\bar{W}^t$, are defined by (32) and (47), and the total welfare change indexes, which incorporate changes in productivity, in the terms of trade and in the trade deficit, T^t and $\bar{T}^t$, are defined by (33) and (50).

the sample period, 1971 and 1974, whereas the U.S. indexes show declines in productivity in many years, including 1969–70, 1975–76, and 1979–82. This is a large portion of a sample that includes only 15 data points. The growth in productivity over the entire sample period for Japan was large relative to the United States and showed a gradual decline from around 6% to 3% per year, although there is a lot of fluctuation around the trend. The worse years for Japan were worse than the worst years for the United States, but those years were very limited. Overall, both countries experienced a decreasing trend in yearly productivity growth over the sample period, but the U.S. decline was more pronounced, and the average level was substantially lower.

The terms-of-trade adjustment indexes also are interesting to compare. Although the A^t indexes are close to 1.0 for Japan, they are even closer to 1.0 for the United States. This is intuitively reasonable because the magnitude of trade relative to GNP is large in Japan as compared to the United States, and because the pattern of export prices as compared to import prices differs more for Japan than for the United States. This difference in price patterns at least partly results because Japan is more dependent on imported raw materials, expecially fuels, than is the United States. For example, the 1974 value of A^t for Japan, .969, is the lowest value over the sample period because of the impact of energy price increases. This value indicates a decrease in potential product of about 3% in response only to the change in the relative prices of traded goods. This corresponds to a U.S. value of .986 in 1974, the second lowest value in the sample, indicating a smaller, 1.4% drop. On average, the Japanese terms-of-trade adjustment values tend to be slightly lower than for the United States and lower than unity; the means are .995 and .977, respectively. This indicates a lower level of welfare overall than is suggested by the pure productivity measures R^t, due to changes in the terms of trade.

Adjustment of the productivity measures by the A^t indexes to derive the W^t indexes has little effect on the comparative welfare found for Japan and the United States. The overall tendency is that the welfare indicators remain similar to the productivity indexes, although welfare growth is slightly lower than productivity growth, especially for the later years and for Japan.

To conclude, it should be recognized that productivity measures, although important, may obscure significant contributions to short-run welfare that are obtained by international trade. In this paper, we have outlined a method, following a more extensive treatment by Diewert and Morrison (1986), that can distinguish these additional "welfare" changes, resulting from changes in the terms of trade and the deficit, from productivity changes. To develop this approach we have used a production theory–based framework similar to that which provides a basis for much of the productivity literature.

This framework is used to construct productivity, terms-of-trade adjustment, and welfare indexes for the United States and Japan as combinations of individual comparative statics indexes representing the effects of output production, domestic output price, input use, the deficit, and export and import price changes on growth in domestic production or sales.

These indexes show that Japan's productivity from 1968 to 1982 has been significantly greater than that of the United States and, in fact, has been strongly positive in almost all years, whereas increases in productivity and welfare have been relatively low in the United States. An interesting implication of these numbers is that Japan's productivity growth appears not to have been declining as significantly as that of the United States; Japan experienced a minimal number of very poor productivity growth years around the first OPEC energy price shock and then snapped back relatively quickly, although not completely. In addition, adjusting for the relative terms-of-trade faced, and the deficit incurred, by the countries has a greater impact for Japan than for the United States.

These implications are obviously only a small subset of those which these indexes provide, but they highlight the richness of the information available from our procedures. Application of these procedures to later and more complete data for these and other countries should provide very useful indications of the effects of trade patterns on economic welfare.

Notes

1. For expositions of traditional trade theory, see Dixit and Norman (1980) and Woodland (1982, 165).

2. See Diewert and Morrison (1986, 669).

3. "Welfare" is perhaps best interpreted as potential welfare since we have not specified how the domestic product is to be distributed between various consumer groups.

4. We also require competitive profit-maximizing behavior on the part of producers and the international price vectors p_x^t and p_m^t must be expressed in terms of domestic currency.

5. Two other approximations were also tried for purposes of comparison. These included dividing the compensation of labor series by the "average month hours per worker" to generate a price of labor series and using "cash earnings per regular worker" to approximate a labor price. These two methods resulted in series that bounded the price of labor data used in the study.

6. It appeared important, particularly for mineral fuels, to decompose these indexes to allow for the individual impacts of the different categories to appear; the fuel component of imports exhibited a dramatic jump in value and price in the 1974 data which is important to capture explicitly.

7. This occurs even though the depreciation rate was assumed to be quite high—12.5%. This assumption was made as a result of evidence that replacement investment is a significantly higher portion of total investment relative to the U.S. experience.

8. The Bureau of Labor Statistics (BLS) labor quantity series is an unweighted man/hours series and hence is unsuitable for our purposes. We wish to thank Mike Harper at BLS and Barbara Fraumeni for their help in providing the updated data series.

References

Bank of Japan. 1986. *Economic statistics annual.* Tokyo: Bank of Japan, Research and Statistics Department.

Denny, M., and M. Fuss. 1983a. The use of discrete variables in superlative index number comparisons. *International Economic Review* 24:419–21.

———. 1983b. A general approach to intertemporal and interspatial productivity comparisons. *Journal of Econometrics* 23:315–30.

Diewert, W. E. 1983. The theory of the output price index and the measurement of real output change. In *Price level measurement,* ed. W. E. Diewert and C. Montmarquette, 1049–1113. Ottawa: Statistics Canada.

Diewert, W. E., and C. J. Morrison. 1986. Adjusting output and productivity indexes for changes in the terms of trade. *Economic Journal* 96:659–79.

Dixit, A., and V. Norman. 1980. *Theory of international trade.* New York: Cambridge University Press.

Jorgenson, D. W., and B. M. Fraumeni. 1981. Relative prices and technical change. In *Modelling and measuring natural resource substitution,* ed. E. Berndt and B. Field. Cambridge, Mass. MIT Press.

Kohli, U. J. R. 1978. A gross national product function and the derived demand for imports and supply of exports. *Canadian Journal of Economics* 11:167–82.

U.S. Department of Commerce, Bureau of Economic Analysis. 1981. *The national income and product accounts of the United States, 1929–76, statistical tables* (A supplement to the *Survey of Current Business*). Washington, D.C.: Government Printing Office.

———. 1982. *Survey of Current Business,* vol. 62 (July). Washington, D.C.: Government Printing Office.

———. 1983. *Survey of Current Business,* vol. 63 (July). Washington, D.C.: Government Printing Office.

U.S. Department of Labor, Bureau of Labor Statistics, 1983. *Trends in multifactor productivity, 1948–81,* Bulletin 2178. Washington, D.C.: Government Printing Office.

Woodland, A. D. 1980. Direct and indirect trade utility functions. *Review of Economic Studies* 47:907–26.

———. 1982. *International trade and resource allocation.* Amsterdam: North-Holland.

8   Alternative Measures of Capital Inputs in Japanese Manufacturing

Edwin Dean, Masako Darrough, and Arthur Neef

Students of the Japanese economy who use capital investment and stock statistics are blessed with riches that might arouse the envy of students of other countries. For manufacturing in particular, there are four plausible sources of gross investment data and at least two means of distributing total gross investment among asset categories. Further, to provide measures of net capital stocks, a choice can be made between the use of the perpetual inventory method or an alternative approach utilizing net capital stock statistics from national wealth surveys as benchmarks. Because these alternatives yield different results, however, the researcher may be more embarrassed than blessed by these riches.

This paper examines the various data sources and methods available for measuring net capital stocks, by asset type, in Japanese manufacturing and assesses the merits of the alternatives, particularly from the viewpoint of their ultimate use in measuring multifactor productivity (MFP) growth. In pursuit of these objectives, we examine the differences in levels and growth rates of manufacturing gross investment and net capital stocks, by asset type, that result from using different Japanese data sources.

Edwin Dean is Associate Commissioner, Office of Productivity and Technology, Bureau of Labor Statistics, U.S. Department of Labor. Masako Darrough is professor of accounting, Graduate School of Business, Columbia University. Arthur Neef is chief of the Division of Foreign Labor Statistics, Office of Productivity and Technology, Bureau of Labor Statistics, U.S. Department of Labor.

The authors wish to acknowledge the assistance of the following persons: Charles Hulten for valuable comments in the initial stages of the research and also on the preliminary version of the paper; Alicia Scott for assistance with both concepts and data during the early stages; the late William Waldorf, Michael Harper, and Mieko Nishimizu for valuable comments; John Rhee for translation assistance; James Thomas, Christopher Kask, and Mark Sprecher for assistance in compiling data and/or reviewing the paper in draft form; and Brenda Johnson and Celestia Tobe for typing the manuscript. The authors are grateful to Masahiro Kuroda for useful comments made as the discussant at the conference.

Measures of capital services inputs are needed for computation of multifactor productivity. Capital services input measures are computed from statistics of capital stock of various asset types. Asset detail allows the input measure to reflect changes in the composition of the capital stock, as assets with different service lives grow at different rates. Capital service inputs are computed as weighted averages of the various types of capital stock, where the weights are implicit rental prices of each type of stock.

This paper begins with a statement of the method used for developing measures of Japanese capital stocks in manufacturing. Reliance is placed on use of national wealth surveys to determine average annual rates of discards plus depreciation. The second section of the paper examines the relevance of the approach used and the results obtained to research problems found in a variety of fields of economic research. In the third section, available data sources for capital stocks and annual gross investment are described. The fourth section presents an assessment of the advantages and shortcomings of each of these data sources. In the fifth section, the methods are implemented, using a variety of data sources for gross investment, to estimate net capital stocks for 1955–81. A conclusion summarizes the main findings of the paper. Finally, an appendix presents, for 1955–81, annual data on gross investment from four data sources and the preferred measures of annual net capital stock for three asset types.

8.1 Method

For most countries, measures of capital stock have been computed by the perpetual inventory method. In the absence of reliable measures of capital stock at any point in time, this method relies on statistics of past annual gross investment, estimates of average service lives, and a discard function. For most countries that have developed capital stock measures, the average service lives and discard function used are often little more than educated guesses, resting in part on service lives embodied in tax law (Blades 1983; Ward 1976).

The perpetual inventory method can be expressed as follows:

(1) $$K_{i,j_t} = I_{i,j_t} + (1 - u_{i,j_t})K_{i,j_{t-1}},$$

where K_{i,j_t} is the current year's net capital stock for the jth industry's ith asset, I_{i,j_t} is the current year's gross investment, and u is a proportion that must be applied against the previous year's net capital stock to account for depreciation and discards. Capital stocks in year t-1 and earlier years are computed by accumulating and depreciating long investment series; no benchmark observation of capital stock is required or, in the typical case, utilized.

An alternative method for computing capital stocks has been utilized by students of the Japanese economy. This method, first implemented by Mieko Nishimizu (1974), takes advantage of periodic official Japanese surveys of net capital stock, the national wealth surveys (NWSs). Following Nishimizu, the method has been used by, among others, Nishimizu and Hulten (1978), Norsworthy and Malmquist (1983), and Jorgenson, Kuroda, and Nishimizu (1985).

This method will be referred to as the double benchmark method. It relies on three sets of statistics for each asset: net stocks as measured by two wealth surveys and the annual gross investment for the years between the surveys, all in constant prices. These data are used in a polynomial equation. Provided that the data fulfill certain basic conditions (Nishimizu 1974), the roots of the polynomial equation generate estimates of the average annual rate of replacement (a rate summarizing average annual discards and depreciation) that are functions of opening and closing net stocks and annual gross investment. Where r is the polynomial root and u is the rate of replacement, $u = 1 - r$.[1]

The value of u, and ultimately net stock by asset type for a given year t, can be found by solving the following equation:

$$(2) \qquad K_{i,j_t} = \sum_{s=1}^{t}(1 - u_{i,j})^{t-s}I_{i,j_s} + (1 - u_{i,j})^t K_{i,j_0},$$

where K_{i,j_0} is the benchmark capital stock for the j_{th} industry's i_{th} asset. (It is obvious that eqq. [1] and [2] are consistent, so the double benchmark method is consistent with the perpetual inventory method.)

An attractive feature of this method is that the rate of discards plus depreciation is dictated by the data.[2] An equally important attractive feature is that this method gives a fix on the size of the stock. This is an advantage over procedures that do not use benchmarks. The perpetual inventory method, for example, typically makes use of very long investment series but no benchmark.

On the other hand, the double benchmark method does suffer from limitations and shortcomings. The gross investment and capital stock data must be consistent, by asset type, in their coverage, definition, and methods, as well as accurate. A change in the procedure for estimating net stock between two wealth surveys will yield biased estimates of u, as will inaccuracy in the price deflators. Further, a u determined by using data between two benchmark years may be unsuitable for computing net capital stocks prior to the earlier year or after the later year. However, most of these limitations have their counterparts in the perpetual inventory method.

Despite the shortcomings, this method is used in this study, in part because, in the Japanese case, the requirement of the perpetual inventory method for reliable gross investment series over a lengthy period is particularly difficult to fulfill, due to widespread destruction of assets during World War II (this affected some assets much more than others). Further, net capital stocks as measured through this procedure for estimating u provide a reasonably close approximation to productive capital stocks.[3]

This method for obtaining annual capital stocks, by asset type, in manufacturing is implemented using the 1955 and 1970 Japanese national wealth surveys (NWSs) for the two capital stock benchmarks. Four different series on annual gross investment are used with these two benchmarks. The data sources used to construct these series are the Census of Manufactures (CM), the Economic Planning Agency (EPA), the Annual Report on the Corporate Sector (ARCS), and the Report on the Corporate Industry Investment Survey (RCIS). A description of these data sources is provided in section 8.3 below, following a discussion of this inquiry's relevance to several fields of economic research.

8.2   Relevance to Several Research Fields: Some Illustrations

The estimates of capital stock and u produced by this study may interest economists who specialize in a number of different research fields. Economists who specialize in measurement and analysis of productivity will find these results directly relevant to their work. The results will also interest researchers who study rates of return, for example, and who need estimates of total capital stock and depreciation rates, and those who study investment incentives, who need estimates of effective tax rates.

It is found that use of the four alternative data sources on gross investment produces considerable variation in the level and growth rates of capital stocks and in implied rates of depreciation and discarding. In a series of illustrative examples, it is also found that the variations in capital stocks and rates of depreciation ultimately produce variations in multifactor growth rates, effective tax rates, and other variables. In most cases, the variation in these variables is great enough to affect research conclusions substantially.

8.2.1   Capital Stocks, Depreciation, and Multifactor Growth

The role of capital services input in the measurement of multifactor productivity growth is best explained in the context of the standard multifactor productivity growth model given in (3).

(3)
$$\frac{\dot{A}}{A} = \frac{\dot{Q}}{Q} - S_k \frac{\dot{K}}{K} - S_l \frac{\dot{L}}{L} - S_m \frac{\dot{M}}{M},$$

where

$$S_k + S_l + S_m = 1.$$

In this model, $\dot{Q}/Q$ is the growth rate of gross output, $\dot{K}/K$ the growth rate of capital services input, $\dot{L}/L$ the growth rate of labor input, $\dot{M}/M$ the growth rate of intermediate inputs, and S_k, S_l, and S_m are the shares of capital, labor, and intermediate inputs, respectively, in total expenditures on inputs. Finally, $\dot{A}/A$ is multifactor productivity as computed by performing the subtraction indicated on the right-hand side. The dot notation refers to the change in the variable over time; hence $\dot{Q}/Q$ represents the growth rate of output.[4] It is well known that this measurement model assumes that the underlying production function has constant returns to scale, that inputs are paid the value of their marginal products, and that technical change is neutral (i.e., the relative marginal products of inputs are unaffected by technical change). The $\dot{K}/K$ term is computed using rental price weights to develop a weighted average of the growth rates of individual capital stocks, as was noted earlier.

The relevance of measures of capital stocks to a variety of research fields may be examined by using an alternative productivity measurement model. Unlike equation (3), this alternative model does not develop capital services input measures by utilizing rental price weights. Instead, the alternative model, given by equation (4), uses a direct aggregate of capital asset types. The capital term, $(\dot{K}/K)'$, is simply the summation of capital stocks of all asset types; rental price weights are not used. The capital share, S_k, is the same as the capital share term in equation (3). The new multifactor productivity term, $(\dot{A}/A)'$, is computed using the alternative capital term, $(\dot{K}/K)'$.

$$(4) \qquad \left(\frac{\dot{A}}{A}\right)' = \frac{\dot{Q}}{Q} - S_k\left(\frac{\dot{K}}{K}\right)' - S_l\frac{\dot{L}}{L} - S_m\frac{\dot{M}}{M},$$

where

$$S_k + S_l + S_m = 1.$$

Use of the $(\dot{K}/K)'$ term permits the examination of the influence on calculated MFP growth of alternative capital stock measures alone, without permitting the influence of differing rental prices, resulting from differing estimates of u, to affect the computations. (Eq. [4] is inferior to eq. [3] because it abandons the use of key assumptions concerning marginal products of different capital inputs and producer equilibrium in the use of these inputs.)

To illustrate the impact of alternative estimates of capital stock on calculated MFP, we implement equation (4), using illustrative examples of statistics for the cost shares of the inputs and the growth rates of all inputs, except capital, that are roughly consistent with data for the years 1973–81 from the Japanese national accounts and other sources.[5] Substitution of these figures into a discrete approximation to equation (4),[6] and adoption of several alternative capital stock measures that are produced in later sections of this study, will then yield alternative values for the growth rate of MFP.

Table 8.1 shows the effects on calculated MFP growth, for 1973–81, of using three different alternative capital stocks—directly aggregated in each case—based on gross investment data from three different data sources: CM, EPA, and ARCS. (Data from the fourth source, RCIS, are not used in this table, because, as discussed later in this paper, the authors did not use the RCIS data for years subsequent to 1974.) The results using equation (4) are

Table 8.1   **Effects of Alternative Capital Input Series on Computed MFP Growth Based on Direct Aggregation of Capital Stocks, Average Annual Growth Rates, 1973–81[a]**

	CM	EPA	ARCS
K	3.2	2.4	3.3
MFP	.8	1.0	.8

[a]Compound rates.

shown in this table. For the period 1973–81, total capital stocks, compiled using EPA gross investment data, grew at a 2.4% average annual rate, while they grew at 3.2% and 3.3% annually using the CM and the ARCS data, respectively. MFP grew most rapidly for the computations using the EPA data. MFP grew at 1.0% for the EPA data and at 0.8% for the CM as well as the ARCS data.

Earlier it was noted that the appropriate measure of capital services input is computed as a weighted sum of different types of capital assets, using rental prices as weights. Equation (3), which uses the $\dot{K}/K$ measure of capital services inputs, provides the appropriate measure of MFP growth.

The $\dot{K}/K$ measure of capital services inputs is a weighted sum of the growth rates of all types of capital assets, as follows:

$$(5) \qquad \frac{\dot{K}}{K} = \sum S_{k_i} \frac{\dot{K_i}}{K_i}, \quad (i = 1, 2, \ldots, n).$$

The weights, S_{k_i}, are computed as:[7]

$$(6) \qquad S_{k_i} = \frac{c_i K_i}{\sum_j c_j K_j}, \quad \sum S_{k_i} = 1.$$

The implicit rental prices, the c_i, provide measures of (the usually unobservable) prices of capital services. The equations used to estimate rental prices will vary from country to country depending on the tax structure of the country. For the Japanese case, we use the following rental price equation:

$$(7) \qquad c_t = \frac{1 - [h_t + v_t(1 - h_t)]z_t}{(1 - h_t)(1 - v_t)} \, [r_t p_{t-1} + u p_t - (p_t - p_{t-1})].$$

In this equation, h_t represents the corporate income tax rate in year t, v_t is the business establishment income tax rate (a prefecture tax), z_t is the present value of ¥1 of tax depreciation allowances, r_t is the nominal rate of return on capital, p_{t-1} the price of the asset in year $t-1$, and u is the average annual rate of discards plus depreciation. (This equation represents a simplified version of the Japanese tax structure; it includes the major tax provisions affecting rental prices of capital, while omitting such taxes as the business property tax, the real property acquisition tax, the property tax on automobiles, the inhabitants tax, and an investment tax credit first introduced in 1978.) A comprehensive discussion of measurement of capital services inputs, including the development of rental prices, is presented by the U.S. Department of Labor (1983). Rental prices for use in MFP calculations for Japan are discussed in Nishimizu (1974).

This equation can be implemented, for illustrative purposes, using parameters that are of plausible magnitudes for the period 1973–81. For all variables except u, the values used are identical for the three alternatives.[8] For u, the values for each of the alternatives are those determined using equation (2) above.

Table 8.2 presents a comparison of three measures as determined by using the gross investment series developed from the alternative data sources. The first measure is u, the average annual rate of discards plus depreciation, estimated using equation (2); the second is the rental price, developed using equation (7); and the third is the rental share weights used in aggregation of capital assets, estimated using equation (6). It is possible to develop the first two measures for all four data sources, including the RCIS, while the third variable, the share weights, can be estimated only for the CM, the EPA, and the ARCS data.

Table 8.2   **Effects of Alternative Gross Investment Series on u's, Rental Prices of Capital, and Capital Weights, 1973–81**

	CM	EPA	ARCS	RCIS	Range ÷ Mean
u:					
Buildings and structures	.062	.111	.078	.029	1.171
Machinery and equipment	.173	.288	.199	.117	.880
Other	.281	.459	.317	.206	.801
Rental prices (c):					
Buildings and structures	.116	.191	.141	.066	.973
Machinery and equipment	.278	.433	.313	.203	.750
Other	.458	.685	.504	.363	.641
Capital weights (S_{k_i}):					
Buildings and structures	.175	.221	.183	N.A.	.238
Machinery and equipment	.602	.614	.593	N.A.	.035
Other	.223	.165	.224	N.A.	.289
Total	1.000	1.000	1.000	N.A.	

Note: The u's are those that are developed later in this study, using Census of Manufactures asset proportions (see table 8.8, panel A below). The numbers given for rental prices of capital and capital weights are based on various assumed parameters, as explained in the text, and are presented only to illustrate the effects of alternative gross investment series and the related alternative u's. N.A. = not available.

The values for u vary widely depending on the data set used. The RCIS data yielded the lowest values of u, the EPA data the highest. The EPA values were more than double the RCIS values for every asset and about four times the RCIS value for buildings and structures.

Rental prices also vary widely, solely as a result of the differences in the values of u. The ratio of the range of the four values for rental prices to their mean is 0.8 or more for each asset.

The capital weights also vary substantially, except for machinery and equipment. The variation in capital weights is produced both by the different values of the rental prices and by differences in the asset-type composition of total capital and in the growth rates of the assets in each data set (see eq. [6]). (The variation in share weights might have been greater if estimates had been possible for the RCIS.)

This table provides an illustration of the wide variation in rates of depreciation and discards, capital rental prices, and capital share weights that can be produced by use of different data sets for measuring gross investment.

Table 8.3 illustrates the variation in estimated MFP growth produced by use of alternative measures of capital services inputs, $\dot{K}/K$, which are in turn computed using alternative data sources for gross investment. The use of rental price weights to develop capital service inputs in this case results in wider variation in the growth rates of capital input than does the use of directly aggregated capital stocks. In table 8.3, capital services input growth rates range from 2.3% to 4.2% per year, while in table 8.1—prepared using directly aggregated capital stocks—the growth rate of total capital stock ranges from 2.4% to 3.3%. However, these differences in capital input growth rates do not produce greatly increased differences in MFP growth rates: in table 8.1, the difference between the highest and lowest MFP growth rates is 0.2%, while in table 8.3 the difference increases only to 0.3%.[9]

8.2.2 Effective Tax Rates

Measures of u are of interest to researchers who study investment incentives, because measures of depreciation and discards are needed in the computation of effective tax rates on income from capital. Measures of u are also relevant to researchers who examine profitability or rates of return.[10]

The concept of effective tax rates may be explained by beginning with the

Table 8.3	Effects of Alternative Capital Input Series on Computed MFP Growth Based on Rental Price Share-weighted Aggregation of Capital Stocks; Average Annual Growth Rates, 1973–81[a]		
	CM	EPA	ARCS
K	3.9	2.3	4.2
MFP	.7	1.0	.7

[a]Compound rates.

idea of a tax wedge. King and Fullerton (1984) define the tax wedge as the difference between the rate of return on investment and the rate of return on the savings used to finance the investment. The wedge, then, is

$$w = p - s,$$

where p is the pretax real rate of return on a marginal investment project, and s is the posttax rate of return to the saver who supplied the finance for the investment. The effective tax rate, t, is defined as the tax wedge divided by the pretax rate of return, that is,

$$t = (p - s)/p.$$

The appropriate pretax real rate of return, p, is the return net of depreciation. Hence,

$$p = MRR - d,$$

where MRR is the gross marginal rate of return to an increment to the capital stock, and d is the rate of depreciation. It is often the case, in fact, that the best measure of depreciation must be computed without detailed information on actual depreciation. In the case of Japanese manufacturing, the average annual rates of discards plus depreciation, u, that are computed in this paper may well be the best available estimates of d that can be obtained for macroeconomic studies.

Hence, the effective tax rate may best be estimated as follows:

$$t = (MRR - u - s)/(MRR - u).$$

Estimates of $p = MRR - u$ vary substantially depending on the data source used to estimate u. The alternative estimates of u produced in this paper have large effects on calculated values of p. These effects are shown in table 8.4 for one asset type, machinery and equipment. For this asset, u varies between .12 (from the RCIS) and .29 (from the EPA). Using an assumed and arbitrary value of .35 for the gross marginal rate of return (MRR)—the actual value of MRR is unknown—the resulting values of p vary from .06 (EPA) to

Table 8.4   **Effects of Alternative u's on Pretax Real Rate of Return on Investment in Machinery and Equipment**

	CM	EPA	ARCS	RCIS	Range ÷ Mean
Gross marginal rate of return (MRR)	.35	.35	.35	.35	N.A.
u	.17	.29	.20	.12	.88
Pretax real rate of return (p)	.18	.06	.15	.23	1.10

Note: The 0.35 value used for MRR is assumed and arbitrary. N.A. = not available.

.23 (RCIS). The asset type chosen, machinery and equipment, is used to illustrate the potential impact on p of variation in u because the results are intermediate between those that would be produced by examination of the two other asset types.

For studies of effective tax rates, as for studies of rental prices and MFP, variation in u may be critical. It is important, therefore, to compare values of u produced by using different data sources and to assess the merits of the various data sources.

8.3   Data Sources: Description

The Japanese national wealth surveys (NWSs) were conducted by the EPA in 1955, 1960, 1965, and 1970. The 1965 survey has been dismissed as "meager in scale and quality compared to the other years" (Nishimizu 1974, 108). The 1960 survey contains some figures that are not based on a fresh survey of assets, but rather on the 1955 asset figures adjusted for estimated increases or decreases in stocks based partly on gross investment figures (Japan, Economic Planning Agency 1964). The 1955 and 1970 NWSs are of higher quality and are used in this study.

Gross investment statistics are available or can be derived from four sources: (1) a series produced by the EPA, using the commodity flow method, but which contains no breakdown of depreciable assets, by asset type, for the manufacturing sector; (2) a series resulting from annual surveys of corporations conducted by EPA—the annual Report on the Corporate Industry Investment Survey (RCIS)—which, for the years 1956–74, obtained investment by nine asset categories; (3) a series resulting from the Census of Manufacturers (CM), conducted annually by the Japanese Ministry of International Trade and Industry (MITI), which contains three asset categories; and (4) data resulting from annual surveys of corporations conducted by the Ministry of Finance and published in the Annual Report on the Corporate Sector (ARCS), which provides no breakdown of depreciable assets by asset category. The first two of these series present private-sector investment statistics for all industries (the RCIS presents figures for the corporate private sector only), while the third presents private-sector figures only for manufacturing. The fourth source covers investment in all industries except finance and insurance.

The commodity flow method used by the EPA involves, first, the estimation of the value of production or shipments of over 2,000 goods; next, in order to prepare estimates of goods available for domestic gross fixed capital formation (GFCF) and other uses, adjustment of shipments by inventory change, exports, and imports; allocation of goods to using sectors—including intermediate demand, households, and GFCF; adjustment of values by the appropriate estimated transportation and trade margins; and, finally, allocation of total GFCF to each industry. In this process, use is made of input-output tables. The resulting statistics on GFCF form part of the national accounts (Japan, EPA 1980a, 26–37, 80–83; Japan, EPA 1980b).

Most of these data sets have been widely used by productivity researchers. The NWS capital stock data have been used by, among others, Nishimizu (1974), Nishimizu and Hulten (1978), Norsworthy and Malmquist (1983), Christensen, Cummings, and Jorgenson (1980), Uno (1984), and Jorgenson, Kuroda, and Nishimuzu (1985). Regarding the various annual gross investment series, the EPA series (in an unpublished 1973 version) was used by Denison and Chung (1976); the CM by Norsworthy and Malmquist (1983) and Uno (1984); and the RCIS by Nishimizu (1974) and Nishimizu and Hulten (1978). Jorgenson, Kuroda, and Nishimizu (1985) used all three of these series. Christensen, Cummings, and Jorgenson (1980) used gross investment series from the Japanese National Accounts, which are identical to the EPA series. To our knowledge, the ARCS data have not been used in productivity studies.

The present study examines data only on corporate private-sector manufacturing investment and on depreciable assets. Nondepreciable assets—land and inventories—generally have small (though nontrivial) weights in capital services inputs. The corporate private sector, moreover, is dominant in Japanese manufacturing: in 1970, this sector accounted for almost 97% of total manufacturing gross investment and almost 96% of net capital stock (Economic Planning Agency 1975, 1:134).

In the remainder of this section, two tasks are undertaken: first, the four sources of gross investment data are discussed in detail, and, second, information is presented on the 1955 and 1970 national wealth surveys. In the section that follows, we assess the merits and deficiencies of these various data sources in light of the purposes of this study.

Table 8.5 presents information on the four sources of gross investment data. Three of the four series result directly from surveys; the fourth, the EPA series, is based on the commodity flow method, as noted earlier. Of the three series produced by surveys, only the CM series is based on an annual census of all establishments above a certain small size. The other two, the ARCS and the RCIS, are based on probability samples. The only series that present data by asset category are the CMs (three categories for the entire period covered in this study, 1955–81) and the RCIS (nine categories, but only for the years 1956–74).[11] Therefore, the EPA and ARCS series must be supplemented by information from other sources to obtain gross investment estimates by asset type. For most of the following analysis, CM asset proportions have been applied to the EPA and ARCS totals, since RCIS asset proportions are not available after 1974.

The gross investment data used in the present study were adjusted, by the authors, in the cases of the CM, ARCS, and RCIS data sources. EPA gross investment data for private manufacturing corporations are taken directly from EPA publications.[12]

The adjustments made, for this study, to the CM data were more extensive than those made to the ARCS and RCIS data. The CM data, as published, suffer from several shortcomings: (1) they do not present separate data for

Table 8.5   Characteristics of Four Sources of Data on Gross Investment in Japanese Manufacturing by Private Corporations[a]

	CM	EPA	ARCS	RCIS
1. Producing agency	Ministry of International Trade and Industry	Economic Planning Agency	Ministry of Finance	Economic Planning Agency
2. Data source	Survey	Commodity flow for total investment; expenditure by final user for distribution by industry	Survey	Survey
3. Coverage	Total population covered[b]	Total population estimates	Sample survey: Inflated to total population	Sample survey: Inflated to total population covered[c]
4. Origin of gross investment statistics	Establishments' annual expenditures for fixed assets	Commodity flow method; several data sources	Corporations' reports of depreciation and book value of fixed assets[d]	Corporations' reports of annual expenditures for fixed assets.
5. Inclusion of unincorporated enterprises' investment?	No[e]	No[f]	No	No
6. Inclusion of acquisition of secondhand assets?	Yes[g]	Yes	Yes	Yes
7. Are figures published net of "in process" investment?	Yes[h]	Yes[h]	Yes[h]	No, for most years[i]
8. Are figures published net of investment in residences?	No	Yes	No	Yes
9. Are figures published by asset category?	Yes, 3 asset categories[j]	No	No	Yes, 9 asset categories[k]
10. Are figures in constant or current yen?	Current yen	Constant yen[l]	Current yen	Current yen
11. Are data published for fiscal or calendar year?	Calendar year	Both	Fiscal year[m]	Fiscal year[n]

| 12. | Are data available for all years, 1956–81? | Yes | Yes | Yes | Only for 1956–74 |

Sources: CM: Ministry of International Trade and Industry (various years) *Census of Manufactures, Report by Industries* (Kogyo tokei hyo sangyohen). EPA: Japan, Economic Planning Agency (1977, 1984b). ARCS: Japan, Ministry of Finance (various years), *Monthly Financial and Monetary Statistics; Special Annual Report of Financial Statistics of Corporations;* Ministry of Finance (1976); Office of the Prime Minister (various years), *Japan Statistical Yearbook,* RCIS: Japan, Economic Planning Agency (various years), *Report on the Corporate Industry Investment Survey;* Japan, Office of the Prime Minister (various years), *Japan Statistical Yearbook.*

[a]For the EPA series, "private" corporations; for the ARCS and RCIS, "profit" or "profit-oriented." For the CM, all establishments "excluding those belonging to the government and the public service corporations." These differences in terms probably entail little difference in the coverage of the series.

[b]For 1956–62, population of all establishments with 4 or more persons engaged; for 1963–75, 20 or more persons engaged; and for 1976–81, 30 or more persons engaged. We adjusted the 1963–81 figures to approximate all establishments with 4 or more persons engaged.

[c]Corporations with capital of 10 million yen or more from 1956–72; 100 million yen or more in 1973–74 (see text).

[d]The ARCS data are from annual financial statements of corporations. The authors computed gross investment from published ARCS statistics on end-of-year book values and depreciation as follows: gross investment in fiscal year *t* is the difference between fiscal year *t* and fiscal year *t* − 1 book values (end-of-year book value of fixed assets net of end-of-year book value of "in process" fixed assets) plus regular and special depreciation in fiscal year *t*. Calendar year gross investment was approximated by computing $I_{ct} = 0.75 I_{ft} + 0.25 I_{ft-1}$, where I_c and I_f are calendar year and fiscal year investment. (Throughout the period studied in this paper, the Japanese fiscal year *t* began on April 1 of calendar year *t*.)

[e]Published data include expenditures on fixed assets of incorporated and unincorporated enterprises. Authors eliminated estimated expenditures of unincorporated enterprises.

[f]The EPA publications provide separate figures for unincorporated enterprise gross investment.

[g]Expenditures on acquisition of secondhand assets are separately published for 1957–75 and are estimated by the authors for 1956 and 1976–81.

[h]Published figures on in process investment are also available for most or all years. In process figures are not available by asset category in the CM.

[i]Published figures permit elimination of in process investment by asset category and for the total in 1956, 1957, 1973, and 1974 and elimination of total in process investment in 1958, but not for other years. Therefore, the series used for all years includes in process investment.

[j]Published figures for investment in each asset category were adjusted by the authors to achieve consistency with their estimates for 1956–81 of all gross investment by establishments of four or more persons engaged, including purchases of secondhand assets in all years, after elimination of unincorporated enterprise investment.

[k]For some years, gross investment figures are available for 11 asset categories. This study used only 6 of the 9 major categories: investment in residences is eliminated; investment in "land improvement works" is combined with "other structures;" and "other investment"—a miscellaneous category—is allocated to all other categories (including residential investment) in proportion to each category's percentage of the total.

[l]We have asked the EPA whether current yen corporate gross investment figures are available for manufacturing alone.

[m]An approximation to calendar year investment is used in this study for the ARCS (see n. 4 above). A similar approximation to calendar year investment was not attempted for the RCIS, since the RCIS was not conducted in fiscal year 1955.

corporate and noncorporate investment—and separate figures are needed for the computation of an asset's rental prices (to provide weights for computing capital services inputs); (2) they do not present data for all years on the acquisition of secondhand assets; and (3) the coverage of the census was changed from establishments with four or more persons engaged (1956–62) to 20 or more persons engaged (1963–75) to 30 or more persons engaged (1976–81). The data on total investment and investment by asset category have been adjusted by the authors (1) to eliminate estimated expenditures by unincorporated enterprises; (2) to add estimates for the acquisition of secondhand assets for the seven years for which such data are not reported; and (3) to approximate, for the years after 1962, gross investment of all establishments with four or more persons engaged. Several straightforward adjustments were also needed in the ARCS and RCIS data to provide gross investment series as closely comparable as possible to the CM and EPA series.[13]

Deflators for the three gross investment series in current yen—all of the series except for the EPA series, which is only published in constant yen—were developed from two sources, the Bank of Japan's *Price Indexes Annual* (*PIA*) (various years) and the 1970 National Wealth Survey (1970 NWS). Buildings and structures, whether treated as two separate categories, as in the RCIS, or combined, as in the CM, were deflated by the *PIA*'s construction materials index. Machinery and equipment was deflated with an index computed for this study using elements of the *PIA*'s general machinery and electrical machinery indexes.[14] More complicated procedures were used to compute deflators for the asset category labeled "other." In the CM, "other" assets is a single category, while in the RCIS there are three categories of "other" assets: water transportation equipment, other transportation equipment, and tools and instruments. For the years 1955–70, price indexes published with the 1970 NWS were used. These price indexes were combined using 1970 gross investment weights from the 1970 NWS for broad categories and 1970 net capital stock weights from the 1970 NWS for detailed categories (in the absence of gross investment weights). For 1970–81, *PIA* price indexes were used, with the 1970 gross investment weights from the 1970 NWS for the broad categories and PIA weights for detailed categories.[15]

Table 8.6 shows gross investment in Japanese manufacturing in 1970 prices, for selected years, from the four data sources. Appendix table 8A.1 shows the data for all years, 1956–81. The EPA series on total constant price investment was taken directly from published EPA statistics. For the other three series, current price total gross investment was distributed among asset categories prior to deflation and subsequently deflated and summed to obtain total investment. The three CM asset category proportions were used to distribute the ARCS as well as the CM totals by asset category; the six RCIS asset categories were used for the RCIS.

EPA total gross investment was 6,595 billion yen in 1970. The ARCS, CM, and RCIS total investment figures were 79%, 76%, and 70%, respectively, of

Table 8.6   **Real Gross Investment in Japanese Manufacturing, Selected Years, 1956–81**

Period	CM[a]	EPA[b]	ARCS[a]	RCIS[a]	
Billions of 1970 yen:					
1956	453	490	469	399	686
1970	5,015	6,595	5,200	N.A.	4,605
1973	4,892	6,120	5,418	2,816[c]	4,304[c]
1981	6,023	7,455	7,127	N.A.	N.A.
Average annual growth rates:[d]					
1956–81	10.7	11.5	11.5	N.A.	N.A.
1956–70	18.7	20.4	18.7	N.A.	14.6
1956–73[c]	15.0	16.0	15.5	12.2[c]	11.4[c]
1970–81	1.7	1.1	2.9	N.A.	N.A.

Note: N.A. = not available. CM, EPA, and ARCS exclude in process investment. RCIS includes in process investment. For sources, see table 8.5.

[a]Total gross investment in current prices is divided into three asset categories for the CM and ARCS (for the RCIS, six asset categories) using the asset proportions from the CM (for the RCIS, the asset proportions from the RCIS). Each of the three (or six) categories is deflated by its own deflator. The deflated investment figures, by asset type, are then summed to yield total investment in 1970 prices.

[b]For 1956 and 1970, total gross investment in 1970 prices, as published. The 1973 and 1981 figures result from linking investment as published in 1975 prices to 1970 investment in 1970 prices.

[c]The RCIS statistics relate to corporations with capital of at least 10 million yen prior to 1973 and to corporations of at least 100 million yen beginning in 1973. This affects the levels of the 1973 figures, compared to those for earlier years, and the 1956–73 growth rate.

[d]Compound rates.

the EPA figure. The RCIS investment series, in contrast to the other three series, includes "in process" investment. It would be substantially less than 70% of EPA investment if it were presented excluding the "in process' investment.

The growth rates of gross investment also differ substantially among series. For 1956–70, the growth rate of EPA investment is almost 2% higher than the ARCS and CM growth rates and about 6% higher than the RCIS growth rate. Gross investment growth rates since 1970, though much lower, also differ substantially.

The differences among the four series in the levels and growth rates of individual assets are also substantial. The differences between the CM, ARCS, and RCIS figures for specific assets reflect the differences shown for total investment in table 8.6. The asset proportions used to distribute total investment among asset types would be similar (identical for the CM and ARCS data, since CM asset proportions are used for both in preparing table 8.6) and the deflators would be identical. The same cannot be said for the relation between EPA asset categories and the others. The EPA gross investment series comes already deflated. EPA investment by asset category could be computed (and,

Table 8.7   Net Capital Stock in Japanese Manufacturing, by Asset Category, 1955 and 1970, in Billions of Yen

Asset Category	1955 in 1955 Prices	1955 in 1970 Prices	1970 in 1970 Prices
Total	1,511.3	2,012.7	18,439.8
Nonresidential buildings and structures[a]	603.0	970.2	6,948.8
Nonresidential buildings	481.7	775.1	5,487.0
Structures[a]	121.2	195.1	1,462.8
Machinery and equipment	808.0	951.7	10,003.4
Other assets[b]	100.3	90.8	1,486.6
Water transportation equipment	4.6	4.9	38.9
Other transportation equipment[b]	41.4	47.4	499.8
Tools and instruments	54.4	38.5	947.9

Sources: Economic Planning Agency (1975), 1970 National Wealth Survey, 1:92, 134–38. Economic Planning Agency (1957), 1955 National Wealth Survey, 3:53.
[a]Includes a small amount for land improvement works in 1970.
[b]Includes small amounts for animals and plants.

later in this paper, is computed) using CM asset proportions or, up to 1974, RCIS proportions. Such a procedure implicitly assumes that all assets had the same rates of price change, an assumption that is contrary to the evidence on price changes. Unfortunately, we have not located figures on the EPA price deflator for gross manufacturing investment. Therefore, the effect of differences in price deflators cannot be assessed.

The 1955 and 1970 national wealth surveys, as noted earlier, can be used as two benchmarks of the value of assets. These two surveys provide estimates for the whole economy of the value of assets, by asset type, industry, and institutional sector (private corporate, private noncorporate, and government) as well as some information on the year of acquisition of assets. Both surveys relate to end-of-year stocks (31 December 1955 and 31 December 1970). Assets are valued at replacement cost as of the year of the survey, that is, 1955 and 1970. For the private corporate sector, the corporation was the unit of observation. The 1970 survey provides estimates of both gross and net stocks, the 1955 survey provides net stocks only.

Table 8.7 presents the 1955 and 1970 net capital stocks in manufacturing, with the 1955 stocks valued in both contemporary and 1970 prices, in asset categories similar to those used in the CM (three categories) and RCIS (six categories). All figures in this table exclude "in process" assets.

8.4   Data Sources: Assessment

This section assesses the adequacy of the 1955 and 1970 national wealth surveys for the specific needs of this paper as well as the relative merits of the four gross investment series.[16] It is concluded that the two national wealth surveys are adequate for their tasks. However, because somewhat different methods were used to determine net stocks in the two surveys, it cannot be claimed that they are ideal. It is also concluded that, for the purposes of this study, the CM is the best of the four sources of estimates of gross investment.

8.4.1   The Adequacy of the 1955 and 1970 National Wealth Surveys

In several critical respects, the 1955 and 1970 NWSs are appropriate for the purposes of serving as benchmarks for net capital stocks and the estimation of u. They were well designed to estimate end-of-year net capital stocks at 1955 and 1970 replacement costs. They both used private corporations as respondents for the survey of private corporate assets. They both used stratified probability sampling.

The surveys are less than ideal, for present purposes, in two respects: (1) the sample proportions were small, and (2) the methods used to determine net stocks differed in some respects between the two surveys.

The 1970 NWS surveyed all Japanese corporations with capital of 1 billion yen or more (1,293 corporations). It used stratified sampling, with the strata defined by size of corporate capital assets and geographical area, to select 10,017 of 701,859 remaining corporations. Among corporations with capital between 100 million and 1 billion yen, 100% were selected outside Tokyo and 50% within Tokyo. Smaller proportions of categories with smaller capital size were selcted for the survey (Japan, Economic Planning Agency 1975, vols. 1 and 4). A similar sampling plan was followed for the 1955 NWS.[17]

Both surveys were well designed to measure end-of-year capital stocks at current replacement costs. The methods used were similar in most, but not all, respects.[18] There are grounds to suspect, however, that the 1970 NWS might have underestimated the level of net stocks relative to the 1955 levels.[19] If this is so, the u's developed for this study are overestimates. A sensitivity test, carried out by increasing published 1970 NWS stocks by 10%, yielded substantially lower u's.[20] It appears unlikely that 1970 stock levels would have been as much as 10% higher than the published figures.

8.4.2   Relative Merits of the Four Gross Investment Series

The main characteristics of the four gross investment series are summarized in table 8.5. Analysis of the merits and shortcomings of each of the data sources indicates that, on balance, the CM is the best of the four sources for the purposes of this study. This analysis includes examination of the coverage of the universe of potential respondents; the shortcomings of the use of book value compared to data on expenditures on capital assets; and special problems of the EPA series.

Series Coverage

The CM series is based on a survey of all establishments above a certain relatively small size defined by numbers of persons engaged. The EPA series, constructed using the "commodity flow method," relates to all manufacturing corporations. The ARCS and RCIS are sample surveys inflated to a universe. The universe for the ARCS is all corporations; the universe for the RCIS is all corporations above a minimum capital size.

The ARCS sampled all firms above a minimum size of capital and proportions of firms below this size. Prior to 1959, all corporations with capital of 50 million yen and more were in the sample; between 1959 and 1979, all corporations with capital of 100 million yen and over; and as of 1981, all corporations of 1 billion yen and over.[21] Sample results were used to estimate financial magnitudes for corporations of all sizes.

The RCIS, unlike the ARCS, did not sample firms below a minimum capital size—10 million yen between 1956 and 1972 and 100 milliion yen in 1973 and 1974—and no estimates are made for firms below the minimum cutoff sizes. In 1969, the RCIS sent questionnaires to all corporations with capital above 1 billion yen, while for the same year the ARCS queried all corporations with capital above 100 million.[22] Clearly, the RCIS results are based on a smaller sample than the ARCS and relate only to corporations above the minimum capital size sampled.[23] The weakness of the RCIS from the viewpoint of providing accurate total investment statistics undoubtedly also affects the RCIS figures on investment by asset type.[24]

In sum, the CM provides the most complete coverage of the three sources that make use of surveys, while the RCIS provides the most scanty coverage. The EPA does not use a survey procedure; the method used for the EPA gross investment data are examined below.

Book Values versus Expenditure Data

The CM and RCIS series are based on establishment or corporation reports of annual expenditures for fixed assets whereas the ARCS is based on book values of fixed assets. Expenditure data rather than book values are generally preferred for deriving capital stock estimates.

The usual warnings against the use of book data on fixed assets in studies of capital stock and investment (Mairesse 1972) apply in some measure to the ARCS data. In particular, book value can change without investment or depreciation. Revaluation through interfirm sales can have the effect of changing book value. If one manufacturing corporation acquires assets from another manufacturing corporation at a higher value than shown on the books of the seling corporation, this causes an increase in book value even though no assets are added in manufacturing. Further, a firm may realize all its loss in a plant in one year.

In several respects, however, the ARCS book value data are more appropriate for use as a source of capital formation statistics than is usually the case. Gross fixed investment is the sum of depreciation plus the change in net fixed assets between two years, if there has been no revaluation of the type described above. Any inappropriate procedures for computing depreciation, due, for example, to features of tax law,[25] are effectively eliminated by this method. By adding depreciation to the change in book value, the influence of depreciation practices on original book value levels is simply cancelled. Further, the ARCS investment figures are from corporations' annual financial statements, which have a semiofficial status. Under tax law and accepted accounting principles, corporations are expected not to revalue assets remaining in their possession, even if their market values rise.[26]

Book values are net of retirements of equipment;[27] this permits the annual changes to reflect more accurately the changes in fixed assets actually employed. This feature, an advantage in some contexts (Faucett 1980), is a disadvantage for present purposes. The correct estimation of u requires gross investment figures that are not adjusted for retirements of assets. The CM, EPA, and RCIS figures are all available on this basis. These considerations imply that, ceteris paribus, the u's estimated from the ARCS will be smaller than those estimated from the other three series. However, the u's are larger for the ARCS than for the CM and RCIS (see table 8.2).

The gross investment figures in the CM and RCIS are computed as costs of acquiring assets. This method is likely to yield investment figures more appropriate for present purposes than the methods used for the ARCS.

In sum, the book value concept, which allows for the possibility of revaluation of assets and is net of retirements, is less appropriate for present purposes than the methods used by the CM and the RCIS. Of the three data sources that rely on surveys of respondents, we have so far uncovered important shortcomings in the ARCS and the RCIS but not in the CM.

Special Problems with the EPA Data

The EPA does not publish a current yen counterpart of its constant yen gross investment series.[28] It is necessary, therefore, to obtain investment by asset category by multiplying total constant gross investment by asset category proportions from the CM (or, up to 1974, from the RCIS). This implies that each asset category has had the same rate of price change as total gross investment, which, as noted earlier, is contrary to fact.

The EPA series, as described in section 8.2, is constructed using the commodity flow method. This method has certain advantages. The EPA procedures take advantage of a variety of data sources, including input-output tables, the CM, the ARCS, and other sources (Japan, EPA, 1980a, 26–37, 80–83; Japan, EPA, 1980b). This approach permits comparison of information from various data sources and identification of problems that might not be recognized if only one data source were used.

On the other hand, practitioners of the commodity flow method have noted that commodity flow calculations require a number of decisions that are largely arbitrary. For example, the addition of transportation and trading margins to the cost of producing investment goods requires judgment calls that are little short of guesswork. The EPA itself notes problems related to the trade and transportation margins and allocation of goods to final using sectors (Japan, EPA, 1980a, 26–27).

The CM does not suffer from these disadvantages. It would appear to be the preferred series for total investment. Unlike the EPA, it does not rely on the commodity flow method. Further, among the three sources that use survey procedures, it has the largest coverage and does not use book value. Also, asset proportions for the whole period, 1955–81, are available in the CM, but not after 1974 for the RCIS, and it is appropriate to use total investment information and asset category proportions from the same data set. Finally, it is found below that up to 1974 there is similarity between the CM asset proportions and the proportions that result from aggregation of the six RCIS asset types to approximate the three CM types.

8.5 Net Capital Stocks, 1955–81

8.5.1 Net Stocks and Calculation of u, 1955–70

Table 8.8 presents u, the average annual rate of discards plus depreciation, calculated according to the method described in section 8.1, using the 1955 and 1970 benchmark net capital stocks and 1956–70 gross investment, all in 1970 prices, as presented in table 8.7 and table 8A.1 in the appendix below. In table 8.8, panels A, B, and C present the u's computed using the CM, EPA, ARCS, and RCIS data.[29] Panel A presents u's for three asset categories. For all four data series in panel A, the gross investment figures by asset type are computed using annual proportions based on reported CM expenditures by asset type, as adjusted for this study. Panel B presents u's for six asset types, using RCIS annual asset proportions. Panel C presents results using asset proportions from the RCIS, grouped for consistency with the three CM asset categories. These grouped RCIS asset proportions are quite similar to the three CM asset proportions.[30]

The u's estimated from the EPA data set are the largest, for every asset and in all panels, followed by the ARCS u's; the RCIS u's are the lowest. Regardless of whether the RCIS or the CM asset proportions are used, the rank of the u's by asset category does not vary. Buildings and structures have the lowest rate of discards plus depreciation and "other" assets the highest.

The variation among u's is wide, as is indicated by the range to mean ratios presented in table 8.8. For most assets, the EPA u's are more than double the RCIS u's; for every asset, they exceed the CM u's by over 50%. The relatively large ARCS u's are surprising. The fact that the ARCS gross investment series is net of retirements while retirements are not deducted from the other series leads one to predict that, ceteris paribus, the ARCS u's will be relatively low.[31]

For any asset, the four net stock series constructed for 1955–70, using the four gross investment series and the corresponding u's, will yield different net

Table 8.8   Computed u's, by Asset Type, Based on CM and RCIS Asset Proportions and 1955 and 1970 Benchmarks

	CM	EPA	ARCS	RCIS	Range ÷ Mean
	A. u Computed Using Three Asset Types from CM				
Buildings and structures	.062	.111	.078	.029	1.171
Machinery and equipment	.173	.288	.199	.117	.880
Other	.281	.459	.317	.206	.801
	B. u Computed Using Six Asset Types from RCIS				
Nonresidential buildings	.047	.090	.061	.016	1.383
Structures	.100	.157	.117	.063	.860
Machinery and equipment	.181	.299	.208	.123	.868
Water transportation equipment	.297	.463	.326	.236	.687
Other transportation equipment	.122	.214	.143	.078	.977
Tools and instruments	.342	.560	.384	.252	.801
	C. u Computed Using RCIS Asset Proportions, Aggregated to Three CM Categories				
Buildings and structures	.058	.105	.073	.026	1.206
Machinery and equipment	.181	.299	.208	.123	.868
Other	.257	.432	.291	.183	.856

stocks for the years 1956–69. The benchmark stocks for 1955 and 1970 will be identical, of course, as will the 1955–70 growth rates. This would not be so if the double-benchmark method did not constrain each series.

Table 8.9 illustrates the results of dropping this constraint. It shows the differences in 1970 net stocks and 1955–70 growth rates that are produced by using the four different gross investment series, while accepting a single benchmark (the 1955 net stocks) and a single set of u's (the CM u's). The first column of table 8.9, which is produced using the CM gross investment and the CM u's, yields the 1970 and 1955–70 growth rates implied by the double-benchmark method, that is, using both 1955 and 1970 NWS net stocks.

The EPA 1970 net stocks, produced using EPA gross investment and CM u's, are 21%–39% above the 1970 NWS levels. The ARCS net stocks are all about 7% above and the RCIS net stocks about 10% below the 1970 net stock levels.[32] The differences in average annual growth rates between the CM and the ARCS are not large, but the EPA growth rates are substantially higher than those for the other three series.[33]

8.5.2 Net Stocks, 1970–81

Table 8.10 presents net stocks, by asset type, for 1970, 1973, and 1981. This table is produced using the asset proportions from the CM series (RCIS asset proportions are not available after 1974), identical net stocks in 1970

Table 8.9   Net Capital Stocks in 1970, Computed with CM u's and Own-Series Gross
             Investment[a]

	CM[b]	EPA	ARCS	RCIS[c]
1970 stocks, in billions of yen:				
Buildings and structures (u = .062)	6,949.7	8,420.8	7,447.6	6,240.1
Machinery and equipment (u = .173)	10,003.3	13,226.4	10,763.3	8,972.8
Other (u = .281)	1,486.6	2,069.1	1,598.4	1,343.0
Average annual growth rates, 1955–70[d]				
Buildings and structures	14.0	15.5	14.6	13.2
Machinery and equipment	17.0	19.2	17.6	16.1
Other	20.5	23.2	21.1	19.6

[a]Computed using CM asset proportions, 1955 net capital stocks in 1970 prices (from table 8.3), own-series gross investment in 1970 prices (from table 8.A1), and CM u's (from table 8.8).
[b]Differences in the final digit from 1970 net stock data in table 8.3 result from rounding.
[c]RCIS 1970 levels are computed using RCIS gross investment, which is gross of "in process" investment, and 1955 NWS net capital stock figures by asset type plus a proportionate amount of "in process" stock.
[d]Compound rates.

from the 1970 NWS, and the u's determined in the previous section using the double benchmark method and the CM asset proportions. The u's are those determined specifically for each gross investment series. In the absence of a national wealth survey after 1970, these provide alternative estimates of levels and average annual rates of change in net capital stocks from 1970 forward. The RCIS series is not included in this table.[34]

The differences between the CM, EPA, and ARCS 1973 or 1981 net stocks for buildings and structures are not particularly large. For the other two asset types, the differences are substantial. It was found in section 8.2 above that the differences between the EPA and the two other series in the 1973–81 growth rates are large enough to result in differences in the proportion of output growth attributed to capital inputs, and hence in the growth of multifactor productivity. These differences are nontrivial when the gross output model is used and substantially larger when the value-added model is used.

Dramatic effects on 1981 net capital stocks are produced by using u's from one series and gross investment from another series. Table 8.11 shows the 1981 net stocks, and the resulting 1970–81 growth rates, that arise from using identical 1970 net stocks, u's from the CM data, and own-series gross investment. The EPA net stock series has substantially higher levels and growth rates when computed using the CM u's rather than the EPA u's. The 1970–81 growth rate for EPA buildings and structures is 7.5% when computed with the CM u's (table 8.11) and 4.7% when computed with the EPA u's (table 8.10). Similar large effects are produced on the growth rates of the other two assets. While the 1981 level of EPA stocks for buildings and structures is only 2% higher than the CM level when both are computed with their own u's (table 8.10), it is 36% higher when both are computed using the CM u's. An oppo-

Table 8.10   Net Capital Stocks, 1970–81, Computed with Own-Series *u*'s and
Own-Series Gross Investment, Selected Years, in Billions of Yen[a]

	CM[b]	EPA	ARCS	Range ÷ Mean
Buildings and structures	(*u* = .062)	(*u* = .111)	(*u* = .078)	
1970[c]	6,949.7	6,949.9	6,949.7	0.00
1973	9,148.2	9,040.5	9,061.0	0.01
1981	11,266.5	11,478.0	10,919.4	0.05
Growth rate, 1970–81[d]	4.5	4.7	4.2	0.11
Machinery and equipment	(*u* = .173)	(*u* = .288)	(*u* = .199)	
1970[c]	10,003.3	10,003.4	10,003.5	0.00
1973	13,294.5	11,793.9	13,148.8	0.12
1981	15,877.9	13,256.9	15,936.8	0.18
Growth rate, 1970–81[d]	4.3	2.6	4.3	0.46
Other	(*u* = .281)	(*u* = .459)	(*u* = .317)	
1970	1,486.6	1,486.6	1,486.6	0.00
1973	2,209.9	1,764.6	2,225.2	0.22
1981	4,611.4	2,544.2	4,936.2	0.59
Growth rate, 1970–81[d]	10.8	5.0	11.5	0.71

[a]Computed using CM asset proportions, 1955 net capital stocks in 1970 prices (from table 8.7), own-series gross investment in 1970 prices (from table 8A.1), and own *u*'s (from table 8.8).
[b]Annual data on CM net capital stocks, 1955–81, are presented in table 8A.2.
[c]Differences in the final digit from 1970 net stock data in table 8.7 result for rounding.
[d]Compound average annual growth rate.

Table 8.11   Net Capital Stocks in 1981, Computed with CM *u*'s and Own-Series
Gross Investment[a]

	CM	EPA	ARCS
1981 stocks, in billiions of yen:			
Buildings and structures (*u* = .062)	11,266.5	15,349.3	12,116.6
Machinery and equipment (*u* = .173)	15,877.9	20,168.3	17,799.5
Other (*u* = .281)	4,611.4	3,728.1	5,339.9
Average annual growth rate, 1970–81:[b]			
Buildings and structures	4.5	7.5	5.2
Machinery and equipment	4.3	6.6	5.4
Other	10.8	8.7	12.3

[a]Computed using CM asset proportions, 1970 net capital stocks in 1970 prices (from table 8.7), own-series gross investment in 1970 prices (from table 8A.1), and CM *u*'s (from table 8.8).
[b]Compound rates.

site effect is produced when the EPA u's are used to compute the CM and ARCS stocks; the 1981 stock levels of these two series decrease compared with the levels computed with own-series u's. These comparisons indicate the inappropriateness of using u's from one series and gross investment from another series.

There is widespread evidence of a slowdown after 1973 in productivity growth in the manufacturing sectors, as well as for the total economies, of large industrialized countries (Neef and Dean 1984; Neef and Thomas 1987; Kendrick 1981). The slowdown in manufacturing labor productivity growth in Japan, as in several other countries, began after 1973.[35] Because of this slowdown, it is of interest to compare 1955–73 and 1973–81 growth rates of capital.

Table 8.12, computed using the CM, EPA, and ARCS own-series u's, shows remarkably high growth rates of net capital stock for the period 1955–73. The 1955–73 growth rates for the three series are, of course, fairly close since they are constrained to equality for the 1955–70 period. Dramatic declines in growth rates, reflected in all three capital stock series and affecting all three asset types, occurred in the 1973–81 period. The 1973–81 growth rates for buildings and structures and machinery and equipment were all less than one-quarter of the 1955–73 growth rates for all three series used for table 8.12. This slowdown in the growth of capital stocks almost certainly contributed in a major way to the post-1973 slowdown in labor productivity growth in Japanese manufacturing.[36]

8.5.3   EPA-based Depreciation in an International Perspective

The estimates of u based on the EPA investment data are much higher than the estimates derived from the three other data sets, as is noted above (table 8.8). The EPA-based estimates are higher for all three asset types, but they are especially high for buildings and structures. The four estimates of u for buildings and structures in Japanese manufacturing are compared in table 8.13 with estimates from five studies of depreciation rates for buildings or buildings and structures in the United States, the United Kingdom, and France. The EPA-based rate of 11.1% is more than four percentage points higher than the highest estimate listed for the other countries. Information on depreciation rates of buildings in additional countries can be computed from information on capital service lives in manfacturing presented in Blades (1983). These depreciation rates are also lower than the EPA-based estimate of u for buildings and structures. This reinforces the judgment, reached above without benefit of these statistical results, that the EPA is not the preferred source of investment data for Japanese manufacturing.

The EPA data have been used in a number of studies of Japanese productivity, including Denison and Chung (1976) and Jorgenson, Kuroda, and Nishimizu (1985).[37] The present results indicate that this choice of data sources

Table 8.12   **Growth Rates of Net Capital Stocks, by Asset Type, 1955–73 and 1973–81[a]**

	CM	EPA	ARCS
1955–73:			
Buildings and structures	13.3	13.2	13.2
Machinery and equipment	15.8	15.0	15.7
Other	19.4	17.9	19.4
1973–81:			
Buildings and structures	2.6	3.0	2.4
Machinery and equipment	2.2	1.5	2.4
Other	9.6	4.7	10.5
1973–81 minus 1955–73:			
Buildings and structures	− 10.7	− 10.2	− 10.8
Machinery and equipment	− 13.6	− 13.5	− 13.3
Other	− 9.8	− 13.2	− 8.9

[a]Growth rates are compound average annual rates. Figures computed using CM asset proportions, own-series gross investment in 1970 prices, and own-series u's. The RCIS is omitted from this table because 1973 and 1974 gross investment figures are not fully comparable to those of earlier years, and the series is not used after 1974 in this study.

Table 8.13   **Annual Percentage Depreciation of Buildings, Estimates from Several Studies**

Country/Building Class	Study	Depreciation (%)
Japan: manufacturing buildings		
and structures[a]	CM	6.2
	EPA	11.1
	ARCS	7.8
	RCIS	2.9
United States: industrial buildings	BLS[b]	3.4
	BEA[c]	6.5
	Hulten/Wykoff study[d]	3.6
United Kingdom: buildings	King/Fullerton study[e]	2.5
France: manufacturing buildings		
and structures	King/Mairesse study[f]	5.7

[a]See this study, table 8.8.

[b]BLS is the Bureau of Labor Statistics. First-year decay computed using a hyperbolic decay function. For discussion of the BLS hyperbolic decay function, see U.S. Department of Labor, Bureau of Labor Statistics (1983, app. C.)

[c]BEA is the Bureau of Economic Analysis of the U.S. Department of Commerce. We computed this using the BEA estimate of asset life of industrial buildings and applying the double-declining-balance formula, $d = 2/L$, where d is the computed annual depreciation rate and L is the asset life in years. For a justification of this formula, see King and Fullerton (1984, 29).

[d]Hulten and Wykoff (1981).

[e]King and Fullerton (1984, 46). Computed by King and Fullerton using the double-declining-balance formula.

[f]King and Mairesse (1984). We made computations using the double-declining-balance formula.

may not be the best for the manufacturing sector. However, Jorgenson and his colleagues faced limited alternatives. They examined productivity trends for a number of industries outside manufacturing, and the CM data are not available for these industries. The desirability of using the same source of capital input data for all industries undoubtedly weighed against the use of the CM data for manufacturing. Further, it is noted above that the ARCS and the RCIS gross investment data have their own serious shortcomings.

8.6 Suggestions Regarding Data Collection

As a by-product of the analysis of Japanese capital and investment data for this study, several ideas have occurred to us on current and future data collection practices.

The Japanese national wealth surveys present the researcher with an opportunity without counterpart in any other major country with a large private sector—to undertake studies of capital using an official measure, based on well-designed surveys, of the level of capital stocks. Only in Japan, among the large private enterprise economies, have such surveys regularly been conducted (Ward 1976; Blades 1983).[38] Therefore, only in Japan is the double-benchmark method an attractive alternative to the perpetual inventory method. In light of this situation, the resumption of national wealth surveys—none has been conducted since 1970—would be most useful, despite the relatively small sample sizes of these surveys.[39]

Regarding gross investment series, there are presently four series on total gross investment, one of which is confined to manufacturing. By contrast, only one of the four sources currently provides manufacturing data on investment by asset category, and that is the source that relates only to manufacturing. Balance sheet information on asset distribution is available from reports on more than 1,800 firms listed on the large stock exchanges, including several hundred outside manufacturing.[40] The industrial coverage of these data, however, excludes primary industries, finance, and insurance. Further, the data relate only to large corporations.[41] We suggest that consideration be given to reducing the number of surveys of total investment and introducing data collection on investment by asset category by industry for the whole economy.

It would be most useful if the EPA were to publish a continuous series of total gross investment in current prices, compatible with the EPA constant price series. Finally, it would be interesting to know why the level of total gross investment in current prices in 1970 and 1975, as reported by the EPA, is substantially greater than the levels reported by the other data sources.

We convey these ideas with some hestitation. We are not acquainted with the costs of various types of surveys in Japan. We are, further, unacquainted with the range of client interests that inform present practices; some present data collection practices, for example, may proceed from clients' interests in forecasting.

8.7 Conclusions

The main conclusions of this study are as follows.

1. The double-benchmark method of measuring net capital stocks, an attractive method from a theoretical perspective, is the most appropriate method to use for Japanese manufacturing. As the 1970 NWS becomes more outdated, and if another NWS is not soon undertaken, it may be advisable to estimate capital stocks for recent years using the perpetual inventory method.

2. The Census of Manufactures series, as adjusted for this study, is the best series to use for annual total investment and for investment by asset category for the whole period 1955 to the present. While the RCIS offers information on six asset categories, as opposed to the three offered by the CM, the deficiencies of the RCIS as a survey are serious. The CM is the preferable series even for the years 1956–74, when asset-type data are available from the RCIS.

3. There are substantial differences among the post-1970 growth rates of net stocks computed using the CM, EPA, and ARCS data. These differences are large enough to lead to nontrivial differences in the measured growth of multifactor productivity in Japanese manufacturing.

4. The growth rates of net capital stocks for the period 1973–81 were about one-half to one-quarter of the growth rates for the period before 1973. This decline affected all three asset types and is reflected in the three alternative net stock series used for the post-1973 period. This slowdown in the growth of net capital stocks almost certainly contributed in a major way to the post-1973 slowdown in the growth of labor productivity in Japanese manufacturing.

5. Considerable variation in estimated capital stocks, rates of depreciation and discarding, multifactor growth, and effective tax rates is produced by use of the four alternative data sources on Japanese manufacturing gross investment. The variation in most cases is great enough to affect substantially the conclusions that researchers or policymakers might reach.

This study began by observing that students of the Japanese economy are blessed with statistical riches, and that this blessing might ultimately prove embarrassing. It is perhaps more important to suggest that the different results obtained with these alternative data series provide a sobering lesson to those who would use available data—for Japan as well as for other countries—and announce their conclusions without qualification. If other countries had four sets of data providing information on rates of depreciation or multifactor growth, in how many instances could we expect that the results would be substantially the same for each data set?

Appendix

Gross Investment and Net Capital Stocks in Japanese Manufacturing: Annual Data

Table 8A.1   **Gross Investment in Japanese Manufacturing in 1970 Prices, 1956–81, in Billions of Yen[a]**

Year	CM	EPA	ARCS	RCIS
1956	453	490	469	686
1957	702	797	735	712
1958	717	810	869	565
1959	792	974	777	854
1960	1,145	1,569	1,527	1,235
1961	1,592	2,084	1,574	1,631
1962	1,897	2,385	1,985	1,427
1963	1,873	2,430	1,981	1,417
1964	2,037	2,662	1,954	1,702
1965	2,084	2,445	2,304	1,462
1966	1,883	2,499	2,085	1,556
1967	2,488	3,326	2,723	2,469
1968	3,507	4,746	3,370	3,188
1969	4,266	5,709	4,871	3,824
1970	5,015	6,595	5,200	4,605
1971	5,245	6,077	5,174	4,415
1972	4,840	5,976	5,472	4,162
1973	4,892	6,120	5,418	4,309
1974	4,760	6,141	5,072	4,224
1975	4,160	5,542	4,835	. . .[b]
1976	4,505	5,557	4,673	. . .
1977	4,654	5,621	4,523	. . .
1978	4,389	4,982	5,111	. . .
1979	4,875	5,772	5,590	. . .
1980	5,117	6,851	6,166	. . .
1981	6,023	7,455	7,127	. . .

Note: CM, EPA, and ARCS exclude in process investment; RCIS includes in process investment.

[a]For methods of computation and sources see notes to tables 8.5 and 8.7.

[b]Ellipses indicate that, although total RCIS investment data are available after 1974, investment by asset type is not, and so the total investment data are not used in this study. See discussion in text.

Table 8A.2   Net Capital Stocks in Japanese Manufacturing in 1970 Prices, 1955–81, in Billions of Yen

Year	Buildings and Structures	Machinery and Equipment	Other	Total
1955	970.2	951.7	90.8	2,012.7
1956	1,059.5	1,052.7	103.2	2,215.3
1957	1,214.6	1,291.7	133.9	2,640.2
1958	1,353.1	1,511.7	156.1	3,020.8
1959	1,499.0	1,737.6	186.5	3,423.0
1960	1,776.8	2,101.3	243.5	4,121.6
1961	2,154.9	2,683.0	333.3	5,171.2
1962	2,627.4	3,326.9	421.8	6,376.1
1963	3,033.9	3,851.1	506.4	7,391.4
1964	3,480.3	4,369.7	580.5	8,430.5
1965	3,887.8	4,850.7	640.3	9,378.8
1966	4,145.9	5,140.1	714.6	10,000.6
1967	4,534.6	5,765.1	840.8	11,140.4
1968	5,197.2	6,916.3	1,017.8	13,131.3
1969	5,994.4	8,367.8	1,228.4	15,590.6
1970	6,949.7	10,003.3	1,486.6	18,439.6
1971	7,898.5	11,516.2	1,688.7	21,103.5
1972	8,602.3	12,534.5	1,847.5	22,984.3
1973	9,148.2	13,294.5	2,209.9	24,652.6
1974	9,766.9	13,800.6	2.354.4	25,921.8
1975	10,188.8	13,926.1	2,308.9	26,423.8
1976	10,454.6	14,351.5	2,430.4	27,236.4
1977	10,666.9	14,707.5	2,698.9	28,073.3
1978	10,768.3	14,681.3	3,045.5	28,495.1
1979	10,871.2	14,838.6	3,593.7	29,303.5
1980	11,003.6	15,146.8	4,016.4	30,166.8
1981	11,266.5	15,877.9	4,611.4	31,755.7

Note: Figures are derived from CM data. For methods of computation, see text and esp. notes to tables 8.5, 8.7, and 8.10. Excludes in process investment. Detail may not sum to total because of rounding.

Notes

1. Although u is a constant, its use does not imply acceptance of the hypothesis that the loss-of-efficiency function is geometric. Rather, u is the average rate of discards plus depreciation over the period of time between two surveys of net assets. Underlying this average rate could be any one of a number of loss-of-efficiency functions.

2. The proof that at least one real zero is contained in the set of all zeros for every real polynomial requires that the polynomial be of odd degree (Nishimizu 1974).

3. For a detailed discussion of productive capital stocks, see U.S. Department of Labor, Bureau of Labor Statistics (1983, app. C). While u does not explicitly correct stocks for loss of efficiency, it is estimated in such a way as to correct for any change in the average age of assets between the two benchmark years. Net stocks in both years are measured net of depreciation. So, if benchmark A contains gross stocks that are,

on average, older than the stocks in benchmark B, the net stock to gross stock ratio will be appropriately lower for benchmark A.

4. Eq. (1) is based on a Divisia index with changing weights, which requires continuous data. Multifactor productivity indexes are customarily based on the Törnqvist index number formula, which is a discrete approximation to the Divisia index. See U.S. Department of Labor, Bureau of Labor Statistics (1983). See also Mark and Waldorf (1983).

5. The values adopted are $\dot{Q}/Q$, 2.79% per year (compound average annual rate); $\dot{L}/L$, 0.8% per year; $\dot{M}/M$, 2.2% per year. S_k, 0.147%; s_1, 0.168%; S_m, 0.685%.

6. The discrete approximation involved the use of compound average annual rates of change for the growth rates of Q, K, L, and M.

7. For use in the Törnqvist index number formula, eq. (6) is estimated as:

$$S_{k_i} = \frac{1}{2}(S_{k_{i_t}} + S_{k_{i_{t-1}}}),$$

where

$$S_{k_{i_t}} = \frac{C_{i_t}K_{i_t}}{\sum_j C_{j_t}K_{j_t}},$$

and where $t = 1981$ and $t - 1 = 1973$. For this illustrative exercise, the value of c_i is the same for both years.

8. The magnitudes used are as follows. For all assets, $p = 1.0$, $r = 0.8$, and $[h_t + v_t (1 - h_t)] = 0.47$—and, therefore, $(1 - h_t) (1 - v_t) = 0.53$. For $(p_t - p_{t-1})$, the first difference in price appreciation, average annual rates were assumed to be .066 for buildings and structures, 0.047 for machinery and equipment, and 0.0 for other depreciable assets. For z, the values used were 0.4 for buildings and structures, 0.6 for machinery and equipment, and 0.7 for other assets. For purposes of the present illustration, nondepreciable assets (inventories and land) are ignored.

9. The differences in MFP are much greater when MFP is computed for a value-added growth model instead of a gross output growth model. Eqq. (3) and (4) are gross output models—the output measure is gross output and inputs are capital, labor, and materials. A value-added model uses a value-added measure for output and inputs of capital and labor only. The value-added counterpart of eq. (4)—i.e., when directly aggregated capital stocks are used for capital input—yields MFP measures of 3.3%, 3.7%, and 3.3% when capital input is measured using data from the CM, EPA, and ARCS series, respectively. If rental price–weighted capital stocks are used—i.e., the value-added counterpart of eq. (3)—the resulting MFP measures are 3.0%, 3.8%, and 2.9%, respectively, for the same three data sources. For further discussion of the distinction between value added and gross output MFP models, see Gullickson and Harper (1987).

10. Recent studies of effective tax rates include King and Fullerton (1984) and Jorgenson and Sullivan (1981). A recent study of international comparisons of rates of return is King and Mairesse (1984).

11. The absence of 1955 data from the RCIS presents only minor problems because 1955 stocks are derived from the 1955 National Wealth Survey. It is possible to estimate post-1974 asset category proportions, consistent with the RCIS asset categories, using balance sheet data from all firms whose common stocks are listed on the Tokyo, Nagoya, and Osaka stock exchanges (1,299 firms, of which 964 are in manufacturing). Jorgenson, Kuroda, and Nishimizu (1985) used these data. Gross investment by asset category is also published in the Japanese national accounts, but only for the total economy.

12. Data in 1975 prices were linked to data in 1970 prices at 1970. In 1978, the

EPA revised its estimates of nonresidential business capital investment for 1965 forward, in 1975 prices, in connection with its adoption of a new system of national accounts (Japan, Economic Planning Agency 1980b, 1). The old series is used for the years 1965–70, as well as for the earlier years. After computations used in this paper were completed (in the summer of 1985) the EPA revised its data on capital stock in 1975 prices; later, EPA published data in 1980 prices.

13. For ARCS adjustments, see table 8.5, n.4. Further, "in process" assets for 1954–59 had to be estimated. For 1956–59, the ARCS fixed assets at the end of the fiscal year were multiplied by the ratio of "in process" to fixed assets, at end of fiscal year, from the RCIS. For 1954 and 1955, the ARCS fixed assets were multiplied by a ratio that was a weighted average of the 1956 to 1958 ratios. Special depreciation for 1954–59 was estimated using ratios of special to total depreciation presented in Ratcliffe (1969, 83–91). For RCIS data adjustments, see table 8.5, n. 11.

14. Prices of exported goods and goods produced mainly for consumers were excluded.

15. These procedures were used for the "other" asset deflators because deficiencies in the *PIA* weights and price indexes affect the "other" assets more severely than they affect buildings and structures and machinery and equipment. The *PIA* weights reflect total transactions in the economy and some of the price indexes relate to commodities purchased mainly by consumers (e.g., cars, bicycles, motorcycles, and cameras). It was necessary to use *PIA* price indexes for 1970–81 because no better price indexes were available. The index numbers, for selected years, are as follows:

Year	Buildings and Structures	Machinery and Equipment	Other
1956	.638	.919	1.226
1970	1.000	1.000	1.000
1981	2.178	1.578	.908

An index was also computed for "other" assets from the *PIA*, using *PIA* weights, for 1955–70. The 1956 value for this index was 1.134. It was decided that the indexes published with the 1970 NWS were preferable.

16. The adequacy of the deflators used in this study is not examined, though it is clear that their quality could be improved (see sec. 8.2.). In particular, the index used for buildings and structures could be improved by development of a weighted index of construction materials and construction labor costs.

17. Firms were divided into five size categories. For each of these five categories, 19 subcategories were defined on the basis of geographical area and capital size. Among firms above 50 million yen, 100% were sampled. For some of the smaller size categories, 100% of the corporations in some of the 19 subcategories were sampled (Japan, Economic Planning Agency 1957, vols. 3 and 6).

18. The 1955 NWS took advantage of an extensive revaluation of assets that was carried out following passage of the Asset Revaluation Law, which permitted corporations to revalue their assets as of January 1, 1950. Assets not revalued as of this date, and assets subsequently acquired, were added to the revalued assets. Firms were asked to report time of acquisition and acquisition costs. For depreciable assets in manufacturing and most other industries, assets were depreciated by the EPA, which used asset-specific constant depreciation rates. Price deflators that were specific to type of asset and usage—one price series went back to 1874—were applied to obtain values in 1955 costs. For assets revalued in 1950, the following formula was used: 1955 replacement cost of assets $= V - S + I$, where V is the 1955 value of the assets revalued in 1950 and valued at 1955 prices by application of the appropriate constant depreciation rate and deflator, S is the scrapping of assets valued at 1955 replacement cost, and I is assets

acquired since the revaluation, minus depreciation, valued at 1955 replacement costs. For assets whose time of acquisition or acquisition cost was not known, the EPA used an "assessment value" as of 31 December 1955, based on market prices as of that time. The 1970 NWS methods differed from those of the 1955 NWS in at least one respect: gross stocks in 1970 prices were estimated first and net stocks were then computed using constant depreciation rates. Also, the description of methods used for the 1970 NWS contains no reference to the 1950 revaluation. For both surveys, assets' tax lives were explicitly used for average expected lifetimes. Given the average lifetimes, constant depreciation rates were computed.

19. Tax law changes in 1961 and 1964 reduced substantially the useful lives of assets other than buildings and structures. The lifetimes applicable to buildings and structures were reduced in 1966. (Ratcliffe 1969, 88). Since tax lives were used to depreciate assets in both wealth surveys, it would appear that these tax law changes would have reduced the level of 1970 assets relative to 1955 levels. This impression is somewhat reinforced by statements by the EPA (Economic Planning Agency 1980b, 10). When the EPA was developing its capital series, it initially computed 1956–70 stock levels on the base 1955 by adding post-1955 investment and deducting depreciation and discards. The result was a level of 1970 stocks 7% higher than that in the 1970 NWS. These observations do not conclusively show that 1970 levels were underestimates. It is possible that useful lives of assets did decline after 1955. And EPA itself might have initially overestimated investment and/or underestimated discards and depreciation over the 1956–70 period. The EPA decided to accept the 1970 NWS levels of 1970 stocks as definitive and to recompute its investment, discard, and depreciation series.

20. The u's obtained by increasing published 1970 NWS stocks by 10% using the CM gross investment and asset proportions, are as follows:

	Buildings and Structures	Machinery and Equipment	Other
Item 1: published 1955 and 1970 NWS stocks	.062	.173	.281
Item 2: published 1955 NWS stocks and 1970 NWS stocks plus 10%	.043	.141	.237
Item 1 ÷ Item 2	1.44	1.23	1.19

These lower u's yield higher average annual growth rates for net stocks for the 1970–81 period; these growth rates are as follows:

	Buildings and Structures	Machinery and Equipment	Other
Item 1: published 1955 and 1970 NWS stocks	4.5	4.3	10.8
Item 2: published 1955 NWS stocks and 1970 NWS stocks plus 10%	5.8	5.7	12.0
Item 2 ÷ Item 1	1.29	1.33	1.11

21. In 1981, all corporations below 1 billion yen were divided into six categories, and larger proportions of the categories with the larger firms were sampled. For example, one-fifth of the corporations between 50 and 100 million yen were sampled, but only ⅓₀₀ of the corporations below 2 million yen were sampled (Japan, Ministry of Finance 1982, *Special Annual Report of Financial Statements of Corporations*).

22. In 1969, the RCIS obtained results from 14,956 manufacturing corporations. Surveyed corporations in all industries were estimated to have been responsible for 52% of all private, nonhousehold, domestic gross fixed capital formation and 50% of nonresidential capital formation (Japan, EPA 1970, *Report on the Corporate Industry Investment Survey.*)

23. When the minimum size rose from 10 million yen to 100 million yen in 1973, there was a substantial decline in the population of firms to which the published RCIS investment figures applied. Despite this, published current value investment rose in 1973.

24. In one respect, the RCIS was superior. The RCIS questionnaire was especially well designed to elicit the actual magnitude of annual spending for new capital assets.

25. Hulten and Wykoff (1980), working with U.S. data, find that economic depreciation is less than allowed for in the tax code. They also find, however, that economic depreciation depends on the tax laws; the more rapidly a firm may depreciate a piece of equipment, the more rapidly its resale value declines, because part of the value of any piece of equipment is the present value of the remaining depreciation allowances.

26. Corporations were permitted, by law, to revalue their assets in 1950 and in 1953, before the earliest ARCS data used in this study.

27. This may not be entirely correct. It is possible, for example, that tax law might permit the pooling of assets of certain types into asset classes of a particular year of acquisition for purposes of computing depreciation. This might lead to the retention on the books of some scrapped assets until the whole asset class reaches its service life, as provided in tax law.

28. The EPA does prepare unpublished deflators. Efforts have been made to obtain such unpublished data.

29. The RCIS investment series includes "in process" investment. Therefore, u was computed using 1955 and 1970 net stocks that include "in process" assets, distributed proportionately across asset categories.

30. The averages of the three asset percentages over the years 1956–1974 are as follows:

	CM	RCIS
Buildings and structures	26.0	26.2
Machinery and equipment	61.7	62.0
Other	12.3	11.7

The percentages also compare closely for individual years, except for 1956, the first year of the RCIS. In 1956, buildings and structures accounted for 34.5% of total gross investment according to the RCIS and 24.8% according to the CM. During the years 1957–74, there were only five instances when the percentages for one of the assets differed between the two data sources by as much as three or four percentage points.

31. Some sensitivity to benchmarks is indicated by comparing the RCIS u's in panel B of table 8.8 with u's obtained by Nishimizu (1974, 113), who used benchmarks from the 1955 and 1960 NWSs. For the largest asset categories, machinery and equipment and nonresidential buildings, the u's are close (for machinery and equipment, 0.123 in

the current study and 0.133 in Nishimizu) while for smaller categories they differ greatly (for tools and instruments, 0.252 and 0.127).

32. The uniformity of the RCIS and ARCS percentages by asset category reflects the fact that the same deflators are used for these series. The EPA figures were deflated by EPA. Regarding the levels of the RCIS figures, see table 8.9, n. 3.

33. Apart from the differences in deflators betwen the EPA and the other series, the differences between the series presented in table 8.9 really result indirectly from differences in the four gross investment series. It is the latter differences that produce the differences in the u's.

34. The RCIS was continued after 1974, though that was the last year in which it included questions on asset acquisition by asset type. The post-1974 RCIS results are not used in this study. Analysis presented in section 8.4 indicates that it is not one of the more accurate sources of total annual gross investment.

35. For the United States, France, Germany, and the United Kingdom, see Neef and Dean (1984). In Japan, a dip in labor productivity growth occurred in 1971, followed by a strong recovery that extended through 1973, when growth was over 10%. The average annual compound growth rate for 1955–73 was 9.6%, for 1973–81, 5.5% (unpublished data series underlying Neef and Thomas 1987). The apparent persuasiveness of these figures disguises the difficulty of separating cyclical and long-term trends in productivity growth (Berndt 1984).

36. It is interesting to note that the slowdown in the growth rates of capital stock began before the slowdown in labor productivity. There is little evidence of a slowdown in labor productivity up to 1973. The growth rates of net stock, on the other hand, began to decline around 1970 and, with a few exceptions, dropped steadily during the 1971–74 period. During the 1971–74 period, there were declines in the net stock growth rate every year, or every year but one, in all three CM, all three EPA, and two of the three ARCS series. The ARCS "other" asset category showed increases in two of the four years.

37. Jorgenson, Kuroda, and Nishimizu (1985) also make use of the CM data, for distributing EPA gross investment in manufacturing by industry, and the RCIS data, for dividing gross investment into asset categories. After 1974, stock market information is used for dividing gross investment into asset categories.

38. In the United States, annual gross book value data are compiled by the Bureau of the Census using the Annual Survey of Manufactures and by the Internal Revenue Service for its Statistics of Income series. The Bureau of Labor Statistics is comparing these series, for selected industries, with series compiled using the perpetual inventory method to shed light on cyclical variations in multifactor productivity in the United States. See Powers (1985) and Powers (1988). However, these series have several shortcomings compared with the national wealth surveys: they are not based on asset data of specific vintages and they provide little information by detailed asset type. Further, they suffer from the general shortcomings of book value data discussed above.

39. The Japanese Statistics Council (a permanent advisory organ on government statistics) prepared a report to the Director General of the Management and Coordination Agency entitled "Medium- and Long-Term Plans for Government Statistical Activities," dated 25 October 1985. The council noted that "the economy of Japan has experienced oil-shocks twice since the survey of national wealth was conducted in 1970 and is assumed to have undergone some large changes in the structure of its capital accumulation." The council also stated that "the present situation where the estimation of capital accumulation in later years has to be made with the 1970 National Wealth Survey results as a benchmark creates some arduous problems." The council concluded that "the development of statistics on tangible assets is especially needed" and that "such statistics should urgently be developed." (Management and Coordination Agency 1986, 4).

40. As of the middle 1980s, balance sheet data were available on tape for 1,299 firms, including 335 outside manufacturing, whose common stocks were listed on the Tokyo, Nagoya, and Osaka stock exchanges.

41. The Ministry of Agriculture, Forestry, and Fisheries conducts an annual sample survey that yields information on capital assets in agriculture. The national accounts include tables on gross fixed capital formation for the whole economy, by six asset categories, in current and constant prices.

References

Berndt, Ernst R. 1984. Comment. In *International comparisons of productivity and causes of slowdown,* ed. John W. Kendrick. Cambridge, Mass.: Ballinger.

Blades, Derek. 1983. Service lives of fixed assets. Working Paper no. 4. Organization for Economic Cooperation and Development, Economics and Statistics Department, Paris (March).

Christensen, Laurits R., Diane Cummings, and Dale W. Jorgenson. 1980. Economic growth, 1947–73: An international comparison. In *New developments in productivity measurement and analysis,* ed. John W. Kendrick and Beatrice N. Vaccara. Chicago: University of Chicago Press.

Denison, Edward F., and William K. Chung. 1976. *How Japan's economy grew so fast: The sources of postwar expansion.* Washington, D.C.: Brookings.

Faucett, Jack G. 1980. Comment. In *The measurement of capital,* ed. Dan Usher. Chicago: University of Chicago Press.

Gullickson, William, and Michael J. Harper. 1987. Multifactor productivity in U.S. manufacturing, 1949–83. *Monthly Labor Review* 110 (October): 18–28.

Hulten, Charles R., and Frank C. Wykoff. 1981. The measurement of economic depreciation. In *Depreciation, inflation, and the taxation of income from capital,* ed. C. R. Hulten. Washington, D.C.: Urban Institute Press.

———. 1980. Economic depreciation and the taxation of structures in United States manufacturing industries: An empirical analysis. In *The measurement of capital,* ed. Dan Usher. Chicago: University of Chicago Press.

Japan, Bank of Japan, Bureau of Statistics. Various years. *Price indexes annual* (Bukka shisu nenpo).

Japan, Economic Planning Agency. 1984a. *Annual report on national accounts.*

———. 1984b. *Capital stock of private enterprises* (Minkan kigyo shihon sutokku).

———. 1975. *1970 national wealth survey of Japan* (Kokufu chosa sogo hokoku). 6 vols. Vol. 1: *Summary report.*

———. 1964. *1960 national wealth survey.* (Kokufu chosa hokoku).

———. Various years (annual). *Report on the corporate industry investment survey* (Hojin kigyo toshi jisseki tokei chosa hokoku).

Japan, Economic Planning Agency, Economic Research Institute. 1980a. *A system of national accounts (Definitions—concepts—sources—methods).*

———. 1980b. *Non-residential business capital stock in Japan—concept and methodology.*

Japan, Economic Planning Agency, Economic Research Institute, National Income Department. 1957 (1958 for vols. 1, 2, 4, and suppl. to vol. 3). *1955 national wealth survey* (Kokufu chosa hokoku). 6 vols. and suppl. to vol. 3. Vol. 1: *Summary report;* vol. 3: *Survey report of assets of corporations.*

Japan, Economic Planning Agency, National Income Department. 1977. *Gross capital stock of private enterprises, 1955–75* (Minkan kigyo soshihon sutokku, 30–50).

Japan, Management and Coordination Agency, Statistics Bureau [before 1984, Office of the Prime Minister, Bureau of Statistics]. 1986. *Statistical notes of Japan,* no. 42 (March).

————. Various years. *Annual report on the unincorporated enterprise survey* (Kojin kigyo keizai chosa nenpo).

————. Various years (annual). *Japan statistical yearbook* (Nihon tokei nenkan).

Japan, Ministry of Finance. Various years (annual). *Monthly financial and monetary statistics: Special annual report of financial statements of corporations.*

Japan, Ministry of Finance, Bureau of Securities. 1976. *Statistical yearbook of incorporated enterprises, 1960–74,* vol. 1.

Japan, Office of the Prime Minister, Bureau of Statistics. *See* Japan, Management and Coordination Agency, Statistics Bureau.

Jorgenson, Dale W., Masahiro Kuroda, and Mieko Nishimizu. 1985. Japan-U.S. industry-level productivity comparisons, 1960–1979. Paper presented at the National Bureau of Economic Research Conference on Research in Income and Wealth. Cambridge, Mass., 26–28 August.

Jorgenson, Dale W., and Martin A. Sullivan. 1981. Inflation and corporate capital recovery. In *Depreciation, inflation, and the taxation of income from capital,* ed. C. R. Hulten. Washington, D.C.: Urban Institute Press.

Kendrick, John W. 1981. International comparisons of recent productivity trends. In *Essays in contemporary economic problems: Demand, productivity and population,* ed. William Fellner. Washington, D.C.: American Enterprise Institute.

King, Mervyn A., and Don Fullerton. 1984. *The taxation of income from capital.* Chicago: University of Chicago Press.

King, Mervyn, and Jacques Mairesse. 1984. Profitability in Britain and France, 1956–1975: A comparative study. In *Measuring profitability and capital costs: An international study,* ed. Daniel Holland. Lexington, Mass.: Lexington Books.

Mairesse, Jacques. 1972. L'evaluation du capital fixe productif: Methodes et resultats. *Les collections de l'INSEE,* C. 18–19. Paris: Institut National de la Statistique et des Etudes Economiques (November).

Mark, Jerome A., and William H. Waldorf. 1983. Multifactor productivity: A new BLS measure. *Monthly Labor Review* 106 (December): 3–15.

Neef, Arthur, and Edwin Dean. 1984. Comparative changes in labor productivity and unit labor costs by manufacturing industry: United States and Western Europe. Paper presented at the American Enterprise Institute Conference on Interindustry Differences in Productivity Growth, Washington, D.C. (October).

Neef, Arthur and James Thomas. 1987. Productivity in manufacturing at home and abroad. *Monthly Labor Review* 110 (December): 25–30.

Nishimizu, Mieko. 1974. Total factor productivity analysis: A dissaggregated study of the post-war Japanese economy with explicit consideration of intermediate inputs, and comparison with the United States. Ph.D. diss., Johns Hopkins University.

Nishimizu, Mieko and Charles Hulten. 1978. The sources of Japanese economic growth, 1955–71. *Review of Economics and Statistics* 60, no. 3 (August): 351–61.

Norsworthy, J. R., and David H. Malmquist. 1983. Input measurement and productivity growth in Japanese and U.S. manufacturing. *American Economic Review* 73, no. 5. (December): 947–67.

Powers, Susan. 1985. Cyclical variation in capital stock measures: Implications for multifactor productivity. Ph.D. diss., State University of New York at Binghamton.

————. 1988. The role of capital discards in multifactor productivity measurement. *Monthly Labor Review* 111 (June), 27–35.

Ratcliffe, Charles T. 1969. Tax policy and investment behavior in postwar Japan. Ph.D. diss., University of California, Berkeley.

U.S. Department of Labor, Bureau of Labor Statistics. 1983. *Trends in multifactor productivity, 1948–81.* Bulletin no. 2178. Washington, D.C.: Government Printing Office.

———. 1987. Multifactor productivity measures. BLS News Release, USDL 87-436 (October 13).

Uno, Kimio. 1984. *Investment trends by industry—an industry analysis.* Sakura: University of Tsukuba, Institute of Socio-economic Planning,

Ward, Michael. 1976. *The measurement of capital: The methodology of capital stock estimates in OECD countries.* Paris: Organization for Economic Cooperation and Development.

Comment   Masahiro Kuroda

This paper provides us with a good summary of the gross investment data for Japan. I believe that this research would be a valuable aid in revising capital stock series in Japan, and I would like to add some comments and suggestions. My comments are broadly divided into three points.

First, the evaluation of the capital input is very important, as the authors have stated, in obtaining estimates of multifactor productivity. However, when it comes to measuring multifactor productivity, not only is it important to get accurate data on one input, such as capital, it is also necessary to obtain a whole set of consistent data on labor, capital, and output. However, Dean, Darrough, and Neef do not provide any information on the consistency of the four alternative choices of gross investment with other data needed in the construction of multifactor productivity estimates.

According to my experience, when we measure multifactor productivity in Japan, we have to depend upon input-output tables or on data from the system of national accounts for obtaining data on output, labor compensation, and capital compensation. From the viewpoint of consistency with these output and input measures, I think the EPA measures are preferable, because EPA data are constructed by methods that are consistent with the input-output table and the system of national accounts (the "commodity flow" method).

The authors found the economic rate of depreciation to be much higher using EPA gross investment series than it was using alternative series. When I used EPA gross investment and net capital stock to measure the economic rate of depreciation by the double benchmark method, I also found the estimated rate of depreciation to be overvalued. But, instead of changing the gross investment series, I changed the bench values of capital stock in the benchmark process.

The "gross" value of assets in NWS was estimated by multiplying the nom-

Masahiro Kuroda is a professor of economics, Faculty of Business and Commerce, Keio University.

inal value of each asset at acquisition time by the rate of change in prices between the acquisition time and the survey year. The "net" value was estimated by multiplying the gross value by the remaining value ration in proportion to lifetime and year elapsed from acquisition time. Theoretically, the capital assets used as benchmarks should be measures in net terms since this corresponds to the real flow of capital services. It is, however, somewhat doubtful that the estimates of "net" values in NWS are consistent with the theoretical concept of net capital stock. Therefore, I believe that one should change the benchmark capital stock to a "gross" concept and adjust the overvalued estimates of the economic rate of depreciation. This allows us to use EPA investment data, which is consistent with other data for the measurement of the multifactor productivity.

As a second general point, the authors try to measure capital input in aggregate Japanese manufacturing. As part of this work, they divide capital stock into several asset categories. The change in the relative proportions of different asset types in aggregate manufacturing results in quality change in capital input during the period of rapid economic growth in Japan. However, there were also large changes in the distribution of capital stock among individual manufacturing industries during this period. Thus, when evaluating capital input in Japanese manufacturing, we have to consider not only the changes in the type of capital but also changes among the component industries within total manufacturing.

Finally, it is worth noting that when you estimate the deflators of investment goods, you can use the fixed capital formation matrix, which is consistent with the input-output tables and EPA commodity flow data. These matrices are available for 1970 and 1975 in Japan.

9 The Taxation of Income from Capital in Japan: Historical Perspectives and Policy Simulations

Tatsuya Kikutani and Toshiaki Tachibanaki

9.1 Introduction

In this chapter we will estimate the effective marginal rate of taxation on capital income in Japan over the past twenty years. In a recent paper, Shoven and Tachibanaki (1988) calculated this tax rate for the year 1980 and compared their result for the Japanese case with that for several industrial nations. This chapter builds upon the findings in their paper. First, we pay particular attention to the effect of taxation over the past twenty years. Since the growth rate of the Japanese economy had been a kind of "miracle", ascertaining the impact of the taxation of capital income in those years would aid in determining whether tax policy was effectively used to promote a higher rate of investment activity. We present actual results for the years 1961, 1970, and 1980.[1]

Second, Shoven and Tachibanaki neglected to consider several special characteristics of Japanese tax law. This oversight does not necessarily weaken their result for 1980 because several studies have concluded that the influence of special measures, such as tax-free reserves and special depreciation, has been virtually negligible in recent years. However, these measures must be taken into account when performing investigations for the years 1970 and 1961, during which the economy underwent rapid growth. As will be shown later, several studies suggest the importance of these special tax measures. We also intend to examine the quantitative effect of tax-free reserves and special depreciation, first on the tax burden on capital income and, second, on investment.

Tatsuya Kikutani is lecturer of economics at Kyoto Sangyo University. Toshiaki Tachibanaki is professor of economics at Kyoto University.

The authors are extremely grateful to A. Ando, M. Aoki, A. Auerbach, D. Fullerton, F. Hayashi, C. Hulten, M. King, M. Kitano, K. Kuninori, Y. Noguchi, J. Shoven, E. Tajika, H. Takenaka, Y. Tanigawa, and K. Yoshioka for their helpful advice and comments. It is gratefully acknowledged that C. Hulten edited this paper very carefully. The authors are fully responsible for errors and opinions.

Third, one of the reasons for the low tax rate on income from capital in Japan is the low personal tax rate on savings, as shown by Shoven and Tachibanaki. We will inquire into what the impact of the personal sector has been on the effective tax rate and on capital formation, and how the impact may have changed over time. We will also treat the banking sector in such a way that the actual behavior of banks is reflected. In our analysis the banking sector is of particular importance because the household sector in this study includes banks.

In section 9.2 we briefly explain the methodology used to estimate the effective rates, and in section 9.3 discuss several institutional arrangements that impinge on the corporate and personal tax laws. Section 9.4 gives the effective tax rates in the personal and banking sectors. Estimates of the Japanese effective marginal tax rates are presented in section 9.5 and then compared with the results for the United States. Section 9.6 gives simulation results of proposed tax reforms, given our findings regarding the effective rates, and section 9.7 provides a brief recapitulation.

9.2   Methodology for Estimating the Effective Marginal Tax Rates

This section presents our procedure for estimating the effective marginal tax rates on capital income. The essential concept we use is the tax "wedge" between the rate of return on investment and the rate of return on saving for a series of hypothetical marginal projects. King and Fullerton (1984) have presented a detailed analysis of this tax-wedge formulation, hence our discussion of the methodology is very brief.

The effective tax rate, t, is estimated as

$$(1) \qquad t = \frac{p - s}{p},$$

where p is the pretax real rate of return on the investment project, net of depreciation, and s is the post-tax real rate of return to the saver who supplied the finance for the investment. The post-tax real rate of return to the saver is given by

$$(2) \qquad s = (1 - m)(r + \pi) - \pi - w_p,$$

where m is the marginal personal tax rate on interest income, r is the real interest rate, π is the rate of inflation, and w_p is the marginal personal tax rate on wealth. Equation (2) reflects the fact that it is nominal, not real, income which is subject to personal taxation.

The minimum pretax real rate of return which an investment must earn in order to give an investor a competitive or equilibrium post-tax return is termed "the cost of capital." The relationship between the cost of capital and the interest rate may be represented as

$$(3) \qquad p = c(r).$$

The cost of capital function, $c(r)$, depends on the specifics of the tax code. For a general situation involving a corporate tax, investment credit, and a wealth tax, the expression for the cost of capital is given by

$$(4) \quad p = \frac{1}{(1-\tau)} [(1 - A)(\rho + \delta - \pi) + (1 - d_1\tau)w_c + d_2\tau\nu\pi] - \delta,$$

where τ is the corporate tax rate; A is the present value of any grants, credits, or allowances; ρ is the nominal discount rate; δ is the economic depreciation rate; d_1 is a dummy variable that equals unity if corporate wealth taxes are deductible from the corporate income tax base and zero otherwise; w_c is the tax rate of corporate wealth; d_2 is a dummy variable that is set equal to unity if assets take the form of inventories and zero otherwise; ν is the proportion of inventories taxed on a first-in-first-out (FIFO) basis.

Equation (4) was obtained from equation (5), the rate of return on an investment net of depreciation, and equation (6), the present value of profits:

$$(5) \qquad\qquad p = MRR - \delta,$$

where MRR is the gross marginal rate of return for one unit of investment, and

$$(6) \quad
\begin{aligned}
V &= \int_0^\infty [(1 - \tau)MRR - (1 - d_1\tau)w_c - d_2\tau\nu\pi]e^{-(\rho+\delta-\pi)u}du \\
&= \frac{[(1 - \tau)MRR - (1 - d_1\tau)w_c - d_2\tau\nu\pi]}{\rho + \delta - \pi},
\end{aligned}$$

where V is the present discounted value of profits from a project. To obtain equation (4), we also made use of the equality between V and C (the cost of the project, which is equal to $[1 - A]$).

We must next consider A, the present value of tax savings from depreciation allowances and other grants associated with one unit of investment. We present the special features of the Japanese tax system in detail in the next section. The formulation given there by equation (11) and the subsequent formulations in this chapter differ from the original King and Fullerton formulation.

The final step is to relate the firm's discount rate to the market interest rate, since with distortionary taxes the values are different. The difference depends on the source of finance. For debt finance the relationship is simple, since nominal interest income is taxed and nominal interest payments are tax deductible. For the other two sources of finance, the discount rates are influenced by both the personal and corporate tax systems. Also, the degree of discrimination between retentions and distributions (dividends) in allocating profits plays an important role. See King (1977, chap. 3) and King and Fullerton (1984, chap. 2) for a detailed discussion of these issues.

There are four characteristics that define a hypothetical marginal project. These are (1) the asset in which the funds are invested, (2) the industrial sector, (3) the way in which the project is financed, and (4) the owner of the returns. Each characteristic may be one of three alternatives. The three asset types are machinery, buildings, and inventories; the industries are manufacturing, other industry, and commerce; the sources of finance are debt, new share issues, and retained earnings; and the ownership categories are households, tax-exempt institutions, and insurance companies. The three types of each of the four characteristics yield eighty-one combinations. The mean tax wedge, $\bar{w}$, is calculated by

$$(7) \qquad\qquad \bar{w} = \sum_{k=1}^{81} (p_k - s_k)\alpha_k$$

where α_k is the capital stock weight of the kth combination ($\Sigma\alpha_k = 1$). Using equation (7), we can estimate not only the overall mean marginal tax rate but also the conditional mean marginal tax rates on investment in particular alternatives. For example, we can estimate the conditional mean tax rate in machinery by summing over all the combinations that involve machinery. There are twenty-seven such combinations in all, and empirical results will be discussed mainly on the basis of these combinations later.

Our analysis requires two sets of data: first, the statutory tax rates and the various parameter values; second, the α weights for the proportion of total net capital stock and statistics on financing and ownership. Shoven and Tachibanaki (1988) provided a detailed discussion of these data sets.

9.3 Special Features of the Japanese Tax System

Shoven and Tachibanaki (1988) also provide a brief discussion of the overall Japanese taxation system. Here we focus only on those institutional characteristics that affect the calculation of the effective marginal taxation of capital income in Japan. Those pertaining to corporations are the enterprise tax, special measures for depreciation, and tax-free reserves in the nonfinancial corporate tax system. Those that affect the personal sector include taxation of interest and dividend income, and treatment of banking sectors.

9.3.1 The Corporate Tax Rate and the Enterprise Tax

There are two basic local taxes in Japan, prefectural taxes and city, town, and village taxes. The enterprise tax is one of the local taxes levied at the prefectural level. It is levied on corporations engaged in business that operate an office or other place of business, and individuals engaged in several types of business or professions described by law. Computation of income for the purpose of levying the prefectural-level tax on corporations is almost the same as the computation used at the national level, although the scope of taxable income is somewhat different.

For the enterprise tax, the standard tax rate applied to ordinary corporations for ordinary taxable income is 12 percent, for those firms with an annual income of more than 7,000,000 yen. Although a somewhat lower rate is applied to smaller firms, we will use 12 percent as the statutory rate. The most important feature of the enterprise tax is its deductibility in calculating next year's taxable income. For this reason, the enterprise tax must be considered separately from the usual corporate and local income taxes. Because of its deductibility, the effective tax rate of the enterprise tax is lower than the statutory tax rate. The method of calculating the effective tax rate used in this analysis is as follows.

The amount of deduction in the payment of corporate tax for one unit (yen) of enterprise tax, TD_E is given by

$$
(8) \qquad TD_E = \sum_{t=1}^{\infty} \{(t_C + t_E)(-t_E)^{t-1}/(1 + \rho)^t\}
$$

$$
= \frac{t_C + t_E}{1 + t_E + \rho}, \text{ with } t_C = t_R(1 - d) + t_D \cdot d,
$$

where t_C is the corporate tax rate, not including the enterprise tax; t_R is the corporate tax rate for retained earnings; t_D is the corporate tax rate for dividends distributed; t_E is the enterprise tax rate; d is the distribution rate of dividends in total profits; and ρ is the nominal discount rate.

The total amount of corporate tax, T, when the enterprise tax is taken into account, is given by

$$
(9) \qquad T = (t_C + t_E)Y - \frac{t_C + t_E}{1 + t_E + \rho} \cdot t_E Y
$$

$$
= \frac{(t_R + t_E)(1 + \rho)}{1 + t_E + \rho} Y + \frac{(t_D - t_R)(1 + \rho)}{1 + t_E + \rho} dY,
$$

where Y is taxable income. Equation (9) is used for calculating the burden of corporate tax as the effective tax rate. When the nominal discount rate ρ is small enough, its effect on the outcome is negligible. Thus, in our formula we will eliminate ρ.

We must also derive equations for the corporate tax rate, τ, and the opportunity cost of retained earnings in terms of gross dividends foregone, θ.

The total tax paid by a corporation is given by

$$
(10) \qquad T = \tau Y + \frac{1 - \theta}{\theta} G,
$$

where G is the gross dividends paid. θ may be regarded as the additional dividend shareholders could receive if one unit of post-corporate-tax earnings were distributed. By combining equations (9) and (10), it is possible to obtain equation (11), assuming $dY = G$.

(11)
$$\tau = \frac{t_R + t_E}{1 + t_E}$$

$$\theta = \frac{1}{1 + [(t_D - t_R)/(1 + t_E)]}$$

Equation (11) is the final form of τ and θ used later to estimate the effective marginal tax rate on capital income.

9.3.2 Special Measures for Depreciation

Under the Japanese taxation system, there are two types of special measures for depreciations, namely, increased initial depreciation and accelerated depreciation. Both measures can be used in addition to the ordinary depreciation allowances. The first allows the deduction of a portion of the acquisition cost of an asset for the first accounting period in which such an asset is used. The second permits the deduction of a certain percentage of the ordinary depreciation of an allowable asset for certain consecutive accounting periods. Since the increased initial depreciation is much more important, it is explained here in detail and taken into account explicitly in calculating the effective tax rate.

The increased initial depreciation, or "special depreciation," was initially introduced in 1951 to speed the replacement of destroyed or obsolete machinery and equipment in the aftermath of World War II. In 1952 the scope of special depreciation was enlarged to include more machinery, and it continued to be expanded throughout the decade. The system grew complicated as it expanded until, in 1961, in accordance with the shortened tax lifetimes of machinery and equipment, special depreciation was simplified. The maximum proportion of an allowable asset that could be depreciated in the first year was reduced from one-half of the acquisition cost to one-third. It was reduced to one-fourth of the acquisition cost in 1964, again in accordance with the shortened tax lifetimes. Another reform was introduced in 1973 to allow greater special depreciation for environmental pollution control, savings from energy conservation, the acquisition of machinery and equipment by small- or medium-sized enterprises, etc. For 1980, the maximum proportion of allowable asset we used was one-fifth.

Examination of the history of special depreciation suggests that shortening tax lifetimes and introducing special depreciation in general have had the same effect on an enterprise's capital cost burden. In other words, shortened lifetimes and reduction in the maximum rate of allowable asset in the first year have been used interchangeably to mitigate the excessive effect of either of the two policy tools.

It is noted that the importance of special depreciation, attested to by the degree of utilization, has been in decline in recent years. Table 9.1 shows this trend. The figures in the table are the proportions of the acquisition assets entitled to special depreciation. It is found that the influence of special depreciation was the greatest in 1970 and was less important in 1961. The year

1980 shows the least effect. This does not necessarily imply, however, that the corporate sector's demand for a lighter tax burden has weakened in recent years in Japan. Indeed, the corporate sector has been calling for a reduction in the tax lifetimes of assets. A simulation addressing this issue will be performed later.

It is worthwhile to examine how the actual depreciable periods of machinery and equipment are shortened when special depreciations are applied. Table 9.2 shows the statutory years of tax lifetimes, while table 9.3 indicates the depreciable period of assets to which special depreciations are applied.

Table 9.1   **A Time-series Change in f_2—the Proportion of the Cost of an Asset Qualified for Special Depreciation Allowance—by Industry**

	1961	1970	1980
Manufacturing	0.171	0.274	0.126
Other industry	0.074	0.293	0.132
Commerce	0.063	0.166	0.063

Note: $f_2 = (1/x) \times (SP/I)$, where x is the proportion of special depreciation written off in the first year; SP is the amount of special depreciation; and I is the nominal investment. The estimation of the amount of special depreciation was obtained using only data from machinery because of the difficulty of obtaining data by asset category. The assumption seems justified since the most frequently used assets are machinery.

Table 9.2   **Statutory Useful Lifetime (in years)**

	1961		1970 and 1980	
	Machines	Buildings	Machines	Buildings
Manufacturing	10.48	31.71	9.53	32.60
Other industry	13.78	38.89	11.29	37.16
Commerce	7.40	33.45	6.62	33.44

Source: Economic Planning Agency, *National Wealth Survey,* 1960 and 1970. The figures for 1980 are the same as those for 1970.

Table 9.3   **The Period of Special Depreciation (straight-line method, for machinery only)**

	1961	1970	1980
Manufacturing	6.60	6.89	7.42
Other industry	8.68	8.16	8.78
Commerce	4.66	4.78	5.15

Note: The period L' is calculated as $L' = (1 - x - \alpha)/d$, where d is the depreciation rate; x is the proportion of special depreciation written off in the first year; and α is the salvage value of the assets.

Obviously, the number of years in table 9.3 are all smaller than the tax life-times in table 9.2. A critical factor explaining this difference is that the assets to which special depreciation is applied are depreciated with the same rates as ordinary assets.

Table 9.2 shows that since 1961 the statutory lifetimes for machinery have been shortened, while for buildings there is no significant change. Further reduction is anticipated for the future. Table 9.3 shows that the depreciable period of the assets, due to the accounting basis through which special depreciations are applied, have been prolonged in agreement with the reduction in the proportion of first-year write-offs allowed by special depreciation.

With respect to special depreciation, our final task is to derive the present value of the depreciation allowance, and in particular the allowance due to special depreciation. Let x be the proportion of special depreciation which is in fact written off in the first year. Then, total tax saving from one unit (yen) of investment, A, is given by

$$(12) \qquad A = f_1 Ad_1 + f_2(Ad_2 + x\tau),$$

where f_1 is the proportion of the cost of an asset entitled to the standard depreciation allowance; f_2 is the proportion of the cost of an asset qualified for the special depreciation allowance; and Ad_1 is the present value of tax savings arising from the standard depreciation allowance on a unit of investment. For a qualified asset, $x\tau$ is the tax savings from the first-year write-off by special depreciation, and Ad_2 is the present value of tax savings from the residual after the first-year write-off.

The great majority of Japanese firms elect either the declining-balance method or straight-line method to calculate depreciation. The first method arrives at the current depreciation by multiplying the past residual value by a (the depreciation rate); thus the value of depreciation at time t for one unit of investment is ae^{-at}. The second method gives a constant amount of depreciation, $(1 - \alpha)/L$, where α is the rate of the residual value of the asset and L is the tax lifetime. Let w_d be the proportion of corporations that elect to use the declining-balance method of depreciation, and w_s be the proportion that elect the straight-line method. Thus, Ad_1 is given by

$$(13) \qquad \begin{aligned} Ad_1 &= w_d \int_0^L \tau a e^{-(a+\rho)t} dt + w_s \int_0^L \tau \frac{1-\alpha}{L} e^{-\rho t} dt \\ &= \tau \left[\frac{w_d a\{1 - e^{-(a+\rho)L}\}}{a + \rho} + \frac{w_s(1 - \alpha)(1 - e^{-\rho L})}{\rho L} \right]. \end{aligned}$$

In Japan, w_d is 0.8 and w_s is 0.2. These rates are almost constant during the sample period. The rate of the residual value of the asset α is specified as 0.1 for all allowable assets.

Since the choice of declining-balance or straight-line method is left up to the corporation after the first-year special write-off, it is safe to assume that all corporations choose straight-line depreciation because this method is more advantageous. Thus, Ad_2 is given by

$$(14) \qquad Ad_2 = \int_0^{L'} \tau \frac{1-\alpha}{L} e^{-\rho t} dt = \frac{\tau(1-\alpha)(1-e^{-\rho L'})}{\rho L},$$

where L' is a depreciable period, depending on the accounting basis used, after the first-year special write-off. The value of L' is given by $(1 - x - \alpha)/d$; d is equal to $(1 - \alpha)/L$. See footnote in table 9.3.

The term Ad_2 in equation (12), and more specifically equation (14), indicates the present value of tax savings from the residual after the first-year write-off by special depreciation. This term had been overlooked in Shoven and Tachibanaki (1988).

9.3.3   Tax-free Reserves

There are several types of tax-free reserves allowed under the Japanese taxation system which serve to reduce the corporate tax burden. Noguchi (1985) has proposed that the importance of these reserves increased until the mid-1970s and has been declining since. According to Tajika and Yui (1984), the amount of corporate tax reduced as a result of tax-free reserves has continuously shrunk since the mid-1960s and by 1980 was negligible. On the basis of these findings, tax-free reserves were ignored in Shoven and Tachibanaki (1988). It is, however, advisable to take them into account for the period before 1980, as mentioned earlier.

Tax-free reserves are classified into two categories, namely, *hikiatekin* and *jumbikin*. The *hikiatekin*, roughly speaking, are those reserves justified by generally accepted accounting principles, and are thus provided for in the corporate tax law. The *hikiatekin* consist of reserves for future debts or for such expenditures as retirement payments, bonus payments, and bad debts. The *jumbikin* differ, however, because they are not duly accepted by accounting principles. The *jumbikin* are allowed, in exceptional cases, for reaching certain specific economic goals, such as dealing with the uncertainty of price fluctuations, overseas market development, or investment loss. It is important to note that the reserves are deductible as expenses in one year but are included in gross income in the next. In other words, the reserves are tax deferrals but not tax exemptions.

Several studies have discussed the economic effect of these reserves. The reserves have been found to be effective in reducing the corporate tax burden, and thereby encouraging corporate investment activity (Tajika and Yui 1984; Tajika, Hayashi, and Yui 1987; Noguchi 1985). It has also been argued that these reserves have only benefited larger corporations because they make greater use of reserves than do smaller corporations. In other words, smaller firms do not have any short-term extra funds that could qualify for these tax-free reserves, whereas larger firms do (Shoven and Tachibanaki 1988; Wada 1980). These are important issues, but they are not directly addressed here. However, we will attempt to incorporate tax-free reserves in our estimate of the effective marginal tax rate on capital income.

All of the reserves, except for retirement allowances, are deductible as expenses in each accounting period. The amount credited is added back in full to income in the following accounting period. For retirement allowances, the amount credited to reserves may be deducted up to a limit. The limit is set at an amount equal to the increase in the total amount of retirement allowances claimable by all employees of the corporation. Thus, the amount credited to the reserve for retirement allowance is in fact equal to the amount credited to the reserve for retirement, payable at each accounting period under the system of adding back in full. See Tajika, Hayashi, and Yui (1987) for an interpretation of retirement allowances and formulations.

Let R be the total reserves. The quantity R may be equal to the sum of the reserve for retirement payable at the end of the accounting period and the reserve for systems other than the retirement allowance. Since the rate of corporate tax is τ, a corporation may save the amount τR in one year. However, the amount R is added back in full to income in the next year. Consequently, the net tax saving arising from these reserves is given by

$$(15) \qquad \tau R - \frac{\tau R}{1 + \rho} = \frac{\rho \, \tau R}{1 + \rho},$$

where ρ is the nominal discount rate.

We are interested in the net tax saving derived from one unit of investment (ΔK). The net tax saving due to tax-free reserves for this investment, B, may be written as

$$(15') \qquad B = \rho \tau \frac{\Delta R}{\Delta K} / (1 + \rho).$$

This may be regarded as a subsidy paid by the government to a corporation.

Table 9.4 presents our estimates of the values of $\Delta R / \Delta K$. The values are highest for all three industries in 1970, while the values for 1961 and 1980 differ among industries.

9.4 Estimation of the Effective Tax Rates in the Personal and Banking Sectors

Shoven and Tachibanaki (1988) used, as a first approximation, the average tax rates of interest income and dividend income based on personal income tax data, rather than the weighted-average marginal tax rates. In view of the importance of the tax rates of interest and dividend income, we will attempt to estimate the marginal tax rate.

Table 9.4   **Estimated Values of $\Delta R/\Delta K$ by Industry**

	1961	1970	1980
Manufacturing	0.0037	0.0429	0.0288
Other industry	0.0197	0.0425	0.0186
Commerce	0.0738	0.0778	0.0199

Note: R is the total reserves; *K* is the capital stock.
Source: For *R, Survey of Corporate Firms Viewed from Tax Data* (1970, 1980), Japanese Ministry of Finance. Since the above surveys are unavailable before 1963, the amount of tax-free reserve for 1961 was extracted from *Annual Yearbook of Incorporated Firms* (1961: Japanese Ministry of Finance; in Japanese). Unfortunately, these two sources do not use common industry classifications. Thus, it is possible that the amounts given for 1961 are somewhat underestimated.

This is an extremely difficult task for the following reasons. First, a considerable number of nontaxable forms of saving is legally allowed. Second, both the system of withholding taxation (at a separate rate) within a certain limit and the system of comprehensive income taxation (at a progressive tax rate) for interest and dividends are prepared, at the taxpayer's option. Third, if a household has several members, it can increase nontaxable savings—and it is widely held that nontaxable savings are frequently abused. Fourth, since our framework regards the banking sector as one of the household sectors, it is necessary to consider the tax rate for the banking sector separately, and then to combine it with the tax rate for individuals.

Our estimation methodologies for deriving the weighted-average marginal tax rates for interest and dividend incomes follow. The actual tax rates are estimated on the basis of various reported tax data. Consequently, no adjustment has been made for the abuse of nontaxable savings, such as a fictitious account or false family members.

9.4.1   Dividend Income

There are three institutions in the household sector: individuals, banks, and stock and securities companies. It is safe to assume that the taxation of stock and securities companies is the same as that of individuals, as in Flath (1984). Individuals and banks, however, are taxed differently.

Individuals. Shoven and Tachibanaki (1988) have described a complicated system of dividend income taxation, to which three additional considerations must be added. First, although a progressive comprehensive income tax must be applied in principle for dividend income over a certain amount, in some cases only a 20 percent tax is withheld separately. Second, it is possible to calculate the marginal tax rate of dividend income that is taxed as a comprehensive income. The *Annual Yearbook of Tax*, prepared by the Tax Bureau of the Japanese Ministry of Finance, enables us to estimate each marginal rate, including both national and local taxes, by income class, which takes into account the tax deductibility of dividends received. The weighted average of the estimated marginal tax rates, with weights being the amount of dividend income, is the average marginal rate of dividend income. Since the yearbook does not distinguish between dividend income received by individuals and that received by corporations, the distinction was made according to the amount of stocks held. Third, some complications remain for local income taxes when a separate withholding tax is elected for dividend income at the national level. A 42 percent tax rate is obtained by adding a 35 percent separate tax rate at the national level and a 7.1 percent tax rate at the local level. The estimated marginal tax rate for each source of taxation in 1980 are given in table 9.5. The estimated average marginal tax rate of dividend income is 44.0 percent.

Banking Sector. Dividend income received by corporations is not taxed, purportedly to avoid double taxation. However, when dividends received are higher than dividends paid, one-fourth of the corporate tax rate is applied to the difference. We calculated the difference at about 35 percent, by using data from financial statements of firms listed in *Nikkei Needs.* Since the corporate tax rate is 52.6 percent, the tax rate on dividend income received by banks equals 4.5 percent ($= \frac{1}{4} \times 0.526 \times 0.35$).

Finally, the weighted average of individuals and banks is 27.3 percent, with weights being the number of stocks held. This value is our estimated average marginal tax rate of dividend income in 1980. Incidentally, this value is 18.7 percent for 1961 and 21.7 percent for 1970. Thus, the tax rate of dividend income has been increased over the past twenty years.

9.4.2   Interest Income

Individuals. The estimated marginal tax rates for each source for the year 1980 is given in table 9.6. From the table it can be seen that the influence of nontaxable savings is great and has lowered the tax rate of interest income. The weighted-average marginal tax rate, 12.9 percent, is obtained from the table. We subtract the proportion of checking accounts which yield no interest (about 11.7 percent of total savings) and find the estimated average marginal tax rate to be 11.4 percent in 1980, 10.3 percent in 1970, and 9.9 percent in 1961.

Banking sector. The main activities banks engage in are collecting funds

Table 9.5   The Estimated Marginal Tax Rate on Dividend Income for 1980

	Marginal Tax Rate (in percentages)	Dividend Income (in billions of yen)
Comprehensive income taxation		
Withholding	20.0	159
Progressive taxation	52.4	473
Separate taxation	42.0	77

Source: Annual Yearbook of Tax (1980: Tax Bureau, Japanese Ministry of Finance).

Table 9.6   The Estimated Marginal Tax Rate on Interest Income for 1980

			Marginal Tax Rate (in percentages)	Interest Income (in billions of yen)
Comprehensive taxation	Withholding	Taxable	20.0	4,525
		Nontaxable	0.0	4,292
	Progressive taxation		41.6	30
Separate taxation	Gains from original issue discount on debentures		16.0	711
	Others		35.0	888

Source: Annual Yearbook of Tax (1980; Tax Bureau, Japanese Ministry of Finance).

from individuals and lending those funds to incorporated nonfinancial firms. In general, the main source of profit from banking lies in the difference between the lending rate and the borrowing rate. Banks have various kinds of financial goods to collect funds from individuals which have varying interest rates, and lending rates differ among banks and also according to which corporation is borrowing funds. These variations must be taken into account in our estimate of the difference between lending rates and borrowing rates.

The *Yearbook of Financial Sectors,* published by the Ministry of Finance, provides the necessary data on an annual basis. We thus obtain as the differences, 1.42 percent in 1961, 1.10 percent in 1970, and 0.17 percent in 1980. These figures represent the differences minus banks' operating costs. Thus, the differences may be regarded as the profit due to one unit of savings. Although these are the average rates of profit, it is plausible to assume that they are also the marginal rates of profit because of constant returns to scale in Japanese banking. Assuming that the distribution rate of dividends in total profits is 30 percent, we obtain as final tax rates for banks, 0.66 percent for the year 1961, 0.50 percent for 1970, and 0.08 percent for 1980; and with respect to the calculated corporate tax rates for banks, 46.2 percent for the year 1961, 45.1 percent for 1970, and 49.5 percent for 1980.

Finally, we may obtain the estimated average marginal tax rates of interest income by combining the two sectors. We arrive at estimated figures of 10.6 percent for 1961, 10.8 percent for 1970, and 11.4 percent for 1980. It is apparent that the marginal tax rates of interest income have increased only slightly over the past twenty years.

9.4.3 Capital Gains Taxes

One can reasonably assume that capital gains taxes are effectively zero for the gains from individual transactions. Since, as we have noted, in our framework the household sector includes the banking sector, it is important that we estimate the capital gains tax rate for banks that hold a nonnegligible proportion of the stocks of nonfinancial incorporated firms.

It is extremely difficult to estimate the exact amount of capital gains realized and of transactions of the stocks held by banks. Nevertheless, it is often said that very few transactions take place because of certain features of the capital market in Japan (see, e.g., Aoki 1984). Since the effective tax rate depends upon the duration, it is necessary to assign a value to it. For simplicity we adopt ten years as the value, following King and Fullerton (1984). This is only a first approximation because no data on duration exist for Japan.

The statutory rate of capital gains taxes is equivalent to the corporate tax rate. Since data exist regarding the proportion of stock held by banks, we may estimate the effective tax rate on capital gains for banks by multiplying that proportion and the tax rate. We thus estimate the tax rates as 3.64 percent for the year 1960, 6.17 percent for 1970, and 20.4 percent for 1980. The increase is due mainly to the growing trend of banks holding greater proportions of stock.

9.5   Effective Tax Rates and the Evaluation of Tax Policy

This section gives estimated results for the effective marginal tax rates on income from capital in 1961, 1970, and 1980, and provides tools for evaluating the effects of tax policy on investment. We apply the estimation procedure of the method expounded in King and Fullerton (1984) to assure comparability. As was explained previously, several modifications have been introduced to take Japanese tax laws into account.

9.5.1   Time-series Change in the Effective Rates

Table 9.7 shows the results for 1980, and table 9.8 shows the results for 1970 and 1961. Since the inflation rates during the 1970s were exceptionally high, due mainly to the two oil crises, the results in 1980 are reported for four different inflation rates, 0, 5, 10, and 8.25 percent (the actual inflation rate observed). Because the actual inflation rates were low during the 1950s (1.28 percent) and the 1960s (3.19 percent), only two inflation rates (zero and actual) are considered in those years. Table 9.9 examines the influence exerted on the effective tax rates by institutional arrangements such as special measures for depreciation and tax-free reserves assured by the corporate tax law. Tables 9.10 and 9.11 are presented to show the relative contributions of the corporate and personal sectors to the total effective tax rate, and give useful supplementary information for interpreting tables 9.7 and 9.8.

Zero inflation rate. The overall effective marginal tax rates at zero inflation rate are 27.2 percent for 1961, 22.0 percent for 1970 and 28.7 percent for 1980. These numbers solely reflect the effect of the tax law and do not take into account the effect of inflation. Several reasons can be given for the much lower rate in 1970. First, the corporate tax rate τ in 1970 was lower than in 1961 and 1980, and the discrimination parameter θ was higher. These two values obviously reduce the tax burden of corporations. Second, as table 9.9 clearly shows, the contribution of special measures for depreciation and tax-

Table 9.7   Effective Marginal Tax Rates for 1980 (fixed-p case; in percentages)

	Inflation Rate			
	0%	5%	10%	Actual
Japan				
Asset				
Machinery	25.1	17.9	7.4	11.4
Buildings	25.8	16.2	1.7	7.1
Inventories	35.8	20.1	4.1	9.8
Industry				
Manufacturing	29.3	21.5	10.6	14.7
Other industry	24.4	9.6	−8.6	−2.0
Commerce	32.9	21.1	7.5	12.4
Source of finance				
Debt	1.0	−31.9	−68.0	−55.1
New share issues	54.1	65.9	76.3	72.8
Retained earnings	52.4	60.5	66.1	64.4
Owner				
Households	28.4	17.2	3.0	8.2
Tax-exempt				
institutions	27.4	16.8	3.8	8.6
Insurance companies	30.8	23.1	13.1	16.8
Overall	28.7	18.2	4.7	9.6
United States				
Overall	32.0		38.4	37.2

Note: The U.S. result is based on King and Fullerton (1984).

free reserves was greatest in 1970. A simulation that did not take into account both special depreciation and tax-free reserves and that applied the rates in 1980 for the parameters τ and θ, gave a higher value for the effective rate (i.e., 26.0 percent). As table 9.10 indicates, the effective rate for the corporate sector, 14 percent, the lowest of the three years compared, was the factor contributing most to this low effective marginal tax rate in 1970. Whether government tax policy, in lowering the effective tax rate around 1970, had a positive effect on raising the amount of investment is a topic for future inquiry.

The high effective tax rate in 1961 is somewhat surprising. It had been anticipated that the effective tax rate would be lower for the 1960s because of the high rate of investment activity, characteristic of the rapid economic growth in those years. However, our analysis gives evidence of a heavy tax burden, owing mainly to the high corporate sector rate, as shown in table 9.10. One of the reasons for the corporate sector's heavy tax burden in 1961 was the weak effect of both special depreciation and tax-free reserves.

It is interesting to inquire why a high rate of investment activity was observed despite the relatively high rate of tax on investment in this period. One reason is that relatively favorable investment financing was provided through

Table 9.8   **Effective Marginal Tax Rates for 1970 and 1961 (fixed-p case; in percentages)**

| | Inflation Rate | | | |
| | 1970 | | 1961 | |
	0%	Actual	0%	Actual
Japan				
Asset				
Machinery	19.0	12.8	25.1	24.0
Buildings	22.6	16.1	26.6	24.6
Inventories	28.1	17.6	29.7	25.4
Industry				
Manufacturing	22.6	16.7	29.5	28.3
Other industry	21.8	14.8	25.8	22.4
Commerce	20.1	9.8	27.5	25.2
Source of finance				
Debt	1.3	−15.8	5.8	−1.5
New share issues	48.3	54.7	50.1	52.7
Retained earnings	44.2	48.1	47.1	48.9
Owner				
Households	20.9	13.3	27.3	24.8
Tax-exempt institutions	11.8	−0.1	19.8	15.7
Insurance companies	28.3	24.6	26.0	23.3
Overall	22.0	15.0	27.2	24.7
United States				
Overall	43.8	47.2	44.9	48.4

Note: The U.S. result is based on King and Fullerton (1984).

government financial sources in order to encourage investment activity on the part of private corporations in the iron and steel, electric power, and transportation industries, as Kosai (1985), and Ogura and Yoshino (1985) suggest. This may be regarded as one form of government-initiated industrial policy following World War II. Our study does not estimate the effective marginal tax rate for investment financed through government channels, thus this explanation is offered only as a conjecture, not on the basis of rigorous statistical evidence. Another reason may be the animal spirits of private corporations, who approached investment in these years expecting great prosperity from the Japanese economy, despite a high rate of tax burden for capital income.

Finally, it should be noted that the tax burden for corporations has been considerable in recent years, as is suggested by the result for 1980. There are several reasons for this. First, the influence of favorable institutional arrangements, such as special depreciation and tax-free reserves, has been gradually eliminated, as table 9.9 shows. This is consistent with the findings in Noguchi (1985). Second, since the oil crises, the growth rate of revenues from personal

Table 9.9   **The Effect of Tax-Free Reserves and Special Measures for Depreciation on the Effective Marginal Tax Rates in Japan (fixed-p case; in percentages)**

	Inflation Rate		
	0%	5%	Actual
1980			
Special measures for depreciation	−0.3	−0.3	−0.3
Tax-free reserves	−1.0	−1.7	−2.2
Combined	−1.2	−2.0	−2.5
1970			
Special measures for depreciation	−1.0	−1.2	−1.1
Tax-free reserves	−2.0	−3.4	−2.9
Combined	−2.8	−4.5	−3.9
1961			
Special measures for depreciation	−0.4	−0.5	−0.4
Tax-free reserves	−0.7	−1.4	−0.9
Combined	−1.1	−1.8	−1.3

Notes: The figures give the difference between the effective marginal tax rate when the effect of special measures is not taken into account and the effective marginal tax rate in the standard case. For example, the figures in the first row indicate the contribution of special depreciation to the total effective marginal tax rate in the standard case. Negative values imply that the tax rate is lowered; positive values imply that it is raised.

income taxes has been declining in accordance with the slow growth rate of the economy. The government has had to raise revenues through corporate taxation to compensate for the gradual loss of revenues from personal income tax. Third, it is held that the statutory useful lifetimes of assets are somewhat longer than their real lifetimes in view of rapid technological change.

Actual inflation rates. The actual inflation rates, which are simple averages of the wholesale price index and the consumer price index over the past ten years, were (in percentages); 1.28 in 1961, 3.19 in 1970, and 8.25 in 1980. The extremely high inflation rate in 1980 (the 1970s) was due largely to the two oil crises and subsequent inflationary pressure. The most important finding derived from the consideration of inflation is that effective tax rates decline considerably as the rate of inflation is increased. As figure 9.1 indicates, the decline took place in both the United Kingdom and Japan, but the rate of decline was steeper in Japan.

Also, it is found that the change in the effective rate due to an increase in the inflation rate from 0% to 5% is 10.8 percentage points in 1960, 11.4 percentage points in 1970, and 10.3 percentage points in 1980. In other words, the effective tax rate has always been sensitive to inflation in Japan.

Shoven and Tachibanaki (1988) gave several reasons for the strong effect of inflation. First was the heavy reliance on debt financing for corporate finance in Japan. Debt financing has two effects. One, since nominal interest pay-

Table 9.10 Effective Marginal Tax Rates for the Corporate Sector in Japan and the United States (in percentages)

	Inflation Rate					
	0%		10%		Actual	
	Japan	U.S.	Japan	U.S.	Japan	U.S.
1980						
Asset						
Machinery	15.6	−16.7	−14.3	−18.6	−8.2	−16.5
Buildings	16.4	21.1	−20.4	4.6	−12.8	12.0
Inventories	27.5	40.1	−17.8	11.6	−9.9	20.8
Industry						
Manufacturing	20.3	32.4	−10.2	26.7	−4.1	29.8
Other industry	14.8	−10.1	−32.8	−32.4	−23.6	−23.4
Commerce	24.3	24.1	−13.9	−2.3	−6.8	7.5
Source of finance						
Debt	−11.3	−26.8	−101.2	−98.5	−84.5	−73.2
New share issues	40.5	39.5	39.7	51.8	40.3	48.9
Retained earnings	46.7	39.5	56.2	51.8	55.0	48.9
Owner						
Households	17.9	19.9	−21.8	7.5	−14.2	12.9
Tax-exempt institutions	26.9	15.7	2.5	−2.2	7.4	5.0
Insurance companies	26.8	−3.9	2.3	−46.6	7.2	−31.1
Overall	19.7	17.1	−17.2	1.0	−10.0	7.7
1970						
Overall	14.0	—	−23.2	—	3.2	—
1961						
Overall	19.8	—	−16.4	—	15.7	—

Note: The U.S. result is based on King and Fullerton (1984). A dash means that we have not calculated the rates.

Table 9.11 Effective Marginal Tax Rates for the Personal Sector in Japan and the United States (in percentages)

	Inflation Rate					
	0%		10%		Actual	
	Japan	U.S.	Japan	U.S.	Japan	U.S.
1980						
Asset						
Machinery	9.5	20.6	21.7	41.4	19.6	34.1
Buildings	9.4	14.3	22.1	37.2	19.9	29.1
Inventories	8.3	10.8	21.9	33.9	19.7	26.2
Industry						
Manufacturing	9.0	11.8	20.8	28.3	18.8	22.9
Other industry	9.6	20.1	24.2	48.2	21.6	38.0
Commerce	8.6	13.8	21.4	39.8	19.2	30.7
Source of finance						
Debt	12.3	24.8	33.2	76.3	29.4	56.9
New share issues	13.6	21.5	36.6	52.8	32.5	42.3
Retained earnings	5.7	8.9	9.9	14.7	9.4	13.5
Owner						
Households	10.5	24.2	24.8	54.4	22.4	44.6
Tax-exempt institutions	0.5	−11.7	1.3	−35.0	1.2	−26.5
Insurance companies	4.0	7.9	10.8	90.9	9.6	54.5
Overall	9.2	14.9	21.9	37.4	19.6	29.5
1970						
Overall	8.0	—	—	20.0	—	11.8
1961						
Overall	7.4	—	—	19.7	—	9.0

Note: The U.S. result is based on King and Fullerton (1984). A dash means that we have not calculated the rates.

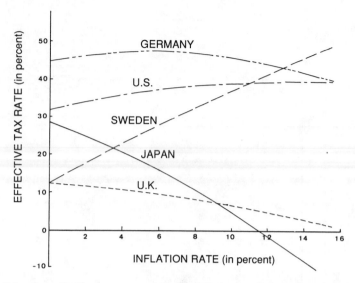

Fig. 9.1   Overall effective tax rates as the inflation rates vary in the U.K., Sweden, West Germany, the U.S., and Japan
*Source:*King and Fullerton (1984) for the first four countries; authors' calculations for Japan.

ments are deductible from corporate income tax, debt financing lowers the discount rate even without inflation, and thus lowers the cost of capital. Two, when the rate of inflation grows, nominal interest payments increase because the nominal interest rate is increased. At the same time, however, it is possible that the tax burden on personal interest income received also grows with an increase in inflation. If this effect were stronger than the effect of the former, the combined tax burden might increase. Since the corporate tax rate is much higher than the tax rate on interest income in Japan, the combined effect in fact *lowers* the effective tax rate of capital income. The second reason given for the strong effect of inflation was the fact that the role of FIFO accounting is relatively weak. Third, the marginal tax rate for personal saving (especially interest income) is low. Fourth, the role of depreciation diminishes in importance as the inflation rate increases. Of the four reasons, the two most important factors are a heavy reliance on debt financing and the low tax rate for saving.

We have conducted a simulation for the Japanese economy in 1980 to verify the above. We replace the proportion of debt financing in Japan by the American one, and the tax rates for savings by the American rates, which are adapted from King and Fullerton (1984). The rate of debt finance in Japan in 1980 was 39.8 percent for manufacturing, 59.8 percent for other industries, and 43.7 percent for commerce, while the rate in the United States was 19.8 percent, 48.5 percent, and 40.0 percent, respectively. The average marginal tax rate on interest income was 11.4 percent in Japan and 28.4 percent in the United States.

Table 9.12 shows the result of the simulation. Row 1 gives the estimated effective tax rates produced by the first replacement, row 2 by the second replacement, and row 3 by the combined simulation. Row 1 indicates that the effective tax rate is lowered because Japanese firms rely heavily on debt financing, and that if the rate of debt in Japan was the same as the U.S. one, the effective tax rate would be raised considerably and the effect of inflation would simultaneously be lowered significantly. Row 2 shows that the effect of inflation becomes weaker because the benefit of the tax deductibility of nominal interest payments lessens and the effect of personal interest income receipt becomes stronger. Row 3 shows the combined effect. Although the declining trend of the effect due to inflation is not reversed by each replacement, the degree of the decline is reduced. Moreover, if we see the result by the combined simulation, we notice that inflation is no longer effective. Thus, it may be concluded that a high reliance on debt financing and a low tax rate for interest income are the most important factors underlying the excessive sensitivity to inflation in Japan, and that the unexpectedly high rate of inflation in the past decade has helped Japanese corporations to reduce the tax burden of capital income.

The last point suggests an interesting interpretation of the excellent performance of the Japanese macroeconomy during and after the oil crises. The performance may be explained by the unexpectedly low rate of corporate tax burden provided by both the high inflation and the oft-mentioned flexibilities in labor and output markets. This is only a speculation and requires more precise verification.

Comparison with Shoven and Tachibanaki. The estimated marginal tax rates for 1980 presented here are about 5–6 percent higher than the rates esti-

Table 9.12   **Estimated Effective Tax Rates from Substituting U.S. for Japanese Rates of Debt Financing and Tax Rates for Saving (in percentages)**

	Inflation Rates		
	0%	10%	Actual
Japan			
(1)	36.2	23.8	29.0
(2)	36.4	25.4	30.0
(3)	41.5	38.2	40.3
United States	32.0	38.4	37.2

Notes: Row 1 is the estimated effective tax rates obtained by replacing the rate of debt financing in Japan by the one in the U.S. Row 2 is the estimated effective tax rates obtained by replacing the tax rate for savings in Japan by the one in the U.S. Row 3 is the combination of rows 1 and 2. The final row gives the original U.S. figures.

mated by Shoven and Tachibanaki (1988), for several reasons. First, the effective tax rate of dividend income is found to be considerably higher because of a more comprehensive treatment of the banking sector and because the marginal calculation with respect to the effective tax rate was used instead of the average calculation. Second, the method of introducing special depreciation is somewhat different. Moreover, we explicitly considered the effect of tax-free reserves in this framework. The first factor raised the effective tax rates of capital income marginally in comparison with the results of Shoven and Tachibanaki, while the second lowered them marginally. Third, while Shoven and Tachibanaki assumed a zero rate of salvage value in calculating depreciation, our method assumed a rate of 10 percent, which is closer to reality. This assumption raised the effective rate considerably.

Comparison with the U.S. results. Both the zero inflation and actual inflation cases show a lower effective tax rate in Japan than in the United States with respect to the overall tax rates. This proved true for all years studied. The most dramatic difference is observed at the actual rate of inflation in 1980. More importantly, the rates in the past (the 1960s and 1970s) are considerably lower, by about half, in Japan than in the United States. Two main reasons can be suggested to account for the difference. First, the Japanese tax rate, in particular the tax rate on interest income, is considerably lower. Second, Japan relied on debt financing more strongly. Several other minor factors also contribute to the difference.

The fact that the effective tax rate of capital income has consistently been lower in Japan than in the United States suggests that one of the principles of the "catching up" process has been in effect in Japan. It may well be that the lower effective tax rate of capital income encouraged more investment and resulted in more intensive industrialization. Thus, the lower tax rate—in particular, a lower tax rate on interest income—may be regarded as one of the industrial policies initiated by the government in the early stage of the rapid economic growth. The other reason for the comparatively low effective rate, namely, heavy reliance on debt financing, is not a government initiative but rather a natural consequence of the capital market's underdevelopment during that period. Firms had to seek their financial resources at banks where a considerable amount of savings were deposited in order to be able to satisfy their strong propensity to invest (see Tachibanaki 1988).

9.5.2   Decomposition of Effective Tax Rates into Corporate Sector and Personal Sector

The previous two sections examined the overall effective marginal tax rate of capital income. In this section we will attempt to decompose these rates into the separate contributions of the corporate sector and the personal sector. The results, shown in tables 9.10 and 9.11 indicate the relative tax burden borne by each sector.

Table 9.10 is obtained by inserting the zero tax rates for the personal sector. The effective rate estimated by this method is in fact the tax rate for the corporate sector. The difference between the previous overall effective tax rates given in table 9.7 and the estimated tax rates for the corporate sector is the estimated effective tax rate for the personal sector. In sum, table 9.10 is the contribution (or decomposition) made by the corporate sector to the overall effective tax rate, and table 9.11 is the contribution of the personal sector. Identical investigations were performed for Japan and the United States to provide a basis for comparison.

Table 9.10 indicates that the effective tax rates for the corporate sector in both Japan and the United States declined as the rate of inflation was increased. This relationship primarily occurs because the deductibility of nominal interest payments has a greater effect than both depreciation at historical cost and FIFO inventory accounting. Thus, in the United States the increase in the overall combined tax rate that occurred as the rate of inflation rose can be attributed to the taxation of nominal capital gains in the personal sector. By contrast, in the Japanese case a high rate of reliance on debt in the corporate sector gave a stronger negative effect from inflation, as described before. When we consider the effective rates by assets, we observe that inventories are affected most by this channel. Among the three categories of industry, nonmanufacturing was affected the greatest.

Although it is true that the effective tax rates at a zero inflation rate are higher in Japan than in the United States, the reverse is true for the effective rates at actual inflation rates. This statement contradicts the belief commonly held in Japan that the tax burden of corporations in Japan is heavier than in the United States. It is possible, however, that the relationship may be currently inverted, because the rate of inflation has declined considerably in recent years and the United States introduced a far-reaching tax reform in the Economic Recovery Act of 1981. This does not necessarily imply, however, that the inversion holds for the overall combined effective tax rate.

In table 9.11, as was seen previously, the tax rate on savings has increased only modestly, from 7.4 percent in 1961 and 9.0 percent in 1980, at the zero inflation rate. The effective tax rates are all lower in Japan than in the United States, except in the ownership categories. It must be emphasized that the dispersion in the tax rates at the zero inflation rate is wider in the United States, from −11.7 to 24.8 percent. In Japan the tax rates in question range from 0.5 to 13.6 percent. When the inflation rate is high, the difference is greater still. There are two reasons for this result. First, tax deductibility is enormous for tax-exempt institutions in the United States, and second, nominal tax deductions for American insurance companies are considerable. As a consequence, the U.S. tax rates on savings may be more distortionary. Since the Japanese tax rates are lower in general, we expect the distortionary effect to be smaller.

9.6   Some Simulation Results

In this section we present several simulation results using current policy issues in Japan. The Ministry of Finance made some tax reforms, both in income tax and corporate tax. See Shoven and Tachibanaki (1988) and Tachibanaki and Ichioka (1990) for discussions of the current policy issues related to tax reform. The simulations contained here scrutinize the economic effect of the tax reforms conceived by the government and proposed by industry.

9.6.1   The Tax Rate on Interest Income

Reform of the tax rate on interest income has been proposed recently. The previous law allowing nontaxable savings had been under criticism for excessively encouraging savings and for only providing an advantage to the rich. One possible reform that was considered was the introduction of a low rate, perhaps 10 or 20 percent, as a separate tax rate for all currently nontaxable interest income. Table 9.13 shows the estimated marginal tax rates resulting from such a reform.[2] It is clear that the effective marginal tax rates are raised considerably. The rate of increase, however, is greater when the rate of inflation is higher. These results suggest that raising the tax rate of interest income in response to the criticisms above may in fact be detrimental to investment activity, because the effective tax rate on capital income would be raised. The simulation provides us an example of the trade-off effects due to tax reform.

9.6.2   Shortening the Tax Lifetimes of Assets

There is a strong demand from industry to shorten the lifetimes of assets in order to reduce the corporate tax burden. Shortening the lifetimes obviously speeds the pace of depreciation. Special depreciation measures have been common in the past. The provision of the special depreciation, however, has been weakened because the measure has not been uniformly applied, enforced only for certain machinery or specific purposes. A demand for shortening

Table 9.13   **Effective Marginal Tax Rates When the Taxation of Interest Income (Separate Taxation) is Introduced (in percentages)**

Tax Rate	Inflation Rates			
	0%	2.5%	5.0%	Actual
10%				
Debt	4.5	−10.1	−25.5	−46.8
Household	30.3	26.0	20.8	13.0
Overall	30.3	26.2	21.1	13.5
20%				
Debt	7.9	−5.2	−19.1	−38.4
Household	32.3	28.8	24.5	17.7
Overall	31.9	28.4	24.0	17.3

lifetimes of all machinery and equipment uniformly is frequently made because rapid technological change requires shorter lifetimes of assets. Also, tax lifetimes in Japan have been somewhat longer than those in the United States in recent years.

In the simulation performed here we reduce the lifetimes for all assets by uniform rates of 10, 15, and 20 percent. We also consider the effect of reducing salvage value (or the residual rate) of assets. In principle it is 10 percent currently, but 5 percent can be chosen at a firm's option and a zero rate may be applied for special assets. Industry frequently calls for a zero percent rate.

Table 9.14 shows the effective tax rates for various combinations of residual rates and percentage reductions in statutory lifetimes of assets at zero inflation. The numbers in parentheses are the estimated corporate income tax rates which would produce the same effective tax rate as that generated from each hypothetical value for the residual rate and the percentage reduction. The table suggests the following results. First, when the salvage value equals 10 percent of the acquisition cost, the effective tax rate is reduced by about one percentage point in proportion to a 10 percent reduction in the tax lifetime. This is equivalent to a 3 percent reduction in corporate income tax. Second, a reduction in the residual rate of assets has a much greater effect than the reduction in lifetimes. Lowering the residual rate from 10 to 5 percent has the same effect as a 5.1 percent reduction in the corporate income tax when we adopt the current lifetimes. Furthermore, the zero percent residual rate brings about the same effect as the 9.6 percent reduction in the corporate tax rate. This is equivalent to a 30 percent reduction in the lifetimes. Third, if we combine the two effects mentioned above, we recognize that a stronger effect is obtained. This is to say, the more the residual rate falls, the higher the corporate tax rate is reduced when the lifetimes are shortened. For instance, when the residual rate is zero, the effective tax rate decreases by 1.3 percentage points, which is

Table 9.14   **Effective Marginal Tax Rates When Changes in the Lifetimes of Assets and in Salvage (Residual) Rates are Introduced**

	Salvage (Residual) Rate		
	10%	5%	0%
Current tax lifetime	28.7	27.1	25.8
	(52.6)	(47.5)	(43.0)
10% Reduction	27.8	26.0	24.5
	(49.6)	(43.7)	(38.8)
15% Reduction	27.3	25.4	23.8
	(48.1)	(41.7)	(36.5)
20% Reduction	26.8	24.8	23.0
	(46.5)	(39.8)	(34.0)

Note: The numbers in parentheses are the estimated corporate tax rates (τ) which are provided by the hypothetical lifetimes and salvage rates.

equivalent to a 4.3 percent reduction in the corporate tax rate in the case of a 10 percent reduction in lifetimes.

The last point has important economic implications because the amendment of both tax lifetimes and residual rates is under way. The amendments would lighten the tax burden of corporations considerably, much more so than would the reduction in the corporate tax rate proposed by the Ministry of Finance.

9.7 Concluding Remarks

The effective marginal tax of capital income was found to be lowest in 1970 at zero inflation, and we conjectured that this low rate encouraged investment activity in the 1960s and the early 1970s, resulting in the rapid growth of the Japanese economies. This conjecture, however, must be verified by a separate study. Several institutional arrangements, such as special depreciations and tax-free reserves, were particularly effective in lowering the marginal tax rates in those years. The effective tax rates were almost equal in 1961 and 1980. For all years studied, the effective rates were found to be lower in Japan than in the United States.

The estimated marginal tax rates were found to be extremely sensitive to inflation throughout the sample period. Thus, the effective rate given actual inflation was lowest in 1980 because the inflation rates in the 1970s were very high. Two reasons for the extreme sensitivity to inflation were the heavy reliance on debt for corporate financing and the low personal tax rate on savings. Simulations were provided to support these explanations more rigorously.

Decomposition analyses were attempted to examine the contributions of the corporate and personal sectors to the overall effective tax rate. It was found that while inflation lightens the tax burden of corporations, it increases the burden on households.

Finally, several simulations were performed to predict the outcomes of several tax reforms which have been implemented quite recently. The following results were obtained on the basis of the simulations. First, abolishing the system of nontaxable savings in the area of personal taxation raised the effective tax rate considerably. This is particularly true during periods of high inflation. Second, shortening the tax lifetimes of assets and eliminating the salvage rate served to reduce the tax burden of corporations, and thus the effective tax rates on capital income.

Notes

1. It was originally planned to perform our analysis for 1960, but difficulty in acquiring data for 1960 and the major tax reform in 1961 led us to consider 1961 instead.

2. In fact, a 20 percent withholding separate tax rate on interest income was implemented, effective April 1988.

References

Aoki, M. 1984. Shareholder's non-unanimity of investment finance: Banks vs. individual investors. In *The economic analysis of the Japanese firm*, ed. M. Aoki, 193–226. Amsterdam: North Holland.

Flath, D. 1984. Debt and taxes: Japan compared with the United States. *International Journal of Industrial Organization* 2:311–26.

King, M. 1977. *Public policy and the corporation*. London: Chapman and Hall.

King, M., and D. Fullerton. 1984. *The taxation of income from capital: A comparative study of the United States, the United Kingdom, Sweden, and West Germany*. Chicago and London: The University of Chicago Press.

Kosai, Y. 1985. Reconstruction period. In *Industrial policy in Japan* [in Japanese], ed. R. Komiya, M. Okuno, and K. Suzumura, chap. 1. Tokyo: University of Tokyo Press.

Noguchi, Y. 1985. Corporate tax burden in Japan [in Japanese]. *Contemporary Economics* no. 61 (Spring): 48–64.

Ogura, M., and N. Yoshino. 1985. Special depreciation, investment funds through government financing and Japanese industrial structure [in Japanese]. *Economic Review* 36(2):110–20.

Shoven, J., and T. Tachibanaki. 1988. The taxation of income from capital in Japan. In *Public policies in Japan and the U.S.*, ed. J. Shoven. Cambridge: Cambridge University Press.

Tachibanaki, T. 1988. Government policies, the working of the financial market, saving and investment in Japan. In *Factors in business investment*, ed. M. Funke. Berlin: Springer Verlag.

Tachibanaki, T., and O. Ichioka. 1990. The Japanese tax reform: Efficiency versus equity. International Monetary Fund, Discussion Paper Series.

Tajika, E., F. Hayashi, and Y. Yui. 1987. Investment. In *An analysis of the Japanese macroeconomy* [in Japanese], ed. K. Hamada, M. Kuroda, and A. Horiuchi. Tokyo: Todai-shuppan-kai.

Tajika, E., and Y. Yui. 1984. Postwar corporate taxation and fixed investment in Japan: Estimation of reduction in corporate tax by industries [in Japanese]. *Contemporary Economics* no. 59 (Autumn):26–40.

Wada, Y. 1980. *Reconsideration of tax policy and reforms in tax systems in Japan* [in Japanese]. Tokyo: Bunsindo.

10 Taxes and Corporate Investment in Japanese Manufacturing

Fumio Hayashi

10.1 Introduction

Postwar Japan's rapid output growth has been characterized by a high level of investment exceeding 30% of gross national product for almost all years. The extent to which this sustained investment boom has been brought about by the Japanese corporate tax system is a very important issue for policy-making and deserves full analytical treatment. This paper attempts to cast the various aspects of the Japanese corporate tax system in the mold of modern investment theory with adjustment costs and to evaluate the role of tax incentives in the postwar capital accumulation of Japanese manufacturing.

Economic theory tells us that investment is governed by the cost and the benefit of incremental capital stock. Financial rate of return and taxes determine the cost of capital, while the benefit is the profitability of capital that depends on market opportunities and technology. The contribution of Hall and Jorgenson (1971) to neoclassical theory lies in showing exactly how taxes influence the cost of capital, whereas the essential feature of the Q theory of investment is that the determinants of investment can be summarized by a single index (called the "tax-adjusted Q") that combines the cost and benefit of capital. In order to understand the high level of investment in Japan, it is necessary to analyze the relative importance of the cost and the profitability of capital and the effect taxes have on them.

The basis of the Japanese corporate tax system is the Corporation Tax Law. In its treatment of depreciation accounting, inventory valuation, and some

Fumio Hayashi is professor of economics at University of Pennsylvania and a research associate of the National Bureau of Economic Research.

An initial version of this paper was prepared for the NBER's Conference on Productivity Growth in Japan and the United States, Cambridge, Massachusetts, 26–28 August 1985. The author is grateful to the Japan Economic Research Foundation for partial financial support.

accruals, it does not differ qualitatively from its U.S. counterpart. One peculiarity of the Japanese system is that the corporate enterprise tax paid in the previous accounting year is tax deductible. Further elaboration of the Japanese corporate tax system is found in the Special Taxation Measures Law, which encompasses scores of tax breaks. The most important of these is probably the prevalent tax-free reserves. The Special Taxation Measures Law lists dozens of reserves and specifies the maximum amount that can be deducted from income and credited to the reserves. The law also provides for additional depreciation over ordinary depreciation, called "special depreciation." Special depreciation is easily accommodated in standard models of investment with or without adjustment costs. However, it is less obvious that the other major feature of the Special Taxation Measures Law, the tax-free reserves, can also be incorporated into the cost of capital and the tax-adjusted Q. In section 10.3, we demonstrate this, building on the expression for the value of a firm obtained in section 10.2. A rigorous derivation of the valuation formula is given in appendix A. Section 10.3 also discloses a close connection between the tax-adjusted Q and the cost of capital for the model that includes adjustment costs. In section 10.4, we calculate the tax-adjusted Q for the Japanese manufacturing sector and evaluate the impact of taxes on investment. Section 10.5 is a brief conclusion.

10.2   Taxes and the Valuation of a Firm

Our task in this section is to incorporate various aspects of the Japanese corporate tax system into a standard model of a firm's value-maximization problem. The next section will derive a one-to-one relationship between the investment-capital ratio and Q adjusted for various tax parameters. For the most part, we will ignore personal taxes and the financial side of the firm. Modifications of the investment-Q relationship that are necessary if those factors are considered will be discussed at the end of section 10.3. Thus for the time being we will consider a 100% equity-financed firm whose investment finance comes from retained profits. The notation will be rather complicated because of the many tax parameters. A glossary of symbols is provided in appendix B.

Consider a firm in period 0 whose objective is to maximize its market value, which is the present value of its net cash flow:

$$(1) \qquad V_0 = \sum_{t=0}^{\infty} C(0,t)(\pi_t - T_t - a_t I_t),$$

where $C(0,t) = (1+r_0)^{-1}(1+r_1)^{-1} \ldots (1+r_{t-1})^{-1}$ is the discounting factor at time 0 for a cash flow t periods hence (so, if the discount rate is constant at r_0, then $C[0,t]$ reduces to $[1+r_0]^{-t}$), r_t is the discount rate in period t, π_t is gross pretax profits (sales minus variable costs), T_t is corporate taxes, a_t is the price of investment goods, and I_t is the quantity of investment. Under Japanese tax law the following are the major items that are deductible from corporate income:[1]

1. *Depreciation allowances.* According to the financial statements filed by corporations with the Ministry of Finance, virtually all corporations employ either the straight-line or the declining-balance method of depreciation.

2. *Special depreciation.* In addition to the ordinary depreciation, the Special Taxation Measures Law lists asset types for which additional depreciation is permitted for the first year (and for some assets, for several succeeding years). Since the cumulative amount of depreciation is unchanged, special depreciation amounts to deferred tax payments.

3. *Investment tax credits.* Currently, for certain types of equipment, corporations can choose between a special first-year depreciation of 30% and a tax credit of 7% of the acquisition cost. Since the amount of the investment tax credit is negligible relative to total investment expenditure, we will ignore it.

4. *Enterprise tax.* The amount of enterprise tax paid in the previous accounting year can be deducted from the current year's income. As seen below, the deductibility of the enterprise tax significantly reduces the "effective" corporate rate.

5. *Tax-free reserves.* The Corporate Tax Law and the Special Taxation Measures Law list a host of tax-free reserves that can be deducted from income. For most reserves, the amount deducted must be added back in to the next year's income. In the formulation below we assume this is the case for all tax-free reserves.[2] Thus tax-free reserves, another vehicle by which corporations may defer tax payments, are essentially a one-year interest-free loan granted by the government. The existence of tax-free reserves will influence firm behavior if the size of the interest-free loan depends on the firm's action.

The reserve for retirement allowances, the largest tax-free reserve, may not at first glance seem to conform to this assumption of adding back in full to the next year's income. Let R_t here be the balance at the end of period t of the reserve for retirement allowances, X_t be the amount credited to the reserve, and Y_t be the amount withdrawn from the reserve. This Y_t equals actual severance payments during period t and this must be added back to income for tax purposes. According to the law, for most of the corporations in Japan, the maximum tax-free amount that is creditable to the reserve (call that X_t') is the smaller of either (*a*) the change over the year in the hypothetical total severance pay that the firm would have to pay if all its employees were to retire (*b*) the difference between some specified amount (currently set at 40% of the hypothetical total severance pay in [*a*]) and $R_{t-1} - Y_t$. Unless the reserve in the previous year (R_{t-1}) is extraordinarily low, due, for example, to a mass exodus of employees, the second criterion is the relevant one because of the factor of 40%. The tax benefit derived from the existence of the reserve results from the decrease in taxable income, which equals $X_t' - Y_t$. Under (*b*) this equals:

$$X'_t - Y_t = (40\% \text{ of the hypothetical severance pay}) - (R_{t-1} - Y_t) - Y_t$$
$$= (40\% \text{ of the hypothetical severance pay}) - R_{t-1},$$

which shows that it is not rational for the firm to let X_t, the actual amount credited to the reserve, exceed X'_t, the legal ceiling on the amount deductible. If it did allow X_t to exceed X'_t, the amount deductible in period $t + 1$ would be less by $(X_t - X'_t)$. Thus it is reasonable to suppose that $X'_t = X_t$. Two conclusions follow from this result. First, the decrease in taxable income $X'_t - Y_t$ equals $X_t - Y_t$, which equals $R_t - R_{t-1}$, which is equivalent to the assumption we made above: the firm can deduct from current income the entire amount R_t but that R_{t-1} must be added back in full. Second, R_t equals 40% of the hypothetical severance pay.

The variable that determines the maximum amount to be deducted from corporate income and credited to the reserve depends on the reserve. For example, for the reserve for retirement allowances it is the hypothetical severance pay, and for the bad debt reserve it is the amount of receivables. We will divide the various tax-free reserves into two groups. The first group is composed of employment-related reserves whose maximum allowable amount is a function of the wage bill. The second group consists of those reserves whose maximum allowable amount is a function of certain other variables pertaining to the firm. We will assume that these variables are a function of the "size" of the firm represented by the reproduction cost of the firm.

The expression for the tax payment T_t that incorporates these features of Japanese tax law is

(2a) $$T_t = (u_t + v_t) \times (\text{taxable income}),$$

(2b) $$\text{taxable income} = \pi_t - \text{DEP}_t - S_{t-1} - (R_t - R_{t-1}),$$

(2c) $$S_t = v_t \times (\text{taxable income}).$$

Here, S_t is the corporate enterprise tax and v_t is the corresponding tax rate. T_t is the total amount of corporate taxes for period t, including the national and local corporate tax and the enterprise tax. The overall tax rate is thus $u_t + v_t$. In the expression for taxable income, R is the maximum amount to be deducted from income and credited to the tax-free reserves in period t.[3] DEP_t is the sum of ordinary depreciation and special depreciation. This can be written as

(3) $$\text{DEP}_t = \sum_{x=0}^{\infty} D(x, t-x) a_{t-x} I_{t-x},$$

where the depreciation formula as of $t - x$, $D(x, t - x)$ includes special depreciation.

It is shown in appendix A that the expression for the value of the firm under equations (1), (2a), (2b), (2c), and (3) can be written as

$$
(4) \quad V_0 = \sum_{t=0}^{\infty} C(0, t)\{(1-\tau_t)\pi_t - (1-z_t')a_t I_t + [\tau_t - \tau_{t+1}/(1+r_t)]R_t\}
$$
$$
+ A_0' - \tau_0(R_{-1} - S_{-1}),
$$

where

$$
(5) \quad y_t = \sum_{n=1}^{\infty} C(t, t+n)(u_{t+n}+v_{t+n})(-v_{t+1})(-v_{t+2}) \ldots (-v_{t+n-1}),
$$

which equals

$$
(5') \quad\quad\quad\quad y_t = (u_t + v_t)/(1 + r_t + v_t)
$$

if

$$
u_{t+n} = u_t, \; v_{t+n} = v_t, \; r_{t+n} = r_t \quad \text{for } n \geq 1,
$$

and

$$
(6) \quad\quad\quad\quad \tau_t = u_t + v_t - y_t v_t,
$$

$$
(7) \quad\quad\quad\quad z_t' = \sum_{x=0}^{\infty} C(t, t+x)\tau_{t+x} D(x, t),
$$

$$
(8) \quad\quad\quad\quad A_0' = \sum_{t=0}^{\infty} \{C(0, t)\tau_t[\sum_{x=1}^{\infty} D(x, -x)a_{-x}I_{-x}]\}.
$$

Some of these rather formidable expressions are standard: z_t' represents the present value of tax savings arising from depreciation allowances on one yen of new investment,[4] while A_0' is the present value of all assets purchased in the past.

Other expressions are new but easy to interpret. The effective tax rate τ is not simply the sum of u and v because of the tax deductibility of the enterprise tax. A one-yen increase in the current enterprise tax results in a tax saving of $u + v$ yen in the next accounting year. But part of the tax saving, v, which is the amount of reduction in the next year's enterprise tax, gives rise to a tax increase of $v(u+v)$ in the year after next. This, in turn, brings about a tax saving of $v^2(u+v)$ in the following year, and so forth. The expression (5') for y is the present value of this tax change on one yen of the current enterprise tax, and the expression (6) for the effective tax rate τ takes this into account. This term is rather important: if $u = 40\%$, $v = 10\%$, and $r = 5\%$, its value is about 43%. That is, for every yen of the enterprise tax paid, the firm recovers 0.43 yen in the present value sense.

The third term in the braces in expression (4)—$[\tau_t - \tau_{t+1}/(1+r_t)]R_t$—represents a subsidy in the form of an interest-free loan through tax-free reserves. By deducting the amount R_t in period t, the firm can reduce the corporate tax in period t by $\tau_t R_t$. Since that amount R_t must be added back to income in period $t+1$, the resulting tax increase in period $t+1$ is $\tau_{t+1}R_t$. The term $[\tau_t - \tau_{t+1}/(1+r_t)]R_t$ is the present value of that change in the stream of corporate tax.

The last term in expression (4) for the value of the firm, $-\tau_0(R_{-1} - S_{-1})$, represents a liability to the government in period 0 due to the tax-free reserves and the enterprise tax incurred in the previous period (period -1). The enterprise tax paid in the previous period of S_{-1} entitles the firm to claim a tax rebate of $\tau_0 S_{-1}$. On the other hand, the amount credited to the tax-free reserves in the previous period of R_{-1} must be added back to current income, which increases current corporate tax by $\tau_0 R_{-1}$.

The expression (4) for the value of the firm neatly divides the effect of taxes (the present value of T_t in [1]) into two components. The first component can influence the firm's action from period 0 on. It is represented by τ_t, z_t', and $[\tau_t - \tau_{t+1}/(1+r_t)]$, which constitute tax incentives for the firm. The second component, represented by the last two terms, $A_0' - \tau_0(R_{-1} - S_{-1})$, is given to the firm in period 0. It is an invisible asset to the firm, and its value is invariant regardless of the behavior of the firm from period 0 and on.

10.3   The Tax-Adjusted Q and the Cost of Capital

We now derive a one-to-one relationship between investment and Q adjusted for various tax parameters for the value-maximizing firm. Assuming that the firm is a price taker, gross pretax profits (before deduction of accounting depreciation) can be written as

$$(9) \qquad \pi_t = p_t F(K_t, L_t, I_t) - w_t L_t,$$

where p is the output price, F is the production function, K is the capital stock, L is labor input, and w is the wage rate. Adjustment costs are incorporated here because output is assumed to be inversely related to investment, that is, $\partial F/\partial I < 0$. "Bolting down" new machines is a resource-using activity; as the quantity of investment increases, a larger fraction of capital and labor has to be directed to the investment activity, which results in lower output.

As we indicated in the previous section, the tax-free reserves are divided into employment-related reserves (RL) and other reserves (RK). The former depends on the wage bill (wL) while the latter are a function of the reproduction cost of the firm (aK):

$$(10) \qquad R_t = RL_t(w_t L_t) + RK_t(a_t K_t).$$

The firm is assumed to maximize its value, given by the expression (4), subject to the capital accumulation constraint

$$(11) \qquad K_t = (1-\delta)K_{t-1} + I_t.$$

Since the last two terms in the expression (4) are predetermined at time 0, the value maximization is equivalent to maximizing the first term subject to equation (11). That is, the firm is assumed to maximize

$$(12) \quad \sum_{t=0}^{\infty} C(0, t)\{(1-\tau_t)[p_t F(K_t, L_t, I_t) - w_t L_t] - (1-z_t')a_t I_t + [\tau_t - \tau_{t+1}/(1+r_t)][RL_t(w_t L_t) + RK_t(a_t K_t)]\},$$

subject to equation (11). Letting $C(0, t)\lambda_t$ be the Lagrange multiplier for (11), we obtain the following first-order conditions:

$$(13a) \quad (1-\tau_t)p_t \frac{\partial F_t}{\partial K_t} + [\tau_t - \tau_{t+1}/(1+r_t)] a_t \frac{\partial RK_t}{\partial(a_t K_t)} - \lambda_t + (1-\delta)\lambda_{t+1}/(1+r_t) = 0,$$

$$(13b) \quad (1-\tau_t)p_t \frac{\partial F_t}{\partial I_t} - (1-z_t')a_t = \lambda_t,$$

and

$$(13c) \quad (1-\tau_t)(p_t \frac{\partial F_t}{\partial L_t} - w_t) + [\tau_t - \tau_{t+1}/(1+r_t)] w_t \frac{\partial RL_t}{\partial(w_t L_t)} = 0.$$

The last condition yields

$$(14) \quad \partial F_t/\partial L_t = w_t^*/p_t,$$

where

$$(15) \quad w_t^* = (1 - \frac{[\tau_t - \tau_{t+1}/(1+r_t)]}{1 - \tau_t} \frac{\partial RL_t}{\partial(w_t L_t)})w_t.$$

This w^* allows for the reduction in wage rate induced by the employment-related tax-free reserves.

If there are no adjustment costs, so that $\partial F/\partial I = 0$, then we have, from (13b), $\lambda_t = (1-z_t')a_t$. Thus from (13a) we obtain the familiar condition that the marginal product of capital equals the *cost of capital*:

$$(16) \quad \frac{\partial F_t}{\partial K_t} = c_t,$$

where

$$(17) \quad c_t = \frac{(1-z_t')a_t - (1-\delta)(1-z_{t+1}')a_{t+1}/(1+r_t)}{(1-\tau_t)p_t} - \frac{\tau_t - \tau_{t+1}/(1+r_t)}{(1-\tau_t)p_t} a_t \frac{\partial RK_t}{\partial(a_t K_t)}.$$

The second term on the right-hand side of equation (17) represents the reduction in the cost of capital arising from the capital-related tax-free reserves. It is easily seen that, if the tax-free reserve RK is ignored, and if static expectations $a_{t+1} = a_t$ and $z'_{t+1} = z'$, are assumed, then equation (17) reduces to the familiar expression for the cost of capital: $(1 - z'_t)a_t(r_t + \delta)/[(1 - \tau_t)p_t]$.[5]

We now reintroduce adjustment costs. Noting that the optimal labor input is a function of w^*/p and solving the condition given in (13b) for investment, we obtain the investment-Q relation

$$(18) \qquad I_t = I_t(Q_t, K_t, w^*_t/p_t),$$

where Q_t is defined by

$$(19) \qquad Q_t = \frac{\lambda_t - (1 - z'_t)a_t}{(1 - \tau_t)p_t}.$$

This Q is referred to as the tax-adjusted Q. It is the real value of the gap between the shadow price of capital λ and the effective price of investment goods $[(1 - z')a]$, grossed up by the corporate tax rate. We note from equation (18) that optimal investment also depends on the adjusted real wage w^*/p. It is clear from the derivation of this optimal investment rule that if the production function F in equation (9) has the separable form $F(K, L, I) = G(K, L) - C(I, L)$, the optimal investment rule does not involve the real wage rate.

There is a simple connection between the tax-adjusted Q and the cost of capital. By definition, the cost of capital c satisfies the conditions

$$(20) \qquad \begin{aligned} &(1 - \tau_t)p_t c_t + [\tau_t - \tau_{t+1}/(1 + r_t)]a_t \frac{\partial RK_t}{\partial(a_t K_t)} \\ &- (1 - z'_t)a_t + (1 - \delta)(1 - z'_{t+1})a_{t+1}/(1 + r_t) = 0. \end{aligned}$$

Subtracting equation (20) from (13a) we obtain

$$(21) \qquad \begin{aligned} &(1 - \tau_t)p_t(\partial F_t/\partial K_t - c_t) - [\lambda_t - (1 - z'_t)a_t] \\ &+ (1 - \delta)[\lambda_{t+1} - (1 - z'_{t+1})a_{t+1}]/(1 + r_t) = 0. \end{aligned}$$

This can be solved for $\lambda_t - (1 - z'_t)a_t$ as

$$(22) \qquad \lambda_t - (1 - z'_t)a_t = \sum_{s=t}^{\infty} C(t,s)(1 - \delta)^{s-t}(1 - \tau_s)p_s(\partial F_s/\partial K_s - c_s).$$

That is, the tax-adjusted Q is the present value of the gap between the marginal product of capital and the cost of capital. Thus, in the model with adjustment costs, the cost of capital continues to be an important channel through which taxes influence investment.

As shown in Hayashi (1982), the shadow price of capital λ in the expression (19) for the tax-adjusted Q can be made observable if we assume that (1) the firm is a price taker and (2) the environment represented by the production function is linearly homogeneous. In the present situation, this latter homogeneity assumption must include the assumption that RL and RK in equation (10), the maximum tax-free accumulation of reserves, are also linearly homogeneous in their respective variables, namely, that

(23a)
$$\frac{\partial RL_t}{\partial(w_t L_t)} = \frac{RL_t}{w_t L_t},$$

and

(23b)
$$\frac{\partial RK_t}{\partial(a_t K_t)} = \frac{RK_t}{a_t K_t}.$$

Under this set of assumptions it seems obvious that the maximized value of expression (12) (which is the first term in [4]) is proportional to the initial capital stock $(1 - \delta)K_{-1}$. Therefore, the *marginal* value of capital λ_0 is equal to the *average* value of capital

(24)
$$\lambda_0 = \frac{V_0 - A_0' + \tau_0(RL_{-1} + RK_{-1} - S_{-1})}{(1 - \delta)K_{-1}}.$$

Thus the tax-adjusted Q as defined in equation (19) is connected to the value of the firm. Furthermore, under the homogeneity assumption the investment-Q relation becomes

(25)
$$I_t/K_t = \phi_t(Q_t, w_t^*/p_t).$$

This yields a new result showing that the connection between the tax-adjusted Q and the value of the firm involves tax-free reserves and the enterprise tax in the previous year.

Until now we have assumed that there is only one kind of capital. The theoretical model can allow for other kinds of capital provided that there are no adjustment costs associated with investment in these other assets. It is fairly straightforward to show that the marginal value of the first asset (with adjustment costs) is given by equation (23) if the market value of other assets (which equals their reproduction cost because there are no adjustment costs for those assets) is already subtracted from V_0. In our empirical implementation in the next section, the first asset is depreciable assets (buildings, structures, and equipment), while the other assets consist of land and inventories.

We close this section by briefly discussing the issue of investment finance. We have assumed an equity-financed firm that finances investment by retained profits. Thus the discount rate r is equal to the expected equity return and the value of the firm is the total equity value. How should we modify the expressions for the tax-adjusted Q? The following results concerning the investment-Q relation have been obtained in Hayashi (1985) for a model of a firm with adjustment costs under uncertainty and with personal taxes in which dividends are taxed more heavily than capital gains: (1) the investment-Q relation can be derived when at least part of incremental investment is financed either by retained profits or by new equity; (2) if new equity is used for investment finance, the value of the firm in the model is simply the sum of equity and debt outstanding; (3) if retained profits are used, the equity value receives a higher weight than debt, provided that the capital gains tax rate is lower than the dividend tax rate; and (4) when incremental investment is financed entirely by debt, the investment-Q relation cannot be derived. A corollary of all these is that if dividends and capital gains are taxed equally heavily or if personal taxes do not exist, then the investment-Q relation holds, with the value of the firm being the sum of equity and debt.

10.4   Empirical Results

The impact of taxes on the incentive to invest can be evaluated by examining how taxes enter the expressions for the tax-adjusted Q and the cost of capital. Since the expressions involve the present value of various forms of tax savings, certain assumptions are necessary concerning how future tax rates and discount rates are anticipated. In our empirical implementation we will assume static expectations for the tax rates (u, v, τ) and the discount rate. Thus z', A', and τ can now be written as

$$(26) \qquad z'_t = \tau_t z_t, \quad \text{where } z_t = \sum_{x=0}^{\infty} (1+r_t)^{-x} D(x, t),$$

$$(27) \qquad A'_0 = \tau_0 A_0, \quad \text{where } A_0 = \sum_{t-0}^{\infty} (1+r_0)^{-t} [\sum_{x=1}^{\infty} D(x, -x) a_{-x} I_{-x}],$$

and

$$(28) \qquad \tau_t = u_t + v_t - (u_t + v_t) v_t / (1 + r_t + v_t).$$

The z here coincides with Hall and Jorgenson's (1971) z. The expression for the tax-adjusted Q (eq. [19] with eq. [24]) becomes

$$(29) \qquad Q = \frac{\left[\dfrac{V - \tau A + \tau R_{-1} - \tau S_{-1}}{a(1-\delta)K_{-1}} - (1 - \tau z) \right] a}{(1 - \tau)p},$$

where the time subscript "0" is dropped for ease of notation.

The measurement of the tax-adjusted Q for the Japanese manufacturing sector as a whole requires data on: V (market value of equity plus debt minus land and inventories), u (corporate tax rate), v (enterprise tax rate), r (discount rate), A (present value of depreciation allowances on past investment), R (tax-free reserves), S (enterprise tax), a (investment goods price), K (capital stock), aI (nominal investment), z (present value of depreciation allowances on new investment), and p (output price). The two principal data sources are the Ministry of Finance (for various fiscal years) and the Tax Bureau (various fiscal years). The Ministry of Finance keeps statistics compiled from financial statements aggregated over all corporations by industry. The aggregation is done by blowing up the sample aggregates by the sampling ratio. These data will be referred to as the financial statements data. The Tax Bureau keeps records of taxes paid by corporations and of tax-free reserves allowed by the Tax Bureau. These data will be referred to as the tax data. Since the time interval for these two primary sets of data is the fiscal year (beginning 1 April and ending 30 March), all calculations that follow are for fiscal years.

The data on V, A, z, al, and K are taken from a study by Homma, Hayashi, Atoda, and Hata (1984), in which the tax-adjusted Q for various Japanese industries was calculated. The study did not, however, take into account tax-free reserves and the tax deductibility of the enterprise tax.[6] The data used covered the period 1955–81, and this determined our own sample period. A brief summary of how the data on V, A, z, al, and K were constructed in their study follows.

The data on nominal investment are taken from the Economic Planning Agency's "Gross Capital Stock of Private Firms" (various years). Although the data include the noncorporate sector, the numbers are very close to the nominal investment series calculated from the financial statements data except that the latter show erratic movements for the first few years of the sample period. The data on the capital stock was taken from the 1970 National Wealth Survey (Economic Planning Agency 1974). Since this survey is only conducted every five years, the "Gross Capital Stock" data are used for interpolation. Using the nominal investment series from the financial statements data and the investment goods price index (see below), we generated a capital stock series by a perpetual inventory method with the rate of depreciation of 8.99%.[7] It turned out that this capital stock series is very close to the EPA capital stock series.

The market value of equity is calculated under the assumption that the ratio of the market value to the book value for all corporations in manufacturing is the same as that for all corporations in manufacturing traded on the Tokyo Stock Exchange. In calculating the market value of equity, the average of daily stock prices over the fiscal year is used. The market value of long-term debt is obtained by dividing the interest payments by a long-term interest rate. The market value of short-term debt is assumed to be the same as the book value. The value of the firm is the sum of the market value of equity and debt. However, the stock market valuation of a firm includes the value of land and inventories, which must be subtracted from the value of equity plus debt to arrive at the financial valuation of the capital stock. A perpetual inventory method is used to calculate the value of land. The price index for land is the "Residential Land Price Index" constructed by the Japan Research Institute of Real Estate (*Nihon Fudosan Kenkyu-Jo*) (various years). The change in the book value of land is assumed to be equal to the change in the market value of land. The market value of land in the base year (1955) is assumed to be equal to the assessment used by the Ministry of Local Administration for the purpose of levying property taxes. The value of inventories is assumed to be equal to the book value because the majority of corporations employ the average method for inventory valuation.

To calculate A and z, the data on the depreciation formula $D(x,t)$ are necessary. The asset life for tax purposes is assumed to be 34 years for buildings, 28 years for structures, and 10 years for equipment in 1970. These figures are taken from the National Wealth Survey. The calculation incorporates the major reductions, in asset lifetimes, reductions made for tax purposes, that occurred in 1951, 1961, 1964, and 1969. The special depreciation permitted by the Special Taxation Measures Law is incorporated into the depreciation formula as follows. The fraction of special depreciation in fiscal year t, $SP(t)$, is defined as the ratio of the amount of special depreciation in the Financial Statements data to nominal investment. If $d(x,t)$ is the depreciation formula implied by a given asset lifetime for a given depreciation method, the depreciation formula $D(x,t)$ adjusted for special depreciation is:

$$D(x,t) = [1 - SP(t)]d(x,t) + SP(t) \quad \text{for } t = 0,$$

and

$$D(x,t) = [1 - SP(t)]d(x,t) \quad \text{for } t > 0.$$

The implicit assumption here is that the ratio of special depreciation, SP, is the same for all asset types. The yield on the Japan Telegraph and Telephone Company's bond is used as the discount rate. Other information necessary for calculating A and z is: (1) the share of respective depreciation methods and (2) the breakdown of nominal investment into the three asset types (buildings, structures, and equipment). The data on the share of respective depreciation methods are taken from the financial statements of corporations traded on the Tokyo Stock Exchange. Since virtually all corporations employ either the straight-line method (about 20%) or the declining-balance method (80%), only the two depreciation methods are considered. This share is assumed to be the same for all asset types. The data on the breakdown of nominal investment are not available on a yearly basis. The breakdown for 1975 (calendar year) is obtained from the capital formation matrix in the *1975 Input-Output Table* (General Management Agency 1979). The breakdown for all years is assumed to be the same as that in 1975.

Our construction of the investment goods price index, a, is as follows. From the capital formation matrix in the *1975 Input-Output Table*, we can obtain the breakdown of nominal investment by industry source. We use this breakdown as a weight to calculate the price index as a weighted average of the relevant components of the wholesale price index. We use the overall wholesale price index for the output price index, p.

Our estimates of u, v, S, and R come from the tax data. The corporate tax rate u is the ratio of national and local corporate taxes to taxable income. The enterprise tax rate v is the ratio of enterprise tax to taxable income. Information on S is obtained directly from the tax data.[8] The measurement of R (tax-free reserves) is more problematic. As of 1981 there are 28 tax-free reserves listed in the Corporate Tax Law and the Special Taxation Measures Law. Since, in some cases, corporations accumulate reserves beyond the maximum amount specified by the tax law without any further tax benefits, the figures given for reserves in the financial statements data are not useful. Furthermore, the financial statements data do not report tax-free reserves separately; some of the figures for tax-free reserves are merged with special depreciation and other reserves that are not tax-free. However the tax data contain figures for six major tax-free reserves beginning in 1963. These are (1) the reserve for bad debts, (2) the bonus reserve, (3) the reserve for retirement allowances, (4) the reserve for price fluctuations, (5) the overseas market development reserve for small- and medium-sized enterprises, and (6) the reserve for overseas investment losses. The amount credited to these reserves (except to the last two, which are minor relative to the rest) must be added back in full in the following accounting year, as assumed in our theoretical model. For lack of alternative data sources, we use the total of these six tax-free reserves for R.

The data thus obtained that are necessary to calculate tax-adjusted Q are assembled in table 10.1. The data for 1955 (fiscal year) are not available because the calculation of Q requires data for the preceding year. Table 10.2 contains the tax-adjusted Q. Since no data are available for R (tax-free reserves) before 1962, our calculation assumes that the ratio of R to aK (the reproduction cost of capital) prior to 1963 is the same as the ratio for 1963. As we can see by comparing the Q series in table 10.2 with the data on the market value of equity in table 10.1, stock prices are the main source of variation in Q.

A basic assumption underlining the formula (29) is that R, the amount deductible from corporate income, is proportional to the capital stock (see eq. [23]).[9] In order to ascertain the validity of this assumption, we examined the financial statements of individual manufacturing firms that are publicly traded. We obtained the relevant data from the *NEEDS Company Data* compiled by the *Nihon Keizai Shimbun* (Japan Economics Daily). From data on accounting depreciation and the book value of depreciable assets, the market value of the reproduction cost of capital, aK, is constructed by a perpetual inventory method for about 620 firms for the fiscal years 1965–81. Although this data set consists mainly of individual financial statements, there is an item that reports the maximum amount to be credited to the reserve for retirement allowances from 1976 on. This amount is regressed on the capital stock for each year. Table 10.3 reports the regression results. Although the intercept term is significant, the capital stock coefficient is very close to that obtained in the regression without the intercept. This finding supports our proportionality assumption about reserves.

The investment-capital ratio and tax-adjusted Q are plotted against time in

Table 10.1   Components of the Tax-Adjusted Q

Year	Equity	Debt	Value	Capital	Investment	Reserve	p_{INVEST}	p_{OUTPUT}	u	v	τ	z
1956	1,041	1,423	332	2,198	535	N.A.	.631	.581	.401	.120	.469	.530
1957	1,553	2,125	602	2,784	867	N.A.	.651	.579	.400	.121	.469	.477
1958	1,912	2,532	1,189	3,370	912	N.A.	.613	.546	.372	.118	.442	.495
1959	2,692	2,502	1,536	3,956	1,158	N.A.	.625	.559	.392	.114	.458	.498
1960	5,019	3,132	3,379	4,542	1,942	N.A.	.626	.560	.400	.115	.466	.495
1961	6,603	3,886	4,431	5,754	2,338	N.A.	.638	.567	.386	.113	.453	.483
1962	7,263	4,220	4,554	6,967	2,486	462	.625	.557	.368	.113	.437	.465
1963	6,459	5,651	3,705	8,179	2,641	561	.622	.569	.368	.111	.435	.543
1964	6,348	6,654	3,309	9,392	2,842	629	.622	.569	.363	.112	.430	.543
1965	6,350	7,899	3,630	10,605	2,453	738	.623	.575	.349	.108	.415	.569
1966	8,591	9,503	6,130	12,615	2,870	914	.648	.591	.344	.111	.413	.604
1967	10,099	10,969	6,625	14,625	4,210	1,118	.659	.599	.342	.112	.411	.593
1968	13,149	13,007	8,811	16,635	5,372	1,602	.664	.603	.340	.113	.410	.579
1969	24,022	15,622	17,948	18,645	6,948	2,062	.683	.623	.344	.113	.414	.574
1970	21,408	18,781	13,853	20,655	7,923	2,223	.696	.637	.356	.113	.425	.565
1971	21,783	23,562	15,570	26,649	6,823	2,540	.686	.632	.349	.109	.416	.593
1972	21,126	29,373	15,950	32,642	7,315	3,090	.720	.652	.362	.109	.427	.620
1973	27,238	31,780	13,136	38,636	8,754	4,058	.877	.800	.379	.113	.445	.576
1974	28,133	33,858	6,265	44,630	9,739	4,458	1.018	.988	.396	.120	.466	.507
1975	38,763	46,364	27,562	50,624	8,890	4,834	.997	1.007	.379	.111	.445	.542
1976	48,535	48,433	35,830	55,502	9,055	5,811	1.032	1.062	.411	.117	.477	.556
1977	45,151	53,055	34,115	60,379	8,916	5,680	1.048	1.066	.413	.120	.480	.591
1978	50,800	58,059	42,809	65,257	8,276	6,098	1.063	1.041	.413	.116	.477	.611
1979	54,740	57,103	36,869	70,135	10,827	6,593	1.150	1.175	.414	.116	.478	.582
1980	60,394	53,820	28,405	75,013	13,316	6,780	1.210	1.331	.422	.116	.486	.549
1981	83,012	63,191	51,437	79,891	14,321		1.195	1.350	.429	.115	.492	.563

Note: Equity = market value of equity; Debt = market value of debt; Value = denominator in (24) of text; Capital = nominal reproduction cost of capital; Investment = nominal investment; Reserve = tax-free reserves (all figures given are in billions of yen). p_{INVEST} = price index of investment goods (normalized to one for the 1975 calendar year); p_{OUTPUT} = price index of output; u = national and local corporate tax rate; v = enterprise tax rate; τ = "effective" tax rate defined by (28); z = present value of depreciation allowances defined by (26).

Table 10.2   **Investment and Tax-Adjusted Q**

Year	I/K	Q
1956	.244	−1.129
1957	.311	−.980
1958	.271	−.598
1959	.293	−.460
1960	.427	1.110
1961	.406	1.061
1962	.357	.437
1963	.323	−.184
1964	.303	−.501
1965	.231	−.590
1966	.227	−.228
1967	.288	−.224
1968	.323	.037
1969	.373	1.445
1970	.384	.623
1971	.256	.060
1972	.224	−.204
1973	.227	−.600
1974	.218	−1.128
1975	.176	−.176
1976	.163	.068
1977	.148	−.101
1978	.127	.084
1979	.154	−.188
1980	.178	−.483
1981	.179	.108

Table 10.3   **Regression of the Retirement Reserve on the Capital Stock**

Fiscal Year	Sample Size	Mean of Capital Stock	With Intercept			Without Intercept
			Constant	Capital Stock	R^2	Capital Stock
1976	626	20,826	759	.062	.69	.064
			(5.5)	(37.8)		(39.6)
1977	626	21,892	1,062	.055	.59	.057
			(5.9)	(29.8)		(31.2)
1978	620	22,362	1,146	.058	.60	.061
			(5.9)	(30.1)		(31.5)
1979	618	23,688	1,165	.058	.62	.061
			(6.0)	(31.5)		(32.9)
1980	616	25,096	1,181	.062	.64	.065
			(5.9)	(33.1)		(34.6)
1981	613	25,247	998	.067	.67	.070
			(5.2)	(35.3)		(37.0)

Note: The dependent variable is the maximum allowable limit on the amount deductible from corporate income as credits to the Reserve for Retirement Allowances. Numbers in parentheses are the *t*-values.

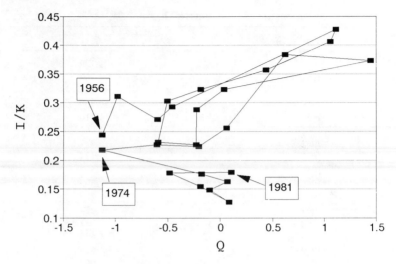

Fig. 10.1   Plot of *I/K* against *Q*: 1956–81

figure 10.1. The two major peaks in investment that occurred in 1960 and 1970, and the sharp trough in 1965, correspond almost exactly to the path of the Q series. This results in a strong positive correlation, until 1974, between I/K and Q. It is thus tempting to fit a regression of I/K on Q to estimate the Q-based investment equation as in expression (25) (with w^*/p dropped under the separability assumption $F[K,L,I] = G[K,L] - C[I,K]$). This gives, for sample period 1956–74,

$$I/K = 0.31 + 0.071\ Q, \quad \text{SER} = 0.040,\ R^2 = 0.65,\ \text{D-W} = 1.27,$$
$$\quad\ (0.009)\ (0.013)$$

where the numbers in parentheses are standard errors, SER is the standard error of the regression, and D-W is the Durbin-Watson statistic. The Q coefficient of 0.071 is, however, biased because Q is an endogenous variable. A larger value of the error term in the investment-Q equation raises investment and hence aggregate demand. It is conceivable that stock prices move up reflecting a boom brought about by the increase in aggregate demand. If this is the case, the ordinary least squares (OLS) estimate of the Q coefficient is biased upward. The same reasoning implies that the correlation between I/K and Q is also consistent with many other theories of investment as long as there is a general equilibrium link between aggregate demand and stock prices. To correct for the simultaneity bias, we use the tax variables u, v, and z in table 10.1 as instruments. The two-stage least squares (2SLS) estimate of the same equation, still for sample period 1956–74, is slightly different:

$$I/K = 0.31 + 0.062\ Q, \quad SER = 0.41.$$
$$(0.010)\ (0.025)$$

This positive association between I/K and Q that remains after the simultaneity bias is removed is certainly consistent with the Q theory.

However, the positive association ceases to hold after 1974. In fact, when the sample period includes the years following 1974, the 2SLS estimate of the Q coefficient is no longer significant at the 5% level. In other words, by historical standards, Q has been too high. Three explanations come to mind for the puzzling behavior of Q after 1974. First, another variable may exist that we failed to take into account in our method. Second, the denominator of Q may have been mismeasured, or third, the numerator may have been mismeasured. The first explanation notes that the relationship between I/K and Q as given in expression (25) involves real factor prices w^*/p, whose components include energy prices. Energy inputs are needed to install new machines within the firm. As energy prices increase, installation activity is depressed, and the I/K–Q relation shifts downward.

The second explanation relies on the heterogeneity of capital. If there is limited ex post substitutability between energy and capital, the financial markets will heavily discount energy inefficient machines when energy prices increase, while our calculation of the capital stock gave the same weight to both energy efficient and energy inefficient machines of the same age. However, if this explanation is correct, Q should have been undervalued in recent years, which has not been the case. The third explanation is that stock prices, which are the main source of the variability in the numerator, contain a bubble that somehow started around 1974 and is responsible for the overvaluation of stocks in subsequent years. Although it appears plausible, this third explanation begs the question of why managers have not taken advantage of the bubble and issued large amounts of new shares to finance investment and pay off debts.

10.5 Conclusion: Taxes and Corporate Investment

Finding a significant relationship between two *ratios* at the aggregate level has been notoriously difficult. The positive relationship between the investment-capital ratio and Q documented in this paper should therefore be taken seriously. According to the Q theory, this relationship is structural in that it is determined by the shape of the adjustment cost function, which is invariant to policy parameters or expectations about future economic variables. Thus we can use this structural investment-Q relationship to evaluate the role of corporate taxes for investment. In order to do this we have to distinguish between the direct and indirect effects of taxes on Q. The direct effect is precisely modeled here: equation (29) indicates exactly how Q should be adjusted for taxes. From table 10.1 we can see that this direct effect accounts for a very small fraction of variations in Q that are dominated by changes in stock prices. The indirect effect operates through the value of the firm, which is not modeled here. However, again from table 10.1, we can immediately see that the tax parameters (u, v, τ, z) have very little to do with changes in the value of the firm. It must be some other factor, such as future profitability, that has been a major determinant of the value of the firm. We conclude that the role played by taxes has been minor for investment in postwar Japan.

We also note from figure 10.1 that the relationship between investment and Q was disrupted precisely when oil prices increased sharply. As argued in section 10.4, this phenomenon is consistent with the Q theory because the adjustment cost could depend on factor prices. However, breakdown of historical relationships during the two oil shocks may not be limited to just investment. Documenting and explaining the impact of the oil shocks on other key macroeconomic relationships are left for future research.

Appendix A
Derivation of the Valuation Formula (4)

Combining (1), (2a), (2b), the value of the firm is written as

$$\text{(A1)} \quad V_0 = \sum_{t=0}^{\infty} C(0, t)[(1 - u_t - v_t)\Pi_t + (u_t + v_t)X_t + (u_t + v_t)S_{t-1} - a_t I_t],$$

where

$$\text{(A2)} \quad C(s, T) = \begin{cases} 1 & \text{if } s = t \\ (1 + r_s)^{-1} \dots (1 + r_{t-1})^{-1} & \text{if } s < t \end{cases}$$

$$\text{(A3)} \quad X_t = DEP_t + (R_t - R_{t-1}).$$

With this notation, (2c) becomes

$$\text{(A4)} \quad S_t = v_t(\Pi_t - X_t) - v_t S_{t-1},$$

which can be solved for S_{t-1} as

$$\text{(A5)} \quad S_{t-1} = v_{t-1} \sum_{i=0}^{t-1} \Psi(i, t-2)Y_i - v_{t-1}\Psi(0, t-2)S_{-1} \quad \text{for } t > 0,$$

where

$$\text{(A6)} \quad Y_t = \Pi_t - X_t,$$

$$(A7) \qquad \Psi(i,j) = \begin{cases} 1 & \text{if } i > j. \\[2ex] (-v_i)(-v_{i+1}) \ldots (-v_j) & \text{if } i \leq j. \end{cases}$$

Substituting (A5) into (A1) we obtain

$$(A8) \qquad \begin{aligned} V_0 &= \sum_{t=0}^{\infty} C(0, t)[\Pi_t - (u_t + v_t)Y_t - a_t I_t] \\ &+ \sum_{t=1}^{\infty} C(0, t)[(u_t + v_t)v_{t-1} \sum_{i=0}^{t-1} \Psi(i, t-2)Y_i] \\ &- \sum_{t=1}^{\infty} C(0, t)[(u_t + v_t)v_{t-1}\Psi(0, t-2)]S_{-1} + (u_0 v_0)S_{-1}. \end{aligned}$$

The second summation can be rewritten as

$$\sum_{t=1}^{\infty}\sum_{i=0}^{t-1}[C(0, t)(u_t + v_t)v_{t-1}\Psi(i, t-2)Y_i]$$

$$= \sum_{i=1}^{\infty}\sum_{t=0}^{i-1}[C(0, i)(u_i + v_i)v_{i-1}\Psi(i, i-2)Y_t] \quad \text{(by interchanging } i \text{ with } t)$$

$$= \sum_{t=0}^{\infty}\sum_{n=1}^{\infty}[C(0, t+n)(u_{t+n} + v_{t+n})v_{t+n-1}\Psi(t, t+n-2)Y_t] \quad \text{(by setting } i = n + t)$$

$$= \sum_{t=0}^{\infty} C(0, t)[\sum_{n=1}^{\infty} C(t, t+n)(u_{t+n} + v_{t+n})v_t\Psi(t+1, t+n-1)]Y_t$$

$$\qquad [\text{since } v_{t+n-1}\Psi(t, t+n-2) = v_t\Psi(t+1, t+n-1)]$$

$$= \sum_{t=0}^{\infty} C(0, t)y_t v_t Y_t,$$

where

$$(A9) \qquad y_t = \sum_{n=1}^{\infty} C(t, t+n)(u_{t+n} + v_{t+n})\Psi(t+1, t+n-1).$$

(The "since" clause bracketed above refers only to the line preceding it.)

Using this y_t, the third summation in (A8) can be rewritten as

$$\sum_{t=1}^{\infty} C(0, t)[(u_t + v_t)v_{t-1}\Psi(0, t-2)]S_{-1}$$

$$= \sum_{t=1}^{\infty} C(0, t)[(u_t + v_t)v_0\Psi(1, t-1)]S_{-1}$$

$$\qquad [\text{since } v_{t-1}\Psi(0, t-2) = v_0\Psi(1, t-1)]$$

$$= y_0 v_0 S_{-1}.$$

Thus (A8) becomes

$$V_0 = \sum_{t=0}^{\infty}[C(0, t)(\Pi_t - \tau_t Y_t) - a_t I_t] - y_0 v_0 S_{-1} + (u_0 + v_0)S_{-1}$$

$$(A10) \quad = \sum_{t=0}^{\infty}C(0, t)[(1 - \tau_t)\Pi_t - a_t I_t] + \tau_0 S_{-1},$$

$$= \sum_{t=0}^{\infty}C(0, t)\tau_t DEP_t + \sum_{t=0}^{\infty}C(0, t)\tau_t(R_t - R_{t-1}),$$

where

$$(A11) \quad \tau_t = u_t + v_t - y_t v_t.$$

Now, it is shown in Hayashi (1982) that the second summation in (A10), the present value of $\tau_t DEP_t$, where DEP_t is defined in (3) in the text, can be decomposed as

$$(A12) \quad \sum_{t=0}^{\infty}C(0, t)(1 - z_t')a_t I_t + A_0',$$

where z' and A' are defined in the text (see eqq. [7] and [8]). Furthermore, it is easy to show that the last summation in (A10) becomes

$$(A13) \quad \sum_{t=0}^{\infty}C(0, t)\tau_t(R_t - R_{t-1}) = \sum_{t=0}^{\infty}C(0, t)[\tau_t - \tau_{t+1}/(1 + r_t)]R_t - \tau_0 R_{-1}.$$

Substituting (A12) and (A13) in to (A10), we obtain the formula (4) in the text.

Appendix B
Glossary of Symbols

A = Present value of accounting depreciation on assets already in existence (see [27]);

A' = Present value of tax saving arising from accounting depreciation on assets already in existence (see [9]);

a = Price of investment goods;

$C(t,s)$ = Discounting factor as of t for income at s (see [1]);

c = Cost of capital (see [17]);

$D(x,t)$ = Depreciation formula as of t on an asset of age x;

DEP = Amount of accounting depreciation (see [3]);

F = Production function;

I = Investment;

K = Capital stock;
L = Labor input;
p = Output price;
Q = Tax-adjusted Q (see [19] and [29]);
RL = Employment-related tax-free reserves;
RK = Other tax-free reserves;
R = $RL + RK$;
r = Nominal interest rate;
S = Enterprise tax;
T = Total corporate tax (see [2a]);
u = Tax rate on corporate income excluding the enterprise tax;
v = Enterprise tax rate;
V = Market value of the firm;
w = Wage rate;
w^* = Wage rate adjusted for the employment-related tax-free reserves (see [15]);
y = Present value of tax changes per yen of the enterprise tax (see [5]);
z = Present value of accounting depreciation on one yen of new investment (see [26]);
z' = Present value of tax saving arising from accounting depreciation on one yen of new investment (see [7]);
δ = Rate of physical depreciation;
Π = Gross pretax profits;
λ = Shadow price of capital;
τ = Effective tax rate (see [6]).

Notes

1. For a good description of the Japanese corporate tax system, see *An Outline of Japanese Taxes* (various years), published by the Printing Bureau under the auspices of the Tax Bureau of the Ministry of Finance.

2. For a few tax-free reserves, the law permits corporations to spread the amount to be added back to income over several years. The tax-free reserves for which the data are available to us are the types described in the text.

3. For the reserve for retirement allowances, R is the amount that has been accumulated.

4. If static expectations about future τ are assumed and if z is the Hall and Jorgenson (1971) z, then z' reduces to τz.

5. The fact that $(1 - \delta)/(1 + r) \cong 1 - \delta - r$ has been used.

6. Kuniaki Hata of the Tax Bureau was in charge of the calculation in this study.

7. This number is obtained as follows. From the capital formation matrix in the *1975 Input-Output Table*, we can obtain the breakdown for manufacturing as a whole of capital inputs by industry source. Take the physical depreciation rates from Hulten

and Wykoff (1981) and take a weighted average with the weights thus obtained. This yields an estimate of δ of 8.99%.

8. Only the total of the corporate enterprise tax collected from all industries is reported. The enterprise tax paid by corporations in manufacturing is obtained by multiplying this total by the manufacturing sector's share of the national corporate tax.

9. Under constant returns to scale, the wage bill is proportional to the capital stock, given factor prices. Thus the proportionality assumption (23) for RL implies that RL is proportional to the capital stock.

References

Economic Planning Agency. 1974. *1970 national wealth survey* (in Japanese). Tokyo: Printing Bureau of the Ministry of Finance.

General Management Agency. 1979. *1975 input-output table* (in Japanese). Tokyo: Printing Bureau of the Ministry of Finance.

Hall, Robert E., and Dale W. Jorgenson. 1971. Application of the theory of optimal capital accumulation. In *Tax incentives and capital spending,* ed. Gary Fromm. Washington, D.C.: Brookings.

Hayashi, Fumio, 1985. Corporate finance side of the q theory of investment. *Journal of Public Economics* 27 (2):261–80.

———. 1982. Tobin's marginal q and average q: A neoclassical interpretation. *Econometrica* 50 (1):213–24.

Homma, M., F. Hayashi, N. Atoda, and K. Hata. 1984. *Setsubitoshi to kigyo zeisei* (Investment and corporate taxes). Research Monograph no. 41. Institute of Economic Research of the Japanese Economic Planning Agency, Tokyo.

Hulten, Charles R., and Frank C. Wykoff. 1981. The measurement of economic depreciation. In *Depreciation, inflation, and the taxation of income from capital,* ed. Charles R. Hulten. Washington, D.C.: Urban Institute.

Ministry of Finance. Various years. *Zeimu tokei kara mita hojin kigyo no jittai* (Facts on corporations seen from tax statistics). Tokyo: Printing Bureau of Ministry of Finance.

———. Various years. *An outline of Japanese taxes.* Tokyo: Printing Bureau of the Ministry of Finance.

11   R&D and Productivity Growth: Comparing Japanese and U.S. Manufacturing Firms

Zvi Griliches and Jacques Mairesse

11.1   Introduction

In economic terms, Japan is a large country with a large internal market in addition to its export potential. In an area that is one twenty-fifth of the United States, Japan has slightly over half of the population of the United States, and more than one-third of its GNP. Japan's manufacturing sector is relatively larger, with total employment in manufacturing around 42% of that in the United States. One of the major differences between the two countries has been the much faster rate of productivity growth in Japanese manufacturing.

Although the oil crises of 1973 and 1979 affected both economies severely and output and productivity growth slowed in both of them, the productivity of labor in manufacturing continued to increase much faster in Japan than in the United States during the 1970s.[1] These events elicited many comments and studies but mostly at the aggregate macrolevel. Also, while there has been much discussion of the possible role of differential R&D policies in these events, there has been little quantitative examination of the R&D-productivity growth relationship; what there has been has focused largely on aggregate data and single-country analysis.[2] It is our intention to look at these issues using Japanese and U.S. company data in an attempt to assess the contribution of R&D to productivity in both countries.

Zvi Griliches is the Paul M. Warburg Professor of Economics at Harvard University and Program Director for Productivity and Technical Change at the National Bureau of Economic Research. Jacques Mairesse is Director of Ecole Nationale de la Statistique et de l'Administration Economique (ENSAE) and Professor at Ecole de Hautes Etudes en Sciences Sociales (EHESS).

The authors are indebted to T. Tachibanaki for providing the Japanese data and assisting with their interpretation, to A. Neff for help with Japanese price indexes, to T. Abbott and M. Sassenou for very able research assistance, and to the National Science Foundation (PRA81–08635 and SES82-08006), le Centre National de la Recherche Scientifique, and the National Bureau of Economic Research Program on Productivity and Technical Change Studies for financial support.

This paper can be viewed as a continuation of our previous work on R&D and productivity growth at the firm level in the United States and in France. In analyzing the data for French and U.S. manufacturing we found that differences in R&D effort do not account for much of the observed difference in the average rate of productivity growth or its distribution across industrial sectors or firms (see Griliches and Mairesse 1983, 1984; Cuneo and Mairesse 1984.) The availability of similar data for Japan led us to extend these comparisons to that country and the United States, between which the contrasts are even larger.

Our work differs from much of the productivity-comparisons literature by taking the individual firm data as its primary focus. Firm data have the virtue of providing us with much more variance in the relevant variables and a more appropriate level of analysis, the level at which most of our theories are specified. By working with microlevel data we escape many of the aggregation problems that plague macroeconomics. On the other hand, these benefits do not come without cost. Our data bases rarely contain enough variables relevant to the specific circumstances of a particular firm, and the available variables themselves are subject to much higher relative error rates, which are largely averaged out in aggregate data.

The basic approach we follow in this paper is to compute simple productivity-growth measures for individual manufacturing firms both in Japan and the United States for the relatively recent 1973–80 period and relate them to differences in the intensity of R&D effort. We start by describing our data sources and the overall pattern of R&D spending in manufacturing in both countries and by reviewing the major trends in productivity growth across different industrial sectors. We then turn to the discussion of regression results that attempt to account for the differences in labor productivity growth by the differences in the growth of the capital-labor ratio and in the intensity of R&D effort across different firms for total manufacturing as a whole and also separately within specific industrial sectors.

Since, as we shall point out in some detail later on, the Japanese R&D data at the firm level turn out to be especially incomplete, we cannot provide a solution to the original puzzle of differential growth rates, but we still have some interesting facts and several new puzzles to report.

11.2 Comparing R&D Expenditures

Before we look at our R&D data at the firm level, it is useful to compare the industrial distribution of R&D expenditures in both countries. Tables 11.1 and 11.2 show comparative statistics on the magnitude and industrial distribution of R&D expenditures for manufacturing in both countries, focusing on the role of "large" firms (firms with more than a 1,000 employees).[3] We look primarily at large firms because they account for most of the R&D in either country and also because these are the firms represented in our microdata sets.

Table 11.1   **R&D Firms in Manufacturing, Japan, 1976: The Relative Importance of Large Firms (1,000 or More Employees) and Their Industrial Distribution**

	No. of Employees in Millions and Percentages	Sales in Units of 100 Billion Yen and Percentages	Company R&D Expenditures in Units of 100 Billion Yen and Percentages	No. of Firms	R&D Sales Ratio[a]
All Firms	8.8	1,244	15.14	85,650	.012
R&D firms	59	69	100	11,950	.018
Large firms	41	52	78	1,120	.018
Large R&D firms	39	50	78	1,030	.019
Large R&D doing firms:					
Total	3.5	623	11.82	1,030	.019
Distribution by industry:[b]					
1. Food & kindred	5.1	9.0	2.2	60	.005
2. Chemicals & rubber	11.0	14.2	16.6	98	.022
3. Drugs	2.3	2.1	5.8	29	.051
4. Primary & fabricated metals	13.7	16.8	9.8	104	.012
5. Machinery	8.0	6.5	6.2	91	.018
6. Electrical equipment	19.1	14.0	30.4	123	.041
7. Transportation equipment	23.7	22.0	20.5	329	.018
8. Instruments	2.1	1.4	2.1	29	.028
9. Other	15.0	14.0	6.4	167	.009

Source: Report on the Survey of Research and Development (Prime Minister's Office 1976).

Note: "Manufacturing" excludes petroleum refining.

[a]Total R&D /total sales (not average of firm ratios).

[b]The numbers in the first three columns are percentages and add up to 100.

Table 11.2 R&D Firms in Manufacturing, United States 1976: The Relative Importance of Large Firms (1,000 or More Employees) and Their Industrial Distribution

	No. of Employees in Millions and Percentages	Sales in Billions of Dollars and Percentages	Company R&D Expenditures in Billions of Dollars and Percentages	No. of Firms	R/D Sales Ratio[a] Total	R/D Sales Ratio[a] Company Financed
1977 All Firms	21.5	1,275	18.00	295,000	.022	.014
R&D firms	62	63	100	2,835	.035	.022
Large firms	65	70	94	1,910	.030	.019
Large R&D firms	56	61	94	1,140	.035	.022
1976 Large R&D firms:						
Total	11.7	672	15.30	1,137	.036	.023
Distribution by industry[b]						
1. Food & kindred	7.6	12.7	2.0	102	.004	.004
2. Chemicals & rubber	9.7	11.4	13.2	112	.030	.026
3. Drugs	2.3	3.5	6.8	29	.063	.062
4. Primary & fabricated metals	13.1	13.0	4.8	165	.009	.008
5. Machinery	6.7	6.1	5.9	135	.023	.022
6. Electrical equipment	20.0	14.8	30.9	159	.077	.047
7. Transportation equipment	18.3	20.6	25.2	90	.065	.028
8. Instruments	3.5	2.6	6.6	55	.066	.057
9. Other	18.8	16.3	4.7	290	.008	.007

Source: Information for all firms in manufacturing from *Enterprise Statistics: General Report on Industrial Organization* (U.S. Bureau of the Census 1977). R&D related numbers from NSF, *Research and Development in Industry*, 1976 and 1977 issues.

Note: "Manufacturing" excludes petroleum refining.

[a]Total R&D/total sales (not average of firm ratios).

[b]The numbers in the first three columns are percentages and add up to 100.

Comparing the two tables we can see that large firms are more numerous in the United States, and that, on average, they are also larger (about 10,000 employees per firm versus 3,500 in Japan). Large firms account for 70% of total sales and 65% of total employment in manufacturing in the United States versus 52% and 41%, respectively, in Japan. Similarly, large firms do almost all of the R&D in the United States—94%—but only about three-quarters in Japan.[4]

Allowing for differences in the size of the countries and the size distribution of firms, there is very little difference either in the intensity or the sectoral distribution of company-financed R&D expenditures in the two countries. There is a big difference, however, in the involvement of government in the financing of R&D performed in manufacturing. In the United States, over a third of total R&D has been federally financed while in Japan the state accounts for less than 2% of the total.[5] Since our micro data reflect only company financed R&D we shall not be able to discuss the role of public R&D support in this context.[6]

While, in absolute terms, large Japanese manufacturing companies spend only about a third as much on R&D as U.S. companies do, the relation of these expenditures to sales is remarkably similar (about 2%) in both countries. The distribution of total company R&D by industry and of the intensity of R&D effort are also very similar in the two countries. Most of the R&D is done in three sectors: electrical equipment, transportation equipment, and chemical industries.[7] The highest R&D to sales ratios are to be found in the drug and electrical equipment industries, the only noticeable difference being the somewhat higher relative R&D expenditure in the U.S. instruments industry.

We turn now to the consideration of our firm-level data sources. In both countries the responses to official R&D surveys are confidential and not publicly available. However, information on individual firms' R&D expenditures is available in their public annual reports or their filings with the respective securities markets regulatory authorities (10K statements in the United States). In Japan such data are collected and organized by the Nihon Keizai Shimbun Corporation and are known as the NEEDS data base. In the United States, the equivalent is Standard and Poor's Annual Industrial Compustat.

We have worked previously with the Compustat data and have created a consistent panel data set based on it.[8] This is, however, our first experience with the NEEDS data, and we had to invest heavily in cleaning them and in trying to understand their construction and provenance. Except for the R&D numbers, as we shall see below, these data seem of comparable quality to the Compustat data for the United States.

The general characteristics of the parallel firm samples that we have constructed are depicted in table 11.3. If we insist on continuous data from 1972 through 1980 with no major mergers or major jumps in the series and require also consistent reporting of R&D expenditures throughout this period, we

Table 11.3 Japan and the United States: 1976 Characteristics of the 1972–80 Continuous Samples

| Variable | Japan[a] | | | | United States | |
| | | R&D Reporting | | | | |
	Total	Original[b]	Corrected[c]	Total	Total	R&D Reporting[d]
N	1,032	394	406	968	525
Average employment, in thousands	2.7	3.4	4.5	68	17
Average sales, in millions of dollars	215	242	345	655	872
Average plant, in millions of dollars	118	128	187	330	434
Average R&D, in millions of dollars	—	3.1	6.9	—	22.7
Average R&D/sales ratio[e]	—	.012	.013	—	.024

[a]From the NEEDS (Nihon Keizai Shimbun) data base. Converted to dollars at $1 = ¥ 300.

[b]In addition to the 394 continuously R&D reporting firms in the Japanese sample, there are also 338 firms that reported nonzero R&D expenditures in one or more years in the 1972–80 period.

[c]The data on largest R&D-performing firms in Japan reported in OECD (1984) were used to fill in some missing values and adjust others for apparent underreporting.

[d]In addition to the 525 continuously R&D reporting firms in the U.S. sample, with no major jumps, there are also 129 firms that reported nonzero R&D expenditures in one or more years in the 1972–80 period.

[e]Average of individual firm R&D to sales ratios.

have complete data for about 400 R&D firms in Japan and slightly over 500 R&D firms in the United States.[9] The U.S. firms are significantly larger, by a factor of four on average. They also seem to be doing much more R&D, even relatively. Here we stumble on our major difficulty with the NEEDS data. The R&D data appear to be badly underreported in this source. If we compare the numbers in table 11.1 with those in table 11.2, we observe that the overall company financed R&D to sales ratio is roughly similar in both countries and only slightly lower in Japan (1.91% vs. 2.3% in the United States for large R&D performing firms), while the numbers in table 11.3 imply that the U.S. firms are twice as R&D intensive.

It does not take very long to convince oneself that indeed the NEEDS data are heavily deficient in their R&D coverage. Table 11.4 reports coverage ratios for 1981 of the NEEDS R&D numbers relative to the official Japanese R&D survey. While the large firms in the NEEDS sample account for close to 80% of the relevant employment and sales totals, the coverage of R&D expenditures is only slightly above one-third.[10] Looking at the distribution by industrial sector we see that coverage varies from good to reasonable for the chemical, drug, and instruments industries, but that it is abysmal for motor vehicles and transportation equipment and poor for the rest of manufacturing. The magnitude of the problem can be appreciated when it is realized that neither Toyota, Hitachi, Nissan, nor Honda report positive R&D expenditures in the NEEDS data base.

Using information published by the Organization for Economic Cooperation and Development (OECD 1984) on the 20 largest R&D performers in Japan in 1979, we find that of the 18 firms that should be within our definition

Table 11.4   Comparison of NEEDS 1981 Data to the Japanese Official 1981 R&D Survey Coverage in Ratios Expressed in Percentages

	Firms	Employees	Sales	R&D Expenditures
All	1.2	30	46	29
R&D reporting	4.2	35	38	29
Large firms (1,000 or more employees)	58	79	78	35
Large R&D-reporting firms, total	45	51	49	35
By sector:				
1. Food & kindred	27	30	45	26
2. Chemicals & rubber	65	70	80	92
3. Drugs	71	92	95	98
4. Metals	60	55	70	42
5. Machinery	46	45	54	27
6. Electrical equipment	51	60	69	26
7. Transportation equipment	38	44	38	14
8. Instruments	42	58	73	75
9. Other	42	48	53	29

of manufacturing and are indeed in the NEEDS file, 10 report no R&D whatsoever, 3 report about the same amount of R&D in both sources, and, what may be even more worrisome, 5 companies report significantly less R&D in the NEEDS data base than is reported by the OECD. For example, the reported R&D expenditures of the Sony Corporation differ by a factor of two. If the OECD information is added to the NEEDS data set, total R&D expenditures come close to doubling, and the coverage ratio rises to a respectable 73%.

Thus the problem we face is not only that R&D is missing for some firms, a problem that we could either ignore or adjust for in some way, but also that the reported figures themselves appear to be inaccurate. They reflect not only real differences in this variable but also differences in reporting practices. Since there was nothing else that we could do at this point, we complemented or adjusted the R&D figures for the 18 very large R&D firms for which we had OECD information and proceeded to analyze these data as if they actually mean what they say. The best we can hope for is that the reported R&D numbers are still acceptable proxies for the true figures.[11] We will come back, however, to this issue in interpreting the results of our analyses.

A few words should be said at this point about the U.S. R&D data. They indeed seem better. Even though they are not exactly conceptually equivalent, the 10K-based reports and the NSF-collected (National Science Foundation, various issues) numbers are not very far apart, especially as far as industry totals are concerned. A recent analysis by the NSF (1985) of data for the 200 largest R&D performers finds the totals in 1981 remarkably close (within 3%), though this covers up significant individual variability. Forty-seven percent of the firms reported totals within 10% in both sources; 22% were within 10% to 25% and only 13% were off by more than 25%. Eighteen percent were not included in the Compustat-based data base, primarily because they were either privately or foreign owned. Using 1976 totals and adjusting for differences in definition and coverage, we ourselves estimated that the Compustat-based universe contained about 85% of total R&D reported to the NSF, with the major discrepancy arising from the above mentioned absence of privately and foreign owned firms in these data.[12] At the same time, our selection of "continuous R&D" firms preserves about 80% of the total R&D reported in the 1976 large Compustat cross section. Thus, roughly speaking, the firms contained in our U.S. sample account for about 70% of the total company financed R&D as reported to the National Science Foundation.

11.3 Comparing Trends in Productivity Growth

Bearing in mind the limitations of the R&D data, we look now at the productivity record of the firms in our samples for both countries during the 1970s. Tables 11.5 and 11.6 list the sample sizes, averages, and standard deviations for some of our major variables by industrial sector and for manufac-

Table 11.5 Continuous R&D-reporting Firms Subsample for Japan, 1973–80 Growth Rates (per Year) and 1973 Levels: Means (and Standard Deviations) for Major Variables

Industry	N	Average Employed, 1976 in Thousands[a]	R/S 1973 (estimated)[b]	Average Growth Rates 1973–80			
				Employed	Deflated Sales per Employee	Adjusted Gross Plant per Employee	Approximate TFP[c]
Total	406	4.5 (9.4)	.010 (.013)	−.021 (.038)	.058 (.046)	.085 (.034)	.036 (.045)
1. Food & kindred	22	2.3 (2.3)	.004 (.006)	−.012 (.028)	.029 (.030)	.090 (.032)	.007 (.026)
2. Chemicals & rubber	82	3.0 (3.8)	.011 (.010)	−.023 (.035)	.026 (.027)	.079 (.037)	.006 (.027)
3. Drugs	31	2.4 (2.4)	.037 (.022)	.006 (.030)	.072 (.037)	.082 (.029)	.051 (.036)
4. Metals	41	5.5 (12.9)	.006 (.006)	−.029 (.031)	.035 (.044)	.078 (.029)	.016 (.042)
5. Machinery	48	1.8 (2.5)	.008 (.008)	−.030 (.035)	.067 (.039)	.081 (.032)	.046 (.037)
6. Electrical equipment	67	7.2 (14.4)	.011[d] (.013)	−.017 (.035)	.105 (.035)	.087 (.037)	.084 (.034)
7. Transportation equipment	33	12.3 (17.5)	.001[d] (.005)	−.006 (.033)	.066 (.034)	.084 (.030)	.044 (.031)
8. Instruments	17	2.3 (2.0)	.015 (.017)	−.015 (.055)	.106 (.040)	.101 (.037)	.081 (.035)
9. Other	65	3.0 (3.5)	.004 (.004)	−.039 (.043)	.041 (.042)	.094 (.028)	.017 (.040)

[a] Average employed, 1976 = arithmetic average.

[b] R/S 1973 (estimated) = 1972 through 1974 average R&D divided by average sales in 1972 and 1974.

[c] Approximate TFP (total factor productivity) = growth in deflated sales per employee − .25 (growth in plant per employee).

[d] OECD data based corrections raise this number to .016 and .009 for electrical and transportation equipment industries, respectively. For the total sample, however, this adjustment raises R/S to only .011.

Table 11.6   Continuous R&D-reporting Firms Subsample for the United States, 1973–80 Growth Rates (per Year) and 1973 Levels: Means (and Standard Deviations) for Major Variables

Industry	N	Average Employed, 1976 in Thousands[a]	R/S 1973 (estimated)[b]	Average Growth Rates 1973–80			
				Employed	Deflated Sales per Employee	Adjusted Gross Plant per Employee	Approximate TFP[c]
Total	525	16.9 (48.9)	.025 (.023)	.019 (.067)	.016 (.038)	.044 (.051)	.005 (.038)
1. Food & kindred	22	17.0 (17.7)	.006 (.005)	.012 (.042)	.022 (.044)	.042 (.036)	.012 (.041)
2. Chemicals & rubber	71	18.3 (32.5)	.026 (.013)	.014 (.052)	.007 (.034)	.048 (.036)	−.005 (.033)
3. Drugs	44	14.6 (15.1)	.038 (.027)	.040 (.066)	.005 (.033)	.044 (.043)	−.006 (.032)
4. Metals	50	9.5 (18.0)	.012 (.010)	.002 (.053)	.001 (.031)	.045 (.042)	−.010 (.032)
5. Machinery	82	7.8 (12.9)	.024 (.021)	.027 (.074)	.002 (.031)	.046 (.054)	−.009 (.030)
6. Electrical equipment	106	19.4 (51.9)	.035 (.024)	.024 (.080)	.044 (.045)	.046 (.068)	.032 (.047)
7. Transportation equipment	34	66.0 (147.8)	.018 (.013)	.004 (.065)	.003 (.032)	.040 (.049)	−.007 (.028)
8. Instruments	39	10.1 (23.6)	.050 (.032)	.047 (.072)	.030 (.025)	.020 (.040)	.024 (.025)
9. Other	77	9.9 (14.0)	.010 (.007)	.001 (.058)	.012 (.027)	.048 (.048)	−.000 (.026)

[a]Average employed, 1976 — arithmetic average.
[b]R/S 1973 (estimated) — 1972 through 1974 average R&D divided by average sales in 1972 and 1974.
[c]Approximate TFP (total factor productivity) = growth in deflated sales per employee − .25 (growth in plant per employee).

turing as a whole. The construction of the major variables is similar for both countries except that in the United States we were able to use 3-digit SIC-level price deflators and business segment information to construct individual firm sales deflators, while for Japan we had to use general 2-digit level deflators.[13] In both countries the gross plant figures were converted from historical to constant prices using the information contained in the net versus gross plant distinction.[14] In neither data set do we have information on hours worked, and materials purchases are available only for Japan.

There are a number of interesting observations to be made on the basis of tables 11.5 and 11.6, some less obvious than others. The major contrast between the two countries is in the employment story and the associated productivity movements. In Japan, total employment declined in eight out of the nine industrial groupings, whereas, in the United States, it rose in all sectors. In fact, real output per firm as measured by deflated sales grew at about the same rate in the United States as in Japan, 3.5% per year on average, with the big difference in the productivity numbers coming essentially from the behavior of the employment series.

The same thing is also true for the growth in the capital-labor ratio, which grew twice as fast in Japan than in the United States, while the capital stock was growing at roughly similar rates in both countries during this same period (about 6.4% per year). It is also interesting to note that in both countries the growth of the capital-labor ratio was very similar for the different industrial groupings, varying much less than the growth in the output-labor ratio. This is consistent with the hypothesis that the ratio of real wages to capital user costs moved differently between the two countries but essentially similarly for the different industries within these countries.

If one estimates total factor productivity growth by assuming that value added and sales vary proportionately and that the capital input weight in value added is constant and equal to 0.25 for all firms in both countries, one finds several commonalities and also some contrasts. In both countries the high R&D industries split in their productivity experience: electric equipment and instruments have the highest productivity growth rates while chemicals are among the lowest ones. The major contrasts occur in the machinery, transportation equipment, and drug industries, where there was significant productivity growth in Japan but not in the United States.[15] Only in the food industry did the United States do better than Japan as far as total factor productivity growth is concerned.

Our numbers are not strictly comparable to similar macroestimates, both because they are unweighted firm averages and because many of the firms in our two samples are multinationals with neither their employment nor productivity restricted entirely to the country of origin. Nevertheless, table 11.7 presents the figures on average growth rates of labor and labor productivity that we have gathered at the industry level and for manufacturing as a whole in the two countries, and the corresponding measures from our two total

Table 11.7   Average Growth Rates, 1973–80, of Labor and Labor Productivity at Company and Industry Level

	Japan					United States				
		Total Sample		National Accounts			Total Sample		National Accounts	
Industry	N	Employed	Deflated Sales per Employee	All Persons	Real Output per Person	N	Employed	Deflated Sales per Employee	All Persons	Real Output per Person
Total	1,032	−.024 (.042)	.055 (.047)	−.005	.038	968	.013 (.066)	.012 (.042)	.007	.004
1. Food	82	−.011 (.035)	.034 (.032)	−.003	.049	63	.020 (.052)	.020 (.042)	−.002	.023
2. Chemicals & Rubber	149	−.019 (.032)	.026 (.031)	−.009[b]	.039[b]	91	.012 (.056)	.009 (.034)	.007	−.002
3. Drugs	37	.005 (.030)	.071 (.043)			52	.035 (.068)	.003 (.032)	.010	.015
4. Metals	149	−.031 (.035)	.036 (.041)	−.007	.026	135	−.004 (.053)	−.008 (.052)	−.005	−.013
5. Machinery	154	−.028 (.044)	.063 (.037)	−.007	.039	113	.028 (.070)	−.000 (.030)	.023[a]	−.004[a]
6. Electrical Equipment	152	−.018 (.036)	.102 (.039)	.003	.083	140	.026 (.081)	.043 (.047)	.022	.051
7. Transportation Equipment	79	−.008 (.040)	.063 (.036)	.010	.065	63	−.004 (.066)	−.001 (.043)	−.005	−.009
8. Instruments	33	−.016 (.045)	.102 (.038)	.007	.062	46	.052 (.073)	.026 (.026)		
9. Other	197	−.044 (.049)	.042 (.047)	−.010	.013	265	−.001 (.059)	.012 (.034)	.006	.000

[a]Machinery and instruments.
[b]Chemicals & rubber, and drugs

samples.[16] There is no striking inconsistency in the two sets of micro- and macroestimates, but rather a rough agreement in terms of the pattern of differences both across industries and countries. For example, productivity growth is clearly the highest for electrical equipment in the two countries and about the lowest for metals; it is also the case that transportation equipment did quite well in Japan contrary to the United States.[17] It is interesting to note, however, that the overall growth in productivity tends to be more rapid for the firms in our samples than for manufacturing as a whole (the differential being as much as 1.7% per year in Japan and 0.8% in the United States), while the contrast in employment experience is even larger: 2.5% slower growth in our firm data in Japan versus the United States, as against only a 0.8% differential in the national-income-accounts-based industry totals.

11.4 R&D Intensity and Productivity Growth at the Firm Level

The model we consider can be thought of as a modified version of the Cobb-Douglas production function in its growth rate form, with labor productivity being a function of the physical capital-labor ratio and research capital.[18] Because we have only a very short history of research expenditures for most of these firms, it is difficult to construct a reliable research capital measure. We use, therefore, the R&D intensity version of this model instead, in which the beginning period R&D to sales ratio is substituted for the unavailable R&D capital variable.

Let the true equation be

$$(q - l) = \lambda + \alpha(c - l) + \gamma k + \mu l + u,$$

where small lettered variables stand for rates of growth (logarithmic changes): $q, l,$ and c represent output, employment, and physical capital, respectively; k is a measure of accumulated research capital; α, β, γ are the elasticities of output with respect to physical capital, labor, and research capital; $\mu = (\alpha + \beta - 1)$ is the economies of scale coefficient; λ is a constant that reflects, among other things, disembodied technical change; and u is a random disturbance standing in for all other unspecified effects affecting measured productivity growth.

The research capital elasticity γ is equal, by definition, to $(dQ/dK)(K/Q)$. Since $k = dK/K$, we can simplify $\gamma k = (dQ/dK)(K/Q)(dK/K)$ to $\rho(R/Q)$, where $\rho = dQ/dK$ is the marginal product of research capital and R is the level of R&D expenditures. Two points need to be made about this type of simplification: it assumes that R, gross expenditures on R&D, is a good proxy for net investment (dK) in R&D capital. This can be true only if there is no or little depreciation of research capital or if we are in the beginning phases of accumulation and the initial stocks of K are small. Also, it is assumed that ρ rather than γ is constant across firms, that the rate of return ρ is the parameter that is more likely to be equalized across firms.[19]

The equations that we estimate are then of the form

$$(q-l) = \lambda + \alpha(c-l) + \mu l + \rho(R/Q) + u,$$

where the rates of growth of $(q-l)$, $(c-l)$, are generally computed over the seven-year period 1973–80.

The adoption of this specification has two important consequences: first, the estimating equation is expressed in terms of rates of growth of productivity (first differences of the logarithms of the various variables) and thus does not relate differences in productivity levels to differences in R&D capital. This has the advantage of protecting the estimates from potential biases due to (correlated) specific effects but at the cost of ignoring the large variability of the data in the cross-sectional dimension. We know from previous work that results based on this dimension (between-firms) are usually stronger than those based only on the time dimension (within-firms) (see, e.g., Griliches and Mairesse [1984] and Cuneo and Mairesse [1984]). A second consequence is that we relate differences in the rate of growth of productivity to differences in R&D to sales ratios (rather than to the differences in the rate of growth of R&D capital stock).[20]

Several alternative measures of R&D intensity, R/Q, were tried with largely similar results. The final variable chosen, AR/S, relates the average amount of deflated R&D during 1972–74 to the mean (geometric) levels of deflated sales for the period as a whole (average of 1973 and 1980 sales). The numerator of this ratio refers to the beginning of the period and allows, implicitly, for an approximate three-year lag in the effects of R&D.[21] The denominator is positioned in the middle of the period to reduce the spuriousness that may arise when a growth rate is based on a ratio whose denominator is in fact the initial level from which the growth rate is measured.[22] Instead of a unique trend term we include, usually, separate industry dummy variables, which allow for differential industrial trends of disembodied technical change, and also for deflator errors and industrywide changes in capacity utilization. Such equations were also estimated separately for each industrial grouping.

Table 11.8 summarizes our main econometric results. The estimated R&D coefficients in the productivity growth equations are of similar magnitude in both countries. They fall substantially when industry dummies (trends) are allowed for, implying, possibly, the presence of significant interfirm R&D spillovers. The major difference is that, in this case, the coefficients for Japan are not statistically significant at conventional significance levels.

Although significant, the contribution of the R&D intensity to the explanation of the variance in productivity growth across firms is rather small, the fit barely improving in the second decimal place. Nor can R&D account for the mean difference in growth rates between the two countries. Both the average R&D intensities and the estimated coefficients are quite close to each other. Nevertheless, if these coefficients are taken at face value, they imply that R&D contributed between 0.4% and 0.6% per year to productivity growth in both countries. This is not a small matter after all.

Table 11.8 Productivity (Deflated Sales per Employee) Growth in Manufacturing at the Firm Level as a Function of Growth in the Capital-Labor Ratio and R&D Intensity: Japan–United States Comparisons, 1973–80

| | Coefficients and (Standard Errors) | | | | | | R^2 and (MSE) | |
| | Japan | | | United States | | | | |
Regression	C/L[a]	L[b]	AR/S[c]	C/L	L	AR/S	Japan	United States
1	.372			.132			.072	.031
	(.067)			(.032)			(.00198)	(.00141)
2	.397		.562	.146		.410	.085	.066
	(.066)		(.229)	(.032)		(.093)	(.00196)	(.00136)
3	.298			.152			.500	.220
	(.051)			(.030)			(.00111)	(.00116)
4	.311		.302	.155		.267	.502	.251
	(.051)		(.214)	(.029)		(.096)	(.00110)	(.00112)
5	.236	−.240	.203	.107	−.080	.248	.531	.265
	(.052)	(.049)	(.209)	(.033)	(.026)	(.096)	(.00104)	(.00110)

Note: Equations 3–5 contain an additional 13 industry dummy variables. Regression 5 includes also the average 1972–74 employment level as a control variable for initial size. Its coefficient is small, positive, and significant for the United States and essentially zero for Japan. MSE is the mean square error of regression residuals.

[a]C/L = growth rate of gross-plant in constant prices per employee.

[b]L = growth rate of employment.

[c]AR/S = average R&D to sales ratio. R&D averaged for the years 1972–74, sales at mid-point of the period: geometric average of beginning (1973) and end-period (1980) sales. Both variables are deflated.

What is most striking in our results is the lower estimated contribution of physical capital to output growth in the United States. It is about half of what is estimated for Japan.[23] In fact, if we apply the coefficients in table 11.8 (regression 3) to the first row of table 11.5, we can account for about half of the Japan–United States difference in productivity growth by (1) the twice-as-fast rate of growth of the capital-labor ratio in Japan, and (2) its twice-as-large effect on productivity there. The reasons for both of these findings remain to be elucidated.

On the other hand, the Japanese data seem also to imply a much sharper rate of diminishing returns. This last estimate (the − .24 coefficient in regression 5) seems rather difficult to believe; it could be due to errors in the Japanese labor variable or to our inability to properly account for the problem of varying capacity utilization and hours of work. In any case, since the Japanese firms reduced their average employment during this period, such "diminishing returns" could not serve as a brake on their productivity growth.

Table 11.9 summarizes our attempts to look at the same issues at the individual industry level. Given the high error rates in the data at the firm level and the relatively small sample sizes, there is little to be seen here. Consistent with our earlier finding that the overall R&D coefficient was not statistically significant in Japan, the individual industry estimates are found to be about half positive and half negative, and only three of them have both the right sign and exceed their estimated standard error. For the United States, the results are only slightly better: seven out of the nine industries have positive R&D coefficients, and three of them are larger than their estimated standard errors. There is little relationship, moreover, in the relative size of these coefficients across the same industry groupings in the two countries (see lower panel of table 11.9).

We made several efforts to improve matters by redefining variables and changing the time periods somewhat, but this had little effect. The results are quite robust to the use of net rather than gross physical capital measures or to changes in the averaging procedures for the R&D data. Changing time periods, however, makes more of a difference. Using the slightly shorter 1974–79 period improves the estimates somewhat in Japan but deteriorates them in the United States.[24] This leads us to a disappointing finding: the instability of the productivity-R&D relationship and its sensitivity to the business cycle and macroeconomic supply shocks.

Table 11.10 presents annual estimates of the R&D coefficients using approximate total factor production (TFP) growth as the dependent variable. We use TFP here to avoid adding another source of variation, which would come from allowing also the physical capital elasticity to vary from year to year.[25] What is striking is that, though the exact timing was a bit different, the oil shock–induced sharp recession of 1974–75 hit the R&D-intensive firms disportionately hard in both countries. It is not clear, however, whether what we see in this table represents a real phenomenon or is just another reflection of

Table 11.9   Distribution of the R/S Coefficients by Industry (Regression 4)

	Coefficients			
	< 0	0–.5	>.5	Total
t-ratios for Japan:				
< 1	3	2		5
>1	1		3	4
Total	4	2	3	9
t-ratios for the United States:				
< 1	1	3	1	5
>1	1	1	2	4
Total	2	4	3	9

	Coefficients for Japan			
	<0	0–.5	>.5	Total
Coefficients for the United States:				
< 0	1		1	2
0–.5	1	1	2	4
> .5	2	1		3
Total	4	2	3	9

Table 11.10   Coefficients of R&D Intensity in TFP Growth Regressions, by Year, Japan and the United States, 1974–80

Year	Japan	United States
1973–74	−.73	1.50
	(.91)	(.38)
1974–75	−.73	−1.48
	(.91)	(.42)
1975–76	.51	−.58
	(.81)	(.33)
1976–77	.85	.65
	(.70)	(.34)
1977–78	1.01	.35
	(.67)	(.27)
1978–79	.60	1.28
	(.64)	(.29)
1979–80	.55	.38
	(.58)	(.32)

Note: Approximate TFP growth is calculated as: (percent growth in deflated sales per employee) − .25(percent growth in gross plant per employee). All equations contain an additional set of industry dummies and a base year (1973) size variable. The R&D intensity variable, AR/S, is calculated as the average of 1972–74 R&D divided by the average (geometric) 1973 and 1980 sales (both deflated). It is the same for all years.

the thinness of our data and our inability to estimate the effects of R&D precisely.[26]

11.5   Tentative Conclusions

Japanese manufacturing firms spent about as much of their own money on R&D, relative to their sales, as did similar U.S. firms; about 1.9% versus 2.3%, respectively, in 1976. On the basis of the econometric analysis of our sample of R&D firms, we cannot reject the hypothesis that the contribution of these expenditures to productivity growth was about the same in both countries. There is no strong prima facie evidence for the hypothesis that differences in either the intensity or the fecundity of R&D expenditures can account for the rather large difference in the observed rates of growth of productivity between the two countries.[27] The reasons for this difference must be looked for elsewhere.

We do find two important differences between Japan and the United States that help to account for some of this difference but require an explanation of their own:

1. In spite of their success in growing and exporting, Japanese firms reduced their employment levels significantly during this period while U.S. firms were increasing theirs. This alone is enough to account for the twice-faster growth in the capital-labor ratio in Japanese manufacturing since the capital stock itself has been growing at roughly similar rates in both countries.

2. For reasons that are not well understood, the estimated effect of growth in the capital-labor ratio on firm productivity in manufacturing appears to be twice as large in Japan than in the United States. An exploration of the reasons for this difference awaits better data, another occasion, and perhaps a different approach to the problem.

There are a number of other puzzling findings that we hope to return to in the future: Why did the chemical industry perform so badly during this period in both countries? Why did the drug industry do so badly in the United States during these same years? Is this a real fact or an artifact of poor deflators? While the oil price shocks provide some explanation for the poor performance of the chemical firms along lines outlined by Bruno and Sachs (1985), it is doubtful that they can also explain the experience of the pharmaceutical firms in the United States. Why does the effect of R&D intensity on productivity growth vary so much over the cycle? Is it because it should only be observable at or near full capacity? How can such consideration be incorporated into a more complete analysis of our data?

An improved analysis of the role of R&D expenditures in the growth of Japanese firms will require better data than are currently available to us. The Japanese Statistics Bureau has collected much more extensive and presumably more reliable data on R&D expenditures of firms for many years but as far as we know these data have not been accessible, nor have they been used in their detailed micro form. In the United States, similarly collected data by the National Science Foundation (NSF) and the Bureau of the Census have been matched for different surveys and brought together in a usable data file. The confidentiality problem was solved by performing all of the major data assembly and cleaning operations within the Census Bureau and by releasing only variance-covariance matrices for the major variables across firms and years without disclosing any individual firm information.[28] It would be certainly interesting to launch a similar effort in Japan. Another way of dealing with the confidentiality requirement is to carry out the econometric analysis within the National Statistical Offices themselves, as was the case for our studies for France.[29]

We cannot expect, however, that having better and more reliable data will solve all the problems. What we are looking for are effects that are at best variable, uncertain, and more or less long term in nature and that are also relatively small in magnitude. This does not mean, of course, that these effects are unimportant or that we should not devote more effort in trying to analyze them. But we cannot expect to account for much of the observed growth in productivity by focusing only on the firm's own R&D investments. The role of research spillovers between firms, sectors, and countries and the impact of other, less formal, ways of generating technical progress, are likely to be quite large and still remain to be measured.

Addendum

After the revision and completion of this paper for this volume, we gained access to new R&D information at the firm level for Japan. We are grateful to Fumio Hayashi for his help in getting these data.

Besides the R&D figures reported in the NEEDS data base and the official R&D survey of the Statistics Bureau of Japan, there exists in fact another R&D survey performed and published by the Nihon Keizai Shimbun Corporation in recent years. This survey is the source of the OECD numbers, which we already used to adjust the NEEDS figures for 18 of the largest R&D firms. In order to check our numbers on a larger scale, we matched these new data to our total sample of 1,032 firms for the fiscal year 1978 or 1979. We found 1,000 firms in common, among which 877 were reporting R&D expenditures. These 877 include our sample of 406 firms that reported R&D consistently from 1972 through 1980 in NEEDS and 471 firms that did not. When we compare the R&D numbers in the two sources for our 406 firms sample, the discrepancy is less than 5% for more than half of the sample; it is less than 50% for another quarter, but it is more than 400% for 48 firms. Contrary to the 18 large R&D adjusted firms, these 48 firms are smaller than average, and it is quite plausible that a major part of their R&D expenditures is external or cooperative and is not declared in NEEDS.

We have adjusted our R&D-intensity variable using the new R&D information (as we already had done with the OECD figures), and we have rerun our main regressions using these adjusted measures for various subsamples: the 406 R&D reporting firms, among which we consider the 48 R&D reporting firms with very large R&D discrepancies separately, and the remaining 358 R&D reporting firms. We have also used the new R&D data for the 471 firms that did not report, or reported intermittently, R&D expenditures in NEEDS. Pooling together this sample and the previous ones, we have two overall samples of 877 (406 + 471) and 829 (358 + 471) firms. The results for the simplest regression (with constant returns to scale and without industry dummies, comparable to regression 2 in table 11.7) are given in table 11A.1.

Using the adjusted R&D-intensity variable does not really improve our estimates. They remain about the same if the 48 firms for which the discrepancies are extreme are excluded, and they look worse if we do include them, the coefficient of R&D being smaller and not significant. Clearly one would like to know more about the 48 problematic firms. The estimates for the additional 471 firms sample and for the pooled 829 firms sample are also very similar to our previous results.

Table 11A.1   **Productivity Growth-R&D Intensity Regressions With and Without R&D Adjusted Measures for Various Samples of Japanese Firms: 1973–80 (Similar to Regression 2 in Table 11.8)**

Various Samples	R&D Measures from NEEDS, Coefficients and Standard Errors			R&D Adjusted Measures, Coefficients and Standard Errors		
	C/L	AR/S	R^2 MSE	C/L	AR/S	R^2 MSE
406 R&D reporting firms	.38	.56	.085	.37	.16	.075
	(.07)	(.23)	.0020	(.07)	(.13)	.0020
48 R&D reporting firms with very large R&D discrepancies	.00	5.22	.090	−.06	.00	.002
	(.20)	(2.53)	.0010	(.21)	(.20)	.0020
358 R&D reporting firms without very large R&D discrepancies (406 − 48)	.42	.48	.101	.42	.58	.109
	(.07)	(.24)	.0019	(.07)	(.21)	.0020
471 nonconsistently R&D reporting firms	. . .	. . .	. . .	.25	.48	.060
				(.050)	(.22)	.0019
877 R&D reporting (consistently and nonconsistently) firms (406 + 471)	. . .	. . .	. . .	.29	.28	.063
				(.04)	(.11)	.0020
829 R&D reporting (consistently and nonconsistently) firms, without firms with very large R&D discrepancies (358 + 471)	. . .	. . .	. . .	.31	.56	.077
				(.04)	(.15)	.0020

On the whole these computations confirm our earlier results. This is reassuring since R&D expenditures are poorly reported in the NEEDS data bank. But it is also unfortunate since one would have hoped for somewhat stronger and more significant estimates with better and more accurate figures. Again the quality of the data is not our only problem.

Notes

1. See, e.g., the *Economic Report of the President* (Council of Economic Advisers 1984, table 3.3).
2. One exception at the macrolevel is Mohnen, Nadiri, and Prucha (1984). After this paper was written we became aware also of the work of Odagiri (1983) and Odagiri and Iwata (1986), who use the same Japanese data base to construct value-added-based TFP growth measures and relate them to firm R&D intensities. Their results for Japan are similar to ours but they make no cross-country comparisons, however.
3. These numbers come from the national R&D surveys conducted by the Statistics Bureau in the Prime Minister's Office (various years) in Japan and the National Science Foundation (various years) in the United States.
4. Some of this contrast may be an artifact of different reporting conventions in the two countries. A perusal of the individual-firm data seems to indicate that there is less consolidation in Japan, with more units, which in the United States would be treated as subsidiaries, appearing as independent firms in the Japanese sources.
5. See Peck (1985) for more discussion of this difference.
6. See Griliches (1980, 1986) for more discussion on this topic.
7. Because we try to have reasonably sized samples in the various "industries," we have aggregated some of the more detailed statistics into nine industrial "sectors." Thus, sector 2 includes chemical and rubber firms, but not pharmaceutical firms, sector 6 includes computers, electrical machinery, and electrical and communication equipment, while sector 9 brings together the textile, paper, wood, glass, and miscellaneous manufacturing industries. Petroleum refining is excluded from our definition of "manufacturing."
8. See Bound, Cummins, Griliches, Hall, and Jaffe (1984) and Hall, Cummins, Laderman, and Mundy (1988) for a discussion of the construction and description of this data set, which includes also a match to the Patent Office data on the number of patents granted to these firms.
9. If we do not require consistent reporting of R&D expenditures we have samples of about 1,000 manufacturing firms in each country. Because of the significant and intermittent nonreporting of R&D one cannot assume that the other firms (the ones not included) are truly "zero-R&D" firms. Thus one cannot separate our samples cleanly into R&D and non-R&D firms and compare the results. This has only been possible in a study for France, because it was conducted within the National Institute of Statistics and we had access to the individual data of the French R&D survey (see Mairesse and Cuneo 1985).
10. The coverage ratios in table 11.4 are for the most recent year that we had data for in both the NEEDS and R&D surveys (1981) but they are not much different in the earlier years. There has been little improvement in R&D reporting in the NEEDS data base. The coverage ratios for the large firms were 30% and 35% in 1976 and 1981, respectively. Firms that do report their R&D in the NEEDS data base do so continuously and apparently on a consistent basis.

11. Even if the total R&D levels are about right (after correction) and comparable in the two countries, if the individual observations are subject to much error and different reporting practices (especially for the smaller R&D performers), our subsequent regression-based estimates of the "importance" of R&D may be significantly biased downward. Actually, however, adjusting the R&D data for the 18 large R&D-performing firms, using the OECD (1984) information, had very little effect on our regression estimates.

12. See Bound et al. (1984) for more detail.

13. The 2-digit deflators for Japan are taken from the Prices Indices Annual issues (Bank of Japan, various years). In previous work, we were able to verify that using 2-digit deflators, instead of more detailed ones, in the case of the United States had very little effect on the regression estimates.

14. See the appendix of Griliches and Mairesse (1984) for more detail on the adjustment of the gross plant numbers for inflation. Using alternative measures for physical capital had little effect on our results.

15. Using a more appropriate price deflator for the drug companies in Japan than one used for the chemical industry as a whole (which was done in an earlier version of the paper) results in a significant rise in their estimated productivity growth, but it has no effect on regression results that allow for separate industry constants.

16. The macroestimates for Japan are taken from the Annual Reports on National Income Statistics. Those for the United States are constructed from output series based on the Survey of Manufactures and from the price indices used in National Accounts— see Griliches and Lichtenberg (1984) for details. Note that table 11.6 is based on total samples, not just the R&D firms. A comparison of tables 11.5 and 11.6 with 11.7 shows only minor differences between our total sample and the R&D firms subsample.

17. Our numbers are also consistent with the macroevidence given in Jorgenson, Kuroda, and Nishimizu (1987).

18. A number of issues are ignored in such a framework, not because they are unimportant, but primarily because there is little that we can do about them here. For example, much of the Japanese progress may be based on imported technology, for which we have no data. However, to the extent that R&D expenditures are required to absorb borrowed or imported technology, this may still be captured, in part, by our measures. We can also do little about the role of government R&D support (there are no data on this at the firm level in either data base) or spillovers in this context (see Griliches 1979 for a discussion of these and other caveats).

19. See Griliches (1979) and Griliches and Lichtenberg (1984) for a related discussion of such models.

20. There are several difficulties in interpreting the estimated coefficient of R&D intensity, ρ, as the marginal product of or rate of return to R&D. The exact meaning of the estimated ρ depends on the measure of R&D intensity, the measure of output, and what else is included in the equation. Since we use an R&D to sales ratio, ρ should be interpreted as a gross marginal product in terms of output. But leaving material inputs out of the equation brings it closer to a value-added interpretation, which would presumably have resulted in a lower coefficient if value added were substituted for sales in the denominator. On the other hand, leaving out the "depreciation" of the existing R&D capital stock would bias the estimated coefficient downward (on the order of a half). It is also the case that the estimated ρ may be affected by the fact that R&D labor and R&D capital are counted twice, once in the available measures of labor and physical capital and again in the measure of R&D. Hence ρ might be viewed as an excess marginal product or rate of return (above the usual remuneration). Such an interpretation must be qualified however, since it does not apply easily to estimates in the time dimension (see Griliches 1979; Schankerman 1981; Griliches and Lichtenberg 1984; and Cuneo and Mairesse 1984 on these matters). Thus the estimated ρ coefficients are only very distant reflections of the relevant "rate of return" concept.

21. We also tried shorter lags, i.e., by defining the R&D measure as of 1976 (the middle of our period) but this produced significantly worse results in both Japan and the United States. We could not really try for longer lags within the framework of our data bases.

22. Using sales in 1973 or an average of 1972 and 1974 sales as a base does indeed make our results look significantly better. Using the $R/S73$ (estimated) ratio (i.e., $2R73/[S72 + S74]$) in eq. 5 of table 11.8 for example, we get for its coefficient .36 with a t-ratio of 2.6 in Japan and .42 with a t-ratio of 5.5 in the United States. These are significantly higher than the comparable numbers in table 11.8. Since the R&D numerator is the same in both measures, this does imply that our worries about potential spuriousness may not be groundless.

23. The higher capital elasticity estimate in Japan is consistent with the higher capital share in output reported by Jorgenson, Kuroda, and Nishimizu (1987).

24. About half the inflation during our seven-year study period of 1973–80 took place in the first year, 1973–74, and in the last one, 1979–80, as a consequence of the two oil shocks of 1973 and 1979. We thought that the potential errors in price deflators and hence in our productivity measures would thus be smaller for the shorter period 1974–79 and hoped for better results over this period.

25. The estimated physical capital elasticity also varies from year to year. But since the growth in the capital-labor ratio and R&D intensity are nearly uncorrelated, the R&D coefficients are almost unaffected by the constraining of the capital coefficient implicit in the TFP equations.

26. Using average rates of growth over a number of years to estimate the relation of productivity to R&D has the advantage of minimizing the possible biases due to measurement errors and to the timing problem. We expected, therefore, to find instability when looking at this relation on a single year basis, but not to such an extent.

27. Given the high standard errors associated with the Japanese estimates, it is not strong evidence against this hypothesis either.

28. See Griliches (1980, 1984) and Griliches and Hall (1982) for more detail on these data and their construction and for results of analyses using them.

29. Since this was first written we have been informed that such efforts are indeed underway by researchers associated with the Economic Planning Agency in Japan. See Goto and Suzuki (1989).

References

Bank of Japan, Research and Statistics Department. Various years. *Prices indexes annual: Input-output price indexes of manufacturing industry by sector.* Tokyo.

Bound, J., C. Cummins, Z. Griliches, B. H. Hall, and A. Jaffe. 1984. Who does R&D and who patents. In *R&D, patents, and productivity,* ed. Z. Griliches. Chicago: University of Chicago Press.

Bruno, M., and J. Sachs. 1985. *Economics of worldwide stagflation.* Cambridge, Mass.: Harvard University Press.

Council of Economic Advisers. 1984. *Economic report of the president.* Washington, D.C.: Government Printing Office.

Cuneo, P., and J. Mairesse. 1984. Productivity and R&D at the firm level in French manufacturing. In *R&D, patents, and productivity,* ed. Z. Griliches. Chicago: University of Chicago Press.

Economic Planning Agency, Government of Japan. Various years. *Annual report on national accounts.* Tokyo.

Goto, A., and K. Suzuki. 1989. R&D capital, rate of return on R&D investment and spillover of R&D in Japanese manufacturing industries. *Review of Economics and Statistics* 71(4):555–64.

Griliches, Z. 1986. Productivity, R&D, and basic research at the firm level in the 1970s. *American Economic Review* 76(1):141–54.

———. 1980. Returns to research and development expenditures in the private sector. In *New developments in productivity measurement and analysis,* eds. J. W. Kendrick and B. Vaccara. NBER Studies in Income and Wealth 44. Chicago: University of Chicago Press.

———. 1979. Issues in assessing the contribution of R&D to productivity growth. *Bell Journal of Economics* 10, no. 1 (Spring): 92–116.

Griliches, Z., and B. H. Hall. 1982. Census-NSF R&D data match project. In *Development and use of longitudinal establishment data.* Economic Research Report ER-4. Washington, D.C.: Bureau of the Census.

Griliches, Z., and F. Lichtenberg. 1984. R&D and productivity growth at the industry level: Is there still a relationship? In *R&D, patents, and productivity,* ed. Z. Griliches. Chicago: University of Chicago Press.

Griliches, Z., and J. Mairesse. 1984. Productivity and R&D at the firm level. In *R&D, patents, and productivity,* ed. Z. Griliches. Chicago: University of Chicago Press.

———. 1983. Comparing productivity growth: An exploration of French and U.S. industrial firm data. *European Economic Review* 21(1–2):89–119.

Hall, B. H., C. Cummins, E. Laderman, and J. Mundy. 1988. The R&D master file documentation. NBER Technical Paper no. 72.

Jorgenson, D. W., M. Kuroda, and M. Nishimizu. 1987. Japan-U.S. industry level productivity comparison, 1960–1979. *Journal of Japanese and International Economics* 1(1):1–30.

Mairesse, J., and P. Cuneo. 1985. Recherche-developpement et performances des entreprises. *Revue Economique* 36(5):1001–41.

Mohnen, P., M. I. Nadiri, and I. Prucha. 1986. R&D, production structure, and rates of return in the U.S., Japanese, and German manufacturing sectors. *European Economic Review* 30(4):749–72.

National Science Foundation. Various years. *Research and development in industry.* Washington, D.C.: Government Printing Office.

———. 1985. A comparative analysis of information on national industrial R&D expenditures. NSF Report 85-311. Washington, D.C.

Odagiri, H. 1983. R&D expenditures, royalty payments, and sales growth in Japanese manufacturing corporations. *Journal of Industrial Economics* 32(2):61–72.

Odagiri, H., and H. Iwata. 1986. The impact of R&D on productivity increases in Japanese manufacturing companies. *Research Policy* 15:13–19.

OECD. 1984. *Science and technology indicators: Resources devoted to R&D.* Paris: Organization for Economic Cooperation and Development.

Peck, M. J. 1985. Government R&D subsidies in the American economy? Discussion Paper no. 35. Economic Research Institute, Economic Planning Agency, Tokyo.

Schankerman, M. 1981. The effects of double-counting and expensing on the measured returns to R&D. *Review of Economics and Statistics* 63(3):454–58.

Statistics Bureau, Management and Coordination Agency. Various years. *Report on the survey of research and development.* Tokyo.

U.S. Bureau of the Census. 1977. Enterprise statistics: General report on industrial organization. ES77-1. Washington, D.C.: Government Printing Office.

Comment   Edwin Mansfield

In this paper, which is a continuation of work they have carried out concerning the United States and France, Zvi Griliches and Jacques Mairesse compare the contribution of R&D to economic growth in Japan and the United States. They conclude that there is no strong evidence "that differences in either the intensity or the fecundity of R&D expenditures can account for the rather large difference in the observed rates of growth of productivity between the two countries."

Before commenting directly on their paper, I would like to summarize some of my own results, which supplement those of Griliches and Mairesse. First, it appears that there are advantages in disaggregating R&D into (1) applied R&D and (2) basic research. Using a model similar to that employed by Griliches and Mairesse, me, and others, there is evidence, based on industry data, that applied R&D in Japan has yielded a higher rate of return than in the United States. This seems reasonable, given Japan's greater emphasis on commercial (rather than government-financed) projects and its reliance on advanced technology from the West, which could be adapted and improved at relatively low cost. On the other hand, my econometric results provide no indication that basic research has been particularly effective in Japan.[1]

Second, it is very important to disaggregate R&D into process and product R&D. The American firms in my sample devote about two-thirds of their R&D expenditures to the improvement of product technology (new products and product changes) and about one-third to the improvement of process technology (new processes and process changes). Among the Japanese firms, on the other hand, the proportions are reversed, two-thirds going for the improvement of process technology and one-third going for the improvement of product technology. It seems likely that Japan's relatively high returns from applied R&D are due in part to its emphasis on process R&D.[2]

Third, there is considerable evidence that the Japanese develop and commercially introduce new products and processes more quickly and cheaply than do their American rivals, although the extent of this difference varies considerably from industry to industry. For innovations based on external technology (i.e., technology developed outside the innovating firm), the Japanese have a big advantage. For innovations based on internal technology (i.e., technology developed within the innovating firm), they have no advantage that I could detect.[3]

Fourth, there is a marked difference between Japan and the United States in the allocation of resources within the innovation process, this difference being undetectable if one looks at R&D alone. The percentage of total innovation cost devoted to tooling and manufacturing equipment and facilities in Japan is almost double that in the United States. This reflects Japan's emphasis on

Edwin Mansfield is professor of economics at the University of Pennsylvania and director of the Center for Economics and Technology.

process engineering and efficient manufacturing facilities. Equally striking is the fact that the percentage of total innovation cost devoted to marketing start-up (i.e., preintroduction marketing activities like market research) in the United States is almost double that in Japan. If American firms could reduce this percentage to the Japanese level (while holding constant the amounts they spend on other stages of the innovation process), it appears that about 60% of the Japanese cost advantage would be eliminated.[4]

Fifth, it is instructive to look at industrial robots, an important industry where Japan is widely regarded as being ahead of the United States. In both countries, high-growth robot producers tend to devote a much higher proportion of innovation costs to tooling and manufacturing facilities than do low-growth robot producers, and the proportion devoted to marketing start-up seems to be much lower among high-growth than low-growth robot producers. Based on the available data, it appears that the more successful firms in both countries, like the Japanese, tend to emphasize manufacturing in the innovation process, not marketing.[5]

Sixth, although the industrial robot was largely an American invention, the rate of diffusion of robots has been slower in the United States than in Japan. In both the United States and Japan, the imitation process can be represented reasonably well by a simple econometric model similar to that in Mansfield (1961). According to the results, Japan's higher rate of imitation can be explained entirely by its later start, which enabled it to utilize earlier experience in the United States and elsewhere. But this does not explain the much higher intrafirm rates of diffusion of robots in Japan than in the United States, which seem to be due in considerable part to differences in the minimum rate of return required to justify investing in robots.[6]

Having provided this brief summary of some of my results in this area, I would like to stress that Japan's relatively rapid rate of technological change has been due largely to the importation of foreign technology. In 1978, the Ministry of International Trade and Industry carried out a survey of Japanese business leaders to determine the relative contributions made by domestic and foreign technologies to product quality and production processes. According to the results, purely indigenous technology accounted for only about 5% of the advances in product quality and about 17% of the advances in processes.[7] While surveys of this sort obviously must be treated with caution, a host of case studies indicate essentially the same thing. For example, in high density polyethylene, Sumitomo Chemical licensed technology from ICI, Mitsui licensed technology from du Pont, and Mitsubishi licensed technology from Gulf Oil.

To a considerable extent, Japan's success in utilizing and obtaining foreign technology has been due to its effectiveness in monitoring foreign technological developments. In 1983, I asked 100 major American firms in 13 industries to rank each major country's firms with regard to their effectiveness in this regard.[8] The consistency with which the Japanese were ranked first is an impressive tribute to the systematic programs carried out by both Japanese firms and government agencies to learn about foreign technology (see table 1).[9] Of course, the effectiveness of the intelligence-gathering activities of a nation's firms depends in part on how much they spend on such activities. As shown in table 2, less than 30% of the American firms in the above survey

Table 1   Average Rank of Five Major Countries by the Perceived Effectiveness of Their Industry in Monitoring Technological Development outside Their Own Country, 1983

Industry	France	Germany	Japan	United Kingdom	United States
Chemicals	3.8	3.0	1.5	4.4	2.2
Pharmaceuticals	4.2	3.1	1.4	4.2	2.0
Petroleum	3.6	2.2	1.2	4.6	3.0
Primary metals	4.2	2.7	1.0	4.6	2.5
Electrical equipment	3.8	2.9	1.0	4.0	3.3
Machinery	3.8	2.7	1.2	4.4	2.8
Transportation equipment	3.7	2.0	1.0	4.7	3.7
Instruments	4.1	2.6	1.4	3.7	3.3
Rubber	3.5	3.0	1.0	5.0	2.5
Stone, clay, and glass	4.0	3.6	1.0	3.8	2.6
Other[a]	4.0	2.8	1.5	4.2	2.4
Average	3.9	2.8	1.2	4.3	2.8

Source: See n. 8.
[a]Includes fabricated metals, food, and paper.

Table 2   Percentage of U.S. Firms Spending at Least as Large a Percentage of Sales on Monitoring Foreign Technological Development as the Average Amount Spent by Their Foreign Rivals, 1983.

Industry	Percentage of U.S. Firms Compared With Firms in			
	France	Germany	Japan	United Kingdom
Chemicals	58	58	42	67
Pharmaceuticals	78	89	33	89
Petroleum	60	40	22	60
Primary metals	60	50	60	80
Electrical equipment	44	33	22	56
Machinery	20	20	10	40
Transportation equipment	67	33	33	67
Instruments	56	67	33	56
Rubber	0	0	0	100
Stone, clay, and glass	60	60	0	80
Other	58	67	67	75
Average	51	47	29	70

Source: See n. 8.

reported that they spent as much (as a percent of sales) on these activities as their Japanese rivals. American firms have been criticized for their "apparent inability to adequately scan and adopt foreign R & D."[10] Perhaps they would do better if they devoted more resources to intelligence-gathering of this sort.

Given the overwhelming importance of the importation of foreign technology to Japan's success story, as well as the less publicized fact that the United States also benefits greatly from imported technology, it should be noted that the model used by Griliches and Mairesse assumes that a firm's rate of productivity increase depends only on its *own* R&D expenditures, not on the amount it spends on foreign technology or on the amount spent on R&D by foreigners. I recognize that it is not easy to include international technology transfer in models of this sort,[11] although a few limited attempts have been made (e.g., Mansfield 1984; and Mansfield and Romeo 1984), but there is the obvious possibility that the omission of technology imports may result in serious specifications errors, particularly in the case of Japan.

Moreover, leaving aside international technology transfer, their model also ignores the impact of one American (or Japanese) firm's R&D on another American (or Japanese) firm's rate of productivity growth. As many econometric analyses and case studies have indicated, these impacts frequently are very substantial. Much of the R&D carried out by the typical firm is aimed at advances in its products, not its processes, and hence may have more effect on the productivity of its customers than its own productivity. For this reason, work during the past decade (see, e.g., Mansfield 1980; Scherer 1982; and Terleckyj 1974) has tended to focus on the total amount of R&D used by a particular industry or firm, rather than the amount of R&D originating in a particular industry or firm. Again, I understand the data problems that Griliches and Mairesse encountered, but it is unfortunate that they were forced to ignore these important interfirm effects.

Also, their model assumes that a firm's government-financed R&D has no effect on its rate of productivity growth. Case studies indicate that major spillovers have occurred from military and other government-financed R&D to the civilian economy. Recent econometric studies by Mansfield and Switzer (1984), Levy and Terleckyj (1983), and others suggest that a firm's government-financed R&D tends to enhance the productivity of its company-financed R&D. While government-financed R&D ordinarily has considerably less effect on a firm's rate of productivity growth than company-financed R&D, there are problems, particularly in a comparison of the United States and Japan, in ignoring it altogether.

In addition, the regressions that Griliches and Mairesse run are subject to identification problems. There is the distinct possibility that firms with relatively high rates of productivity growth tend to have the sorts of managements and other characteristics that lead to relatively high R&D expenditures. Thus, the line of causation may run both ways, and their estimates of the effect of a firm's R&D on its productivity growth may be biased. Further, although relatively little is known about the time lags from R&D to the commercial introduction and diffusion of technical advances stemming from that R&D, the available evidence indicates that these lags frequently are long enough so that R&D in 1973 had effects on productivity that were not felt until after 1980, when the analysis ends.

In conclusion, as Griliches and Mairesse recognize, while it is true that "we cannot reject the hypothesis that the contribution of [R&D] expenditures to productivity growth was about the same in both countries," it is also true that, on the basis of their results, one cannot reject the hypothesis that there is a considerable difference in this regard between the two countries. Obviously, this is not the fault of the authors; as they point out, the data they use are imperfect in a number of ways. I agree with their statement below, that "the omissions arise largely from the state of the available data and are not something we could do very much about." Nonetheless, their study sheds light on an important topic.

Notes

1. For further discussion, see Mansfield (1988a).
2. Ibid.
3. For further discussion, see Mansfield (1988b).
4. Ibid.
5. For further discussion, see Mansfield (1987).
6. For further discussion, see Mansfield (1989).
7. See Okimoto (1986), 544.
8. Each firm included in the survey was chosen at random from a list of major firms in the 13 manufacturing industries in table 1. In general, it was the firm's vice president for research and development who responded, and there was essentially no problem of nonresponse. This survey was part of a larger study I carried out, which was supported by a grant from the National Science Foundation.
9. For an interesting case study in the steel industry, see Lynn (1982). It is important to note in this regard that new technology tends to leak out relatively quickly. See Mansfield (1985).
10. Report of the Conference on U.S. Competitiveness, Harvard University, 1980.
11. For some relevant discussion, see Mansfield et al. (1982).

References

Levy, David, and Nestor Terleckyj. 1983. Effects of government R and D on private R and D, investment, and productivity. *Bell Journal of Economics* 14:551–61.
Lynn, Leonard. 1982. *How Japan innovates*. Boulder, Colo.: Westview.
Mansfield, Edwin. 1989. The diffusion of industrial robots in Japan and the United States. *Research Policy* 18:183–92.
———. 1988a. Industrial R and D in Japan and the United States: A comparative study. *American Economic Review* 78 (May):223–28.
———. 1988b. The speed and cost of industrial innovation in Japan and the United States: External vs. internal technology. *Management Science* 34 (October):1157–68.

————. 1987. Innovation, R and D, and firm growth in robotics: Japan and the United States. Paper presented at Symposium on Research and Development, Industrial Change, and Economic Policy, University of Karlstad, Sweden.

————. 1985. How rapidly does new industrial technology leak out? *Journal of Industrial Economics* 34 (December):217–24.

————. 1984. R and D and innovation: Some empirical findings. In *R&D, patents, and productivity*, ed. Zvi Griliches, 127–48. Chicago: University of Chicago Press.

————. 1980. Basic research and productivity increase in manufacturing. *American Economic Review* 70 (December):863–73.

————. 1961. Technical change and the rate of imitation. *Econometrica* 29 (October):741–66.

Mansfield, Edwin, and Anthony Romeo. 1984. Reverse transfers of technology from overseas subsidiaries to American firms. *IEEE Transactions on Engineering Management* EM-31 (August):122–27.

Mansfield, Edwin, and Lorne Switzer. 1984. Effects of federal support on company-financed R and D: The case of energy. *Management Science* 30 (May):562–71.

Mansfield, Edwin, et al. 1982. *Technology transfer, productivity, and economic policy.* New York: W. W. Norton.

Okimoto, Daniel. 1986. The Japanese challenge in high technology. In *The positive sum strategy*, ed. R. Landau and N. Rosenberg. Washington, D.C.: National Academy Press.

Scherer, F. M. 1982. Inter-industry technology flows and productivity growth. *Review of Economics and Statistics* 64 (November):627–34.

Terleckyj, Nestor. 1974. *Effects of R and D on productivity growth of industries.* Washington, D.C.: National Planning Association.

Reply   Zvi Griliches and Jacques Mairesse

In his comment, Mansfield reports on several aspects of his own work in this area which indeed make a valuable contribution to our limited knowledge of these matters; he notices a number of omissions and ambiguities in our work. The omissions arise largely from the state of the available data and are not something that we could do very much about. What we tried to do is to analyze, to the best of our abilities, the data that do exist and to which we had access. Admittedly, they are incomplete, but progress is made, we believe, by trying to comprehend an imperfect world in imperfect ways.

We have only a few comments on some of the points raised by Mansfield. While monitoring technological developments elsewhere is clearly an important activity for any technologically "active" firm, it is not entirely obvious how this should impinge on measured productivity numbers. Even though France has the second worst record in this regard in Mansfield's table 1 above, much worse than the United States, French firms nevertheless experienced a significantly higher rate of productivity growth in the 1970s than their U.S. counterparts (Griliches and Mairesse 1983).

Knowledge spillovers are indeed a major omission in our analysis. It is not a topic that can be handled easily at the individual-firm level, unless one has a much richer data base that would allow the construction of some differential measure of technological "connectedness" between firms. Otherwise, this is an effect that would be common to all firms within an industry. In the United States, where we have had access to more detailed data, it has been possible to construct a measure of technological distance between firms and make more progress on the measurement of spillover effects (see Jaffe 1986).

We did ignore governmentally financed R&D expenditures because there were no data on them in our sources. The evidence on the effect of such expenditures on the magnitude and productivity of privately financed R&D is mixed. Griliches (1986) finds only small effects, while Lichtenberg (1984) interprets the stimulating effect of governmentally financed R&D as reflecting the rent-seeking behavior of firms, stimulated by governmental defense procurement activities, rather than a direct productivity spillover.

It is obvious that lags and differences in lag structures are an important aspect of the R&D story. Our functional form, which relates differences in average growth rates to differences in R&D intensity, is, however, not well adapted to looking at this question. We have some scattered evidence showing that moving the R&D dating from 1972–74 to 1976 in analyzing 1973–80 growth rates deteriorates our results somewhat. Thus, there is an indication here that there may indeed be nonnegligable lags in this process.

The causality issue is also very important and has been discussed by us in other contexts. Here, the best we could do is to relate "subsequent" growth (1973–80) to "early" (1972–74) R&D intensity. To do more, will require a full-fledged theory of R&D investment, a topic on which some of us have been working in recent years (Mairesse and Siu 1984; Pakes 1985; Hall and Hayashi, 1989; Lach and Schankerman 1989; and Griliches, Hall and Pakes 1990).

There are also a number of difficulties not mentioned by Mansfield, especially problems associated with the measurement of total factor productivity, the measurement of output and price in technologically sophisticated and changing industries, and the associated problems of making international comparisons that may overshadow the other issues discussed by Mansfield and us. Nevertheless, something is to be learned from looking at the data as they are and then trying to improve on them. Our work is only a first step in this direction and a progress report from a continuing quest for understanding. We have, indeed, benefited from the comments of Mansfield and other participants in this discussion and we hope that this will reflect itself in our future work on this range of topics.

References

Griliches, Z. 1986. Productivity, R&D, and basic research at the firm level in the 1970s. *American Economic Review* 76(1):141–54.
Griliches, Z., B. Hall, and A. Pakes. 1990. R&D, patents, and market value revisited:

Is there a second (technological opportunity) factor? *Economics of Innovation and New Technology* 1(1). In press.

Griliches, Z., and J. Mairesse. 1983. Comparing productivity growth: An explanation of French and U.S. industrial firm data. *European Economic Review* 21(1–2):89–119.

Hall, B. H., and F. Hayashi. 1989. R&D as an investment. NBER Working Paper no. 2973.

Jaffe, A. 1986. Technological opportunity and spillovers of R&D. *American Economic Review* 76(5):984–1002.

Lach, S., and M. Schankerman. 1989. Dynamics of R&D investment in the scientific sector. *Journal of Political Economy* 97(4).

Lichtenberg, F. 1984. The relationship between federal contract R&D and company R&D. *American Economic Review* 74(2):73–8.

Mairesse, J., and A. Siu. 1984. An extended accelerator model of R&D and physical investment. In *R&D, patents, and productivity,* ed. Z. Griliches. Chicago: University of Chicago Press.

Pakes, A. 1985. On patents, R&D, and the stock market rate of return. *Journal of Political Economy* 93(2):390–409.

12 Compositional Change of Heterogeneous Labor Input and Economic Growth in Japan

Hajime Imamura

12.1 Introduction

In this paper I evaluate the role of labor input during the rapid expansion period of the Japanese economy and in the years following the oil crisis, in order to measure the contribution of labor quality to productivity growth. Two factors influence the quality changes in labor input. One is a demographic factor, which is basically exogenous and which determines the endowment of a heterogeneous labor input. The other is an economic factor, which includes the technological conditions and the market conditions of the economy. Therefore, quality change in labor input can be defined as the result of rational behavior among economic entities under given market conditions, a given level of technology, and fixed-factor endowment.

A framework that treats the above factors as endogenous variables is the most preferable, but unfortunately we lack precise data as to what factor has the greatest impact on quality changes in labor input. The contributing factor at the outset of an enterprise may not remain the same as the stages of economic development progress. Also, we lack sufficient insight into the relationship between economic growth and quality change, particularly on account of compositional shifts in heterogeneous labor. In this paper I hope to more accurately determine the interdependent economic mechanisms underlying quality change in labor input. In addition, I undertake comparative analysis of the United States and Japan to ascertain how quality change in labor input differs in these two countries, which have had dissimilar patterns of economic development.

Hajime Imamura is an associate professor of economics at Toyo University, Tokyo, Japan.

This paper was developed from a joint research project between Keio University and Harvard University. The author wishes to thank H. Shimada and M. Kuroda for invaluable advice in preparing this paper, and W. Oi and a referee for their thoughtful comments.

Under the assumption of weak separability between labor inputs and other factor inputs, we can posit the existence of an aggregator function of heterogeneous labor inputs. This enables us to analyze the sources of quality change in labor input independently of other factor inputs. In aggregating labor inputs, we utilize Divisia indices, which are consistent with transcendental logarithmic aggregator functions. Based on the neoclassical theory of production, we measure labor quality on the premise of equality between wage rates and the value of marginal productivity.

Before proceeding we will briefly review previous research on this subject. The representative works are Watanabe and Egaizu (1968), Denison and Chung (1976) and Tachibanaki (1973). Watanabe and Egaizu measured quality change in labor input for the period 1951–64 and compared it with results for other developed countries. Their results showed quality change in labor input in Japan to be relatively low, because of an imitation lag in technological progress. They considered technological change at that time to be embodied in imported capital goods, and, as a consequence, the need for highly qualified workers employed in the development of original technology remained low. In concluding, they forecasted that, after the 1960s, a great degree of quality change in labor input would be brought on by the process of catching up technologically with the United States and Western Europe; it would be a prerequisite for original technological development.

Denison and Chung's (1976) assertion about quality change in labor input, especially the effect of education, was the opposite of Watanabe and Egaizu's (1968) results. For the period 1953–71, Denison and Chung estimated the contribution of the education effect to economic growth (10.4% per annum) as 0.41% per annum. Watanabe and Egaizu had estimated it as 0.06%– 0.18%. In their framework, Denison and Chung cross-classified their data only by age and sex. Education was not cross-classified. This, then, imposed the restriction that the education effect must be almost identical in all age-sex categories.

Tachibanaki (1973) measured the quality change in labor input for 1956– 70. He found the major source of quality change to be education and, especially, experience. However, his framework of analysis treated the number of employees of a company as one of the measures of quality of labor, and he measured labor input only by the number of persons, assuming hours were constant throughout the observation period.

As a continuation to this research, I measure quality change in labor input in 29 industries using the Divisia index, a method that is consistent with the neoclassical theory of production under some necessary assumptions. In addition to one-dimensional effects, a great number of multidimensional effects are considered, enabling us to understand quality change in labor input more systematically than in previous research. Second, I compiled large amounts of data on labor inputs cross-classified into age, sex, education, occupation, and industry. Such data have never before been developed consistently in time series. Third, I compare quality change in labor inputs in the United States and Japan in a more decomposed manner than in other previous research. I also assess the causes of the difference in productivity change for the United States and Japan in a precise way.

12.2 Theoretical Framework for Measuring Labor Input

12.2.1 Measurement of Total Factor Productivity and the Divisia Index

Let us consider the ith industrial sector. Suppose that there exists a production function with constant returns to scale.

$$(1) \qquad Z_i = F_i(X_i, K_i, L_i, t).$$

Differentiating equation (1) logarithmically with respect to time, we obtain

$$(2) \qquad \frac{d\ln Z_i}{dt} = \frac{\partial \ln Z_i}{\partial \ln X_i}\frac{d\ln X_i}{dt} + \frac{\partial \ln Z_i}{\partial \ln K_i}\frac{d\ln K}{dt} + \frac{\partial \ln Z_i}{\partial \ln L_i}\frac{d\ln L_i}{dt} + \frac{\partial \ln Z_i}{\partial t}.$$

Under perfect competition, the value-marginal product equals the real factor price.

$$(3) \qquad \begin{aligned} P_{Z_i}(\partial Z_i/\partial X_i) &= P_{X_i} \\ P_{Z_i}(\partial Z_i/\partial K_i) &= P_{K_i} \\ P_{Z_i}(\partial Z_i/\partial L_i) &= P_{L_i}. \end{aligned}$$

Then, output elasticity is equal to the value share of each factor.

$$(4) \qquad \frac{d\ln Z_i}{dt} = V_X^i\frac{d\ln X_i}{dt} + V_K^i\frac{d\ln K_i}{dt} + V_L^i\frac{d\ln L_i}{dt} + V_t^i,$$

where V_X^i represents the value share of intermediate input in the ith industry, V_K^i represents the value share of capital input in the ith industry, and V_L represents the value share of labor input in the ith industry. And, $V_t^i = \partial \ln Z_i(X_i, K_i, L_i, t)/\partial t$.

Under the assumption of weak separability between each factor input, we can define constant returns to scale aggregator functions for each factor input.[1]

$$(5) \qquad \begin{aligned} X_i &= X_i(X_{1i}, X_{2i}, \ldots, X_{ni}) \\ K_i &= K_i(K_{1i}, K_{2i}, \ldots, K_{pi}) \\ L_i &= L_i(L_{1i}, L_{2i}, \ldots, L_{qi}), \end{aligned}$$

where $X_{ji}, (j = 1, \ldots, n)$ represents the n intermediate inputs from the jth sector, $K_{ki}, (k = 1, \ldots, p)$ represents the p capital inputs, and $L_{li}, (l = 1, \ldots, q)$ represents the q labor inputs.

Differentiating equation (5) logarithmically with respect to time under the assumption of perfect competition in factor markets, the elasticities of each aggregate, with respect to the individual inputs, equal the shares of each individual input in the corresponding aggregates; then, we obtain

$$\frac{d\ln X_i}{dt} = \sum_{j=1}^{n} \frac{\partial \ln X_i \, (X_{1i}, \ldots, X_{ni})}{\partial \ln X_{ji}} \cdot \frac{d\ln X_{ji}}{dt} = \sum_{j=1}^{n} V_{Xj}^{i} \frac{d\ln X_{ji}}{dt}$$

(6)
$$\frac{d\ln K_i}{dt} = \sum_{k=1}^{p} \frac{\partial \ln K_i(K_{1i}, \ldots, K_{pi})}{\partial \ln K_{ki}} \cdot \frac{d\ln K_{ki}}{dt} = \sum_{k=1}^{p} VE_{Kk}^{i} \frac{d\ln K_{ki}}{dt}$$

$$\frac{d\ln L_i}{dt} = \sum_{l=1}^{1} \frac{\partial \ln L_i(L_{1i}, \ldots, L_{qi})}{\partial \ln L_l} \cdot \frac{d\ln L_{li}}{dt} = \sum_{l=1}^{q} V_{Li}^{i} \frac{d\ln L_{li}}{dt},$$

where V_{Xj}^{i}, $(j=1, \ldots, n)$ represents the share of the n intermediate inputs, V_{Kk}^{i}, $(k=1, \ldots, p)$ represents the share of the p capital inputs, and V_{Li}^{i}, $(l=1, \ldots, q)$ represents the share of the q labor inputs. These are the growth rates of the Divisia indices of intermediate, capital, and labor inputs, respectively.

Here, we should comment on the data available to economic analysis. The discussion above was made in the hypothetical world of continuous data, but data in the real world can only be obtained in discrete form. To cope with a discrete data system, discrete approximation is needed. Equations (4) and (6) can be rewritten as follows.

(7) $\ln Z_i(t) - \ln Z_i(t-1) = \bar{V}_X^i[\ln X_i(t) - \ln X_i(t-1)]$

$$+ \bar{V}_K^i[\ln K_i(t) - \ln K_i(t-1)] + \bar{V}_L^i[\ln L_i(t) - \ln L_i(t-1)] + \bar{V}_t^i,$$

where

$$\bar{V}_X^i = \frac{1}{2}[V_K^i(t) + V_X^i(t-1)],$$

$$\bar{V}_K^i = \frac{1}{2}[V_K^i(t) + V_K^i(t-1)],$$

$$\bar{V}_L^i = \frac{1}{2}[V_L^i(t) + V_L^i(t-1)],$$

$$\bar{V}_t^i = \frac{1}{2}[V_t^i(t) + V_t^i(t-1)],$$

(8) $$\ln X_i(t) - \ln X_i(t-1) = \sum_{j=1}^{n} \bar{V}_{Xj}^i[\ln X_{ji}(t) - \ln X_{ji}(t-1)],$$

where

$$\bar{V}_{Xj}^i = \frac{1}{2}[V_{Xj}^i(t) + V_{Xj}^i(t-1)].$$

$$\ln K_i(t) - \ln K_i(t-1) = \sum_{k=1}^{p} \bar{V}_{Kk}^i[\ln K_{ki}(t) - \ln K_{ki}(t-1)],$$

where

$$\bar{V}^i_{Kk} = \frac{1}{2}[V^i_{Kk}(t) + V^i_{Kk}(t-1)].$$

$$\ln L_i(t) - \ln L_i(t-1) = \sum_{l=1}^{1} \bar{V}^i_{Ll}[\ln L_{li}(t) - \ln L_{li}(t-1)],$$

where

$$\bar{V}^i_{Ll} = \frac{1}{2}[V^i_{Ll}(t) + V^i_{Ll}(t-1)].$$

These discrete-type Divisia indices are in fact exact and superative index numbers of a translog aggregator function. Proof for this approximation is given by Diewert (1976).

12.2.2   Measurement of the Quality Change in Labor Input

To calculate an aggregate index that takes into account the heterogeneity of labor input, we use equation (6) or (8) (the discrete approximation of [6]). We then divide the index into a man-hour index and a quality index. Further, we can decompose the quality index with respect to individual quality factors.

Let us assume there are only four quality factors of labor input, sex(s), occupation(o), education(e) and age(a).[2] We can define the growth rate of the Divisia index of labor input employed in the ith industry as follows:

(9)
$$\frac{\dot{L}_{it}}{L_{it}} = \sum_s \sum_o \sum_e \sum_a V_{soea,it} \frac{\dot{H}_{soea,it}}{H_{soea,it}},$$

where

$$V_{soea,it} = \frac{W_{soea,it} H_{soea,it}}{\sum_s \sum_o \sum_e \sum_a W_{soea,it} H_{soea,it}},$$

$W_{soea,it}$ is the hourly wage rates of the $soea$th labor input of ith industry and $H_{soea,it}$ is the quantity of labor input in terms of total hours worked of the ith industry.

The quantity of labor input, $H_{soea,it}$, can be rewritten as the product of total hours worked by all workers employed in the ith industry, H_{it}, and the proportion of hours worked by the $soea$th-type of labor input in the ith industry($d_{soea,it}$).

(10)
$$H_{soea,it} = d_{soea,it}H_{it}.$$

Differentiating equation (10) logarithmically with respect to time and substituting into equation (9) yields

$$\frac{\dot{L}_{it}}{L_{it}} = \sum_s \sum_o \sum_e \sum_a V_{soea,it} \left(\frac{\dot{d}_{soea,it}}{d_{soea,it}} + \frac{\dot{H}_{it}}{H_{it}} \right)$$

(11)
$$= \sum_s \sum_o \sum_e \sum_a V_{soea,it} \frac{\dot{d}_{soea,it}}{d_{soea,it}} + \frac{\dot{H}_{it}}{H_{it}} \cdot \sum_s \sum_o \sum_e \sum_a V_{soea,it}$$

$$= \sum_s \sum_o \sum_e \sum_a V_{soea,it} \frac{\dot{d}_{soea,\,it}}{d_{soea,it}} + \frac{\dot{H}_{it}}{H_{it}}$$

The growth rates of the Divisia indices are now expressed as the sum of quality change and growth rates in hours of work. The first term of the right-hand side of equation (10) accounts for the quality change in labor input, and the second term accounts for the growth rate in hours of work of labor. Hence, at any time period *t*, the quality change in labor input is due to the shift in the work force to jobs with higher marginal productivities. The improvement in the individual worker is reflected in the intertemporal change in each individual labor's share.[3]

By using discrete approximation, equation (11) can be rewritten as follows:

(12)
$$\ln L_i(t) - \ln L_i(t-1) = (\ln H_i(t) - \ln H_i(t-1)$$
$$+ \sum_s \sum_o \sum_e \sum_a \frac{1}{2} [V_{soea,i}(t) + V_{soea,i}(t-1)]$$
$$\cdot [\ln d_{soea,i}(t) - \ln d_{soea,i}(t-1)].$$

12.2.3 Decomposition of Quality Change in Labor Input

A Simple Model of Quality Decomposition

In the previous section, I showed that the Divisia index of labor input increases through upward movement of quality composition even though there is no increase in total hours worked. In reality, heterogeneity of labor input should be expressed not by one dimension, for example, education, but by multiple dimensions of education, sex, age, and occupation. This is because individuals with a given educational attainment must be either male or female and of a certain age. We cannot treat those measures of quality independently.

The next question is, Among those four factors, which contributed the most to the upward movement of quality change in labor input? To that end I have decomposed quality change into its individual factors. First, I illustrate the simple model of this framework and subsequently explain the entire model applied in our empirical analysis.

The simple model in figure 12.1 is used to explain this multiplicity in the quality of labor. Here, we assume that there are only two identifiable measures of quality: education and age. We also assume that there are only two cate-

	Age		Total
	old	young	
Education high	(W_{ho}, H_{ho})	(W_{hy}, H_{hy})	(W_h, H_h)
low	(W_{lo}, H_{lo})	(W_{ly}, H_{ly})	(W_l, H_l)
Total	(W_o, H_o)	(W_y, H_y)	(W, H)

Fig. 12.1   A simple model of labor input classification in two dimensions
Note: W = hourly wage ratios; H = quantity of labor input in terms of the total hours worked by workers in each category.

gories for each: highly educated(h) and less educated(l); and young(y) and old(o) workers.

In figure 12.1, H represents the quantity of labor input in terms of the total hours worked by workers in each category, W represents hourly wage rates, and suffixes correspond to each category of classification. H without a suffix denotes total hours worked by all workers; W without a suffix denotes the average hourly wage of all workers.

Let us assume three different types of labor aggregator functions.

(13) $$L_1 = L_1(H_h, H_l),$$

(14) $$L_2 = L_2(H_o, H_y),$$

(15) $$L_3 = L_3(H_{hy}, H_{ho}, H_{ly}, H_{lo}).$$

Equations (13) and (14) are one-dimensional aggregator functions, each of which includes only one of the two measures, assuming there is only one measure that makes a difference in the value of the marginal productivity of labor input. Equation (15) is the multidimensional aggregator function that includes all (two) measures.

Differentiating the above equations logarithmically with respect to time yields,

(16) $$\frac{d\ln L_1}{dt} = \sum_e \frac{\partial \ln L_1}{\partial \ln H_e} \frac{d\ln H_e}{dt},$$

(17)
$$\frac{d\ln L_2}{dt} = \sum_a \frac{\partial \ln L_2}{\partial \ln H_a} \frac{\partial \ln H_a}{dt},$$

(18)
$$\frac{d\ln L_3}{dt} = \sum_e \sum_a \frac{\partial \ln L_2}{\partial \ln H_{ea}} \frac{d\ln H_{ea}}{dt}.$$

Assuming a linear homogeneous aggregator function and perfect competition, the output elasticity of the individual factors in each equation equals the value share of the individual factor, and using discrete approximation, we can rewrite the above equations as follows:

(19)
$$\Delta \ln L_1 = \sum_e \bar{V}_e \, \Delta \ln H_e,$$

(20)
$$\Delta \ln L_2 = \sum_a \bar{V}_a \, \Delta \ln H_a,$$

(21)
$$\Delta \ln L_3 = \sum_e \sum_a \bar{V}_{ea} \, \Delta \ln H_{ea}.$$

where $\bar{V}$ represents the value share in the labor aggregate of the period, and Δ denotes the first-order difference operator.

Equation (21) is the growth rate of the total Divisia index of labor input by discrete approximation. However, equations (19) and (20) are kinds of Divisia indices, but they do not include all measurable categories of labor input. So, let us call equations (19) and (20) the partial Divisia indices of education and age (discrete approximation case).

We can calculate the amount of quality change in labor input by subtracting the growth rates of total hours worked by all workers, $\Delta \ln H$, from the growth rate of labor input calculated from the above equations:

(22)
$$q_e = \Delta \ln L_1 - \Delta \ln H,$$

(23)
$$q_a = \Delta \ln L_2 - \Delta \ln H.$$

We shall call these quality changes calculated from partial Divisia indices the main effects of education or age, respectively.

From equation (21), we can calculate quality change, including both age and education. Let us define the interactive effect of education and age as follows:

(24)
$$q_{ea} = \Delta \ln L_3 - \Delta \ln H - q_a - q_e.$$

Next, the net contribution of age to the quality change in labor input can be calculated by subtracting the one-dimensional quality change of education (the main effect of education) from the two-dimensional quality change (total quality change). Then resulting net contribution is defined as marginal effect of age:

(24') $$q_a + q_{ea} = \Delta \ln L_3 - \Delta \ln H - q_e.$$

Full Framework of Empirical Analysis for Quality Decomposition

In our actual empirical analysis in this paper, we use a four-dimensional classification of labor: sex(s), occupation(o), education(e), and age(a). The growth rates of total hours worked by all employed workers is

(25) $$\Delta \ln H = \Delta \ln \sum_s \sum_o \sum_e \sum_a H_{soea},$$

where

> s = sex classification (male and female);
> o = occupation (blue and white collar);
> e = education (junior high school, senior high school, junior college, and university graduates);
> a = age (less than 17 years old, 18–19, 20–24, 25–29, 30–34, 35–39, 40–44, 45–49, 50–54, 55–59, 60–64, and over 65 years old.

We define five types of growth rates of Divisia indices, the first-order partial Divisia growth rate of labor input:

(26) $$\Delta \ln L_i = \sum_i \bar{V}_i \, \Delta \ln \sum_j \sum_k \sum_l H_{ijkl},$$

where

$$i = s, o, e, a,$$

and

$$j, k, l = s, o, e, a \ (j, k, l \neq i);$$

the second-order partial Divisia growth rate of labor input:

(27) $$\Delta \ln L_{ij} = \sum_i \sum_j \bar{V}_{ij} \, \Delta \ln \sum_k \sum_l H_{ijkl},$$

where

$$i, j = s, o, e, a \ (i \neq j),$$

and

$$k, l = s, o, e, a \ (k, l \neq i, j);$$

the third-order partial Divisia growth rate of labor input:

(28) $$\Delta \ln L_{ijk} = \sum_i \sum_j \sum_k \bar{V}_{ijk} \, \Delta \ln \sum_l H_{ijkl},$$

where

$$i, j, k = s, o, e, a \ (i \neq j \neq k),$$

and

$$l = s, o, e, a \ (l \neq i, j, k);$$

and the total Divisia growth rate of labor input

(29) $$\Delta \ln L_{ijkl} = \sum_i \sum_j \sum_k \sum_l \bar{V}_{ijkl} \Delta \ln H_{ijkl},$$

where

$$i, j, k, l = s, o, e, a \ (i \neq j \neq k \neq l),$$

and where $\bar{V}$ represents the value share of the period and Δ denotes the first-difference operator.

Using these growth rates of Divisia indices, we define the main effects and interactive effects for the quality change in labor inputs:
the main effects for sex, occupation, education, and age are

(30) $$q_i = \Delta \ln L_i - \Delta \ln H \quad (i = s, o, e, \text{ and } a);$$

the first-order interactive effects for quality change are

(31) $$q_{ij} = \Delta \ln L_{ij} - \Delta \ln H - q_i - q_j \quad (i, j = s, o, e, a)(i \neq j);$$

the second-order interactive effects for quality change are

(32) $$\begin{aligned} q_{ijk} &= \Delta \ln L_{ijk} - \Delta \ln H - q_i - q_j - q_{ij} - q_{ik} - q_{jk} \\ &(i, j, k = s, o, e \text{ and } a); \end{aligned}$$

the third-order interactive effects for quality change are

(33) $$\begin{aligned} q_{ijkl} &= \Delta \ln L_{ijkl} - \Delta \ln H - q_i - q_j - q_k - q_l \\ &\quad - q_{ij} - q_{ik} - q_{il} - q_{jk} - q_{jl} - q_{kl} \\ &\quad - q_{ijk} - q_{jkl} - q_{ijl} - q_{ikl}, \\ &(i, j, k, l = s, o, e \text{ and } a), \end{aligned}$$

and the total quality change in labor input is

(34) $$\begin{aligned} \Delta \ln L_{ijkl} - \Delta \ln H &= \text{main effects } (q_i + q_j + q_k + q_l) \\ &+ \text{first-order interactive effects } (q_{ij} + q_{ik} + q_{il} + q_{jk} + q_{jl} + q_{kl}) \\ &+ \text{second-order interactive effects } (q_{ijk} + q_{ikl} + q_{jkl} + q_{ijl}) \\ &+ \text{third-order interactive effect } (q_{ijkl}). \end{aligned}$$

Finally, we can define the marginal effects for each category as the effect of the nth factor added to the $(n-1)$ factor of labor quality.
Marginal effects of labor quality change for

$$
\begin{array}{ll}
\text{sex} & q_s + q_{so} + q_{se} + q_{sa} + q_{soe} + q_{soa} + q_{sae} + q_{soea}, \\
\text{occupation} & q_o + q_{so} + q_{oe} + q_{oa} + q_{soe} + q_{soa} + q_{oea} + q_{soea}, \\
\text{education} & q_e + q_{se} + q_{oe} + q_{ea} + q_{soe} + q_{sea} + q_{oea} + q_{soea}, \\
\text{age} & q_a + q_{sa} + q_{oa} + q_{ea} + q_{soa} + q_{sea} + q_{oea} + q_{soea}.
\end{array}
\tag{35}
$$

12.3   Data Compilation

The primary data source for full-time Japanese workers employed in non-agricultural industries is the Basic Wage Structure Survey (BWSS). We obtained data for the numbers of employees, average hours worked, and wages and bonuses cross-classified by sex, occupation, education, and age. Industries for which data were available are mining, construction, 20 two-digit level manufacturing industries, and six two-digit level service industries. We also obtained subaggregated BWSS data for motorized vehicles, bringing the total number of industries for which data were available to 29. Data for agriculture, forestry, and fishery are available from another source, the Labor Force Survey (LFS), which is only classified by sex. The time period for which we considered our index construction was 1960–79.

It is useful to take note of how the BWSS defines full-time and part-time employees.[4] Full-time employees are defined as those employees whose hours of work are the usual daily contractual hours, while part-time employees work less than that. Since part-time employees are not cross-classified by sex, occupation, education, age, and industry, our analysis mainly focuses on full-time employees.

According to the classification described in equation (25), we obtained data for 192 ($2 \times 2 \times 4 \times 12$) categories of heterogeneous labor for each of the 29 industries. However, in the process of data construction, the BWSS made a few estimates using the LFS and the Census of Manufactures.

12.4   Empirical Results

In what follows, I discuss the magnitude of the contribution of quality change in labor input to sectoral productivity change. I observe the changes of labor input in agricultural, manufacturing, and service sectors. The number of industries studied is 29. Second, I undertake a decomposition of quality change in labor input. In this analysis I subaggregate manufacturing industries into three categories: light, material, and fabricated manufacturing; all service industries are treated as a single service industry.[5] On the basis of these results, we will examine the characteristics of human capital accumulation during the process of economic development in Japan. Finally, the characteristics of quality change in labor input in Japan will be further clarified by a comparative analysis of the United States and Japan.

Table 12.1   **Average Annual Growth Rates of Labor Input by Industry (in % per calendar year)**

Industry	1960–65	1965–70	1970–73	1973–79	1960–73	1960–79
1. Agriculture	−6.67	−3.12	−3.08	−1.29	−4.48	−3.47
2. Mining	−8.87	−3.75	−14.27	−5.81	−8.15	−7.41
3. Construction	14.06	4.49	5.72	3.59	8.45	6.92
4. Foods	8.49	2.89	2.34	1.23	4.92	3.75
5. Textiles	1.27	.18	−3.45	−5.39	−.24	−1.86
6. Fabricated textiles	10.35	5.27	5.81	3.41	7.35	6.11
7. Lumber	4.39	.02	.36	−3.53	1.78	.10
8. Furniture	4.67	4.23	2.42	2.13	3.98	3.40
9. Paper	5.61	1.81	.62	−.51	2.99	1.89
10. Printing	6.76	2.43	.73	.84	3.71	2.80
11. Chemicals	4.55	3.45	−1.00	−1.08	2.85	1.61
12. Petroleum and coal	2.60	9.29	−1.00	1.54	4.34	3.46
13. Rubber	−.26	6.88	−1.63	−.29	2.17	1.39
14. Leather	4.65	1.71	−3.77	3.48	1.58	2.18
15. Stone and clay	5.79	3.81	1.26	.27	3.99	2.81
16. Iron and steel	1.35	5.22	−2.41	−2.10	1.97	.68
17. Nonferrous metals	4.07	4.93	−.14	−.23	3.43	2.27
18. Fabricated Metal	10.84	6.08	.37	−1.82	6.59	3.93
19. Machinery	9.01	3.73	−.46	−1.77	4.79	2.72
20. Electrical machinery	6.69	10.21	1.16	.83	6.77	4.89
21. Motor vehicles	13.53	7.32	3.66	2.36	8.86	6.81
22. Transportation equipment	1.65	5.03	2.58	−7.51	3.16	−.21
23. Precision instruments	7.10	5.56	4.43	.56	5.89	4.21
24. Miscellaneous manufacturing	5.94	6.35	.62	2.34	4.87	4.08
25. Transportation and communication	7.09	2.64	1.71	1.41	4.13	3.28
26. Utilities	2.38	3.01	2.71	1.14	2.70	2.21
27. Trade	14.19	4.20	5.53	2.49	8.35	6.50
28. Finance	9.94	3.28	2.60	3.60	5.68	5.02
29. Real estate	20.25	14.18	7.36	2.12	14.94	10.89
30. Services	10.80	5.68	5.41	5.03	7.59	6.78
31. Government services	−6.28	−1.41	2.72	.52	−2.33	−1.43
Average	5.67	4.05	.93	.24	3.96	2.78

12.4.1   Annual Growth of Sectoral Labor Input

Here I shall highlight some of the main features of our results presented in tables 12.1–12.3. As should be expected for Japan, we observe negative average annual growth rates of labor input for the following two industries: agriculture-forestry-fishing and mining. For the entire period 1960–79, labor input in agriculture-forestry-fishing declined at a rate of −3.47% per year and at −7.41% per year in the mining industry. In contrast to these, the rest of the industries exhibit growing labor input for the 1960s. This indicates that the mobility of labor from traditional industries to the modern industrial sector is one of the main features of Japanese economic growth in the 1960s. In the 1970s however, we can observe negative growth of labor input, particularly in

Table 12.2   **Average Annual Growth Rates of Labor Quality by Industry (in % per calendar year)**

Industry	1960–65	1965–70	1970–73	1973–79	1960–73	1960–79
1. Agriculture	− .10	.31	3.39	1.00	.87	.90
2. Mining	.45	.59	− .10	.19	.37	.32
3. Construction	.64	.39	.59	.82	.53	.63
4. Foods	.03	1.51	.58	.70	.72	.72
5. Textiles	.22	1.68	1.54	.98	1.08	1.05
6. Fabricated textiles	− .17	1.48	.06	.47	.52	.51
7. Lumber	− .58	.23	.66	.28	.02	.10
8. Furniture	− .32	.53	.71	1.14	.24	.53
9. Paper	.30	1.64	1.02	1.04	.98	1.00
10. Printing	.21	1.77	1.94	1.26	1.20	1.23
11. Chemicals	− .02	1.51	1.19	1.57	.85	1.07
12. Petroleum and coal	.83	1.35	.14	1.42	.87	1.04
13. Rubber	2.70	1.21	1.68	1.37	1.89	1.73
14. Leather	− .52	.78	1.11	.37	.36	.36
15. Stone and clay	.06	1.16	.67	.87	.62	.70
16. Iron and steel	.45	.95	1.17	1.11	.81	.90
17. Nonferrous metals	− .07	1.35	1.18	1.07	.76	.86
18. Fabricated metal	.85	1.30	1.24	.69	1.12	.98
19. Machinery	.41	1.26	1.21	1.27	.92	1.02
20. Electrical machinery	.52	.86	1.21	1.86	.81	1.14
21. Motor vehicles	− .83	1.51	1.67	1.41	.64	.88
22. Transportation equipment	.19	.82	− 1.20	.57	.11	.25
23. Precision instruments	.02	1.62	.92	1.24	.84	.97
24. Miscellaneous manufacturing	.90	2.11	1.48	.99	1.49	1.34
25. Transportation and communication	.09	.71	1.07	.91	.55	.67
26. Utilities	1.08	.61	.11	.25	.68	.54
27. Trade	1.07	1.10	2.14	1.29	1.33	1.32
28. Finance	− .77	.94	.44	.79	.17	.36
29. Real estate	.86	1.25	.91	.56	1.02	.88
30. Services	− .35	1.47	.65	.35	.58	.51
31. Government services	.44	− .12	.62	− .05	.27	.17
Average	.28	1.09	.97	.90	.75	.80

heavy industry, which is a symptom of the first oil crisis. In contrast to the manufacturing sectors, tertiary industries, such as trade, finance, and service show a relatively stable and positive growth in labor.

The uppermost two diagrams of figures 12.2–12.5 show the index for ordinary labor input, the index for man-hours worked, for average hours worked, for labor quality during the period 1960–79 in light, material, and fabricated manufacturing and in tertiary industries. In the figures, $\bar{L}$ represents the index of man-hours worked, and $\bar{Q}$ the index for labor quality. Finally, L_s stands for the composite index of quantity $\bar{L}$ and quality $\bar{Q}$ for labor input. In terms of man-hours worked, the growth rate for manufacturing industries gradually begins to level off at the end of the 1960s and experiences a sudden decrease after the oil crisis in 1974. On the other hand, the growth rate of man-hour labor input increases throughout the entire period 1960–79 in tertiary indus-

Table 12.3   **Average Annual Growth Rates of Man-hour Labor Input (in % per calendar year)**

Industry	1960–65	1965–70	1970–73	1973–79	1960–73	1960–79
1. Agriculture	−6.58	−3.43	−6.47	−2.29	−5.34	−4.38
2. Mining	−9.32	−4.34	−14.17	−6.00	−8.52	−7.73
3. Construction	13.42	4.10	5.12	2.77	7.92	6.30
4. Foods	8.46	1.38	1.75	.53	4.18	3.04
5. Textiles	1.04	−1.50	−4.99	−6.37	−1.33	−2.92
6. Fabricated textiles	10.52	3.78	5.75	2.93	6.83	5.60
7. Lumber	4.98	−.22	−.30	−3.81	1.76	.01
8. Furniture	5.00	3.70	1.71	1.00	3.74	2.87
9. Paper	5.30	.17	−.41	−1.56	2.01	.88
10. Printing	6.55	6.72	−1.21	−.42	2.50	1.58
11. Chemicals	4.57	1.94	−2.19	−2.64	2.00	.53
12. Petroleum and coal	1.77	7.94	−1.14	.12	3.47	2.41
13. Rubber	−2.96	5.67	−3.31	−1.66	.28	−.33
14. Leather	5.17	.94	−4.88	3.11	1.22	1.82
15. Stone and clay	5.74	2.65	.59	−.60	3.36	2.11
16. Iron and steel	.90	4.27	−3.58	−3.21	1.16	−.22
17. Nonferrous metals	4.13	3.60	−1.32	−1.30	2.67	1.41
18. Fabricated metals	9.99	4.77	−.87	−2.52	5.48	2.96
19. Machinery	8.60	2.47	−1.67	−3.04	3.87·	1.69
20. Electrical machinery	6.17	9.35	−.04	−1.03	5.98	3.75
21. Motor vehicles	14.36	5.81	2.00	.96	8.22	5.92
22. Transportation equipment	1.45	4.21	3.78	−8.08	3.05	−.46
23. Precision instruments	7.08	3.94	3.52	−.68	5.05	3.24
24. Miscellaneous manufacturing	5.04	4.24	−.85	1.35	3.37	2.73
25. Transportation and communication	7.00	1.93	.65	.50	3.58	2.61
26. Utilities	1.29	2.41	2.59	.89	2.02	1.66
27. Trade	13.12	3.10	3.39	1.20	7.02	5.18
28. Finance	10.71	2.34	2.16	2.81	5.52	4.66
29. Real estate	19.39	12.93	6.46	1.56	13.92	10.01
30. Services	11.15	4.21	4.77	4.68	7.01	6.27
31. Government services	−6.72	−1.29	2.10	.57	−2.60	−1.60
Average	5.40	2.96	−.03	−.65	3.21	1.99

tries. Although these latter underwent a slight decrease after 1974, they recovered to the historical trend level in 1979.

Quality changes both in manufacturing and tertiary sectors maintain a stable rate of growth during the entire period. The growth rate of labor quality in the manufacturing sectors is higher (0.87%–1.02%) than in the tertiary sector (0.68%). In the tertiary sector, the improvement in labor quality started at the end of the 1960s.

Average annual growth rates of the index for sectoral labor quality are shown in table 12.4 below. Average annual growth rates during the period

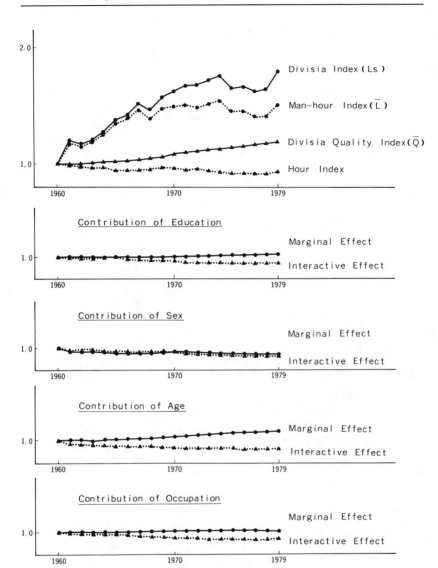

Fig. 12.2   Decomposition of labor quality change—light manufacturing industry

1960–79 are positive in all sectors. The average annual growth rate of 3.39% found in agriculture-forestry-fishing during the period 1970–73 is extraordinarily high. In fact, the magnitude of quality change offsets almost half of the decrease in man-hour labor input in that sector. As shown in table 12.3, average annual growth rates of man-hours worked turned negative in 16 manufacturing industries during the third and the fourth subperiod. On the other hand, in almost all of these industries, average annual growth rates of labor quality

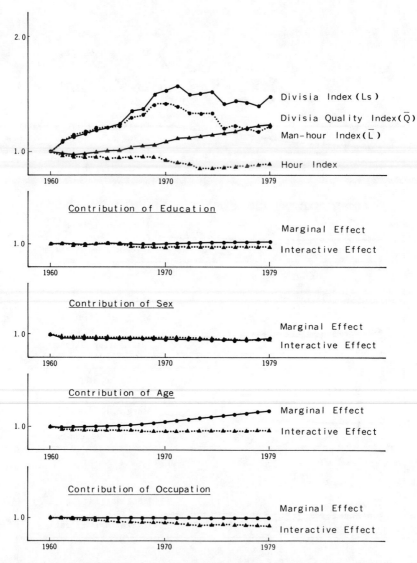

Fig. 12.3   Decomposition of labor quality change—material manufacturing industry

rose for these periods. Although quality of labor input usually plays a relatively minor role in contributing to total change in labor input, the earlier observations in agriculture-forestry-fishing and many of the manufacturing industries show that the magnitude of quality change was, in many cases, large enough to offset the decline in man-hours worked.

It is well known that many Japanese firms benefit from the institution of

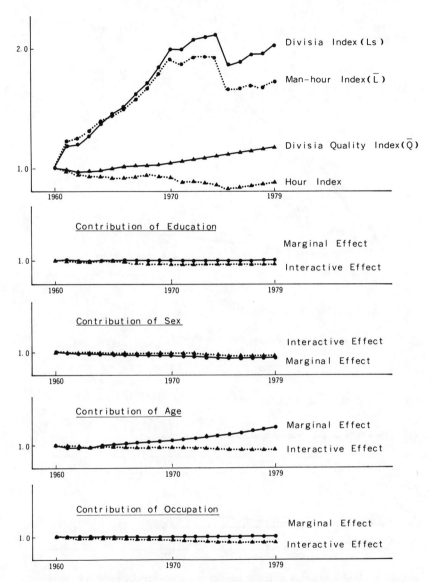

Fig. 12.4 Decomposition of labor quality change—fabricated manufacturing industry

"lifetime employment," which guarantees low labor turnover. The labor market in Japan is also structured so that most new workers are hired immediately upon finishing school at the beginning of each fiscal year (which coincides with the academic year). This implies that the age classification in our data base with its detailed disaggregation is an acceptable proxy for the experience

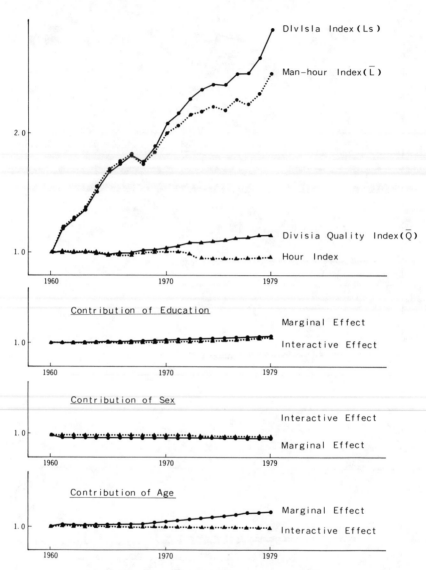

Fig. 12.5   Decomposition of labor quality change—service industry

or the on-the-job training component of all labor types. Under those considerations, if a Japanese industry exhibits a relatively low or negative rate of growth in man-hours worked, it implies a change in the age distribution of its labor force toward older workers with greater accumulated experience. Since older workers' wage rates are higher, our assumption of producer equilibrium associates higher productivity with these older workers; hence we should observe an increase in the quality of the labor force. Thus it is not surprising that our estimates show an inverse relationship between the quality change in labor input and the change in man-hours worked.

12.4.2   Decomposition of Quality Change in Labor Input in the Manufacturing Sector

A summary of growth rates of quality decomposition is given in table 12.4, and its time-series movement is shown in the lower part of figures 12.2–12.5. Here we examine the results of decomposition by individual category: sex, education, age, and occupation.

The Sex Effect

Table 12.4 shows that, during the period 1960–69, the main effect of sex in light, material, and fabricated manufacturing sectors was, respectively, -0.07%, -0.13%, and -0.24% per annum. In light and material manufacturing sectors, it turned positive more than 0.45% and 0.27%, respectively, after 1969, while in fabricated manufacturing it remained negative until 1973. After the oil crisis the effect was positive in all manufacturing sectors, of which the main effect of sex accounts for more than 30% in light manufacturing, 10% in material manufacturing, and 3% in fabricated manufacturing. This suggests that the growth rate of female labor force decreased after the oil crisis.

The sum of interactive effects in terms of sex was -0.36%, 0.008%, and -0.08% per annum in each manufacturing sector during the period 1960 to 1979. The minus sign persisted during the whole period for sex education as well as for sex and age in all manufacturing, indicating an expanding proportion of female workers and less-educated younger workers.

The Education Effect

The main effect of education is fairly high for all manufacturing sectors. It explains more than 20% of total quality change in labor input, on average, during the period 1960–79. The interactive effect between education and age increased gradually, while the interactive effect between education and occupation decreased. The increase of the education-age effect reflects the increasing proportion of older and highly educated workers in the labor force, while the decrease of the education-occupation effect represents the increase in the proportion of highly educated blue-collar workers.

In postwar Japan, the proportion of highly educated workers has increased as the result of reforms in the educational system and changes in human capital investment behavior on the part of the workers themselves. This latter trend brought about an increase in highly educated older workers, while the excess supply of highly educated younger workers caused an increase in highly educated blue-collar workers.

Relative prices among heterogeneous labor have had a great influence based

Table 12.4 Summary Table of Quality Change in Labor Input (in % per calendar year)

	1960–69	1969–73	1975–79	1960–79
Light manufacturing industry:				
Main effect:				
s	−.0680	.4536	.3024	.1283
e	.4279	.3974	.3427	.3985
a	.9411	.9088	.4966	.8359
o	.5044	.5435	.0450	.4037
Interactive effect:				
se	−.1169	−.1122	−.0987	−.1077
sa	−.4949	−.2980	−.1107	−.3510
so	−.0734	−.0674	−.0460	−.0625
ea	−.2213	.0497	.1205	−.0570
eo	−.3668	−.3225	−.2199	−.3176
ao	−.3681	−.1280	−.0274	−.2135
sea	.1476	.0068	−.0155	.0674
seo	.0643	.0758	.0529	.0624
sao	.1798	−.0107	−.0003	.0857
eao	.1794	.0218	−.0063	.0863
seao	−.1139	.0204	.0133	−.0571
Man-hour	4.3365	.7047	1.0402	2.1439
Hour	−.4178	−.8936	.5426	−.4234
Quality	.6214	1.4984	.8487	.9018
Divisia	4.9579	2.2031	1.8689	3.0457
Material manufacturing industry:				
Main effect:				
s	−.1259	.2775	.1611	.0329
e	.2369	.2342	.1508	.2213
a	.8281	.9956	.9413	.8961
o	.3995	.4531	−.0572	.3002
Interactive effect:				
se	−.0498	−.0454	−.0347	−.0454
sa	−.3193	−.1620	−.0372	−.2165
so	−.0068	.0810	.0053	.0178
ea	.0270	.2972	.3436	.1737
eo	−.2861	−.2242	−.1017	−.2262
ao	−.2382	.0739	−.0310	−.1138
sea	.0519	−.0104	−.0628	.0083
seo	−.0323	−.0076	.0033	−.0162
sao	.0754	−.0968	−.0127	.0115
eao	.0338	−.1291	−.0589	−.0262
seao	.0038	−.0037	.0176	.0055
Man-hour	3.8531	−1.6828	.0999	.9713
Hour	−.4500	−1.5974	1.0555	−.6056
Quality	.5982	1.7335	1.2266	1.0229
Divisia	4.4513	.0507	1.3265	1.9942

Table 12.4 (continued)

	1960–69	1969–73	1975–79	1960–79
Fabricated manufacturing industry:				
Main effect:				
s	−.2389	−.0738	.0406	−.0328
e	.2481	.1876	.1439	.2083
a	.6099	1.3264	1.0296	1.9314
o	.3583	.4458	.0001	.3091
Interactive effect:				
se	−.0157	−.0169	−.0364	−.0235
sa	−.1929	−.2656	−.0505	−.1962
so	.0291	.0894	.0287	.0359
ea	−.0975	.0991	.1696	.0384
eo	−.2893	−.2304	−.1951	−.2520
ao	−.1485	−.1264	−.0500	−.1255
sea	.0335	.0132	−.0253	.0066
seo	−.0007	−.0075	.0283	.0084
sao	.0113	−.0561	−.0172	−.0092
eao	.0661	−.0030	.0208	.0331
$seao$	−.0129	−.0066	−.0003	−.0084
Man-hour	6.5869	1.9528	1.1172	2.9387
Hour	−.7552	−1.6631	1.7134	−.6436
Quality	.3598	1.3753	1.0860	.3739
Divisia	6.9467	3.3281	2.2031	3.3125
Service industry:				
Main effect:				
s	−.3760	.1951	−.0249	−.1188
e	.1584	.1898	.1694	.1545
a	.4534	.9192	.6049	.6283
o				
Interactive effect:				
se	.0148	.0659	.0189	.0280
sa	−.0546	−.1320	−.0177	−.0824
so				
ea	−.0107	.1705	.2033	.0805
eo				
ao				
sea	.0046	−.0272	−.0187	−.0089
seo				
sao				
eao				
$seao$				
Man-hour	6.3940	4.3901	3.5894	4.9464
Hour	−.1113	−.4567	.4769	−.2708
Quality	.1399	1.3831	.9282	.5820
Divisia	7.0840	5.7731	4.5176	5.6284

on the Divisia index of labor input. Shimada (1981) pointed out that wage differentials in Japan were largely affected by years of experience (or age as a proxy) and years of education, and that interactive effects of education and age to wage differentials were quite high. My observation of the large main effect of education and the movement of the education-age and education-occupation interactive effects must be affected by such characteristics of wage profiles in Japan.

The Age Effect

The main effect of age explains more then 80% of quality change in labor input in Japan. This is extremely high compared to the other main effects. Interactive effects in terms of age were fairly small during the whole period, which means that the effect of age universally influenced all categories of labor as a demographic factor. The main cause of this strong age effect in all categories of labor input is the demographic trend of an aging population in Japanese society.

Under the assumption of perfect competition, the observed upward-sloping age-wage profile is interpreted to reflect the differential of marginal productivity of labor input for different age classes, which is equivalent to assuming that older people are always more productive than younger people insofar as wages increases according to age. This may appear a peculiar assumption, but, as we discussed earlier, if we regard age as the proxy for experience or the accumulation of some other relevant know-how in a company under the lifetime employment system, we cannot refute, a priori, the existence of such an equality between wages and the value of marginal productivity.

The Occupation Effect

The main effect of occupation was of almost equal magnitude as the main effect of education. It accounted for more than 40% of quality change in 1966–69, while it explained less than 40% or almost nothing of quality change in 1969–73 and in 1975–79. This means that the proportion of white-collar workers increased in the period 1966–69, but in subsequent periods it failed to increase by as much.

12.4.3   Decomposition of the Quality Change in the Service Sector

Table 12.4 also shows the summary of quality changes in the service sector. Since the service sector in the BWSS data is not classified by occupational category, we cannot observe quality change in terms of occupation. Among the remaining three categories, the age effect was the dominant factor in quality change, just as it was in the manufacturing sector. Also, the interactive effect of education and age (*EA*) began to exhibit a positive trend in the 1969–73 period, while the interactive effect of sex and age was slightly negative in the whole period.

12.4.4 Quality Change in Labor Input and Economic Growth

Comparison of the amounts of quality change in labor input reveals that quality change in the manufacturing sector has always been larger than in the service sector, as have been the main effects of age and education and the interactive effects of education and age. On the other hand, the trend of the man-hour index was leveled off after the 1969–73 period and fell into an apparent negative trend during 1973–79. These results suggests that the manufacturing sector attained a high level of labor productivity through the combination of reduction in man-hours and substitution of highly qualified workers. For the service sector, which still remained the labor absorption sector, both man-hour and quality change increased, but the degree of quality change was not so large as that of the manufacturing sector. However, if a more decomposed industry analysis were performed, it might be found that certain service industries have increased the pace of quality change and the age effect. The quality change in the service industries after the oil crisis is a topic that merits further research.

The period covered by our analysis has been 1960–79, a time in which the Japanese economy was catching up with the technology of the United States and Western Europe. From table 12.5, it is clear that quality change in labor inputs occurred continuously after the 1960s, and, as previously stated, the primary sources of quality change have been the main effects of age and education and the interactive effects of education and age. All of these effects are contributing factors to technological development, because a high level of technological development requires positive quality change in labor input, especially in education and age. Education represents the amount of general training, and age represents experience and company-specific skills. We may conclude that these distinctive features of quality change in labor input were the critical factors for the Japanese economy's productivity growth during the rapid expansion period and, in particular, for those industries that made major contributions to productivity growth by introducing highly developed technologies.

Watanabe and Egaizu (1968) estimated the quality change in labor input in Japan for 1951–64. They concluded that quality change in labor input in Japan was lower than that in other developed countries, and one reason given for this was the existence of an imitation lag in technology with respect to the United States and Western Europe. At that time, Japan depended on imported technology, so that technological progress was embodied in capital input. Therefore, the demand for high-quality labor was limited, which resulted in a low level of quality change. Watanabe and Egaizu indicated that there would be a high level of quality change in labor input as Japan's technology level reached that in the United States and Western Europe.

The result of my analysis is consistent with Watanabe and Egaizu's (1968) predictions. Although both their framework and my own treated technological

Table 12.5   **Quality Change in Labor Input in the United States**

	1959–63	1963–67	1967–71	1971–74
Main effect:				
Sex (s)	− .05	− .24	− .22	− .06
Class (c)	.14	.04	.05	.09
Age (a)	− .07	− .22	− .20	− .29
Education (e)	.72	.85	.81	.67
Occupation (j)	.37	.14	.40	− .11
Total	1.11	.57	.84	.30
Interactive effect:				
First-order:				
sc	.14	.17	.00	.02
sa	.13	.12	.02	− .01
se	.13	.13	.03	.02
sj	.17	.15	.07	− .03
ca	.12	.04	− .01	− .03
ce	.06	− .20	− .04	− .02
cj	.07	− .51	.03	− .05
ae	.12	.03	− .01	− .07
aj	.09	.00	.04	.06
ej	− .18	− .36	− .35	− .05
Total	.85	− .43	− .22	− .16
Second-order:				
sca	− .09	− .07	− .00	− .01
sce	− .10	− .11	− .00	− .01
scj	− .15	− .20	.01	− .01
sae	− .09	.00	.02	.01
saj	− .09	− .07	.00	− .01
sej	− .17	− .12	− .05	− .04
cae	− .06	− .02	.02	.02
caj	− .11	.00	− .01	.01
cej	− .08	.04	− .01	− .02
aej	− .12	− .05	− .01	.02
Total	− 1.06	− .60	− .03	− .04
Third-order:				
$scae$	.11	.03	.00	.00
$scaj$	.10	.04	.00	.01
$scej$	.10	.13	.00	.00
$saej$	.10	.03	− .01	.01
$caej$	− .02	.07	.03	.00
Total	.48	.26	− .01	.02
Fourth-order:				
$scaej$	− .11	− .03	.00	.00
Quality change	1.27	− .23	.58	.12
Total hours	− .03	2.54	.26	2.55
Divisia index	1.24	2.31	.84	2.67

Source: Chinloy (1980).

change as an exogenous factor, the results suggest that we should further investigate the relationship between technological development and quality change in labor input, especially as regards the age and education effects.

Of all the sources of quality change in labor input, the age effect is the most controversial one. In the period of our analysis, the main demographic trend has been the increase of middle-aged workers, which corresponds to an upward-sloping age-wage profile. That trend has influenced the significance of the age effect as a source of quality change in labor input. But, in the near future, as the middle-aged population enters old age, this trend will tend to correspond to a downward-sloping age-wage profile. Other things being equal, the age effect will stagnate or even become negative in the future. This will result in a stagnation in quality change. However, analysis of this problem requires a more interdependent framework, one in which the age-wage profile is treated as an endogenous factor arising from the behavioral adjustment of economic agents.

12.4.5 Comparison of Quality Change in Labor Input in Japan and the United States

We draw on Chinloy (1980) for a similar analysis of the United States (see table 12.5). He has reported some specific features of quality change in labor input in the United States which we may compare with the same phenomenon in Japan.

1. In the United States, the main effect in terms of sex was negative for the entire period 1959–74, which is the opposite of the result obtained for Japan. In Japan, the main effect in terms of sex was positive for 1966–69, on average.

2. The main effect in terms of age was negative in the United States. On the other hand, it was positive in Japan, where it accounted for more than 80% of all quality changes.

3. The main effect in terms of education was positive both in the United States and Japan. It ranged from 0.67%–0.85% in the United States, which was somewhat higher than that in Japan.

4. The interactive effect between education and occupation was negative in the United States. During the periods 1963–67 and 1967–71, its magnitude was more than 40% of total quality changes. On the other hand, the interactive efect between education and age was negligible in the United States, which is a difference between the two countries.

5. In the United States, the kinds of quality change found were the result of recent shifts within the labor force as the amounts of female and younger workers increased. Such changes consequently worsened improvements in the quality of labor inputs. On the other hand, the effect of education contributed to the improvement of labor quality, although a negative interactive effect between education and occupation offset this improvement to some extent. Chinloy explained this situation as "overeducation" in the United States.

6. Finally, quality changes in the United States, on average, were smaller than those in Japan. In the United States, quality change was 1.27% per year in 1959–63, 0.23% in 1963–67, and 0.58% in 1967–71, while in Japan quality change was greater than 1.0% per year throughout the whole period.

The characteristics of quality change are the cause of the differences in productivity performance in the U.S. and Japan. We may conclude that the high degree of quality change of labor input in Japan favorably affected the development of technology, which resulted in high labor productivity. The low level of quality change of labor input in the United States slowed the growth of labor productivity.

12.5 Summary and Conclusion

Our analysis started with an observation of sectoral changes in labor input. Agriculture showed a constant reduction in man-hours, whereas the service sector exhibited a stable increase. The manufacturing sector, including mining and construction, showed a positive trend at first, but this turned negative after the 1969–73 period. In addition, quality change in labor input in the manufacturing sector was always larger than that of the service sector. Consequently, this quality change influenced the relatively high level of labor productivity in the manufacturing sector.

Further, we decomposed quality change in labor input using Divisia indices, which are consistent with transcendental logarithmic aggregator functions under certain assumptions. The results showed that total quality changes in labor inputs in Japan were always positive through 1960–79 and that the sources of these quality changes were mainly an age effect, an education effect, and the interactive effects of education-age and education-occupation (only for the secondary industries). Causes for these effects were the increase in experienced middle-aged workers, the growing proportion of highly educated workers, a reduction in less-educated young workers, an increase in better-educated older workers, and the decrease in less-educated blue-collar workers.

During our observation period, the Japanese economy was catching up with the technology of the United States and Western Europe. If we assume that a high technology level requires highly qualified workers, the results of this paper concerning quality change in labor inputs are consistent with this "catching-up" process. The coincidence of quality change in labor input and technological development has been the most distinctive feature of the rapid productivity change in the Japanese economy.

Among sources of quality change, the age effect provided the most significant contribution. This is because of an increase in the proportion of experienced middle-aged workers whose wages are on the upward slope of the age-wage profile. In the future, if the number of older workers whose wages are on the downward slope of the age-wage profile increases, the age effect will stagnate or even become negative, all else being equal. This eventuality depends on whether the shift of the age-wage profile for older workers will be upward or downward.

The comparison between the United States and Japan apparently showed that quality change in labor input in the United States was small compared to that of Japan, especially in terms of the sex and age effects. Only the education effect turned out to have significantly positive value; however, its impact was reduced when an adjustment for occupation was made. These comparative results suggest there are different input structures for the United States and Japan. Above all, quality change in labor input has not been a contributing factor to productivity change in the United States, while it has contributed significantly in Japan.

My analysis in this paper is part of larger research work investigating the interdependent mechanisms governing the relationship between input structure, economic growth, and technological progress. Further investigation of other factor inputs, such as capital and intermediate inputs is needed, as well as of the interaction among labor, capital, and intermediate inputs.

Notes

1. Under this restriction we can obtain path-independent indices of labor, capital, and intermediate inputs. See Berndt and Christensen (1973) and Hulten (1973).

2. In the empirical analysis section, I use these four categories as the measures of labor quality.

3. I should also note here that the Divisia index is biased if wages do not equal the value of the marginal product. However, in Japanese companies there are frequent retraining programs, such as job-rotation systems, accompanied by on-the-job training, and off-the-job training for middle management and executives. The frequency of retraining will generally increase to keep pace with technological development, especially for the period of rapid expansion of the Japanese economy. Consequently, under the existence of the internal training and promotion system in the Japanese company, it is not unwarranted to assume that the equality between wages and the value of marginal productivity. We cannot refute, a priori, the existence of such an equality between wages and value of marginal productivity.

4. The definition of employees in the BWSS is as follows: (a) workers without a particular contract regarding period of employment; (b) workers with contracts for more than three months; (c) temporary and daily workers employed in the same enterprise for more than 18 days per month in the preceding two months.

5. Industries are classified as follows: (1) light manufacturing (mining; construction; food and related products; apparel and textiles, furniture and fixtures, rubber, stone, clay, and glass products; textile mill products; lumber and wood products; printing and publishing; leather and leather products; fabricated metal products); (2) material manufacturing (paper and allied products; petroleum refining and related products; nonferrous metals; chemicals and chemical by-products; iron and steel; miscellaneous manufacturing); (3) fabricated manufacturing (machinery; transportation equipment; electrical machinery; precision instruments); (4) service industry (transportation and communication; wholesale and trade; real estate; public utilities; finance and insurance; services).

References

Berndt, E. R., and L. R. Christensen. 1973. The internal structure of functional relationships: Separability, substitution and aggregation. *Review of Economic Studies* 40:403–10.

Chinloy, P. 1980. Sources of quality change in labor input. *American Economic Review* 70:109–19.

Denison, E. F., and W. K. Chung. 1976. *How Japan's economy grew so fast: The sources of postwar expansion.* Washington, D.C.: Brookings.

Diewert, W. E. 1976. Exact and superlative index numbers. *Journal of Econometrics* 4:115–45.

Hulten, C. R. 1973. Divisia index numbers. *Econometrica* 41:1017–25.

Management and Coordination Agency, Statistics Bureau. Various years. *Roudouryoku chousa houkoku* (Labor force survey).

Ministry of International Trade and Industry. Various years. *Kougyou toukei hyou* (Census of manufactures). Tokyo: Ministry of Finance Bureau of Printing.

Ministry of Labor. Various years. *Chingin kouzou kihon toukei chousa* (Basic wage structure survey). Tokyo: Institute of Labor Law.

Shimada, H. 1981. *Earnings structure and human investment.* Tokyo: Keio Economic Observatory.

Tachibanaki, T. 1973. Quality change in labor input and wage differentials: A study of Japanese manufacturing industries. Ph.D. diss. Johns Hopkins University.

Watanabe, T., and N. Egaizu. 1968. *Rodoryoku no shitu to keizai seicho—sengo Nippon ni tsuite* (Improvement of labor quality and economic growth—postwar Japan's experience). *Economic Studies Quarterly* 19:38–52.

Comment   Walter Y. Oi

Robert Sproull, in assuming the presidency of the University of Rochester stated, "Technology and capital investment have increased productivity in other areas, notably manufacturing, but has been of little help to universities as counters to inflation. Thus, it is remarkable that for four decades or more, the price of a year at the University of Rochester including board and room has remained about equal to the price of a full-sized Chevrolet (*Rochester Review* [Spring, 1975], 3). He did not go on to say that most families do not buy four new Chevys in successive years. Further, a 1974 Chevy is not the same as a 1936 Chevy. In addition, the quality of education supplied by the University of Rochester had also changed over that 40-year span. Data from the *Historical Statistics of the United States* and the 1983 *Statistical Abstract of the United States* provide another irrelevant comparison. In 1936, a new car was equal to 996 hours of work by a typical factory worker, but, by 1974, it took only 826 hours to pay for a new car. My colleague immediately pointed out that "an hour of work in 1974 embodied more human capital than an hour

Walter Y. Oi is the Elmer B. Milliman Professor of Economics at the University of Rochester.

of work in 1936." This new-car numeraire illustrates the difficulties that we encounter in measuring economic growth and in making welfare comparisons when the qualities of outputs and inputs are both changing.

The ultimate aim of this paper is to measure the contribution of the labor input to the growth of Japanese output. Labor is heterogeneous, and the composition of the Japanese work force has varied over the two decades covered in this study. In addition, the makeup of industry-specific labor forces has also varied. Imamura has quantified these changes to arrive at estimates of the quality-adjusted labor input for each of 29 industries. He recognized that quality is endogenous, but he does not develop a formal analysis that can explain quality changes.

The methodology is a familiar one. Suppose that the heterogeneity could be described by two traits, say, sex i and education j. If I let asterisks denote logarithms and denote man-hours by H_{ij}, I obtain the following counterparts to Imamura's equations:

(1)
$$dH^* = H_t^* - H_{t-1}^*, \quad H_t^* = \ln \Sigma\Sigma H_{ij,t},$$

(2)
$$dL_i^* = \sum_i V_i dH_i^*, \quad [H_i = \sum_j H_{ij}],$$

(3)
$$dL_{ih}^* = \sum_i \sum_j V_{ij} dH_{ij}^*.$$

Here, (1) is the man-hours index, (2) demonstrates the first-order main effect, and (3) is the second-order interactive effect. The main effect of the ith trait on the quality-change index is given by

(4)
$$Q_i = dL_i^* - dH^* \quad Q_j = dL_j^* - dH^*.$$

(5)
$$Q_{ij} = (dL_{ij}^* - dH^*) - Q_i - Q_j.$$

Thus, the total quality change in this example can be decomposed into two main effects plus one interactive effect.

(6)
$$Q = dL_{ij}^* - dH^* = Q_{ij} + Q_i + Q_j.$$

Imamura identified four traits; sex, $s = 2$, occupation, $o = 2$, education, $e = 4$, and age, $a = 12$ for a total of 192 cells for each industry over the 20 years in his sample.

He also assembled data on employment, hours, and pay (the sum of earnings plus annual bonuses) of regular employees from the Basic Wage Surveys, 1960–79. These data were used to develop the Divisia index of the labor input L^s shown in table 1. If capital and labor inputs are not adjusted for quality changes, then technical progress (total factor productivity) accounted for 50% of the growth rate of annual output, but this figure drops to 25% after quality-change adjustments. Indexes of man-hours, quality-adjusted labor inputs, and the quality-change index Q are calculated for each industry and are summarized by growth rates in tables 2, 3, and 4. Table 5 illustrates the decomposition of the growth rate in the labor input for four industries. Comparisons of labor quality changes in the U.S. and Japan are shown in tables 4 and 5.

Imamura's estimates indicate that the quality of the labor input improved at an annual rate of 1% a year in Japan, which is substantially higher than the rate of improvement in the United States. Age and education are mainly responsible for this improvement. He chose to present all of his empirical results in terms of indexes and growth rates. In table 1, I show the educational distribution of regular (full-time) Japanese employees in 1980 classified by age, sex, and firm size for all industries and for males in manufacturing in 1970 and 1980. The latter comparison reveals the upward shift in the educational attainment in manufacturing, while the top panel reveals that educational at-

Table 1   **Percentage Distribution of Regular Employees in Japan, by Education**

	Employment (000)	Lower Secondary School	Upper Secondary School	Junior College	College
All industries, 1980:					
Males, all firms	13,704.2	32.68	44.42	3.26	19.65
Small	4,882.4	41.21	43.46	3.40	11.94
Medium	4,533.6	29.70	44.44	3.62	22.23
Large	4,288.2	26.10	45.49	2.71	25.69
Females, all firms	6,214.5	33.32	53.57	10.16	2.94
Small	2,529.3	41.42	47.24	9.04	2.30
Medium	2,077.6	34.88	52.25	9.27	3.59
Large	1,607.7	18.55	65.24	13.10	3.11
Manufacturing, 1980:					
Males, all firms	5,603.6	40.38	44.11	1.90	13.61
Small	1,675.8	52.33	39.27	1.66	6.73
Medium	1,841.8	37.28	44.97	2.12	15.62
Large	2,086	33.49	47.23	1.90	17.38
Females, all firms	2,408.8	52.25	43.11	3.52	1.13
Small	1,016.1	61.42	35.97	1.95	0.66
Medium	902.5	51.82	43.60	3.28	1.29
Large	490.3	34.00	56.99	7.20	1.79
Manufacturing, 1970:					
Males, all firms	5,821.8	53.69	35.73	1.81	8.76
Small	1,650.6	65.90	28.74	1.47	3.89
Medium	1,759.9	51.29	37.12	1.94	9.64
Large	2,411.2	47.09	39.52	1.94	11.46
Females, all firms	2,843.3	65.14	34.86	.00	.00
Small	1,021.8	72.09	27.91	.00	.00
Medium	962.8	66.11	33.89	.00	.00
Large	858.7	55.81	44.19	.00	.00

Source: Basic Wage Survey, Japan.
Note: Small = 10–99; medium = 100–999; large = 1,000 + .

Table 2   **Percentage Distribution of Employed Persons and Employees by Sex and Age, 1970 and 1980**

	1970			1980		
	Both	Male	Female	Both	Male	Female
A. Employed Persons:						
15–19	5.8	4.7	7.5	2.5	2.0	3.4
20–24	15.5	13.8	18.3	9.6	7.9	12.2
25–34	24.2	26.8	20.2	25.4	27.8	21.7
35–44	23.9	24.3	23.3	24.8	25.0	24.6
45–54	15.9	14.8	17.5	21.5	21.2	22.0
55–64	10.1	10.5	9.6	11.1	10.8	11.7
65+	4.5	5.1	3.6	4.9	5.3	4.4
Total (in Millions)	50.94	30.91	20.03	55.36	33.94	21.42
B. Employees:						
15–19	7.8	5.4	12.6	3.2	2.3	5.0
20–24	20.6	16.5	28.9	12.4	9.3	18.2
25–34	26.6	30.2	19.4	28.3	30.9	23.4
35–44	20.9	22.3	18.1	24.9	25.6	23.6
45–54	15.2	15.5	14.6	20.1	20.3	19.9
55–64	6.8	7.5	5.4	8.4	8.7	7.9
65+	2.0	2.4	1.1	2.6	2.9	1.8
Total (in Millions)	33.06	22.10	10.96	39.71	26.17	13.54

Source: Japan Statistical Yearbook (1983), table 3-2.

tainment is higher for men and for workers in large firms. The main effect of education was, however, stronger in the United States as a factor improving labor quality. Imamura argues that for regular employees, age is a good proxy for job tenure and hence for firm-specific human capital. Reference to the Basic Wage Surveys reveals, however, that it is an imperfect proxy, especially for females and, to a lesser extent, for males in small firms. The data in table 2 show that the percentage of all employed persons and of paid employees who were under 35 years of age fell sharply between 1970 and 1980. This shift in the age distribution of employees (putting more toward the peak of the age-earnings profiles) was the most important contributor to the quality gains in the Japanese labor input. In the United States, the fraction of employees in the youngest age groups rose so that age made a negative contribution to the quality of the U.S. labor input.

The measurements in this study pertain to the quality of regular employees who made up only 49.9% of all employed persons in 1960 and 64.8% in 1980; see the data in table 3. Regular employees tend to work longer hours, so that they probably accounted for a larger share of total man-hours and of quality-adjusted man-hours. The declining importance of self-employed and unpaid family workers is due, in part, to sectoral shifts out of agriculture, fisheries, and aquaculture. The omission of these workers, whose remuneration is either in kind or as a residual claimant, is serious. Table 4 shows that, in manufac-

Table 3   Percentage Distribution of Employed Persons by Employment Status and Sex

Employment Status	Both Sexes			Males	
	1960	1970	1980	1970	1980
Employed persons (in millions)	44.36	50.94	55.36	30.91	33.94
Percentage who were:					
1. Self-employed	22.7	19.2	17.2	22.4	19.4
2. Family workers	23.9	15.8	10.9	6.0	3.3
3. Paid employees	53.4	64.9	71.3	71.5	77.1
4. Paid regular employees	49.9	59.3	64.8	67.4	73.0

Source: Japanese Statistical Yearbook (1983), table 3-3, pp. 72–73.

Table 4   Paid Employees and Females as Percentage of Employed Persons by Industry, 1980

Industry	Employed Persons[a]	% Paid Employees	% Female Employees
All industries	55,665	71.8	37.9
Agriculture	5,426	2.7	50.7
Fisheries	459	37.5	21.6
Mining	111	94.6	10.8
Construction	5,364	77.0	13.0
Manufacturing	13,145	85.1	36.1
Wholesale/Retail Trade	12,633	65.8	45.4
Finance	1,604	96.1	48.6
Real Estate	433	70.4	34.0
Transportation/Communication	3,476	94.8	11.6
Electricity	348	100.0	14.1
Services	10,346	79.4	49.7
Government	2,023	100.0	21.3
Miscellaneous	119	47.1	43.7

Source: Japan Statistical Yearbook (1983), table 3–5, pp. 74–75.
[a]In thousands.

turing, only 85.1% of all employed persons were wage and salaried employees (some of whom were casual or temporary day workers) and only 65.8% in wholesale/retail trade. I suspect that the quality changes of these omitted workers did not follow the same time path as quality changes of regular employees. Finally, we find that paid employees make up a larger share of all employed persons at younger ages. We clearly need to learn more about the productivity and returns to these unpaid workers.

The quality change in the labor input is decomposed into four main effects and interactive effects for sex, occupation, education, and age. The author has, however, ignored the classification by firm size that can be obtained from the Basic Wage Survey. Monthly wages and annual bonuses are substantially higher in large firms, suggesting that labor productivity is also greater. Workers in larger firms have more formal schooling (as shown in table 1) and longer job tenures. Some economists have argued that these higher wages are supported by larger investments in general and firm-specific human capital. My research on this topic leads me to conclude that the higher wages in larger firms are due in large part to a greater effort intensity of work. Employees in the larger manufacturing firms receive less time for breaks, time off for personal business, and so on, and are obliged to maintain a faster work pace. A shift in the distribution of employed persons from small to large firms will thus be accompanied by a rise in labor productivity. It would be useful to see how big a difference this firm-size adjustment would make in the quality-change component of the labor input.

The author correctly argues that labor quality is endogenous. His conjectural hypothesis is that a faster rate of technical progress will induce a higher rate of quality improvement. I presume that the technical progress will raise the returns to human capital leading to this outcome. The rate of total factor productivity growth varies over time and across industries. These variations could be correlated with labor-quality changes to test this hypothesis, and this is surely an obvious direction for future research.

My closing comments go beyond the Imamura paper to criticize the received methodology of Divisia indexes in measuring technical progress. Each industry or sector presumably supplies a single product that is related to input flows via a translog production function. Over the last 40 years, nonproduction worker employment has grown relative to the input of blue-collar production workers. A translog production function interprets this rise in the ratio of nonproduction to production worker man-hours as a substitution of the former for the latter in producing a given product, say Wheaties. Every manufacturing firm is, however, a multiproduct firm that jointly supplies Wheaties at the factory doorstep, packing crates, delivery services, advertising, and insurance. The postwar growth in nonproduction worker employment can largely be explained as an expansion of the manufacturing firm's activities into finance, insurance, distribution, and so on. In short, the parameters of a translog production function must surely depend on the firm or industry's "output mix." The maintained assumption of stable parameters is untenable.

This methodology also assumes that factor markets are perfectly competitive. The wage is the "price" of labor. Labor is homogeneous within each type or grade of labor. Labor services are exchanged in spot markets where marginal-value products are equated to wages in each period. The validity of this neoclassical model has been questioned at both the theoretical and empirical levels. Contract and search theories rest on the assumption that workers and jobs are *not* interchangeable. There is something to be gained from estab-

Table 5   Average Monthly Labor Cost per Regular Employee in Japan by Industry, Size of Enterprise, and Kind of Labor Cost

	Total Pay[a]	Earnings	Other Labor Costs[a]	Required Welfare	Pension	Fringe Benefits	Hiring and Training
Year:							
1975	198.0	86.38	27.0	44.9	22.9	27.0	5.3
1977	242.1	85.33	35.5	45.3	24.5	25.5	4.7
1978	263.8	84.58	40.7	44.4	26.0	25.2	4.4
1979	279.0	84.81	42.4	45.5	25.7	23.4	5.5
1980	294.5	85.13	43.8	47.4	23.2	23.3	6.1
1981	311.3	84.39	48.6	47.9	21.5	25.6	5.0
By firm size:[b]							
30–99	242.1	86.10	33.7	59.7	14.9	21.9	3.5
100–299	262.3	85.85	37.1	55.4	16.9	23.0	4.7
300–999	304.7	85.15	45.3	51.1	20.4	22.9	5.6
1,000–4,999	355.3	83.76	57.7	44.3	24.1	26.1	5.6
5,000 or more	400.1	82.25	71.0	38.7	25.8	30.4	5.2
By industry:[b]							
Mining	405.7	74.41	103.8	40.3	36.6	20.7	2.3
Construction	309.5	84.16	49.0	58.6	14.3	23.2	3.9
Manufacturing	311.8	84.25	49.1	47.1	22.2	26.2	4.6
Apparel	202.9	86.57	27.3	54.3	18.4	21.9	5.5
Iron and Steel	416.1	81.53	76.9	40.1	25.6	30.0	4.4
Fabricated metals	291.1	84.49	45.1	54.0	19.3	23.1	3.6
Transportation Equipment	342.9	85.17	50.9	50.9	16.2	27.7	5.2
W/R Trade	276.8	85.49	40.2	47.9	18.2	27.0	6.8
Wholesale	317.4	84.96	47.7	46.3	20.4	27.8	5.5
Retail	232.8	86.28	31.9	50.67	14.6	25.7	9.0
Finance	404.5	83.29	67.6	36.7	25.6	31.8	5.9
Transportation and Communication	336.1	84.81	51.1	54.2	23.8	18.2	3.8
Electricity	437.0	78.05	95.9	29.3	39.7	24.6	6.5
Services	260.1	86.14	36.1	51.0	16.5	26.4	6.1

Source: Japan Statistical Yearbook (1983), table 3-38, p. 109.
[a]Total pay and other labor costs are expressed in thousands of yen per month.
[b]1981.

lishing durable employment relations. Given an implicit contract, wages can diverge from marginal-value products so long as the present values of the two are equated at the time that the contract is "signed." At an empirical level, total employee conpensation and total labor costs include more than cash earnings. In table 5, I reproduce data from the 1983 *Japan Statistical Year-book*. In 1981, obligatory (required) contributions to welfare programs, employer contributions to retirement (pensions), voluntary contributions to employee welfare (fringes), and recruiting, training, and miscellaneous other labor costs accounted for 15.61% of total pay of regular employees. These "other labor costs" are growing relative to cash earnings as evidenced by the secular decline in the ratio of cash earnings to total pay shown in the second column of table 5. Cash earnings are seen to comprise a larger share of total pay in smaller firms. The ratio of obligatory contributions to welfare (payroll taxes) to cash earnings rose from 7.07% in 1975 to 8.86% in 1981. This ratio, (payroll taxes/cash earnings) is inversely related to the size of enterprise varying from 9.65% in firms with 30–99 employees to 8.34% in firms with 5,000 or more employees. The data in table 5 also reveal a wide dispersion in the relative costs of pensions, recruiting/training costs, and fringe benefits. Some studies have acknowledged the presence of these "other labor costs" by replacing the hourly wage by an hourly total pay that includes the *average* hourly cost of fringes and taxes. This is *not* the right way to incorporate these other labor costs. The "correct" price of labor should measure its marginal cost per incremental hour worked and not per hour paid. Then labor costs, C, are related to man-hours, H, in a nonlinear fashion: $C + g(H)$, rather than $C = WH$. The marginal labor cost, $C' = g'(H)$, should be used to calculate the proper value shares appearing in equations (16)–(19). Imamura, Jorgenson, Christiansen, and others compute value shares by assuming that the wage W is the marginal labor cost; thus, their value shares for the ith type of labor are $V_i = W_i H_i / \Sigma W_i H_i$. If C' is the marginal labor cost per incremental hour, the correct value share is $V_i' = C_i' H_i / \Sigma C_i' H_i$. One should also question the separability of materials from labor and capital inputs. At the 1985 NBER conference, "Productivity Growth in Japan and the United States," Kurosawa stated that casual and temporary day workers are significant in many industries. Moreover, their labor costs are often put into the account for purchased materials. If true, material costs, as measured, are not separable from labor costs.

The indexes of the labor input developed by Imamura represent a major improvement over earlier series. There is room for further research, especially in measuring the contribution of nonwage employees (the self-employed and family workers), who constitute a significant fraction of all employed persons in agriculture, wholesale/retail trade, and services. Studies of the U.S. labor market have shown that labor productivity is higher in unionized firms, which also happen to be larger firms. Kurosawa pointed out that in Japan, labor productivity in large firms was substantially higher than that in small firms within the same industry. I believe that the higher productivity in large firms is not the result of firm-specific training and human capital, but rather a more intensive level of work effort demanded by the large firms. If workers in large firms have to cope with a speedier assembly line, take shorter rest breaks, and conform to a disciplined work environment, they are, in a very real sense, supplying man-hours of labor that are of a higher quality than the hours supplied by employees working in smaller firms. A shift of man-hours toward employment in larger firms is just as much of an improvement in labor quality as a shift in the mix of workers from younger to prime-age males. The differences in wages and productivity across firm-size categories are large enough to warrant further investigation if we are to understand the sources of productivity growth.

13 Technical Change and Human Capital Acquisition in the U.S. and Japanese Labor Markets

Hong W. Tan

The contribution of education to productivity growth is widely accepted among economists and is reflected in its inclusion in growth accounting studies. Less well understood is the role played by postschooling investments in human capital, such as training or informal learning on the job. What kinds of training are most important for productivity growth? Do these tend to be general skills or firm-specific skills? How do labor markets provide price signals to induce investments in the appropriate kinds of training? What kinds of employment relationships and compensation schemes are needed to encourage investments in skills required by technical change? Answers to these questions should provide insights into how labor markets function to facilitate technical change and productivity growth.

In this regard, a comparison of how U.S. and Japanese labor markets operate, and the way in which they facilitate productivity growth, is particularly interesting. Some observers in the past have sought to explain higher rates of productivity growth in Japan than in the United States in terms of differences in labor market organization, contrasting Japan's unique institutions of lifetime employment (*syushin koyosei*) and seniority-based wage compensation (*nenko joretsu seido*) with a spot-market characterization of the way U.S. labor markets operate. These institutions, they argue, instill loyalty and motivate increased work effort and training among Japanese workers, and reduce workers' opposition to introduction of new technologies. In contrast, weak worker-firm attachment and high labor turnover in the United States may retard work incentives and investments in training and inhibit innovation.

Neither characterization of U.S. and Japanese labor markets appears well

Hong W. Tan is an economist in the Economics and Statistics Department of the RAND Corporation.

Views expressed in this paper are the author's own and are not necessarily shared by RAND or its research sponsors.

founded. The culturally based argument for Japan is at odds with evidence that these labor practices are concentrated only among larger firms, that they are of recent origin (after the 1920s), and that they arose with the onset of modern economic growth. Recent studies indicate that long-term jobs are also prevalent in the U.S. labor market (Hall 1982). However, jobs are typically of shorter duration and have slower rates of wage growth with seniority as compared to Japan (Hashimoto and Raisian 1985). Explanations for these cross-national similarities and differences in employment and wage practices offer potentially important insights into how labor markets operate to facilitate technological change.

This paper presents a model of technology-specific skills that seeks to explain why these labor market practices are found in some firms but not others, and how such practices may be related to productivity growth in the two countries. The model hypothesizes that technological change is associated with a greater demand for firm-specific investments in learning about new technologies and, to the extent that more-educated workers are better adept at learning, with a greater demand for a better educated work force as well. If the potential for technical change differs across industries, differences in specific training and the resulting returns to such investments should be reflected in interindustry wage-tenure profiles (and schooling returns), which vary systematically with the rate of total factor productivity growth. Given the technology gap between the two countries (see Jorgenson, Kuroda and Nishimizu 1985), learning opportunities are also greater in Japan and, if translated into increased training investments, should be reflected in cross-national differences in wage profiles as well. Another implication of the model—that long-term jobs are more common in technologically progressive industries—follows from skill specificity, since neither workers nor employers have any incentive to invest in specific training in the absence of a durable employment relationship. This prediction, though not explicitly addressed in this paper, may explain why jobs in Japan tend to be of relatively longer duration.

The paper also addresses the complementary hypothesis that rapid growth itself may induce increased firm-specific training. For a given commodity or product class, the derived demand for skills specific to that particular production technology is larger the more rapid the output growth of that industry. To the extent that demand growth outstrips the supply of these skills in the open market, employers must devote increased resources to developing these technology-specific skills in-house. Cross-national differences in the rate of output growth—over 8% in Japan and about 3.5% in the United States over the 1960–79 period—may account for both greater training investments and more frequent internalization of training in Japanese companies than in American firms. The technology-specific skills and output-growth hypotheses are jointly tested in the paper.

Tests of these hypotheses use the May 1979 Current Population Survey for the United States and the 1977 Employment Status Survey for Japan. Both surveys are broad-based nationally representative samples of the labor force in the two countries, containing similar information on schooling attainment, work experience, years of tenure on the current job, and earnings. To these data are merged industry indices of total factor productivity growth estimated by Jorgenson, Gollop, and Fraumeni (1986) for the United States and unpublished estimates by Kuroda (1985) for Japan. Because information on firm size is available, the analysis also explores variations in the postulated relationships across firm sizes. Previous studies, both in the United States and in Japan, have found systematic variations in earnings and job tenure across firm size (e.g., Shimada 1981; Mellow 1982; Hashimoto and Raisian 1985). Though these differences could reflect differential investments in firm-specific training (Kuratani 1973), they may also reflect the idiosyncratic nature of production in large firms (Oi 1983) or problems of monitoring worker performance that are exacerbated in larger firms.

The last point highlights a potential difficulty in distinguishing between firm-specific training explanations on the one hand and a broad class of implicit labor contract theories on the other. Both predict steeply rising wage-tenure profiles, though the implicit contract theories make no assumptions about training. Instead, steeply rising wage profiles are offered by employers to reduce incentives to shirk (Lazear 1981) or to attract workers with low quit propensities (Salop and Salop 1976). Another difficulty, raised by several recent papers (Abraham and Farber 1987; Altonji and Shakotko 1987), is in the interpretation of wage-tenure profiles. They argue (and demonstrate) that the estimated tenure coefficient in cross-sectional wage models is upward biased by the omission of measures of job-match quality. Both issues are addressed for the U.S. case, using information on reported training, and evidence is found to support the maintained hypothesis that wage-tenure profile differences are attributable primarily to specific training investments.

Section 13.1 provides the justification for the technology-specific skills model and reviews both U.S. and Japanese labor-market research for insights into the link between technical change and human capital investments. Section 13.2 describes the U.S. and Japanese data and the specification of the earnings models to be estimated. Section 13.3 presents the empirical results and discusses the similarities and differences in the relationship between technical change and skill acquisition in the two labor markets. Several qualifications about the interpretation of wage-tenure profiles are also addressed here. The conclusions are summarized in section 13.4.

13.1   The Link between Technical Change and Human Capital

The relationship between technical change and skill acquisition is based on an economic model of technology-specific skills (Tan 1980). This model draws upon, and integrates, elements from the technical change literature, human capital theories (Becker 1975), and the allocative efficiency of schooling hypothesis (Welch 1970). The hypotheses are that individuals working with new technologies acquire new and more productive skills specific to that technology, and that better-educated labor are more adept in this learning. The theoretical justification for these hypotheses are developed below.

13.1.1 The Technology-Specific Skills Model

First, consider the notion that skill acquisition is greater in more technologically progressive firms. We know from microeconomic studies of the innovative process that much of the productivity gains from introducing a new technology comes from making cumulative small modifications in it, essentially through an intensive learning-by-doing process (Enos 1962; Hollander 1965). Indeed, the Horndal effect—a phenomenon in which labor productivity increases of 2%–4% per annum are observed in plants with fixed facilities—may be a consequence of these learning and innovative activities. If so, then innovative firms have an incentive to motivate increased worker investments in learning about new technologies and to monopolize the new information embodied in workers' skills.

They can do this by sharing in the costs of skill acquisition and paying workers out of that component of productivity that is specific to the innovating firm. The familiar bilateral monopoly problem associated with skill specificity (Becker 1975) arises here as well. On the one hand, workers have few incentives to learn about new technologies since skills acquired may not be readily transferred to alternative uses; furthermore, such skills are subject (presumably) to more rapid rates of obsolescence when innovation is high. Employers, on the other hand, are denied any innovative rents since new technologies cannot be used effectively without these skills. The solution is for worker-firm sharing of the costs and returns to specific training (Hashimoto 1979). "Lifetime employment" guarantees could allay concerns about risky skill investments and encourage increased training and retraining as older skills become obsolescent over time.

Innovative firms are also more likely to use highly educated and technically skilled workers, especially at the outset of a new technology when experience is so limited. This assertion is based on the argument that better-educated workers are more adept at critically evaluating new information, and therefore learn more (Welch 1970). The evidence from U.S. farming appears to support the hypothesis about schooling's "signal-extraction" effects. The schooling attainment of farmers is positively correlated with farm incomes and the speed with which farmers allocate resources in a dynamically changing environment (Schultz 1975). Several case studies also document the decline in the industrial demand for educated workers as technologies become routinized and widely diffused (Setzer 1974). More broadly based empirical research by Bartel and Lichtenberg (1987) reveal that the relative demand for educated workers across manufacturing industries declines as the capital stock (and presumably the technology embodied in it) ages.

These perspectives provide the basis for the model's predictions about the relationships between technical change, specific training, and schooling. Unlike firm-specific human capital, which is thought to be idiosyncratic, technology-specific skills are hypothesized to be firm-specific only in so far as the company retains exclusive access to that technology. Over time, these embodied technology-specific skills become general as that technology diffuses to other firms; accordingly, the quasi rents that these skills command also fall. However, firms that innovate faster than the rate at which their technologies diffuse to others can continue to generate new skills and quasi rents. Thus, this model predicts systematically higher returns both to specific training and to schooling in firms experiencing rapid technical change.

Rapid economic growth may also lead to increased firm-specific training. For a given product, the derived demand for skills specific to that particular production technology is likely to vary systematically with the rate of output growth. To the extent that demand growth outstrips the ability of the labor market to supply these skills (firms can either develop these skills internally or hire workers away from competitors using the same production technology), employers must devote increased resources to developing these technology-specific skills in-house. Thus, holding technical change constant, this ancillary hypothesis predicts that firms in rapidly growing industries invest more in specific-training than do slow-growing firms.

Another implication of the model—that long-term jobs are likely to be found in more technologically progressive industries—follows from skill specificity. In essence, neither workers nor employers have any incentive to invest in specific training in the absence of a durable employment relationship. Though we do not explicitly examine this implication of the model, it is useful to briefly review several recent studies that seek to explain Japanese lifetime employment and wage practices in terms of technological change.[1]

13.1.2 A Selective Review of Japanese Research

A major focus of labor-market research in Japan has been on explaining "dualism" in the wage and employment practises of large and small firms. Large firms in Japan not only pay higher wages but also extend the guarantee of lifetime employment to workers; this in contrast to small firms, where pay is lower and labor turnover higher. One explanation for this dualism is that it is technology induced. Taira (1970) dates the origin of lifetime employment and *nenko-joretsu* (seniority-based) wage practices in Japan at some time during the 1920s or 1930s. These practices were adopted primarily by large firms—who were the major importers of foreign technology—to reduce high rates of labor turnover (by present-day standards) among skilled workers. Dualism exists, he argued, because of the coexistence of large firms using modern technology and small firms using traditional (indigenous) production methods.

Yasuba (1976) extends this line of argument to examine the model's implication that firm-size wage differentials in an industry increase with the induction of foreign technology but subsequently diminish with its diffusion to other firms in the industry, including small firms. For four cross sections in time from 1909 to 1951, he allocates industries to either a "dualistic" or a "homogeneous" category on the basis of the coefficient of variation (to measure wage spread) and the size elasticity of wages (to measure the association of high wages and firm size). With information on which industries had purchased foreign technology and when, Yasuba finds considerable support for this hypothesis. For example, the period preceding World War I was a period of rapid foreign-induced technical change in textiles, and six of ten dualistic industries were textile related. In later years, the dualistic industries were no longer concentrated in textiles, and, in fact, for the apparel and hosiery industries, firm-size wage differentials narrowed in the face of generally widening trends. Iron and steel, bricks and tiles, and printing industries all experienced rapid technical change after World War II and appeared in the dualistic category. These findings suggest that firm-size wage differentials in dualistic industries may be associated with quasi rents from the use of foreign technology by large firms, rents that disappear when technology is widely diffused to other firms.

Research by Saxonhouse (1976) also establishes a link between the nature of technology and labor turnover. He speculates that the use of identical technology contributed to high labor turnover in the Japanese cotton-spinning industry at the turn of the century. He rejects the hypothesis that employers had few incentives to retain workers because no productivity advantages were gained by increased tenure in the firm. Estimating a translog production function whose parameters are explained by variables such as schooling, years of tenure, and the number of trained engineers, he finds that increases in these variables had large productivity effects. This finding leads him to conclude that the uniformity of technical practices among firms using identical English looms inhibited incentives to train workers since skills were easily transferred to other competing firms. Some skills, it appears, are specific to particular production technologies and not necessarily to the firm. As such, incentives to invest in training workers are diminished unless institutional arrangements—such as lifetime guarantees or seniority-based wage and promotion practices—are developed to cement worker-firm relationships.

A study by Tan (1980) suggests that interindustry differences in the rate of technical change are related systematically with some components of earnings but not others. Using data from the 1961 Basic Wage Survey, a document comprising male workers in 11 manufacturing industries for which independent estimates of technical change were available, Tan estimated separate wage models for schooling, occupation, and education group by industry.[2] From the estimated wage profiles, present values of specific training (ST) and general training (GT) returns were calculated for each group of workers, assuming continuous employment in the same firm for 35 years. These wage components were regressed on estimates of industry rates of technical change (TFP) and a set of controls for structural factors such as unionization (UNION), market concentration (CON), profitability (PR), and the share of wage bill in value added (WB). These regression results are reported below:

$$ST = 8,334 + 1,496* \text{ TFP} + 677 \text{ HS} + 525 \text{ JC} + 4,351* \text{ UNIV} - 11$$
$$CON - 47 \text{ PR} - 36 \text{ WB} - 81 \text{ UNION,} \quad (R^2 = 0.525),$$

$$GT = 3,917 - 233 \text{ TFP} + 826 \text{ HS} + 7,088* \text{ JC} + 7076* \text{ UNIV} + 23$$
$$CON + 224 \text{ PR} + 77 \text{ WB} - 14 \text{ UNION,} \quad (R^2 = 0.771),$$

where HS, JC, and UNIV are dummy variables for completion of high school, junior college, or university, respectively, and an asterisk denotes statistical significance at the 1% level. From these results, Tan concluded that higher rates of technical change in an industry are associated with an increase in specific training as measured by the present value of specific training returns (ST), but not with general training (GT). In other empirical specifications, which considered the simultaneous determination of ST and TFP, this relationship remained very robust.[3]

To summarize, extant research appears to provide corroborative evidence for some of the predictions of the technology-specific skills model, at least for Japan. The issue examined below is whether these perspectives carry over to the U.S. labor market and to cross-national comparisons of U.S. and Japanese labor markets in a more recent period.

13.2 Data and Model Specification

The data used for the analysis come from two sources: the May 1979 Current Population Survey (CPS) for the U.S. and the 1977 Employment Status Survey (ESS) for Japan. Both surveys are broad-based representative samples of the labor force in each country. The data are also from approximately the same time period and, in terms of the business cycle, in the recovery phase following the international recession of the mid-1970s. Most important, both surveys contain similar kinds of information on earnings, job tenure in the current firm, establishment size, schooling attainment, occupation, and industry. Thus, the same model specifications can be used in studying the determinants of earnings in both countries.

In both data sets, analysis is limited to males between the ages of 18 and 65 years engaged full-time in nonagricultural wage and salary employment. For the CPS, responses to questions on usual weekly earnings and hours worked are used to construct an hourly wage variable, W. For the ESS, the corresponding wage variable is created from annual earnings, which include both contractual wages and semiannual bonus payments,[4] as well as from usual weekly hours worked.[5] To mitigate labor-supply effects on earnings, only those who worked full-time full-year are included in the Japanese sample. The vector of personal attributes included years of schooling attainment (S), prior work experience (EXP), and job tenure (TEN).[6] Indicator variables were also defined for white-collar occupations (WCOLAR), geographic location, and residence in metropolitan areas. A common definition of firm size was used in both data sets: small firms with less than 100 employees, medium-size firms with 100–999 employees, and large firms with over 1,000 workers. The CPS also contained information on union membership not found in the Employment Status Survey.

Measures of industry rates of total factor productivity (TFP) growth estimated by Jorgenson, Gollop, and Fraumeni (1986) for the United States and by Kuroda (1985) for Japan are merged into the two data sets by industry of current employment.[7] The U.S. TFP series is for the 1966–79 period and that for Japan for the 1966–77 period. These measures have several advantages over alternative proxies for technical change. First, both measures of technical change derive from a common methodological approach, which facilitates comparison of their effects on earnings across countries. Second, because these measures already adjust for changes in the quality of human capital inputs, the estimated correlations between technical change and the returns to technology-specific skills can be interpreted as reflecting the relationships of interest rather than a spurious correlation between wages and labor quality in the unadjusted technical change measure.

Two other industry attributes are merged into the data by industry of current employment: rate of output growth (IGR) and output variability (IVAR). Separate regressions of output on a quadratic specification of time were run for each two-digit industry, using annual output data for the United States (1960–79) and Japan (1960–77). The coefficient of the linear trend variable is used as a measure of output growth; the mean squared error of the regression is used as a proxy for the degree of cyclical variability around trend output growth. Though not central to the major thrust of this paper, IVAR is used to control for possible compensating wage effects for employment in industries with predictably high cyclical output variability.

Table 13.1 summarizes some of the variables of interest for the U.S. and Japan, both for the aggregate sample and separately by firm size. Several cross-national differences are noteworthy. First, the sample of U.S. workers have more schooling (about two extra years), they spend approximately the same amount of time working for other firms prior to joining the current employer, and on average they have shorter job tenure. The Japanese sample is older, possibly because those who were not working full-time full-year (predominantly youth) were dropped from the sample (see sample selection criteria). For this sample, however, the fraction of total work experience spent in the current firm (job tenure divided by total work experience) is slightly higher in Japan than in the United States. Second, for both countries, workers in large firms are characterized by higher average schooling attainment, longer job tenure, and a smaller fraction of total work experience spent in

Table 13.1   **Comparisons of Worker and Industry Attributes in the United States and Japan by Firm Size**

Worker and Industry Characteristics	Aggregate Sample	Small Firms	Medium Firms	Large Firms
A. U.S. sample:				
Log(hourly wage)	1.906	1.816	1.974	2.119
Schooling	12.883	12.745	12.901	13.358
Previous experience	8.778	9.490	8.394	6.848
Job tenure	8.070	6.409	9.580	11.470
TFP, 1966–79	−.198	−.286	−.130	.005
IGR, 1960–79	2.195	2.473	1.893	1.715
IVAR	.036	.029	.040	.052
B. Japanese sample:				
Log(hourly wage)	−.141	−.312	−.102	.138
Schooling	11.014	10.423	11.518	11.681
Previous experience	8.072	10.173	7.841	4.455
Job tenure	12.150	11.165	11.241	14.654
TFP, 1966–77	1.571	1.132	1.822	2.164
IGR, 1960–77	4.004	4.511	3.786	3.260
IVAR	.093	.097	.092	.085

Note: TFP = Industry total factor productivity growth; IGR = industry output growth; IVAR = industry output variability.

previous jobs. Finally, note that the average industry rate of technical change imputed to individuals rises with firm size in both countries, suggesting that industries with high rates of technical change tend on average to be made up of a higher proportion of larger firms. In contrast, rapidly growing industries appear to have a disproportionately higher proportion of smaller firms.

13.2.1 The Wage Model

The technology-specific skills hypothesis may be tested using an expanded specification of the conventional cross-sectional wage model. Consider the following wage model where, for expositional simplicity, quadratic experience terms are suppressed (these, and other interacted terms, are included in the empirical analysis):

$$(1) \qquad \ln W_i = \alpha_1 + \alpha_2 S_i + \alpha_3 \text{EXP}_i + \alpha_4 \text{TEN}_i,$$

where for individual i, $\ln W$ = logarithm of hourly wages, S = years of schooling, TEN = years of tenure with the current employer, and EXP = years of previous labor-market experience, defined as age minus S minus 6 less years of current job tenure.

This specification of the wage model has been used by a number of recent studies to decompose earnings into the returns to specific and general skill components (Chapman and Tan 1980; Mincer and Jovanovic 1981). The rationale is that, when skills are completely general, no distinction need be made about where experience is acquired and general training returns are adequately captured by the coefficient of total labor market experience, EXP + TEN. On the other hand, if specific training increases a worker's productivity more in the current firm than elsewhere, the two experience measures should be entered separately. The added wage effects of TEN over and beyond those of EXP (i.e., $\alpha_4 - \alpha_3$) may be interpreted as reflecting the returns to firm-specific training on the current job.[8]

Equalization of the present values of training costs and returns requires an inverse relationship between initial wages and subsequent rates of wage growth with tenure. Since investments in specific training are hypothesized to increase with technical change (TFP), the model predicts that starting wages are negatively related to TFP while wage-tenure profiles are positively related to TFP. Furthermore, controlling for TFP growth, investments in specific-training are predicted to increase with the rate of output growth (IGR) so a similar pattern of lower starting wages and higher rate of wage-tenure growth varying with IGR is predicted. Finally, the proposition that schooling returns increase with TFP is tested in a straightforward fashion through an interaction term between schooling and the rate of technical change, $S \times TFP$.

The following wage specification, where general training returns are constrained to be equal across firms, permits tests of these predictions:

$$(2)\ \ln W_{ij} = \beta_1 + \beta_2 S_i + \beta_3 S_i x TFP_j + \beta_4 EXP_i + \beta_5 TEN_i + \beta_6 TFP_j + \beta_7 TFP_j x TEN_i + \beta_8 IGR_j + \beta_9 IGR_j x\ TEN_i,$$

where j subscripts industry and i the individual. The technology-specific skills hypothesis is supported if firms experiencing rapid technical change have low starting wages (negative β_6), higher rates of wage growth with tenure (positive β_7) coefficients, and a corresponding pattern of wage effects for output growth (negative β_8 and positive β_9). Furthermore, a positive coefficient on the interaction between schooling and TFP (β_3) would provide support for the "allocative efficiency of schooling" hypothesis.

13.3   The Empirical Findings

Two specifications of a log-linear wage model are estimated, where the logarithm of hourly wages (one U.S. dollar or 100 Yen for Japan) is related to a common set of regressors in each country. In specification (1), these include years of schooling, quadratic forms of prior work experience, and years of tenure with the current firm, an interaction between prior experience and tenure,[9] controls for firm size, union membership (United States only), occupation and location. Specification (2) adds industry estimates of total factor productivity growth (TFP) and their interactions with schooling and job tenure, output growth (IGR) and IGR interacted with job tenure, and a control for the degree of industry output variability (IVAR).

Table 13.2 reports the results of estimating these ordinary least squares

Table 13.2   **Results of Wage Regressions for the United States and Japan**

Variable Name	United States		Japan	
	(1)	(2)	(1)	(2)
Constant	.817	.772	−1.572	−1.511
	(30.41)	(25.74)	(62.08)	(47.14)
Schooling (S)	.042	.046	.051	.051
	(22.73)	(24.75)	(36.77)	(29.29)
Prior experience	.031	.030	.044	.044
	(22.22)	(21.94)	(39.19)	(38.78)
Experience^2	−.0006	−.0006	−.0008	−.0008
	(16.18)	(15.75)	(30.33)	(30.16)
Experience × tenure	−.0012	−.0011	−.0013	−.0013
	(17.06)	(16.49)	(26.49)	(26.03)
Tenure	.043	.038	.063	.057
	(26.28)	(14.91)	(51.64)	(20.33)
Tenure^2	−.0008	−.0006	−.0009	−.0008
	(16.39)	(9.31)	(28.75)	(10.66)
Medium-size firm	.085	.066	.158	.146
	(8.74)	(6.69)	(19.92)	(18.06)
Large-size firm	.158	.115	.310	.290
	(12.88)	(8.98)	(39.76)	(35.36)
IVAR		1.699		.287
		(9.67)		(1.78)
TFP × schooling		.0065		.0003
		(4.96)		(.41)
TFP		−.1344		−.0092
		(7.27)		(1.06)
TFP × tenure		.0046		.0016
		(4.14)		(2.49)
TFP × tenure^2		−.0001		−.00001
		(3.13)		(.55)
IGR3149		−.0331		−.0144
		(6.27)		(3.63)
IGR × tenure		.0026		.0008
		(2.86)		(1.43)
IGR × tenure^2		−.00005		−.00002
		(2.02)		(1.09)
R^2	.3162	.3415	.4776	.4808

Note: Region, metropolitan residence, occupation, and union membership (United States only) controls included but not reported. Dependent variable is log(hourly wage). Absolute value of t-statistics are in parentheses.

(OLS) wage models for the two countries. The estimated coefficients of specification (1) are broadly similar in the two countries and resemble those reported elsewhere in the literature (e.g., see Hashimoto and Raisian 1985). Generally, they suggest a pattern of wage growth increasing with schooling attainment and with both prior work experience and years of tenure. In both countries, tenure on the current job is on average rewarded more highly than prior work experience, a result we interpret as tentative evidence for the presence of firm-specific training.

Nonetheless, hourly wages in the two countries differ in several important respects. First, Japanese firms appear to reward education more highly than U.S. firms (5% vs. 4%). Second, both measures of work experience are associated with more rapid wage increases in Japan than in the United States—4.4% versus 3.0% for outside experience, 6.3% versus 4.3% for job tenure, respectively. These results imply not only greater skill investments (both general and firm specific) in Japan than in the United States, but also a greater firm-specific component in Japanese training. To see this latter point, note that the relative returns to tenure and prior work experience are 1.43 (.063/.044) in Japan and 1.38 (.043/.031) in the United States. Finally, hourly wages across firm size are much more highly differentiated in Japan than in the United States. Comparing the largest firm size (over 1,000 employees) to small firms employing less than 100 workers (the omitted category), large employers in Japan pay wages that are over 30% higher; the corresponding figure in the United States is about 16%. (Results are reported separately by firm size in table 13.4 below.)

The second wage model addresses the issue of whether interindustry wage-tenure profiles vary systematically with the industry rate of TFP growth and IGR. As hypothesized, higher industry rates of technical change are associated with lower starting pay (as measured by the coefficient of TFP) and higher rates of wage growth with job tenure (coefficient of tenure interacted with TFP). Controlling for TFP, industry wage-tenure profiles also appear to vary systematically with IGR, with lower starting pay and higher rates of wage growth with tenure in rapidly growing industries. The estimated parameters for the U.S. sample are statistically significant at conventional levels; while individual parameters for Japan attain statistical significance, the relationships of interest are not measured very precisely. The interaction between schooling and technical change is also positive and statistically significant for the U.S. sample, which is consistent with the "allocative efficiency" hypothesis. It is interesting that no support for this hypothesis is found for Japan—while positive, the coefficient of S interacted with TFP is not statistically different from zero. We speculate that this result may reflect the relatively unspecialized nature of public education in Japan or, alternatively, the greater emphasis placed on team production in which individual contributions (of more educated workers) are not easily identified.

Table 13.3 provides a convenient summary of the estimated results by comparing the predicted wage-tenure profiles under several different assumptions about TFP and IGR. A convenient starting point is at the mean level of TFP and IGR (case 1). Ignoring the quadratic term (which is very similar in both countries), the steeper wage-tenure profile in Japan implies that Japanese companies on average invest over 50% (5.22/3.29) more in their workers' specific training than their American counterparts. For the United States, a

Table 13.3   **Predicted Wage-Tenure Profiles in the United States and Japan for Alternative TFP and Output (IGR) Growth Assumptions**

Country/Wage-tenure growth profile	Mean TFP and IGR (1)	1 SD, TFP Increase (2)	1 SD, IGR Increase (3)
United States			
Intercept[a]	1.9818	1.9237	1.9343
Linear wage growth	.0329	.0384	.0367
Quadratic term	−.00081	−.00087	−.00084
Japan			
Intercept	−.3349	−.3503	−.3632
Linear wage growth	.0522	.0549	.0537
Quadratic term	−.0009	−.0009	−.0009

Source: Table 13.2 above.
Note: SD = standard deviation.
[a]Excluding tenure and its interactions with TFP and IGR, the intercept is evaluated at the sample means of the explanatory variables, plus half the standard error of log(hourly wage).

standard deviation increase in TFP (case 2) is associated with a steepening of tenure-wage growth from 3.29% to 3.84%; a standard deviation increase in output growth (case 3) increases wage growth to 3.67%. The corresponding increases in Japanese firms are, at best, marginal given the poor fit of the model. Part of the reason for this, as we shall see below, is attributable to aggregation across firm size in the Japanese sample.

Table 13.4 presents separate estimates of equation (2) for the three firm size groups in the two countries. Though qualitatively similar to the previous results, several systematic differences across firm sizes and between countries are noteworthy. First, consider the returns to schooling. Large firms in both countries reward schooling more highly than small firms—in going from the smallest to the largest firm size category, the returns to schooling increase from 4.3% to 5.0% in the United States, and from 4.3% to 5.7% in Japan. Second, like the previous results, a systematic effect of TFP growth on schooling is found in the United States but never in Japan. Furthermore, in U.S. industries characterized by rapid TFP growth, highly educated workers in large firms are paid more than "similar" employees in small firms. To see this, compare the $S \times$ TFP coefficient in large firms (1.2%) and in small firms (.05%). Third, wage-tenure profiles in small U.S. firms appear to be steeper than those in large firms (4.5% vs. 3.3%), a difference that is further amplified in industries with high TFP growth (the tenure-TFP interaction is .0075 in small firms and .0033 in large firms). In contrast, the tenure-TFP coefficients only attain statistical significance for the largest firm-size category in Japan. Finally, the effects of output growth, IGR, on wage-tenure profiles are most pronounced (and statistically significant) for medium-size and large firms in the United States and, again, only for the largest firms in Japan.

Table 13.4   **Wage Regressions for the United State and Japan by Firm Size**

	U.S.			Japan		
Variable Name	Small	Medium	Large	Small	Medium	Large
Constant	.739	.903	.984	− 1.3492	− 1.4289	− 1.2566
Schooling (S)	.043	.047	.050	.043	.058	.057
	(16.63)	(14.28)	(1 .35)	(16.87)	(15.86)	(17.02)
Prior experience	.031	.028	.028	.039	.046	.046
	(7.12)	(10.76)	(7.43)	(23.96)	(20.24)	(20.97)
Experience^2	− .0006	− .0005	− .0005	− .0007	− .0008	− .0008
	(12.56)	(7.62)	(4.86)	(20.01)	(15.55)	
Experience × tenure	− .0012	− .0010	− .0010	− .0011	− .0015	− .0015
	(11.85)	(8.91)	(5.84)	(14.45)	(13.52)	(16.30)
Tenure	.045	.034	.033	.052	.061	.051
	(10.31)	(8.74)	(6.89)	(11.41)	(11.41)	(11.28)
Tenure^2	− .0008	− .0005	− .0006	− .0008	− .0007	− .0006
	(6.78)	(5.00)	(4.67)	(6.73)	(5.12)	(5.27)
IVAR	2.324	1.273	1.602	− .338	− .312	.833
	(7.69)	(4.80)	(4.60)	(1.12)	(1.01)	(3.74)
TFP × S	.0055	.0071	.0118	.0015	− .0015	.0004
	(2.94)	(3.15)	(3.47)	(1.42)	(1.13)	(0.36)
TFP	− .1198	− .1468	− .2035	− .0111	0.0124	− .0133
	(4.57)	(4.59)	(3.93)	(.81)	(.65)	(.81)
TFP × tenure	.0075	.0035	.0033	− .0003	.0025	.0028
	(4.29)	(1.82)	(1.31)	(.32)	(1.67)	(2.33)
TFP × tenure^2	− .0002	− .0001	− .0001	.0000	− .0001	− .0000
	(3.67)	(1.10)	(.90)	(1.16)	(1.72)	(1.23)
IGR	− .0231	− .0404	− .0373	− .0088	− .0150	− .0431
	(2.93)	(4.53)	(3.13)	(1.45)	(1.86)	(5.75)
IGR × tenure	.0003	.0040	.0038	.0007	.0004	.0037
	(.19)	(2.62)	(2.16)	(.82)	(.38)	(3.69)
IGR × tenure^2	− .0000	− .0001	− .0000	− .0000	− .0000	− .0001
	(.37)	(1.96)	(1.08)	(.21)	(.05)	(2.38)
R^2	.3004	.3390	.3239	.3488	.4862	.5034

Note: Region, metropolitan residence, occupation, and union (U.S. only) controls included but not reported above. Dependent variable is log(hourly wage).
Absolute value of t-statistics are in parentheses.

To summarize, on the most general level these results suggest that firms in technologically progressive industries invest more in their workers' specific skills, and that Japanese firms on average invest more heavily in training workers than do their American counterparts. These results appear to stem from two sources—from increased skill investments in industries where learning possibilities are greater; and, for a given technology, from increased specific-training investments induced by rapid output growth.

The firm-size comparisons suggest some intriguing differences between the United States and Japan. Taken together, the estimated partial effects of TFP and IGR on wage-tenure growth suggest that specific-training investments in small U.S. firms are more responsive to technological possibilities, while training decisions in larger firms are driven more by output growth, given existing technology. In Japan, on the other hand, both factors are operative but only in the largest firm size category. In small Japanese firms, some part of training appears to be firm-specific, but it is neither related to TFP nor IGR. Small Japanese firms' use of technologically standardized machinery, or reliance on large firms for technical expertise (many are subcontractors to large firms), may mean that small Japanese firms invest relatively little in new, more productive skills of the kind that are related to technical change.

13.3.1   What Do These Earnings Differences Reflect?

The previous results, while suggestive, are nonetheless subject to two qualifications. First, do steeply rising wage-tenure profiles really reflect firm-specific training or are they the outcome of wage incentive schemes suggested by implicit contract theories that make no assumptions about training? Second, are wage-tenure effects a meaningful measure of specific training returns or simply a statistical artifact of an omitted firm-worker match variable in a cross-sectional wage equation? These two qualifications are addressed below.

Specific Training and Implicit Contract Interpretations

The problem of distinguishing between the firm-specific training and recent implicit contract theories has been noted by Parsons (1986) and others. These models share a common feature: they predict rapid growth of wages in the current firm relative to opportunity wages elsewhere. Denote this pattern of relative wage growth with tenure t by $W(t)$. In one approach, workers forgo high initial wages to invest in firm-specific training that only increases their productivity, $VMP(t)$, and future wages, $W(t)$, in the current firm. Since both firms and workers share initial specific training costs, subsequent returns are also shared so that $W(t) < VMP(t)$. In the agency and self-selection models, employers initially pay workers less than their value-marginal product but offer them wage-tenure profiles that are steeper than their productivity growth, that is, $W(t) > VMP(t)$. Such back loading of wages relative to spot marginal product serves to reduce incentives to shirk (Lazear 1981) or to attract workers with low quit propensities (Salop and Salop 1976). If early job separation occurs, workers forfeit the difference between their initial value-marginal product and wage; in effect, workers post a bond guaranteeing their nonshirking on the job or their employment stability. In these models, then, $W(t)$ grows with years of tenure even if $VMP(t)$ is constant over time. Individual data on $W(t)$ and $VMP(t)$ needed to distinguish between the competing theories are rarely available to the analyst.

An alternative way of empirically distinguishing between the competing models is with data on worker training. If a positive association between company training and TFP growth is found, we may, given the previous results, infer a causal relationship between increased firm-specific training and steeper wage-tenure profiles in high TFP industries. For the United States, we can draw upon the findings of a recent study of the determinants of private-sector training by Lillard and Tan (1986). Using self-reported measures of training in the National Longitudinal Surveys (NLS) of young men and mature men, they estimated separate probit models of the likelihood of training from company training programs, business and technical schools, and miscellaneous other sources. Each probit model included a common set of regressors on schooling, race, labor force experience, the industry rate of technical change, and labor-market conditions.[10] The TFP variable was interacted with five levels of schooling attainment to allow different technical change effects on the likelihood of training for more and less educated workers.

Table 13.5 reports selected results for the effects of technical change on the likelihood of training from each source, holding other factors constant. For both the young men and mature men samples, company training was significantly more prevalent in industries characterized by higher rates of TFP growth, especially among the more highly educated. In contrast, the likelihood of training outside the firm of current employment—from business and technical schools and miscellaneous other sources—was lower in high TFP industries, with the more educated being significantly less likely to get such training. These results are consistent with the view that rapid technical change leads to increased reliance on in-house training, possibly because technology-

Table 13.5   Effects of Technical Change on the Probability of Training: NLS Young Men and Mature Men

Industry TFP Growth and Schooling Interaction	Source of Training		
	Company Training	Business and Technical Schools	Other Sources
A. NLS young men			
<12 years	4.250	18.005**	7.035
12 years	1.250	−4.796*	−5.062*
13–15 years	.283	−3.219	−7.542**
16 years	9.866**	−6.554	−8.612*
16+ years	16.877**	0.302	−13.354**
B. NLS mature men			
<12 years	.767	6.104	−.554
12 years	−5.976	8.708	−3.273
13–15 years	−1.232	−6.039	−17.600**
16 years	−4.346	−17.591	−15.266**
16+ years	32.111**	−16.564	−5.786

Source: Lillare and Tan (1986), table 3.6.
Note: TFP indices are from Gollop and Jorgenson (1980).
NSL = National Longitudinal Survey.
*$p \leq .05$
**$p \leq .10$

specific skills are not readily available elsewhere, and to greater demand for educated workers who may adapt more readily to new technologies. The results thus provide independent confirmation for the maintained hypothesis that steeply rising wage-tenure profiles reflect specific-training investments, and not just a pure incentive scheme.

Comparable data on training are not available in Japan, which makes it difficult to verify the assertion that steeper wage-tenure profiles in Japan reflect more intensive specific training in that country than in the United States. Anecdotal information, however, suggests that Japanese firms invest more heavily in the enterprise-specific skills of their workers. For example, in a comparison of male workers in auto assembly plants in Detroit and Yokohama, Cole (1979) finds that Japanese workers received a higher proportion of training courses that were company oriented as compared to their U.S. counterparts. A recent study comparing U.S. firms and Japanese firms operating in the United States finds striking differences in their hiring and training practices (Mincer and Higuchi 1988). Compared to U.S. firms, Japanese firms in this country spend more on screening new hires, provide company training to a higher fraction of their American workforce (24% vs. 13%), and, consistent with the firm-specific training model, have wage-tenure profiles that are steeper than those found in the U.S. sample.

Specific Training and Job-Match Quality

The second problem is whether positive tenure-wage effects reflect specific-training returns or the quality of the job match. This issue is at the heart of several recent papers, including those by Altonji and Shakotko (1987) and Abraham and Farber (1987). They argue that the positive cross-sectional association between job tenure and earnings does not imply additional increases in earnings with seniority over and above the returns to general work experience, but may actually reflect the unobserved returns to a good job match. Indeed, the Abraham-Farber results show that inclusion of a measure of completed job duration (an instrument for job-match quality) substantially reduces the returns to job tenure. If the effects of unobserved job-match quality are important, few inferences can be drawn from our wage models of the United States and Japan because of potential omitted variable bias in the estimated tenure coefficients.

The effects of job-match quality, however, may operate through the joint decisions of workers to get (and employers to provide) job training. A standard prediction of human capital theory is that firm-specific training increases with expected time on the job N (or expected job duration) since there is a longer period over which to amortize firm-specific investments costs. A higher quality job match (and longer N) should therefore also result in a greater likelihood of firm-specific training, other things equal. Since job-match quality and training decisions are linked inextricably, it follows that the Abraham-Farber findings cannot be interpreted as a rejection of the firm-specific training hypothesis; they may simply reflect the omission of job-training measures.

A recent paper by Tan (1988) follows this line of reasoning using comprehensive training information contained in a matched January–March 1983 sample of 4,660 males from the CPS. Two types of training variables were considered: (1) "in-house training," which combined participation in company training programs and informal on-the-job training and (2) "outside training," from all other external sources such as traditional schools, and business, and technical institutions. Training and earnings equations were estimated using a two-stage procedure suggested by Barnow, Cain, and Goldberger (1981). In essence, the procedure involved estimating separate probit models for each source of training and including their fitted values as instruments in the earnings model, which was then estimated by a two-stage least squares method. The specification of the wage model is similar to that used earlier, except that two indices of TFP growth estimated by Jorgenson, Gollop, and Fraumeni (1986) are used, one for the 1947–73 period, the other for 1973–79. TFP growth was separated into two time periods to investigate whether long-run TFP or short-run TFP had a more important effect on current earnings growth.

Table 13.6 presents selected results from the two-stage wage model and, for comparison, OLS regression results from a wage model with training treated as exogenously determined. Note that the size of the tenure coefficient is reduced dramatically from .026 to .0023 in the two-stage model, and the variable loses statistical significance. This result suggests that, if the quality of the job match is responsible for the widely reported cross-sectional wage-tenure coefficient (as suggested by Abraham and Farber), it appears to operate entirely through worker and employer training decisions. If this is the case, then wage-tenure profiles estimated from conventional cross-section data without training information may still provide a useful first approximation of investments in firm-specific training.

Several other points are noteworthy. First, the effects of training on earnings are large, especially training from in-house sources. In going from the single equation to the two-stage results, not only do the coefficients on training increase, but their relative rankings change as well, so that in-house training increases earnings more than training from outside sources, which is more plausible. Secondly, consistent with the results reported earlier, the effects of technical change (1973–79) on wage-tenure profiles remain largely unchanged in the two-stage model, with lower starting wages and higher rates of wage-tenure growth in technologically progressive industries. In fact, the effects of TFP on wage-tenure growth becomes even larger, the tenure coefficient rising from .0012 in the single equation model to .0019 in the two-stage model. Finally, contemporaneous earnings growth is only affected by recent TFP growth—the interactions between long-run TFP growth and tenure are never statistically significant. This result is intuitively plausible if older, vintage job skills are rendered obsolete by rapid technical change.

Table 13.6   **Selected Results of Ordinary Least Squares (OLS) and Two-Stage Wage Models with Training**

Variable Names	OLS Model	Two-Stage Model
Constant	4.6782**	4.2205**
Years of schooling	.01619**	.01261*
Labor-market experience	.07645**	.05866**
Experience^2	−.00147**	−.00089**
Years of tenure	.02614**	.00227
Tenure^2	−.00043**	−.00004
TC 1947–73	.00711	−.00857
TC 1947–73 × tenure	.00076	.00027
TC 1973–79	−.04420**	−.03906**
TC 1973–79 × tenure	.00120**	.00193**
In-house training	.13942**	2.02830**
Outside Training	.21293**	1.04400**

Source: January–March 1983 matched Current Population Survey.
Note: Other control variables not reported here include race, location, and state unemployment rate. The training probit models included marital status, categorical schooling indicators, and training needed to get the current job as identifying variables. $N = 4{,}171$ observations; dependent variable is log-weekly wage (mean = 5.845). TC = technical change.
*$p \leq .05$.
**$p \leq .10$.

13.4   Summary and Conclusions

The starting point of this paper was the proposition that many employment and wage practices found in the United States and in Japan may actually reflect rational labor-market responses to the exigencies of technological change. New technologies, before they can be used effectively, require extensive modification and learning; less than optimal amounts of learning may result because of the bilateral monopoly issue associated with these new and more productive specific skills. By clarifying the property rights of employers and workers to these efficiency gains, long-term employment relationships and seniority-based wage and promotion practices create a context that induces the appropriate investments in learning. By viewing the emergence of these institutions as demand induced, it follows that, where there was less need to develop technology-specific skills, these labor-market practices did not arise or were not retained.

To test this proposition, we presented a model of technology-specific skills that yielded several (refutable) predictions about the relationships between industry rates of technical change and output growth on one hand, and wage-tenure growth and schooling on the other. These predictions were tested using comparable labor-market data for the United States and Japan. The hypotheses were strongly supported in the U.S. sample, both in the aggregate and by firm size, and among Japanese workers employed in large firms. The first hypothesis, that rapid technical change induces increased investments in specific skills, found support in steeper rates of tenure-wage growth in technologically more progressive industries. Holding the level of productivity growth constant, rapid output growth was also associated with faster wage growth with tenure. A related hypothesis—that better-educated workers have better "signal extraction" abilities—also found support in the positive interaction between schooling attainment and technical change, but only in the U.S. sample.

Several competing interpretations for the empirical findings were also evaluated using information (some anecdotal) on training. Evidence was presented for the United States that indicated that rapid technical change leads to increased reliance on in-house training—possibly because technology-specific skills are not readily available elsewhere—and to a lower demand for training from outside sources. These findings were interpreted as providing independent confirmation for the hypothesis that steeply rising wage-tenure profiles reflect specific-training investments, and not the (pure) incentive schemes derived from implicit labor contract theories. The findings of several recent papers on job-match quality—which indicated a potential bias in estimated wage-tenure profiles—were also shown not to be inconsistent with a specific-training interpretation. Results were presented that suggest that the wage effects of job-match quality may actually operate through the joint decisions of workers to get (and employers to provide) job training. By implication, wage-tenure profiles estimated from conventional cross-sectional wage models without training information may provide a useful first approximation of specific-training returns.

Overall, the cross-national comparison has provided some insights into how U.S. and Japanese labor markets operate to provide the human capital skills required for productivity growth. Surely, part of the Japanese success of rapid economic growth is attributable to more intensive job training, of both general and specific types, as revealed in higher returns to both general work experience and job tenure in Japan than in the United States. Our empirical analyses were successful in explaining only part of the systematic interindustry and cross-national variation in wage profiles, and there, more successfully for the U.S. than for Japan. In this regard, the preliminary results reported here raise more questions than they answer. For example, how do we explain differences between the United States and Japan in the responsiveness of small and large firms to productivity growth? Why is schooling more productive in technologically progressive industries in the United States but not in Japan? Further refinement and tests of the technology-specific skills model are needed to address these (and other) issues.

Notes

1. For interested readers, Tan (1982) provides a comprehensive survey of the recent literature on wage determination in Japan.

2. The wage specification (and justification) used for the decomposition of earnings

into general training and specific training components is similar to that discussed in section 13.2.

3. Simultaneity might arise if the residual measure of TFP included specific training as one component of unmeasured labor quality so that TFP and ST were positively correlated. This possibility of simultaneity bias was addressed by formulating a structural model of ST and TFP, in which TFP is determined by ST and other inputs into the innovative process including the number of imported technology licenses, R&D spending, investments in new plant and equipment, and research staff. Allowing for the endogenous determination of ST and TFP reduced, but did not change, the positive effects of technical change on specific-training investments.

4. Semiannual bonuses are an important component (as much as one-third) of total wage compensation in Japan. Hashimoto (1979) argues that these bonus payments represent the worker's share of specific-training returns.

5. In the ESS, the variable for weekly hours worked is reported in broad categories that may result in some (unknown) measurement error in the construction of hourly wage rates.

6. Unlike the CPS, where schooling attainment is continuous, this variable is categorical: middle school (8 years), high school (12 years) and college (16 years) graduates.

7. I am grateful to Masahiro Kuroda for kindly providing unpublished estimates of industry rates of TFP growth in Japan, as well as the input series used to create the TFP measures. Similar thanks go to F. M. Gollop and D. W. Jorgenson for the companion TFP series for the United States.

8. A problem (which we discuss later) is that steeply rising wage-tenure profiles may also reflect wage schemes designed to reduce incentives to shirk (Lazear 1981) or to attract workers with low quit propensities (Salop and Salop 1976).

9. This interaction term adds flexibility to the model specification since the returns to job tenure are allowed to vary with prior work experience. We would expect lower investments in specific training for those with long prior experience since the remaining time on the current job is correspondingly shorter.

10. The TFP measures in that study referred to the period between 1966 and 1973, and were derived from Gollop and Jorgenson (1980).

References

Abraham, Katharine, and Henry Farber. 1987. Job duration, seniority, and earnings. *American Economic Review* 77 (June):278–97.

Altonji, Joseph, and Robert Shakotko. 1987. Do wages rise with seniority? *Review of Economic Studies* 54 (179):437–59.

Barnow, Bart, Glen Cain, and A. Goldberger. 1981. Issues in the analysis of selection bias. Typescript. University of Wisconsin-Madison, Department of Economics.

Bartel, Ann, and Frank Lichtenberg. 1987. The comparative advantage of educated workers in implementing new technology. *Review of Economics and Statistics* (February).

Becker, Gary S. 1975. *Human capital,* 2d ed. New York: Columbia University Press.

Chapman, Bruce, and Hong Tan. 1980. Specific training and inter-industry wage differentials in U.S. manufacturing. *Review of Economics and Statistics* 62 (August):371–78.

Cole, Robert E. 1979. *Work, mobility, and participation.* Berkeley and Los Angeles: University of California Press.

Enos, John L. 1962. Invention and innovation in the petroleum refining industry. In *The rate and direction of inventive activity,* ed. Kenneth Arrow. Princeton, N.J.: Princeton University Press.

Gollop, Frank M., and Dale W. Jorgensen. 1980. U.S. productivity growth by industry, 1947–1973. In *New developments in productivity measurement and analysis,* ed. John W. Kendrick and Beatrice N. Vaccara. NBER Studies in Income and Wealth 44. Chicago: University of Chicago Press.

Hall, Robert. 1982. The importance of lifetime jobs in the U.S. economy. *American Economic Review* 72 (September):716–24.

Hashimoto, Masanori. 1979. Bonus payments, on-the-job training and lifetime employment in Japan. *Journal of Political Economy* 87 (October):1086–1104.

Hashimoto, Masanori, and John Raisian. 1985. Employment tenure and earnings profiles in Japan and the United States. *American Economic Review* 75 (September): 721–35.

Hollander, Samuel. 1965. *The sources of increased efficiency.* Boston: MIT Press.

Jorgenson, Dale, Frank Gollop, and Barbara Fraumeni. 1986. Productivity and growth of sectoral output in the United States, 1948–1979. Discussion Paper no. 1217, Harvard University, Harvard Institute for Economic Research, February.

Jorgenson, Dale, Masahiro Kuroda, and Mieko Nishimizu. 1985. Japan-U.S. industry level productivity comparison, 1960–1979. Paper presented at the NBER Conference on Research in Income and Wealth. Cambridge, Mass., 27–30, August.

Kuratani, Masatoshi. 1973. The theory of training and employment: An application to Japan. Ph.D. Diss., Columbia University.

Lazear, Edward. 1981. Agency, earnings profiles, productivity and hours restrictions. *American Economic Review* 71 (September):606–20.

Lillard, Lee, and Hong Tan. 1986. Training: Who gets it and what are its effects on employment and earnings. R-3331-DOL. The Rand Corporation (March).

Mellow, Wesley. 1982. Employer size and wages. *Review of Economics and Statistics* 64:495–501.

Mincer, Jacob, and Yoshio Higuchi. 1988. Wage structures and labor turnover in the U.S. and Japan. *Journal of Japanese and International Economies* 2:97–133.

Mincer, Jacob, and Boyan Jovanovic. 1981. Labor mobility and wages. In *Studies in labor markets,* ed. Sherwin Rosen. Chicago: University of Chicago Press.

Oi, Walter. 1983. The fixed employment costs of specialized labor. In *The measurement of labor cost,* ed. Jack Triplett. Chicago: University of Chicago Press.

Parsons, Donald. 1986. The employment relationship: Job attachment, work effort, and the nature of contracts. In *Handbook of labor economics,* ed. O. Ashenfelter and R. Layard, chap. 14. Amsterdam and New York: Elsevier Science Publishers.

Rosen, Sherwin. 1972. Learning and experience in the labor market. *Quarterly Journal of Economics* 86 (August):326–42.

Salop, Joanne, and Steven Salop. 1976. Self-selection and turnover in the labor market. *Quarterly Journal of Economics* 90 (November):619–27.

Saxonhouse, Gary. 1976. Country girls and competition among competitors in the cotton spinning industry. In *Japanese industrialization and its social consequences,* ed. Hugh Patrick. Berkeley and Los Angeles: University of California Press.

Schultz, Theodore. 1975. The value of the ability to deal with disequilibria. *Journal of Economic Literature* (September):827–46.

Setzer, Francis. 1974. Technical change over the life of a product: Changes in skilled inputs and production processes. Ph.D. diss., Yale University.

Shimada, Haruo. 1981. *Earnings structure and human investment: A comparison between the United States and Japan.* Tokyo: Keio University.

Taira, Koji. 1970. *Economic development and the labor market in Japan.* New York: Columbia University Press.

Tan, Hong W. 1980. Human capital and technological change: A study of wage differentials in Japanese manufacturing. Ph.D. diss., Yale University.

————. 1982. Wage determination in Japanese manufacturing: A review of recent literature. *Economic Record* (May), 46–60.

————. 1988. Productivity growth, training, and earnings. Working paper. RAND Corporation, April.

Welch, Finis. 1970. Education in production. *Journal of Political Economy* 78 (January–February):350–66.

Yasuba, Yasukichi. 1976. The evolution of the dualistic wage structure. In *Industrialization and its social consequences,* ed. Hugh Patrick. Berkeley and Los Angeles: University of California Press.

Comment   Romesh Diwan

1. The revised version of this paper has successfully incorporated some of the specific suggestions I made at the NBER conference where it was originally read. There are still a number of issues that merit discussion.

2. One of the basic limitations of the paper follows from the model itself. The stated objective of the paper is to develop and quantify a model of technology-specific skills in order to explain differing, and different, labor market practices. However, in its final form, the model in Tan's equation (1) ends up in attempting to explain *partial* changes in wage profiles by three factors that measure labor quality, namely, (i) level of education, (ii) level and growth in prior job experience, and (iii) level and growth in the job, that is, experience with a particular employer or tenure. The model is able to explain *only* partial changes in wage profiles because it is not based on any theories of supply of or demand for labor. The statistical results confirm this *partial* explanation.

3. In equation (2), the model is augmented by the introduction of technical change and industrial growth, both factors existing at the industry level while the rest of the model is at the firm/enterprise level. Technical change is measured by total factor productivity (TFP) at the industry level. The estimated single equation in table 13.2 is given a *selective* translog form. Thus, there are variables for experience^2 and tenure^2 but no term for schooling^2. Similarly, there are interaction terms: experience $\times$ tenure, TFP $\times$ schooling, TFP $\times$ tenure, IGR $\times$ tenure, but there are no variables for schooling $\times$ experience, TFP $\times$ experience, IGR $\times$ experience; IGR $\times$ schooling. Again, there are two additional variables for TFP-tenure squared and IGR-tenure squared. It is not clear, or explained, why some square and interaction variables are included and others omitted.

There are two sets of problems here. One, the *selective* use of the translog

Romesh Diwan is professor of economics at Rensselaer Polytechnic Institute, Troy, New York, and a member of the NBER Conference on Research on Income and Wealth.

form has resulted in the omission of a number of interaction variables. Unless the interaction effects are small, such omission has the effect of biasing the estimated coefficients. Fortunately, the value of the interaction effects, as estimated below, are quite small. Two, measurement of TFP poses all sorts of difficulties, conceptual as well as quantitative. By and large, TFP has been estimated as a "residual" so that it is highly sensitive to model specification. As a residual, TFP can be meaningfully interpreted *only* with the reference to the model of which it is a residual. To treat TFP as a variable, in and of itself, even if it has been estimated by experts such as Gollop and Jorgenson and Kuroda, is to stretch the argument, the logic, and the estimates a little too far.

4. Given the *selective* translog form, one can develop an alternative interpretation of the estimated parameters. In view of the square and cross-product terms in the estimated equation, one can distinguish the following *four* effects: (i) first-order effects, (ii) second-order effects associated with the square terms, (iii) interaction effects derived from cross-product terms, and (iv) total effect, which is the sum of the three effects. We have calculated these four effects for the tenure variable for both the United States and Japan. These are given in table 1.

These calculations suggest that the totality of interaction effects are similar for both the United States and Japan. Furthermore, these effects are rather small. The major effect is given by the first-order term.

5. There are two stories that we in the United States tell to each other: one about United States and the other about Japan. The story about the United States is that it does not pay to stick with one firm or company. Instead, one gains in wages/salaries by regularly switching jobs from one company to the other. Based on the market philosophy, the "theory of exit" is recognized, respected, and well practiced. There is ample evidence to prove it.

The story about Japan that we tell in the United States is just the opposite. In Japan it pays to stick with one company. One does not gain in wages/salaries by switching jobs from one company to the other. Instead, job switching is discouraged. The celebration in Japan is of lifetime employment with one company. The theory that is practiced is of "loyalty," not of "exit." Quite a large number of experts have written about it.

The story that emerges from these results is that the wage changes are most

Table 1   First-Order, Second-Order, Interaction, and Total Effects of Tenure

Country	Effects			
	First Order	Second Order	Interaction	Total
United States	.038	− .0048	− .0050	.0282
Japan	.057	− .0097	− .0048	.0425

Note: The second-order effects and interaction effects have been calculated at the average values for the aggregate sample given in table 13.1 above.

affected by the initial situation, whether it is prior experience or job tenure. Given the initial situation, additions to years in tenure and/or a combination of tenure with other qualitative variables does not help in the rate of change of the wage rate. These results conform with the story about the United States. They seem to be at odds with the story about Japan. These results point out to the similarities rather than differences between the United States and Japan. Given much of the information about the differences between the United States and Japan, these results suggest that the search is not over.

14 Labor Disputes and Productivity in Japan and the United States

Alice C. Lam, J. R. Norsworthy, and Craig A. Zabala

14.1 Introduction

The quantity of effective labor in the work force depends not only on the number of workers employed but on how hard they work. Many explanations of the superior performance of the Japanese economy stress this fact. Japanese workers seem more dedicated and motivated than their American counterparts. We examine this phenomenon by comparing the effects of worker attitude on productivity and production costs in the U.S. and Japanese manufacturing sector. The findings suggest that worker attitude affects economic growth.[1]

In analyzing the effects of worker behavior on automobile industry performance—total factor productivity, labor productivity, and total unit cost—for the 1959–76 period, we simulated the effects of a 10% improvement in worker attitudes on industry performance (Norsworthy and Zabala 1985b). We found that positive changes in attitudes would have resulted in substantial cost savings over the last two decades. In 1976, for example, the estimated cost savings for automobile manufactures were approximately $5.0 billion. We also investigated worker-attitude effects on the shadow value of total capital input, assuming a significant capital-using effect from negative worker behavior in auto plants (Norsworthy and Zabala 1985c). A 10% improvement in worker behavior would save between $1.0 billion and $6.0 billion between 1959 and 1979. Thus, poor worker attitudes caused a large capital-using bias in technology and, thus, increased capital requirements. These results are

J. R. Norsworthy is professor in the Department of Economics and School of Management at Rensselaer Polytechnic Institute in Troy, New York. Craig A. Zabala is assistant professor and research fellow in the School of Management at Rensselaer Polytechnic Institute. Alice C. Lam is research scientist at the Suntory Toyota International Center for Economic and Related Disciplines (STICERD), London.

411

strong and suggest consideration of similar patterns in other models of production.

In this paper, we extend our method to study the aggregate manufacturing sectors of Japan and the United States using comparable worker-behavior data. We expect significant differences between these two countries in behavioral effects on productivity and costs because of differences in industrial relations, management systems, and other institutions. We also expect to find significant differences in investment behavior that affects productivity and cost performance, as found in Norsworthy and Malmquist (1983).

In the following sections, we first discuss differences in institutional settings and industrial relations practices. Second, we introduce the variables used to depict workers' attitudes toward their jobs; these variables reflect institutional and systemic differences between the two countries and describe the cost and output data. Third, we introduce the translog cost function model, which is used to estimate the effects of worker behavior on the cost of production. Fourth, we present the estimation results and compare the estimated influences of worker attitudes on manufacturing productivity in the two countries.

14.2   How Worker Attitudes Affect Productivity and Costs

Worker attitudes affect not only labor productivity but also the productivity of other input factors. The mechanisms by which worker attitudes affect productivity and costs is important. The transaction-costs literature discusses deals with "shirking" or output restriction by workers and argues that without very close supervision—in the limit, one supervisor per worker—the worker has discretionary control over the quality, and even the quantity, of effort and concentration applied to his job. There is scope for the worker to manifest dissatisfaction in various forms of low-grade sabotage (Zabala 1983, 1989), which may take the form of breakage (increasing materials costs), letting machines break down through inattention, omitted adjustment or maintenance (increasing maintenance and/or materials costs), and absenteeism (increasing labor costs). These behaviors will typically increase the costs of supervision. While some of behavior of this type may be partially unintentional, there is little reason to doubt that dissatisfaction or alienation will generally give rise to more of it, resulting in higher costs and possibly a reduction in the quality of output.

14.3   Institutional Setting of Industrial Relations

Many institutions created for the resolution of labor-management conflict in Japan and the United States have similar outward forms, due in large measure to U.S. influence on Japan's reshaping of its economic institutions in the decade following World War II (Hanami 1981). However, the Japanese union movements and their respective relations with management are quite different and, consequently, have different historical experiences that may result in different workplace behavior. (Shimada 1982a). In Japan, there are two major labor federations with social as well as political agendas, while in the United States there is one major labor federation, linked principally, although not formally, to one national political party. Some 25%–30% of Japanese workers, mostly in manufacturing, are aligned with the conservative majority in the Diet. Public-sector unions are more militant and aligned with the minority left-of-center political parties.

There are other important differences between Japanese and U.S. institutional structures for managing labor-management conflict. While many U.S. manufacturing industries are organized by industrywide unions, such as the United Auto Workers, United Steel Workers, International Association of Machinists, and so on, Japanese manufacturing workers are represented by unions that typically cover only one large enterprise. Among small- and medium-sized firms, the pattern is different and more similar to the one in the United States. Under these circumstances, the Japanese union has less bargaining leverage in terms of political power. Outside manufacturing, industrywide unions are more common, and many are considerably more militant than the unions in the manufacturing sector.

Since the early 1970s, annual nationwide wage negotiations, called the *shun-to* (spring offensive), set general wage levels across industries; typically, the largest unions in industry negotiate rates at their firm. This is followed by pattern bargaining at other firms. Instead of mass strikes and production stoppages, the *shun-to* is accompanied by mass demonstrations, intended to show power and solidarity, and by public bargaining between unions and employers that is reported in the national press. This public debate provides information and time for nonadversary bargaining when both parties sit down face to face. The *shun-to* is also used to set the nation's social agenda. For example, in the early 1970s a movement emerged, in response to changing demographics, demanding that the government raise the retirement age for Japanese public-sector workers from 55 to 60 years of age. Militant public-sector unions raised these demands in the *shun-to*. This in turn shaped a national debate that spilled over into Japanese manufacturing with the demand to raise the retirement age for all full-time Japanese workers. The debate extended beyond collective bargaining to concerns about income support programs—an inadequate social security system and nonexistent private-sector pension programs for an aging Japanese labor force with an increasing life expectancy (from 50 years in 1947 to 70 years in 1973 for men)—and future expectations of labor shortages.

While its present widespread influence is rather recent, the *shun-to* has affected the data for Japan in the last few years. In the United States, triennial industrywide pattern bargaining is a major influence on labor policy development. In Japan, social and political agendas of the main federation in the labor movement are more widely publicized and discussed than in the United

States, where a tradition of business unionism continues to exert strong influence. Finally, overt labor-management conflict in Japanese labor relations is uncommon in the manufacturing sector (Lam 1983), compared to the adversarial nature of U.S. collective bargaining.

Differences in national institutions can be expected to result in different patterns of labor-management conflict and in different structures and processes of nominally similar institutions in workplace bargaining. The time required for final adjudication of disputes in the two countries is dramatically different: the process takes much longer in Japan. The empirical evidence we have developed is consistent with the proposition that Japan's system of conflict resolution is more effective, but it is also consistent with lower levels of latent conflict in labor-management relations in Japan's manufacturing sector.

14.4   Structure and Processes in Dispute-Resolution Procedures

Dispute adjustment and resolution of unfair labor practices in the manufacturing sector are similar in both countries.

14.4.1   National Dispute-Resolution Institutions in the United States

The National Labor Relations Board (NLRB), created and guided by the National Labor Relations Act (NLRA or Wagner Act, 1935, which was amended by the Taft-Hartley Act, 1947), collects U.S. dispute resolution data routinely and reports them in the *Annual Report of the National Labor Relations Board*. The board does not initiate cases but acts only on those cases submitted by the company, union, or employee to administer of the basic laws governing the relationships between management and trade unions. Dispute-adjustment cases include representation disputes, for example, for determining collective bargaining representatives, changes in union affiliation, advisory opinions on the board's jurisdiction in regional or state agency or court disputes, unit clarification disputes involving employee classifications in existing bargaining units, or jurisdictional disputes and union deauthorization cases. Unfair labor practices include charges by unions and employees that employers interfered with, restrained, or coerced employees in exercising their legally sanctioned rights of self-organization; dominated or interfered with either the formation or administration of unions; discriminated in hiring or tenure of employment or discourage membership in a labor organization; discharged or otherwise discriminated against an employee because the employee filed unfair labor practice charges or offered testimony against company actions under the National Labor Relations Act; or refused to bargain collectively with elected representatives of their employees.

Conversely, employers can bring charges of unfair labor practices against unions if unions restrained or coerced employees who were exercising their rights to engage in or refrain from engaging in collective bargaining; caused employers to discriminate against employee to encourage or discourage union membership; refused to bargain in good faith; participated in certain types of strikes and secondary boycotts; charged excessive or discriminatory union initiation fees or union dues; or caused employers to pay for labor services not performed (i.e., featherbedding).

Arbitration cases include disputes that cannot be resolved within the bilateral grievance procedure. After all bilateral steps in the grievance procedure have been exhausted, management and labor select an impartial outsider to decide the dispute. Often, this persons' decision is stipulated in the contract to be final and binding upon both parties (Zabala 1983).

The five-member board, appointed by the U.S. president, acts as a quasi-judicial body to decide cases on formal records, and it employs administrative law judges to hear and decide cases. All cases heard at the national level begin in regional offices, where regional directors process and investigate disputes. Appellate procedures exist within the board at the regional and national levels. Although the NLRB has no independent statutory power to enforce its decisions and orders, it may seek enforcement in the U.S. Court of Appeals. Grievants may also appeal board decisions to the federal judicial system. Arbitration cases are administered and heard by the Federal Mediation and Conciliation Service and other private associations, including the American Arbitration Association.

The volume of disputes is high, nearly doubling between 1958 and 1974. The year 1980 had record levels, with 24,411 total disputes filed with the board. In 1981, the NLRB closed 52,804 cases, with 25,211 pending, and a record $37,617,144 was reimbursed to employees for illegal discharges or discriminatory representation. In many U.S. industries, such as the automobile industry, a large proportion of arbitration cases in recent years involved disciplinary layoffs and firings. An overwhelming number of these cases result in reinstatement and backpay.

Unfair labor practice disputes, or charges of unlawful acts by employers or unions or both, increased dramatically throughout the 1958–81 period, doubling by 1969 and with a maximum of 19,246 cases in 1980. In 1981, the board closed 41,020 unfair labor practices cases. Most cases are resolved informally: 90% of unfair labor practice cases are disposed of within 40 days without formal litigation, and only 3% of the cases require an NLRB decision. Strikes ended in 205 of the cases closed in 1981, and collective bargaining commenced in 2,028 cases.[2]

14.4.2 Japanese Dispute-Resolution Institutions

The Japanese system has a strong resemblance to the U.S. system. This is because U.S. institutions served as models for many postwar economic institutions established in Japan. Japanese statistics on dispute adjustment and unfair labor practices are collected at the prefecture level and reported in the *Annual Report of the Labor Relations Commissions*. A network of local commissions operating under central direction and review by the Central Labor

Relations Commission (LRC) is the primary institution for the resolution of labor disputes and data collection in Japan; grievance and other dispute-adjustment mechanisms at the enterprise level are more limited than in the United Sates. Thus, the Labor Relations Commission (LRC) has an active role in administering and developing Japanese labor relations.

Dispute adjustment includes conciliation, mediation, and arbitration, as well as a semijudicial function that resolves unfair labor practice disputes. Moreover, LRCs perform major fact-finding activities prior to informal and formal negotiations. Lam (1983) has characterized the LRC's dual function as a government conciliation agency and a labor court. Unlike the U.S. system, the LRC system often extends collective bargaining agreements to other trade unions and industries. The LRC system operates at the national level (Central Labor Relations Commission [CLRC]) and in each prefecture (Local Labor Relations Commcssions [LLRC]) and for the maritime industry (Seamen's Labor Relations Commission [SLRC]).

The CLRC presides over interprefectural cases, cases of "national importance," and other appeals. The LLRCs preside over intraprefectural and prefectural disputes. (Hereafter, we refer to the total system as the LRC.) Unlike the U.S. NLRB, tripartite membership on LRCs includes equal numbers of representatives of employers, labor, and government. Consequently, LRCs are not formally subject to direct ministerial control. Revisions to the LRC legislation in 1949 limited authority in final LRC decisions in unfair labor practice disputes to public officials, because of adversarial company-union relations.

Although most dispute cases in Japanese manufacturing are handled by conciliation and then mediation, in recent years differences between the two processes have largely disappeared. Conventional arbitration, which explicitly acknowledges the adversarial relationship between parties, settles few disputes, since this technique does not conform to the Japanese tradition of compromise between bargaining parties. Unfair labor practice disputes include an employer's refusal to bargain, interference in union administration, or dismissals of union leaders due to union activities. The role of LRCs in unfair labor practice disputes borrows more from civil court proceedings than does the U.S. system, which has cumbersome legal proceedings dominated by lawyers at all steps of negotiations. The average length of time to resolve disputes is substantial: for example, it took 635 days for LLRCs to resolve 1976 disputes and 774 days for those filed in 1980.

14.4.3   Comparisons between U.S. and Japanese Trade Unions

Typically, Japanese trade unions initiate dispute-adjustment cases, as in the United States. Some Japanese scholars have argued that a major difference between the U.S. and Japanese systems is that the level of informal dispute adjustment in Japan is much higher, although informal negotiation in the United States is also widespread. Since Japanese unions in the manufacturing sector are usually enterprise unions, we expect weak workplace bargaining, where Japanese-style dispute adjustment is a viable alternative. Japanese unions also use dispute adjustment to obtain satisfactory wage settlements as well as to make statements on social issues of national importance.

Shimada (1982a) and Lam (1983) have pointed out that Japanese workers and their unions behave much like American workers and unions in formulating their economic demands. Wage demands and demands to reduce the length of workdays and increase the number of holidays increased substantially during the period of rapid economic growth in the 1960s. In fact, until 1975, wage disputes constituted 50% of all cases and declined only as economic growth slowed. With slower economic growth came decreased wage demands, reflecting job security fears and demands for "noneconomic" policies. This behavior is similar to patterns in U.S. collective bargaining.

In the United States, a formal, four-step grievance procedure is clearly specified and used to resolve disputes at unionized firms. This procedure is used to a lesser extent at nonunionized firms, and arbitration is used only as the final step to resolve conflicts (Zabala 1983). In Japan, the industrial relations system does not include four-step grievance procedures at the plant level. LRCs replace workplace bargaining, an act that centralizes the dispute process but also creates inefficient settlements in terms of timeliness and presumably policies that improve worker morale (Zabala 1983). Thus, we expect that the low volume of LRC cases reflects at least partial disenchantment among Japanese workers with this form of dispute resolution.

In our previous work in the U.S. automobile industry, we used plant-level grievance data. As stated above, we analyze different dispute data for U.S. and Japanese manufacturing. Based on our earlier research, we suggest the following typology. *Type 1* grievance data are labeled grievance rates (per 100 employees), open grievance rates (e.g., unresolved grievances), and so on, collected by plant personnel as measures of shop tensions. *Type 2* grievances are arbitration cases, which are primarily shop worker grievances, involving step-four grievance rates, based upon the failure of labor and management to resolve the disputes at the first three steps of the formal grievance procedure (Zabala 1983). *Type 3a* grievances are dispute-adjustment cases, including representation complaints and collective bargaining process complaints by unions. *Type 3b* grievance data are unfair labor practice cases. *Type 3a, 3b* grievance data are described above and are consistent between the two countries.

There is a systematic nonrepresentativeness in similar Japanese data series since the trade unions most prone to use dispute-adjustment procedures are those in the small- and medium-sized enterprises. Among the medium- and small-sized enterprises, there are more conventional adversary disputes common to the United States. Hanami (1981) describes these relationships: "Industrial relations are conducted without established rules, governed by emotional elements, and developed amid treacherous antagonism and misunderstanding." Also, dispute rates are higher among smaller firms because young trade unions are fighting for new rights or new terrain for policies before labor-management relationships are routinized. It is not surprising that in the small- and medium-sized firms, worker grievances often involve general economic and social discontent rather than plant-specific policies. Thus, the mediation of the LRCs is crucial for the resumption of consensual labor relations.

Nonrepresentativeness of the dispute data also occurs in the structures and processes of collective bargaining within each country. In the United States, adversarial collective bargaining includes substantial *union voice* for rank-and-file workers. In Japan, consensus decision making involves union, managers, work teams, and individual workers. The Japanese industrial relations system includes high levels of participation and formal and extensive information sharing. Disputes are minimized and problem-solving activities emphasize production management, rather than policy development and implementation in the collective bargaining framework. Joint problem solving takes place in formal and informal, regular and irregular meetings, quality circles, and work groups. Bilevel union representation involves (1) managers and union bargaining over basic pay rates, fringe benefits, working hours, and so on; and (2) joint consultation in strategic planning and corporate performance. There is some overlap however since bonus rates based on performance are determined in formal collective bargaining. Joint consultation meetings occur regularly at all levels of the enterprise—shop floor, plant, division, and corporate levels (Shimada and MacDuffie 1986). In the United States, grievances are policy devices used to interpret, revise, or develop new labor policies with attitude effects. In Japan, nonadversarial collective bargaining at the shop-floor level aids production and is not used for policy formation and implementation. We cannot test Kamata's thesis that Japanese workers have weaker shop-floor representation than American workers who labor in similar production environments but have dissimilar collective bargaining environments. We note the differences for future research.

The number of labor disputes that bubble up to the national level in Japan need not be large if changes in the number indicate widespread changes in worker attitudes, with associated effects on costs. This is an empirical problem: If the small number of disputes represent nothing but noise with respect to worker behavior, there will be very weak or no association with the cost of production; if the disputes correspond to significant cost and productivity-related manifestations of worker attitude, then the effect will be captured in the cost function.

The number of dispute-adjustment cases in Japan declined dramatically during the recession that followed the energy crisis. During this period, the major type of dispute shifted to broader issues, such as working conditions, employment levels, and, notably, job security. There has also been a greater tendency for trade unions to bargain directly with the government over general economic policy, as is done in Western Europe. This fact partly accounts for declines in wage disputes. At a deeper level, unions and management may have lost confidence in the LRC over time and, thus, turned to the central labor movement to provide satisfactory labor policies. With the changing nature of disputes, the variety of worker demands, and the maturation of workplace bargaining, unions, in particular, have found the LRC's principle of compromise and delay ineffective in resolving worker grievances and discontents. Our findings in earlier studies suggest that worker-attitude indicators, for example, number of fact-finding cases, and enterprise grievance rates would be useful.

14.5   Data

For this paper, we use *type 3a* (dispute-adjustment cases) and *type 3b* (unfair labor practice disputes) grievance data, strikes, and quits (United States only) as our behavioral data set to illuminate the relationships between worker attitudes and productivity in U.S. and Japanese manufacturing since the late 1950s. Our decisions on data were based on availability and comparability between countries. We described the grievance data above. For Japanese manufacturing, the strike data are collected and published annually by the Ministry of Labor. For the United States, strike and quit data are collected and published annually by the Bureau of Labor Statistics. We believe that this set of behavior variables accurately depicts the sate of labor relations within the manufacturing sectors of both countries and can be used as attitude proxies to measure the impact of worker behavior on productivity and cost performance.[3]

Data limitations prevented analysis of other behavior data. Shimada (1982b) challenges popular stereotypes of Japanese workers with his findings that Japanese labor turnover is quite high, and Levine and Koji (1980) argue that some part of turnover results from latent industrial conflict. These findings suggest that Japanese workers are not unlike their counterparts in U.S. industry and that "exit voice" might be a significant indicator of worker attitudes, and might proxy for their effects on productivity and costs in Japan. Although we use quits data in our model of the U.S. production process, we were unable to obtain satisfactory quit data for Japan. We were also unable to obtain absenteeism series for either country. We expect that these variables would be good indicators of attitudes for our models of production. Thus, we are unable to compare various "exit voice" data between countries in this research.

Type 1 grievance data—actual grievance rates in unionized U.S. plants and the number of fact-finding cases by LRCs in Japanese plants—might provide useful information in our estimations, although U.S. coverage would account for less than 25% of all plants since the late 1970s because of declining unionization rates. These data were not available for this paper. We also believe that introducing positive measures of worker behavior—participation rates in team meetings, number of innovations and suggestions, voluntary participation in training programs—would provide useful information in our model of production; but we were unable to obtain these data.

The worker attitude indicators in the augmented cost function we estimate below are quits, Q (for the United States only); strikes, Z; dispute-adjustment cases, A; and unfair labor practices disputes, U. The variables Q and Z are published for U.S. manufacturing by the Bureau of Labor Statistics and for Japanese manufacturing by the Ministry of Labor. The variables A and U are compiled for U.S. manufacturing enterprises by the NLRB and for Japanese industry by the LRC, an autonomous agency of the Ministry of Labor. These data represent full coverage and are reasonably representative of worker attitudes at this level of aggregation; they are routinely collected for both union and nonunion enterprises, although actions from unionized establishments dominate the NLRB's agenda. The importance of the variables Q and Z as indicators of worker attitudes has been argued in earlier work by Norsworthy and Zabala (1985a, 1985b, 1985c).

Cost data for Japan are from Norsworthy and Malmquist (1983). Capital input is a Törnqvist (Divisia) aggregate of structures, transportation equipment, other equipment, land, and inventories. The aggregation is based on capital service prices computed using an internal rate of return following Gollop and Jorgenson (1980). Capital stocks were developed from investment data taken from the Census of Manufactures, using the perpetual inventory method with geometric decay. Depreciation rates were taken from Nishimizu (1979).

The only difference between the data for Japan in that study and this one is that the labor input here is disaggregated to production worker and nonproduction worker components. We believe this separation is appropriate for the study of worker attitudes since the two groups are affected differently by technology and output growth. Energy and materials inputs and further details about data construction are provided in the earlier study.

For the U.S. manufacturing sector, we have used a preliminary version of the new Berndt-Wood data set, which permits us to add the years 1978–81 to the data for U.S. manufacturing used by Norsworthy and Malmquist (1983). Capital stock data are for equipment and structures only, and energy input includes feedstocks, unlike the U.S. data in the earlier paper.

In both countries, there are delays between the onset of a labor dispute and its final resolution. For the United States, we entered adjusted disputes for the following year to reflect delays in settlements. We used unfair labor practice disputes for the following year and dispute-adjustment cases for the second following year for Japan to allow for the effects of delays in dispute resolution.

14.6 The Model

The translog cost model has been used widely in a variety of studies in the last decade and has clearly surpassed the Cobb-Douglas function and the constant elasticity of substitution specifications as the model of choice for representing the production process.[4] For this application, we use an equilibrium unit cost function model to estimate the effects of worker attitudes: an equilibrium formulation because the appropriate valuation of capital input in disequilibrium is open to debate and a unit cost model (which imposes constant returns to scale) because scale effects are difficult to identify in aggregate time-series models. In general, the equilibrium translog model usually tracks the estimation period reasonably well, although it has its detractors.[5] The translog cost function is a logarithmic approximation to an arbitrary twice differentiable cost function based on a Taylor series expansion around the point $\ln C = 0$. We recognize five input factors: capital (K), production-worker labor (L), nonproduction-worker labor (N), energy (E), and materials (M).

Thus, the general cost function may be written:

$$C = C(Y, P_k, P_l, P_n, P_e, P_m, T),$$

where Y is output, P_i is the price of input i, and T is a time trend, often described as an index of technical change. Denoting logs by lower case characters, the translog cost function is written

(1)
$$\begin{aligned}
\ln C_o = a_o &+ \Sigma_i a_i p_i + \tfrac{1}{2}\Sigma_i \Sigma_j a_{ij} p_i p_j \\
&+ s_t T + \Sigma_i s_{Ti} p_i T + \tfrac{1}{2} s_{TT} T^2 \\
&+ a_y y + \Sigma_i a_{iy} p_i y + \tfrac{1}{2} a_{yy} y^2, \\
&i, j = K, L, N, E, M.
\end{aligned}$$

For the unit cost function, we restrict $a_y = 1$, $a_{iy} = a_{yy} = 0$. For convenience, we then subtract Y from both sides, thus

$$\ln C = \ln C_0 - Y,$$

denotes the logarithm of the total unit cost of production. Further, to save estimated parameters (a concern because there are so few observations for manufacturing in Japan), we impose the restriction

$$s_{TT} = 0.$$

Homogeneity of degree one in input prices is imposed by the following parameter restrictions:

$$\begin{aligned}
\Sigma_i a_i &= 1, \\
\Sigma_i a_{ij} &= \Sigma_j a_{ij} = 0, \\
\Sigma_i s_{Ti} &= 0.
\end{aligned}$$

Under the assumption of cost minimization, Shephard's lemma implies that the equations for the shares of each input factor in total unit production cost are equal to the elasticities of total cost with respect to the input prices:

(2) $s_i = \partial \ln C / \partial p_i = a_i + \Sigma_i a_{ij} p_j + s_{Ti} T, \quad i = K, L, N, E, M.$

The conventional practice is to estimate the cost function jointly with all but one of the share equations. This, then, is the form for estimating the standard translog cost function models.

To include the effects of worker attitudes, we augment the cost function by inserting (the logs of) the worker-attitude indicators discussed above, just as we would introduce any other nonpurchased inputs that might affect the production process.[6] The augmented unit cost function then becomes

$$C = C(p_i, R_k, T),$$

where

$$R_k, k = A, U, Q, Z,$$

respectively, denote adjusted disputes (A), unfair labor practices (U), quits (Q), and strikes (Z), where $r_k = \log (R_k)$.

Then, the translog approximation to this unit-cost function is:

(3)
$$\begin{aligned}
\ln C = a_0 &+ \Sigma_i a_i p_i + \tfrac{1}{2} \Sigma_i \Sigma_j a_{ij} p_i p_j \\
&+ s_T T + \Sigma_i s_{Ti} p_i T \\
&+ \Sigma_k c_k r_k + \tfrac{1}{2} \Sigma_k \Sigma_l c_{kl} r_k r_l \\
&+ \Sigma_l \Sigma_k c_{ik} p_i r_k,
\end{aligned}$$

where

$$\begin{aligned}
i &= K, L, N, E, M, \\
k &= A, Q, U, Z.
\end{aligned}$$

Thus, the indicators of worker attitude have first- and second-order influences on production costs just as do the conventional inputs, and the indicators interact with the inputs as well as with each other.

Under this specification, the share equations then become

(4) $$s_i = a_i + \Sigma_j a_{ij} P_j + s_{Ti} T + \Sigma_k c_{ik} r_k.$$

The augmented cost function is then estimated jointly with four of the five share equations. Zabala (1983) has found that behavioral expressions of worker attitude in response to the work environment typically operate with a lagged effect. Thus, it is labor policies and work conditions of the recent past that give rise to behaviors in the present. While acute changes in conditions have more immediate results, this generally lagged effect reduces the problem of simultaneous determination of attitudes and the quantities of input factors (input prices are assumed exogenous). Vestiges of bias from simultaneous determination can certainly remain in the estimates we present below.[7]

Given estimates of the augmented cost functions, we may determine the elasticity of the cost of production with respect to each of the attitude indicators by

$$(5) \qquad e_{ck} = \partial \ln C / \partial r_k = C_k + \Sigma_k C_{kl} \, r_k + \Sigma_i C_{ik} \, p_i,$$

where

$$i = K, L, N, E, M,$$
$$k = A, Q, U, Z.$$

The effects on marginal cost of indicator r_k is then given by

$$(6) \qquad \partial C / \partial R_k = C/R_k \times \partial \ln C / \partial \ln r_k.$$

Finally, we may construct a measure of the effects of attitudes on production costs by weighting the indices of the attitude indicators by their respective marginal costs and summing. Thus,

$$(7) \qquad I_w = C \times (\Sigma_k \partial \ln C / \partial \ln r_k \times 1/R_k), \quad k = A, Q, U, Z.$$

In any year, the proportional change in production costs due to negative attitudes—which is the negative of the corresponding change in total factor productivity—will be

$$(8) \qquad d = I_w/C = \Sigma_k \, d \ln C / dr_k$$

To avoid the difficulties of comparing the productivity and cost differences between the two countries in common currency terms, we will simply use the annual values of d from equation (8) for comparison.

14.7 Empirical Analysis

14.7.1 Estimation Results 1

The augmented cost function models were estimated for the manufacturing sectors of Japan and the United States for the periods 1965–78 and 1958–80, respectively. The results for Japanese manufacturing are shown in table 14.1. Due to homogeneity restrictions, the cost function parameters associated with materials (M) are not estimated directly; similarly, the second-order parameters for strikes, Z, are not estimated, but are inferred from existing parameters.

Table 14.2 shows the estimated own-Allen partial elasticities of substitution, and table 14.3 the cost elasticities associated with each of the worker attitude indicators. Tables 14.4, 14.5, and 14.6 show corresponding results for U.S. manufacturing. Table 14.7 below shows the total cost elasticities for the two manufacturing sectors for their respective estimation periods.

Table 14.1   **Estimated Cost Function Model, Japanese Manufacturing, 1965–78**

Parameter Name	Estimated Value	Standard Error	t-statistic
AO	11.1011	.014988	740.631
AK	.265802	.009219	28.8306
AL	.087381	.001692	51.6274
AN	.029563	.000622	47.4553
AE	.021912	.001630	13.4397
AKL	−.036751	.005984	−6.14067
AKN	−.021098	.003334	−6.21779
AKE	.011714	.004494	2.60624
ALN	.021316	.012364	1.72426
ALE	.018580	.004498	4.13002
ANE	.092085	.001818	5.06482
ST	−.012916	.002807	−4.59982
STK	.068900	.001929	3.57173
STL	.092177	.001357	.67909
STN	.001638	.000666	2.45800
STE	−.004338	.000793	−5.46565
ALL	−.019278	.013726	−1.40445
ANN	−.029958	.014451	−2.07308
CA	−.131481	.046428	−2.83191
CU	.083229	.053591	1.55302
CZ	.111858	.054941	2.03593
CAU	.152060	.057921	2.62528
CAZ	.140907	.033932	4.15259
CUZ	−.202413	.140785	−1.43377
CKA	.052999	.016864	3.14265
CKU	−.058823	.016082	−3.65769
CLA	.031360	.0036767	3.70004
CLU	−.009759	.0037954	−2.57127
CNA	.003314	.0014169	2.33965
CNU	−.002601	.0014674	−1.77245
CEA	−.009982	.0031332	−3.18601
CEU	.012355	.0027863	4.50542

Note: Key to parameter names: K = capital; L = production-worker labor; N = nonproduction-worker labor; E = energy; A = disputes adjustments; U = unfair labor practices; Z = strikes.

In preliminary estimates of the cost functions without the worker-attitude indicators, both sectors exhibited nonconcavity in early years for capital and energy prices. Concavity was imposed by restricting the a_{kk} and a_{EE} parameters to zero. For Japan, this had the added benefit of reducing the number of parameters to be estimated. In consequence, all the own-Allen partial elasticities of substitution have the correct sign, and the corresponding input factor demand schedules are downward sloping.

In Japan, the average annual rate of cost change, given by the s_T parameter, is −.0129, corresponding to total factor productivity growth of 1.29% per

Table 14.2   **Own-Allen Partial Elasticities of Substitution for Japan, 1965–78**

Year	Capital	Production-Worker Labor	Nonproduction-Worker Labor	Energy	Materials
1965	− 3.19715	− 14.9715	− 91.8636	− 31.7277	.699319
1966	− 2.88712	− 14.0569	− 82.6761	− 37.3110	.759410
1967	− 2.83564	− 14.1467	− 84.7511	− 38.1942	− .765745
1968	− 2.89788	− 15.0820	− 88.5929	− 37.4315	− 740769
1969	− 2.94922	− 14.9954	− 88.0302	− 35.8958	− .734760
1970	− 2.88089	− 14.8450	− 80.9179	− 37.4542	− .570955
1971	− 3.26449	− 14.4085	− 73.4642	− 34.2569	− .699768
1972	− 2.76220	− 12.9708	− 67.1035	− 44.6362	− .801840
1973	− 3.02002	− 12.8735	− 62.7135	− 37.0063	− 767647
1974	− 3.30986	− 13.0715	− 60.1869	− 27.0552	− .744338
1975	− 3.27200	− 12.5813	− 55.5272	− 26.6714	− 765644
1976	− 3.27539	− 12.6501	− 56.5135	− 26.4505	− .763571
1977	− 3.64671	− 12.3814	− 51.8016	− 24.9059	− .724170
1978	− 3.39022	− 12.3100	− 51.8388	− 28.1690	− .750163

Table 14.3   **Cost Elasticities for Attitude Indicators for Japan, 1965–68**

	Disputes Referred to LRCs	Unfair Labor Practice Charges	Strikes
1965	− .077932	.135806	.0114178
1966	− .159589	.169528	.0575843
1967	− .187181	.196407	.0571942
1968	− .110320	.110666	.0661729
1969	− .123840	.134979	.0538747
1970	− .938256	.0750949	.0810498
1971	− .002877	.0542922	.0124814
1972	− .131481	.0932289	.111858
1973	− .038643	.0478906	.0432072
1974	.122801	− .0429827	− .0464368
1975	.106955	− .0195364	− .0558456
1976	.106401	.0083032	− .0869417
1977	.140026	.0562864	− .169113
1978	.088802	.0717245	− .129844

year. The trend in relative input factor utilization not accounted for by other factors in the model—often called biased technical change—is positive for capital and production and nonproduction worker labor, and negative for energy and materials.

For the United States, the average annual rate of total factor productivity growth is 0.7% per year, and unexplained trends in relative factor intensity are positive for capital, nonproduction labor, and materials, and negative for production worker labor and energy.

Table 14.4   **Estimated Cost Function Model for U.S. Manufacturing, 1958–80**

Parameter	Estimated Value	SE	t-statistic
AO	6.65346	.0164108	405.433
AK	.019490	.012274	1.58793
AL	.289242	.005911	48.9267
AN	.081622	.008199	9.95484
AE	.062455	.005647	11.0584
AKL	−.058193	.007444	−7.91687
AKN	−.066572	.004707	−14.1405
AKE	.031369	.003553	8.56311
ALN	.005487	.005186	1.05808
ALE	−.014506	.005917	−2.45165
ANE	.031923	.002911	10.9644
ST	−.007080	.002273	−3.11453
STK	.004050	.001683	2.40576
STL	−.001519	.000804	−1.88807
STN	.001888	.001121	1.68377
STE	−.001996	.000782	−2.55326
ALL	.094837	.014917	6.35745
ANN	−.002821	.004528	−.62310
CA	−.004804	.049558	−.09694
CU	−.021224	−.03061	−.69333
CQ	−.040594	.016846	−2.40973
CZ	.158377	.037786	4.19134
CAU	.009580	.249915	.38335
CAZ	.348573	.113167	3.08016
CUZ	.000040	.046656	.00087
CAQ	−.104289	.044527	−2.34212
CUQ	.111645	.021427	5.21035
CQZ	.167533	.049301	3.39812
CKA	.044169	.21321	2.07164
CKU	−.071363	.022534	−3.16678
CKQ	.020346	.010753	1.89206
CLA	.000898	.009380	.09580
CLU	−.008909	.010234	−.87052
CLQ	.013794	.005043	2.73494
CNA	.025954	.014041	1.84840
CNU	−.042870	.014845	−2.88783
CNQ	.016772	.007154	2.34445
CEA	−.020889	.010317	−2.02464
CEU	.037555	.108701	3.45495
CEQ	−.023857	.004933	−4.83613

Note. Q = quits; for other parameters, see table 14.1 above. SE = standard error.

Table 14.5   **Own-Allen Partial Elasticities of Substitution for the United States, 1956–80**

	Capital	Production-Worker Labor	Nonproduction-Worker Labor	Energy	Materials
1958	− 13.0789	− 1.38246	− 8.46371	− 20.8431	− 1.19678
1959	− 13.3746	− 1.38973	− 9.61571	− 19.7145	− 1.10188
1960	− 13.9458	− 1.35576	− 8.31190	− 23.8269	− 1.19009
1961	− 14.2307	− 1.37053	− 8.59380	− 22.1218	− 1.16641
1962	− 14.6426	− 1.36390	− 8.58289	− 23.0257	− 1.15887
1963	− 16.2070	− 1.34402	− 8.37832	− 23.7549	− 1.15918
1964	− 17.4828	− 1.35057	− 8.62148	− 22.3701	− 1.13221
1965	− 14.5656	− 1.36023	− 8.74267	− 25.3102	− 1.13999
1966	− 12.7360	− 1.34296	− 8.17741	− 32.2869	− 1.19170
1967	− 13.8096	− 1.33280	− 8.04691	− 30.7266	− 1.19285
1968	− 15.2027	− 1.34620	− 8.73380	− 26.3132	− 1.13808
1969	− 16.0053	− 1.30455	− 7.98864	− 29.1096	− 1.19553
1970	− 20.1943	− 1.31052	− 8.25295	− 23.1352	− 1.15776
1971	− 22.9103	− 1.33241	− 8.74542	− 19.5600	− 1.11722
1972	− 19.9003	− 1.36750	− 9.85762	− 19.6281	− 1.06015
1973	− 14.2169	− 1.37694	− 9.19305	− 21.9709	− 1.13272
1974	− 11.9761	− 1.45099	− 8.66048	− 15.9872	− 1.19708
1975	− 13.4311	− 1.45047	− 8.26527	− 13.8791	− 1.22186
1976	− 13.4141	− 1.49092	− 9.49470	− 12.5652	− 1.14427
1977	− 15.7005	− 1.47753	− 9.65428	− 11.7283	− 1.13247
1978	− 13.0729	− 1.46812	− 9.57869	− 12.2343	− 1.14343
1979	− 13.8871	− 1.49505	− 9.36756	− 11.1454	− 1.17406
1980	− 14.5727	− 1.55272	− 10.1319	− 9.22754	− 1.12755

14.7.2   Estimation Results 2

The first-order effects of the attitude indicators are measured by the parameters c_A c_O, c_Z, and, in the United States, c_Q. Second-order effects are measured by the parameters c_{AD}, c_{AZ}, and c_{SZ} (with additional terms for Q in the U.S. model) and interactions with input factors by c_{ir}; that is, c_{KA} is the partial effect of adjusted disputes on capital requirements, and so on.

The overall cost effects of each of the indicators are shown in tables 14.3 and 14.6, and of their sum in table 14.7. In overall terms, the effects in the United States of attitudes as manifested in production costs and productivity were to raise production costs and reduce total factor productivity by about 8% in the late 1950s and 1960s, rising more rapidly in the 1970s to about 11% in the late 1970s. The effects in Japan were to raise costs and to reduce total factor productivity by nearly 7% in 1965. This effect declines slowly to 1973 and rather sharply thereafter to about 3% in 1978. These rates are not especially large, compared to the U.S. auto industry where total cost elasticity with respect to better indicators of worker attitude was .24.

Table 14.6   Cost Elasticities for Attitude Indicators for the United States,
                    1958–80

Year	Disputes Referred to NLRB	Unfair Labor Practice Charges	Quit Rate	Strikes
1958	.090266	.0075699	.0217394	−.036681
1959	.068860	.0053790	−.0067716	.014494
1960	−.009884	.0137394	.0386882	.117814
1961	−.003617	−.0098877	−.0114907	.108095
1962	.012163	.0020485	−.0225933	.916150
1963	−.020722	−.0069601	−.0289838	.139392
1964	−.013556	−.0130771	−.0237373	.133747
1965	.006031	.0099952	−.0482822	.116357
1966	.008164	.0513433	−.0939478	.119848
1967	.025306	.0360233	−.0673207	.091344
1968	.076332	.0293724	−.0487660	.029308
1969	.094563	.0419415	−.0448769	−.003863
1970	.075721	.0106047	−.0724908	.019357
1971	.071379	−.0317793	.0240316	.026299
1972	−.004804	−.0212241	−.0405943	-.158377
1973	.009712	.0153951	−.0673164	.137910
1974	.146048	.0155280	.0139675	−.073272
1975	.024073	−.0451165	.0418093	.094710
1976	.055679	−.0481791	.0394685	.059970
1977	.119205	−.0505240	.0717341	−.031496
1978	.036554	−.0360443	.0148252	.096051
1979	.085484	−.0334776	.0421227	.021725
1980	.056910	−.688292	.0658762	.065809

This contrast between worker-attitude effects through time in Japan and the
United States corresponds to the finding in Norsworthy and Malmquist (1983)
that total factor productivity rose in U.S. manufacturing somewhat more
slowly (.7%–1.0%) before 1973 but slowed down in the United States to about
.5% per year after the energy crisis of 1973, while it accelerated in Japan to
about 1.4% per year.

In the U.S. automobile industry, Norsworthy and Zabala (1985b), using
similar methods, found a strong cyclical component to worker attitudes—the
negative effects of worker attitudes were stronger in expansions and weaker in
recessions. No such pattern appears in the aggregate U.S. manufacturing sector in this study. In Japan, however, there is a substantial reduction in the
negative effect of attitudes after 1973. In the pre-1973 period, output was
growing rapidly in Japan's manufacturing sector—about 12% per year, and
employment of production and nonproduction workers was slowly increasing.
Between 1974 and 1978, however, labor input in Japan was reduced by more
than 10%, and output grew far more slowly than before. It is reasonable to
conclude, therefore, that similar cyclical forces that restrained the overt
expression of worker attitudes in cost-increasing and productivity-reducing

Table 14.7   **Total Cost Elasticities for Worker-Attitude Indicators, The United States and Japan**

Year	United States	Japan
1958	.0825843	
1959	.0819522	
1960	.0829811	
1961	.0830990	
1962	.0832336	
1963	.0827259	
1964	.0833753	
1965	.0841020	.0692909
1966	.0854080	.0675235
1967	.0853532	.0664205
1968	.0862477	.0665192
1969	.0877652	.0650138
1970	.0888898	.0623191
1971	.0899309	.0638965
1972	.0917536	.0636063
1973	.0957011	.0524545
1974	.0102271	.0333817
1975	.0105476	.0315735
1976	.0106940	.0277625
1977	.0108919	.0271993
1978	.0111386	.0306832
1979	.0115855	
1980	.0119767	

behaviors in the U.S. auto industry also had that effect in Japanese manufacturing after 1973. Indeed, if there is a mystery in the conclusions of this study, it must be: Why were the negative effects of worker attitudes in U.S. manufacturing *not* damped by the post-1973 recession?

The answer may simply be that we do not have a sufficiently sensitive model of U.S. manufacturing to capture these effects. Or that, unlike autos, formal shop dispute-resolution processes are less efficient, and manufacturers rely more on arbitration and mediation services for outside intervention in labor relations.

In particular, the statistics of the national dispute-resolution process in Japan may reasonably well reflect the attitudes of Japanese workers, because it is the primary formal organization for managing labor-management conflict. In the United States, by contrast, considerable use is made of the grievance machinery in unionized plants. In the U.S. automobile industry, we found grievance statistics to be sensitive indicators of productivity- and cost-related worker attitudes, and the same may be true for other unionized sectors, with the result that statistics of formal submission of labor disputes to third parties are less useful in the United States than in Japan as indicators of worker attitude.

14.8   Recent Developments in Labor Relations and Productivity in Japan

Despite vast differences between the Japanese and U.S. economies, fashions in U.S. economic policies, national and corporate, are often communicable and, at times, highly contagious for Japan. For example, Japan is currently undergoing waves of deregulation of industry and of privatization of government-operated enterprises similar to that which began in the United States in the late 1970s. Similarly, in the United States, the Japanese style of management has been widely discussed, and many U.S. firms have experimented with different labor and general management practices, for example, the team concept management system.

Anything in Japanese management connected with productivity or product quality quickly obtains the attention of American business.

One set of concerns that seems important is based not on the Japanese mystique, but on demographic trends: while the rate of growth of the Japanese economy has slowed down considerably in recent years, the widespread practice of early retirement (between ages 55 and 60 for many large enterprises) is straining the capacity of those enterprises to retire members of the cohort now reaching retirement age. Japan, virtually alone among major industrial countries, had a "baby boom" in the 1930's, and that group would normally retire between 1985 and 2000. This is the same large group that has recently passed through its most productive years. Throughout the late 1960s and the 1970s, while the U.S. labor force (1) grew younger and less experienced by absorbing the postwar U.S. baby boom and (2) increased in female participation, the Japanese labor force was growing older and more experienced. In conventional labor quality terms (see, e.g., Gollop and Jorgenson, 1980), the Japanese labor force was improving while the U.S. labor force was declining in productive capacity. Those trends are now reversing. The Japanese baby boom cohort is due for retirement even as the U.S. baby boom cohort is just entering its most productive years. Other things equal, this portends well for productivity in the United States relative to Japan. The demographic pattern mentioned above created another type of stress in the Japanese system that may tend to worsen worker attitudes. Rapid output growth—in excess of 10% per year in manufacturing—created employment and promotion opportunities even when accompanied by rapid labor productivity growth. Slower growth, and the somewhat delayed retirement of the Japanese workers approaching retirement age, has slowed down the growth of jobs, particularly in high quality, management-tracked jobs, even as Japanese universities are producing highly qualified graduates in record numbers. The scarcity of good jobs and promotion opportunities may lead to somewhat less favorable attitudes on the part of new labor force entrants. Indeed, some Japanese businessmen have been saying for several years that younger workers take for granted the pay and working conditions that their predecessors found very satisfying.

14.9 Summary

Compared to U.S. manufacturing, we find lower effects in Japan of negative attitudes. Japanese manufacturing plants are also characterized by nonadversarial collective bargaining, with lower grievance rates, fewer unresolved grievances, fewer strikes, and higher in-process quality audits.

The empirical evidence concerning the effects of worker attitudes on productivity in Japan and the United States is consistent with the widespread idea that Japan's system of conflict resolution—for the manufacturing sector, at least—is more efficient than the U.S. system in terms of productivity and costs. An alternative interpretation is that there is less potential for conflict in labor-management relations in Japanese manufacturing. Our finding of lower negative effects cannot distinguish these explanations. Another hypothesis to test is that, in future years, as Japanese business experiences the usual cycles, top-heavy bargaining will cause erosion in both trade union and employee commitment, as that which occurred at Nippon Steel Corporation in 1979 and the early 1980s.

Notes

1. Our work to date has focused primarily on the U.S. automobile industry, where we have forged a quantitative link between *worker attitudes,* measured in an objective and reproducible way, and the *productivity* and *cost of production* (Norsworthy and Zabala 1982; 1985a, 1985b, 1985c). That link is quantitatively important, and the worker-attitude index is robust, as we have shown for different econometric specifications (Norsworthy and Zabala 1990). We are currently engaged in a cross-sectional plant-level study of the U.S. Postal Service that studies a more limited set of worker-attitude indicators, but includes the effects of selected management policies on worker-attitude formation as well as the effects of worker attitude on productivity and costs (Norsworthy and Jang 1989).

2. We should point out that there are significant policy shifts in dispute outcomes in an agency whose leading members change with each new administration, suggesting four-year cycle effects (Sockell and Delaney 1987). We do not account for these effects in this paper.

3. Type 3a and 3b grievance data cannot be described as worker-attitude proxies since they include disputes by management as well as trade union and employees. See discussion of *shun-to* in sec. 14.3 above; also see sec. 14.4 above. A pure type 3 worker-attitude variable should be purged of disputes sent to the NLRB by management. We could not obtain such a measure for this paper. The other behavioral data are consistent with our earlier research with worker-attitude data.

4. Binswanger (1974) presents an exceptionally clear description, which we will not repeat here.

5. The counterculture in production modeling claims (with some merit) that the equilibrium model tracks well because the (ex post) service price of capital adjusts to a level consistent with the quantity of capital input, rather than the reverse. Norsworthy

and Zabala (1985c) hold that an explicit disequilibrium model is preferable for measuring the effects of worker attitudes on the level and value of capital input.

6. Norsworthy and Zabala (1985b); see also F. R. Lichtenberg (1981).

7. The instrumental variables solution is an approach to dealing with the simultaneity issue. A preferred solution would be to augment the model with explicit representation of the formation of worker attitudes by labor policies based on technology, and other conditions of work. For the total manufacturing sector, it would be very difficult to develop any but the most general attitude-formation model. At the industry and plant levels, it may be possible to measure some of the important determinants of worker attitudes required to extend the production model to encompass attitude formation.

References

Binswanger, H. P. 1974. The measurement of technical change bias with many factors of production. *American Economic Review* 64 (6):964–76.

Central Labor Relations Commission. 1977. *Rodo iinka: Nenpo,* vol. 3.

Gollop, F. M., and D. W. Jorgenson. 1980. U.S. productivity growth by industry. In *New developments in productivity measurement and analysis,* ed. John W. Kendrick and Beatrice Vaccara. NBER Studies in Income and Wealth, vol. 44. Chicago: University of Chicago Press.

Hanami, T. 1981. Labor relations in Japan today. Tokyo: Kodansha.

Lam, A. C. 1983. Labour dispute settlement in Japan: Analysis and evaluation of the labour relations commissions dispute adjustment functions, 1946–1980. M.A. Thesis, Waseda University, Japan.

Levine, S. B., and Koji, T. 1980. Interpreting industrial conflict: The case of Japan. In *Labor relations in advanced industrial societies: Issues and problems,* ed. Benjamin Martin and Everett M. Kassalow. New York: Carnegie Endowment for International Peace.

Lichtenberg, F. R. 1981. Training, tenure, and productivity. Doctoral diss., University of Pennsylvania.

Nishimizu, M. 1979. An international comparison of sectoral changes in productivity. Doctoral diss., Johns Hopkins University.

Norsworthy, J. R., and S. L. Jang, 1989. Worker behavior and its effects on productivity and costs in the U.S. Postal Service. Presented at the meeting of the American Economics Association (December).

Norsworthy, J. R. and D. H. Malmquist. 1983. Input measurement and productivity growth in Japanese and U.S. manufacturing. *American Economic Review* 73 (6):947–67.

Norsworthy, J. R., and C. A. Zabala. 1982. A note on introducing a measure of worker attitude in cost function estimation. *Economic Letters* 10:185–91.

———. 1985a. Responding to the productivity crisis: A plant-level approach to labor policy. In *Productivity growth and U.S. competitiveness.* ed. William Baumol and Kenneth McLennan, pp. 103–18. New York: Oxford University Press.

———. 1985b. Worker attitude, worker behavior, and productivity in the U.S. automobile industry, 1959–76. *Industrial and Labor Relations Review* 38 (4):544–57.

———. 1985c. Effects of worker attitudes on production costs and the value of capital input. *Economic Journal* 95 (4):992–1002.

———. 1990. Worker attitudes and the cost of production: Hypothesis tests in an equilibrium model. *Economic Inquiry* 28(1):57–78.

Satoshi, K. 1982. Japan in the passing lane: An insider's account of life in a Japanese auto factory. New York: Pantheon.

Shimada, H. 1982a. Japan's postwar industrial growth and and labor-management relations. *Proceedings of the American Industrial Relations Association, 1982* 241–48 (December).

———. 1982b. Perceptions and the reality of Japanese industrial relations: Role in Japan's postwar industrial success. *Keio Economic Studies* 19 (2):1–21.

Shimada, H., and J. P. MacDuffie. 1986. Industrial relations and "humanware." Working paper. Sloan School of Management, Massachusetts Institute of Technology.

Sockell, D., and J. T. Delany. 1987. Union organizing and the Reagan NLRB. *Contemporary Policy Issues* 5(4):28–45.

Zabala, C. A. 1983. Collective bargaining at UAW Local 645, General Motors Assembly Division, Van Nuys Assembly Plant, 1976–1982. Doctoral diss., University of California, Los Angeles.

———. 1986. Recommendations for human resource data collection in the Census of Manufactures. Subcommittee on Human Resource Data Development, Strategic Productivity Task Force, Assistant Secretary of the Office of Productivity, Technology and Innovation, U.S. Department of Commerce, *Working Papers Series.* Troy, N.Y.: Rensselaer Polytechnic Institute, 1–14.

———. 1989. Sabotage at General Motors' Van Nuys assembly plant, 1975–1983. *Industrial Relations Journal* 20 (1): 16–32.

Comment   Mary Jean Bowman

This paper—along with others published by Norsworthy and Zabala since 1982 and on up to the present time—starts with the proposition that worker attitudes affect total cost, cost structures, and productivity and that attitude indicators should be added to conventional production functions. This they do for manufacturing in Japan over the years 1965–78 and in the United States over the years 1958–80. Their analysis makes use of an equilibrium translog cost function and its production dual, entailing the crucial assumptions of cost minimization and constant returns to scale.

The availability and selection of attitude indicators is critical to such an endeavor. So also, in the present case, are the institutional contexts and their implications for interpretation of those indicators. The contribution by Lam et al. provides an essential and insightful comparison of the Japanese and U.S. systems for settlement of industrial disputes.

Attitudes are measured indirectly, using observable forms of behavior as indicators. This is not a study of what explains the behavior—let alone the unobserved "attitudes" and how these relate to the systems for settlement of disputes. Empirically, it is in fact the latter that are entered in the regressions, as the title of this paper, though not its underlying argument, suggests. For

Mary Jean Bowman is professor emeritus, Department of Economics and Education, University of Chicago.

both Japan and the United States the "attitude indicators" are: A, disputes referred for solution to the LRCs in Japan and the NLRB in the United States; U, unfair labor practice charges; Z, strikes. Only in the United States did they have quit rates, Q.

The cost function in the basic model, without worker attitudes, incorporates five input variables (physical capital, production workers, nonproduction workers, energy, and materials). Time trend T is taken to represent technological change, which is interacted with the other input variables. Attitude variables are then inserted, interacting these variables with each of the conventional inputs, and the estimated cost function is estimated jointly with four of the five share equations. This provides the basis for estimating the elasticity of the total cost of production with respect to each of the attitude indicators. Finally, the authors construct an overall measure of effects of attitudes on production costs by weighting the attitude indicators by their respective marginal costs.

I have two questions relating to methodology. First, the assumption of constant returns to scale and the assumption that time trend T stands for technological change evade the perennial problem of sorting out economies of scale and technological change stressed earlier by Nadiri. This is common enough. But we must ask, nevertheless, What in fact may T be saying? Perhaps there is a special problem here in view of the changes that have occurred over the years covered in the experiences and roles of the LRCs in Japan. Has the assumption that T is exogenously determined technological change blocked thinking about interactions between changing structures and the attitude indicators?

Second, even setting aside unavoidable problems in making cross-national comparisons, a problem is created in the inclusion of Q for the United States but not for Japan. This would seem to invalidate the comparisons of "total" attitude effects in the two countries. But even if Q were available for Japan there would be a dilemma here. Although turnover is considerably higher in Japan than often is assumed, the lack of data on quits in Japan may not be accidental, and especially, perhaps, with reference to manufacturing industry over the years covered. Furthermore, dissatisfaction would have had to be more intense in Japan than in the United States before a Japanese worker would take the costly alternative of quitting. Differing age structures will be important in this respect as well.

Some of the other findings raise questions that would seem to call for comment by the authors relating back to the systems of dealing with conflicts in Japan and in the United States and their histories. Putting tables 14.1 and 14.4 side by side highlights, for example, the contrast between Japan and the United States in elasticities on nonproduction workers and on their interaction with physical capital. Does the shifting emphasis in LRC activities with increased white-collar involvement say something here? Also interesting are contrasts between the two countries in elasticities on the variable A, which, taken alone, is more strongly negative in Japan than in the United States but becomes more strongly positive in interaction with production labor in Japan than in the United States.

The authors point not only to the decline in total cost elasticities for worker-attitude indicators in Japan in the 1970s (not surprising) but also to a puzzling lack of such a change (even a slight increase in those elasticities) in the United States. I share their puzzlement, but this raises another question. Does using an optimizing constant-cost model create more of a problem in short-term shifts of capacity utilization in relation to worker behavior in the United States than in Japan? For that matter, what about the very different situations with respect to unemployment insurance in the two countries as a factor in these differences?

While I still have some concern that contrasts between the situations and systems in Japan and in the United States may raise greater problems for empirical comparisons than the authors explicitly recognize, this most recent version of their paper is a big improvement in this respect. Moreover, the importance of contrasts in demographic changes and associated time paths of aggregate productivity is now made explicit, albeit without explicit attention to the associated processes of in-firm human resource development. Do such considerations not weaken somewhat the case for incorporating attitudes in production functions, whatever their indicators?

Very much to its credit, a study such as this raises many basic questions that go beyond anything that could be asked of the authors in one investigation. As they recognize, "industrial conflict" is only one part of a broader interplay of incentive structures, rules of the game, how shirking is monitored, and personnel and human resource development policies generally in their relationships to worker attitudes and behavior. The sorting out of some of the commonalities and differences between Japan and the United States (and within each of these countries) in these respects is a challenge that may prove to be of rising importance in the future.

Contributors

Ernst R.Berndt
Sloan School of Management
Massachusetts Institute of Technology
50 Memorial Drive
Cambridge, MA 02139

Mary Jean Bowman
Department of Economics
University of Chicago
1126 East 59th Street
Chicago, IL 60637

Masako Darrough
Business School
Columbia University
International Affairs Building
New York, NY 10027

Edwin Dean
Bureau of Labor Statistics
U.S. Department of Labor
441 G Street, NW
Washington, DC 20212

W. Erwin Diewert
Department of Economics
University of British Columbia
Vancouver, British Columbia V6T 1W5
Canada

Romesh Diwan
Department of Economics
Rensselaer Polytechnic Institute
Troy, NY 12180

Melvyn Fuss
Department of Economics
University of Toronto
150 St. George Street
Toronto, Ontario M5S 1A1
Canada

Zvi Griliches
National Bureau of Economic Research
1050 Massachusetts Avenue
Cambridge, MA 02138

Fumio Hayashi
Department of Economics
The University of Pennsylvania
3718 Locust Walk
Philadelphia, PA 19104

Charles R. Hulten
Department of Economics
University of Maryland
College Park, MD 20742

Hajime Imamura
Department of Economics
Toyo University
28-20, 5 Chome, Hakusan
Bunkyo-ku, Tokyo 112,
Japan

Dale W. Jorgenson
Department of Economics
Harvard University
Littauer Center 122
Cambridge, MA 02138

437

Tatsuya Kikutani
Faculty of Business Administration
Kyoto Sangyo University
Motoyama, Kamigamo, Kita-ku
Kyoto 606, Japan

Masahiro Kuroda
Faculty of Business and Commerce
Keio University
15-45, Mita 2-chome
Minato-ku, Tokyo 108
Japan

Alice C. Lam
Suntory Toyota International Center
London School of Economics and Political Science
London WC24 2AE, United Kingdom

Jacques Mairesse
Institut National de la Statistique et des Etudes Economiques
18, Boulevard Adolphe-Pinard
75675 Paris Cedex 14
France

Edwin Mansfield
Department of Economics
Wharton School
University of Pennsylvania
Philadelphia, PA 19104

Shunseke Mori
Department of Economics
Science University of Tokyo
Tokyo, Japan

Catherine Morrison
Department of Economics
Tufts University
Medford, MA 02155

M. Ishaq Nadiri
National Bureau of Economic Research
269 Mercer Street, 8th floor
New York, NY 10003

Arthur Neef
Bureau of Labor Statistics
U.S. Department of Labor
441 G Street, NW
Washington, DC 20212

J. R. Norsworthy
Department of Economics
Rensselaer Polytechnic Institute
Troy, NY 12180

Walter Y. Oi
Department of Economics
University of Rochester
Rochester, NY 14627

Ingmar R. Prucha
Department of Economics
University of Maryland
College Park, MD 20742

Hikaru Sakuramoto
Faculty of Business and Commerce
Keio University
15-45, Mita 2-chome
Minato-ku, Tokyo 108
Japan

Takamitsu Sawa
Kyoto Institute of Economic Research
Kyoto University
Sakyo-ku
Kyoto 606, Japan

Robert M. Schwab
Department of Economics
University of Maryland
College Park, MD 20742

Toshiaki Tachibanaki
Kyoto Institute of Economic Research
Kyoto University
Sakyo-ku
Kyoto 606, Japan

Hong W. Tan
The Rand Corporation
1700 Main Street
P.O. Box 2138
Santa Monica, CA 90406

Leonard Waverman
Department of Economics
University of Toronto
150 St. George Street
Toronto, Ontario M5S 1A1
Canada

David O. Wood
Center for Energy Policy Research
Massachusetts Institute of Technology
One Amherst Street (E40-437)
Cambridge, MA 02139

Kanji Yoshioka
Keio Economic Observatory
Keio University
15-45, Mita 2-chome
Minato-ku, Tokyo 108
Japan

Craig A. Zabala
School of Management
Rensselaer Polytechnic Institute
Troy, NY 12180

Author Index

Subject Index